THE ILLUSTRATED ENCYCLOPEDIA OF
WEAPONS
OF WORLD WAR I

THE ILLUSTRATED ENCYCLOPEDIA OF
WEAPONS
OF WORLD WAR I

A Comprehensive Guide to Weapons Systems,
including Tanks, Small Arms, Warplanes, Artillery,
Ships and Submarines

General Editor
CHRIS BISHOP

amber
BOOKS

Published by
Amber Books Ltd
74–77 White Lion Street
London
N1 9PF
United Kingdom
www.amberbooks.co.uk
Appstore: itunes.com/apps/amberbooksltd
Facebook: www.facebook.com/amberbooks
Twitter: @amberbooks

ISBN: 978-1-78274-141-1

Project Editor: Michael Spilling
Design: Brian Rust
Picture Research: Terry Forshaw
Images: Courtesy of Aerospace Publishing Ltd.

Printed in China

Contents

German tank crew sit astride a captured British tank following the occupation of Armentieres in April 1918.

Armoured Vehicles of World War 1

A Tank Mk IV (Male) with short 6-pdr guns displays the 'No have eyes, how can see?' insignia possibly bestowed by Chinese labourers in France. This tank was presented to the Tank Corps by the President of the Federal Council of the Malay States.

Armoured vehicles of World War I were not particularly good as fighting machines. Wheeled vehicles could not handle the terrain, and those using the recently-invented continuous track were slow and prone to breakdown. Yet the German High Command were to claim in 1918 that armoured vehicles, particularly the tank, were a major factor in the Allied victory.

The weapon that was to become widely known as the tank was virtually forced upon the armies of World War I by the very nature of the terrain over which the embattled armies had to operate. After the end of 1914 the war settled down to what was practically a siege campaign, but on a scale that no one had ever conceived possible. The German army and its French and British opponents faced each other across a strip of country in northern France that was swept by the firepower produced by the machine-gun and massed artillery. The opposing armies lived a miserable life in their trenches and dugouts, and from time to time made an effort to break the stalemate by laying on mass attacks presaged and supported by huge artillery concentrations. It was all to no avail.

Every time an attempt was made by either side to cross the contested strip of land known as the Western Front the result was slaughter on a massive scale. No matter how intensive or how thorough the artillery's preparatory bombardment, there was always a flank from which machine-gun fire could be delivered and there was always a machine-gun somewhere that was able to survive the shell-fire. To the soldiers of the day there seemed to be no answer to this deadlock and all they could contrive was to make the preparatory bombardment that much more intense and concentrated. But the machine-gun always survived and the casualty tolls continued to lengthen.

The answer to all this destruction of life was so straightforward that we now wonder why it was neglected so long. The answer was a simple layer of armour plate and light armament carried on a powered chassis that we now call the tank. These new vehicles had to be able to cross the devastated terrain that the French country had become between the lines, cross the deep trenches in which the hapless infantry lived and died, and get through to the open country beyond. Once the tanks had got there, the theorists proposed, fluid warfare and the destruction of the enemy could progress once more. What those proponents did not realize was that they had created a new weapon with which all future wars were to be fought.

A Tank IV (Female) in the ruined streets of Peronne during the German attacks of March 1918. The small sponsons for the machine-guns can be clearly seen, and the tank carries an unditching beam over the rear tracks; this was used to help the vehicle clear a trench if it was unable to do so using the tracks alone.

Minerva armoured car

The story of the Belgian **Minerva** armoured cars is now little known outside Belgium, which is a pity as in many ways the Belgians were the progenitors of armoured car warfare and demonstrated to others how such vehicles could be used, so anticipating a type of mobile combat that was not to realize its full form until World War II.

Almost as soon as the Germans invaded Belgium in August 1914 cavalry sweeps ahead of the main body of the German army were encountered by the Belgians. Usually the Germans heavily outnumbered the Belgians, who soon took to using the mobility of the motor car as a counter against German numbers. By the end of the month two Minerva touring cars were provided with improvised armour at the Cockerill works at Hoboken and sent into action. These early cars were simply commercial models with sheets of 4-mm (0.16-in) armour plating around the engine and sides, and with the top left open for a Hotchkiss machine-gun mounting. Before very long the first two cars were followed by further examples with a more formal armoured hull but retaining the same basic layout. With this small force the Belgians showed what armoured cars could do: acting originally as a form of motorized cavalry they carried out long reconnaissance missions, gathered intelligence of the enemy's movements, gave fire and other support to infantry attacks when possible, and also carried out long disruption missions behind the lines of the German advance. It was perhaps the last type of mission that attracted most attention, for at that stage of the war the Germans were advancing or marching

in open order across open country or along roads. The single machine-gun of a Minerva armoured car could create havoc in such conditions, and frequently did just that.

But this period did not last long. By October 1914 the line of trenches had reached the Yser region, and there the Belgian army remained until 1918. The area was too wet and boggy for armoured cars to achieve anything useful and their period of immediate action passed. But during the few weeks they had been in action they had demonstrated to all who cared to learn what the armoured car could achieve. The Belgian example was copied directly by the British Royal Naval Air Service squadrons and the

Germans also went ahead with their own designs for armoured cars.

While the Western Front was 'out' as far as Belgian armoured car units were concerned, a special Belgian armoured car unit was formed for service in Russia against the Germans. There the Belgian cars performed sterling service until they were shipped home in 1918. Once back in Belgium the units re-equipped, and in 1919 there appeared yet another version of the basic Minerva armoured car, this time with an armoured turret. But the old 1914 Minervas were retained in service, usually for use by the Gendarmerie, with which some were still in use as late as 1933.

A section of Belgian Minerva armoured cars operates near Houthem in September 1917. The cars are all armed with Hotchkiss machine-guns, and the design had by 1917 been sufficiently formalized for spotlights to become standard.

Specification
Minerva
Crew: 3 to 6
Weight: 4 tons
Powerplant: one unknown petrol engine
Dimensions: length 4.90 m (16 ft 1 in); width 1.75 m (5 ft 9 in); height 2.30 m (7 ft 6½ in)
Performance: maximum speed 40 km/h (25 mph); range not known

Austin-Putilov armoured cars

Although the vehicles known as the **Austin-Putilov** armoured cars had British origins they may be assumed to be Russian, as most of them were produced and used there; another point is that their size was such that they might also be termed armoured trucks.

In 1914 the Russian army was so short of equipment that it had to turn to the United Kingdom to supply armoured cars. Various types were involved but one of these was an Austin design, a fairly massive design with twin turrets and solid-tyred wheels. Two types of hull were supplied, one of which had the armour over the driver's position arranged in such a way that it restricted the traverse of both of the gun turrets, each of which mounted a single Maxim machine-gun. This early arrangement was soon altered in favour of a lower cab, but on this model the weight was increased by 1.16 tons. This weight increase was brought about mainly by the use of thicker (maximum 8 mm/0.315 in) chrome-steel armour and a revision of the driving arrangements. The original British design could be steered from the front only, but the Russians wanted steering from the rear as well and the revisions required to accommodate this requirement added to the weight. This was not the only rearrangement demanded by the Russians, who soon found that the harsh Russian conditions were too much for the British vehicles, which broke down frequently.

Despite such problems orders were

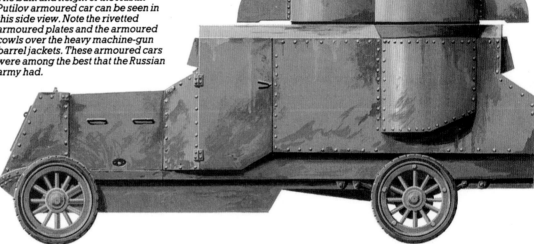

The bulk and height of the Austin-Putilov armoured car can be seen in this side view. Note the rivetted armoured plates and the armoured cowls over the heavy machine-gun barrel jackets. These armoured cars were among the best that the Russian army had.

placed for 200 Austin armoured cars, but not many were ever delivered. The main reason was that Austin was already stretched to the limit to supply vehicles for the British army and had few facilities to spare for the Russians. Instead of complete armoured cars they supplied bare chassis instead direct to the Putilov works, where the Russians were able to add whatever strengthening they thought necessary and make some of their own modifications to the hull. This mainly involved staggering the twin turrets so that

although each still covered only a 270° traverse they could together cover a slightly wider field of fire. A later innovation was the introduction of tracks in place of the rear wheels which converted the vehicle into a half-track; eventually Putilov ceased production of the armoured cars at its St Petersburg plant and concentrated on the half-track version. There was even a plan to produce half-tracks in place of any more armoured cars but the revolution of 1917 occurred before this could be carried out.

From 1914 to 1917 the Russians used many types of armoured car, ranging from direct imports to local improvisations, but the most important type was the Austin-Putilov. It was numerically and mechanically the best the Russians had to hand and eventually proved to be far more suited to the rough conditions under which the Russians had to fight. During 1917 many became involved in the internal fighting that accompanied the events leading to the October Revolution, and the type can frequently be seen in photographs of the period. Some were used by Poland after 1918 and a few even ended up in Japan.

Specification
Austin-Putilov
Crew: 5
Weight: 5.3 tons
Powerplant: one 50-hp (37.3-kW) Austin petrol engine
Dimensions: length 4.88 m (16 ft 0 in); width 1.95 m (6 ft 4¾ in); height 2.40 m (7 ft 10½ in)
Performance: maximum speed 50 km/h (31 mph); range 200 km (125 miles)

German troops examine a captured Austin-Putilov armoured car, probably in search of loot. Note the prominent Czarist insignia and the height of these vehicles, which can be assessed by comparison with the soldiers standing around.

 UK
Tank Mk I

There is no space in these pages to provide a full account of the development of the vehicles that led to the **Tank Mk I**. Suffice to say that the Mk I was the production and service model of the prototype vehicle known as 'Mother', which was the eventual outcome of a series of development models that were originally based on the use of a Holt tractor chassis. By the time 'Mother' was produced, the original Holt design had been submerged by operational requirements that called for prodigious trench-crossing capabilities that the Holt concept could never achieve. Lieutenant W.G. Wilson was in the main responsible for the final design of 'Mother' after a great deal of committee and experimental work, and it was he who conceived the idea of using the large and high track outline with its characteristic shape that came to be the classic tank outline of World War I.

'Mother' was demonstrated in January and February 1916, and soon after this the first production order was placed. A separate arm was established in March 1916 to use the new vehicle, which was named the 'tank' purely as a cover, though the name stuck and is still in use. The first production vehicles were issued to the Heavy Section, Machine-Gun Corps in mid-1916, and the first crews were assembled and trained. The Tank Mk I was a large and heavy beast powered by a single Daimler 105-hp (78.3-kW) petrol engine carried in an armoured box slung between the two massive lozenge-shaped continuous tracks. Originally it had been intended to mount a turret on the top but this would have made the design unstable so instead the main armament of two 6-pdr (57-mm) guns was placed in one sponson on each side. The sponsons each had a single Lewis or Hotchkiss machine-gun, and a third such gun was fitted for extra defence. The 6-pdr (57-mm) guns were ex-Admiralty weapons as the army would not supply an armament when requested. The vehicle was protected by armour plate (ranging in thickness from 6 mm/ 0.24 in to 12 mm/0.47 in) riveted to steel joists, but in action this proved unsatisfactory as bullet 'splash' found its way through the armour seams and

caused casualties so that the crews took to wearing chain mail facial armour. The Tank Mk I could cross trenches up to 2.44 m/8 ft wide, and steering was at first accomplished by using external twin-wheel 'steering tails' that proved to be unnecessary: in action they were frequently damaged, yet the tanks could still be steered.

Almost as soon as the first tanks appeared in France in mid-1916 they were ordered into action, despite the fact that the vehicles were still full of mechanical 'bugs' and their crews were barely trained. Thus the first Tank Mk Is went into action on the morning of 15 September 1916 at Flers-Courcelette in a vain attempt to provide some impetus to the flagging Somme Offensive that had been under way since July. Although they were used locally in ones and twos, the tanks did manage to make some local breakthroughs and created panic when they appeared. But the sad truth was that too few actually got into action. Many of the planned 50 that were supposed to make the attack simply broke down on their way to the front, and others were quickly bogged down in the mud that prevailed everywhere. Individual tanks did make deep impressions into

Above: A Tank I (Male) moves up into action near Thiepval in September 1916. Items to note are the anti-grenade wire mesh screen over the hull and the clumsy steering 'tail' at the rear; these steering devices were discarded after a short while as they proved to be of limited value.

Below: This Tank Mk I (Female) was photographed coming out of the battle near Flers-Courcelette on 15 September 1916 after the first-ever tank action took place there. Note the armoured cowls over the machine-guns and the frame for the anti-grenade screen.

the German line but they were too few in number to make any major impact. The Mk I was produced in two versions: the **Tank Mk I (Male)** described above, and intended for the primary offensive mission; and the **Tank Mk I (Female)** with larger sponsons and an armament of four Vickers and two Lewis machine-guns, and intended for the anti-infantry support of the Tank Mk I (Male). Other variants were the **Mk I Tank Tender** with mild steel boxes in place of the sponsons, and the **Mk I Wireless Tank** without sponsons but with a tall aerial mast.

Thus the Tank Mk 1 made history by being the first tank to be used in combat, but it was something of a fiasco as far as the action was concerned. What the type did achieve in the long term was to impress on the British military hierarchy the fact that the tank did have potential, more funds and facilities being thereafter diverted towards the 'Tank Corps' which was duly established in July 1917.

Specification
Tank Mk I (Male)
Crew: 8

Weight: 28 tons
Powerplant: one 105-hp (78.3-kW) Daimler petrol engine
Dimensions: length with tail 9.91 m (32 ft 6 in); length of hull 8.05 m (26 ft 5 in); width over sponsons 4.19 m (13 ft 9 in); height 2.45 m (8 ft 0½ in)
Performance: maximum speed 6 km/h (3.7 mph); range 38 km (24 miles)

UK
Medium Tank Mk A

When the first tanks were designed they were intended to be little more than 'machine-gun destroyers' capable of crossing rough country. As a result they were huge lumbering beasts that could cross trenches but could not move very fast over good ground. By 1916 the idea of using the tanks as a form of cavalry that could exploit any breakthroughs brought about by the heavy tanks began to take root. It was proposed that a new design of light tank with few obstacle-crossing attributes but capable of speed across good ground should be designed and built, and such a product was developed by Mr (later Sir) William Tritton, who had been instrumental in the development of the early 'landships'.

For the new design, soon nicknamed **Whippet**, Tritton reverted to his early 'Little Willie' layout in which flat rather than lozenge-shaped tracks were used. A front-mounted engine bay was slung between the tracks, and this housed two Tylor 45-hp (33.6-kW) London bus engines, one to drive each track; steering was effected by speeding or slowing each track. Towards the rear was the driver on the left, with the fighting compartment to his right. Originally this latter was to have been a turreted affair, but this was changed to a rigid superstructure mounting one Hotchkiss machine-gun in a special mounting on each face. Armour ranged in thickness from 5 mm (0.2 in) to 14 mm (0.55 in).

The prototype of the Whippet was ready by February 1917, and was ordered into production in the June of that year. But production took time and it was not until late 1917 that the first examples appeared. Even then they did not reach France quickly, and it was March 1918 before they saw action. The official name for the new tank was the **Medium Tank Mk A**, but to everyone it was the Whippet. The type proved to be difficult to drive as the driver had to juggle constantly with each engine clutch to control the machine, and in action many were lost when they went out of control. But the Whippet soon proved to be reliable enough, and once on good ground it could notch up speeds greater than that of horsed cavalry.

At first the Whippets were used to plug gaps in the line during the major German advances, but it was when the time came for counterattack that they came into their own. Some made deep forays behind the enemy lines creating havoc as they went. One, the famous 'Musical Box', spent nine hours cruising German rear areas and gunning down unsuspecting rear echelon troops before it was finally knocked out by a field gun.

By the time of the Armistice the Whippet or Mk A was well established, but it did not remain in service

A Medium Tank Mk A, the famous 'Whippet'. This vehicle was armed with two Hotchkiss machine-guns and had a rigid turret superstructure. Armour was 14-mm (0.55-in) thick at best.

long after that date. A few saw service during the Irish 'Troubles' and a batch was sent off to Japan in 1920 to become the first Japanese tanks. The Japanese were not the only foreign operators, however, for before the Armistice the Germans had captured enough for them to take the Medium Mk A into their own service, though the numbers were not large.

Specification
Medium Tank A
Crew: 3 or 4
Weight: 14 tons

Powerplant: two 45-hp (33.6-kW) Tylor four-cylinder petrol engines
Dimensions: length 6.10 m (20 ft 0 in); width 2.62 m (8 ft 7 in); height 2.74 m (9 ft 0 in)
Performance: maximum speed 13.4 km/h (8.3 mph); range 257 km (160 miles)

Right: In this photograph of a Medium Tank Mk A the prominent recognition stripes at the front are red and white. Note the complex shape of the turret superstructure and the large mud chutes under the track tops, which reflect the muddy Western Front conditions.

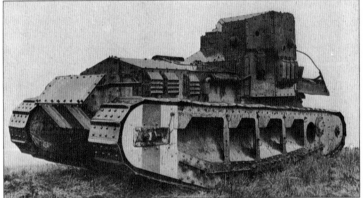

Below: Whippet tanks of the 3rd Battalion Tank Corps move up into action near Maillet Mailly on 26 March 1918. This was the first action in which the Whippet tanks were used, and when they charged a force of 300 German infantry they took many prisoners and routed the remainder. They later took part in several skirmishes in the area.

British Tank Development

Written about since the days of Leonardo, the armoured 'land ship' did not come to fruition until the development of the internal combustion engine and the invention of the caterpillar track coincided with the needs of armies floundering in the mud of Flanders. Few could know that those early experimental vehicles would lead to the massive armoured forces of World War II and after.

The idea of the armoured 'landship' was quite well established in fiction before 1914, and proposals to construct such a machine had been made to nearly every major army in Europe, including the British War Office. None of these proposals was taken up for the simple reason that there seemed to be no requirement for such a machine, but after 1914 that changed. Some far-sighted soldiers and others realized that the conditions existing on the Western Front could only be overcome by the use of mobile armoured machines.

One of these early prophets was Colonel E.D. Swinton, who used his position of influence to interest government officials in the concept. Accordingly a War Office committee was set up to investigate some proposals, but its efforts came to nothing. Not deterred, the Royal Navy took a hand as its Royal Naval Air Service armoured car squadrons had at least had some experience of armoured warfare in 1914. From their experience came a number of proposals that involved the use of a 'big wheel' vehicle with massive wheels that could cross trenches. At this point Winston Churchill became more than interested and set up what was to become known as the Landship Committee to investigate ways of crossing the French battlefields.

The 'big wheel' machine was given the construction go-ahead, and the attention of the committee was drawn to another device known as the Pedrail which used a wide central track carrying any load or powerplant above it. This too was ordered for trials, and more machines of the caterpillar track form were ordered for experimental work. There were several of these such as the Killen-Strait tractor, a Bullock Creep Grip tractor and a peculiar purpose-built machine that embodied the wheels of a Daimler-Foster tractor and was known as the Tritton Trench-crossing Machine. None of these machines was deemed suitable for the task, the same verdict befalling the Pedrail, which proved to be far too cumbersome a vehicle to cross rough ground.

The Bullock tractor seemed to offer more promise, two such vehicles being specially obtained from the United States. Being primarily an agricultural machine, the Bullock could not be classed as intrinsically suitable, but its tracks did offer a way through mud and wire. Accordingly Mr William Tritton (later knighted for his services) of Foster's of Lincoln was asked to redesign the tractor. This man was the one who had been involved in the design of the Tritton Trench-crossing Machine after the 'big wheel' design had been abandoned.

Tritton accordingly used the Bullock track and suspension and built the 'No. 1 Lincoln Machine'. This design was far more promising, but the track was too narrow and gave constant trouble. A new track and some other improvements led to the vehicle later known as 'Little Willie' in December 1915.

'Little Willie' was the first British tank, although at that time the term had not been coined. Although it appeared to meet the Landship Committee requirements, 'Little Willie' was still too unstable and had virtually no obstacle-crossing capabilities, so a Lieutenant Wilson, who had been working with Tritton at the behest of the Landship Committee, conceived the idea of greatly enlarging the tracks into an 'all-round' form that came to resemble the lozenge shape that epitomized the tanks of World War I. The box body of 'Little Willie' was accordingly altered to accommodate the new track outline and the machine became 'Mother'.

With 'Mother' the War Office once more became interested, and after demonstrations held in Hatfield Park in January 1916 the design was approved. The Landship Committee was then revised to become the Tank Supply Committee, for in an effort to hide the intended role of the new machine the codename 'water carrier' and eventually 'tank' was applied; the latter term was the one that stuck.

'Mother' was used as the prototype for the vehicles that later became the Tank Mk I. An order for 100 was placed in February 1916 and the tank had arrived.

The American Holt tractor was obtained for use as a heavy artillery tractor but also served as the inspiration for the trials vehicles that led eventually to the tank. The tracks were very similar to those adopted for use on 'Little Willie'.

Above: 'Little Willie' in pristine form at the William Foster and Co works in Lincoln, complete with the original form of wheeled steering tail. This body form was later adapted with the large 'lozenge' tracks to form the basis of 'Mother', the first of the real combat tanks. 'Little Willie' is now in the Tank Museum at Bovington, Dorset.

Below: 'Mother' shows her paces in Poppleton's Field, Lincoln, on 14 January 1916. Other such obstacles were later constructed in Hatfield Park for demonstrations in front of the Landship Committee and other VIPs. 'Mother' took them all in her stride, and the vehicle was ordered into large scale production.

Tank Mk IV

The **Tank Mk IV** was the most numerous type used during World War I, and benefited from all the many design and tactical lessons that had been so desperately hard-won since the service debut of the Tank Mk I. Only relatively small numbers of the **Tank Mk II** and **Tank Mk III** had been built (50 of each), and most of these were converted to stores carriers and special-duties. The Mk II featured a wider track shoe at every sixth link, and the Mk III had better armour. When the Mk IV appeared in March 1917 it was the forerunner of a batch of 1,000 that had been ordered in the previous year, the design originating in October 1916.

The Mk IV had several changes over the previous three marks, which differed only in small detail. The main change operationally was the introduction of better armour (ranging in thickness from 6 mm/0.24 to 12 mm/ 0.47 in), first used on the Mk III, which had to be introduced as the Germans had quickly developed special anti-tank rifles and armour-piercing ammunition. Another change was to armament. The ex-naval 6-pdr (57-mm) guns of earlier marks were 40 calibres long, and were frequently bent or embedded into the ground when trench-crossing. They were replaced in the Mk IV by much shorter guns only 23 calibres long, and these thereafter remained the standard tank guns for many years. Secondary armament was four Lewis machine-guns. The sponsons for the guns were also made smaller and for transport they could be pushed into the vehicle on rails, whereas on the early marks the sponsons had to be removed altogether for transport. Numerous internal mechanical changes were introduced and an 'unditching' beam was placed ready for use above the hull.

The Mk IV carried over an armament concept that was introduced originally on the Mk I. This was the concept that certain tanks carried four primary machine-guns (two in each sponson) and two secondary guns, the 6-pdr (57-mm) guns being omitted. These were used for direct infantry support and trench-clearing, the variant being known as the **Tank Mk IV (Female)** in differentiation from the gun-armed **Tank Mk IV (Male)**. There was also a variant with machine-guns in one sponson and a 6-pdr (57-mm) gun in the other and known as the **Tank Mk IV (Hermaphrodite)**.

It was the Mk IV that was used to such good effect at Cambrai and many of the tank battles thereafter, and after 1918 the Mk IV was retained by the Tank Corps for many years. Some were used in the Palestine battles and after the war they were used during the internal 'Troubles' in Ireland. A few were handed over to the Italians but perhaps the greatest users after the British were the Germans; almost inevitably many Mk IVs fell into the hands of the Germans, who then used them against the British, naming the type the **Beutepanzerwagen IV** (captured armoured vehicle). Like the British, the Germans used more Mk IVs than any other armoured vehicle. Other Mk IV variants were the **Mk IV Supply Tank**, the **Mk IV Tadpole Tank**, with length increased by 2.74 m (9 ft) at the rear for better trench-crossing, and the **Mk IV Fascine Tank**, fitted to carry trench-filling fascines (chain-bound wood bundles some 1.37 m/4 ft 6 in in diameter). There was also a crane version for salvage duties.

A Tank Mk IV (Female). The early tanks used water-cooled Vickers machine-guns, but these were soon replaced by air-cooled Hotchkiss machine-guns. Some Mk IVs, known as Hermaphrodites, were Female on one side and Male on the other with a 6-pdr gun to provide a more balanced weapon arrangement.

Specification
Tank Mk IV (Male)
Crew: 8
Weight: 28 tons
Powerplant: one 105- or 125-hp (78.3- or 93.2-kW) Daimler petrol engine
Dimensions: length 8.05 m (26 ft 5 in); width over sponsons 3.91 m (12 ft 7 in); height 2.49 m (8 ft 2 in)
Performance: maximum speed 6 km/h (3.7 mph); range 56 km (35 miles)

Tank Mk V

The **Tank Mk V** was the last of the classic lozenge-shaped tanks to serve in any numbers, and embodied all the improvements introduced on the Mk IV together with the Wilson epicyclic gearbox that enabled the tank to be driven by one man, the earlier marks depending on the actions of two men and a great deal of team-work for steering. The Mk V also had a purpose-built engine, the 150-hp (112-kW) Ricardo, which not only gave more power but made life for the engineers inside the confines of the hull a great deal easier. Another innovation was the introduction of a cupola for the commander and at long last provision was made for communication with the outside world by the mounting of semaphore arms on the back of the hull. Until then a tank crew was virtually isolated from other troops not only by the great noise produced by the engine but by poor vision devices and no method of passing messages in or out. The early tanks could communicate only by sending pigeons to the rear if required. Main armament of the male version was two 6-pdr (57-mm) guns, supplemented by four Hotchkiss machine-guns, and the armour varied in thickness from 6 mm (0.24 in) to 14 mm (0.55 in).

About 400 Mk Vs had been built in Birmingham by the time of the Armistice, but even by then the mark had begun to sprout variants. The first introduced was a new 1.83-m (6-ft) section into the hull to improve trench-crossing capabilities and also to provide more internal space for personnel (up to 25 troops) or stores. This was the **Tank Mk V***, which was converted in the field, while the comparable but much improved **Tank Mk V**** was introduced on the production lines. As with the Mk IV, this improved vehicle was produced in **Tank Mk V (Male)** and **Tank Mk VI (Female)** forms.

The Mk V was also the first American tank. Enough Mk Vs were passed to the newly-arrived US Army partially to equip a battalion together with some French FT 17s.

Post-war the Mk V was used as the standard equipment of the Tank Corps, and although there were several designs based on the Mk V, none was produced or used in any numbers. The Mk V was used for all manner of experiments that ranged from bridge-laying to mine-clearing with variations of the **Tank Mk V** (Tank RE)**, but never in any great numbers for the years after 1918 were not financially conducive to such innovations. Numbers of Mk Vs were passed to armies such as that of Canada, where they remained in use into the early 1930s.

The Mk V never had the chance to replace the earlier Mk IV, although it arrived on the Western Front from about mid-1918 onwards. It proved to be far more reliable and easy to use than the earlier marks, but the war ended before it could take part in the massive armoured operations that had been planned for 1919. Those plans called for the massed use of Mk Vs along with some special tanks that never left the drawing board (supply tanks, armoured recovery vehicles etc.) along chosen sectors of front. They were to be used in a manner in which the infantry was to have little part to play as the tanks alone would sweep all before them and achieve the big 'breakthrough' that had been sought for so desperately and expensively since 1914. But the Armistice thankfully put paid to 'Plan 1919' and the world had to wait until 1939 and 1940 for the envisaged *Blitzkrieg*.

Using a cable, a Tank Mk V (Male) assists another tank out of difficulties in August 1918. The Mk V carries red-white-red recognition stripes at the front. The rails over the top are for unditching beams.

Specification
Tank Mk V (Male)
Crew: 8
Weight: 29 tons
Powerplant: one 150-hp (112-kW) Ricardo petrol engine
Dimensions: length 8.05 m (26 ft 5 in); width over sponsons 4.11 m (13 ft 6 in); height 2.64 m (8 ft 8 in)
Performance: maximum speed 7.4 km/h (4.6 mph); range 72 km (45 miles)

The Mk IV and Mk V in Action

First introduced in June 1917, the British Mk IV and its Mk V successor were to become the workhorses of Allied tank operations, being used in large numbers during the offensives of 1918.

When the first Mk I tanks were ordered into action along the Somme in the autumn of 1916 they were unprepared as regards training and as to the mechanical efficiency of their machines. As if this were not enough, the tanks were called upon to perform miracles. They were dispersed in ones and twos along the front but were still expected to provide the magic punch that would break the German lines. To do this they were asked to make their way across shell-torn ground which was so wet that it swallowed artillery trains without trace, and to top it all in some places the tanks were expected to cross swollen rivers and streams. The tank officers pleaded in vain for some sort of sense to be instilled in their orders, but the military mind of the day was such that attrition had become the standard tactic, and the tanks were just another handy weapon for this system.

The Somme offensive shuddered to a bloody halt in the last days of 1916. A great opportunity to use the tank to good effect had been wasted along the Somme, and already the Germans were studying the few tanks captured along the Somme and developing a special armour-piercing bullet to penetrate the armour. By the time the Mk I and the few new Mk IIs went into action again at Bullecourt in the snow of 11 April 1917, these new armour-piercing rounds were in use, proving effective to the extent that some tanks were lost. Thereafter each German soldier carried at least five rounds of the new 'K' ammunition and machine-gunners got much more.

The arrival of this new ammunition was duly noted by the British, who already had some ideas for future tank improvements as a result of the dearly-won lessons of 1916. One lesson was that the method of securing the armour onto the tank hull would have to be revised. Even conventional bullets fired against the armour found their way into the interior in the form of lead 'splash' that could cause some nasty wounds for the crew. When combined with the thicker armour that was proof against the German 'K' rounds, the construction of the new Mk IV promised far better protection; and coupled with the improved interior ventilation life for the tank crews looked far more promising, experience gained during the first Mk IV battle seeming to bear this out.

The Mk IVs went into action at Messines on 7 June 1917. Messines was one of those massive set-piece battles favoured by the British in view of the masses of semi-trained infantry provided by a citizen's army which proved to be inflexible in military skills. The battle started with the usual preliminary artillery bombardment, which was followed by a relative novelty, a series of large mines under the German lines being detonated all at the same instant. The tanks were to be used in their usual role: accompaniment for the infantry to knock out machine-gun nests.

Some 76 of the new Mk IVs were to be used, of which 72 were in the immediate front line ready for the off the night before. In nearly all the tank battles the tanks were placed on their starting lines the previous night. This involved a great deal of preparation and many difficulties, for the tank crews had poor vision at the best of times and in the dark things were much worse. The noise of the engines prevented voice communications, so there was usually no other recourse but to lay down, well in advance, markers such as white tapes or posts to guide the way. The tank crews had to rely on these or guides who walked in front, but all too often the guides never turned up or the tapes were knocked down by artillery fire. Thus the crews had to navigate using large-scale maps, a special tank compass and their intuition. After a while the tank crews grew to be very good at finding their own way in the dark, to the extent that the infantry grew to rely on their guidance rather than the other way round. But it was a slow and tiring business that often took all night, and the crews were exhausted before the battle even began.

Messines was no different. Once the mines went up the tanks lumbered forward along with the infantry waves. The front lines were taken from the German infantry, who were dazed by the blast and shock of the mines, and the tanks lumbered on to the next objective. One Mk IV earned itself a great deal of praise by knocking out machine-gun posts in the village of Wytschaeta (White Sheet to the British) and making things easy for the infantry. Some tanks then got stuck in the mud that prevailed across the battlefield, but were able to act as static pillboxes and provide supporting machine-gun fire.

First blood

The battle then petered to the usual halt, for the tanks had been assigned secondary objectives in a battle that overall had only limited objectives. They had generally proved themselves effective and the new armour of the Mk IVs proved to be able to stand up to the German 'K' armour-piercing ammunition.

Thereafter the Mk IVs were called upon to provide support in two more minor affairs before they were duly given their big chance. For some time the tank staff officers had been har-

A Tank Mk IV in use by the Germans – note the circular flame-thrower pack in the foreground. To the Germans such tanks were known as 'beute Panzer', and the Germans used more of them in action than their own A7V. This appears to be a Mk IV Male.

rying the general staff to allow them to wage a battle on terms that would suit the tanks, over ground that had not been churned up by repeated artillery bombardments, and with the tanks massed in numbers that would overwhelm the opposition. At last the tanks were given their chance and they then fought the epic battle that history has dignified as the 1st Battle of Cambrai, on 20 November 1917.

For a number of reasons the Cambrai sector had not attracted the attentions of the artillery as had some other sectors. The general lie of the country is flat and open, but it was made difficult in 1917 by no less than three lines of deep trenches. The tanks would have to cross these, and the tank crews accordingly devised a drill whereby three tanks worked in teams and used bundles of timber known as fascines to cross the trenches. Each tank in turn would drop its fascine into a trench and the others would then cross. To make the going easier for

A Tank Mk V and triumphant New Zealand infantry soon after the capture of Grevillers on 25 August 1918. Some troops are hitching a lift on the tank, which belonged to the 10th Battalion Tank Corps and appears to be moving up into action again.

The Mk IV and Mk V in Action

the tanks no previous artillery bombardment was to be made, and this would also add the element of surprise.

No fewer than 378 combat tanks were to take part in the battle, plus a further 98 supporting vehicles such as Mk Is fitted out with radio to provide the rear with the details of the events as they unfolded. There were also numbers of supply tanks carrying ammunition and fuel. The Royal Flying Corps was to be involved in scouting and the subsequent artillery observation.

Everything was ready on the morning of 20 November, and at 06.00 the battle started. The tanks were led into action by their commander, General Hugh Elles, and they soon advanced into the mist and crossed the front trenches. The drills and practice then paid off, for not only did they cross the first trenches but the second and third line as well. The effect of the tanks appearing out of the mist was too much for many of the hapless German infantry, who in

many cases simply left their trenches and ran to the rear, but in many locations isolated machine-gunners stayed at their posts until they were literally crushed by the tank tracks. Once past the trenches the tanks were in open country and they advanced no less than 8 km (5 miles) at one point, far more than the advances of all the Somme battles in five months during the year before.

The tanks did not have it all their own way, for at one point a single German field gun was able to knock out several tanks. Others came to grief in deep ditches, and others again were knocked out as they tried to charge directly against German batteries. But in general all the objectives were reached and the wire was cleared for the promised cavalry to storm through.

The cavalry did not arrive, and in the resultant and expected German counterattacks all the ground that had been gained was lost. The main cause of this failure was later traced to the higher staff levels where the promised success of the Tank Corps was treated with a great deal of scepticism: they did not expect the tanks to be successful, and thus the reserves available were too far away from the scene of the action to be of any use in holding the gains won by the tanks. The tanks could not hold the ground alone, and had to be withdrawn to regroup and replenish their supplies; the infantry who had advanced with them were too few in number to hold the large areas taken. Thus Cambrai ended with no tangible gains in terms of territory, but the tanks had proved their point. Provided they were able to operate on terms that suited them and in sufficient numbers they could carry the day and the battle. Their point had been made and thereafter the higher echelons should have heeded that point.

But that lesson was not immediately learned. The next major action in which the tanks played a part was once again on the Somme, in a battle that was being planned even before

This photograph purports to show American Mk Vs attacking German trenches during October 1918, but it has that undefinable air of a 'posed' shot; pictures of tanks actually in action are rare. The Americans used the Mk V along with some French Renault FT 17 light tanks in their first armoured units.

To the ordinary German soldier, used to mass infantry attacks, the slow, ponderous approach of seemingly invulnerable tanks had a terrifying effect.

Cambrai. Once again the tanks were dispersed in small numbers along a wide front, so although they were able to provide local support and knock out local strongpoints, they could not prevail. This time the battle had been planned by the Germans, and was the first in the series of breakthrough battles that started on 21 March 1918. The Germans broke through in many places and as they advanced the few tanks available locally provided support for the retreating British units. Many tanks were lost during this period, more from lack of fuel than any operational reason, and eventually the German advances ground to a halt, but not before they had thoroughly rattled the Allied commanders.

Allied strength increases

Although it was not apparent at that time, the March battles were the last major efforts the Germans could produce. Worn down by years of economic blockade and lack of essential supplies, the German army was growing short of men and munitions. For the Allies things were at last going the other way. The Americans were arriving in appreciable numbers and were instrumental in halting the German advance at Château-Thierry. And to add to future prospects the first of the new Mk Vs arrived in France ready to go into action in July. The number of tanks and trained crews was also increasing in leaps and bounds, and by mid-1918 no fewer than 15 complete battalions were ready for use.

In the series of battles that culminated in the Armistice one small example stands out as a text-book specimen of inter-arm co-operation and planning. This was the action at Hamel on 4 July 1918, when for the first time Australian infantry worked with the tanks. In this limited-objective action aircraft flew over the front as the tanks assembled and a brief but effective artillery barrage presaged the attack. The tanks then advanced, supporting their Australian partners right up to the planned objective. Once this had been reached, supply tanks came forward with enough supplies to ensure that the troops could hold the ground; and the tanks remained around long enough to knock out any machine-guns that had escaped their previous attentions. The result was an action in which there were, for the Western Front, very small casualties; the five tanks knocked out were all later recovered.

The largest of all the tank battles was the Battle of Amiens which started on 8 August 1918. The number of tanks involved was no fewer than 450, but some of these were held as reserves and to back up this main strength there were a further 118 supply tanks. The tanks were organized in 12 battalions, eight of them equipped with the Mk V, two with the Mk V* and two with the Medium Mk A Whippet.

At Amiens there were no half measures. As the tanks assembled their noise was masked by low-flying aircraft and artillery, and in the morning light the tanks moved forward along the British 4th Army's front. The breakthrough

was soon made, and the German lines crumbled. As the tanks advanced they were joined by an armoured car battalion that was helped across the battlefield by the tanks, and once in the open the armoured cars spread out and struck deep into the German rear. One armoured car even managed to shoot up a train and capture its crew. The disruption was total, the first advance penetrating as deep as 12 km (7½ miles). Numerous tanks were knocked out, mainly by the field guns that were emerging as the tanks' only major counter-weapon, but many of these casualties were recovered for later use.

This time the cavalry did move forward, but once past the lines soon proved incapable of advancing against even single machine-guns and of moving at the same speed as the Whippets. If proof was needed that the cavalry was no longer viable in modern warfare, the Battle of Amiens provided that proof.

The advances were held and the next blow was prepared. This fell during a series of actions at Bapaume, Arras, Epéhy, Cambrai (again), Catelet-Bony and Selle. These battles usually involved the tanks advancing in close co-operation with the infantry as the artillery supplied support and aircraft scouted above. The degree of co-operation was total, to an extent that was not relearned until well after 1940, and the results rolled up the German lines and sent the Germans gradually back towards Germany. The Armistice was declared finally on 11 November and World War I ended.

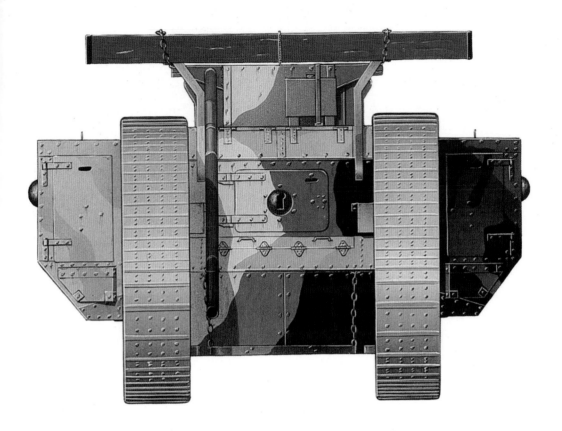

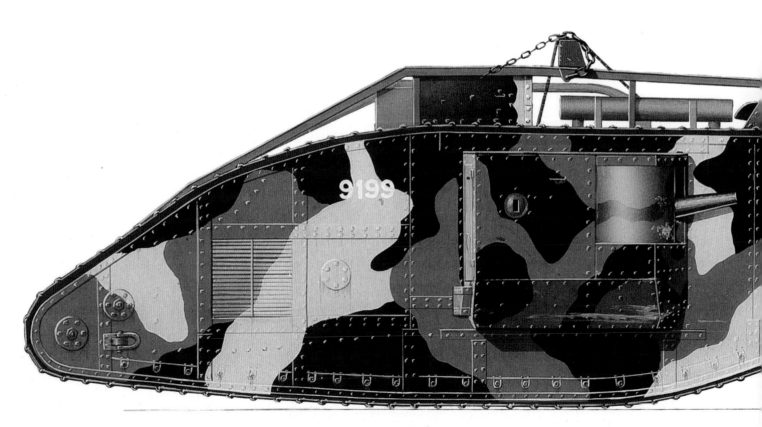

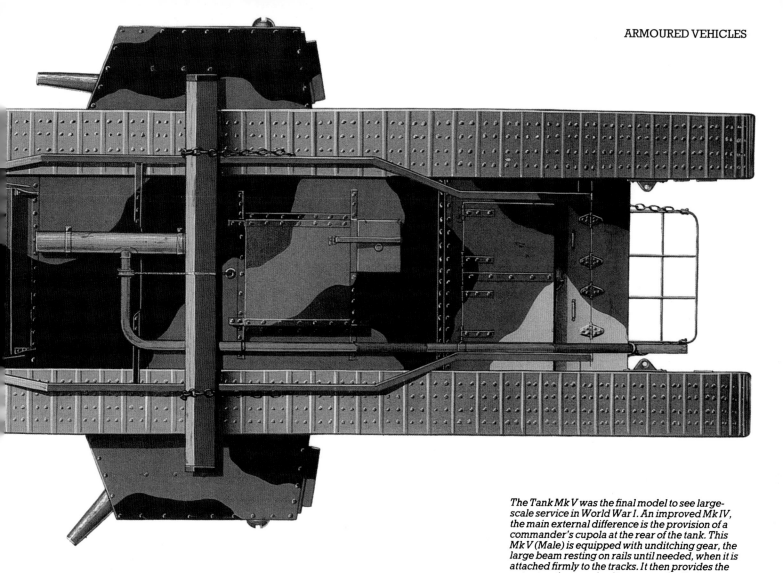

The Tank Mk V was the final model to see large-scale service in World War I. An improved Mk IV, the main external difference is the provision of a commander's cupola at the rear of the tank. This Mk V (Male) is equipped with unditching gear, the large beam resting on rails until needed, when it is attached firmly to the tracks. It then provides the extra traction required to get out of a ditch.

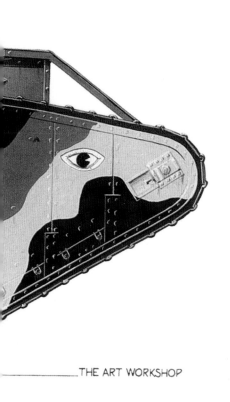

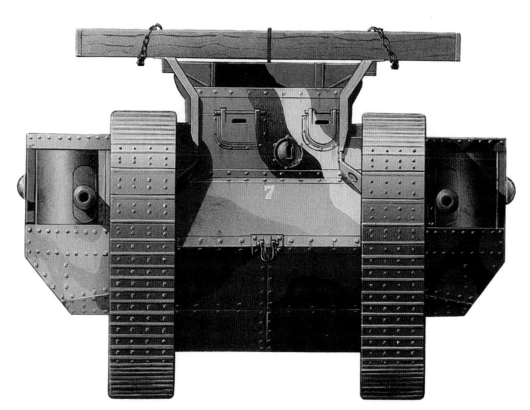

THE ART WORKSHOP

Rolls-Royce armoured car

When the Royal Naval Air Service went to war in 1914 it sent a variegated squadron of aircraft and vehicles to France and Belgium. Once there, some of the naval officers noted the way in which the Belgians were using armoured cars to harry the advancing Germans and to carry out raiding and other missions, and decided to join in. Within a few days some of the **Rolls-Royce Silver Ghost** touring cars used by the RNAS were converted in Dunkirk to carry armour plating on the sides. A single machine-gun was carried behind the driver. The Admiralty noted the success of the conversion and gave its sanction to the design of proper armoured cars based on the Silver Ghost chassis, and the first of these official designs was in France by the end of 1914.

The official Rolls-Royce armoured car, sometimes known as the **Armoured Car, Rolls-Royce (1914 Admiralty Turreted Pattern)**, was a straightforward conversion of the civilian Silver Ghost tourer with a turret and armour added. The springs were strengthened to take the extra weight but that was all the modification required on the chassis. The armour extended all around the chassis, and the turret, which mounted a Vickers or Maxim machine-gun, had peculiar sloping sides rather like the shape of a bishop's mitre. The radiator had an armoured door and the roof armour on the turret could be removed if required. A small area behind the turret was left open to carry stores and a ground-mounted machine-gun. Once in service the Rolls-Royce armoured cars proved very successful, remaining in service until 1922. Maximum armour thickness was 9 mm (0.35 in).

By March 1915 the first RNAS armoured car squadrons were in being in France, most of them equip-

This 1914 Rolls-Royce armoured car has the original Admiralty pattern turret, mounting a Vickers 7.7 mm (0.303 in) machine-gun. These cars provided sterling service throughout the war and many remained in use for years afterwards, especially in India and the African colonies.

ped with the Rolls-Royce. Before that the RNAS armoured cars carried out some patrols and reconnaissance work along the French and Belgian coastal areas until the 'Race to the Sea' reached the Channel Coast and trench warfare became the norm. Once that was in progress there was little enough for the Rolls-Royces to do and as more squadrons were established they

A Rolls-Royce armoured car and its crew are shown at a Guards Division casualty evacuation point near Guillemont during September 1916; the Somme Offensive was at its height. Note the anti-mud chains around the tyres of the rear wheels and the lack of front mudguards.

were used for anti-invasion patrols along the east coast of England. When the first formal armoured car squadrons were sent to France they had little to do, so eventually these RNAS armoured car squadrons were disbanded, the car being handed over to a generally uninterested British army.

Rolls-Royce armoured cars were thereafter used on other fronts and in the overseas theatres of war such as the North West Frontier in India, at Gallipoli (where they could accomplish nothing), German South West Africa (where they accomplished much during a campaign about which little is known) and in Uganda. It was in the Western Desert and the Arabian peninsula that the Rolls-Royce

Street scene in Arras, April 1917, with Rolls-Royce armoured cars and their crews awaiting a move. All the cars are well loaded with the crews' gear and equipment, and the ever-present muddy conditions have dictated the use of tyre chains on the rear drive wheels.

armoured cars and a number of similar armoured tenders (like the armoured car but without the turret and used for carrying stores or personnel) made their greatest impact. There they proved to be remarkably reliable, fast and capable of crossing some very rough country.

The Rolls-Royce armoured cars soldiered on until 1922 when they began to be replaced by a modernized version, the **Armoured Car, Rolls-Royce (1920 Pattern)**. Even so, some of the old Pattern 1914 cars lasted until well into World War II in India.

Specification
Armoured Car, Rolls-Royce (1914 Admiralty Turreted Pattern)
Crew: 3 or 4
Weight: 3.5 tons
Powerplant: 40/50-hp (30/37.3-kW) Rolls-Royce petrol engine
Dimensions: length 5.03 m (16 ft 6 in); width 1.91 m (6 ft 3 in); height 2.55 m (8 ft 4½ in)
Performance: maximum speed 95 km/h (60 mph); range 240 km (150 miles)

Lanchester armoured car

After the Rolls-Royce armoured car, the **Armoured Car, Lanchester (Admiralty Turreted Pattern)** was the most numerous in service with the Royal Naval Air Service (RNAS) armoured car squadrons that had sprung up by the end of 1914. Originally these armoured cars were supposed to provide support for the air bases and to retrieve downed airmen, but it was not long before they were used in more offensive roles. By the beginning of 1915 they were being

organized into formal armoured car squadrons as part of a larger Royal Naval Armoured Car Divisions.

In appearance the Lanchester armoured car was very similar in layout to the Rolls-Royce and also had a turret with sloping sides. However, the Lanchester had sloping armour over the front of the bonnet in place of the more angular bonnet of the Rolls-Royce. It was originally a civilian touring car but by the time the Admiralty designers had been at work little of the

original bodywork remained. However, the engine was retained for not only did it provide a useful 60 hp (44.7 kW) but it had many advanced design features for its day, along with a very advanced epicyclic gearbox.

When the Royal Navy armoured cars were handed over to the army in August 1915 the latter decided that the collection of designs it received was too varied for logistic and operational comfort. It thus decided to standardize the Rolls-Royce design, and the Lan-

chesters were put to one side. They did not remain neglected for long for in October 1915 they were gathered together in England. The following year they were organized as No. 1 Squadron of the Royal Naval Armoured Car Division and sent to Russia. Once there they took part in no end of campaigns about which little has been recorded. For much of the time the Lanchesters had to travel on their own wheels across country where few roads existed, and were used in Persia, Romania and Galicia, operating in climates that varied from desert heat to near-Arctic conditions. But they kept going. For much of their operational life the Lanchesters were used in a manner that anticipated what was later to become the norm in armoured warfare. They acted as the spearhead of large motorized columns carrying troops on armoured lorries and personnel trucks that ranged far and wide over the wastes of southern Russia and the Iraq deserts. They acted as scouts, fire-support vehicles and general raiders, roles in which the Lanchesters proved reliable and fast.

The Lanchester remained with the Russians until the final failure of the Brusilov Offensive in mid-1917. Thereafter Russian sank into the throes of internal disruption and revolution, and there was no part the Lanchester squadron could play in such internal conflicts. Thus they were shipped back to the United Kingdom with well over 53,000 miles added to their speedometer clocks.

Above: A Lanchester armoured car in 1914 RNAS markings. These vehicles never gained the fame accorded to the Rolls-Royce armoured cars, but at the time were just as important in service. Many were later used in Russia from 1916 to 1917 with Royal Navy crews.

Right: Royal Navy Lanchester armoured cars in Russia during 1917. These vehicles motored thousands of miles in support of the Russians fighting the Germans and carried out scouting and raiding operations that covered many miles on all parts of the Russian front, including the Brisilov Offensive in mid-1917.

Specification
Armoured Car, Lanchester (Admiralty Turreted Pattern)
Crew: 4
Weight: 4.8 tons
Powerplant: one 60-hp (45-kW) Lanchester petrol engine
Dimensions: length 4.88 m (16 ft 0 in); width 1.93 m (6 ft 4 in); height 2.286 m (7 ft 6 in)
Performance: maximum speed 80 km/h (50 mph); range 290 km (180 miles)

Autoblindo Mitragliatrice Lancia Ansaldo IZ

The first **Lancia modello IZ** was not an armoured car but a small truck that mounted on the rear a form of expanding fireman's ladder which was used by 102-mm (4-in) artillery units for the observation of fire. While this was certainly a military function it was not long after, in 1915, that the truck was drastically adapted to become an armoured car known as the **Autoblindo Mitragliatrice Lancia Ansaldo IZ**. For its day the IZ was quite an advanced design. Its layout was conventional, with the engine forward and the main driver's position behind a fully armoured sloping plate. The main fighting compartment was in a box structure at the rear which mounted a squat round turret with a single machine-gun. On some later versions this turret arrangement was revised to accommodate a second but smaller turret on top of the first, enabling another machine-gun to be carried. A further variation that was almost universally adopted was to place two machine-guns in the lower turret so the IZ was quite heavily armed for a vehicle of its size.

Prominent on the IZ were the twin steel rails that extended from the driver's position to a point below and in front of the wheels. These rails were intended for wire-cutting. Later versions had even more protection against wire by an extension of the armour over the wheels both at the front and rear. Armoured shutters were used to protect the radiator at the front. Firing ports were provided around the top of the hull, and there was provision for another machine-gun at the rear of the hull. The rear of the hull also had provision for a rack to

hold a bicycle if required. Maximum armour thickness was 9 mm (0.35 in).

For much of the war the Italian armoured car units could contribute little to the campaigns against Austria-Hungary as most of the fighting took place in mountainous regions where wheeled vehicles had little chance to operate. A small force of 39 IZ armoured cars did a certain amount of reconnaissance along the Piave during the fighting along that front, and contributed to the limited period of fluid fighting in the aftermath of the Austro-German breakthrough of 1917. After that there was little enough they could

do and some were sent over to North Africa for policing duties. By 1918 about 120 such cars had been produced, and these remained in use for some years thereafter. A few were handed over to Albania during the post-war period and long remained the sole equipment for the small armoured element of the new nation.

The Autoblinda Mitragliatrice Lancia Ansaldo IZ, one of the better armoured car designs of World War I, mounted a twin machine-gun armament in its circular turret. These cars proved to be remarkably durable; some were still in use during the Spanish Civil War of 1936-8 in Italian army hands.

Specification
Autoblindo Mitragliatrice Lancia Ansaldo IZ
Crew: 6
Weight: 3.8 tons
Powerplant: one 35/40-hp (26/30-kW) petrol engine
Dimensions: length 5.40 m (17 ft 8⅔ in); width 1.824 m (6 ft 0 in); height with single turret 2.40 m (7 ft 10½ in)
Performance: maximum speed 60 km/h (37 mph); range 300 km (186 miles)

Char d'Assaut Schneider

The basis of the **Char d'Assaut Schneider** (or Schneider CA) was developed under the aegis of General Estienne, who envisaged an armoured tractor to tow armoured sledges carrying troops across the Western Front batlefields in a surprise assault on German trenches. For the basis of his armoured tractor Estienne proposed using the track and chassis of the American Holt agricultural tractor which was then (1915) becoming widely used as an artillery tractor. By going direct to General Joffre, the French commander-in-chief, Estienne was able to obtain support for his proposal, and the armament concern Schneider became involved as the development agency.

The original proposals called for 200 Schneider CAs by the end of 1916, but development and production were so slow that it was not until the middle of 1917 that appreciable numbers were ready for use. The Schneider CA emerged as what was basically an armoured box mounted over a virtually unaltered Holt tractor suspension and track. The box mounted two machine-guns and a short 75-mm (2.95-in) gun to one side forward. The engine developed 55 hp (41 kW) and was fed from two petrol tanks that were situated near the machine-gun mountings. These tanks proved very vulnerable to enemy fire, to the extent that a single armour-piercing bullet could set the tank on fire, a fate that befell many Schneider CAs once they moved into action. Maximum armour thickness was 11.5 mm (0.45 in), increased to 19.5 mm (0.77 in) on late vehicles. The idea of the armoured personnel-carrying sledge had been dropped, and the Schneiders were used mainly for infantry support in the manner of the day. They proved to be less than successful in this role for their cross-country capabilities were severely restricted. By May 1917 some 300 had been produced, but thereafter the gun version was replaced in production by the **Schneider Char de Ravitaillement** stores-carrying version, on which the right-hand gun position was replaced by a door opening into the stores-carrying area. Extra 8-mm (0.31-in) armour was added to the sides of most examples as the result of experience in action, and perhaps the greatest

Schneider tanks move up to the front near L'Eglantiers on the Oise. The short 75-mm (2.95-in) gun was on the right of the superstructure, but one machine-gun ball mounting can be seen on this side. The crew are riding on top to avoid the uncomfortable heat of the engine inside.

contribution made by the Schneider CA was that as the result of hard experience the French army learned how to use and maintain armoured vehicles in the field. The French set up their first armour school at Champlieu in October 1916 and soon learned that lack of maintenance and lack of spares could remove a vehicle from the field as thoroughly as enemy action. Some of the early operations were fiascos as the result of lack of training and maintenance, typical of these being the attack on the Chemin des Dames in April 1917, when 76 out of a total of 132 Schneider CAs taking part were lost.

The last Schneider CA was delivered in August 1918, but by then attrition and a move towards the Renault FT 17 had reduced the numbers in service to under 100. Most of these were the unarmed supply version but the gun Schneiders had taken their part in a number of operations during 1918, enjoying a degree of success in some. But the Schneider CA was an unstable and indifferent performer on the Western Front and proved too prone to catching fire when hit. The best that can now be said of them is that they taught the French army a great deal about the limitations and possibilities of armoured warfare.

Specification
Char d'Assaut Schneider

The Char d'Assaut Schneider proved less than effective when first introduced to the field. The short tracks and the long body combined to give a bad obstacle-crossing capability, even with the extra 'nose and tail' ramps. The armour was thin and the vehicle burned easily.

Crew: 7
Weight: 14.6 tons
Powerplant: one 55-hp (41-kW) Schneider four-cylinder petrol engine
Dimensions: length 6.0 m (19 ft 8 in); width 2.0 m (6 ft 6⅔ in); height 2.39 m (7 ft 10 in)
Performance: maximum speed 6 km/h (3.7 mph); range 48 km (30 miles)

Char d'Assaut St Chamond

The development of the Schneider CA had by-passed the normal French army supply channels, which miffed some of the normal supply authorities to the extent that they decided to proceed with their own tank design. Using one Colonel Rimailho as the designer, the French army set about producing its own original design, and by early 1916 the first prototype had been built at the Saint Chamond factory at Homecourt, from which the new vehicle became generally known as the **Char d'Assaut St Chamond**. As with the Schneider CA, development and production were slow, so it was not until May 1917 that the first service examples were in action.

Even for a 'first try' the St Chamond CA had several unusual features. Like the Schneider CA it was based on the suspension, track and chassis of the Holt tractor, but on the St Chamond CA the track was lengthened to provide more track length on the ground. The drive to the track was unusual in that a petrol engine was used to drive an electric transmission. While this petrol-electric transmission worked, it was also a heavy and bulky system that meant the projected design weight was exceeded by over 5 tons. This overweight feature was not assisted by the configuration of the hull, which extended both forward and to the rear of the track to the extent that whenever the vehicle had to traverse rough ground or cross even the shortest trench it became stuck as the hull dug in. In service this proved a considerable drawback, for the Germans soon learned of the St Chamond CA's poor

trench-crossing performance and widened their trenches accordingly. The St Chamond CA mounted a conventional Modèle 1897 75-mm (2.95-in) field gun in the front of the hull, and it was possible to mount as many as four machine-guns around the hull. Maximum armour thickness was 17 mm (0.67 in).

The poor cross-country performance of the St Chamond CA so severely restricted its use in action as 1917 progressed that the type was gradually replaced by the newer Renault FT

17, and many were converted to **St Chamond Char de Ravitaillement** supply carriers. They took part in their last major action as gun tanks in July 1918, when 131 took part in a counter-attack near Reims. By the end of the war there were only 72 out of the production run of 400 left in service. Although the St Chamond CA had many novel features that pointed the way ahead (the forward-mounted 75-mm/2.95-in gun, the petrol-electric drive and the lengthened track), it was basically an unsound design of poor cross-country capability, and in action proved to have only limited value.

Specification
Char d'Assaut St Chamond
Crew: 9
Weight: 23 tons
Powerplant: one 90-hp (67-kW) Panhard four-cylinder petrol engine powering a Crochat-Collardeau electric transmission
Dimensions: length with gun 8.83 m (28 ft 11¾ in); length of hull 7.91 m (25 ft 11½ in); width 2.67 m (8 ft 9 in); height 2.34 m (7 ft 5⅔ in)
Performance: maximum speed 8.5 km/h (5.3 mph); range 59 km (36.7 miles)

Above: The Char d'Assaut St Chamond was even longer and clumsier than the Schneider, and the long hull so restricted its use in action that it was often relegated to the supply tank role. It had a powerful weapon potential, having four machine-guns and a 75-mm (2.95-in) gun, and had an advanced petrol-electric drive.

Right: Char d'Assaut St Chamond tanks move forward near Moyennville on the Oise in 1917. This picture provides a good indication of the great bulk and shape of these tanks compared with the limited length of track run; note also the limited ground clearance under the hull.

FRANCE
Renault FT 17

The little **Renault FT 17** was without a doubt one of the most successful of all the World War I tanks. It had its origins in the proposals put forward in 1915 by the far-sighted General Estienne, who saw the need for a light armoured vehicle to support infantry operations directly. It was not until mid-1916 that Renault became involved and with a potential order for well over 1,000 examples in prospect the Renault company started to produce a design.

By the end of 1916 the design was ready. It emerged as a two-man tank armed with a machine-gun, and did not meet with general approval at the time. The design was considered too cramped and too lightly armed, but an order was pushed through, and it was not long before a further order for 2,500 was placed. By then the armament had been increased to a 37-mm gun, but many examples were produced with only a single machine-gun.

The FT 17 design was the first of what can now be seen as the classic tank design. It had its armament in a small turret with a 360° traverse, and the thin hull had the tracks on each side. There was no chassis as such, the components being built directly onto the armoured hull. The engine was at the rear, the tracks each had a large forward idler wheel that proved ideal for obstacle clearing, and to enhance trench-crossing capability a frame 'tail' was often fitted to the rear.

Renault were unable to produce the numbers required so production batches were farmed out to other concerns. Even the Americans became involved, but as they insisted that their FT 17s would be built to American standards and methods none arrived in France before the Armistice. In France the original cast armoured turret was often replaced on the produc-

tion lines by an octagonal design using flat armour plates. The 37-mm gun became the virtual norm (**Char-canon FT 17**), although machine-guns could be fitted (**Char-mitrailleuse FT 17**). It was not long before a self-propelled gun version mounting a 75-mm (2.95-in) gun was produced as the **Char-canon Renault BS**, and there was even a special radio version, the **Char Renault TSF**. Maximum armour thickness was 16 mm (0.63 in).

The first FT 17s were delivered to the French army in March 1917 but it was not until May 1918 that they were first used in action. By then the French tactics were to use them en masse but this was not always possible in the face of the constant German attacks under way at that time. At first they were used in relatively small numbers, but by July things had settled down to the point where 480 could be concentrated for a counterattack near Soissons. Here

they were successful, and thereafter the type was used to great effect. One constant worry was maintenance, for the FT 17 had been designed with little thought for repairs and long-term spares holdings, so at any one time hundreds were out of action with various faults. But many more were in the line as the various manufacturers duly delivered the ordered thousands. Some were passed to American troops. As the war ended there were 1,991 FT 17s fit for combat but another 369 were under repair and another 360 out of use.

After 1918 FT 17 remained in large-scale service and was produced or converted to suit a number of new roles such as mobile bridging, more self-propelled artillery, radio versions and so on. In 1939 there were still large numbers in use, and the Germans took over many after the French collapse of 1940. They retained some for their own

The Renault FT 17 was one of the most successful of the World War I tanks. They were produced in thousands, mainly as infantry support light tanks, but many other uses were found for them. Turret armament was either a machine-gun or a short 37-mm (1.45-in) gun, and it had a crew of two.

use until 1944 when many were used by the Germans in the Paris fighting.

Specification
Renault FT 17
Crew: 2
Weight: 6.485 tonnes
Powerplant: one 35-hp (26-kW) Renault four-cylinder petrol engine
Dimensions: length with tail 5.0 m (16 ft 5 in); width 1.71 m (5 ft 7⅓ in); height 2.133 m (7 ft 0 in)
Performance: maximum speed 7.7 km/h (4.8 mph); range 35.4 km (22 miles)

The Specials

Following the introduction of the tank to the shell-smashed battlefields of the Western Front, it became obvious that armour and infantry had to be supported and supplied across no-man's land. Yet no lorries or logistic vehicles could handle the terrain. The problem was, what could keep up with a tank?

One of the features of armoured fighting vehicle design is that almost as soon as a tank is designed it is converted to carry out no end of special purposes. The same thing happened in the years before 1918, for no sooner had the first Mk Is been issued and put in service than they were converted for all manner of other roles.

These other roles usually involved working with the tanks themselves, and many of the conversions made during the early days were made by the troops in the field. The very first of these conversions was to alter Mk I, Mk II and Mk III vehicles from gun tanks into supply tanks. Among the early experiences gained on the Somme battlefields was that when the tanks went forward with their supporting infantry, the securing of an objective (if it were reached) meant that surviving tanks were in need of fuel, ammunition, food and water. As the tanks were the only means of crossing the ravaged ground, it was tanks that had to carry all this despite their limited internal volume.

Thus the supply tanks were created simply by removing the armament from some vehicles and using the space for supplies instead. To add to the load that could be carried a cargo tray was slung between the tracks at the rear and experiments were carried out with towed sledges. In a very short time these supply tanks became an integral part of tank operations on the Western Front, and at Amiens the idea was taken one stage further: if supplies could be carried, why not men? The Mk V* tanks were specially lengthened to increase obstacle-crossing capability, and as a bonus there was more internal space. At Amiens it was decided to carry machine-gun teams to take up positions on the forward objectives and as a result some of the tanks in the first waves carried up to 10 extra men plus their machine-guns. The experiment was not a success, for the heat and fumes inside the tanks proved too much for the unprepared soldiers who were deposited at their allotted locations in no fit state to do anything other than recover. The experiment was not repeated, a later generation of armoured vehicles being needed to bring it to fruition.

The supply tank concept became so accepted that special vehicles were designed for the role. This was the Mk IX supply tank, commonly known as the Pig. It could carry up to 10 tons of stores or (a carry-over from the Amiens experiment) up to 30 men instead of stores. They never got a chance to prove

A Gun Carrier Tank ('Harwich'), with its intended transportable gun removed, is being used as a supply tank near Arras in August 1918. These tanks were mainly used to transport ammunition, as each could carry 200 152-mm (6-in) shells, replacing a carrying party of 300 men. Even so, such employment was a waste of their potential as artillery carriers.

themselves, for the first such vehicle did not arrive in France until October 1918 and took no part in any of the fighting.

Another special tank that came to nothing was the Gun Carrier Tank Mk I. It was developed for the simple reason that the artillery of the day could not be hauled across the rough ground of the Western Front battlefields without a great deal of difficulty. As any advances had to be provided with fire support, the guns had to be got forward somehow to hold any territory that might be won, and this often took too long, the inevitable counterattack being launched before the guns were in position. It seemed that a possible answer lay in carrying the guns on some form of tank and depositing them once they were at their chosen position. Accordingly a special design was put forward in October 1916 and the first example arrived in France in July 1917.

This Gun Carrier Tank Mk I used the mechanical interior of a Mk I allied to a long and low track. The gun, either a 60-pdr or a 152-mm (6-in) howitzer, was carried slung between the two front track horns. The wheels were removed and slung on the vehicle sides and the driver and brakesman sat in two armoured boxes set well forward in front of the gun. The old steering tail of the Mk I tank was retained. A total of 48 of these gun carriers was ordered, and some were used in the 3rd Battle of Ypres; they were little used apart from that. On at least one occasion a carrier was used to carry a 152-mm (6-in) howitzer along various sectors of the front and fire a few harassing rounds, but that was all. Instead the gun carriers were used as supply tanks, carrying forward ammunition. The concept of using the vehicles as gun carriers was simply too novel for the time.

A few Mk Is and some other of the early tank marks were fitted with crane jibs or lifting gantries at some of the huge base workshops that sprang up behind the Allied lines, and a very few were fitted with radios to supply battle information to the rear during actions.

Above: This unusual experiment with a Mk IV tank is using an electromagnet on a 3-ton crane jib to clear unexploded ammunition from the path of intended advances or from ranges. This Mk IV was a salvage tank with its armament removed, and was probably converted at the Erin tank depot.

Above: This Mk IV salvage tank was converted at the Erin tank depot by the addition of sheerlegs and a Weston purchase to become a repair tank.

Above: The Gun Carrier Tank Mk I used the engine and power train of a Mk I tank allied to a new and longer track. It carried a 60-pdr gun or a 152-mm (6-in) howitzer with the wheels removed and slung on the sides. Despite its potential, this tank was little used in its intended role.

Right: This Mk IV has a 'tadpole tail' fitted to improve trench-crossing performance. A platform was added between the tails to increase rigidity, and could be used to carry stores such as the 152-mm (6-in) trench mortar shown here. These tails proved to be unsatisfactory and were not widely used.

FRANCE
Peugeot armoured cars

The first **Peugeot** armoured cars were produced as rather hasty improvisations in 1914, and were typical of their period in that they were based on a commercial model, the 4×2 Peugeot 153. These early conversions used a centrally-mounted machine-gun on a pivot in the centre of the open rear body, but once the design had been formalized this armament was increased to a 37-mm gun. The early slab-sided armour plates (5.5 mm/0.216 in thick) were also revised to provide better all-round protection, but the top was left open.

By the time the purpose-designed Peugeot armoured cars were in service the vehicle scarcely resembled the early improvisations. A sloping armour plate now covered the driver's position and the engine was also armoured. The radiator was protected by steel shutters but the wheels remained as they originally were with their wire spokes, even though the extra weight caused by the armour was partially balanced by the use of dual wheels at the rear. Although a machine-gun could be carried on the central pintle, the more usual weapon was a 37-mm gun behind a curved steel shield. This gun was a half-size version of the famous Modèle 1897 field gun, and could fire a useful high explosive shell. This gave the Peugeot armoured car a modest firepower potential that was sometimes used to support infantry attacks. An alternative to the mix of a 37-mm gun and a machine-gun was a pair of machine-guns. After the end of 1914 there was little enough for these armoured cars to do on the Western Front. A few were used for patrols to the rear of the front, but they could do little else until the relatively small number that remained in use in 1918 were able to take their part in containing the large-scale Ger-

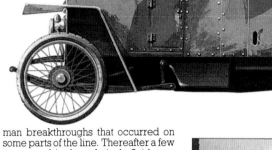

The fully-developed form of the Peugeot armoured car used a short 37-mm (1.45-in) infantry gun as the main armament. Although later replaced in their infantry support role by the FT 17 light tank, they remained in use through World War I and were then passed on to the new Polish army.

man breakthroughs that occurred on some parts of the line. Thereafter a few were used in the relatively fluid warfare that developed. But most of this fighting was carried out by tanks, particularly the FT 17s which prove to be of more use over rough country than the Peugeots with their narrow wheels.

When the war ended the French army still had 28 Peugeot armoured cars in service, but most of these were later handed over to Poland, where they remained in use for some years.

Specification
Autoblindé Peugeot
Crew: 4 or 5
Weight: 5 tons
Powerplant: one 40-hp (30-kW) Peugeot petrol engine
Dimensions: length 4.80 m (15 ft 9 in); width 1.80 m (5 ft 11 in); height 2.80 m (9 ft 2¼ in)
Performance: maximum speed 40 km/h (25 mph); range 140 km (87 miles)

A French army Peugeot armoured car provides fire support for British infantry near Meteran during the Battle of the Lys in April 1918. In such *flat open country these armoured cars were able to provide useful fire support with their gun, but they were often restricted to the available roads.*

GERMANY
Sturmpanzerwagen A7V

For a nation that was normally well to the fore of military technology, Germany was surprisingly slow in appreciating the potential of the tank and, despite some early and far-sighted proposals put forward by various individuals, no interest was taken in any form of armoured vehicle other than armoured cars. That was rectified soon after the first British tanks had made their debut on the Somme battlefields, when a committee was formed to design and produce a German equivalent.

Like so many other designs produced by a committee under time constraints the result of this venture was not a great success. The vehicle be-

came known as the **Sturmpanzerwagen A7V**, the A7V coming from the committee's departmental abbreviation. The design was based on that of the readily-available Holt caterillar track and suspension, but Joseph Vollmer did introduce some suspension modifications to the original that improved the possible speed, these efforts being negated by the location on the basic chassis of a large armoured box structure that held a crew of no fewer than 18 men. This box

had large slab sides with nose and tail arrangements that extended under the body to such an extent that the ground clearance was only about 40 mm (1.57 in). The length of track on the ground was also rather short and the overall result was a vehicle that was inherently unstable and with a very poor cross-country performance. The

main armament was a captured 57-mm Russian gun (mounted at the front) and six machine-guns, each with a crew of two. The one advantage the A7V had over the British tanks was the armour thickness used, ranging from 10 mm (0.39 in) to 30 mm (1.18 mm). By the time production had begun the Germans had developed their own armour-piercing ammunition, and the A7V's armour was proof against this new projectile.

The first A7V was ready by October

The A7V was a large and bulky vehicle with a crew of 18 and carried six machine-guns. The main armament was a 57-mm (2.24-in) gun in the front hull. The A7V proved to have a poor cross-country performance and its height made it rather unstable, and only about 20 were ever produced. Many of these were pressed into action during 1918.

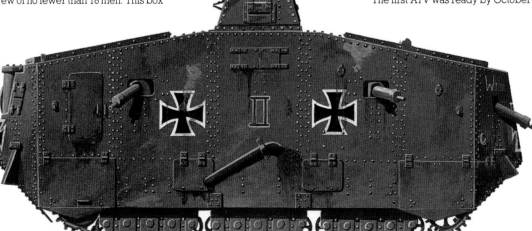

1917, and in December that year 100 were ordered. Production of the A7V involved several firms, all of them already hard put to meet existing production requirements, with the result that by the end of the war only about 20 A7Vs had been produced. In March 1918 the first A7Vs went into action. When used over good going as mobile fire support units they proved successful enough, but over rough ground they proved to be less than successful and some of the first examples soon revealed shortcomings in their special armour plate. The A7V's lack of trench-crossing ability often left the tank behind the infantry it was supposed to support, and all too often when opposed by field artillery firing over open sights the type was easily knocked out.

Three A7Vs took part in the first tank-versus-tank combat on 24 April 1918. This took place at Villers-Bretonneux when three Mk IVs (one Male and two Females) encountered three A7Vs. The two Females were soon damaged and had to retire but the sole Male was able to hit and knock out one of the A7Vs. More tank-versus-tank combats took place later before

the Armistice, but the A7Vs rarely shone. In fact the Germans favoured the various British tanks they were able to capture in place of the A7V, mainly because of the poor cross-country performance of the latter.

Despite the slow production of the A7V the Germans produced an unarmoured supply version with an open top, the **Uberlandwagen**, and even went so far as to attempt to produce the **A7V/U** version with the 'all-round' tracks and sponsons of the British tanks. This venture came to naught, as did the **A7V/U2** and **A7V/U3** projects,

the former having smaller sponsons and the latter being a 'female' version armed only with machine-guns.

Post-war a few took part in the internal German power struggles and a few more were used by the new Polish army for some years.

Specification
Sturmpanzerwagen A7V
Crew: 18
Weight: 33 tons
Powerplant: two 100-hp (74.6-kW) Daimler petrol engines
Dimensions: length 8.0 m (26 ft 3 in);

Two A7Vs as seen from a sector of the French lines in June 1918. The cloud of smoke came mainly from the twin Daimler-Benz petrol engines, but some was no doubt dust thrown up by the tracks. Some of the machine-guns are visible, but the main 57-mm weapon is obscured in the smoke.

width 3.06 m (10 ft 0½ in); height 3.30 m (10 ft 10 in)
Performance: maximum speed 12.9 km/h (8 mph); range 40 km (25 miles)

Panzerkraftwagen Ehrhardt 1915

The very first German armoured cars were in fact special large car or truck chassis adapted to carry a skyward-looking artillery piece for use against observation balloons. There were several of these weapons, collectively known as *Ballon Abwehrkanonen* (BAK), but although some were used for army trials none was taken into large-scale use. It was left to the Belgians in 1914 to demonstrate to the Germans the potential of the armoured car in warfare when the latter were hindered by the hit-and-run raiding carried out by the Minervas and other converted touring cars. The Germans, having suffered somewhat at the hands of the Belgians, decided to produce their own equivalent but having no practical experience of their own to fall back upon approached the design problems in typically Germanic style.

During 1915 the Germans produced prototypes of three different armoured cars. The manufacturers were Ehrhardt, Daimler and Büssing, who all chose to ignore the fact that the Belgian cars were little more than converted touring cars and went instead for what they thought were more suitable vehicles. All three turned out to have one feature in common, in that they were massive. The largest of the three was the Büssing, which used a 'double-ended' layout that could at least boast a high ground clearance. The other two designs were roughly the same and had the armoured engine at the front and a large box-like body at the rear with a turret or cupolas on its top. They were both high clumsy-looking vehicles that were far too heavy for their operational tasks. Some indication of this fact is provided by the knowledge that the Daimler and Ehrhardt designs each had to use double wheels on each side at the rear. All three cars had a crew of eight or nine men and carried at least three machine-guns. Maximum armour thickness was 7 mm (0.28 in).

The three prototypes were formed

The Panzerkraftwagen Ehrhardt 1915 was one of the first examples of a type of high and flat-sided armoured car design that the Germans were to use until almost World War II for internal policing duties. It weighed nearly 9 tons, had a crew of eight or nine men and an armament of up to three machine-guns.

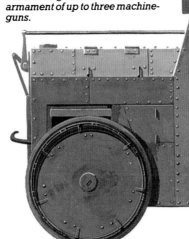

into one unit along with some improvised conversions and sent at first to the Baltic and then to the Western Front. Conditions on both fronts were such that the armoured cars could do little, and eventually they were sent to Russia where they could at least use their mobility to some effect. It was at this stage that more cars were needed, and as Büssing and Daimler were already overextended on war work, Ehrhardt received the contract, being asked to produce a further 20 armoured cars. These were 1.72 tons lighter than the original **Panzerkraftwagen Ehrhardt 1915**. This batch, known as the **Panzerkraftwagen Ehrhardt 1917**, had revised frontal armour, and the vehicles were sent to the Eastern Front until the end of the

fighting there in 1917. Thereafter they appear to have kept within Germany for internal policing duties, in which role they were so successful that a further 20 were produced specifically for the purpose in 1919. The Ehrhardt design was in fact considered just what internal policing required for its weight was such that it towered above crowds and enabled police units to control riots and the like that much better. Vehicles of the Ehrhardt type were in use until World War II.

The requirement for armoured cars was such that by 1918 the Germans were forced to employ large numbers of captured Rolls-Royce and other such vehicles, and the Ehrhardts, clumsy and high though they were, were never around in sufficient numbers. On the

Eastern Front the small numbers involved were never able to make much impression, so the design is now little known and few operational details have survived.

Specification
Panzerkraftwagen Ehrhardt 1915
Crew: 8 or 9
Weight: 8.86 tons
Powerplant: one 85-hp (63.4-kW) petrol engine
Dimensions: length 5.61 m (18 ft 5 in); width 2.0 m (6 ft 6½ in); height not known
Performance: maximum speed 59.5 km/h (37 mph); range 250 km (155 miles)

Field Guns of World War 1

Field artillery played a crucial role in shaping the course of World War I. The hail of shell produced by quick-fire field artillery helped force the armies on the Western Front to shelter in the trenches, where they remained until 1918. Lack of field guns gravely hampered the vast Russian armies, while aggressive artillery tactics were an important element in the Germans' success in the East.

During World War I field guns were the most numerous type of artillery in use. All of it had been developed and produced to take part in the fluid type of warfare that had been the norm during the previous century, in which large armies wheeled about the battlefields of Europe and the field artillery provided them with fire support. The conditions of warfare during World War I did not allow such artillery to behave in its accustomed mobile manner, for after a period in which it seemed that the old conditions of manoeuvre and open battle would prevail, it was not long before trench warfare set in all along the battlefronts.

The firepower of the new QF guns drove the infantry to take cover in trenches but it could not destroy earthworks. Only the howitzer could make any useful contribution, with its high angle of firing elevation and the near-vertical descent of its projectile. Only howitzers could reach out into the enemy trenches, and only the heavy howitzers could be of any real use. But the armies had large numbers of field guns and light field howitzers, so these had to be used. They could do but little against even the most lightly-protected defences, especially as during the early stages of World War I much of their ammunition was restricted to shrapnel intended for use against an enemy in the open. Shrapnel could not enter dug-outs or cut wire, so gradually it was replaced as a type by HE.

Why then was field artillery present in such quantity? The answer to that can be seen in production facilities and the continual search for

A 60-pdr field gun is seen in action at Cape Helles during the Dardanelles campaign, July 1915. The large guns had to be manhandled into position, but once in place were invaluable due to their projectile weight and long range. This gun is at full recoil; note the dust kicked up by the muzzle blast.

some form of strategic breakthrough. Once that had been achieved the field guns could once more come into their own, whereupon the static and heavy siege guns that had gradually come into use along every battle front could be left behind. The production facility reference is explained by the fact that field artillery could be relatively easily manufactured in large quantities, while the production of heavier weapons took much more time and money. So field artillery it had to be for much of the time.

Not all World War I warfare was restricted to the trenches. In Russia, the Middle East and in the Balkans the fluid warfare envisaged by the pre-1914 military planners did take place, and here field artillery could play its proper role of supporting the other arms in the field. But the main theatre of World War I was the Western Front, and there the field artillery was massed to provide what support it could, and the gunners of all nations did their best.

A British Army 18-pdr field gun fires under typical Western Front conditions during the Battle of Pozières Ridge in late July 1916. The stack of spent cartridge cases gives an indication of the volume of fire that the gun was called on to produce day after day, testing the fitness of the gun and its crew.

ITALY
75-mm field gun

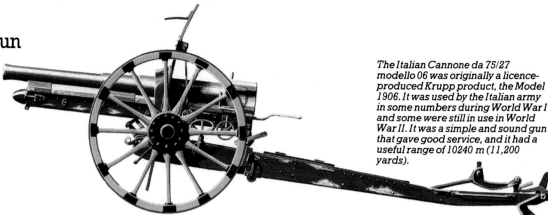

The Italian Cannone da 75/27 modello 06 was originally a licence-produced Krupp product, the Model 1906. It was used by the Italian army in some numbers during World War I and some were still in use in World War II. It was a simple and sound gun that gave good service, and it had a useful range of 10240 m (11,200 yards).

Although the **Cannone da 75/27 modello 11** was designed by a Frenchman it was produced only in Italy and may thus qualify as an Italian weapon. The designer was named Deport, who conceived the idea of a recoil mechanism that could stay fixed in a horizontal plane while the barrel could be elevated to any angle desired. The advantages of this system are rather obscure, but the Italian army certainly took to the idea to the extent that they produced the modello 11 in large numbers.

The modello 11 was a relatively small field piece, as a result mainly of the fact that it was originally ordered for cavalry use. In time it was issued to other arms and became a standard field gun. Apart from the unusual (an uncopied) recoil system, the modello 11 also had one other novel feature for its day. This was split trail legs which gave the gun an unusually wide traverse by contemporary standards, and also enabled the barrel to be elevated to a maximum of 65° allowing the gun to be used in mountainous areas if required. In action the trails were spread and instead of the more usual trail spade the legs were held in place by stakes hammered through slots at the end of each. This certainly held the gun steady for firing, but there were two disadvantages to this system. One

was that any large change of traverse could not be made until the stakes had been laboriously removed from the ground; the other was that on rocky or hard ground it took time to hammer in the stakes. For all these potential troubles the Italians used the stake securing method on many of their artillery designs, large and small.

The modello 11 was a handy little weapon with a good range: its 10240-m (11200-yard) capability was well above that of many of its contemporaries. However, for its size it was rather heavy, which was no doubt a factor in its change from the cavalry to the field artillery. In action it had a crew of at least four men although a full detachment was six, the extra two looking

after the horses.

It is known that some of these guns were used by the Italian maritime artillery militia within the Italian coastal defence organization. The modello 11s appear to have been used as light mobile batteries that could be used for close-in beach defences of likely landing spots. Many of the modello 11s were still in use in this role after 1940, and many other modello 11s were in service with the field artillery. In fact so many were still on hand in 1943 that many came under German control, with the designation **7.5-cm Feldkanone 244(i)**, for use by the German occupation forces in Italy. By that time many modello 11s had been modified for powered traction by conversion of

the old wooden spoked wheels to new steel-spoked wheels and revised shields; these modernized equipments used pneumatic tyres.

Specification
Cannone da 75/27
Calibre: 75 mm (2.95 in)
Length: of barrel 2.132 m (83.93 in)
Weights: in action 1076 kg (2,372 lb); travelling 1900 kg (4,189 lb)
Elevation: −15° to +65°
Traverse: 52°
Muzzle velocity: 502 m (1,647 ft) per second
Maximum range: 10240 m (11,200 yards)
Shell weight: 6.35 kg (14 lb)

UK
Ordnance, QF, 13-pdr Gun

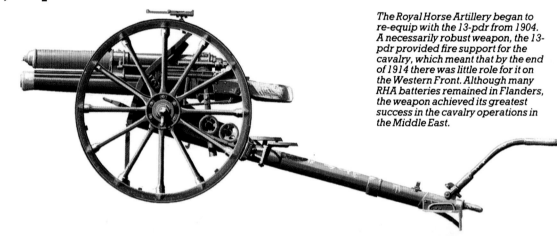

The Royal Horse Artillery began to re-equip with the 13-pdr from 1904. A necessarily robust weapon, the 13-pdr provided fire support for the cavalry, which meant that by the end of 1914 there was little role for it on the Western Front. Although many RHA batteries remained in Flanders, the weapon achieved its greatest success in the cavalry operations in the Middle East.

In the aftermath of the Boer War the Royal Artillery decided that its ageing gun park was in great need of overhaul, and so launched a search for replacements. Field guns were one new type of equipment sought, but the final selection was difficult. The choice was between a design known as the **Ordnance, QF, 13-pdr Gun**, which was an amalgamation of the best features of Woolwich Arsenal and Vickers submissions, and the gun known as the Ordnance, QF, 18-pdr. Deliberations went on for some time before the decision was made to acquire the 13-pdr for the Royal Horse Artillery and the 18-pdr for the field regiments.

The first 13-pdr guns entered service in 1904. The numbers of these weapons were never as great as those of the 18-pdr, for the Royal Horse Artillery was much smaller than the rest of the Royal Artillery. Some 13-pdr guns were sent to India, but most stayed in the United Kingdom, ready to move to France in 1914. It was a 13-pdr gun that fired the first British shot of World War I, and almost as soon as they arrived these guns were involved in the epic gunner battle of Nery. Thereafter the 13-pdr weapons were generally overshadowed by the 18-pdr guns, to the extent that at one point some 13-pdr pieces were withdrawn to be converted to rudimentary anti-aircraft guns.

The 13-pdr had a calibre of 76.2 mm (3 in), and in the light of Boer War experience much of the ammunition fired was shrapnel. This was not shrapnel as it is known today (fragments produced

The British 13-pdr (calibre 76.2 mm/ 3 in) was used by the RHA and was produced in far fewer numbers than the 18-pdr. The rope-bound tube over the barrel contained the hydro-spring recoil system.

by the detonation of the shell) but rather a form of carrier shell which contained a small explosive charge (detonated when the shell was still in the air) to blow out from the front of the shell a large number of lead or steel balls that spread out to act as anti-personnel weapons. Against an enemy in the open shrapnel was a very effective weapon, but against defended troops under cover it was virtually useless, and not much use at cutting through barbed wire. It took some time for appreciable amounts of high explosive shell to get to the gunners in France, so after the initial period of the war the 13-pdr guns were of only limited use in France. Instead many were sent to the Middle East where they were used in the various campaigns against the Turks.

Although not used in such large numbers as the 18-pdr, the 13-pdr was a good gun of its type and well suited to the horse artillery tactics of the era before World War I. The problem for the 13-pdr was that those tactics did

not last long under the trench warfare conditions of World War I. But the design was basically sound, so sound that apart from the departure of some for use as anti-aircraft guns, the 13-pdr remained virtually unchanged throughout its service life. That service life is still not over, for the 13-pdr is still used by the King's Troop of the Royal Horse Artillery for its well-known ceremonial and display duties in London and elsewhere.

Incidentally, the shell fired by the 13-pounder did not weigh 13 lb (5.9 kg), but rather 12.5 lb (5.67 kg).

Specification
Ordnance, QF, 13-pdr Gun
Calibre: 76.2 mm (3 in)
Length: of barrel 1.86 m (73.25 in)
Weight: complete 1014 kg (2,236 lb)
Elevation: −5° to +16°
Traverse: 8°
Muzzle velocity: 511 m (1,675 ft) per second
Maximum range: 5395 m (5,900 yards)
Shell weight: 5.67 kg (12.5 lb)

This photograph, taken near Inexent in June 1918, shows exactly how robust horse-towed field guns had to be. The 13-pdr was light enough to be towed at speed by a six-horse team, and to this day 13-pdrs can still be seen towed by the King's Troop, Royal Horse Artillery, during their dramatic displays.

Ordnance, QF, 15-pdr Gun

The **Ordnance, QF, 15-pdr Gun** should not be confused with the Erhardt 15-pdr field gun, which was a much more modern weapon than the British 15-pdr. The original British 15-pdr was a pre-Boer War piece that used the old system of a spring-loaded spade to absorb much of the firing recoil. This spade was under the axle and the main 'springing' came from a rope connected to a spring contained in a tube on the trail spade. This system worked, but it was cumbersome and inefficient, demanding a lot of work from the gun team. So in the aftermath of the Boer War, rather than simply dispose of the large numbers of guns in service, they were converted to take a hydro-spring recoil system over the barrel. The old 15-pdr breech was modified to a more modern form and other alterations were made. Once ready for use in 1907 they were issued to the Territorial Army batteries.

The 15-pdr was really too heavy for the field gun role and had an indifferent range capability, but it proved to be an excellent training weapon that could be provided at a relatively low cost. The new recoil system was efficient enough, but it was something of a fitter's headache as numerous marks of the old 15-pdr had been used for the conversions, and interchangeability of parts between guns was difficult.

The 15-pdr guns did not move to France until 1915, by which time the supply of 13-pdr and 18-pdr guns was becoming difficult. Only a few Territorial batteries took their 15-pdr equipments to France, but on arrival there was little they could do, for the only ammunition they had was shrapnel, which was of little use against a well dug-in enemy under top cover as was the case all along the Western Front by 1915. A few 15-pdr guns were present during the 1915 Battle of Loos, where they could add little to the proceedings as a result mainly of their lack of suitable projectiles.

After that brief flurry of activity the 15-pdr was retired to act as a training gun once more. A few were sent to South Africa, where they were used

Above: The 15-pdr field gun could trace its origins back to the 1890s, for it was an old field-gun design altered to use a new hydro-spring recoil system plus some other changes. The result was heavy and cumbersome, and by 1914 most were used by the Territorial Army who took them over to France in 1915. They were replaced as soon as possible.

during some of the campaigns against the Germans in East Africa, but most of the rest were used to fire off their large stocks of ammunition as burst-producing delivery systems for the training of artillery observers, both on the ground and in the air. They continued in this role for a remarkably long time, for some Royal Artillery batteries in India were still using 15-pdr guns for this same purpose as late as the mid-1930s.

The 15-pdr is still one of the lesser-known guns of World War I, but it had its small part to play. It was certainly distinctive enough. The recoil system added to the weapon during the conversion from the original sprung spade configuration gave the gun a very distinctive appearance, as it was contained in a metal shroud that covered the entire upper length of the barrel.

Specification
Ordnance, QF, 15-pdr Gun
Calibre: 76.2 mm (3 in)

Length: of barrel 2.345 m (92.35 in)
Weight: complete 1339.5 kg (2,953 lb)
Elevation: −9° to +16°
Traverse: none
Muzzle velocity: 484 m (1,590 ft) per second
Maximum range: 5258 m (5,750 yards)
Shell weight: 6.35 kg (14 lb)

The original 15-pdr the World War I field gun evolved from was still employed by the Indian Army in 1914, who used them during some of the early campaigns in German East Africa. This example is seen firing during a training camp exercise in India in July 1915.

The Battle of Neuve Chapelle

By Christmas 1914 the armies on the Western Front found themselves in a line of trenches stretching from the Channel coast to Switzerland: it was siege warfare on a continental scale. The first attempt to break the deadlock was launched by the British Expeditionary Force in March 1915 in the form of a limited offensive aimed towards the town of Lille.

The high hopes with which Europe went to war in 1914 had largely evaporated by the end of that year. No one was going to be 'home for Christmas' after all, and no one in the immediately foreseeable future was going to hold any triumphant victory parades, for the war on the Western Front was set into an apparent stalemate, though neither of the high commands was prepared to accept this as anything but a temporary situation.

But how to break it?

The British in particular were unhappy about it all; unhappy because their famous cavalry was unoccupied, unhappy because none of their vast experience of warfare gained on every frontier of their empire (especially those of India) seemed relevant in these dank and muddy conditions, and especially unhappy because a fundamental axiom of British military life (that British soldiers and especially their officers all possessed an innate 'eye for country') was totally nullified here. The British sector of the line ran a twisting 45 km (28 miles) from a point near Ypres in the north down to the area of La Bassée through ground as flat as a plate, with visibility rarely over 100 m (110 yards), and what little raised ground there was was in the hands of the enemy. A fat lot of use an 'eye for country' was here.

High ground

But there was one sector of the British front where, if the stalemate could be broken, great advantage might accrue. Opposite this sector lay the small village of Neuve Chappelle, and beyond it lay the Aubers Ridge from which good observation (and indeed command)

could be obtained of the town of Lille, that essential focus for the great breakout which would sweep the Germans back out of Belgium and behind their own frontiers.

Here, certainly, an attack might be mounted. At the very least an advance up Aubers Ridge would get General Sir Douglas Haig's 1st Army out of the sodden, waterlogged mud where it had spent the last weeks, and up into drier and thus more comfortable conditions.

Planning the offensive

Preparations began in the last days of February 1915, and ran immediately into unforeseen problems. It had become accepted that the generals would have to command in the field far larger armies than ever before, and now the staffs were finding themselves confronted with tasks of far greater magnitude and complexity than either they or their instructors had ever envisaged. Moreover, this offensive was to be the first ever launched from a trench system; there was no previous experience of any kind upon which to draw.

At least there was going to be no shortage of either men or matériel. Three whole brigades (the 23rd and 25th Brigades, and the Garhwal Brigade of the Indian Corps) were being made available, to crash through a mere 2745 m (3,000 yards) of trench between the 'Moated Grange' on the left and the 'Port Arthur' cros-

This photograph tells more than mere words how dreadful the conditions in the trenches were by March 1915. Even simple tasks such as writing home were turned by the mud and cold into a major operation.

sroads on the right, and according to intelligence there would be reinforcements of only 4,000 German rifles by the end of the day that the attack was launched, plus 12,000 more only by the end of the second day. The German front-line strength at the time of the assault was some 1,400 rifles.

Even more important, artillery was to be used on a scale hitherto unimagined, working to a timetable giving each battery a definite task, and with specific targets for each phase of

A 6-in (152.4-mm) 30-cwt Siege Howitzer registers its fire prior to the Battle of Neuve Chapelle. These heavy and cumbersome howitzers were used by the single Siege Brigade formed by the Royal Artillery at that time, and had a range of only 4755 m (5,200 yards).

the bombardment. This was in itself a new departure, but even more innovatory was the decision to use in front of the advancing infantry a 'creeping barrage', which would lift to more distant targets as the infantry approached. This was an experiment which would be watched carefully by gunners everywhere.

The entire artillery of two corps was secretly moved into position and most guns had begun a carefully-controlled registration programme by 5 March, 340 guns altogther, including batteries of 119-, 152- and 233-mm (4.7-, 6- and 9.2-in) weapons at the rear, and 119-, 152- and 233-mm howitzer batteries at the front. Two more 152.4-mm howitzer batteries arrived on 9 March and were fitted into position in the northern half of the attack line, and the fact that they had no time for registering or even practising their main task (the cutting of enemy wire to their front) did not particularly worry the Scottish Rifles or the Middlesex battalion about to go over the top in front of them.

Dawn attack

By 04.00 on the raw, damp morning of 10 March all the assaulting infantry was in position: the 2nd Middlesex, 2nd Scottish Rifles, 2nd Lincolnshires, 2nd Royal Berks and the Garhwalis, with behind them in immeditate support the 2nd West Yorks, 2nd Devons, 1st Royal Irish Rifles, 2nd Rifle Brigade, and 1st Seaforth Highlanders with the Indians; and the 5th Cavalry Brigade waited impatiently at GHQ for the magic word that the breakthrough was open for them to sweep through and exploit.

The waiting men were cold, though they had had a hot meal during the night, and now they were keyed up with excitement and enthusiasm.

Artillery barrage

A few ranging shots went over between 06.00 and 07.15, there was a brief pause, and then at 07.30 opened the loudest and heaviest bombardment any of them had ever experienced. The air above was filled with the roar and scream of passing shells, the known German positions in front erupted in gouts of mud and earth, and stakes flew through the air trailing masses of wire, occasionally laden with gruesome remnants of bodies; and back towards the British lines drifted the thick, sickening fumes of Lyddite explosive. The whole earth quivered momentarily as in an earthquake, then the bombardment steadied, the barrage lifted from the German trenches opposite to the village of Neuve Chapelle itself, and the men clambered out of their trenches and went forward.

Early success

On the right, the Garhwalis reached the lines opposite with very little trouble, although their right-hand companies had veered too far right and left a gap to be plugged by the Seaforths behind them; on their left the Berkshire and and Lincolnshire men were into the German trenches by 08.20, and the Rifle Brigade and the Royal Irish Rifles came through and stormed straight on into the village as the barrage lifted to the far side. Everywhere they found German troops dazed and shocked by the bombardment, hardly able to comprehend the situation, let alone offer resistance; by 09.00 nearly 300 prisoners had been shepherded back. A few survivors were seen making their way towards some woodlands behind the village.

On the left, however, the Middlesex had been shot to pieces. The newly arrived howitzers had failed to cut the wire in front of them, the defending company of a Jäger battalion was virtually unscathed and its machine-guns had annihilated the leading Middlesex waves, enfilading the Scottsh Rifles next to the Middlesex and blocking the entire assault.

British reaction was remarkably quick: at 09.40 a second bombardment was ordered opposite the Middlesex position, and this proved exceeding accurate and efficient; as the second wave of the Middlesex attack began, an officer and 60 men of the Jägers climbed out of their trenches and walked forward to give themselves up! By noon all initial objectives of the attack had been achieved and visions of reaching the commanding heights of Aubers Ridge beckoned; the support troops moved up, the whole of the 7th Division to the north was alerted, and the 5th Cavalry Brigade moved to Estaires, 9.7 km (6 miles) north.

But now the problems of communication made themselves felt, for runners and message pads were still the chief means: it was five hours before the next advance could be mounted, five hours in which the Germans had moved reserves up into their second defence lines, had resited their machine-guns and buttressed the more obvious of their weak points. And now the British infantry were moving through thickening dusk into wet and muddy country of which they knew nothing, and into which their artillery could no longer drop preplanned and accurately-registered cover.

There were no successful advances during that evening, and by morning the Germans had had even longer to strengthen their defences, bring up more reserves and even plan a counterattack. This, however, was beaten off on the morning of 12 March, for the British and Indians had also been working on the defences in their

This wrecked machine-gun position was only destroyed in the second bombardment after it exacted a heavy toll of the attacking infantry, but all too often the machine-guns and gunners survived to wreak havoc against the advancing British battalions.

A German gunner peers into the sights of a 21-cm (8.26-in) howitzer. The Germans had a powerful siege park which made short work of the Belgian forts but was initially inadequate to defeat extensive trench systems.

new positions, and by that evening it was obvious that the stalemate was back. So the battle ceased.

The British had lost 583 officers and 12,309 other ranks, and the Germans approximately the same numbers, of whom 1,687 had been taken prisoner. The area of ground newly in British hands measured about 3660 m by 915 m (4,000 yards by 1,000 yards) deep, and most of it had been captured during the first three hours. It was, in fact, almost exactly the area covered by that first, meticulously-planned artillery schedule.

The day of the Master-Gunner had dawned.

Ordnance, QF, 18-pdr Gun

The first **Ordnance, QF, 18-pdr gun Mk I** was issued to the Royal Artillery in 1904, and in the years after that it was also issued to many other Commonwealth armies, so that by 1914 the 18-pdr was the standard field gun of the British and Commonwealth armies; some were even being produced in India. The 18-pdr had no single parentage, but was an amalgam of design ideas produced by Woolwich Arsenal, the Elswick Works and Vickers. The barrel was wire-wound, had a simple single-action breech, and was mounted on a pole trail carriage. The usual shield was fitted, and as was common at that time the ammunition fired was almost entirely shrapnel.

It was not long before the original design was being modified. The first change was to allow a barrel liner to be replaced when worn, but when the 18-pdr went to war in 1914 it was still basically the same as it was when first issued. The trials of battle soon highlighted what was to become known as the 18-pdr's weakest point: the recuperator springs, which returned the barrel back to the firing position after recoil, could not put up with the stresses that continued firing produced and broke under the strain, leaving the gun useless. At first all the gun fitters could do was keep changing the springs, a hazardous and time-consuming operation until a modification that could be adopted in the field was developed. This was an entirely new hydropneumatic recoil system that fitted inside the existing spring housings: this did the trick and the 18-pdr became much more reliable.

However, the 18-pdr was to undergo one more major change during World War I. The original carriage used a pole trail which was useful enough for horse traction, but as it went right under the breech it limited elevation angles, and thus range. This led to what became known as the **18-pdr Gun Mk IV** (the other marks were development models, apart from the original Mk I). This was virtually a new design: for a start the Mk IV was fitted with a box trail which allowed the barrel to be elevated much further to provide the required range increase, the breech mechanism was changed to a new form known as the Asbury type, and the recoil system was moved to an entirely new position under the barrel. The new recoil system used a 'floating piston' that employed oil and compressed air to provide a much smoother and more reliable movement. The cradle was redesigned to take the loads imposed by these new features, and the result was a much better all-round gun. Not only did it have a far better range, but it was far more stable in action and proved to be capable of very high rates of fire: 30 rounds a minute in the hands of a well-trained team was not unusual.

The 18-pdr Mk IV was just getting into full production as the war ended, and it became the preferred weapon of the Royal Artillery in the inter-war years. By then the 18-pdr was in use

The 18-pdr Mk I field gun entered service in 1904, and in 1914 was in widespread use by the British and some Commonwealth armies. It had a pole trail for horse traction and the original recoil system proved prone to breakage, but it was regarded as a good and sound gun design that was used throughout the war.

Right: An 18-pdr (calibre 83 mm/ 3.3 in) is seen in action near St Leger aux Bois in the Oise region during August 1916. The pole trail is clearly visible, as is the one-piece round that was almost the same size as one of the old quart beer bottles.

outside the British and Commonwealth armies. The US Army had taken over large numbers commencing in 1917, and other nations that later used the 18-pdr were Ireland, some of the Baltic States and China. Many 18-pdr guns were used during World War II and the last of the type did not leave Irish service until the 1970s.

Specification
Ordnance, QF, 18-pdr Gun Mk I
Calibre: 83.8 mm (3.3 in)
Length: of barrel 2.463 m (96.96 in)
Weight: complete 1280 kg (2,821 lb)
Elevation: −5° to +16°
Traverse: 8°
Muzzle velocity: 492 m (1,615 ft) per second
Maximum range: 5966 m (6,525 yards)
Shell weight: 8.39 kg (18.5 lb)

Right: 18-pdr field guns come into action in a remarkably open fire position during the Battle of Thiepval Ridge in September 1916. The gun off the road to the rear is ready for action, while the team in the foreground is just about to drag off an empty ammunition limber.

An 18-pdr is manhandled from a waterlogged gun position near Zillebeke during the Flanders offensive of August 1917, providing a graphic indication of why that offensive failed to achieve anything and got bogged down.

UK
Ordnance, QF, 4.5-in Howitzer

The **Ordnance, QF, 4.5-in Howitzer** used by the British army throughout World War I was another weapon developed in the aftermath of the Boer War. During that colonial conflict the Royal Artillery learned the hard way that its field howitzers were too heavy, too slow in action and generally too cumbersome, so they asked for something better. For some reason the usual state arsenals were asked to submit their new designs at the same time as private manufacturers, and in the end a private manufacturer, the Coventry Ordnance Works, was awarded the contract.

This welcome change from what had up till then been a virtual state monopoly meant that when the BEF went to France in 1914 it took what was then thought to be the best field howitzer in the world. It was able to outperform all its contemporaries, and yet was handy enough to operate alongside the 18-pdr guns in a normal field artillery regiment. This result was achieved mainly by making the basic design simple and robust, and the weapon was so sound it required only one modification throughout its long service life: the rounding off of some of the sharper corners of the breech mechanism to prevent cracking after prolonged firing. As with the 18-pdr the 4.5-in (114.3-in) howitzer was also issued to many Commonwealth armies including those of Canada, Australia and New Zealand. During the war the 4.5-in howitzer was also passed on to Russia, as by 1916 the Tsarist armies were in a rather poor state, and the British government handed over 400 4.5-in howitzers. These were destined to have an eventful life, for they took part in the Russian defeats of 1917, and also played their part in the events surrounding the revolutions of 1917 and the subsequent civil war. Many were still on hand when the Germans invaded in 1941, captured examples being designated **11.4-cm leichte Feldhaubitze 363(r)**.

During World War I the 4.5-in howitzer was towed into action by a team of six horses. The full gun team was 10 men although fewer actually served the gun in action, the rest acting as ammunition and horse handlers. In common with most other weapons of the period the 4.5-in howitzer was sup-

posed to make great use of shrapnel, but high explosive was soon found to be much more useful, though it was in short supply in 1914 and 1915, a shortage that lead to a political storm known as the 'shell scandal'. The ammunition also featured in another political uproar, this time after World War I, for the fuses used on the shells were a clockwork type first produced by Krupp in Germany. After the war Krupp took the British government to an international court to extract royalties due on every fuse fired, and won the judgement!

By the time World War I ended, 3,177 4.5-in howitzers had been produced in addition to the 182 completed before 1914. After 1918 these howitzers

were retained in British army service to be used again during the early campaigns of World War II. By then their original wooden spoked wheels had been replaced by new items with pneumatic tyres for powered traction. The Germans used 96 captured equipments in the Atlantic Wall with the designation **11.4-cm leFH 361(e)**. The last 4.5-in howitzers to be used as service weapons were those of the Irish army, the final examples not retired until the late 1970s.

Specification
Ordnance, QF, 4.5-in Howitzer
Calibre: 114.3 mm (4.5 in)
Length: of barrel 1.778 m (70 in)
Weight: complete 1365 kg (3,010 lb)

The 4.5-in (114-mm) field howitzer was one of the best of the British Army field pieces, as it was light, handy and fired a useful shell. Its design was to remain virtually unchanged from its first use in 1914 until World War II, when it once more was taken over to France. Many were sent to Russia in 1916 and more were used by Commonwealth armies.

Elevation: −5° to +45°
Traverse: 6°
Muzzle velocity: 308 m (1,010 ft) per second
Maximum range: 6675 m (7,300 yards)
Shell weight: 15.876 kg (35 lb)

An Australian battery of 4.5-in (114-mm) field howitzers are seen in action during the open warfare of late August 1918, somewhere near Hamel. The high elevation of the short barrels enabled their shells to fall almost vertically into enemy earthworks.

 UK
BL, 60-pdr

During the Boer War some 4.7-in (119-mm) naval guns were converted to the field role, and these provided the Royal Artillery with an idea of what they would need in the future. From this example the Royal Artillery gunners asked for a long-range gun firing a shell weighing 27.2 kg (60 lb) for use by divisional heavy batteries, and the Elswick Ordnance Company was asked to produce a design, the first example of which was accepted.

This gun became known as the **BL, 60-pdr Mk I**, and it was a large and handsome gun with a long barrel, two prominent recoil cylinders over the barrel, and a heavy trail. In order to make the gun more manageable the barrel could be drawn back over the carriage for towing, and the large wheels were based on traction engine wheel designs to help spread the loads over soft ground. The trail was a heavy

affair made from large slabs of steel and with a large towing bracket at the end.

Soon after the war began in 1914 it was found that the 60-pdr was a most useful weapon. More were demanded, but it was not an easy gun to manufacture quickly. Some short cuts had to be made to speed matters, so the facility to draw back the barrel for towing was removed, and some other expedients were introduced. The result was a carriage that was heavier, but at least more equipments could be sent to France. There it was soon discovered that trying to move these large guns around with horse teams was an almost impossible task, so Holt tractors were

introduced instead, making the 60-pdr one of the first British weapons of its kind to be towed by powered traction. But even with the Holt tractor the Mk II carriage with its fixed barrel was a cumbersome load, leading to the Mk III carriage in which the barrel could

The British 60-pdr Mk 1 had a calibre of 127 mm (5 in) and fired a shell weighing 27.2 kg (60 lb) to a range of 11,247 m (12,300 yards). Its carriage used traction engine road wheels to spread the weight, and the trail was very heavy for firing stability. This made it so heavy that only Holt tractors could tow the gun.

once more be withdrawn, but this time the method used was much simpler: the barrel was disconnected from the recoil mechanism and pulled back.

The 60-pdr was initially supplied mainly with shrapnel shell, but this was changed to high explosive once trench

 31

warfare had set in. Thereafter, wherever the British army went the 60-pdr went with it, from France to Mesopotamia. The 60-pdr gave sterling service, although it was always a brute to move, but in action it was steady, reliable and accurate. New streamlined shells were provided to increase range, but the only real long-term answer to producing even more range was to develop a new gun. This duly appeared during the last few months of World War I in the shape of the **BL, 60-pdr Mk II**, which introduced a new type of carriage and recoil system, a longer barrel and many other detail changes. None of these 60-pdr Mk II guns was in service before the war ended.

Along the Western Front the 60-pdr guns were used mainly for counterbattery work or for demolishing strongpoints. They were also used at times for what is now known as harassing fire, i.e. firing off odd rounds deep into the enemy rear to land around road junctions, railway stations etc. generally to disturb the enemy's movements. To do this effectively the guns had to be moved up to close behind the front lines, no easy task in view of the bulk of the 60-pdr.

Specification
BL, 60-pdr Mk I on Carriage Mk III
Calibre: 127 mm (5 in)
Length: of barrel 4.268 m (168.05 in)
Weight: complete 4470 kg (9,856 lb)
Elevation: −5° to +21.5°
Traverse: 8°
Muzzle velocity: 634 m (2,080 ft) per second
Maximum range: 11247 m (12,300 yards)
Shell weight: 27.2 kg (60 lb)

Above: 60-pdrs fire at Turkish positions near Samarra in 1918. These guns have Mk 3 carriages, which were much lighter than the previous marks using traction engine wheels. Recognition features of the 60-pdr were the two recoil cylinders over the long barrel and the large and heavy carriage trail.

A 60-pdr fires near La Boiselle in March 1918. These guns had a range that allowed them to be sited well back from the trench lines and thus needed digging in only during long spells in one position.

FRANCE

Canon de 75 mle 1897

The claim to being one of the most famous guns of all time can be truly made by the French '75', the well-known 'soixante-quinze' or **Canon de 75 mle 1897**. Over the years this gun earned for itself an almost legendary reputation, but in historical terms it deserves fame as being one of the first true quick-firing guns. This was achieved by the introduction of a novel hydraulic recoil system that rendered contemporary mechanisms (based upon the use of springs alone) virtually obsolete overnight. This mechanism, allied to the introduction of the Nordenfeld breech mechanism that could be opened and closed by the flick of a lever, enabled the '75' to fire shells at rates of up to 28 rounds per minute, which in its day was truly revolutionary.

The '75' was a government design first produced at the Atelier de Bourges, but it was not long before the type was being made elsewhere, especially by Schneider & Cie at Le Creusot. This company's production

was so prolific that the design was sometimes attributed to Schneider. The first models appeared in 1897 (hence mle 1897) and were kept under wraps for a considerable time as they were regarded as highly secret weapons. Much was expected of them, for they were seen as the main support weapons for the French doctrine of the attack, in which the offensive spirit was supposed to overcome any opposition. The high fire rate of the '75' was intended to overcome the relatively light weight of HE shell fired, 6.195 kg (13.66 lb). This doctrine was to cost the French army dearly in 1914, but throughout the 'Great War' the '75' remained the standard field piece of the French army.

The hydraulic recoil system of the '75' produced a relatively long recoil action, so long in fact that two 'ears' were fitted under the muzzle to engage lugs on the recoil housing at full travel to take some of the barrel loads off the pistons. These 'ears' provided the '75' with an easy recognition fea-

ture. The breech mechanism used a simple lever and interrupted-thread action that was swiftly and easily operated to allow the one-piece ammunition to be fed into the chamber. A box-section pole trail was used, limiting the maximum angle of elevation and consequently the range, but this undesirable feature was not rectified until well after World War I. Many '75s' had a fuse-setting machine fixed to the trail leg when in action.

The '75' was produced in thousands during World War I, and it was issued to armies other than the French. The US Army adopted the type in 1917 and even commenced production of its own version. So many '75s' were produced that they were used for a variety of other purposes. The armament of the first French tanks was the '75', and the '75' was also used as an anti-aircraft gun, either mounted on some dreadful lash-ups involving metal frames or on self-propelled mountings on de Dion lorries. Some were used as coastal defence weapons and when a 37-mm

(1.456-in) trench gun was required in 1916 the result was a half-scale '75'.

The '75' went on to a long post-war career after 1918, and was later produced in some strange guises, but it is as one of the most widely-used guns of World War I that the '75' will be best remembered. Examples used by the Germans in World War II were designated **7.5-cm Feldkanone 231(f)**, but a more common name was **7.5-cm FK97(f)**.

Specification
Canon de 75 mle 1897
Calibre: 75 mm (2.95 in)
Length: of barrel 2.587 m (101.85 in)
Weights: in action 1140 kg (2,514 lb); travelling 1970 kg (4,343 lb)
Elevation: −11° to +18°
Traverse: 6°
Muzzle velocity: 575 m (1,886 ft) per second
Maximum range: 11000 m (12,030 yards)
Shell weight: 6.195 kg (13.66 lb)

The Legend of the French `75´

The '75' was the pride of the pre-war French army. A truly innovative weapon, it completely outclassed the field guns of all other armies when it was introduced at the turn of the century. The secrecy surrounding its design and development endowed the gun with a mystique that was to prove enduring, and the soixante-quinze gave sterling service.

The 75-mm (2.95-in) mle 1897 was also used as an anti-aircraft gun on both fixed and mobile mountings, as seen here. This mobile gun is manned by newly-arrived US Army gunners who took over a great deal of French and British equipment once they arrived, as they had little of their own at that time.

The gun that was to become internationally-known as the '75' had its origins in a French army project of the 1890s. By that time the breech-loading gun was commonplace, but it suffered from the factor that had affected artillery weapons ever since black-powder days: when a gun was fired the recoil forces forced the gun barrel and carriage back out of position, and they had to be replaced before another round could be fired. If some method of absorbing this recoil could be found, rapid rates of fire would be possible as there would be no need to keep manhandling the guns back to their firing position after every shot. The solution seemed to lie in the field of hydraulics, for a German firm had developed a way of making a piston attached to the barrel move through a thick fluid as it recoiled, and by careful design this absorbed the recoil forces. This principle was applied to some large static coastal guns, but to make the idea work on a much smaller and lighter field gun was another matter. Most of the major European powers set their designers to work on the problem, but the French found the answer first.

The French solution was a simple extension of the original German piston and fluid idea; they simply made it smaller and with holes in the piston so that a mixture of water and glycerine could pass through the holes at a set but slow rate. This would absorb recoil forces to the extent that none, or virtually none, would be passed to the carriage. Thus the mle 1897 was born and the French army immediately put a strict security clamp on it. No one outside the immediate circle of user gunners was allowed even to see the weapon, and not even the gunners had any real idea of how the recoil system actually worked.

Unfortunately for the French army, this desperate secrecy attracted attention and it was not long before the workings of the recoil system were out. By that time the other major European powers had decided that if the French were to have a new quick-firing weapon with an efficient recoil system, then they had to have one as well. Thus their designers duly came up with other but basically similar solutions. Some of these solutions were even better than that of the mle 1897, for to ensure that the French system worked efficiently the barrel had to recoil a considerable distance, some 1.22 m (48 in). This made the barrel move so far that the centre of gravity and thus carriage stability could be affected, and the stresses on the recoil cylinder piston rods were so considerable that 'ears', engaging in lugs under the recoil housing, had to be fitted under the muzzle to take some of the strain. This did not materially affect the rate of fire of the mle 1897, which could be as high as 28 rounds per minute with a trained crew. The barrel used a Nordenfeld breech mechanism that could be rapidly opened using a simple lever and a flick of a trained wrist, and the ammunition was loaded in one piece, shell and propellant case joined together.

By the time 1914 arrived the general secret of the mle 1897 was well known, although the French still retained some security restraints on the internal details. The French army expected great things of the '75', for it exactly suited their philosophy of the attack. In this view any enemy would simply be swept away by massed infantry attacks with batteries of '75s' producing vast supporting barrages at high rates of fire. The relatively light shell weight was overlooked, it being stated that

high fire rates would overcome that slight problem. Thus when the French infantry advanced to the Battles of the Frontiers in August 1914, they advanced in front of massed batteries of '75s' firing over open sights at the German enemy.

The Battles of the Frontiers soon showed that French ideas on the strength of the attack were of no avail in the face of machine-guns, magazine loading rifles and well-concealed enemy artillery. The '75s' did indeed prove to be very useful and handy weapons, but their overall

British gunners watch a French battery firing their 75-mm (2.95-in) mle 1897 field guns near Domart, April 1918. The '75s' had a high rate of fire, but their light shells could do little more than scrape the ground surface from the terrain and help create the Western Front landscape.

The Legend of the French '75'

lack of shell weight made them no match for the heavy German howitzers and they suffered almost as much as the infantry during the opening battles of World War I. The protagonists reeled apart and started to entrench themselves for the peculiar state of siege warfare that was to last the next four bitter years. Here the '75' was not to shine for it fired in a low trajectory only, and against trenches and even lightly-defended field fortifications it was of very limited value. All it could do was scrape slight depressions into the terrain and produce some small measure of the semi-desert landscape that was to mark the Western Front.

Public craze

But before 1914 was out the '75' was already famous. To disguise the measure of their defeats on the Frontiers some French propagandist hit upon the idea that the '75' was the gun that 'saved' France. The French public seized upon the notion and the '75' became a public craze almost overnight. Songs were published lauding the gun, and the media used every method to promote the idea. Even jewellery and lapel badges depicted the '75', and a legend was born.

The troops on the battlefields no doubt had other ideas. The only way the '75' could be used along the Western Front was well forward, just behind the front lines and well within enemy artillery range. To make up for the light shell weight of the '75' the guns had to be massed together in large numbers: at one point in the 1916 battles at Verdun one entire valley was filled with '75s' massed wheel to wheel and kept constantly firing. Sheer numbers had to make up for the overall lack of firepower until heavier weapons reached the front, and it was no consolation to the French gunners to know that their shells could have little effect on the enemy trenches and earthworks.

During World War I the '75s' rolled off the production lines at Bourges and elsewhere in large numbers, but the mle 1897's recoil system was not an easy thing to make. Because of the close tolerances involved each system had to be virtually hand-made. Despite this so many guns were produced that some were soon being diverted to other uses than field artillery. The first French anti-aircraft guns were simply '75s' placed on steel frameworks and pointed skywards, while some were placed on mobile truck mountings. When the tank appeared the first French examples mounted the '75' as their main armament. Other '75s' were mounted on pedestals to defend French harbours and ports, or were placed into forts to replace guns stripped out during 1914 and 1915. Throughout this period the legend of the '75' persisted, to the extent that when the US Army arrived in France in 1917 without artillery it asked to be

given batteries of '75s'. It duly got them, and so influenced were the Americans that they decided to produce a version as their standard field piece. The problem for them was that the French manufacturers would not give them the production drawings. In typical American style an mle 1897 was shipped to the USA and stripped down to the smallest component. The manufacturers were soon dismayed, for they saw that each mle 1897 was virtually a hand-built weapon produced at great cost in material and manpower. Yet the Americans wanted to mass produce the '75', so they set about revising the basic design to suit their production methods, and in so doing made the '75' a much cheaper (and better) weapon.

The '75' saw out World War I and in the years after the war there was no hope of the French army even thinking of replacing it: it was too much a symbol of the French victory of 1918. But some detail improvement could be made. For a start the box-section trail was eliminated, for that restricted elevation and extended range. A new box trail (through which the breech could be lowered as the barrel was elevated) was designed, but only a few were made. The reason seemed to be that as the '75' had seen the French through World War I it was good enough for the next, and no funds were forthcoming for such expensive changes. Changes did come with the introduction of pneumatic tyres so that the weapon could be towed behind trucks, but that was in the late 1930s and before long another war was looming. Once again the '75' would have to be put ready to save France.

World War II use

So when World War II started in September 1939 the '75s' were at the ready, often still on their original carriages, complete with wooden-spoked wheels. The old anti-aircraft guns were still emplaced on their elevated frames and on their original World War I trucks. Some (but not many) new equipments had been produced. A new form of '75' was used to arm a few of the Maginot Line forts, and

A pre-1914 photograph of a Model 1897, taken at a time when the French army expected to fight mobile battles over open terrain. The battles of 1914 drove the armies into the trenches where the 75 was unable to reach them but it remained the standard French field gun of World War I.

some French tanks used the short-barrelled '75' as their main armament. It was all for nothing, as not even the '75' could withstand the Panzer hordes that swept across France in May 1940. Huge piles of all manner of French war booty fell into German hands, and with them went the '75s'. The '75' thus became a German gun, used to arm the Atlantic Wall and some garrison units in France and elsewhere. It even became an anti-tank gun in 1942 when the increasing number of Soviet T-34s proved to be impervious to the existing German anti-tank guns. The '75s' were dragged out from the booty stockpiles and fitted with new muzzle brakes and strengthening bands around the barrels. New armour-piercing ammunition was issued, and the gun became the 7.5-cm Pak 97/38, the '38' denoting that the Pak 38 carriage was used. It seemed to be the last indignity the '75' could suffer.

But even as that was happening the '75' was doing its bit across the Atlantic. The Americans had mastered production of the '75' just as World War I ended, but in the years after then they used the gun as their standard weapon. They also used it as the starting point for many other projects. For instance, when a tank gun was wanted in the late 1930s the '75' was taken virtually unchanged to arm the new medium tanks, later to become the M3 Lee/Grant and the M4 Sherman. The idea of a tank-busting airborne gun was mooted by the US Army Air Force so a '75' was fitted to a North American B-25 Mitchell bomber. Development gradually reduced the gun weight to the point where B-25s carried the '75' as an anti-shipping weapon in the Pacific. The weight of this airborne gun was low enough to be used as a light tank gun to arm the M24 Chaffee series. And all this occurred while the old American '75' field guns were used to train the new US Army ready for war. Some even saw action during the early stages of the Pacific war, and more were passed to the British army during the grim days of 1940 and 1941.

Thus the old '75' was still doing its bit to save France again, but this time in different hands. The '75' can still be found in many French cities adorning war memorials as a reminder of past glories. It remains one of the most famous guns ever produced.

Part of a French army mle 1897 battery in a field position near Elberfeld in 1915. Within a few short months positions such as these had been driven to shelter in trenches as the Western Front 'hardened' and artillery fire grew heavier. Scenes such as this were not to occur again until the battles of August 1918.

Above: An interested audience watches a 75-mm (2.95-in) mle 1897 in action near Steinbach. The gunners have dug a pit for the carriage trail to provide the barrel with more elevation and thus more range. Note the gunner by the breech waiting to close the breech block by a rapid hand movement once the round is loaded.

Canon de 75 mle 1897

Right and below: The famous French '75' was supposed to be one of France's war-winners prior to 1914, and it had an unequalled rate of fire of up to 28 rounds a minute. It was also light in action and easy to handle. Its main claim to fame was its novel recoil mechanism that returned the barrel to its firing position after every shot, allowing the high rate of fire, but its shell weight was too light for the conditions prevalent on the Western Front after 1914 and its line of fire was too flat to reach into trenches or dug-outs. But the French had many of them, using them throughout the war and for long afterwards.

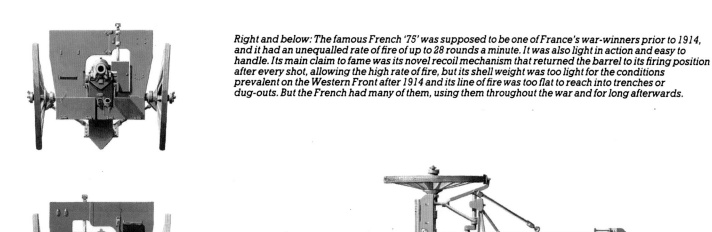

Canon de 105 mle 1913 Schneider

During the early 1900s the French Schneider & Cie took over much of the assets of the Russian Putilov concern, including the latter's arsenal at St Petersburg. When Schneider officials looked around the works they discovered a rather large and handsome gun chambered for the standard Russian 107-mm (4.21-in) round. Subsequent investigations demonstrated that this equipment fired a useful shell to a good range, and the Schneider representatives decided that it would be a good gun to offer the French army. The design was subsequently taken back to France and rechambered for the French 105-mm (4.134-in) calibre; few other changes were necessary.

Unfortunately for Schneider & Cie the French army was not impressed. It already had large numbers of '75s' and there was no need for anything heavier, despite the fact that the 105-mm gun was not being offered as a field gun alone but more as a medium support weapon. Even so it took a great deal of lobbying and persuasion before the French army relented and purchased a relativley small batch in 1913. Thus this new French gun became the **Canon de 105 mle 1913 Schneider**, or more commonly in the service abbreviation of the time the **L 13 S**.

The first batch was duly delivered, but the French army remained unenthusiastic until after the start of World War I in 1914. After the Battle of the Frontiers and the arrival of trench warfare the shortcomings of the '75' became painfully apparent as it lacked shell weight and any significant effect on field fortifications, including trenches. But the L 13 S fired a much heavier shell and could have a considerble effect on such structures, and was thus soon in great demand. It was true that it fired its shell in a relatively flat trajectory that often prevented it from reaching down into trenches, but as a counterbattery weapon it was very useful. It was not long before Schneider was churning out the L 13 S as fast as it could.

In action the L 13 S was a much more cumbersome weapon than the handy '75'. the long box trail was rather heavy, but it kept the gun stable when firing for prolonged periods. The overall design was basically simple and there were no frills, a carry-over from its Russian origins. The interrupted-screw breech was easy to operate but the ammunition took a bit of handling, especially after a prolonged period in action: the HE shell weighed 15.74 kg (34.7 lb). The L 13 S was often towed into action behind an eight-horse team with a small limber taking the weight of the trail, and in action the gun team could be as large as eight men, most of them handling the ammunition.

Numbers of L 13 S guns were handed over to the Belgian army during World War I and they were used among the Belgian positions on the River Lys. After 1918 L 13 Ss were handed over or sold to Italy (**Cannone da 105/28**) and Yugoslavia, and some ended up with the new Polish army. Most of these World War I veterans were still in use when 1939 came around and the L 13 S then took part in a new war. Most of the French L 13 S guns ended up in German hands after 1940 and many were used for beach defence as part of the Atlantic Wall, with the designation **10.5-cm Kanone 331(f)** or **K 333(f)**.

Specification
L 13 S
Calibre: 105 mm (4.134 in)
Length: of barrel 2.987 m (117.6 in)
Weights: in action 2300 kg (5,071 lb); travelling 2650 kg (5,843 lb)
Elevation: −5° to +37°
Traverse: 6°
Muzzle velocity: 550 m (1,805 ft) per second
Maximum range: 12000 m (13,123 yards)
Shell weight: 15.74 kg (34.7 lb)

Above: French gunners take a rest close to their 105-mm (4.14-in) mle 1913 (L 13 S) somewhere in the Argonne region. Ammunition limbers are ready to the left of the gun, which has not yet been fired as the trail spade is not dug into the ground.

Below: A French battery near Amiens in April 1918 is armed with Schneider 105 mm mle 1913 heavy field guns, also known as the L 13 S. Originally derived from a Putilov design, they were among the best of the French artillery and were powerful enough to demolish German field works.

Skoda 149-mm Modell 14 and Modell 14/16

In many ways the **Skoda 149-mm Modell 14** can be regarded as the medium howitzer equivalent to the 100-mm (3.94-in) Model 1914. The 149-mm (5.87-in) weapon was much larger and heavier, however, and was intended for use at higher artillery command levels than the 100-mm howitzer used by the field artillery: the 149-mm howitzer was used at regimental level and upwards, including corps artillery. The Modell 14 was intended for the destruction of major enemy emplacements and field works, and could be a very powerful weapon.

The Modell 14 was intended for use as a field howitzer only, and there was no facility to break the weapon down into loads as was the case with the smaller-calibre weapons. Instead the Modell 14 featured a large box trail, so heavy that a special trail lifting lever had to be fitted over the spades. This was used to effect large changes of traverse, and it required two men to lift the lever and move the carriage. The Modell 14 had a large shield (sometimes curved and sometimes straight), and the recoil mechanism under the barrel was large and heavy. In fact weight seemed to be the watchword of

The Skoda 149-mm (5.87-in) Model 14 was one of the standard Austro-Hungarian Army howitzers of World War I. It fired a 41-kg (90.4-lb) shell to a range of 6900 m (7,546 yards) and could demolish even large field fortifications. Many were later captured by the Italian army and used by them for many years, even through World War II.

the Modell 14, and it required a large horse team to move the weapon. Despite all this weight the Modell 14 did not have a particularly good range: 6900 m (7,546 yards) was the maximum, even if the HE shell was quite destructive.

During 1916 a new version of the Modell 14 began to appear on the Skoda production lines. This was the **Modell 14/16**, which featured a slightly longer barrel and to provide more range fired a shell that was lighter than that of

the Modell 14. The original Modell 14 ammunition could still be fired, and the Modell 14/16 shell could be fired from the Modell 14 if required, but this meant such a change in range tables and training etc. that this was rarely done. The new barrel and ammunition meant a range increase to 8790 m (9,613 yards) which was a help, but these were not the only changes. The Modell 14/16 had a new carriage design which was stronger and more stable than the original, but also

heavier.

Both the Modell 14 and Modell 14/16 were used throughout World War I by the Austro-Hungarian armies, and gave good service. Many passed into Italian use, so many in fact that they were still the standard Italian medium howitzers in 1940, with the designations **obice da 149/12 modello 14** and **obice da 149/13**. After 1914 the howitzers were used by the Czech (**hruba houfnize vz 14** and **vz 14/16**), Austrian and Hungarian armies for many years,

An Austro-Hungarian Skoda Model 1914 149-mm howitzer is seen in action with Italian forces on the northern Italian front. These howitzers were used by both sides during the war, with the Italians capturing their stocks from the Austro-Hungarians – so many, in fact, that this model became a virtually 'Italian' gun during World War II.

and the Modell 14/16 in particular was the subject of a gradual series of improvements and modifications to keep it as up-to-date as possible. This involved the usual replacement of the wooden-spoked wheel with pressed steel wheels fitted with rubber tyres, but in addition new ammunition was introduced and the Hungarians went so far as to virtually rebuild their **M.14/ 35** howitzers, a programme that even involved the fitting of muzzle brakes to reduce recoil forces on the carriage when new ammunition was fired.

Both the Modell 14 and Modell 14/16 were sound and sturdy weapons, but they were rather heavy and, compared with many contemporary designs, lacked range. However, they were produced in such large numbers that many were on hand in 1939 ready for use in another war. Examples in German service were designated **15-cm schwere Feldhaubitze M.14 (Skoda)**, while ex-Italian equipments were **15-cm sFH 400(i)** and **sFH401(i)**.

Austro-Hungarian Skoda 149-mm (5.87-in) Model 1914 heavy field howitzers in a battery position at Wolhynie. The changes from the battery lay-outs of the Western Front are very apparent, although shelters for men and ammunition have been prepared near the guns.

Right: British and Italian transport pass captured Austro-Hungarian artillery on a road near the Val d'Assa in November 1918. The gun in the immediate foreground is a Skoda 149-mm (5.87-in) Model 1914 field howitzer, one of many that fell into Italian hands to become one of the standard Italian artillery weapons of World War II.

Specification
Modell 14
Calibre: 149.1 mm (5.87 in)
Length: of barrel 2.09 m (82.3 in)
Weights: in action 2344 kg (5,168 lb); travelling 3070 kg (6,769 lb)
Elevation: −5° to +43°
Traverse: 5°
Muzzle velocity: 300 m (984 ft) per second
Maximum range: 6900 m (7,546 yards)
Shell weight: 41 kg (90.4 lb)

Modell 14/16
Calibre: 149.1 mm (5.87 in)
Length: of barrel 2.1 m (82.7 in)
Weights: in action 2765 kg (6,097 lb); travelling 3340 kg (7,365 lb)
Elevation: −5° to +70°
Traverse: 6°
Muzzle velocity: 350 m (1,148 ft) per second
Maximum range: 8790 m (9,613 yards)
Shell weight: 40.33 kg (88.9 lb)

GERMANY
Ehrhardt field guns

Although less well known outside Germany, the Ehrhardt concern of Düsseldorf was one of the more important German steel and weapons manufacturers, although it was often overshadowed by the giant Krupp concern. In time it underwent a series of mergers and take-overs that resulted in the Rheinmetall-Borsig AG conglomerate that was to become as big and as important as Krupp, but during the early 1900s it had to struggle to get what orders it could. One of these early 1900 orders was from the UK, no less, which was at that time still enmeshed in the 2nd Boer War, a war in which the UK's farmer opponents were better off for modern field artillery than the British army. In 1901 the British ordered 108 Ehrhardt field guns that were known to the British as the **Ordnance, QF, 15-pdr**. These guns had a calibre of 76.2 mm (3 in) and were regarded very much as stopgap equipment until something better came along, when the Ehrhardt guns were handed over to the Territorial Army field batteries. Some of these TA batteries still had their 15-pdr guns when they were ordered to travel to France during 1915, and for a while these were used until enough 18-pdr guns were on hand to replace them in 1916. A few more batteries of 15-pdr guns were sent to Egypt but these saw little, if any, action.

The 15-pdr guns were typical Ehrhardt designs as they prominently featured one of the main Ehrhardt trademarks, the pole trail carriage. Ehrhardt used the pole trail to enable the gun to be towed easily by horses as it combined strength with lightness. The company soon learned, however, that the pole trail restricted elevation

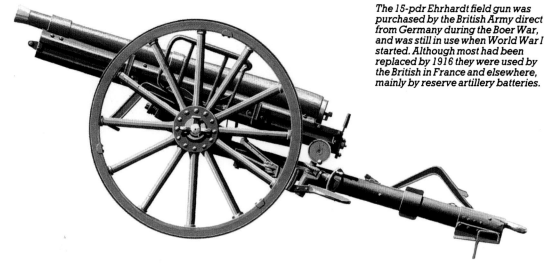

The 15-pdr Ehrhardt field gun was purchased by the British Army direct from Germany during the Boer War, and was still in use when World War I started. Although most had been replaced by 1916 they were used by the British in France and elsewhere, mainly by reserve artillery batteries.

(and thus maximum range) so later Ehrhardt guns featured what became known as the split pole trail. This had two tubular pole trail legs reaching back from the carriage cradle to a point well behind the breech at full recoil. A connecting tube then joined the two poles at right angles and to this connecting piece the single pole trail ran back to the trail spade and towing eye. This combined the lightness of the pole trail with the ability of the barrel to elevate as much as required, and this feature became a virtual Ehrhardt trademark, being used on many Ehrhardt mountain gun designs.

The British 15-pdr guns had the ordinary pole trail, and the first versions even had two seats over the axle

to carry two gun crew members on the move. These were later replaced by a shield, and the original gun wheels were replaced by British service items. The Royal Artillery was not very impressed with the 15-pdr guns and, as already mentioned, they were replaced by 18-pdr guns as soon as possible.

1901 was a good sales year for Ehrhardt, for in that same year it received an order for 132 field guns from the Norwegian army. These guns were of 75-mm (2.95-in) calibre and differed in many details from the British 15-pdr pieces. Although Norway was not directly concerned with World War I, its **7.5-cm Feltkanon L631 M/01** Ehrhardt guns were kept in service

throughout the war years and many of them were still in use when the Germans invaded Norway in 1940, whereupon they were designated **7.5-cm FK246(n)**.

Many other Ehrhardt guns were sold to South American nations.

Specification
15-pdr
Calibre: 76.2 mm (3 in)
Length: of barrel 2.286 m (90 in)
Weight: in action 1030.5 kg (2.272 lb)
Elevation: −5° to +16°
Traverse: 6°
Muzzle velocity: 510 m (1,674 ft) per second
Maximum range: 5852 m (6,400 yards)
Shell weight: 6.35 kg (14 lb)

GERMANY
7.7-cm field gun

During the 1890s the German army asked Krupp to produce a field gun with a calibre of 77 mm (3.03 in). This odd calibre was chosen as it was realized that most potential enemies used field guns with calibres of 75 mm (2.95 in), namely France or 76.2 mm (3 in), namely Russia. Thus any captured guns could be bored out to take German ammunition but an enemy would be unable to do the same with captured German guns: this is an early example of this nation's thorough approach to war. In order to save manufacturing potential the new gun was to be mounted on the howitzer carriage of the day.

This gun was known as the **Feldkanone 96 n/A** (n/A for *neues Art*, or new model). It was the standard field gun of the German artillery arm when World war I began in 1914, and many served until 1918. The **FK 96 n/A** was a sound Krupp design, but the German gunners gradually came to appreciate that it lacked range and asked for improvements. New ammunition was introduced, but the main range increment came during 1916 with the introduction of a new and longer barrel; the carriage continued to be the original C/96 howitzer carriage and the breech mechanism of the FK 96 n/A was retained. This new field gun became known as the **7.7-cm Feldkanone 16** or **FK 16**, and it was rapidly adopted as the standard German field gun, replacing as many of the older models as possible.

The 7.7-cm (3.03-in) Feldkanone C 96 n/A (neues Art – new model) was the standard German field gun of the early war years. Built by Krupp, it was a rugged and very reliable gun but lacked range and was later replaced by the 7.7-cm FK 16, which had a longer barrel and some other small changes to the field carriage and shield.

The FK 16 introduced considerable range increase. With the old type ammunition the FK 96 n/A could manage only about 7000 m (7,655 yards) firing light shrapnel projectiles. The new FK 16 firing new streamlined shells could reach 10300 m (11,264 yards), which was a considerable in-

A German 7.7-cm (3.03-in) Feldkanone (FK) C 96 n/A is shown in action in the Champagne region with the barrel at maximum recoil. As the loader stands by with a fresh round the soldier at the end of the carriage trail prepares to make any laying corrections the layer next to the shield might call for.

crease. Some of this range increase had to be offset by an increase in overall weight but this price was borne willingly. The FK 16 could fire a wide range of ammunition types, all of them loaded separately, i.e. the shell and charge case were loaded as two items. As well as the usual shrapnel and high explosive (HE), the FK 16 was also used to fire various forms of gas shell. Compared with the earlier short projectiles, the improved ammunition for the FK 16 was much longer and more streamlined, offering less drag in flight. These shells were usually HE only; there were also smoke and illuminating projectiles.

Ammunition for the FK 16 was carried into action on a gun limber. A six-horse team was used to pull the gun and limber into action, but late in the war other animals such as oxen had to be used. The normal gun crew was six or seven men but often less were used once the gun was emplaced in a forward position; the rest then acted as ammunition handlers.

After 1918 the FK 16 was one of the

few weapons allowed to the rump of the old German army. Others were handed out as war reparations to nations such as Belgium, and the Netherlands also received a number. Many of these FK 16s were converted to take 75-mm (2.95-in) barrels, including the German examples, so that when World War II came around there were virtually no 77-mm versions left other than a few training equipments. Many of the re-barrelled FK 16s were used throughout World War II.

Specification
FK 16
Calibre: 77 mm (3.03 in)
Weights: in action 1422.5 kg (3,136 lb); travelling 2286 kg (5,040 lb)
Length: of barrel 2.70 m (106.3 in)
Elevation: −9.5° to +38°
Traverse: 8°
Muzzle velocity: maximum 600 m (1,968 ft) per second
Maximum range: 10300 m (11,264 yards)
Shell weight: streamlined HE 5.9 kg (13 lb)

Above: A German army 7.7-cm (3.03-in) C 96 n/A field gun in action in Poland during the 1915 summer campaign. The gun sight can be seen above the lowered gun shield flap and some ammunition carriers lie in front of the gun muzzle.

Below: German gunners train with 7.7-cm (3.03-in) C 96 n/A field guns on ranges somewhere in Germany during World War I. These guns, although replaced by the FK 16 in the field batteries after 1916, were still in use for training or by reserve batteries until the war ended in 1918.

Above: Detail of the breech of a captured FK 16 shows the sliding breech block, which was by 1916 a standard feature of German field artillery design.

Above: German gunners engaged in urban fighting against Bolshevik forces near Nariva, March 1918. The guns are 7.7-cm (3.03-in) FK 16s and the layer is aiming the gun over open sights. Note how the gun crew used the ammunition limber to obtain extra cover.

The 7.7-cm (3.03-in) Feldkanone 16 was based on the C 96 n/A, but had more range and was more suited to Western Front conditions. Maximum range was 10300 m (11,264 yards).

RUSSIA
76.2-mm Field Gun Model 00/02

In 1914 the Russian army was desperately short of up-to-date field artillery, but this was not due to lack of production facilities or technological backwardness, as might be supposed. On the contrary, from 1906 vast sums of money were expended on artillery but were used to modernize the armament of the fortresses which protected the western frontiers of the Empire. These

fortresses, which absorbed so large a proportion of the defence budget, proved to be of little use when the German army finally invaded, while the lack of modern field guns in the armies was a serious handicap.

Since the 1860s Russia had used field artillery based on Krupp designs. Although unable at first to afford the steel barrel construction of the Ger-

man weapons, Russia demonstrated to the world the superiority of metal carriages over conventional wooden ones during the Russo-Turkish war in 1877. The campaign in Bulgaria revealed many shortcomings in the Russian army but probably saw the Tsarist army at the peak of its efficiency. Thereafter, its fortunes declined as vigorous officers like Skoboleff were

passed over for political reasons.

Russian field artillery continued its reliance on Krupps, and its main field piece of World War I owed much to Krupp designs. The 76.2-mm Field Gun Model 00 was based on an older Krupp weapon, and had no recoil system other than a sprung spade under the axle. It had not been in service long before a more modern recoil system was fitted to produce the Model 00/02. This gun was produced at the Putilov arsenal at St Petersburg, which was the most modern facility in Russia at the time. Thus the Model 02 was very like many other Krupp designs of the period. The barrel was 30 calibres long and the usual Krupp steel section trail was copied almost exactly. A shield was provided, but this was often removed and replaced by two seats over the axle. One small feature that was to become a virtual Putilov trademark was to be seen at the front of the recoil mechanism cylinder: this was a peculiar embossed pattern that appeared on almost every subsequent Putilov product.

The quantities of field guns required by the massive Tsarist armies were so large that when World War I broke out many batteries were still using field guns that dated back to the 1870s. There were never enough Model 02s to go around, and the German victories

of 1914 and after usually resulted in the guns that there were to hand being added to the pile of German war booty. All the Putilov workers could do was attempt to churn out as many Model 02s as they possibly could. Thus the Model 02 was kept in production for long after 1917, and so many were still in use by 1930 that a programme to modernize them was instituted. Thus when 1941 arrived the Model 02 was still in service as the **Model 02/30**, and captured examples were designated **7.62-cm leFk 294(r)** by the Germans.

Specification
Field Gun Model 00/02
Calibre: 76.2 mm (3 in)

Length: of barrel 2.286 m (90 in)
Weights: in action 1040 kg (2,293 lb); travelling 1965 kg (4,332 lb)
Elevation: −5° to +16°
Traverse: 5.5°
Muzzle velocity: 588 m (1,929 ft) per second
Maximum range: 6400 m (7,000 yards)
Shell weight: 6.5 kg (14.33 lb)

Russian Putilov 76.2-mm (3-in) Model 00 (1900) field guns were converted for the anti-aircraft role on modified garrison carriages and used by the Germans on the Western Front. This trio was captured at Chateau Thierry in July 1918.

107-mm Field Gun Model 1910

Soon after production of the 76.2-mm (3-in) Model 00/02 got under way at the Putilov arsenal, the designers had an opportunity to assess what other artillery weapons would be needed by the Tsarist armies. At that time many of the heavy field batteries were equipped with a motley array of weapons, mainly of Krupp origins, and the Putilov designers decided to see what they could produce using their own talents. They soon demonstrated a real flair for designing modern artillery that was to come to full flower during World War II, for they produced a gun known as the **107-mm Field Gun Model 1910**.

This Model 1910 was one of the best designs of its generation. It was well-balanced and good-looking with an excellent all-round performance, and as time was to show it had a considerable amount of built-in growth potential. As was only to be expected, features from existing weapons (especially from some Krupp sources) were evident in the design, but it was innovative and demonstrated a good balance of weight and performance. The shell weighed 16.4 kg (36.15 lb) and could be fired to a very useful 12500 m (13,670 yards). The gun was towed by eight horses.

It was at this stage, just after production of the Model 1910 had commenced, that the Putilov concern got itself into severe financial difficulties. The state of the Russian economy was at best parlous, and the demands made upon it by rapidly expanding

industries such as the defence concerns made it even shakier. The only way out the Tsarist officials could see was to attract foreign finance into such industries, and the French defence manufacturers descended on Russia like hawks. The massive Schneider & Cie concern soon took over the Putilov arsenal and poured in huge amounts of hard cash. In return it took what it could to bolster its own sales efforts, and the Model 1910 caught the French eye. The result was the 105-mm (4.134-in) Model 1913, or L 13 S.

Even with the financial backing of Schneider, production of the Model 1910 at St Petersburg never got anywhere near meeting demand until well into the war years. But by 1917 Model

1910s were flowing off the lines in considerable numbers, so many in fact that when the line closed in the period after the revolution of 1917 there were many Model 1910s for the new Red Army to use during the civil war and for years after. In 1930 the type was one of several chosen to be updated in an attempt to modernize the Red Army gun park. For the Model 1910 this meant a new and longer barrel and new ammunition; this produced the **Model 1910/30**. This gun was one that the Germans came to prize after the events of 1941, for it made an excellent weapon for use in the Atlantic Wall with the designation **10.7-cm K352(r)**. Thus the Model 1910/30 was used there alongside numbers of captured French L 13

S guns, and the two weapons that originated in St Petersburg many years before ended their service lives together.

Specification
107-mm Field Gun Model 1910
Calibre: 106.7 mm (4.2 in)
Length: of barrel about 2.99 m (117.7 in)
Weights: in action 2172 kg (4,788 lb); travelling 2486 kg (5,480 lb)
Elevation: −5° to +37°
Traverse: 6°
Muzzle velocity: 570 m (1,870 ft) per second
Maximum range: 12500 m (13,670 yards)
Shell weight: 16.4 kg (36.15 lb)

A Russian army 107-mm (actually 106.7-mm/4.2-in) Field Gun Model 1910 in action with Armenian gunners in Mesopotamia. This gun was the originator for the Schneider 105-mm (4.14-in) L 13 S used by the French army, and a modernized version was used in World War II.

Heavy Artillery of World War 1

To the sentry standing his pre-dawn duty in the trenches of the Western Front, the sight of a jagged line of light on the opposite horizon cannot have been comforting, for behind such a line lay the fire of the largest concentration of artillery pieces in history.

Heavy artillery of World War I had few mechanical aids for handling heavy ammunition. Particularly on the older models, shells weighing over 1000 kg (2205 lb) would have to be manhandled into the breech, as happened with this French 400-mm equipment.

World War I was an artillery war and, while large numbers of field guns were involved in all the major battles of that conflict, it was the heavy artillery that ultimately won or lost battles. It was only the heavy artillery that had the shell power to destroy the earth or concrete protection upon which each side came to rely for survival in the front line, and it was only the heavy artillery that could smash a way through the lines of defences behind which each side sheltered.

By 1914 most European powers had built up large gun parks that contained artillery of increasingly heavy calibres and power. These were necessary to demolish the rings of fortifications that all the major powers used to protect their territories against the intrusions of others, but once those fortresses had been bypassed by the events of the first year of the war the same heavy artillery was equally useful in the strange conditions of the Western Front, where trench lines imposed their own peculiar method of warfare.

This short survey cannot include all the many and various models of heavy artillery that were used during World War I. What has been attempted is a general indication of the many types involved, and included here are some of the models that might be considered the most important. Thus the Paris Gun and 'Big Bertha' are included along with the British 234-mm (9.2-in) guns and 305-mm (12-in) howitzers, but

weapons such as the German 21-cm (8.27-in) mortars have had to be left out for space reasons. Space has been found for some of the smaller examples of heavy artillery, such as the British 152-mm (6-in) howitzer and the German 15-cm (5.9-in) Kanone 16, but the main emphasis is on the really heavy weapons, for it is they that now attract the most attention and interest.

The 'Great War' was the heyday of heavy artillery. In the purely static conditions that existed along the Western Front the heavy guns and howitzers could be carefully emplaced with few thoughts of dramatic or rapid moves, and they could be fed with their heavy projectiles for as long as the required logistic machinery remained in being. They had plenty of targets as each side burrowed deep into the earth to survive the storm that daily flew over their heads. The only way to harm such burrows was by the use of heavy projectiles that could smash their way through such protection as there was, and these heavy projectiles could only be delivered by the heavy artillery.

Once the war had settled down to a face-to-face confrontation between deeply entrenched forces, the howitzer came to the fore as the main offensive weapon of the various artillery arms. The monstrous 42-cm M-Gerät (known as 'Big Bertha') was used by the Germans at Liège and Namur.

15-cm Kanone 16

The inclusion of a gun with a calibre of only 150 mm (5.9 in) may seem out of place in a description of heavy artillery, but the German 15-cm (5.9-in) guns were really in a class above that of normal field artillery. Quite apart from their size and weight, they were intended for use as corps artillery capable of long-range counterbattery and 'interdiction' employment, and thus came into the heavy artillery category.

By 1916 the long-range German artillery in use on the Western Front was mainly of a makeshift nature, being derived from a policy of placing coastal defence or naval gun barrels on to improvised field carriages. While this was adequate as a stopgap measure, the gunners needed something more suitable and manageable for their long-term equipment, and consequently the German general staff made a special plea to its artillery designers for a world-beater. Both Krupp and Rheinmetall took up the challenge, and as things turned out their individual submissions were virtually identical. Both guns were named 15-cm Kanone 16 or 15-cm K 16, but in the long term it was the Krupp 15-cm K 16 Kp submission that was produced in the greater quantities. The Rheinmetall 15-cm K 16 Rh was produced in some numbers as the demands from the front were so great, but never in the numbers that Krupp was able to churn out.

The 15-cm K 16 was a long and large gun. The overall design was entirely orthodox for the time apart from the fact that the barrel was extraordinarily long (L/42.7 in the Krupp design and L/42.9 in the Rheinmetall offering) for the size of the wheeled carriage. The carriage was a fairly simple box-trail design fitted with a large shield for the gun crew. Heavy spoked wheels were fitted as the gun had to be towed by horse teams as motor traction was by that stage of the war (it was 1917 before appreciable numbers of the guns actually reached the front) at a premium and reserved mainly for the really heavy guns. The weights involved meant that the 15-cm K 16 had to be

Above: In contrast to most of the artillery involved in World War I, the German 15-cm pieces were not howitzers. With their long range, the weapons were feared in the counterbattery role, and could only be opposed by much larger and less mobile Allied weapons.

towed in two loads, the barrel and the carriage. The carriage was usually towed on a special four-wheeled limber which also had some seating for the crew members, who also operated the brakes.

On the Western Front the 15-cm K 16 became one of the most feared of all the German counterbattery guns. The long range (22000 m/24,060 yards) of the gun meant that it could reach well into the rear areas behind the Allied lines to destroy gun batteries, road and rail junctions and generally to lay down harassing fire that could not be countered by anything other than the heaviest and longest-ranged Allied guns (railway artillery or specially emplaced weapons). This entailed a great deal of effort on the part of the Allies, for despite its weight and bulk, the 15-cm K 16 was still more mobile than its potential opposition.

After 1918 numbers of 15-cm K 16s were handed out to various nations as war reparations (Belgium was a major recipient) but the gun was one of the few allowed to remain on the strength of the small post-Versailles German army. Thus for nearly two decades it acted as a training weapon for a new generation of gunners who, re-equipped and with a new military philosophy, went to war once again. Even then the 15-cm K 16 was used during some of the early World War II campaigns.

Specification
15-cm K 16
Calibre: 149.3 mm (5.88 in)
Length of barrel: 6.41 m (21 ft 0.4 in)

The 15-cm Kanone 16 was manufactured by both Krupp and Rheinmetall, the latter (as seen here) being made in smaller quantities. The equipments were still in limited use during the early campaigns of World War II, as it was one of the few military items permitted to Germany after Versailles.

Weight: in action 10870 kg (23,964 lb)
Elevation: −3° to +42°
Traverse: 8°
Muzzle velocity: 757 m (2,484 ft) per second
Maximum range: 22000 m (24,060 yards)
Shell weight: 51.4 kg (113.3 lb)

German 28-cm howitzers

By 1914 the growth of the German navy had ensured a corresponding increase in the number and power of the coastal batteries that were built to defend the various German dockyards and harbours. Coastal defence was the responsibility of the German navy, and as a general rule it adapted naval guns to carry out the coast defence role. But following the general fashion elsewhere it also adopted the high-trajectory howitzer, and for this it had to turn to the army for advice.

By the turn of the century the German navy thus had an adaptation of an army 28-cm (11.02-in) howitzer known as the 28-cm Küstenhaubitze (coast howitzer). The army weapon was the 28-cm Haubitze L/12, and both of these heavy weapons were products of the prolific Krupp armament works at Essen in the Ruhr. Both howitzers were intended mainly for the static role: the army howitzer had been designed primarily for fortification-smashing, in which a lengthy emplacement period was of no real importance. Thus the squat barrel of the howitzer rested in a

cradle mounted on a large and heavy carriage which was in its turn located on a turntable connected to a heavy firing platform dug into the ground. Both howitzers had features from an earlier age: at the rear was a crane for raising ammunition to the level of the breech, while most of the recoil forces were absorbed by the barrel and cradle sliding along short rails when fired, the rest of the forces being absorbed by the mass and weight of the carriage.

Even by 1914 standards the 28-cm (11.02-in) howitzers were obsolescent. Their weight and bulk rendered them virtually immovable, and the relatively short ranges possible (11400 m/12,465 yards) made them somewhat uneconomical in terms of

The 28-cm Küstenhaubitze was an extremely unwieldy weapon, its weight and bulk fixing it to one spot and the relatively short range making it uneconomical in terms of manpower and resources. In spite of this, many served throughout the war.

mic in terms of manpower and travelling requirements. Moreover, each howitzer took three or four days to emplace and as long to remove, and was extraordinarily difficult to move. For transport the howitzers were broken down into the usual loads: the army version travelled in four loads, while the coastal version had to be virtually dismantled and reassembled each time. The most unusual feature of these howitzers was that they used bagged-charge propellants: for many years the German artillery designers had used some form of cartridge case allied to a sliding-block breech mechanism, but the 28-cm (11.02-in) howitzers used bagged charges allied to a screw breech.

During World War I these howitzers were dragged up and down the length of the German lines in France whenever and wherever there appeared worthwhile targets for their power. Both the army and navy versions were used at Verdun and during many of the other major German artillery battles, and most survived the war to be hidden away in various secret stockpiles. Thus both models were to hand when 1939 came around. They were once more pressed into service, this time somewhat modified for traction by half-track vehicles, and they were used during the siege of Sevastopol in 1942 and later during the savage crushing of the Warsaw Rising of 1944. Thereafter they faded from view. It

was a wonder that they lasted so long.

Specification
28-cm Küstenhaubitze
Calibre: 283 mm (11.14 in)
Length of barrel: 3.40 m (11 ft 1.9 in)
Weight: in action 63600 kg (140,214 lb)

Elevation: 0° to +65°
Traverse: 360° on turntable
Muzzle velocity: 350-379 m (1,148 to 1,243 ft) per second
Maximum range: 11400 m (12,465 yards)
Shell weight: 350 kg (771.6 kg)

The massive foundation and turntable necessary for the 28-cm (11-in) howitzers made moving them a considerable task, and yet the huge weapons were dragged up and down the Western front throughout the war.

M-Gerät or 'Big Bertha'

The Schlieffen Plan that was intended to secure the German defeat of France, by wheeling armies through Belgium to take the French armies in the flank, was conceived during the 1890s and honed almost to perfection during the years up to 1914. It entailed the invasion of a neutral state (Belgium) and the rapid destruction of the forts at Liège and Namur, both of them among the most powerful in Europe. Heavy artillery was needed, so Krupp was involved.

Throughout earlier years Krupp had been responsible for a long string of super-heavy guns and howitzers, but to defeat the Belgian forts it had to produce something special. It undertook a series of trials with heavy-calibre weapons that ultimately led to a 420-mm (16.54-in) howitzer known as **Gamma**, a prodigious beast that proved to be very accurate when firing a heavy projectile capable of destroying any fortification. But Gamma was a static weapon, designed to be taken apart for moves and reassembled piece by piece after rail transportation. While the German staff planners appreciated the power of Gamma, they asked for a weapon that could be towed on roads and the obliging Krupp designers looked to their research and came up with the answer. This was an enlarged and modified wheeled carriage originally intended for a 305-mm (12-in) howitzer. Thus was born the **M-Gerät** (Gerät means equipment).

All this development took place right at the last possible moment, and it was not until August 1914 that the huge howitzers moved off to war. The type was soon known as the *dicke Bertha* (Fat Bertha, but more commonly translated 'Big Bertha') to its crews and the

name stuck. The crews belonged to a special unit known as kurz Marine Kanone 3, and initially only two howitzers went into action against the Belgian forts. They moved on the roads in a series of tractor-towed loads, five to each gun. The carriages had been designed to enable the howitzers to be assembled with a minimum of labour and time. Special armour-piercing projectiles as well as the conventional high explosive types were available.

The impact of these huge howitzers has now passed into history. Within a few days the mighty Liège forts were smashed and forced to capitulate, soon to be followed by the Namur forts. The 420-mm (16.54-in) shells were able to plunge deep into the earth before exploding and the resultant shock waves shook the forts to their foundations. They had a tremendous morale as well as destructive effect, and after a few days of steady bombardment the occupants of the fort had been reduced to a state of collapse.

After deployment in Belgium the battery moved to the Russian front, where it repeated its successes. The howitzers were soon joined by more examples from the Krupp works, and

yet more were used on the Western Front. However, it was soon learned that the type's accuracy fell off as the barrel became worn after even a limited period of firing and that, consequently, destructive impact was reduced. Although the 'Big Berthas' had a maximum range of 9300 m (10,170 yards), their best accuracy was obtained at around 8680 m (9,490 yards). Another problem came painfully to light when it was discovered that the projectiles were very prone to detonating while still inside the barrel the instant after firing, and many barrels were destroyed in this fashion.

The 'Big Berthas' had their maximum impact against the Belgian forts. Thereafter their importance fell away, and a measure of this can be seen in the fact that although they were used extensively during the Verdun battles French reports make virtually no mention of their effects, a sign that their day was already past. None remained after 1918, though the Gamma howitzers, used in the development of the towed 'Big Berthas', did survive. At least one saw action in 1942, when it was used in the siege of Sevastopol.

Specification
M-Gerät
Calibre: 420 mm (16.54 in)
Length of barrel: 6.72 m (22 ft 0.7 in)
Weight: in action 42600 kg (93,915 lb)
Elevation: 0° to +65°
Traverse: 20°
Muzzle velocity: about 426 m (1,400 ft) per second
Maximum range: 9300 m (10,170 yards)
Shell weight: 810 kg (1,786 lb)

The mighty 420-mm howitzer known as 'Big Bertha' was used by the German army to nullify the threat of the Belgian forts at Liège and Namur. It was a fearsome weapon, powerful and accurate (at least while the barrel was new).

Moving the Big Guns

World War I was fought in the early years of motor transport, often using massively heavy equipment and over the most difficult terrain. While it was appreciated that the new engines could be of the greatest of use, supply was still slow, and the old standby of manpower and horsepower came into play.

In an age in which mass-produced mechanical transport devices are commonplace, it comes as something of a surprise to realize how scarce such devices were during the early days of this century. Before World War I a great deal of power was generated by the simple application of manual labour assisted at times by the power of the horse, and this has to be remembered in the context of heavy artillery. At that time mechanical traction and powered lifting devices were unusual, so when it came to moving and handling heavy artillery there was often little more than brute force available.

Throughout the centuries gunners have learned to handle even the heaviest of their charges using only what is to hand. This has always involved a complicated system of timbers, joists, pulleys, levers and hard work, and while this can on its own move even the heaviest field gun and its carriage, such methods can have only a limited utility in the movement of large-calibre weapons. Fortunately the monsters in service during World War I had generally been designed at a time when metallurgy and mechanics were beginning to reach an advanced state, so designers were often able to build into these weapons some form of handling system that required only a minimum of physical effort and also offered a greater degree of safety to all concerned. The various systems usually involved built-in rails and winches that enabled a howitzer or gun barrel to be removed or withdrawn on to its transport carriage without the need for special jigs and overhead structures. Some heavy artillery had inbuilt cranes for the same purpose, while some designers simply decided that the best way to assemble and disassemble guns was by supplying a mobile crane that was issued as part of the weapon's standard equipment.

So by the time of World War I the emplacement of a heavy artillery piece was often not quite the problem it might have been, but usually there was still a great deal of work to be done. Pits had to be dug to accommodate the heavy firing platform needed by most weapons of the period, and in some cases earthboxes had to be filled to counteract the forces produced on firing. Heavy subassemblies still had to be manhandled on occasion, and this necessity often led to the allocation of only the largest men to heavy artillery units.

Putting the weapons together or taking them apart was only one aspect of the labour involved in moving heavy artillery. Once the weapon had been broken down into a number of loads, each load had somehow to be pulled to where it was required. Before World War I this usually involved the horse or other draught animal, but the largest weapons required so many teams of horses that any real efficiency was impossible. Some of the less advanced nations had to rely on the horse, but the more advanced nations came to rely upon powered traction in the form of the internal combustion-engined tractor, the steam traction engine and even railways.

Traction engines were very often normal commercial models impressed into military service, and they rarely required any modifications for their new role.

The Holt tractor was very successful in the task of hauling heavy equipment through the mud of the Front. It eventually gave rise to the caterpillar-tracked fighting vehicle, otherwise known as the tank.

With the motor tractors things were different, however. The motor vehicle was still a relatively simple vehicle, and very often the power generated by the engines was relatively low. The only way to gain the power required to tow heavy artillery was by the enlargement of engines to massive proportions. This in turn led to large and heavy wheels to carry the engines and transmit the power, with the result that the specialist artillery tractors of World War I resembled nothing more than huge bonnets carried on large wheels. In such examples the driver appeared to be a mere appendage to the vehicle. Typical of these monsters were the many designs produced in Austria and Germany, such as the Austro-Daimlers and their ilk.

But it should not be forgotten that all too often the motor tractor and traction engine could not be used for the simple reason that even under war production conditions there were rarely enough to meet all the demands made upon the numbers available. All too often the gunners had to rely on the horse for their traction purposes, and if horses were not available they had to call upon such beasts as draught oxen or even camels. The difficulties involved in using huge teams of such animals to tow heavy and awkward artillery loads across the shattered terrain of World War I battlefields can barely be imagined, but for the gunners who had to carry out such tasks we can now only offer our admiration.

Above: The field version of the 42-cm Skoda could be disassembled for travel, but with a weight of over 100 tonnes, movement was not easy.

Below: The 38-cm model 16 from Skoda was also designed for road transport, to be towed by large wheeled tractors in sections.

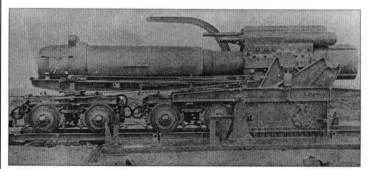

Above: Very often the assembly and disassembly of these heavy pieces required special equipment. Here the barrel of a 370-mm French mortar (howitzer) is suspended prior to fitting onto the firing platform. Often the crane was issued as part of the equipment.

Right: The terrain-crossing ability of the tank was put to good use during the battle of Cambrai. This German 15-cm (5.9-in) gun was captured and towed back across the battlefield.

The Paris Gun

March 1918 saw the final major German offensive of the war, with an all-out assault which caught the Allies by surprise. One of the aims of the German general staff was to create as much confusion behind the lines as possible; to this end, a Krupp project was put into effect, and one of the most unusual weapons of the war entered service.

At 07.30 on 23 March 1918 there occurred in the Quai de Seine (in the north east of Paris) an explosion for which no cause could be found. About 20 minutes later there was a similar explosion in the crowded Boulevard de Strasbourg and this time, when the crowds cleared, it was found that eight unfortunates had been killed and a further 13 injured. Again the cause of the explosion was not apparent but some steel fragments were found, suggesting an aerial bomb. But no aircraft had been seen, nor were any noticed when a third explosion occurred in the Rue de Château-Landon, where a building was partially demolished. By this time the Paris officials were deeply anxious to discover the actual cause of the explosions, and investigators began to piece together such evidence as there was. Almost as soon as they began there was a fourth explosion, this time in the Rue Charles-Cinq, and yet another person was killed.

It was not long before more fragments were found and this time there were enough to indicate that they came from artillery shells. But where was the gun that had fired them? More mystery shells landed as the investigators worked and a general alarm was sounded, sending the people of Paris to their shelters. By the eighth explosion the investigators had already decided that the shells were from a 208-mm (8.19-in) gun and even hinted at a possible location for the gun involved. Their prediction was that the gun was somewhere in the Crépy region, but Crépy was 120 km (75 miles) from Paris!

The Germans obviously had some sort of long-range gun of a kind hitherto only imagined. It was all too much for the citizens; as more and more of these mystery shells fell in and around Paris the population simply left the city. Over the next few days shells contined to

land in a sporadic pattern, causing limited damage and some casualties, but much worse was to come. On Good Friday, 29 March, a shell fell into the church of St Gervais on the Ile de France right in the centre of the city: 82 people were killed and 68 more injured. The mystery gun had caused its biggest casualty toll to date. But what was the gun that had caused all this carnage?

The answer was complicated, and began with German ballistic trials in which the projectiles travelled much further than anticipated. The cause was found in the fact that the projectiles had left the thicker strata of the Earth's atmosphere; as air friction was greatly reduced for much of the trajectory, range was enhanced. To take advantage of this effect a special gun was designed. A 380-mm (14.96-in) naval gun barrel was relined with a new and much longer 210-mm (8.27-in) barrel (about 40 m/131.2 ft overall), for which special charges and projectiles were developed. The new gun was an oddity with its very long barrel that protruded some way out of the original naval gun. It weighed no less than 142 tonnes, but it had a range of 132 km (82 miles) and it could be made to work consistently, if only at a price. Each time the gun was fired the shell passing along the barrel produced so much wear that the internal calibre actually increased, and successive shells had to be of larger diameter than the one before. The long barrel tended to droop under its own weight so external bracing had to be provided.

As always, a Krupp designer was the man behind all this advanced ballistic technology, the same man in fact who was responsible for the 420-mm (16.54-in) 'Big Berthas'. The whole project absorbed a great deal of Krupp's facilities but there was a reason behind it all. In early 1918 the German general staff intended to

Towering over the other products of the Krupp works, the Paris gun nears completion. The gun was such a challenge to the technology of the time that a fair proportion of even such a large firm's resources was taken up by the project.

make a series of attacks along the Somme that were intended to win the war and the new long-range gun was to play its part in harassing the Paris area and generally causing confusion and disruption. This is the reason for the popular name 'Paris Gun' for what was officially designated the lange 21-cm Kanone in Schiessgerüst (long 21-cm gun in firing platform). Later versions of the gun used a basic calibre of 232 mm (9.13 in) when the original barrel was

The barrel of the Paris gun is test-fired. Such were the stresses of firing upon the metal of the barrel that each discharge appreciably increased the bore of the weapon.

The Paris Gun

bored out, but it must be stressed that each shell that was fired enlarged the barrel calibre, so carefully manufactured shells had to be fired in the correct sequence.

The firing platform for the Paris Gun was of naval origin, with a turntable under the forward end and racers running on tracks at the other. The gun and its carriage were carefully emplaced near Crépy on a solid timber base and the surrounding area was carefully concealed in the centre of a wood. So careful was the concealment that the German gunners even went to the trouble of planting extra trees and replacing them if they wilted.

French reaction

But as the drizzle of shells continued to fall on Paris the French reacted. They moved heavy railway guns into the area closest to Crépy and began to fire into the area where they suspected the gun might be located. This came at a time when the degree of barrel wear in the German gun was so great that its accuracy was becoming extremely erratic and range was falling away. The barrel life was learned to be of the order of only 60 rounds, and a new barrel was fitted to the gun while it was still in its location in the Crépy woods.

Away to the north of the gun the advancing German armies were pushing forward with great success. They had virtually eliminated one British army, and by 30 March had advanced as far as Montdidier. It had already been decided that the Paris gun should then be moved to the Bois de Corbie, which is even closer to the French capital than Crépy. The gun then launched a second bombardment of Paris that was far more accurate than the first as the gunners were not firing at the extreme limits of its range. More and more barrels were changed, but once again the Paris gun attracted the attention of French army railway guns and airborne spotters to the extent that life on the new site became very unhealthy. Casualties were inflicted on the gun crew by

On the proofing range the Paris gun is prepared for firing. The external support was necessary to ensure accuracy in the long and slender barrel. The unprecedented range was purchased at the expense of weight of shell.

near-misses and even by one shell exploding in the gun: the shell had apparently been loaded in the wrong sequence and did not fit the barrel correctly.

By this time the Parisians, or rather those who were left, had begun to get used to the idea of being constantly shelled. Paris was a big place and shells could not fall everywhere so a form of normal life was resumed. On occasion one would land in a vulnerable spot, such as a Metro station, but on many more occasions they fell on open roads or empty buildings, causing few casualties. The German advance on the Marne by the end of May caused much more concern.

The Paris gun was eventually moved to a new position at Beaumont in order to escape the attentions of French railway guns, and from there the third bombardment was started. This was a very carefully prepared position with a steel bed for the carriage turntable and rail access for the ammunition on a lavish scale (the earlier gun positions had possessed rail access, but not on the scale of the Beaumont site). By this time the 232-mm (9.13-in) barrel was in use and was shooting very well, but already the gun was having less and less effect. The mighty land battle that was taking place to the north had reached the stage where the main German thrust had been contained, so the chances of the Germans having any major success before the American armies arrived in force had passed. The Paris gun could do little to remedy this state of affairs, and could merely keep up the harassing fire to create as much nuisance as possible. The ebb and flow of the battle led to a new gun location at a site in the Bois de Bruyères, and by 5 July it had resumed its bombardment of Paris. But it was all to no avail. By August the Allies were once more on the move. The German attacks had finally come to an end and in the process the German army had exhausted its last reserves of men and energy. All along the line they fell back towards Germany, abandoning all the gains they had made in the early months of the year. As they retreated they moved well out of range of Paris and the guns were dismantled and withdrawn. By that stage there was more than one gun (perhaps as many as three) though only one was used in action at any one time.

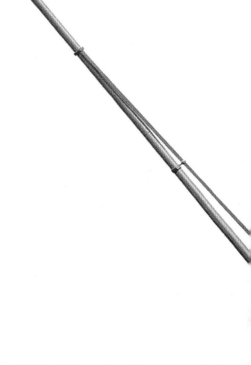

An impression of the Paris gun (officially known as the 'lange 21-cm Kanone in Schiessgerüst'), on location in the forest of Crépy.

Exactly what happened to the Paris guns in the aftermath of the war is still a mystery. None ever fell into Allied hands, although some firing platforms were found and carefully recorded for history. It seems safe to say that they were cut up to prevent the Allies from learning their secrets, but a great deal of ballistic data was accrued and carefully hidden away ready for a later generation of German artillery designers. At least one German World War II weapon, the 21-cm Kanone (Eisenbahn), owed more than passing influence to the Paris gun, and perhaps others did as well.

But for all its brilliant technical success, the Paris gun was a failure. It was intended to make Paris a dead city and render it useless to the Allies as a centre of industry and communications, but apart from a brief initial period of panic this never happened. Paris was too large a city for even a constant drizzle of shells to have anything more than local effect, and once the Allied advance had placed the city out of range the Paris gun could have no other application.

Special ammunition had to be developed to make best use of the potential range of the weapon. Illustrated below are two types of shell together with two charges (by varying the charge, range could be altered without changing elevation) and the case in which the charges were placed.

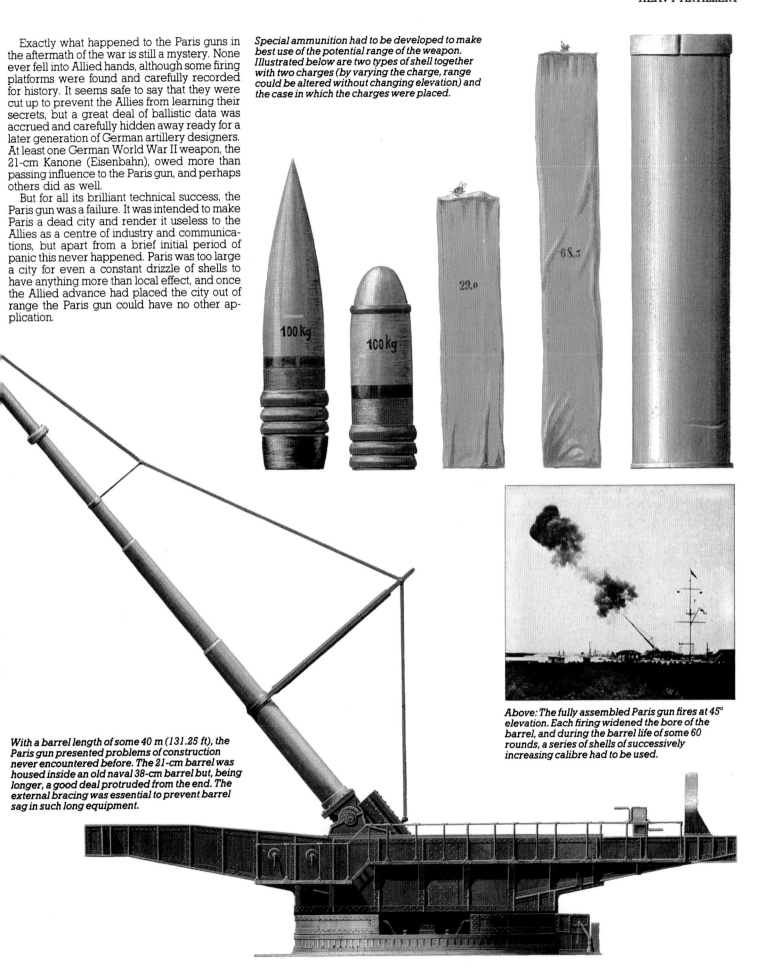

Above: The fully assembled Paris gun fires at 45° elevation. Each firing widened the bore of the barrel, and during the barrel life of some 60 rounds, a series of shells of successively increasing calibre had to be used.

With a barrel length of some 40 m (131.25 ft), the Paris gun presented problems of construction never encountered before. The 21-cm barrel was housed inside an old naval 38-cm barrel but, being longer, a good deal protruded from the end. The external bracing was essential to prevent barrel sag in such long equipment.

6-in 26 cwt BL Howitzer

The **6-in 26 cwt BL Howitzer** is one of those weapons that just scrapes into the category of heavy artillery, although its 6-in (152.4-mm) calibre would seem to categorize it more as an ordinary field artillery piece. However, the type was frequently used as heavy artillery by the British during World War I for the simple reason that on many occasions there was nothing else to hand. Thus the 6-in 26 cwt had to fill a gap, though it must be admitted that it filled that gap very well.

When the British army went to war in 1914 its Royal Artillery siege batteries were equipped with an elderly piece known as the **6-in 30 cwt BL Siege Howitzer**. This was very much a relic of earlier times, had a very limited range and lacked such refinements as an effective recoil mechanism. It was also too heavy for the conditions encountered in France, so a new piece was demanded. This was produced in a remarkably short time, design beginning in early 1915 and the first examples being ready soon after the middle of the same year. By the end of 1915 nearly 700 were in the hands of the troops.

The new howitzer was named the 6-in 26 cwt BL Howitzer to differentiate it from its predecessor. It proved to be a remarkably efficient weapon, and its employment was confined almost completely to the front lines for the demolition of enemy earth works, trenches and bunkers. It had a short stubby barrel that could be elevated to provide the plunging fire that was required in such tasks, such elevation being made possible by the use of a heavy box trail. The recoil mechanism was particularly effective, so effective in fact that it was used many years afterwards as the mechanism for the World War II 5.5-in (139.7-mm) gun-howitzer, a piece still in use in many places. A further measure of the success of the design can be seen in the fact that once in service the weapon remained virtually unchanged apart from some minor modifications, no designation higher than Mk I being required.

By 1916 the 6-in 26 cwt was one of the most important and numerous heavy guns in the British inventory, and its use spread to many other Allied and Commonwealth armies. Two types of projectile were fired, one weighing 45.36 kg (100 lb) and the other weighing 39 kg (86 lb). The maximum range with the lighter shell was 10425 m (11,400 yards). Millions of rounds were fired from these howitzers but many were in active use when

The 6-in 26-cwt BL Howitzer was a very effective artillery piece, light enough to serve at the front as field artillery, and firing a large enough shell to be pressed into service as heavy artillery when necessary.

Right: 6-in 26-cwt howitzers of the V Brigade, Royal Garrison Artillery parked in the Grande Place, Peronne, on 17 March 1918. By this time, motor transport was a relatively common feature of the British Army.

the war ended, and were retained in service until World War II. Some saw action during the early North African battles. Exports were made to Belgium, Italy and the Netherlands, where the weapon was designated **Obusier de 6″**, **Obice da 152/13** and **Houwitzer 6″** respectively. Weapons taken over by the Germans from these sources in World War II were thus the **15.2-cm sFH 410(b)**, **15.2-cm sFH 412(i)** and **15.2-cm sFH 407(h)**, while pieces captured from the British were **15.2-cm sFH 412(e)**.

Incidentally, the 6-in 26 cwt was the subject of one of the first attempts to produce a self-propelled artillery platform. In late 1916 some Mk I tanks were converted to carry 6-in 26 cwt howitzers on two forward 'horns', but despite the potential of this arrangement they were little used.

Specification
6-in 26 cwt BL Howitzer Mk I
Calibre: 152.4 mm (6 in)
Length of barrel: 2.22 m (7 ft 3.55 in)
Weight: in action 3693.5 kg (8,142 lb)
Elevation: 0° to +45°
Traverse: 8°
Muzzle velocity: 429 m (1,407 ft) per second
Maximum range: with light shell 10425 m (11,400 yards) and with heavy shell 8685 m (9,500 yards)
Shell weight: 39 or 45.36 kg (86 or 100 lb)

1 July 1916, and the battle of the Somme is under way. This 6-in howitzer is in action during the action around Albert. Note the cleats fitted to the wheels in an attempt to aid traction in the Flanders mud.

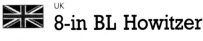

8-in BL Howitzer

When the BEF went to France in 1914 it was, like most combatants, ill-equipped with heavy artillery. It did not take long for the British to realize that they would need heavy artillery in great quantities and in a very short time, but there were few sources for such weapons. Unlike their German and French counterparts, the military planners were unwilling to strip the coastal defences, and there were few forts from which to remove the armament, so an alternative had to be produced quickly. The answer was the 152.4-mm (6-in) naval gun, already in production for both Royal Navy and

The first 8-inch howitzers in action were re-bored naval 6-in weapons with cut-down barrels. The carriage was hastily built in railway workshops, and the wheels were originally produced for traction engines.

coast-defence purposes, but a 152.4-mm (6-in) projectile was not thought heavy enough.

The answer was to obtain a quantity of barrels from old 152.4-mm (6-in) guns from stockpiles all over the country. These barrels were generally well worn, but this did not matter for they were considerably shortened by cutting off a length from the muzzle and boring out the barrel and chamber to a new calibre of 203 mm (8 in). The resultant barrel was then mounted on a hastily devised carriage produced at numerous railway workshops throughout the UK, and to complete the makeshift nature of these guns they were mounted on traction engine wheels for ease of movement.

The 8-in BL Howitzer was a ponderous load and a bulky weapon, but it was at least something to issue to the troops in France. Initially 100 were ordered, but these were soon followed by more, the first entering service in February 1915. These initial howitzers ran to no fewer than five marks with as many marks of carriage, all of them differing in some way or another from the rest. These were soon followed by an 8-in BL Howitzer Mk VI, which was a purpose-built weapon with a longer barrel than the earlier five marks for improved range. In its turn this was replaced in late 1916 by the 8-in BL Howitzer Mk VII, which had an even longer barrel. A later 8-in BL Howitzer Mk VIII differed only in details.

The Mk VII and VIII howitzers were excellent weapons that formed the basis for a family of 203-mm (8-in) guns that are in service to this day. The later marks had a much more sophisticated carriage than the early marks, and were thus easier to handle and to move to the extent that they can be considered as different guns. Some of these late howitzer marks were handed over to the US Army when it arrived in France in 1918, and it is via them that

the modern 203-mm (8-in) guns have been derived.

After 1918 the early Mks I-V were withdrawn (if they had not been retired already) but the Mks VII and VIII were retained by the British army and some others (including the US Army). In 1939 they were still on hand for the early campaigns of the war and later many were converted to a new calibre of 183 mm (7.2 in). Examples captured

in France by the Germans during 1940 were redesignated 20.3-cm sFH 501(e) but saw little use.

Specification
8-in BL Howitzer Mk VII
Calibre: 203 mm (8 in)
Length of barrel: 3.77 m (12 ft 4.3 in)
Weight: in action 9017 kg (19,880 lb)
Elevation: 0° to +45°
Traverse: 8°

By May 1918, when this example was in action at Wagonlieu, the 8-in BL howitzer had evolved through several marks, and had become an excellent weapon.

Muzzle velocity: 457 m (1,500 ft) per second
Maximum range: 11245 m (12,300 yards)
Shell weight: 90.7 kg (200 lb)

 UK
9.2-in BL Siege Howitzers

In 1914 the British army was not entirely devoid of heavy artillery, for the Royal Artillery had in service a heavy weapon known as the 9.2-in BL Siege Howitzer Mk I. This had its origins in a staff requirement dated 1910, but it was not until 1913 that the first examples were produced. The type was cleared for service in 1914. As its designation implies, the 233.7-mm (9.2-in) howitzer was intended as a siege weapon for the demolition of fortifications, and was accordingly constructed as a purely static weapon mounted on a large and heavy firing platform. On the road the howitzer was carried in three loads. Emplaced, the Mk I appeared to be a rather complex weapon, but closer examination soon showed that it was really very simple.

The short howitzer barrel was mounted in a cradle that contained the hydro-pneumatic recoil system. This cradle was carried on two large side-frames that in their turn sat on a segment-shaped firing platform supplied with platforms on which the crew could work. The entire unit was in turn mounted on an emplaced firing base. The recoil mechanism was of fairly limited efficiency, and thus there was provision in front of the carriage for what must have been the 9.2's most

unpopular feature. This was a large steel box, open at the top to allow it to be filled with earth. The weight of the filled box provided more stability when the weapon was fired at low angles of elevation, for without it the entire howitzer and carriage could rear upwards and to the rear on firing. Filling this box with earth took time and labour, and before the howitzer could be moved it all had to be emptied out again.

The Mk I had only a limited range of 9200 m (10,060 yards). It was not long therefore before the Royal Artillery started to request a similar weapon with more range, and this duly appeared during late 1916. It was known as the 9.2-in BL Siege Howitzer Mk II, and differed mainly in that it had a longer barrel providing a range of 12740 m (13,935 yards), but for the gunners the main importance was that the recoil system was enlarged to absorb the recoil forces to such an extent that the unloved heavy earth box was no longer necessary. Otherwise the Mk II followed the same general lines as the Mk I in both general appearance and construction. As before, the Mk II was carried in three loads, but there was an overall increase in weight of each load by about 1 tonne.

Production of both marks of 233.7-mm (9.2-in) howitzer ran to 812 by the time the war ended in 1918, and many of these were either stockpiled or passed on to other nations. The US Army had been provided with some equipments when it arrived in France during 1918, but others went to Commonwealth armies and after 1918 others ended up in such nations as Belgium, the newly-formed Baltic States and even the White Russian forces. In 1939 the weapon was still in Royal Artillery service, but many were lost during the events of May and June 1940, which was just as well as ammunition for these howitzers was in increasingly short supply and there were no facilities to manufacture more.

The major heavy artillery piece in British service in 1914 was the 9.2-in Siege Howitzer. As its name suggests, it was designed to be used from a fixed position, and movement involved breaking the equipment down into three sections.

Specification
9.2-in BL Siege Howitzer Mk II
Calibre: 233.7 mm (9.2 in)
Length of barrel: 4.33 m (14 ft 2.51 in)
Weight: in action 16460 kg (36,288 lb)
Elevation: +15° to +50°
Traverse: 60°
Muzzle velocity: 488 m (1,600 ft) per second
Maximum range: 12470 m (13,935 yards)
Shell weight: 131.5 kg (290 lb)

12-in BL Siege Howitzers

By 1915 World War I was well under way, and the pattern of the battles that were to rage for the next three years had already been set. Also established was the need for yet more and heavier artillery, and the Elswick Ordnance Company was requested to produce a heavy weapon for delivery into the line as soon as possible. Elswick simply took the existing 233.7-mm (9.2-in) howitzer design and scaled it up to a new 305-mm (12-in) calibre. In general the new howitzer resembled the earlier weapon, but the recoil mechanism was much revised and by early 1916 the first examples were ready.

The **12-in BL Siege Howitzer Mk I** was intended for a railway mounting, but a version for road use was also required. Here Vickers became involved, and it too took the 233.7-mm (9.2-in) weapon as a starting base and enlarged it accordingly. This resulted in the **12-in BL Siege Howitzer Mk II**, which in appearance closely resembled the 233.7-mm (9.2-in) equivalent right down to the retention of the massive earth box. On the 305-mm (12-in) version this required no less than 20 tons of earth to prevent the recoil overcoming the stability of the carriage at low angles of elevation. Being larger than the 233.7-mm (9.2-in) weapon, the 305-mm howitzer had to be transported in six loads (barrel, cradle, bedplate, carriage, earthbox and accessories). Assembly was carefully thought out and accomplished by a system of girder ramps, winches and jacks, but it was a lengthy process and all for a maximum range of only 10370 m (11,340 yards).

The **12-in BL Siege Howitzer Mk III** was another railway mounting, so it was not until the appearance of the **12-in BL Siege Howitzer Mk IV** in 1917 that the field gunners got their required range increase, which had been requested almost as soon as the Mk I reached the batteries. The Mk IV was a lengthened Mk II which provided a range of 13120 m (14,350 yards), but other changes were incorporated at the same time. A new Asbury breech mechanism was introduced and the carriage was beefed up all round, but to the dismay of the gunner the earthbox in front of the carriage was carried over, so the spade work had to continue. A power rammer was provided, which no doubt took away a considerable workload from the gun crews, and extra ammunition handling jibs were provided at the rear. The overall effect of all these additions was to provide an increase in the rate of fire.

On the move the Mk IV was originally towed by steam traction engines in six loads, as had been the case with the Mk II. After 1918 heavy trucks were introduced for towing, and this arrangement was still in service in 1939 when the BEF took some Mk IVs over to France. There the weapons took up so much room on the road system that they were known as '12-in Road Hogs'. They did not last long, for when the Germans invaded France in 1940 their tactical initiative rendered the 305-mm (12-in) howitzer's lack of mobility a major disadvantage. Events simply swept around them, and all were either destroyed or captured,

leaving a tiny handful in the UK for training purposes only.

The **12-in BL Siege Howitzer Mk V** was another railway mounting.

Specification
12-in BL Siege Howitzer Mk IV
Calibre: 305 mm (12 in)
Length of barrel: 5.65 m (18 ft 6.5 in)
Weight: in action 57915 kg (127,680 lb) with earthbox loaded
Elevation: +20° to +65°
Traverse: 60°

Muzzle velocity: 447 ft (1,468 ft) per second
Maximum range: 13120 m (14,350 yards)
Shell weight: 340 kg (750 lb)

The breech of a 12-in howitzer, showing the cradle for the massive shell together with some of the shell-handling equipment. Later models employed a mechanical ramming device to insert the shell into the barrel.

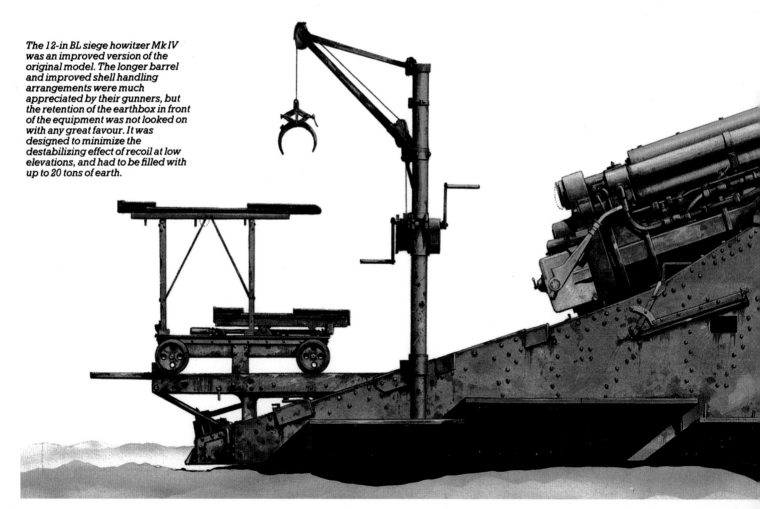

The 12-in BL siege howitzer Mk IV was an improved version of the original model. The longer barrel and improved shell handling arrangements were much appreciated by their gunners, but the retention of the earthbox in front of the equipment was not looked on with any great favour. It was designed to minimize the destabilizing effect of recoil at low elevations, and had to be filled with up to 20 tons of earth.

Above: May 1918, and a 12-in howitzer is firing somewhere near Louez. Note that the blast has kicked up dust from an area several yards around the equipment. The longer barrel gives the howitzer a greater range than earlier models.

Above: A typical artillery position of 1917. From the number of 12-in shells ready for use, it would seem that a pre-offensive barrage is being prepared, possibly for dawn the next day. The camouflage was necessary to prevent aerial observation.

15-in BL Siege Howitzers

The British army at no time requested a 381-mm (15-in) howitzer, but was presented with such a weapon. Exactly how this came about is an odd story, but it had its origins in the Coventry Ordnance Works, which as a private venture took the 233.7-mm (9.2-in) howitzer as a starting point and enlarged it. One of the directors of the Coventry Ordnance Works was a recently retired senior naval officer, who contacted the Admiralty in order for them to pass on the news of the existence of the enlarged weapon to the War Office, rather along the lines of the 'Old Pals Act'. Instead the news fell upon the ears of the then First Lord of the Admiralty, Winston Churchill, whose ever-active mind soon thought up a role for the big howitzer as part of a Royal Navy presence on the battlefields of the Western Front, and a single example of the Coventry gun was obtained.

Thus arrived on the military scene the **15-in BL Siege Howitzer**. In a very short time the howitzer was in France in the hands of a Royal Marine Artillery crew and in action. A further 11 were then ordered and delivered into Royal Marine hands. The Royal Navy made much of the howitzers' capabilities, but experience soon showed that it had fathered something of a problem.

The main difficulty was that the 381-mm (15-in) howitzer was a large and ponderous brute that lacked the range that would be expected from such a large-calibre weapon. It was true that it could fire a projectile weighing no less than 635 kg (1,400 lb) with dreadful effects on the receiving end, but the maximum range was a mere 9870 m (10,795 yards). The howitzer required a crew of no less than 12 men on the gun, and even more were involved in the weighty task of ammunition supply.

In 1916 the Royal Navy apparently tired of the whole scheme and withdrew, presenting the 12 howitzers to an unwanting Royal Artillery, which had to accept them with good grace for inter-service political reasons. But once the Royal Artillery had time to examine its new charges it lost no time in announcing that it was none too pleased about performance. The Royal Artillery considered the howitzers to be too large and too heavy for the results and range that could be obtained. And at the ranges involved they were obvious targets for counter-

battery work, so disproportionate care and consideration was required for their siting in locations close to the front lines. But the weapons had to be put to some form of use, so they saw the war out at odd times and locations whenever targets could be found in situations where the howitzers' dire lack of range was of little account. As soon as the war ended they were quickly withdrawn from use and disposed of, apparently to the White Russian forces during the Russian Civil War of the early 1920s.

Specification
15-in BL Siege Howitzer
Calibre: 381 mm (15 in)
Length of barrel: 4.19 m (13 ft 9.05 in)
Weight: in action not known

Above: Arising from a private venture, the 15-in BL siege howitzer first saw action in the hands of the Royal Navy contingent on the Western Front. Maximum range was limited to less than 10000 m (10,936 yards), but the projectile weighed some 635 kg (1,400 lbs).

Elevation: +25° to +45°
Traverse: 25°
Muzzle velocity: 340 m (1,117 ft) per second
Maximum range: 9870 m (10,795 yards)
Shell weight: 635 kg (1,400 lb)

The 15-in howitzers were all transferred to the Royal Artillery, who were not enthused with their performance. Here a shell is being loaded into the breech of a 15-in near Ypres in September 1917.

Skoda howitzers

During the years that led up to World War I the Skoda concern, based at Pilsen in what is now Czechoslovakia, was well to the fore in the development and manufacture of super-heavy artillery. Like so many other nations in Europe during that era, Austria-Hungary faced the prospect of having to smash through the rings of massive fortifications that protected the main centres of the empire's potential foes, and as the fortifications grew heavier so did the weapons to defeat them. By 1911 Skoda had already produced a 305-mm (12-in) howitzer that was the equal of any comparable weapon in Europe, and this stubby howitzer fired a 382- or 287-kg (842- or 633-lb) shell capable of penetrating the heaviest protection of any fort.

This **Skoda Model 1911** was an im-

portant design in that it was one of the first of such heavy howitzers to be designed from the start with motor traction in mind. Each of the howitzers could be broken down into three main loads, the barrel, the firing platform and the main carriage. The barrel and the main carriage could be towed by a massive Austro-Daimler tractor along roads at a ponderous but steady pace over considerable distances. By 1911 such tractors were not unusual, though the designing of a heavy howitzer for such traction was novel and so attracted much attention. The howitzers were organized into two-howitzer batteries with two gun-carriage tractor loads and another tractor pulling the two firing platforms. On each towed load sat crew members to operate the brakes, while further tractors pulled

The Skoda model 1914 was produced as a coast defence howitzer, but during the campaigns in northern Italy the 4.2-cm piece was used as a fortress smasher. Rate of fire was only two shells per hour.

The Skoda model 1911 305-mm howitzer was one of the first heavy artillery pieces to be designed with motor traction in mind. The equipment broke down into three parts comprising barrel, gun carriage and firing platform.

ammunition, assembly cranes, tools and even a special mobile workshop. More trucks carried items such as fire-control instruments, the battery's rations and offices and so forth. Mobile batteries such as these were used in the crushing of the Belgian forts in 1914 (along with the Krupp 42-cm/16.54-in 'Big Berthas') and were later used during the Verdun battles and the campaign in Italy.

Once World War I was well under way the need for even heavier artillery became apparent and Skoda went on to produce larger-calibre weapons. The first of these was ready in 1914, although it was not a field howitzer but a coastal artillery piece intended for use inside armoured turrets. The calibre of this **Skoda Model 1914** was 420 mm (16.54 in), the same as that of the Krupp howitzers, but despite the Model 1914's intended employment the type was used on occasion as a weapon to demolish heavy fortifications during the campaigns along the border with northern Italy. Some survived as coastal artillery weapons until World War II. Moving the massive 420-mm (16.54-in) howitzer was a huge task, so in 1916 Skoda introduced a more formal howitzer design for use in field conditions. Even so this was still a very hefty 420-mm (16.54-in) howitzer that took days to emplace or to move, and it was not until 1917 that a 420-mm (16.54-in) design intended from the outset for relatively easy movement and emplacement was ready. This was the **Skoda Model 1917**, which was in many ways the same piece as the

Model 1916 but designed so that the individual loads could be towed by large wheeled tractors. The total weight of the emplaced Skoda Model 1917 was well over 100 tonnes, and on the road the combined loads came to far more than that. The rate of fire was only about one or two rounds per hour, but the heaviest shell weighed no less than 1000 kg (2,205 lb) and the maximum range was 14,600 m (15,965 yards).

Skoda also produced in 1916 a **Skoda Model 1916** 380-mm (14.96-in)

howitzer which was nicknamed 'Barbara'. It too was designed for motor traction, but few such weapons were actually built.

After 1918 the 305-mm (12-in) howitzers still around were distributed among the new nations that grew out of the old Austro-Hungarian Empire. Most went to Hungary and Czechoslovakia, but Italy also received some along with a few of the 420-mm (16.54-in) coastal howitzers.

Specification
Skoda Model 1911
Calibre: 305 mm (12 in)
Length of barrel: 3.03 m (9 ft 11.3 in)
Weight: in action 20830 kg (45,922 lb)
Elevation: +40° to +70°
Traverse: on carriage 16°
Muzzle velocity: with heavy shell 340 m (1,115 ft) per second
Maximum range: with light shell 11300 m (12,360 yards) and with heavy shell 9600 m (10,500 yards)
Shell weight: 287 or 382 kg (633 or 842 lb)

FRANCE

Canon de 220 L mle 1917 Schneider

Before 1914 the French military philosophers who dictated the nature of the French army training and tactics decided that as fast attack was to be the main strength of the French army there would be little need for heavy artillery, whose main purposes were defence or slow attack. The 75-mm (2.95-in) mle 1897 field gun was all that would be needed as massed French infantry swept all before them, so scant attention was given to the provision of heavy weapons before the start of World War I. The 1914 Battle of the Frontiers demonstrated in a terrible fashion the fallacies behind such thinking, and the battered French army withdrew behind the trench lines that were to be the virtual 'trade mark' of World War I.

Once in its trenches, the French army soon discovered that heavy artillery was sorely needed. The concentration on the '75' as a weapon for all tasks proved to be a major blunder, for against protected earthworks field guns such as the '75' were virtually useless. Heavier-calibre weapons were needed to destroy trench lines and bunkers, and the French army had but few. The only sources for such weapons were from the batteries situated all around the French coastline, and from the nation's ancient forts. Heavy guns were stripped from these sources and it was with these elderly weapons that the French army withstood the rigours of the dreadul Verdun battles of 1916.

Better weapons were demanded, but it took time for these to be produced for the French designers had to work virtually from scratch. Develop-

ing and manufacturing new heavy weapons took years and it was not until 1917 that Schneider was able to deliver the first of its heavy offerings, a gun known as the **Canon de 220 L mle 1917** or the **Can 220 L 17 S**. It had a calibre of 220 mm (8.66 in) and was a derivative of a naval gun design. It had a long slender barrel and was mounted on a long heavy carriage in such a way that the barrel slid in its cradle back along the length of the carriage when the gun was fired. The L 17 S was a heavy weapon that had to be towed in two loads (the barrel and the carriage) but it had a very good range of 28,800 m (24,935 yards) and fired a shell weighing 104.75 kg (231 lb).

In action the L 17 S proved to be an excellent heavy weapon but it arrived on the battlefields of France only just in time. By mid-1917 the French army was in such a state following the lethal maulings of the Verdun battles that large sectors openly mutinied and refused to fight further. For some reason the Germans never got to hear of the mutinies, and for long periods were held at bay only by the artillery. The French artillery arm was relatively untouched by the mutinies and fought on using the L 17 S and other such heavy weapons until the troubles were resolved and the French army once more settled down to face the enemy. Thus the L 17 S may be regarded as the gun that helped to save France in the desperate troubles of 1917, but went on to play its part during the battles of 1918.

By 1918 the L 17 S was one of the better of the many types in the French

artillery gun park and it was retained until 1940, when the many examples still around fell into the hands of the Germans, who used them as coastal guns emplaced in the Atlantic Wall. Some saw action again during the Normandy landings of June 1944.

The Schneider Canon de 220 L mle 1917 was derived from a naval weapon. The long-barrelled gun was the first new design to enter French army service in place of the largely obsolete coastal artillery, which had been a stopgap in 1914.

Specification
Can 220 L 17 S
Calibre: 220 mm (8.66 in)
Length of barrel: 7.67 m (25 ft 2 in)
Weight: in action 25880 kg (57,055 lb)
Elevation: −10° to +37°
Traverse: 20°

Muzzle velocity: 766 m (2,513 ft) per second
Maximum range: 22800 m (24,935 yards)
Shell weight: 104.75 kg (231 lb)

Canon de 240 L mle 84/17 St Chamond

One of the early candidates considered for stripping from the French fortifications of an earlier era was a heavy gun known as the mle 1884. This was a St Chamond design with a calibre of 240 mm (9.45 in), but in the early part of 1915 the weapon was generally considered too heavy for field use by conventional means and was thus mounted on special railway gun carriages. As such the weapons were as successful as any of the other extemporized French railway guns of the period. But railway guns have a habit of not always being able to get to the locations where they are most needed, and this lesson was driven home during the Verdun battles of 1916, which settled down to a slogging match between the opposing artillery, and under such circumstances the heavier calibres were often of more use than the longer-ranged guns. Thus a call went out to mount the St Chamond 240-mm (9.45-in) guns on to some form of field carriage.

The new carriage was delivered during 1917 and the gun and carriage combination became known as the **Canon de 240 L mle 84/17 St Chamond** or **Can 240 L 84/17 St Ch**. By that time there were few of the original mle 1884 guns available, so the guns were placed back in production (these were known as **Can 240 L mle 1917 St Ch**). The best that could be said of the resultant weapon was that it was a ponderous item. The gun barrel had to be towed separately from the carriage, and on the road both were long and awkward loads. The usual towing vehicles appear to have been steam tractors; these endowed the weapon with a very limited cross-country capability unless special roads were laid, and the time to assemble or dismantle the gun often had to be considered in days.

Because of its age, the range of the L 84/17 was limited to 17300 m (18,920

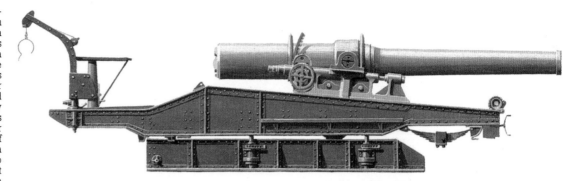

Above: The Canon de 240 L mle 84/17 St Chamond was originally a fortress weapon dating from 1884. First attempts at making the weapon mobile involved a railway mounting, but by 1917 a field mounting had been developed.

Right: The barrel of the Canon de 240 L mle 84/17 was easily detachable from the carriage. Movable in two loads, the great length of the equipment made for an extremely awkward load, and setting up a position could take several days.

yards), but the ordnance fired a 161-kg (355-lb) shell of considerable power. The numbers produced during 1917 and after appear to have been limited, no doubt as a result of the time required to manufacture the large barrel and carriage. The new barrels produced in 1917 were slightly longer than the original but had the same performance, so they were still relatively unworn when the Armistice was signed in November 1918. At least two or three batteries were retained up to

1940, but in that year the Germans demonstrated that the L 84/17 was a leftover from another era by destroying all the remaining weapons with Stuka dive-bombers, most of them while they were still on their road carriages.

Specification
Can 240 L St Ch
Calibre: 240 mm (9.45 in)
Length of barrel: mle 84/17 6.70 m (22 ft) and mle 1917 7.00 m (22 ft 11.6 in)
Weight: in action 31000 kg (68,343 lb)
Elevation: 0° to +38°
Traverse: 10°
Muzzle velocity: 575 m (1,886 ft) per second
Maximum range: 17300 m (18,920 yards)
Shell weight: 161 kg (355 lb)

Mortier de 280 mle 14/16 Schneider

The years up to 1914 were not entirely devoid of heavy artillery activity for the French armaments industry. The large Schneider concern continued with its full range of artillery development, mainly funded from internal sources in order to keep abreast of design influences elsewhere and to remain ready to seize upon any possible sales opportunities that might arise. Thus in 1914 it had ready to hand a design for the 280-mm (11.02-in) **Obusier de 280 mle 1914 Schneider** that was soon accepted for service by a French army eager to improve its heavy artillery holdings.

It was two years before Schneider could deliver the first examples, however. By then the howitzer's designation had been decided as **Mortier de 280 mle 14/16 Schneider**, the term *mortier* (mortar) in place of *obusier* (howitzer) being a typical piece of European terminology as on the Continent heavy howitzers were frequently

The Mortier de 280 mle 14/16 was a ponderous piece designed for siege warfare. Range was limited, which placed the howitzer well within the range of German long-range guns. Indeed, many suffered from counter-bombardment.

called mortars. As the type was ordered 'off the shelf', the French army had to take what they got and what they got was a very ponderous weapon. The original mle 1914 as produced by Schneider had been designed as a heavy artillery piece that would be used for siege warfare, in which plenty of time would be available for the move to the battlefield and more time for the emplacement. Thus the mle 14/16 had to be broken down into no less than four loads for travelling and in position for firing rested on a heavy metal firing platform. Ammunition was delivered to the breech by means of a little crane which lifted the shell on to a small trolley that ran along

a pair of rails to the breech. Ramming the shell into the breech was carried out by a chain-driven rammer.

Once the assembly lines for the mle 14/16 had been established the units were churned out in relatively large numbers. Many suffered from enemy counterbombardment as the range was only 10950 m (11,975 yards), putting the type well within the reach of many of the German long-range guns. The mle 14/16 was nonetheless a very useful weapon for destroying trench systems and underground installations, though it cannot have been a very popular weapon with the French gunners. Every move, however short, entailed the lengthy and involved job

of breaking down the howitzer into four loads, and once on site a pit had to be dug for the heavy steel platform, together with a deeper pit to allow the barrel to recoil when the howitzer was fired at high angles of elevation.

After 1918 the mle 14/16 was one of the types selected to remain in service. Thus some were still around in 1940. By then they belonged to a past generation and had no chance for effective use as the German Panzers rolled across France. Many mle 14/16s were captured intact and were added to the German army 'siege train', being used once again during the siege of Leningrad and later during the siege of Sevastopol, where their weight and

bulk were no disadvantage. Thus the mle 14/16 ended up in the hands of the enemy it was originally procured to defeat.

Specification
Mortier de 280 mle 14/16 Schneider
Calibre: 280 mm (11.02 in)
Length of barrel: 3.35 m (11 ft 0 in)
Weight: in action 16000 kg (35,274 lb)
Elevation: +10° to +60°
Traverse: 20°
Muzzle velocity: 418 m (1,371 ft) per second
Maximum range: 10,950 m (11,975 yards)
Shell weight: 205 kg (452 lb)

FRANCE
Mortier de 370 Filloux

The **Mortier de 370 Filloux** had its origins in a requirement for a coastal artillery weapon capable of producing plunging fire to pierce the relatively thin protection of warship decks. By 1913 a number of these short howitzers that fired at high angles of elevation had been produced, but in 1913 the 370-mm (14.57-in) weapon was produced and this remained thereafter the largest of all these French specialist weapons.

In appearance the Mortier de 370 Filloux was a deceptively small weapon. In fact it was a brute. It had originally been designed for use in static coastal emplacements where (in theory at least) it was to have been delivered, emplaced and thereafter left. What actually happened was that in the period following the early carnage of 1914, the French army rushed whatever it could find in the heavy artillery line to the areas behind the trenches in order to have some trench-crushing capability, however limited. Fortunately for the French, when the Mortier de 370 was delivered it came with special handling gear of two kinds. One was for use on railway trucks and the other for road transport and both had handling gantries, cranes and special rigs. The largest of these rigs was for the barrel, which was carried slung under a special wheeled gantry; the other loads were carried slung in a similar fashion. In all there were three main loads with more for the ammunition and the various accessories.

If moving the Mortier de 370 was not enough, emplacing the thing was worse. The preparation began with the digging of a large pit into which was lowered the main firing platform: this had a series of vertical spades on its underside which were intended to absorb some of the barrel recoil. More of the recoil was taken by the heavy carriage, which was mounted on the platform and featured a rudimentary recoil cylinder system coupled to the trunnions of the barrel. The emplacement and assembly of all this took a considerable time and a great deal of labour, but it was a price the French had to pay in order to put some form of heavy artillery in the front line during 1915.

Once in the line the ammunition for the howitzer was gradually changed from the original armour-piercing pattern to a heavy blast-producing type; the last of these projectiles was introduced into use during 1917. There

Above: A French 370-mm howitzer in position in the Ravin de la Baraquette west of Foucaucourt, seen in September 1916. The great battles of that year saw artillery become the great mankiller of an already murderous war.

were two of these 1917 type projectiles, the heavier weighing 489 kg (1,078 lb). But with this the range was only 8100 m (8,860 yards), which made all the labour involved rather a waste of potential. But for a considerable period it was all that there was to hand and the unfortunate French gunners just had to put up with it all.

After 1918 the Mortiers de 370 Filloux were placed into storage to be dragged out again during the 'Phoney War' of 1939-40. There then appears to have been some indecision as to exactly where they were to be emplaced, and in the event most of them were apparently destroyed by Luftwaffe attacks.

Specification
Mortier de 370 Filloux
Calibre: 370 mm (14.57 in)
Length of barrel: 3.31 m (10 ft 10.3 in)
Weight: in action between 29000 and 30000 kg (63,934 and 66,139 lb)
Elevation: −6° to +65°

Traverse: 6°
Muzzle velocity: with light shell 370 m (1,214 ft) per second and with heavy shell 316 m (1,037 ft) per second
Maximum range: with light shell 10400 m (11,375 yards) and with heavy shell 8100 m (8,860 yards)
Shell weight: 413.5 or 489 kg (911.6 lb or 1,078 lb)

Simple in appearance, the Mortier de 370 Filloux was a brute to handle, and its heaviest projectiles had a range of only 8100 m (8858 yards). As was true of so many heavy artillery pieces of the period, the 370-mm was originally a coast defence weapon.

Verdun 1916

The titanic struggles of 1916 have gone down in history as perhaps the most tragic waste of human life the world has seen. Arising out of a need to overcome strong defences by frontal assault, attrition was appalling, decimating a generation and looming large in the memories of those who survived. Of the campaigns of World War I, it is Verdun which probably casts the darkest shadow.

The Battle of Verdun lasted from February 1916 until it finally petered out in the December of the same year. It can be regarded as one of the greatest battles of all time, for although other battles involved more men and equipment, or produced greater results for one side or the other, the Battle of Verdun was a conflict that maintained its ferocity and scope through many months to reach a pitch where it seemed that the very vitality and honour of the two combatant nations was being put to the test. The result was horrific in the extreme for the unfortunate soldiers sucked into the maelstrom of the area around the old city of Verdun: they existed and died in a hell on Earth where they were rarely able to catch a glimpse of their prime adversaries, for these were the guns.

The Battle of Verdun had its origins in the mind of the German Chief of the General Staff, General Erich von Falkenhayn. By the end of 1915 the German and the Allied armies faced each other across the trench lines of the Western Front with little immediate prospect of either ever being able to break the stalemate, though neither side would admit it at the time. The war by then had already regressed into a state of attrition where the only way either side could win was by reducing the manpower and equipment strength of the other by sheer weight of repeated destruction. In effect this meant the use of artillery, for infantry alone could make little impression against the powerful defences of the other side. But Germany was not in a position to win such a war, mainly as a result of the Allied blockade of raw materials, so Germany had to make some sort of move to destroy a major part of the Allied strength during 1916 or face the prospect of a possible defeat.

Falkenhayn devised the notion of a gigantic 'mincing machine' battle that would destroy the French army. His idea was simple in the extreme but horrific in its execution: the German forces would make limited attacks against the salient around Verdun to suck in more and more of the French army, which would then be gradually destroyed by the German artillery on a chosen killing ground. Falkenhayn's concept was logically sound in a terrible way, but as things turned out the concept of his own army's limited attacks were somehow never imparted to his subordinate commanders,

among whom was the Kaiser's son. Additionally, he and his staff regarded the attacks in this area as a matter of honour in that Verdun should be taken. Thus as more French troops were sucked into the fighting so too were more German troops, until the point was reached where as many Germans were being fed into the 'mincing machine' as there were French, and in this way the two armies slugged it out through many dreadful months.

The Verdun battlefield was divided into two almost equal halves by the River Meuse. Falkenhayn originally dictated that his 'limited attacks' should take place on the east bank only. The opening attacks were to be preceded by a barrage from the largest concentration of artillery yet seen on the Western Front, for Falkenhayn had gathered together no less than 1,220 artillery pieces to lay down fire on a front only 13 km (8 miles) long. Of these there were 542 heavy pieces and 306 field guns along the immediate front to be attacked, together with 152 heavy mine projectors. The rest of the artillery force was assembled along the flanks.

Largest in calibre of all this massed artillery were 13 420-mm (16.54-in) 'Big Berthas'. Much was expected of these weapons, but in the event their accuracy was less than anticipated. But this was to matter little, for hidden away in the covering branches of the Bois de Wapremont were two of the massive 380-mm (14.96-in) guns taken from coastal defences away in the Baltic. Further forward were 17 of the 305-mm (12-in) Skoda howitzers that had done so well against the Belgian forts in 1914. When it came to the smaller calibres the numbers of artillery pieces began to grow. Next down from the 305-mm (12-in) howitzers were the 210-mm (8.27-in) *Mörser* (mortars or howitzers) that were to become one of the most widely used German weapons of the Verdun battles. They were greatly feared by the French soldiers, who had an equal dislike for the 130-mm (5.12-in) heavy guns that were really naval pieces mounted on field carriages. Their high muzzle

A battery of German 210-mm howitzers. Once troops began burrowing into the ground on the western front, the howitzer came into its own. Its high angle of fire enabled it to drop shells right into a trench or bunker, with even a near miss able to collapse a position.

velocity was such that the projectiles arrived on target with no presaging sound signals. The mine projectors were essentially short-range weapons that fired huge canisters of explosives (packed with all manner of scrap metal to enhance their nastiness), while more short-range support was supplied by the 105-mm (4.13-in) and 77-mm (3.03-in) field pieces of the field artillery. If all this was not enough there was also the might of the massive 420-mm (16.54-in) Gamma howitzer hidden away with the 'Big Berthas' behind the hills of Morimont and Romagne.

All this massed firepower opened up on the morning of 17 February 1916. The 420-mm (16.54-in) mortars were used to fire against the ring of forts that surrounded Verdun, and from that day onward they worked their way over and around the individual forts, though with far less effect than they had obtained against the Belgian forts in 1914. The 380-mm (14.96-in) naval guns opened up a harassing fire against the city of Verdun itself and its approach routes, at times managing 40 shells per day from each gun. But it was the lesser calibres that were used against the hapless French lines, the 210-mm (8.27-in) howitzer batteries being especially notable. In places they were situated at intervals of one battery to every 150 m (165 yards) of opposing trench, and they wrought fearful havoc. The French trench lines in certain sectors simply ceased to exist, along with their unfortunate defenders.

At the same time as short-range fire fell upon the trenches, the longer-range artillery began to spray the recognized French artillery positions with gas. So meticulous had the German artillery preparation been that they even had reserve 150-mm (5.9-in) batteries standing by to open fire on any French battery that might not have been spotted or that somehow evaded the initial gas saturation. They had little enough to do. At that stage of the war the use of gas was still a relative novelty and the French were ill-equipped to deal with its effects.

The overall effect of the initial bombardment was dramatic: large holes were punched through the French lines through which the advancing infantry could pass, but here and there some French positions had somehow survived the hail of steel and put up a fierce resistance. It was a harbinger of what was to come. No matter how fiercely the artillery fired there were always some positions left undamaged, and from these the occupants could crawl to open fire on the attackers, as happened time and again in the long days, weeks and months that lay ahead. But 17 February was a foretaste of what was to come, for the artillery that had been so carefully amassed by Falkenhayn was to remain in place almost throughout the battle.

By 23 February the Germans had made their breakthrough, although at that stage reinforcements were carefully husbanded and fed into the battle at a limited rate in order to lure the French into the 'killing ground'. But it was not long before this carefully planned sequence began to run out of control. By the end of the month the mighty Fort Douaumont had fallen into German hands almost by default, and as Douaumont was one of the king pins of the armoured ring around Verdun this was heralded as a major victory. Thereafter things began to increase in intensity, if such a thing were possible, for a breakthrough to Verdun itself seemed increasingly likely.

This impression was enhanced by the close investment of Fort Vaux, which in the event

managed to hold out for weeks until 7 June. From Fort Vaux the suburbs of Verdun appeared to be almost within reach but it was around this stage that the battle took on a tempo of its own. In order to turn the conflict into a major German victory more and more units were thrown into the attack and the fighting spread to the west bank of the Meuse following a bombardment similar to that which opened the battle. This attack also came to a halt on the slopes of the aptly named hill called Le Mort Homme and Côte 304.

But they got little further as the battle raged on, absorbing ever more men while at the same time producing increasingly less in the way of gains. As the German infantry attempted to edge further forward across ground churned into a morass by the rain of incessant shelling they found advances more difficult to obtain. Instead, the guns continued their constant barrage from both sides, for soon after the initial German attacks the French had brought up more of their own artillery, in places denuding their front in order to supply weapons. The French had few really heavy weapons to emplace. Instead they relied on huge volumes of fire from their famous '75' field guns backed up by numbers of 105-mm (4.13-in) field guns and 155-mm (6.1-in) guns and howitzers. Only later were they able to bring up railway guns and heavier pieces.

A matter of honour

Ammunition for all these French batteries was a constant headache for the French staff officers, for they had only one logistic road as the Germans commanded the others. This road was the famous Voie Sacrée to Souilly and Bar-le-Duc, and along it had to pass all the supplies and reinforcements for the French front. It was a road that many French soldiers took only once, for vast numbers died at Verdun: French official figures later put the casualties at 377,231, although the true total was probably much higher at 542,000. On the German side most references seem to agree on a figure around 434,000, the combined total of casualties being around 976,000. Many of these were caused by the artillery alone, for thousands died without even seeing the enemy they sought so desperately to fight. And they did want desperately to fight, for by mid-1916 the battle of Verdun had assumed the nature of a gigantic struggle between two ancient foes, in which the outcome became a matter of national

Despite the enormous weight of fire directed at Vaux, the fort's structure survived, the garrison only surrendering when their water ran out. The French concluded that if a fort was well provisioned it could hold out indefinitely, leading to the philosophy of the Maginot Line.

A border fortress for centuries, Verdun was no stranger to attack. The increasing power of artillery forced the French to build a chain of forts to keep enemy guns out of reach of the city, but by 1916 artillery ranges had increased again and Verdun was shelled heavily.

Verdun 1916

pride and honour. Throughout it the artillery fired almost without cease, all the time pouring shells on to the forward and rear areas alike. The soldiers went underground whenever they could, taking shelter in such locations as railway tunnels and the basements and cellars of the villages like Douaumont and Fleury, villages that were simply wiped off the map by the artillery from both sides. The infantry emerged on occasion only to fight off the infantry attacks from the other side, and then went back to ground to attempt to avoid the shells they knew would come.

By June the battle was in a state of crisis. By sending in yet more men the Germans had advanced to Fleury after further artillery saturations of high explosive and gas. But this was the high point of their advance. During the conflict the original concept of the 'mincing machine' had been lost as events, rather than Falkenhayn, dictated the battle, and thereafter

Poilus (French soldiers) in a captured German position near Douaumont. The alien landscape created by the millions of shells fired at Verdun was a danger in itself, liquid mud made movement very difficult, and shell holes often contained hidden pockets of gas.

A French 370mm heavy mortar battery rains high explosive on German positions at Verdun.

the Germans were forced to fall back. By mid-July the French had somehow managed to push the Germans back to a line that was to remain until almost the end of the war. Fort Douaumont was retaken by 24 October, with the supporting fire of two 400-mm (15.75-in) railway guns and sporadic local attacks continued until December.

It had been a holocaust, dominated throughout by the artillery. Later references state that throughout it all the German guns fired off around 22 million rounds while the French returned about 15 million rounds. The result was a battle that haunted the minds of a whole generation of French and German people, caused the deaths of hundreds of thousands and has a dreadful effect on the minds of many to this day. The immediate result was that a few square kilometres of French soil changed hands, but the final results may never be fully assessed.

Fort Vaux under bombardment. The defenders of Vaux were subjected to some of the most intensive shelling of the war. They sheltered underground, protected by the massive concrete casemates, but the sheer volume of noise in the darkened tunnels was appalling.

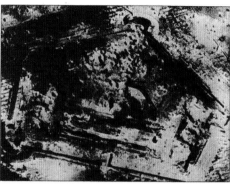

Douaumont, February 1916. Down below, a series of underground levels were the scenes of some of the most ferocious fighting in French history. During an attempt to retake the fort, hundreds of Germans were entombed by an explosion caused by leaking flamethrowers.

Canon de 240 sur affut-truc Modèle 93/96

When the French army decided to adopt railway guns during World War I it used a large number of 240-mm (9.45-in) barrels culled from all manner of places, but when it decided to use the Modèle 93/96 coastal defence gun for the role it soon found that such a relatively modern and powerful gun had to have a more complex type of carriage than the more hasty improvisations produced to suit the less powerful weapons of the same calibre. Consequently the Modèle 93/96 guns were placed on well platforms mounted fore and aft on six-axle bogies with an arrangement that allowed the gun platform to be lowered onto the track for the firing proper. On the move the **Canon de 240 sur affut-truc Modèle 93/96** gun and carriage was dismantled into three main sections.

Up to 1918 the Modèle 93/96 was used for a variety of purposes, ranging from long-range counterbombardment close to the trench lines to act as a mobile reserve for coast defence. After 1918 most of the remaining equipments were diverted almost entirely to the coast-defence roles, in which they generally remained at various central depots for long periods at a time with little practice firing and often very little maintenance. In 1939 that changed and the surviving guns were quickly renovated and new crews were trained so that by the time the Germans invaded France several guns in good condition

were ready for the Germans to take over after the fall of France.

With the Germans the Modèle 93/96 started a new career, this time as the **24-cm Kanone (E) 558(f)** or **24-cm Kanone (E) Modell 93/96(f)**. For a while they were retained as railway guns to equip a few training units, but by 1943 most of these had been scrapped or diverted for use as coastal defence guns. In this role the guns were completely removed from their railway mountings altogether. They were emplaced on fixed turntables that were securely based in concrete foundations, and once in place there they stayed. By late 1943 only eight of these guns were still in full-time use although some others were kept in reserve at various points. Of these eight, four were emplaced near the important U-boat port of St Nazaire, two at La Bats and the other two at Prefailles. The other four guns were sent off on a long foray to Norway, where all four were emplaced at Ofoten near the important naval base at Narvik. So far as is known none of these guns ever had to fire a shot in anger, and as soon as the war was over they were scrapped. However, it now seems that the Norwegians, not wanting to see good guns go to waste in 1945, kept the four at Ofoten in service for some years and it is far from certain that they were ever removed. It may well be that the old French guns are still there, though Norwegian security sensitivities make any con-

firmation of this very difficult to determine.

Incidentally, Schneider produced a 240-mm (9.45-in) railway gun with a L/51 barrel in 1928 and sold it to Japan. It was still around in 1941 but what subsequent use was made of it is now not known and no records survive of it being used in any action.

Specification
Precise calibre: 240 mm (9.45 in)

A characteristic of many French railway guns dating from World War I is that the gun and carriage were separated while travelling. Here a Canon de 240 Modèle 1903 is shown.

Length of barrel: 9.60 m (31 ft 6 in)
Weight complete: 140000 kg (308,640 lb)
Weight of shell: 162 kg (357 lb)
Range: 22700 m (24,825 yards)

Canon de 240 sur affut-truc Modèle 93/96 in travelling configuration. These guns, formerly coast defence weapons, needed a more complex mount than less powerful weapons of the same calibre.

French 320-mm railway guns

When the French army started to produce large numbers of railway guns during World War I it used a large number of what had been considered obsolete naval guns or odd items from the manufacturers' stockpiles. Among these were guns with calibres of 274 mm and 285 mm (10.79 in and 11.22 in), some of which were still in use during the early days of World War II. Some of these passed into German service for a while, but generally speaking they were mainly 'one-offs' of limited military value so they were often used for training or else scrapped – their limited stocks of ammunition were used land mines and roll-bombs to bolster beach defences.

However, the next calibre up the French scale was 320 mm (12.6 in), and

here there were several models of guns pressed into action, nearly all of naval origins. All of them dated originally from 1870 but to complicate matters nearly every barrel had been provided with an updating programme in different years thereafter and consequently no two barrels were exactly alike. For instance there were the **Modèle 70/80**, the **Modèle 70/84** and the **Modèle 70/93**. To make things even more complicated, the last model had an elongated chamber to accommodate a larger charge introduced to boost performance, so it was nonstandard to the others. And as if that

were not enough the same carriage, which had a sliding platform to absorb the considerable degree of recoil produced on firing, was also used to mount a much more modern gun, based on the Modèle 1870 series but manufactured in 1917 specially for the railway role. This was the **Canon de 320 T 17**,

320-mm 70/93 being taken into action in 1939 by French army troops, who are apparently not expecting air attack. After the fall of France these weapons were used by the Germans for coastal defence.

which transformed the elderly Modèle 1870 into a good modern equipment with a useful range. Nearly all these guns, being naval in origin, used an interrupted screw thread, opened and closed by a worm-gear cranking system, and, being originally intended for use in turrets, guns were not uncommonly found with their breech blocks opening to either the right or the left.

With the fall of France in 1940 the various 320-mm (12.6-in) railway guns fell into German hands. In fact so many were captured intact and in good working order that the Germans took

them into their own service. The old Modèle 1870 series of guns became the **32-cm Kanone (E) 651(f)**, with a special **32-cm Kanone (E) 651/1(f)** designation to denote the guns with the enlarged chambers and thus a special ammunition supply arrangement. The more modern 1917 guns became the **32-cm Kanone (E) 652(f)**. They spent the rest of the war years being trundled around the French coastlines and were used on occasion as propaganda weapons when they were towed through some of the major French cities in shows of force. At least one

was based in the south of France. The weapons appear to have made little impression during the invasions of the Normandy coast or the south of France (both in 1944) and many of them were later captured in a wrecked condition.

Specification
Modèle 1870 series
Precise calibre: 320 mm (12.6 in)
Length of barrel: 10.112 m (33 ft 2.1 in)
Weight complete: 16200 kg (357,145 lb)
Weight of shell: 387 kg (853 lb)
Range: 20500 m (22,420 yards)

Canon de 320 T 17 showing overhead gantry for ammunition handling. Sharing the same carriage as much older designs dating from the previous century, Modèle 1917 was derived from naval designs.

Specification
Modèle 1917
Precise calibre: 320 mm (12.6 in)
Length of barrel: 11.82 m (38 ft 9.4 in)
Weight complete: 178000 kg (392,415 lb)
Weight of shell: 392 kg (864 lb)
Range: 26200 m (28,655 yards)

FRANCE
French 340-mm railway guns

As with the French 320-mm (12.6-in) railway guns, there was more than one type of 340-mm (13.4-in) gun converted to the railway gun role, usually from barrels that were either naval in origin or design. To complicate matters further, there were two types of carriage in use for a single barrel type, the **Modèle 1912**.

The first type of mounting that should be considered is the sliding mount. This was a simple concept in which the central section of the gun carriage was either lowered onto the railway tracks or chocked into place on them in such a way that the recoil forces were absorbed by the carriage sliding along the track, usually not very far in view of the large weights and masses involved. While being simple to design, produce and use, this type of carriage had the disadvantage that there was no form of traverse control, the gun being trained by accurate positioning on a curve of railway track. As the gun had to be winched or pushed back into a carefully surveyed point on the track after every shot, the rate of fire was very slow and the whole system most laborious. However, the gun and carriage combination was produced in a very short time by Schneider et Cie of Le Creusot and the type was still around in 1939.

The 340-mm (13.4-in) barrels used originally had a form of rifling that limited the potential power of the guns and the rifling was subsequently altered to capitalize on this potential. But this considerably increased the stresses produced on firing, to the extent that a new type of carriage had to be evolved. This new carriage had a cradle type of gun barrel support that enabled recoil cylinders and recuperators to be used to absorb the increased firing stresses. This new carriage was produced by the St Chamond concern, but even as it was entering service Schneider was still pro-

ducing the original sliding mounts for the unaltered barrels. Thus there emerged a quartermaster's nightmare in the form of variable guns, carriages and their ammunition, all in service at the same time. At one point there were four different types of gun variation in use at one time on the sliding mounts alone.

With the coming of peace in 1918 many of these supply difficulties were resolved by a rationalization of types in service. None of the 340-mm (13.4-in) guns remaining saw much use between the wars, but in 1940 many were still available to fall into German hands. Nearly all of them entered German army service either as fully operational guns based in France or kept to provide spare parts for others. Four had a special destination. These were known to the Germans as the **34-cm Kanone-W-(E) 674(f)**, with the W (*Wiege*, or cradle) denoting that the guns were of the cradle-carriage pattern. These four were removed from their railway carriages and carried on road transporters to a coastal defence site at Plouharnel, near Quiberon in Brittany. Once emplaced they stayed there until they were removed for scrap after the war, but their large gun pits can still be found there among the sand dunes.

Specification
Modèle 1912 (cradle mount)
Precise calibre: 340 mm (13.39 in)
Length of barrel: 15.30 m (50 ft 2.4 in)
Weight complete: 164000 kg (361,550 lb)
Weight of shell: 432 kg (952 lb)
Range: 44400 m (48,555 yards)

Schneider Modèle 1912 railway gun, dismounted from its carriage onto a turntable and extensively camouflaged. In 1918, when this photo was taken, French quartermasters had the difficult task of supplying ammunition for the four variants of the barrel then in service.

Schneider Modèle 1912 railway gun captured by the German army in 1940 and later used by them as part of the Atlantic Wall. Based in Brittany, near Quiberon, the dismounted barrels saw little in the way of action.

Matériel de 400, Modèle 15 ou 16 sur affut-truc à berceau

The French 400-mm (15.75-in) railway howitzer was the largest of their practical railway weapons, and was produced in the usual rush in 1916 to take part in the Battle of Verdun. The first two examples were ready in time to smash their way through the carapace of Fort Douamont just before the French army retook the fort from the Germans and thereafter the **Matériel de 400, Modèle 15 ou 16 sur affut-truc à berceau** was one of the most favoured of French heavy artillery pieces used during World War I.

The 400-mm (15.75-in) railway howitzer was a product of St Chamond arsenal, and the first howitzer had been produced by simply boring out a worn Modèle 1887 340-mm (13.4-in) naval gun barrel to 400 mm (15.75 in) and placing it on a special carriage. The resultant howitzer was just over 25 calibres long on a simple, clean and open carriage with an unusual method of pivoting the rear of the platform to allow a degree of traverse. Behind the breech of the howitzer was a long open platform for the loading crew, an overhang at the rear mounting a loading crane. In action this crane lifted the shells direct from an ammunition waggon onto a loading tray that delivered the shell into the interrupted-screw breech. There was one factor that slowed the speed with which the equipment could be brought into action, and that was the fact that a recoil pit had to be provided under the breech. At full recoil the barrel moved so far that without the pit the breech would have struck the track, and to complicate matters further provision had to be made for a buried recoil spade arrangement against which the full carriage could move on firing. Without this recoil spade the whole carriage moved backwards on firing

and then had to be winched or pushed back to the firing point. This would have reduced the rate of fire even more from the normal one round every five minutes or so.

The ability of the 400-mm (15.75-in) howitzer shell to smash its way through almost any fortification was much used by the French army up to the end of 1918, but thereafter the type was retained as a preferred type which grew in importance as the 1930s advanced and it became apparent that it might have a task to fulfil against the German *Westwall*. In the event the equipments were never given a chance, for by the end of June 1940 the French 400-mm (15.75-in) railway howitzers were in German service, this time as the **40-cm Haubitze (E) 752(f)**. In all the Germans took over eight examples. Two of them were kept as reserves and to provide spare parts for the other six. These six were distributed three each to Eisenbahnbatterien 686 and 693. As far as can be determined neither of these batteries was deployed outside France, and they do not appear to have survived after mid-1944. However, at least one of these howitzers was used for a time during 1943 by German experimenters to fire special armourpiercing 'Röchling' shells against an old French fort to test their penetration qualities.

Specification
Precise calibre: 400 mm (15.75 in)
Length of barrel: 10.65 m (34 ft 11.3 in)
Weight complete: 140000 kg (308,640 lb)
Weight of heavy shell: 900 kg (1,984 lb)
Range: 15000 m (16,405 yards) with heavy shell

A Matériel de 400 Modèle 15 at maximum elevation in action with a crew of American soldiers in late 1918; the Americans used only one of these howitzers, which was later replaced by American equipment.

Hand-ramming a 400-mm (15.75-in) projectile into the breech of a 400-mm French railway howitzer, probably a Modèle 16. Thought in the 1930s to be the answer to German border fortifications, in fact they were taken over after the fall of France without seeing action.

British 9.2-in railway guns

When the British army started to demand railway guns in 1915, the well-established 234-mm (9.2-in) coastal defence gun was an obvious candidate for consideration. Not only did production facilities exist for the gun, but there were also well-established ammunition supply lines on tap and, probably more important at the time, there were trained gunners already in service who both knew the gun well and were aware of all its attributes and drawbacks. Unfortunately the urgency of the times produced a large crop of odd extemporized gun and carriage combinations to the extent that by the time the war ended the whole 234-mm (9.2-in) railway gun scene had to be drastically curtailed to impose some measure of order into what had become a chaotic situation.

In the end only one type of gun and carriage was retained for possible future use. This was the **9.2-in Gun Mk 13 on Mounting Railway Truck Mk 4**, which by that time was a very different beast from the original coastal guns

placed on simple flat-bed trucks. The Mk 13 gun was purpose-built for the railway gun task and was a very good specimen of its type. The carriage had three axles fore and aft supporting a flat steel-bedded platform, at the centre of which was a large turntable. On this turntable were mounted the gun mounting proper and the firing platform. As with other designs the firing platform for the gun crew extended well to the rear of the breech and mounted an ammunition-handling crane to raise the heavy shells from ground level to the breech level. The firing platform could traverse through 360° along with the gun, but to provide some measure of stability when firing four outriggers (two on each side) could be lowered to the ground from outrigger arms. Some mountings retained the **Mk 10** gun, which was kept in service long after 1918 to the extent that it was still around in 1939, but the Mk 13 gun was the preferred type.

Between the wars the 234-mm (9.2-in) railway guns were little used apart

from the odd demonstration shoot on special occasions. Most were wrapped and coated in grease, and then placed in strange corners around the United Kingdom, to the extent that when war broke out in 1939 no-one appeared to know where they all were. The equipments had to be searched out by special parties, who found

A 9.2-inch howitzer is brought into action on its field carriage in 1917, clearly showing the advantages of mounting such heavy pieces on railway mountings.

them in some very odd places indeed, but by early 1940 enough had been found to equip the British army's re-

formed School of Railway Artillery at Catterick, an establishment mainly staffed by old railway gunners from World War I. They provided the crews and the equipment for two 9.2-in railway guns that were sent to France to back up the British Expeditionary Force, but there was no ammunition to send with them. The outcome of this sorry state of affairs was that both guns were unable to contribute anything to

A 9.2-inch gun and its full detachment 'somewhere in the Dover area' during 1941. Not all these men would actually be on the gun in action.

the conflict, and were captured near Dunkirk during May 1940.

After Dunkirk the remaining 234-mm (9.2-in) railway guns were moved south to the Dover area, where they

A 9.2-inch railway gun firing during a practice shoot at the School of Railway Artillery at Catterick. The mounting is a Mk 5; note the extra chains used to restrain the recoil.

spent the next few years as part of mobile anti-invasion defence. From time to time they were fired to impress visiting dignitaries, but they could do little else and by 1944 they had been

withdrawn, their crews sent to other tasks, and eventually all were scrapped.

Specification
Precise calibre: 233.7 mm (9.2 in)
Length of barrel: 8.509 m (27 ft 11 in)
Weight complete: 88400 kg (194,885 lb)
Weight of shell: 172.4 kg (380 lb)
Range: 20665 m (22,600 yards)

British 12-in railway howitzers
UK

While the tale of the 305-mm (12-in) railway howitzers followed the same general lines as that of the 234-mm (9.2-in) railway guns the overall story was much simpler, at least as far as the World War I period was concerned. The first model was the **12-in Howitzer on Mounting Railway Truck Mk 1**, produced by the Vickers Elswick company, but this design had some in-service limitations and it was soon replaced in use by the **Mk 3**. This in turn was supplemented by the later **Mk 5**. The Mk 3 and Mk 5 both mounted the same type of howitzer but varied mainly in their types of mounting. The Mk 3 was theoretically capable of firing through 360° of traverse, but in practice this had to be limited to within 20° of the centreline on each side. The Mk 5 could fire through 360° of traverse, but again it was often deemed sensible to place extra supports or ties to add stability when firing directly to the flanks.

The carriages for the 305-mm (12-in) howitzers consisted of two two-axle bogies, one at the front and one at the rear. These bogies supported a well-decked platform in the centre of which was the turntable surmounted by the firing platform. The firing platform had ample room for the loading and laying

Right: An impressive row of three 12-inch railway howitzers at the School of Railway Artillery, 1940. These howitzers were moved to the Dover area, where they remained until 1943.

Below: The 12-inch BL (breech-loading) Railway Howitzer Mk 3, with the barrel at its maximum 65-degree elevation to give maximum plunging fire.

members of the crew and the usual ammunition-hoisting jib was provided at the rear. The long loading platform also acted as a counter-weight to balance the forward weight of the barrel.

By 1918 only the Mk 3 and the Mk 5 were still in use and these were almost immediately placed into store, where they were forgotten about until 1939. They once more came to light after the usual search and became part of the equipment of the army's School of Railway Artillery at Catterick Camp. From there four complete equipments were sent to France to support the British Expeditionary Force, but they proved to be of no avail against the rapid tank attacks of the German army and all four of them fell into German hands. At least two of them appear to have been 'spiked' to prevent any further use and in this the gunners' efforts appear to have been successful for the type, although appearing in a list of captured equipment, does not appear to have

been used by the Germans.

Back in the United Kingdom, the remaining 305-mm (12-in) railway howitzers moved south to the English Channel coast to become part of the mobile defences but like the 234-mm (9.2-in) guns alongside which they served, they had little to do other than be rolled out to impress visiting VIPs. By 1944 there were no such equipments left in the Channel area for the threat of invasion had long since diminished. Most were put back into their protective wraps and their crews were dispersed to other duties. When the war ended they were scrapped.

Specification
Mk 3
Precise calibre: 304.8 mm (12 in)
Length of barrel: 5.715 m (18 ft 9 in)
Weight complete: 61976 kg (136,630 lb)
Weight of shell: 340 kg (750 lb)
Range: 13715 m (15,000 yards)

Specification
Mk 5
Precise calibre: 304.8 mm (12 in)
Length of barrel: 5.715 m (18 ft 9 in)
Weight complete: 77220 kg (170,240 lb)
Weight of shell: 340 kg (750 lb)
Range: 13715 m (15,000 yards)

A factory-fresh 12-inch BL Mark 5 Railway Howitzer, the last 12-inch howitzer design used throughout the early days of World War II. They were of no use in France, faced with the rapid German tank advance.

 UK
British 13.5-in railway guns

The story of the British **13.5-in railway guns** began in 1916, when it was decided to mount 356-mm (14-in) naval gun barrels onto a new type of railway mounting to provide the British army in France with a really powerful long-range gun of the type the French army was just beginning to bring into service. The 356-mm (14-in) naval gun barrels came from a batch originally intended for export to Japan, and the first of these was mounted onto its carriage at the Elswick Works at Newcastle-upon-Tyne during late 1917. It was early 1918 before the first two equipments were sent to France, one named 'Boche-Buster' and the other 'Scene-Shifter'. Once in France both did sterling work until the war ended.

Back in the United Kingdom during 1919 the two guns were sent off to store, 'Scene-Shifter' being hidden away at an ordnance depot at Chilworth minus its barrel. The same fate awaited the other two carriages that had been ordered, both of which were stored away without their intended barrels as soon as they were finished. There they remained until 1940 when the need for some form of counterbombardment gun was urgently needed in the Dover region to deal with the long-range batteries being constructed in the Pas de Calais area. The Prime Minister, Winston Churchill, took a personal hand in the measures that

A side view of the 13.5-inch Railway Guns ready for loading. The design of this carriage was the last ever produced for a British railway gun, and was considered to be among the best ever produced anywhere, but only a few were produced in 1918 and none after that.

provided a new role for the World War I gun carriages and he personally kept in touch with all stages of the guns' return to service.

The 356-mm (14-in) guns that were originally intended for the carriages had been declared obsolete in 1926 and had subsequently been scrapped. Replacement barrels were sought and found, tucked away in Royal Navy stores, in the form of a number of 343-mm (13.5-in) guns taken from the old 'Iron Duke' class of battleship. These barrels were in reasonable condition and their dimensions were such that they could be fitted into the 356-mm (14-in) railway carriages without too much trouble. Thus the conversions were made and the old carriages were provided with a thorough renovation and update.

The 343-mm (13.5-in) guns were manned by men from the Royal

Marines Siege Regiment and the first of them, HMG (His Majesty's Gun) 'Scene-Shifter' was ready in November 1940. Soon after it was joined by HMG 'Piece-Maker' and HMG 'Gladiator'. Distributed along various railway lines in the hinterland of Dover, these three guns then went into action at times, firing the odd shell in the general area of the Pas de Calais. Unfortunately the fall of these shells could only rarely be observed so their effectiveness was often uncertain. The three guns also had an anti-invasion role as their considerable ranges enabled them to cover a considerable length of coastline, but thankfully they were never called upon to undertake that task.

In November 1943 the guns once more came under army control and went into training for some possible task involved with the invasion of

One of the three 13.5-inch railway guns firing. The background suggests that this was a shoot over the Catterick ranges rather than the general Dover area.

Europe. It was intended that they would follow up the invasion forces to knock out the Pas de Calais defences from the rear, but in the event they were not required. The war ended with the three guns still in the United Kingdom, and in 1947 they were finally declared obsolete and scrapped. Today nothing of them remains.

Specification
Precise calibre: 342.9 mm (13.5 in)
Length of barrel: 15.90 m (52 ft 2 in)
Weight complete: 244590 kg (539,920 lb)
Weight of shell: 567 kg (1,250 lb)
Range: 36,575 m (40,000 yards)

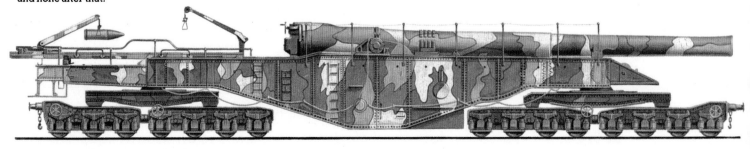

Machine-Guns of World War 1

World War I differed in kind and degree from any previous human conflict. It was the first true industrial war, in which more men were killed in battle than ever before. The two paramount weapons were artillery and – the scourge of no-man's land – the machine-gun.

Indian Army soldiers in France fire a Hotchkiss Mk 1 from a position very like the sangars of the North West Frontier. The strip feed used on the Hotchkiss machine-gun can be clearly seen, as can the cooling fins around the barrel.

During World War I the machine-gun dominated the battlefields in a manner that is now difficult to comprehend. In fact it would be safe to say that the machine-gun dictated the very way in which World War I was fought, and this dominance of a tactical situation by a single weapon spurned the development of novel weapons to counter that same machine-gun.

Throughout World War I military planners sought desperately to overcome the power of the machine-gun. Time and time again prolonged artillery bombardments battered an enemy defensive system until it seemed that nothing could survive, but every time the hapless infantry moved forward from their trenches there seemed always to be a machine-gun that could prevent further progress. Thus it was that the artillery destroyed while the machine-gun killed. But in tactical terms many of these machine-guns were large and heavy weapons that could not be moved easily or rapidly, and a new family of lighter machine-guns was devised even as the war continued. It was these light machine-guns that were partly able to break the pattern of static emplacements and massed frontal assaults, by allowing the evaluation of a new tactical

situation in which relatively mobile infantry could supply a fair proportion of their own fire support where and when it was most needed. Even so, it should not be forgotten that despite all the dreadful success of the machine-gun it was the arrival of the tank that finally did away with the mincing-machine apparatus of trench warfare on the Western Front.

Included in this study are some superb examples of machine-gun design, ranging from the magnificent Vickers machine-gun and the sturdy PM1910 to the dreadful Chauchat. All the weapons included here used some mechanical devices that tested the skills of designers and metallurgists alike, and the results were often technical marvels of their day. Many of the weapons mentioned here would still be viable in any form of combat were it not for the fact that they have been replaced by new and yet more powerful generations of weapons.

French and British soldiers operate together, with a Hotchkiss mle 1900 ready to provide fire support. This 1918 scene reflects the return to mobile warfare which preceded the end of the war and at last brought the machine-gun out of the trenches. It would have been inconceivable only six months before.

Hotchkiss mle 1909

In the years up to 1914 the French army was trained in the tenet that the attack (or the offensive) was the key to victory in any future war. The infantry and cavalry were trained to attack at all times, overcoming any opposition by the force of their onslaught and by their determination. In this optimistic scenario the machine-gun hardly featured, but at one point in the early 1900s it was thought that some form of light Hotchkiss machine-gun would be useful for cavalry units, and might also be portable enough for attacking infantrymen to carry.

The result of this suggestion was the **Fusil-mitrailleur Hotchkiss mle 1909**, which used the basic gas-operated mechanism of the larger Hotchkiss machine-guns, though for some reason the ammunition feed was complicated further by inversion of the ammunition feed strip mechanism. When it was introduced the cavalry units did not take to the weapon at all and it proved to be too heavy for infantry use, so the numbers produced were either relegated to use in fortifications or stockpiled. However, export sales of the mle 1909 were more encouraging for the weapon was adopted by the US Army who knew it as the **Benét-Mercié Machine Rifle Model 1909**; it was used mainly by cavalry units.

When World War I began the mle 1909 was once more taken from the stockpiles, and it was even adopted by the British army as the **0.303-in Gun, Machine, Hotchkiss, Mk 1** in an attempt to get more machine-guns into service. The mle 1909 was produced in the United Kingdom chambered for the British 7.7-mm (0.303-in) cartridge and in British use many were fitted with a butt and a bipod in place of the original small tripod located under the centre of the gun body.

However the mle 1909 was not destined to be used very much in the trenches: the ammunition feed was a constant source of troubles and gradually the Hotchkiss was diverted to other uses. The mle 1909 in its several forms became an aircraft gun and it formed the main armament of many of the ear-

ly tanks such as the British 'Female' tanks with their all-machine-gun armament, and the little Renault FT17. On the tanks the ammunition feed strips sometimes limited the traverse available inside the close confines of the tank mountings, so many guns, especially those of the British, were converted to use the three-round linked strips intended for use on the larger Hotchkiss mle 1914. Some of these guns were still in British army use in 1939, and more were later taken from the stockpiles for use as airfield defence weapons and for arming merchant shipping.

The mle 1909 was one of the first light machine-guns, but it had little impact at the time, although it was used in quite large numbers. Its main disadvantage was not so much a technical difficulty as a tactical problem, for the tactics involved in trench warfare of the period and the lack of appreciation of the potential of the weapon never gave the mle 1909 a chance to shine. As a tank weapon it made its mark on history, but it was less successful as an aircraft gun, the feed strip mechanism proving a definite drawback in an open aircraft cockpit.

Specification
Fusil-mitrailleur Hotchkiss mle 1909
Calibre: 8 mm (0.315 in)

Above: The Hotchkiss mle 1909 was used by the French, the British (as the Hotchkiss Mk 1) and also by the US Army, who knew it as the Benét-Mercié.

Below: A drummer of the 1/7th Lancashire Fusiliers demonstrates a Hotchkiss Mk 1 to newly-arrived US Army soldiers in France in May 1918.

Lengths: overall 1.19 m (46.85 in); barrel 600 mm (23.62 in)
Weight: 11.7 kg (25.8 lb)
Muzzle velocity: 740 m (2,428 ft) per second
Rate of fire: (cyclic) 500 rpm
Feed: 30-round metal strip

Hotchkiss medium machine-guns

In the 1890s the only viable machine-guns were those produced by Maxim and Browning, both of whom wrapped their products in a tight wall of patents to prevent others enjoying the fruits of their invention. Many armament concerns were desperate to find some way of getting around the patent wall, and one of these was the French Hotchkiss company. Thus when it was approached by an Austrian inventor who described to them a novel method of gas operation to power a machine-gun, the invention was quickly purchased and developed by Hotchkiss.

The first Hotchkiss machine-gun was the **Mitrailleuse Hotchkiss mle 1897**, and although this model was hardly a viable service weapon it was the first gas-operated machine-gun. This was followed by the **mle 1900** and later by the **mle 1914**, the latter being the model mainly used in World War I. These models all had air-cooled barrels, but as these tended to overheat the company very quickly introduced a feature that was to remain as a virtual 'trademark' of the Hotchkiss machine

gun: this consisted of five prominent 'doughnut' collars around the end of the barrel closer to the receiver. These rings (sometimes brass and sometimes steel) enlarged the surface area of the barrel at the point where it became hottest and thus provided greater cooling.

For operating, gas was tapped off from the barrel and used to push back a piston to carry out all the various extracting and reloading operations. It was a system that worked well and reliably, and was soon to be used in one form or another by many other machine-gun designers. The weapon had its first exposure to action during the Russo-Japanese War of 1904-5, in

French and British infantry at the Battle of the Aisne in 1918 in the follow-up to the Allied advance. The gun is a Hotchkiss mle 1900 mounted on the mle 1916 tripod, with ammunition boxes close to hand behind the gunner. To the left of the gun are two ammunition handlers ready to assist.

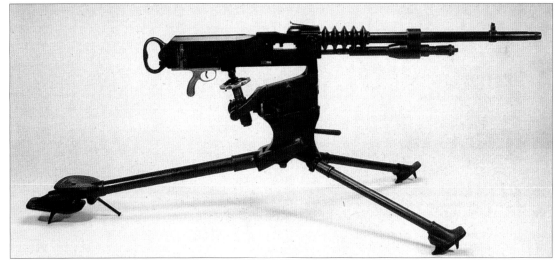

Easily recognized by the large doughnut cooling rings around the barrel, the Hotchkiss mle 1914 became the standard French heavy machine-gun of World War I. Although heavy, it was well made and generally reliable, but the strip feed sometimes gave trouble. It fired an 8-mm (0.315-in) round.

which it performed well enough though one feature did cause trouble. This was the ammunition feed, the Hotchkiss using a method whereby the rounds were fed into the gun mounted on metal strips; originally brass strips were used, but these were later replaced by steel strips. These strips carried only 24 or 30 rounds, which severely limited the amount of sustained fire that could be produced. On the mle 1914 this was partly overcome by redesigning the strip system to give three-round strips linked together to form a 249-round 'belt'. Even in this form the strips were prone to damage and any dirt on them tended to cause jams. The feed mechanism was thus the weakest point in an otherwise reliable and serviceable design.

There were some variations on the basic design. Versions for use in fortifications had a downwards 'V'-shaped muzzle attachment that was supposed to act as a flash hider, and several types of tripod were in use during World War I, including a mle 1897 mounting that had no provision for traverse or elevation.

The Hotchkiss machine-guns were used mainly by the French army during World War I, but in 1917 large numbers were handed over to the American Expeditionary Force when it arrived in France. The Americans continued to use them until the war ended.

Specification
Mitrailleuse Hotchkiss mle 1914

Calibre: 8 mm (0.315 in)
Lengths: overall 1.27 m (50 in); barrel 775 mm (30.51 in)
Weight: gun 23.6 kg (52.0 lb)
Muzzle velocity: 725 m (2,379 ft) per second
Rate of fire: (cyclic) 400-600 rpm
Feed: 24- or 30-round strip, or 249-round strip in 3-round links

---

Chauchat

Officially known as the **Fusil-Mitrailleur mle 1915**, the **Chauchat** or **CSRG** is one of the more unpleasant weapon production stories of World War I. It was intended as a light machine-gun, and was created by a commission of designers in 1914, the result being a long and awkward weapon using a mechanism known as 'long recoil' in which the barrel and breech block moved to the rear after firing, the barrel then being allowed to move forward while the bolt is held and released later to feed the next round. This mechanism works, but is rather complicated and the movement inside the gun makes aiming difficult.

The Chauchat was apparently intended for ease of manufacture, but when the design was rushed into production in 1915 its manufacture was hived out to a large number of firms, some of whom had virtually no weapon-manufacturing experience. The result was a horror, for many manufacturers used the Chauchat simply as a means of making maximum profit and so used cheap and unsuitable materials that either wore out quickly or broke in action. Even when the materials were suitable the service versions of the Chauchat were still bad: the weapon handled badly and tended to jam at the slightest excuse. The half-moon magazine under the body did little to make the weapon easier to carry, and the light bipod was so flimsy that it bent very easily. The French soldiers hated the weapon, many later proclaiming that the manufacturers' greed for profits had caused the deaths of many French soldiers, as they no doubt had.

Unfortunately, the manufacturers were not alone in their search for weapon production profits. When the Americans entered the war some French politicians prevailed upon the US Army to adopt the Chauchat, and the unsuspecting Americans agreed. They accepted over 16,000 Chauchats and a further 19,000 were ordered of a version chambered for the American

The Fusil-Mitrailleur mle 1915 or 'Chauchat' was one of the worst machine-guns ever built and was reviled by the soldiers who had to use it in action.

7.62-mm (0.3-in) cartridge; this model had a vertical box magazine instead of the French half-moon magazine. Neither of these versions proved to be any better in American hands than they were in French hands. The Americans often simply cleared jams by throwing the jammed weapon away and taking up a rifle, especially when the rechambered weapons reached their ranks. The American cartridge was more powerful than the French 8-mm (0.315-in) round and made the gun components break even more rapidly.

In the end existing production contracts were allowed to run their course, but the resultant weapons were usually stockpiled to be dragged out and later dumped upon unsuspecting post-war markets. In France some parliamentary investigations were made into the Chauchat affair in an attempt to determine exactly how and where the profits ended, but by then

so many parliamentarians and industrialists were involved that the whole affair gradually fizzled out.

Most references state that the Chauchat in all its forms was one of the worst machine-guns of World War I in all aspects. From basic design to manufacture and the materials used, it was a disaster, but what now appears worse is the fact that the whole programme was not controlled at all. The result was that many soldiers suffered from having to use the weapon while others pocketed the profits their greed had generated.

Specification
Chauchat
Calibre: 8 mm (0.315 in)
Lengths: gun 1.143 m (45.0 in); barrel 470 mm (18.5 in)
Weight: 9.2 kg (20.3 lb)
Muzzle velocity: 700 m (2,297 ft) per second
Rate of fire: 250-300 rpm
Feed: 20-round curved box magazine

Below: A French soldier fully attired in his horizon bleu *uniform and greatcoat holds his Chauchat in the prescribed drill book manner for use in the assault.*

Light Machine-Gun Tactics 1915-1918

The first machine-guns were not the most mobile of weapons, being emplaced in battle rather like pieces of artillery. It did not take long for the troops on the Western Front to appreciate how effective a machine-gun could be, advancing with them into battle, and so the light machine-gun was born.

When World War I started the light machine-gun was virtually unknown. Belgian troops did carry into action a number of Lewis Guns, but these were used at that time in exactly the same way as conventional heavy machine-guns, i.e. they were carefully emplaced before an action and used to provide supporting or covering fire. As the troops moved forward into an attack the machine-guns stayed where they were, being considered too heavy to be carried forward.

This was unfortunate, for in the Lewis Gun the Belgians had an excellent infantry weapon that was quite capable of taking on a new role. This new role was indicated during 1915 when the first of the setpiece attacks along the German lines began, with their massive artillery overtures and the subsequent confusion and carnage when the planned infantry attacks stalled either on the barbed wire or in front of emplaced heavy machine-guns. At times like these there was no way in which the infantry could get themselves out of their predicament. Using their rifles alone they could rarely produce enough firepower to make an enemy machine-gunner keep his head down, and there was no way that artillery or machine-gun support could be called upon, for radio was in its infancy and telephone wires were soon cut. For this reason all artillery and machine-gun fire plan support had to be prepared beforehand using rigid fire plans on a timetable basis. If an enemy machine-gun intervened there was no way any supporting fire could be diverted from the fire plan, and the 'poor bloody infantry' thus had to suffer.

Fire support

But by the end of 1915 the first inklings of how supporting machine-gun fire could be produced to counter this problem had been suggested by a few forward-looking officers. It was 1916 before their ideas came to the hardware stage: the overall solution to the crossing of no man's land was of course the tank, but an interim solution was found with the service introduction of the Lewis Gun. This had been adopted by the British army for economic rather than tactical reasons: the expanding British armies clearly had to be equipped with machine-guns, and it was found that five or six Lewis Guns could be churned out in the time that it took to produce one of the heavier and more complex Vickers machine-guns. Initially there were four Lewis Guns to a battalion, to replace the Vickers machine-guns that had been passed to the newly-formed Machine Gun Corps. By mid-1916 this allotment had been increased to eight, and a month later a further four were added. By the end of 1916 there was one Lewis Gun to every four platoons, and by the end of the war every two platoons shared one Lewis Gun. By that time there were even four Lewis Guns in every battalion dedicated to the anti-aircraft defence role. This rapid growth in numbers was pushed through by a realization that in the Lewis Gun the long-suffering infantry battalions could have their own local fire support weapons. No longer did the infantry have to rely upon Vickers machine-guns emplaced away to the rear for local fire support. If a target presented itself the Lewis gunners operating right up in the front lines with the first waves of infantry were on the spot to throw themselves down and open fire right away. In this way isolated pockets of resistance left behind by the artillery bombardment could be overcome as quickly as possible. Some units even devised a drill whereby the Lewis Guns were moved forward by two men in the first wave of attackers. One man held the Lewis Gun by looping his arms around the barrel. The other man fired the gun at anything that presented itself. In this manner the gun could be fired without the gunner having to adopt the prone position and fire could also be opened up all the more rapidly.

But these tactics were not universal. Despite the firepower potential of the Lewis Gun, the men that used it were just as vulnerable to enemy fire as the rest, and all too often the Lewis gunners were among the first to be picked off by the carefully-emplaced defenders. In time the infantry tactics changed: they had to, for men were simply not able to walk through a hail of enemy fire to carry out an attack. Instead of proceeding forward in a sedate manner, the infantry instead adopted a method whereby small sections of men rushed forward one after the other. As each section moved forward the other sections provided covering fire over the trench system being attacked. The French adopted this method after suffering from its effects when it was used by the Germans at Verdun in 1916.

French infantry operate in the Vosges mountains, with the unfortunate soul in the foreground carrying a Hotchkiss mle 1900 on his back; others would have to carry the tripod and the boxes of ammunition strips. Note that all have rifles or carbines to carry as well while most carry their packs.

Above: This Indian cavalryman is seen as he would have been on the Western Front during 1914-5. The Lewis Gun was ideal for use with cavalry as it was relatively light.

Left: The German MG 08/15 was an air-cooled machine-gun developed from experience gained during World War I. Designed by Rheinmetall, it had an 'all-in-line' layout and a novel form of locking mechanism.

Above: Any enemy aircraft flying within range of this array of Lewis Guns would have been in for a nasty shock. These Indian Army guns are shown somewhere in Mesopotamia and are fitted with 47-round magazines. Some have slings for ease of carrying their 11.8 kg (26 lb) bulk.

Above: A section of the Gordon Highlanders is seen in action during March 1918 near the Somme, with their Lewis Gun being used in the classic supporting fire role. The figure in the tree is probably spotting for targets for the Lewis team and shouting down fire corrections.

The British were reluctant to assume this form of tactics mainly because of the overall poor standard of training they were able to provide for their mass armies, but gradually the soldiers themselves devised methods for the mutual support of sections by other sections. It was here that the Lewis Gun came into its own, for the firepower potential of the weapon was such that a single Lewis Gun could assume the support role of a whole section of riflemen. Thus infantry sections reached the point where a single Lewis Gun team of two men could cover the forward progress of almost an entire platoon.

As ever, by this time the Germans were already one stage ahead. They had seen the requirements for a portable machine-gun as early as 1915 and had devised the MG 08/15 Maxim gun for a new array of infantry tactics. Using experience gained on the Eastern Front, the Germans had already designed a new system of infantry warfare employing the same balanced mutual fire support role that had been tentatively evolved by the Allies. However, the Germans took it one stage further. Realizing that infantry alone could not hope to take control of a Western Front trench system, they did not even attempt to take a trench by storm. Instead the German infantry were divided up into small assault teams that were trained simply to pass around any strongpoints they might encounter: so rather than attempting to attack any defensive emplacements that might be in their path, they moved away to the flanks and filtered round into the rear areas. Once there they could disrupt the movement of men and supplies to the forward trenches, attack command posts and generally disrupt the enemy's rear areas. If necessary, troublesome strongpoints could be attacked from the rear.

In this type of combat the light machine-gun had many roles to play. The most important was still that of providing supporting or covering fire while the other sections moved, but the Germans' activities were hampered by a shortage of MG 08/15s. Supply of this weapon could not meet demand, so captured Lewis Guns were pressed into German use. Stretcher bearers became involved in this process of obtaining enemy weapons, some units ordering their stretcher bearers to carry back to the rear as many Lewis Guns as they could find on the battlefield, each one carried on a stretcher along with a casualty.

By 1918 light machine-guns were being used in defence as well as attack. As the German army fell back during the later months of 1918 it worked out a method whereby small light machine-gun teams were used to cover the withdrawal of much larger bodies of men. At times a single MG 08/15 would be used to hold up a whole battalion advancing across open ground, the gun team simply packing up and carrying its gun away to the rear, ready for another holding action, as soon as the Allied assault forces came uncomfortably close to their position.

Above: The MG 08/15 was converted from its aircraft role for the ground role during World War II, again a carry-over from World War I when many weapons were similarly converted. This conversion involved the fitting of a light bipod and a rudimentary butt, but the end result was not very successful.

Right: A Schütztruppen NCO holds an ammunition box for his MG 08. A critical shortage of artillery made the machine-guns of the German army in East Africa doubly important.

Saint-Etienne

The Hotchkiss was a commercial design, and the French military authorities wanted to have their own design of machine-gun to match. Unfortunately their efforts were not a success, and indeed were not helped by the fact that the gas-operated mechanism devised by Hotchkiss was protected by a long list of patents that were almost impossible to circumvent. Not deterred, the French attempted to produce a model known as the **mle 1905** or **Puteaux**. It was so unsuccessful that it was withdrawn from use within two years, the basic design being used for another attempt that was known as the **Mitrailleuse mle 1907** or **Saint-Etienne**, after the arsenal at which it was manufactured.

The French military designers decided to use a gas mechanism based on the Hotchkiss, but to reverse the overall process. Instead of gases in the barrel pushing back a piston, the Saint-Etienne used a system whereby the gases were tapped forward where the piston compressed a spring. The compressed spring was then released to power the rest of the operation. This system worked, but only at the expense of complication and of the use of more pieces that could break or go wrong, so in practice the whole idea was simply not worth the trouble involved. The mle 1907 had an inherent source of ammunition and other jams, and the return spring that was supposed to do all the work got so hot that it either lost its tempering and ceased to operate or else simply broke. In the end the designers could do nothing more than leave the spring exposed to the elements, which aided cooling but also allowed dust and dirt to enter the workings and so produce more jams.

Despite all these inherent troubles, the mle 1907 Saint-Etiennes were used during World War I for the simple reason that the French army became so desperate for weapons that it used

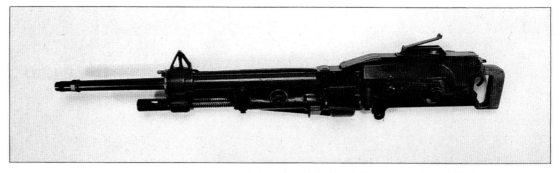

Above: The French mle 1907 was a state-produced machine-gun intended to improve upon the basic Hotchkiss designs. It was less successful, many being sent to the colonies or relegated to fortress use.

anything it could obtain. The tribulations of the mle 1907 simply had to be borne, and as late as 1916 attempts were made to eradicate some of the more obvious faults. None of the modifications was of any use, and gradually the mle 1907s were phased out in favour of the far more reliable Hotchkiss guns. The mle 1907s were shunted off to the French colonies, where they were used to arm local levies and police units. Others were issued to fortress units.

All in all the Saint-Etienne was not a success; indeed, it even carried over the failings from other models. The mle 1905 Puteaux had already indicated the impracticality of some of the mle 1907's features, and the troublesome ammunition feed strip method of the Hotchkiss guns was adopted even when it was known that it should have been phased out in favour of a better method. The result was that in the dreadful conditions of the Western Front trenches the Saint-Etienne often failed.

A mle 1907 St Etienne machine-gun team poses for a publicity photograph on one of the levels of the Eiffel Tower in an attempt to

prove that Paris was able to defend itself against German air raids. The mle 1907 was no more successful in this role than it was in any other.

Specification
Mitrailleuse Saint-Etienne mle 1907
Calibre: 8 mm (0.315 in)
Lengths: gun 1.18 m (46.46 in); barrel 710 mm (27.95 in)

Weight: 25.4 kg (56.0 lb)
Muzzle velocity: 700 m (2,297 ft) per second
Rate of fire: 400-600 rpm
Feed: 24- or 30-round metal strip

Browning M1917

Almost as soon as the Colt-Browning Model 1895 was in production, Browning was already at work on a recoil-operated weapon. Unfortunately for Browning, at that time the American military authorities had no interest in any more machine-guns: they considered they had enough already, and anyway funds to purchase more were few. Thus virtually nothing happened until 1917 when the USA found itself at war with few modern weapons and even fewer serviceable machine-guns. In a very short space of time the 'new' Browning machine-gun was ordered into production in large numbers as the **Machine-Gun, Caliber .30, M1917**.

Externally the M1917 resembled other machine-guns of the time, especially the Vickers Gun. In fact the M1917 was quite different: it used a mechanism known as the short recoil system, in which the recoil force produced on firing the cartridge pushes back the barrel and breech block to

The Colt Model 1917 was the first of many successful Browning-designed machine-guns that are in use to this day. Chambered for the American 0.30-in (7.62-mm) cartridge, they were used by the US Army in France.

the rear of the gun; after the barrel and bolt have travelled back together for a short distance, the two components part and the barrel movement is halted; a swinging lever known as an accelerator then throws the bolt to the rear, and as it travels a series of cams move the belt feed mechanism to insert another round; a return spring then pushes forward the bolt to the barrel and the whole assembly is then returned for the cycle to start again. This basic mechanism was retained for all future Browning machine-gun designs, from the air-cooled 7.62-mm (0.3-in) to the large 12.7-mm (0.5-in) M2 weapons.

One component that differentiated the M1917 from the Vickers machine-gun (apart from the internal workings) was the firing grip: the Vickers used two spade grips, but the M1917 used a pistol grip and a conventional trigger. Close inspection between the two types will soon reveal many other differences, but the pistol grip is easily noticed.

The M1917 was rushed into production at several manufacturing centres and was churned out in such numbers that by the time the war ended no less than 68,000 had been made. Not all of these reached the troops in France, but after 1918 the M1917 became one of the standard American heavy machine-guns and remained in service until well after World War II. Also after 1918 some slight alterations were introduced as the result of combat experience, but these changes were slight. More drastic changes came after 1918 when the water cooling jacket was removed altogether to produce the **M1919**.

In service the M1917 proved to be relatively trouble free, and despite the rush with which it was placed in service few problems appear to have been recorded. Relatively few M1917s actually reached France before the Armistice, but many were on their way. Those which did arrive were extensively used, for the M1917s were among the few purely-American

weapons that were issued to the American troops: up until then all they had from home were their Springfield rifles and a few other sundry items. It was just as well that the M1917 turned out to be an excellent weapon design.

Specification
M1917
Calibre: 7.62 mm (0.3 in)
Lengths: gun 0.981 m (38.64 in); barrel 607 mm (23.9 in)
Weights: gun less water 14.79 kg (32.6 lb); tripod 24.1 kg (53.15 lb)
Muzzle velocity: 853 m (2,800 ft) per second
Rate of fire: 450-600 rpm
Feed: 250-round belt

Completely unprepared for a major conflict, the US Army was compelled to rely on Britain and France for much of the equipment for its Expeditionary Force. One honourable exception was the Browning M1917, a fine weapon destined to enjoy a long career.

USA
Colt-Browning Model 1895

John Moses Browning started design work on a machine-gun as early as 1889, at a time when the American armed forces were still heavily involved with the hand-operated Gatling Gun and when Maxim had already patented his recoil-operated machine-gun. Browning was thus directed towards a gas-operated mechanism, which he gradually refined until it reached the point where the Colt Patent Firearms Manufacturing Company built some prototypes, one of which was demonstrated to the US Navy. It was 1895 before the US Navy decided to purchase a batch chambered for the Krag-Jorgensen 7.62-mm (0.3-in) cartridge, but later this was altered to the .30-06 cartridge that was to remain in use for two world wars.

The **Colt-Browning Model 1895** was a gas-operated weapon that used gases tapped off from the barrel to push down a piston. This in turn pushed down a long lever that swung below the gun body to operate the gun mechanism. It was this lever that gave the weapon the nickname of 'potato digger', for if the gun was mounted close to the ground a small pit had to be dug into which the lever could move, otherwise it would hit the ground and cause stoppages. This drawback was partially offset by the fact that being based on a mechanical operation the movements were very definite and precise, and so able to provide a smooth and trouble-free action. Ammunition was fed into the weapon in 300-round belts.

The Model 1895 first went into action with the US Marine Corps during the Cuban campaign of 1898. The US Army took over a few, and some sales were made to Belgium and Russia. By the time that World War I came around the Model 1895 was already regarded as obsolete, but since by that time the US Army was largely starved of funds to procure more modern weapons the Model 1895s were all that were available and were retained for training. Some did make the journey to France in 1917 and 1918 but few were used in action; instead the Americans took over numbers of French and British

machine-guns. The Model 1895 did remain in production for a while during World War I: production was switched to the Marlin-Rockwell Corporation, which modified the weapon by designing out the lever action and replacing it by a more orthodox gas piston system. The result was known as the **Marlin Gun**. It resembled the Model 1895 but was much lighter and was a better weapon overall. Many were produced for the US Army air service as aircraft weapons, and some were produced to become the standard machine-gun for tanks produced in America. In the event the war ended before many of the Marlin Guns could reach the front in sizable numbers, and the bulk of the production run was stockpiled, only to be sold to the United Kingdom for home defence in 1940.

Despite its awkward underbody lever that swung down during firing, the Colt Model 1895 was selected for use as a weapon for early combat aircraft such as this Voisin. This was mainly due to its relatively light weight and air-cooled barrel, though it was not used as such for long.

The Belgian and Tsarist Russian armies used the Model 1895 throughout World War I, some of the Russian weapons being prominent during the political upheavals of 1917. A few of the Russian Model 1895s were still being used as late as 1941.

Specification
Colt-Browning Model 1895
Calibre: 7.62 mm (0.3 in)
Lengths: gun 1.20 m (47.25 in); barrel 720 mm (28.35 in)

The Colt Model 1895 was known to the troops as the 'potato digger' because of the arm that swung down under the body when the gun was firing. This weapon was still in use when the Americans entered the war in 1917 and was used in France.

Weights: gun 16.78 kg (37 lb); tripod 29.0 kg (64 lb)
Muzzle velocity: 838 m (2,750 ft) per second
Rate of fire: 400-500 rpm
Feed: 300-round belt

Browning Automatic Rifle

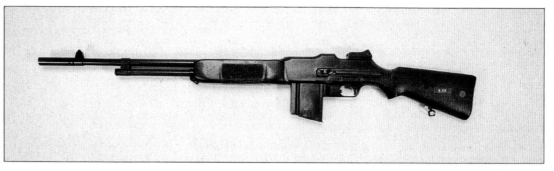

In 1917 Browning demonstrated two new automatic weapon designs to the Congress in Washington: one was the heavy machine-gun that was to become the M1917, and the other a weapon that is still regarded by many as a hybrid and which became known to all as the **Browning Automatic Rifle**, or **BAR**. The BAR was in an odd category, for to many the weapon was a light machine-gun but to the US Army it was an automatic rifle, in some ways an early assault rifle. It was a light and portable weapon that could fire single shot or automatic, and it could be carried and used by one man.

By early 1918 the BAR was in production at several centres, but as Colt held the Browning patents at that time it produced the drawings and gauges that the other centres were to use. It was September 1918 before the BAR actually reached the stage where it was used in action, but it made a tremendous impact on the American soldiers who soon grew to value the weapon highly, so highly in fact that they were still using the BAR during the Korean War of the 1950s. Exactly why the Americans went so overboard regarding the BAR was (and still is) rather difficult to determine. The first BARs, as used in World War I, were simply hand-held weapons. There was no bipod or any form of support for use when the weapon was fired on automatic in the prone position, and as the box magazine held only 20 rounds the

length of bursts was strictly limited. As a light machine-gun the BAR was really too light, and as an automatic rifle it was too large and heavy.

But the American soldiers took to the BAR very well, no doubt as a relief from having to deal with the dreadful Chauchat. Apart from the Springfield rifles, the BAR was one of the first 'all-American' weapons to reach them, and no doubt they wanted to demonstrate the quality of American small arms. The BAR was certainly an impressive-looking weapon. It was excellently made, was provided with well-finished wooden furniture, and was capable of taking hard knocks. The mechanism was gas operated and so arranged that at the instant of firing the mechanism was locked in place by the bolt engaging in a notch in the top of the receiver. This notch was the

source of the 'hump' on top of the gun just in front of the rear sights. For maintenance and repairs the BAR could be rapidly and easily stripped down to its 70 component parts and reassembled just as easily.

In the field the US Army devised some combat drills for the BAR. One that did not last long was a drill whereby attacking infantry would fire one shot every time the left foot touched the ground. In fact most of the tactical drills involving the BAR were formulated after 1918, when the lessons of the few months of combat that the US Army had to endure were analysed. Along with the drills the BAR itself changed by the addition of a bipod and a shoulder strap for carrying, and the BAR became more of a section support weapon that could deliver automatic fire in support of riflemen rather than

The Browning Automatic Rifle, or BAR, was a cross between a heavy machine rifle and a light machine-gun. Its magazine held only 20 rounds and there was no bipod on the first models. The US Army found it a very useful weapon and used it in large numbers.

the assault-type weapon role it had been used for in the trenches.

Specification
BAR
Calibre: 7.62 mm (0.3 in)
Lengths: overall 1.194 m (47 in); barrel 610 mm (24 in)
Weight: 7.26 kg (16 lb)
Muzzle velocity: 853 m (2,800 ft) per second
Rate of fire: (cyclic) 550 rpm
Feed: 20-round box magazine

Vickers Gun

The UK was among the first to adopt the Maxim gun following demonstrations held in the country as early as 1887. A manufacturing line for various models was set up at Crayford in Kent by a company that came to be known as Vickers' Sons & Maxim Limited, and from this factory Maxim guns went to the British armed forces and to many other countries. The Vickers engineers realized the virtues of the Maxim gun but considered that some weight savings could be made by a redesign, and by careful stress studies much of the mechanism was gradually lightened and the basic action inverted so that the toggle lock invented by Maxim could be made lighter.

The result came to be known as the **Vickers Gun**. In relative terms it was not all that much lighter than a comparable Maxim machine-gun, but the operating principles were much refined making the weapon more efficient. It was approved for British army service in November 1912 as the **Gun, Machine, Vickers, 0.303-in, Mk 1**, and all production initially went to the British Army, where the machine-gun was still regarded with such suspicion that the rate of issue was only two per infantry battalion.

Once World War I started that allotment changed drastically. New production centres were soon opened, some of them located in Royal Ordnance Factories, but the basic design remained unchanged throughout its long production life. The last Vickers machine-gun was very like the first and changes were confined to details. Like most machine-guns of its period, the Vickers was subject to jams, most of them induced by the ammunition, and a series of drills were devised to

clear the weapon rapidly. These drills took a bit of learning so in time a new Machine Gun Corps was formed within the British Army so that experience and skills could be confined within a relatively small body and not spread throughout all the regiments of the expanding armies. The Machine Gun Corps also raised its own esprit de corps, and that enabled the machine-gunners to use their weapons with a little extra spirit; their cap badge was two crossed Vickers machine-guns.

In action a Vickers could be kept firing for as long as ammunition could be fed into it. The water in the cooling jacket had to be kept topped up, and after early experiences where steam from the jacket gave way the gun's position a special condenser system

(using a hose fed into a water can) was introduced to conceal the steam. After a while the water could be replaced in the jacket.

The Vickers machine-gun was usually mounted on a heavy tripod. Variations on the basic gun included air-cooled versions for use on aircraft, usually on fixed installations only. Many more variations were produced between the two world wars, and the Vickers is still in service with some armed forces to this day; it did not pass from British service until the 1970s. The Vickers machine-gun was, in the opinion of many authorities, one of the best of all the World War I machine-guns, and would still be a very useful weapon today.

Specification
Vickers Gun
Calibre: 7.7 mm (0.303 in)
Lengths: gun 1.156 m (45.5 in); barrel 721 mm (28.4 in)
Weights: gun 18.14 kg (40 lb); tripod 22.0 kg (48.5 lb)
Muzzle velocity: 744 m (2,440 ft) per second
Rate of fire: 450-500 rpm
Feed: 250-round fabric belt

This Vickers is an American-built version mounted on the British Mk 4B tripod. It was the standard British machine-gun and was even used as the badge of the Machine-Gun Corps, a formation whose very creation underscores the importance of the machine-gun during World War I.

The Vickers in Action

Hiram Maxim produced one of the most successful of early machine-guns, variants equipping many of the armies taking part in World War I. The modified Maxim produced by Vickers, still in service today, became one of the finest machine-guns of the 20th century.

When the first Vickers machine-guns entered service in 1907, few British army officers knew exactly what to do with their new charges. Few appreciated the potential power of the weapon, and those few who did were regarded as eccentrics.

The initial rate of issue of the Vickers machine-gun was two to an infantry battalion; few cavalry battalions took to the weapon and only a few carried them across to France in 1914. Once there they soon learned that the machine-gun was a powerful weapon and the first to suffer were the cavalry units. A single machine-gun hidden away on a distant horizon could keep an entire cavalry battalion immobile for as long as it kept firing. The Battle of Loos further reinforced the lesson for the British, and they began to look at the Vickers weapon in a different light.

The Vickers machine-gun was developed from the earlier Maxim Gun. Vickers had manufactured the Maxim Gun at its Crayford factory in Kent, and although the Maxim had sold very well to many customers, the Vickers design engineers thought that they could improve upon the basic concept to produce a lighter and more efficient weapon. This they did by reversing the Maxim toggle lock device so that it opened upwards instead of downwards. This can perhaps be better explained by going through the sequence of operations involved in the Vickers short recoil mechanism.

At the moment a cartridge was fired the toggle mechanism, formed from two levers, was in an all-in-line position with the central hinge in line with both levers. This gave the mechanism a very positive and strong lock, for the only way to break the toggle joint was by an upward movement. This was not imparted at the moment of firing, for the recoil forces tended to push the breech block (the lock) backwards in a straight line. As the bullet left the muzzle the gases expanded in a small muzzle chamber and forced back the barrel which in turn provided more impetus for the breech block. Together they moved to the rear, but as they did so the rear of the two toggle levers struck a fixed post, the lever being so arranged that it was then pushed upwards. This broke the positive lock and the breech could then move separately to the rear, taking with it the spent case from the chamber. At the same time the reloading operation could start: as the breech block moved to the rear it placed a load on a spring known as the fuzee spring, which would eventually return the breech block back to the original position. This operation would continue for as long as the trigger in front of the firer's spade grips was pressed.

Prolonged firing made the barrel very hot, so it was cooled by water contained in a metal jacket around the barrel. This jacket held 3.98 litres (7 pints) of water, which would boil after three minutes of sustained fire at the rate of 200 rounds per minute. At first this boiling assisted the cooling process as minute air bubbles helped to carry the heat away from the barrel, but soon the heat caused the water to evaporate as steam. In the early days this was allowed to escape from the top of the jacket, but it was soon noticed that the cloud of steam gave away the gun position and invited retaliatory fire, so an easy solution was found by diverting it via a flexible pipe into a can of water where it could condense harmlessly back to water and eventually be returned to the jacket. This last was important in areas where water was scarce.

Seated in front of his Vickers machine-gun, with the tripod reversed to allow the barrel to be elevated for anti-aircraft use, this Anzac soldier is taking a quick break. Using the Vickers in this role could be successful – Australian soldiers claimed responsibility for shooting down von Richtofen's Fokker triplane.

Despite the water cooling system the barrel had to be changed every 10,000 rounds. As it was possible to fire 10,000 rounds in an hour it often became a drill that in action a barrel was replaced every hour on the hour. A well trained crew could accomplish this in about two minutes with no loss of water other than that which entered the barrel as it was pushed in from the rear. In fact it was this type of operation that led to the use only of specialists on the Vickers machine-gun. At first men from ordinary battalions were assigned to the weapons, but the need

An Australian soldier demonstrates the drill-book method of packing a Vickers machine-gun onto a packhorse or mule. The special harness carried a complete machine-gun and tripod along with ammunition, water, spares and sighting equipment, even including spare barrels.

Vickers machine-gunners keep their gun in action during the aftermath of a chemical attack in July 1916. The primitive respirators of the time caused severe restriction on vision but were just adequate. Note the strap around the barrel that was used for rapid movement in an emergency.

The Vickers Gun Mk 1*

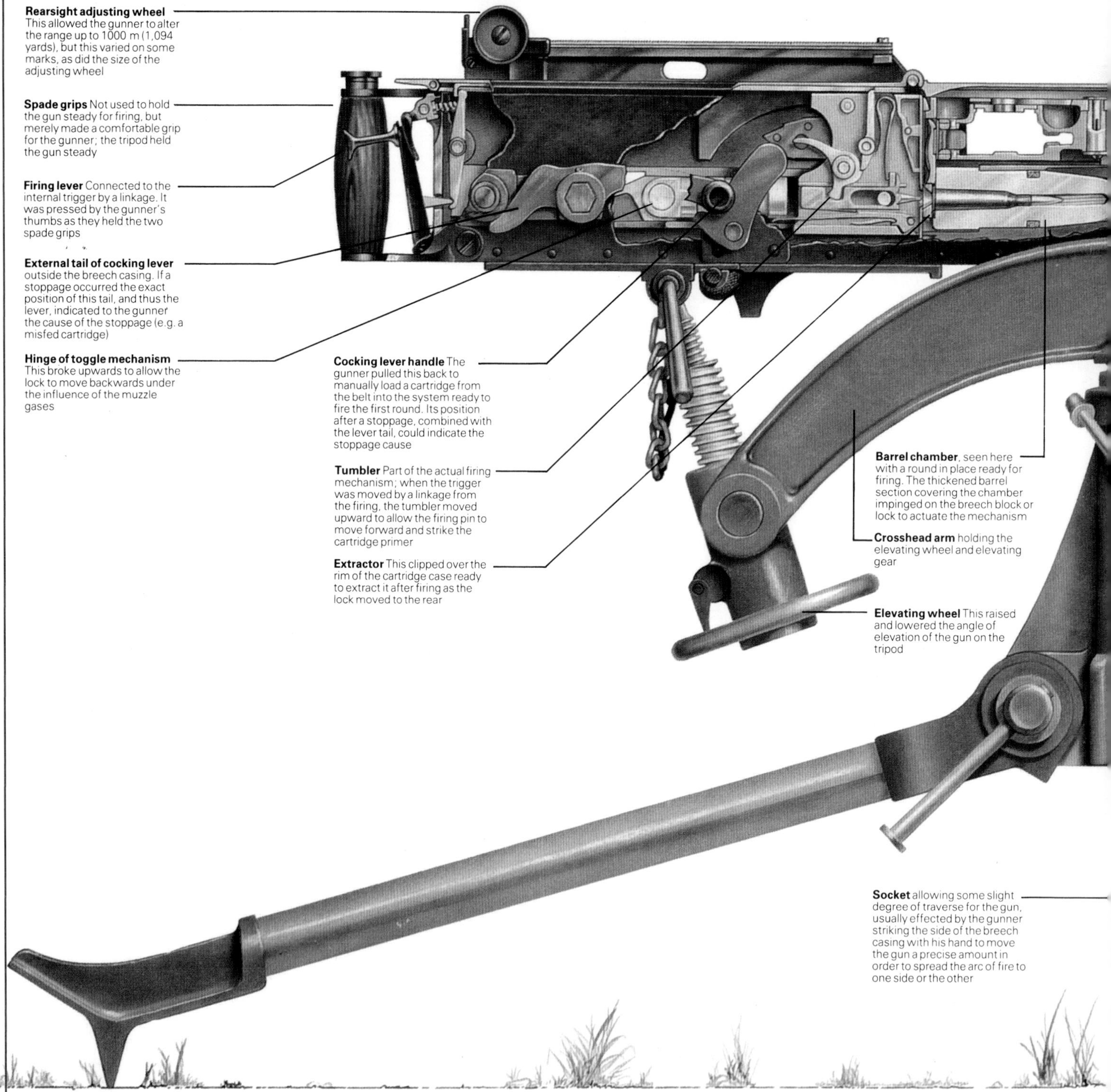

Rearsight adjusting wheel This allowed the gunner to alter the range up to 1000 m (1,094 yards), but this varied on some marks, as did the size of the adjusting wheel

Spade grips Not used to hold the gun steady for firing, but merely made a comfortable grip for the gunner; the tripod held the gun steady

Firing lever Connected to the internal trigger by a linkage. It was pressed by the gunner's thumbs as they held the two spade grips

External tail of cocking lever outside the breech casing. If a stoppage occurred the exact position of this tail, and thus the lever, indicated to the gunner the cause of the stoppage (e.g. a misfed cartridge)

Hinge of toggle mechanism This broke upwards to allow the lock to move backwards under the influence of the muzzle gases

Cocking lever handle The gunner pulled this back to manually load a cartridge from the belt into the system ready to fire the first round. Its position after a stoppage, combined with the lever tail, could indicate the stoppage cause

Tumbler Part of the actual firing mechanism; when the trigger was moved by a linkage from the firing, the tumbler moved upward to allow the firing pin to move forward and strike the cartridge primer

Extractor This clipped over the rim of the cartridge case ready to extract it after firing as the lock moved to the rear

Barrel chamber, seen here with a round in place ready for firing. The thickened barrel section covering the chamber impinged on the breech block or lock to actuate the mechanism

Crosshead arm holding the elevating wheel and elevating gear

Elevating wheel This raised and lowered the angle of elevation of the gun on the tripod

Socket allowing some slight degree of traverse for the gun, usually effected by the gunner striking the side of the breech casing with his hand to move the gun a precise amount in order to spread the arc of fire to one side or the other

for experience (not only in the actual servicing of the weapon but its tactical use and resupply over prolonged periods) led to formation of the Machine Gun Corps in October 1915. Gradually the heavy machine-guns assigned to divisions were reallocated as companies of this new corps, and its ultimate importance can be seen in the fact that when World War I ended it contained 6,432 officers and 124,920 other ranks. These men gradually improved the art of using machine-guns in battle by formulating procedures whereby they were fired not in isolation but as part of a mutually-supporting fire plan. Steadily they improved these fire plans so that at times the machine-gun fire plans resembled those of the artillery. Indeed, on occasions machine-guns were used to harass the enemy in much the same way as artillery.

However, it was soon discovered that if machine-guns were given the task of providing prolonged fire support, they required not only highly trained crews but also a highly organized supply system. The Vickers machine-gun could devour ammunition at a prodigious rate, and considerable ammunition supplies had therefore to be kept in the supply line at all times. One snag soon encountered was that of transport: there were few places in the front lines of 1914-8 where supply vehicles could get anywhere close to the forward trenches, so the

ammunition had to be carried over considerable distances by manpower alone. Once on site the ammunition could not be simply loaded into the gun. The rounds were supplied in metal cases that often held the ammunition in the form of small cardboard cartons each containing 100 rounds, as being intended for use by many types of weapon (Lee-Enfield rifles, Lewis Guns and so on) and it was not possible to provide the rounds already loaded into their fabric belts, and this had to be done before they could be fed into the gun. This was often done by hand, which was a time-consuming process, though later a special loading machine was devised and issued.

So there was more to using the Vickers machine-gun in action than simply pressing a trigger and watching the enemy tumble. In time the members of the Machine Gun Corps became every bit as proficient as their German counterparts when it came to using machine-guns in action, and were sometimes much more imaginative in the tactical use of their weapons.

An example of this can be found in the instance when 10 Vickers machine-guns of the 100th Machine Gun Company played their part in the battle to secure High Wood on 24 August 1916, as part of the battle now known as the Battle of the Somme. This was a dour slogging match that lasted months under the most

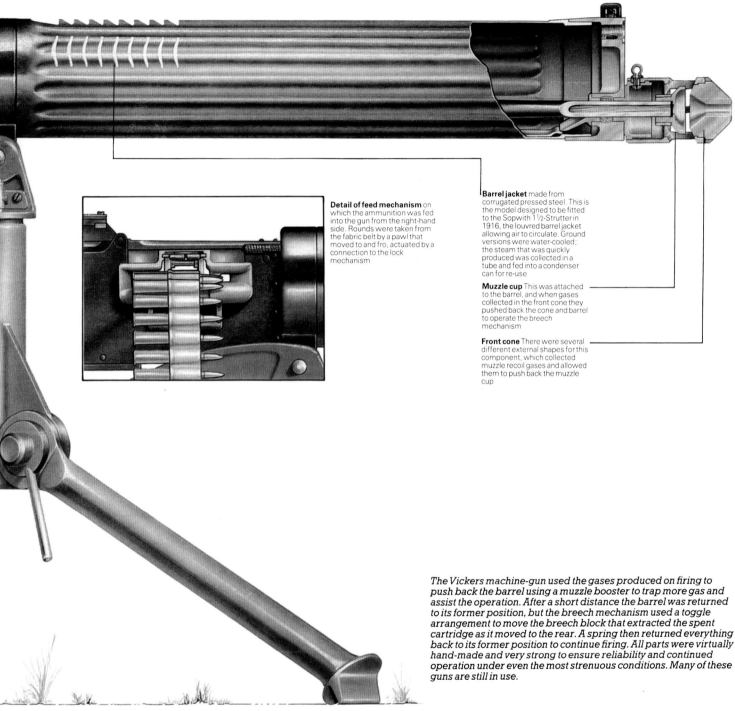

Detail of feed mechanism on which the ammunition was fed into the gun from the right-hand side. Rounds were taken from the fabric belt by a pawl that moved to and fro, actuated by a connection to the lock mechanism

Barrel jacket made from corrugated pressed steel. This is the model designed to be fitted to the Sopwith 1½-Strutter in 1916, the louvred barrel jacket allowing air to circulate. Ground versions were water-cooled; the steam that was quickly produced was collected in a tube and fed into a condenser can for re-use

Muzzle cup This was attached to the barrel, and when gases collected in the front cone they pushed back the cone and barrel to operate the breech mechanism

Front cone There were several different external shapes for this component, which collected muzzle recoil gases and allowed them to push back the muzzle cup

The Vickers machine-gun used the gases produced on firing to push back the barrel using a muzzle booster to trap more gas and assist the operation. After a short distance the barrel was returned to its former position, but the breech mechanism used a toggle arrangement to move the breech block that extracted the spent cartridge as it moved to the rear. A spring then returned everything back to its former position to continue firing. All parts were virtually hand-made and very strong to ensure reliability and continued operation under even the most strenuous conditions. Many of these guns are still in use.

dreadful conditions, with the British attacking most of the time. After an attack in the High Wood area it was noted that an earthwork known as Savoy Trench offered a good fire position that commanded the German front line about 1830 m (2,000 yards) distant. It was decided that the next foray on the German front line would be supported by the machine-guns of the 100th Company; once this had been completed the inevitable German counterattack would be halted by keeping the area behind the front-line trenches covered by machine-gun fire lasting 12 hours.

Such a formidable fire plan called for considerable preparation. The night before the attack two infantry companies were needed to move forward the ammunition and the water for the guns. The guns were carefully emplaced and camouflaged under netting and made ready for the battle ahead.

As the attack went in the machine-guns opened fire and kept firing for the next 12 hours. At intervals the gunners were changed, along with the faithful ammunition numbers who were responsible for guiding the ammunition belts into the gun to prevent them from twisting or dragging along the ground and so picking up dirt. The firer had little to do other than keep down the trigger between the two spade grips; he could feel little of the firing recoil, which was

mostly absorbed by the heavy tripod. From time to time he gave the side of the gun a sharp tap to move the barrel slightly to cover a wider area and a few moments later another tap would move the barrel again.

When necessary the water in the cooling jackets was topped up with some of that so carefully stockpiled during the previous night. Barrels were changed every hour. All through the 12-hour period a party of men was kept busy moving ammunition from the dump built the previous night to two men who kept a loading machine in constant action. From the loading machine another party took the full belts to the guns. By the time the action ended the 10 guns had managed to fire just 250 less than one million rounds. Throughout that period only two guns gave any trouble, one with a broken extractor pawl and another that had something wrong with its lock mechanism and so suffered random jams. All the stockpiled water had been consumed, and the guns had only been kept going by use of the company water bottles and the crews' personal resources. But in the end it all worked. The enemy front-line trenches had been taken and the anticipated counterattack had not taken place, for the simple reason that no German soldier could cross the area of ground beaten by the fire of the 10 Vickers machine-guns of the 100th Machine Gun Company.

Above: An Australian Army Vickers machine-gun team engages a low-flying enemy aircraft. This usually involved reversing the tripod head to provide the required barrel elevation and some care with the ammunition feed, but this anti-aircraft method could be highly effective against the German ground attack aircraft which appeared in large numbers in 1918.

Right: A Vickers machine-gun is hidden in farm buildings near Haverskerque during the period of relatively fluid warfare that followed the German offensives of early 1918. As always, one man directs the gunner's fire and another guides the ammunition belt into the gun. The condenser hose is fitted to the jacket.

Left: A sergeant of the Machine Gun Corps uses his Vickers machine-gun at close range (note the rearsight in the 'down' position). He is personally armed with a revolver, and on his arm can be seen the machine-gun proficiency badge, awarded only to the most skilful machine-gunner who knew the Vickers backwards.

Below: Vickers machine-gun teams operate from specially-prepared positions somewhere among the Flanders battlefields. This photograph provides an indication of the field conditions the Vickers had to operate in during World War I, but the guns could absorb all manner of hard and mud-infested use.

🇩🇰 DENMARK
Madsen machine-guns

The first Madsen machine-gun was produced in Denmark by the Dansk Industri Syndikat in 1904 and the last in 1950. The Madsen series was really a long string of near-identical models produced in a very wide array of calibres to suit the requirements of many export customers all around the world.

Although it was not fully realized at the time that the first were produced, the **Madsen 8-mm Rekytgevaer M1903** machine-gun was one of the very first of the light machine-guns, and even featured the world's first overhead box magazine of its type. The weapon used a unique operating principle that has been used in no other design and which even for its time was expensive, complex and difficult to manufacture. This was a system that used the Peabody-Martini hinged block action, an action familiar on small-calibre match rifles. What Madsen did was to convert this essentially manually-operated action to a fully automatic. By using a combination of the recoil plus the movement of a plate moving on cams and levers, the action opened and closed the hinged block, but as this block had no integral bolt action (as with a normal breech block) a separate rammer and extractor mechanism had to be used. It sounds and was complicated, but the system had one major attribute and that was that it worked very reliably under a wide range of conditions and with all sorts of ammunition, although rimmed ammunition such as the British 7.7 mm (0.303 in) was not so successful.

As well as being produced in many calibres for customers as far away as Thailand, the Madsen was also manufactured in a wide variety of forms. Having an air-cooled barrel the Madsen was not ideally suited for the sus-

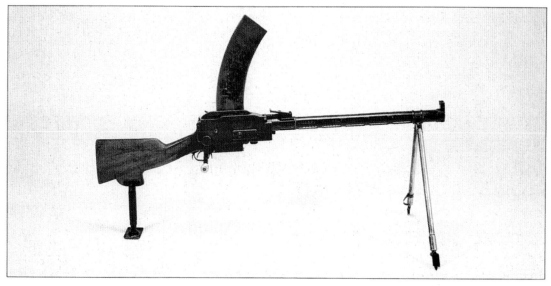

tained-fire role, but various types of heavy tripod were produced. The more usual mounting was a bipod secured just under the muzzle though some models, including those for the Danish armed forces, had a short pedestal under the barrel for resting the barrel on parapets in houses or fortifications. A carrying handle was often fitted. One feature that promoted the Madsen's reliability was the type's excellent manufacture using the best materials available, which no doubt added to the overall costs.

During World War I the Madsen was not an official weapon used by any of the major protagonists, but all the same many Madsens appeared in nearly every continental army. The Madsen was one of the first weapons

used by both sides for early experiments in aircraft armament, although it was soon passed over in favour of other weapons. It was also used in small numbers by German troops experimenting on the Eastern Front with their *Sturmtruppen* tactics, and more were used by some of the Central European armies, again in small numbers only. When the light machine-gun concept became more widely accepted the Madsen was investigated by many nations, and the British even attempted to use it in 7.7-mm calibre. Unfortunately this cartridge was rimmed and it was one that did not work well in the Madsen mechanism; the guns were thus put by only to be issued again in 1940, this time to the new Home Guard.

The Madsen machine-gun was one of the first light machine-guns, and used a complex falling block locking system. It was produced in many calibres and models and was widely used throughout World War I. This version was used for a while by the British Army chambered for 0.303-in (7.7-mm) ammunition.

Specification
Rekytgevaer M1903
Calibre: 8 mm (0.315 in)
Lengths: overall 1.145 m (45.0.8 in); barrel 596 mm (23.46 in)
Weight: 10 kg (22.05 lb)
Muzzle velocity: 825 m (2,707 ft) per second
Rate of fire: (cyclic) 450 rpm
Feed: 20-round box magazine

RUSSIA
Pulemet Maksima obrazets 1910

The first Maxim machine-guns for Russian service were ordered direct from Vickers in the early 1900s, but it was not long before the Russians were producing their own models at the state arsenal at Tula. The first 'Russian' model was the **Pulemet Maksima obrazets 1905** (Maxim gun model 1905), which was a direct copy of the original Maxim gun but produced with a typical Russian flourish in the bronze water jacket. In 1910 this bronze jacket was replaced by a sheet steel jacket and this was known either as the **obr 1910** or the **PM1910**.

The PM1910 was destined to be the longest-produced version of all the many Maxim gun variants, for it remained in full-scale production until 1943. Although there were several variants over the years, the basic PM1910 was a solid piece of equipment that served very well under even the most drastic conditions and all extremes of climate, a fact which suited the Russians very well considering their far-flung empire. This reliability had to be purchased at a cost, and that cost was weight. The PM1910 and anything to do with it was very heavy, so heavy in fact that the usual carriage resembled a small artillery field carriage. On this carriage, known as the Sokolov mounting, the gun was usually protected by a removable shield. The gun rested on a large turntable for

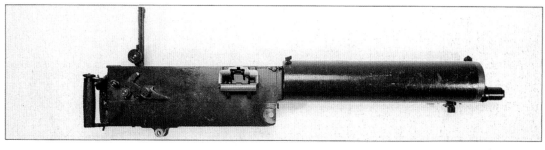

traversing and was elevated by a large wheel-operated screw. The turntable was carried on two spoked steel wheels and the whole arrangement could be towed by hand using a U-shaped handle. On many of these early Sokolov mounts there were two side legs that could be extended forward to raise the entire weapon and carriage for firing over parapets; on later models these legs were omitted.

The weight of the PM1910 complete with the mounting was no less than 74 kg (163.1 lb). This meant that at least two men were required to drag the weapon (more across rough ground, for which drag ropes were provided). A special sledge mounting was available for use during the winter months, and the weapon could also be carried on the widely-available peasant carts used all over Russia. To offset this

weight penalty, the PM1910 could be kept firing for as long as belts were fed into the mechanism. It required next to no maintenance, which was just as well for the state of training in the Tsarist armies usually meant that no servicing (other than rudimentary cleaning) was provided.

PM1910s were produced in vast numbers until 1917, by which time production had spread to centres other than Tula. The only change made during World War I was that the original smooth water-cooling jackets were replaced by corrugated jackets to increase the surface area slightly and thus increase cooling. At times the heavy shields were left off to decrease the weight slightly. During World War I the amount of rough handling the PM1910 could absorb became legendary, so much so that the Germans

used as many as they could capture, though only on the Eastern Front.

Specification
PM1910
Calibre: 7.62 mm (0.3 in)
Lengths: overall 1.107 m (43.58 in); barrel 720 mm (28.35 in)
Weights: gun 23.8 kg (52.47 lb); mounting with shield 45.2 kg (99.65 lb)
Muzzle velocity: 863 m (2,831 ft) per second
Rate of fire: (cyclic) 520-600 rpm
Feed: 250-round fabric belt

Originally built by Vickers for the Russian army, the Maxim gun was soon being manufactured in the Imperial Arsenal at Tula, outside Moscow. It was to remain in quantity production until 1943.

Lewis Gun

The **Lewis Gun** is put into an international category for although its origins were American it was first produced and manufactured in Europe. Its inventor was an American, one Samuel Maclean, but the basic concept was developed further and 'sold' by Colonel Isaac Lewis, another American. The American military authorities were unenthusiastic about the new gun, so Lewis took the design to Belgium where it was accepted and put into production for the Belgian army. That was in 1913, and in the following year production was switched to the UK where Birmingham Small Arms (BSA) took over the programme.

The Lewis Gun was put into production at BSA as the **Lewis Gun Mk 1** for the British Army for the simple reason that five or six Lewis Guns could be produced in the time it took to produce a single Vickers machine-gun. The fact that the Lewis was light and portable was secondary at that time, but once in service the Lewis proved to be a very popular front-line weapon with a host of mobile tactical uses. The Lewis Gun was one of the first of the true light machine-guns and with its distinctive overhead drum magazine it was soon a common sight on the Western Front. The Lewis Gun was a gas-operated weapon, gas being tapped off from the barrel on firing to push a piston to the rear; the piston pushed back the breech block and mechanism and also wound up a coil spring under the gun which was used to return everything to the start position. The mechanism was rather complex and took careful maintenance, but even then was still prone to an alarming number of jams and stoppages, some of them introduced by the overhead drum magazine, which was a constant cause of trouble especially when only slightly damaged. The barrel was enclosed in a special air cooling jacket that was supposed to use a forced draught system of cooling, but experience showed that the jacket's efficiency had been over-rated and the gun worked quite well without it. Versions of the Lewis Gun intended for use on aircraft did not have this complex cooling jacket.

Only after the Lewis Gun had been produced in thousands in Europe did the American military authorities finally realize the potential of the weapon, and it went into production for the US Army (and air corps) chambered in the American 7.62-mm (0.3-in) calibre. Thus the Lewis Gun became truly international, especially as the Germans were in the habit of using as many captured examples as they could to bolster their own machine-gun totals. Some Lewis Guns were used on the early tanks and more were used by naval vessels. A similar role cropped up again in World War II when stockpiled Lewis Guns were distributed for the defence of merchant shipping and for Home Defence in the hands of the Home Guard and Royal Air Force airfield defence units.

The Lewis Gun was a complex

Above: The Lewis Gun was widely used by the British Army but it was originally produced in Belgium. It was easily recognizable from its bulky air-cooling jacket and the flat pan magazine, here holding 47 rounds.

weapon, but in service it made quite an impression in a way that was not possible using the heavy machine-guns. The Lewis Gun was the first of the true light machine-guns in more ways than one.

Specification
Lewis Gun Mk 1
Calibre: 7.7 mm (0.303 in)
Lengths: gun 1.25 m (49.2 in); barrel 661 mm (26.02 in)
Weights: 12.25 kg (27 lb)
Muzzle velocity: 744 m (2,441 ft) per second
Rate of fire: 450-500 rpm
Feed: 47- or 97-round overhead drum magazine

A British Lewis Gun team in action shows the ready-filled ammunition pans still in their box. The fins of the air-cooling jacket can be seen under the ammunition pan on the gun; these fins were supposed to force air along the barrel, but were superfluous.

A British Army Lewis gunner firing his Lewis Gun as if it were a rifle, no doubt at some hastily-presented target. Firing the Lewis Gun in this fashion was usually inaccurate, for the weight of the gun was too high for prolonged firing and the recoil soon shook the aim off the target.

The Somme

That fine July morning in 1916 gave no hint to the men in the trenches of the Somme the scale of the ordeal to come. Within minutes they were to bow their heads into a storm of machine-gun fire, and were to die like cattle in their thousands.

No battle in World War I was as shaped by the machine-gun as the British 1916 summer offensive, the Battle of the Somme. The impact of the German MG08 'Spandau' and Bergmann guns has remained long after the 'day of breathtaking summer beauty', as Siegfried Sassoon described 1 July 1916, the opening day of the Battle of the Somme. The image of the skirmish lines of khaki infantry, Lee Enfields at the high port position, cut down in the barbed wire has shaped not only the West's perception of modern war, but of modern life itself. More than infantrymen fell to the machine-guns on the Somme. The structured, progressive pre-1914 world died there as well.

The heavy losses inflicted on attacking troops by German machine-guns at Neuve Chapelle and Loos in 1915 shaped the British plan for the Somme. The lesson that the British drew from those battles was that they had to use their artillery to deliver even more tons of high explosive onto the machine-guns before the infantry assault was committed. Enough shells, it was reasoned, would result in no more machine-guns.

Dugout survival

The British preliminary barrage was supposed to defeat the machine-guns. The infantry would then, according to plan, simply occupy the ground. But despite the length of the British barrage, the German machine-guns on the Somme showed that firepower cannot win a battle by itself. The front-line machine-guns survived the barrage in their deep dugouts. This lesson of the machine-guns on the Somme was relearned by the US Marines on Tarawa in 1943 and countless times during the Vietnam War. Massive firepower (even the seven-day barrage that preceded the opening of the Somme) will not defeat an entrenched defender by itself. Later in the war the barrage became the short, tremendously intense 'hurricane', often using extensive gas for suppression. The barrage before 1 July also suffered from a high dud

rate and a lack of heavy guns that could penetrate the deep bunkers where the German machine-guns and machine-gunners were waiting until the 10-minute period, just before 07.00, between the moment the barrage lifted and the whistles blew for the British infantry to go over the top.

The 1915 battles showed that a single machine-gun could defeat an attacking battalion if allowed to fire unsuppressed. On 1 July 1916 battalion after battalion found that the power of the machine-gun had not been overestimated. For example, the 7th Battalion, Green Howards and the 10th Battalion, West Yorkshire Regiment attacking the village-fort of Fricourt (the German defence was based around these village-forts, connected by trenches) were both cut up within three minutes by a single machine-gun. The 16th Battalion, Northumberland Fusiliers attacked towards Thiepval with great bravery, dribbling a football across no man's land. There were four machine-guns opposite the battalion, and only 11 men from the assault companies walked back. The story was repeated throughout the day up and down the British front. The casual-

The mine explodes under the Hawthorn Redoubt 10 minutes before the attack on Beaumont Hamel. This mine heralded the Battle of the Somme and removed one of the major German strongpoints in the path of the planned British advance. It was one of a series of mines exploded along the German lines.

ties (57,470 men, of whom 19,240 were killed or died of wounds) amounted to half of the other ranks, and three-quarters of the officers, who went over the top on 1 July. The vast majority of this carnage was done by about 100 machine-guns.

The machine-gun was able to determine the course of the Battle of the Somme in a way that would not have been thought possible two years earlier. Most armies recognized the value of the machine-gun in 1914, but it was under conditions of trench warfare that it showed its potentially decisive importance.

All the mud and discomfort of the trenches is epitomized in this photograph of a ration party of the Royal Irish Rifles waiting to move up on the fateful day of 1 July 1916. Despite the awful conditions some of these soldiers can still raise a smile for the camera, but for how long?

The Somme

Since the industrial revolution, tactics have often lagged behind technology. Just as the British army tactics were inadequate to deal with opponents armed with Mauser magazine rifles at the start of the Boer War, or the Israeli army was surprised by the anti-tank guided missile at the start of the 1973 Middle East War, the machine-gun mandated a new era in battlefield tactics.

Fire and movement

On the Somme the machine-gun was primarily a defensive weapon. Because the Germans were on the overall defensive their machine-guns had a greater opportunity to shape the battle. The two basic elements of tactics are fire and movement. Tripod-mounted medium machine-guns are hard to move and cannot fire while doing so. Both the British and the Germans had recognized this in 1914, and had deployed light machine guns (the British Lewis Gun and the German Bergmann gun) that allowed attacking infantry to carry their machine-guns forward where the medium machine-guns could not go. Light machine-guns saw extensive use on the Somme.

The British were the first to realize, however, that if you want to make a machine-gun that is truly capable of both fire and movement, it had to be put in a self-propelled armoured mount capable of moving over the battlefield: in short, a tank. These vehicles first appeared in the later stages of the battle, on 15 September 1916. The machine-gun had created the problem of trench warfare. It also provided a solution.

Machine-guns, especially the tripod-mounted medium machine-guns, are most effective on the defensive to a large part because, even if they are pushed forward, it is hard to replace the tremendous quantities of ammunition they consume in action. The German machine-guns on 1 July all had large stores of pre-positioned ammunition, whereas ammunition for the Lewis guns the British brought with them had to be carried across no man's land by carrying parties.

The machine-gun not only fires more rapidly than a rifle but it is much easier to direct and control. In action it is hard for officers and NCOs to direct the fire of riflemen, much easier to direct a single machine-gun. In modern warfare riflemen are frequently reduced to the position of bystanders by the feeling that their own weapons are inadequate: in World War II, US Brigadier-General S.L.A. Marshall found that often only 10 to 15 per cent of riflemen

actually fired their rifles in combat. Machine-gunners, however, almost always fired.

The machine-gun crews of World War I knew they were the primary target for all the firepower that could be directed against them. They also knew that few infantrymen took machine-gunners prisoner. Yet the German machine-gunners on 1 July manned their weapons until they repulsed the attacks aimed against them or perished under the sword bayonets of the Lee Enfields. In the words of Lieutenant-Colonel A. Carton de Wiart, VC, 'The German machine-gunners were outstanding, almost invariably very brave men and the pick of the German Army'. The British Army called its Machine Gun Corps 'The Suicide Club'. Their German counterparts might well have done the same.

The nature of the Somme emphasized the German use of machine-guns, but this did not mean that the British did not use their machine-guns effectively as well. Technically, they were more advanced than the Germans in some regards, as was demonstrated by their capability for delivering supporting fire over the head of advancing troops. In the later stages of the battle, Vickers guns would fire extensive 'barrages', often ranged in like artillery to fire indirectly, to protect the flanks of advancing units and to interdict German movement.

German defensive tactics on the Somme were based on counterattacking any British penetration of their defences almost immediately, before the British could bring in their reserves and consolidate the position. These counterattacks resulted in heavy German losses but time after time pushed the British back from hard-won objectives including, on 1 July, the Schwaben Redoubt and Thiepval Wood, where the 36th Ulster Division was repulsed. These counterattacks would have been more successful were it not for the Lewis guns carried by assaulting British troops. While Lewis guns (unlike the heavier tripod-mounted Vickers) could be carried into an attack, they were not very effective against dug-in positions. It was in support of infantry cleaning out strongpoints and in defeating counterattacks that the Lewis showed its value on the Somme, and the numbers of Lewis guns carried by British infantry was increased as a result.

The Somme showed not only the power of the machine-gun, but also some of the tactical and technical countermeasures that were evolved in response to its dominance of the battlefield. This could be seen in the offensive tactics used on the French sector of the front on 1 July. Benefiting from the costly lesson of Verdun, the French used more flexible and fluid formations than the long British skirmish lines. The French suffered fewer casualties than the British and gained some of the Allied successes of 1 July. The British not only deployed the tank as an answer to the machine-gun (which it remains today) but also started to emphasize 'creeping' artillery barrages to suppress the machine-guns until the attacking infantry was within a bayonet's reach. In the later stages of the battle the British shifted to dawn attacks (such as that which took much of Bazentin Ridge on 14 July), dusk attacks (as on the Ancre Heights on 1 October), and night attacks (as that on Delville Wood on 22/23 July, the wood being secured by 26 July). The effectiveness of the machine-gun put an increased premium on operations at night and in decreased visibility, which is why in June 1982, the British Army launched their attack on the Argentine defences around Port Stanley at night.

Machine-guns are just as deadly today as they were on the Somme. The British Expeditionary Force of 1916 shows that all the bravery in the world cannot triumph by itself against the hard realities of modern warfare. By using tanks, more effective and responsive artillery to suppress the machine-guns, less vulnerable infantry tactics, attacking in conditions of reduced visibility, there has never been a repeat of 1 July 1916.

At 7 pm on 1 July 1916 the 7th Dragoon Guards and the Deccan Horse launched a classic cavalry charge, the last of its kind to be seen on a Western European battlefield. Their target was high wood, through which the Germans had retreated as their trenches in Bazentin were pounded by British artillery. A personal reconnaissance by senior officers had found the wood empty during the morning, but it was decided to wait for the cavalry rather than advance with the available infantry. Thus the Germans had all afternoon to recover, and by early evening their machine-guns were re-positioned to cover all the approaches. The first waves of horsemen were mown down by guns firing from the top of the ridge and in front of the wood. Here a machine-gun team works their MG 08 from amongst the tall crops before the wood as cavalry pass on either side to avoid the hail of bullets. Incredibly the cavalry carried the front of the wood and killed and captured many of the defenders.

Above: In action the Machine Gun Corps was not averse to using captured weapons, as shown by this photograph of a British team using a sMG 08. The team in the foreground are using a Vickers machine-gun. Using the Maxim mechanism of the sMG 08 presented no problems to Vickers-trained machine-gunners.

Below: This illustration of a section of captured German trench near the Albert-Pozières road shows the deep bunkers in which the German machine-gunners sheltered during an artillery attack, and from which they emerged to set up their machine-guns once the attack lifted to herald the infantry attack.

Below: A German view of the British infantry advancing over the open terrain near Mametz on 1 July 1916. Presented with such a target the German machine-gunners could not fail to halt such an attack in its tracks, especially when the advancing lines moved across the path of enfilading fire from both sides.

Above: Troopers of the Deccan Horse await their chance to advance during the action at Bazentin Ridge on 14 July 1916. The call never came, and all the cavalry were able to do was clutter the rear areas and make undue demands on the supply lines for fodder for their horses. They were unable to advance against machine-guns.

GERMANY
Maschinengewehr 08

Contrary to general belief, the German army was not an avid proponent of the machine-gun when Hiram Maxim started to demonstrate his product around the European capitals in the 1890s. His gun aroused some interest but few sales, and the first made to the German army were actually paid for out of the private funds of Kaiser Wilhelm II. Thereafter things began to look up and gradually a licensing agreement was made between Maxim and the German army. From this agreement Maxim machine-guns were soon being produced by both commercial concerns and the Deutsche Waffen und Munitionsfabriken at Spandau, near Berlin. Several models were produced before the 'standard' weapon appeared in 1908 as the **schwere Maschinengewehr 08**, or **sMG 08**. It fired the standard 7.92-mm (0.312-in) rifle cartridge of the day.

As a machine-gun the sMG 08 differed little from many other Maxim guns, and the Maxim recoil-operated mechanism was used unchanged. Construction was very solid, and once in service the **'Spandau'** proved to be very reliable under the most demanding battlefield conditions. Where the sMG 08 did differ from other machine-guns of the time was the mounting.

The schwere Maschinengewehr 08 (sMG 08) was the standard German machine-gun of World War I and used the basic Maxim system unchanged. It was a very heavy weapon capable of a prodigious amount of fire. Emplaced in well-constructed dugouts protected by dense thickets of barbed wire, it took a fearful toll of Allied troops.

Even the early German Maxims used a type of mounting known as a *Schlitten* (sledge) that was intended to be dragged across country when folded with the gun on top. As an alternative this mounting could be carried by two men as if it was a stretcher. The mounting, known as the Schlitten 08, provided a stable firing platform but was very heavy, to the extent that in 1916 an alternative tripod mounting known as the Dreifuss 16 was introduced.

During World War I the sMG 08 took a fearful toll of the Allies' manpower strengths. It was usually the sMG 08 that was responsible for mowing down the massed infantry attacks of 1914 to 1917, for after 1914 the numbers of machine-guns used by the German army increased greatly and (probably more important) the Germans learned to use them widely. Instead of simply placing a machine-gun to face directly across no man's land, the Germans learned to set them up firing to a flank so that one gun could enfilade and break up an infantry attack to much better effect, while at the same time providing more cover for the gun crew. The German machine-gunners were picked men who often maintained their guns in action to the last, and they were highly trained in all aspects of their task. They knew the sMG 08 backwards and could carry out repairs in the front line if need arose.

At times two or three men using a single sMG 08 could break up entire Allied infantry battalions once the latter had left the shelter of their trenches. The slaughter of Neuve Chapelle, Loos, the Somme and all the other costly infantry carnages can be traced to sMG 08s and their determined crews.

After 1918 the sMG 08 was maintained in German service, and many were still in use when 1939 came around, but by by then they had been relegated to second-line duties.

Specification
sMG 08
Calibre: 7.92 mm (0.312 in)
Lengths: gun 1.175 m (46.26 in); barrel 719 mm (28.3 in)
Weights: gun complete with spares 62 kg (136.7 lb); sledge mount 37.65 kg (83.0 lb)
Muzzle velocity: 900 m (2,953 ft) per second
Rate of fire: 300-450 rpm
Feed: 250-round fabric belt

Bulgarian machine-gun teams in action use Maxim Model 1908 machine-guns purchased from Vickers in the United Kingdom. These guns fire an 8-mm (0.315-in) cartridge and were very similar to the German sMG 08.

Above: The heavy tripod-mounted guns in service in 1914 had to be broken down into several loads for prolonged marching. Here a Jäger (light infantryman) in 1914 service kit shoulders the burden of the sMG 08.

Maschinengewehr 08/15

By 1915 the German army had come to appreciate that there was a need for some form of light machine-gun for front-line use. While the sMG 08 was an excellent heavy machine-gun, it was too heavy for rapid tactical moves and trials were held to determine what type of weapon would suffice. Among weapons tested was the Danish Madsen, and light Bergmann and Dreyse machine-guns, but the choice fell upon a lightened form of the sMG 08. This emerged as the **MG 08/15** and the first examples of the type were issued in 1916.

The MG 08/15 retained the basic mechanism of the sMG 08 and the water cooling system, but the water jacket was smaller; the receiver walls were thinner, some detail parts were eliminated, a bipod replaced the heavy sled mounting, and a pistol grip and butt were added; some changes were also made to the sights. By no stretch of the imagination could the MG 08/15 be called light, for it still weighed a hefty 18 kg (39.7 lb), but it was portable and could even be fired from a standing position with the weight taken by a sling. A shorter fabric belt was introduced to make handling easier, or a belt drum could be fitted to the side of the weapon to prevent feed belts dragging in the mud.

The choice of the basic sMG 08 mechanism meant that no additional training was required to use the lighter weapon, and there was a fair degree of spares interchangeability. Late in the

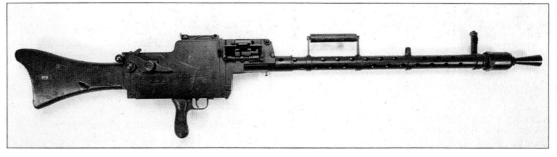

war the designers went one stage further and did away with the water-cooling jacket altogether to produce the **MG 08/18**. The war ended before this version could be widely used, the few that were produced being issued to the more mobile units of the German army; few actually reached the front-line infantry.

There was one further variant of the MG 08/15 known as the **LMG 08/15**, where the L denoted *Luft* (air). This version was one of several air-cooled machine-guns used in fixed mountings by the new German air arm and was basically an MG 08/15 with a perforated water jacket to allow air-cooling of the barrel. The guns were fired via a cable and were synchronized so as not to shoot through the aircraft propeller. Ammunition was fed into the gun from a drum and another spring-loaded drum was often used to prevent the used fabric belt flapping around in the

slipstream. Some of the early Maxim aircraft guns had been lightened sMG 08 models known as the **LMG 08**, but these passed out of use once the LMG 08/15 was established.

The ground-used MG 08/15 equipped front-line troops at company level and below, while the heavier sMG 08 was retained at battalion level or even deployed in special heavy machine-gun companies. The portability of the MG 08/15 enabled it to be used by the *Sturmtruppen* of 1917 and 1918, but it was never a handy weapon to use in action: in comparison with other light machine-guns of the period it was much larger and bulkier. But it remained every bit as reliable in action as its large counterpart and the German troops were well trained in its use. Perhaps the most effective use was made of the MG 08/15 during the latter stages of the 1918 campaign, when the retreating German army used small

The MG 08/18 was the last of the World War I versions of the sMG 08 to see service. It used an air-cooled barrel without the usual large casing and was an attempt to provide German troops with a light machine-gun.

MG 08/15 teams to cover its withdrawals, single weapons sometimes holding up whole battalions and preventing the Allied cavalry from taking part in any action.

Specification
MG 08/15
Calibre: 7.92 mm (0.312 in)
Lengths: overall 1.398 m (55.0 in); barrel 719 mm (28.3 in)
Weight: complete 18 kg (39.7 lb)
Muzzle velocity: 900 m (2,953 ft) per second
Rate of fire: 450 rpm
Feed: 50-, 100- or 250-round fabric belt

Schwarzlose machine-guns

The first indigenous Austro-Hungarian machine-gun was invented by one Andreas Schwarzlose in 1902, and was later manufactured at the Waffenfabrik Steyr. The first model was the **Schwarzlose Maschinengewehr Modell 07**, soon followed by the **MG Modell 08** and the full standard model, the **MG Modell 12**, to which standard the two earlier models were later converted by the Austro-Hungarian armed forces. There was little of note to mention between all these various models, for they all used an identical method of construction and the same operating principle.

The Schwarzlose machine-guns were all heavy belt-fed and water-cooled weapons working on an unusual principle, namely that known as delayed blow-back, in which the recoil forces impinge to the rear upon a heavy breech-block held in position (with the spent case still in the chamber) by a levered mechanism. Only after a short period of time has elapsed do these levers move sufficiently for the breech block to travel to the rear; this time is just long enough for the bullet to leave the muzzle and for the pressure in the barrel to fall to a safe limit. But the system means that the barrel length is limited: too long a barrel and the breech opens before the bullet has left the muzzle. So the operating system is a compromise between cartridge propellant strength, barrel length and the delayed-action lever timing.

In practice the Schwarzlose machine-guns worked well enough, but the barrel used was really too short for the standard Austro-Hungarian 8-mm (0.315-in) cartridge of the period,

and this resulted in excessive muzzle flash. As a result a long tapering flash hider had to be fitted, and this became one of the distinguishing features of the Schwarzlose. Another design feature of the series was the feed, which was amongst the first to use a drive sprocket to carry a cartridge into the system in a very precise manner. This added to the overall reliability of the Schwarzlose weapons.

Between 1914 and 1918 the main operators of the Schwarzlose were the Austro-Hungarian armies, but later in the war Italy had also become a major user, mainly by means of captured weapons. The Netherlands was another major buyer, but was a neutral during World War I. By 1914 nearly all the versions in use were the 07/12, 08/

12 and 12 models. The original Modells 07 and 08 used lubricated ammunition, but on the Modell 12 this feature was eradicated and the earlier models were modified up to Modell 12 standards. There was also a **Modell 07/16** intended for use on aircraft and featuring a rudimentary system of air-cooling, but this was not a great success and not many were produced.

All the Schwarzlose machine-guns were large and heavy weapons notable for the excellence of their manufacture. Indeed, they were so heavy and well made that few appear to have worn out, so that many were still in service during 1945 in Italy and Hungary. The delayed action blow-back system has not been widely copied, and is now regarded as an oddity.

The Austro-Hungarian armies used the heavy Schwarlose machine-gun in several forms, most of them looking very like this M 07/12. It used the blow-back principle for operation and was very reliable even though early models used an oil pump to lubricate the ammunition.

Specification
Modell 07/12
Calibre: 8 mm (0.315 in)
Lengths: gun 1.066 m (41.97 in); barrel 526 mm (20.71 in)
Weights: gun 19.9 kg (43.87 lb); tripod 19.8 kg (43.65 lb)
Muzzle velocity: 620 m (2,034 ft) per second
Rate of fire: (cyclic) 400 rpm
Feed: 250-round fabric belt

Rifles of the Great War

The introduction of the magazine-loading rifle gave the infantryman more firepower than ever before, but the appearance of quick-fire artillery and machine-guns combined to produce a bloody stalemate.

The years from 1914 to 1918 were very much a period of purgatory for the ordinary foot soldier. He was confined to a miserable life of trench warfare interspersed by periods when attacks were made through barbed wire in the face of massed machine-gun fire. The artillery ruled his existence and his military skills were few.

But every one of the unfortunates who led this odd life had one thing in common. He was equipped with a standard service rifle which was supposed to be his main weapon. In the event the individuals rarely got the chance to use these weapons, apart from the frantic and frenzied periods when an infantry attack actually reached the enemy's trenches. There the rifle's bayonet could be more useful than its bullet, and if all else failed the rifle became a very effective club. This close-quarter warfare was far from what the rifle designers had envisaged, namely accurate fire at long ranges. What the soldiers wanted was something that worked when required, very often at close ranges, and it was this fact that differentiated the true service rifle of World War I from the target rifles their designers thought they wanted. Under trench conditions the rifles that were able to withstand the rough-and-tumble of service life were much more favoured than the designers' dreams. Thus rifles such as the German Gewehr 98 and the British No. 1 Mk III fared much better than refined products such as the Canadian Ross or the British/American No. 3 Mk I.

The Western Front was not the only battleground of World War I. Elsewhere the Austro-Hungarians and Italians fought it out with Mannlicher modello 1895s and Mannlicher-Carcano modello 1891s. The Rus-

Serbian soldiers are seen in April 1916, with the man laden with trophies in the foreground carrying his 7-mm (0.275-in) rifle carefully wrapped against the mud. Part of his booty is a Mannlicher-Carcano carbine. Elaborate decoration of rifles was a Balkan tradition dating back to the 16th century.

sians carried what Mosin-Nagant Model 1891s they could produce through the long series of campaigns against the Germans and Austro-Hungarians, while the French had a variety of weapons, some of them with colonial-warfare origins. Nearly all of these rifles used some form of magazine in which extra rounds could be carried ready to fire, and all of them carried long and wicked bayonets that reduced the rifle to little more than a long-range pike as carried in warfare for hundreds of years.

Nearly all the major types of rifle used by both sides in World War I are mentioned in this study. The men that carried them have now nearly all passed away, all of them remembering every last detail and feel of the weapons that they very often carried to their deaths. They are now part of history, but a surprising number of these rifles survive, not all of them in museums, for many are now collected by enthusiasts who treasure their design and robust construction. If they can fire them the enthusiasts are often agreeably surprised by the high degree of accuracy many are still capable of producing.

The disparity between the length of the Lebel mle 1886/93 in the foreground and the No. 1 Mark III held by the British soldier can be readily appreciated here. The Lebel was typical of most World War I rifle lengths, while the much shorter No. 1 Mark III was far easier to carry and use in action.

Mauser Gewehr 1898

The first Mauser rifle approved for German army service was the **Mauser Modell 1888**. This used a Mauser bolt action that has remained virtually unaltered to this day, but with it a rather dated 8-mm (0.315-in) cartridge. Trials led to the adoption of a new 7.92-mm (0.312-in) cartridge, and a new rifle to fire it became known as the **Gewehr 1898** or **Gew 98** (Rifle Model 1898). This new rifle was destined to be one of the most widely used and successful weapons of its type, and it was produced in large numbers. Many later rifles could trace their origins back to the Gewehr 1898. It was the classic Mauser rifle, handsome and rather long, but well-balanced and with everything excellently designed and in general nicely made. The term 'in general' is used advisedly, for once World War I was into its stride the standards of manufacture had to be relaxed and some comparatively rough specimens were issued to the troops. But most were very well-made with good quality wooden furniture that was emphasized by the use of a pistol-type grip behind the trigger to assist holding and aiming. The original rear-sight was a very elaborate affair with sliding ramps and other niceties that needed experience for effective use, but some larger versions were simpler. The bolt action retained the usual Mauser front-lug locking systems, with the addition of an extra lug to make the number up to three for added safety with the new and more powerful cartridge. The bolt used a straight-pull action which was and still is rather awkward to use quickly and smoothly but in service generated few problems. The integral box magazine held five rounds loaded from a charger clip.

While the Gewehr 1898 was produced primarily for the German armed forces, it was also the starting point for a multitude of rifle designs that spread all over the world. Spain was an early user of the basic Mauser action and versions produced there differed little from the Gewehr 1898. The output of Mauser models from Germany and Spain were soon encountered all over the world in nations as far apart as China and Costa Rica. The Mauser action accrued an enviable reputation for reliability, strength and accuracy, and the arguments rage even today as to whether or not the Gewehr 1898 and its various cousins were the finest service rifles of their time. Many still state that they were but there are many other contenders to the title. What is certain is that during the years 1914 to 1918 the Gewehr 1898 served the German army well. The front-line soldiers had to take care of

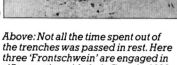

Above: Not all the time spent out of the trenches was passed in rest. Here three 'Frontschwein' are engaged in rifle practice with their Gewehr 1898s.

Left: Years of trench warfare radically altered the appearance of the German soldier. Carrying the Gewehr 1898K, he wears the distinctive 'coal scuttle' helmet. Note the wirecutters tucked into the belt.

them but usually this extended no further than keeping the bolt area covered with a cloth at all times when the rifle was not in use. Some versions such as sniper rifles appeared with special sights, including various forms of optic-

al sight, and the weapon still has the claim to fame that it was one of the very first, if not the first, anti-tank weapon. This came about by the chance discovery that the armour of the first British tanks could be penetrated by the simple expedient of reversing the bullets used in the Gewehr 1898 before they were fired: the blunt end simply punched a hole through the armour before the bullet could warp.

The standing figure watches the target and shouts out the score to be marked down by the seated soldier on the right. The date is May 1917.

Specification
Mauser Gewehr 1898
Calibre: 7.92 mm (0.312 in)
Length: overall 1.25 m (49.2 in); barrel 0.74 m (29.1 in)
Weight: 4.2 kg (9.26 lb)
Muzzle velocity: 640 m (2,100 ft) per second
Magazine: 5-round integral box

The German army's Gewehr 1898 was one of the more important Mauser rifles, as it was the standard German service rifle of World War I. It was very well made with a strong bolt action, and fired a 7.92-mm (0.312-in) round using a five-round magazine. It served as the model for many later rifles.

Ross Rifles

The first Ross rifle appeared during 1896 and was produced, like the later models, at Sir Charles Ross's own arms factory in Quebec, Canada. Ross was a keen marksman of the old 'Bisley School', and longed for what he considered to be the ideal service rifle: one that would consistently provide accuracy. In pursuit of this ideal he concentrated on items such as barrels and sighting systems as opposed to the more mundane aspects of design that are essential to the true service rifle.

Thus although his products were superb target weapons, they revealed themselves to be less than ideal under the rough-and-tumble of service conditions.

The number of types of Ross·rifle runs to well over a dozen. Many of the types produced were often minor modifications of the preceding model and to list them all would be unhelpful. The main service model was known to the Canadian army as the **Rifle, Ross, Mk 3** and may be taken as typical. It

was a long-barrelled rifle to provide accurate long-rifle fire, and used an unusual straight-pull bolt system allied to a box magazine holding five rounds. In common with other Commonwealth armies of the day the Canadian army adopted the British 0.303-in (7.7-mm) cartridge, and this led to the British army taking numbers of Ross rifles in 1914-5.

The Canadian army adopted the Ross after about 1905, and the first Canadian troops to travel to France in

1914 were equipped with them. It was not long before the Ross rifles were found wanting once they encountered the mud of the Western Front trenches, for their bolt actions clogged with remarkable ease once even small amount of debris had entered the system. In his search for accuracy Ross had overlooked that service rifles need to be tolerant of rough conditions, and the Ross rifle required dedicated maintenance and care in handling. The bolt action frequently jam-

med and the resultant clearing revealed another nasty drawback to the design: the bolt had to be put together in a very precise manner, and if it was re-assembled in the wrong way after cleaning or repair it could still fire the rifle even though the locking lugs that held its bolt in place were not engaged. As the Ross used a straight-pull bolt the part could fly back and hit the firer in the face. Thus the Ross soon fell from grace and was replaced by the British No. 1 Mk III. Quite apart from the bolt problems, the length of the Ross rifle was too great for ease of use in the trenches.

The Ross was not completely withdrawn from service use. Fitted with a telescopic sight it was used very suc-cessfully as a sniping rifle, a role in which its accuracy was most prized. Trained snipers could also provide the weapon with the extra care it required. To this day the Ross is still a much-prized target rifle. Many were used during World War II by various British second-line units, including the Home Guard, but the Ross never overcame the reputation for problems that it gained during its introduction to the trenches during 1914 and 1915.

Specification
Rifle, Ross, Mk 3
Calibre: 7.7 mm (0.303 in)
Length: overall 1.285 m (50.6 in); barrel 0.765 m (30.15 in)
Weight: 4.48 kg (9.875 lb)
Muzzle velocity: 792 m (2,600 ft) per second
Magazine: 5-round box

The Canadian Ross rifle (this is a Mk 2) was an excellent target rifle, but less successful in service, as mud and dirt tended to clog the straight-pull bolt action. Although used in France, the Canadians later exchanged it for the No. 1 Mk III, and the Ross rifles were used for training.

Canadian armourers maintain their Ross rifles on Salisbury Plain in September 1914. The armourers had the job of maintaining bicycles as well as guns. When well maintained, the Ross was a formidably accurate rifle and remained a prized sniper's weapon.

After the Ross rifle was withdrawn, some were used for training and some were issued to British armed trawler crews to provide them with some form of defence against German aircraft or even U-boats operating in the North Sea; they were better than nothing.

UK
Rifle No. 3 Mk I

Despite their eventual success, when first introduced the No. 1 Mk III rifles were deemed to lack the features required by some military pundits. In case the new SMLE did not meet requirements a 'back-up' design was put forward, one chambered for a new 7-mm (0.276-in) cartridge and employing a Mauser bolt action. Being only a back-up design at first, this rifle did not appear until 1913 under the general title **P.13**. At the time the design was taken no further and work on the new 7-mm cartridge ceased. Thus things were in abeyance just as the war began in 1914, and by then the P.13 had become the **P.14**.

In 1915 the overall shortage of rifles for the expanding British and Commonwealth armies was such that at one point rifles were being ordered from places as far away as Japan. It was accordingly decided that the P.14 could be ordered from the United States, but chambered for the standard 7.7-mm (0.303-in) cartridge. Several firms, including Winchester and Remington, became involved in production of the P.14, which was known to the British army as the **Rifle No. 3 Mk I**, and the results were shipped eastwards across the Atlantic.

When they arrived they were hurriedly issued and rushed into combat. They did not fare very well, for the No. 3 rifle was a product of what became known as the Bisley School of rifle thought. To the Bisley School long-range accuracy was the touchstone of all combat rifle worth. Soldiers were expected to hit man-sized targets at ranges of over 914 m (1,000 yards), and if a rifle could not attain these standards it was reviled. It was exactly this factor that drew so much criticism to the SMLE when it was first issued in 1907, for the SMLE was never a perfect target rifle. With the No. 3 the Bisley School had been given full rein and the result was not unlike the ill-fated Canadian Ross rifles. The No. 3 was quite simply not a good service rifle: it was long and awkward to use under combat conditions, encumbered by a long bayonet it was ill balanced and even less handy, and the bolt action took considerable maintenance. It was withdrawn from service when enough No. 1 Mk IIIs were to hand.

The No. 3 Mk I did have one saving grace; it was as accurate as the Bisley School had intended. Thus the No. 3 was used mainly for the sniping role, in which it was very successful.

The No. 3 Mk I had one more task to perform in World War I, and that came when the Americans entered the war in 1917. They were even more desperate for service rifles than the British and as the production lines were still producing No. 3s for the British they were changed to manufacture the same rifles chambered for the American 7.62-mm (0.3-in) cartridge. Thus the No. 3 became the **M1917**, known to most Americans to this day as the 'Enfield'. In American hands the M1917 (or **P.17** to some) fared no better than it had with the British, and in 1919 the entire output was placed into store, only to be dragged out again in 1940 and sold to the United Kingdom to arm the new Home Guard.

Specification
Rifle No. 3 Mk I
Calibre: 7.7 mm (0.303 in)
Length: overall 1.175 m (46.25 in); barrel 0.66 m (26 in)
Weight: 4.35 kg (9.6 lb)
Muzzle velocity: 762 m (2,500 ft) per second
Magazine: 5-round box

The P.14 was a Mauser rifle produced in case the No. 1 Mk III failed to come up to specification. A 0.303-in (7.7-mm) version was ordered from the USA, and this was later adopted by the US Army as the Model 1917. It was an excellent and accurate weapon.

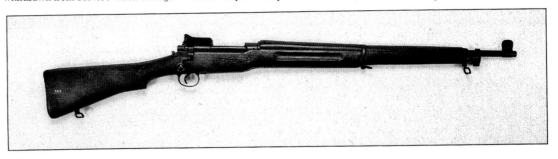

Mons-the Making of a Legend

Before the war, the tiny size of the British Army was a source of amusement to our enemies and anxiety to our allies. But when the German armies swept through Belgium in 1914, it fell to the British Expeditionary Force to stem the flood. Every man a volunteer, the BEF dug itself in around the little town of Mons and awaited the German onslaught.

At the outbreak of World War I, two gigantic military plans were put into action: Plan 17 by the French armies under command of General Joffre, and the Schlieffen Plan by the Germans under the slightly hesitant command of the younger General von Moltke.

Plan 17 collapsed almost immediately, the élan and 'Spirit of the Offensive' of the French troops upon which it was to such a great extent based proving ineffective in the face of the realities of rifle and machine-gun fire, plus the refusal of the German commanders to act in strategic accordance with French pre-conceptions. Instead of driving forward into the gigantic trap set by the French in the Trouée des Charmes, between Nancy and Belfort, the Germans swung huge armies in a wide arc along the traditional military routes through the Low Countries, in an endeavour to outflank their main enemy and eventually entrap the hostile armies against their own frontier defences.

However uncertain von Moltke's grasp might eventually prove to be, during those opening weeks of the war all movements were strictly controlled by the firm precepts laid down years before by his predecessor in office, the omnipotent Graf von Schlieffen. Those precepts dictated not only the overall pattern of movement, but also the distribution of forces necessary to carry it out; Schlieffen's dying words had been 'Make the right wing strong!' and so, despite von Moltke's doubts, the German 1st Army (under the coldly efficient General von Kluck) smashed forward like a gigantic hammerhead through Belgium and northern France, the 2nd, 3rd and 4th Armies to its left acting as the shaft, the whole weapon pivoting on the French fortress of Verdun.

So during those long, hot August days of 1914 it appeared to the eyes of an astonished world that the battle was indeed progressing in accordance with the plans of the deceased von Schlieffen. The huge fortress of Liège fell within the first few days, its supposedly impenet-rable steel cupolas shattered by the plunging fire of huge siege weapons, the largest and heaviest guns so far used in warfare, the garrisons dazed and disoriented by shock and deafened by explosion. To the south the battles of the frontier were being fought and won by armies under Crown Prince Wilhelm and the Duke of Würtemberg, and once Liège had fallen General von Bülow's 2nd and General von Hausen's 3rd Armies drove on down the Meuse, taking Huy, Namur and Dinant, pressing back the French armies along the whole length of the assault, disrupting the desperate attempt of the French 5th Army under General Lanrezac to drive northwards and block or at least cut off von Kluck's implacable advance.

For it was the German 1st Army which was making the most spectacular and impressive gains. To this army had fallen first Louvain and then Brussels itself, and by the end of 18 days' campaigning the 200,000 men and 40,000 horses had advanced 160 km (99 miles), dragging their thousand-odd pieces of artillery and other military impedimenta with them. They marched all the way, fighting quite a lot of it through countryside peopled sometimes by actively hostile troops, mostly by sullenly hostile civilians and on occasion by groups of insidious treacherous *francs tireurs*, despite the immediate and severe punishment meted out

The superbly disciplined troops of the BEF were trained to fire 15 aimed rounds per minute, and when the Germans attacked, their close formations were swept away in a hail of bullets. Many Germans were convinced that they were facing a line of machine-guns.

on the spot to them and their associates when caught.

But success and the sense of victory were enough to sweep away all doubt and fear, to revivify tired muscles and aching bones; the 1st Army consisted, after all, of young soldiers, well-trained and hardened in willing service to the Fatherland, and on the morning of 23 August they were further heartened by the repetition of an old joke which made its way along the columns. There had been rumours for the last 24 hours that there were British troops (possible the whole British army) in front of them, and von Kluck was said to have repeated Bismarck's remark made so many years before: the German soldiers need not concern themselves with the English, for he was sending the police to arrest them!

The British army was, of course, a joke. German comic papers had long portrayed its soldiers as figures of fun in their short scarlet tunics with small caps set at an angle on their heads or with bearskins with the chin-straps under their lip, and the first sight of them on that fateful morning did little to dispel the impression. Hauptmann Walter Bloem, commandng a fusilier company of the 12th Brandenburger Grenadiers, was approaching a group of farm buildings on the outskirts of Tertre, just north of the canal which runs from Condé sur l'Escaut eastwards to the small town of Mons, when he turned a corner and saw in front of him a group of fine-looking horses, all saddled up.

He had hardly given orders for their capture when 'a man appeared not five paces away from behind the horses – a man in a grey-brown uniform, no, in a grey-brown golfing-suit

with a flat-topped cloth cap. Could this be a soldier?'

Surely not!

But it was. It was an officer from A Squadron, 19th Hussars, the cavalry regiment attached to the 5th Division of the British Expeditionary Force (BEF), and behind this reconnaissance patrol on the far side of the 20-m (66-ft) wide canal, waited the infantry of one of the 5th Division's brigades, the 14th. Other brigades flanked this on either side: on the west to just past Conde sur l'Escaut, and on the east to the Mons salient, where they linked with the left-hand brigade of the 3rd Division, these two divisions comprising the British II Corps under command of General Sir Horace Smith-Dorrien. The divisions of I Corps under General Sir Douglas Haig then continued the line eastwards towards the left flank of Lanrezac's army.

The British advance

The British Expeditionary Force of two infantry corps and a cavalry division under Major-General Sir Edmund Allenby had begun embarkation from Dublin and Southampton on 12 August, crossed the Channel that night, spent a few days in tented reception camps near Boulogne, Le Havre and Rouen, travelled by train as far as Le Cateau and then spent the next five days marching into Belgium along rough pavé roads and in sweltering temperatures. It was a journey which had at first exacted a price in blistered feet and sweating exhaustion (especially among the newly-recalled reservists) but which by the previous evening (22 August) had brought them to a satisfactory state of physical and morale fitness.

The Londoners, Scots, Irish and Welsh; the men from Surrey, Suffolk, Lincolnshire, Wiltshire, Kent, Cornwall and South Staffordshire; the Guardsmen, the Fusiliers, the privates and troopers, the NCOs and officers were now fit and relaxed, settled into their allocated positions, some dug in along the flank or around the Mons salient, most of them lying easily behind the bank of the canal or hidden in the barns and outhouses close to the 16 bridges that crossed it, their Lee-Enfield rifles, their Vickers machine-guns (two per battalion) and their Webley revolvers all cleaned, checked and to hand.

And they waited for what 23 August would bring.

It brought at first in the early morning the sights of ordinary small-town and village life continuing unconcernedly among the narrow streets and lanes, between the numberless slag heaps and pit heads of this small coal-mining community. Church bells rang, sombre-coated villagers responded to their summons, a small train filled with holiday-makers chuffed away towards the coast, the scent of newly-ground coffee was everywhere; and the sudden explosion of a shell in the outskirts of Mons itself, among the Royal Fusiliers, was so unexpected that the whole world seemed to hold its breath in astonishment.

If the Allied armies were to extricate themselves from the German trap, the BEF had to hold off von Kluck's First Army for at least 24 hours. The Germans along the British front were soon pinned down by withering rifle fire, but it was not long before they began to work their way around the flanks of the BEF's position.

Two British infantrymen carrying full packs probe forward along a Belgian hedgerow. When the German cavalry patrols discovered the British position they were driven off by rapid and accurate rifle fire. Before long the British outposts fell back to the main position as the German attack began.

Elements of the Indian Army soon joined the BEF, and the 129th Baluchis, seen here at Wytschaete in October 1914, were some of the most experienced soldiers in the theatre. Indian troops later provided the bulk of British Imperial Forces fighting the Turks in Mesopotamia.

But not for long. As the sound and smoke died away, the rifles came up and the appearance of a German cavalry patrol opposite caught no one unawares except themselves: the first volley of the Fusiliers emptied all their saddles, and very shortly afterwards Oberleutnant von Arnim of the Death's Head Hussars was brought in swearing profusely with a smashed knee.

By now the whole of the British line was alert and waiting, though hardly for what next happened. Before their astonished eyes, the woods, hedges and buildings stretching before them 1.6 km (1 mile) away across the canal and the flat water-meadows beyond, began erupting solid columns of grey-uniformed men, moving unhurriedly towards them in a solid mass like a football crowd after a match.

Watching the grey ocean lapping across the fields, one British officer asked another to pinch him in case he was dreaming, and his wonder was palpable as along 26 km (16 miles) of dead straight canal the British infantry waited while thousands of men walked with apparent innocence and unconcern towards almost certain death. At least 12,000 Lee-Enfield rifles, each held by a soldier expert in the famous British 'rapid fire', waited behind the embankment of the canal, augmented by 24 Vickers machine-guns; and it would seem that hardly one of them was fired until the German front ranks had come within 550 m (600 yards), the range over which the Lee-Enfield fired a flat trajectory.

When fire was opened, the slaughter was immediate – and horrific.

Within minutes whole German battalions were wiped out, junior officers found themselves the only officers left to a regiment bereft of all warrant or non-commissioned ranks and the majority of the men. Walter Bloem and his company were immediately pinned down in a water-meadow and decimated, the survivors held where they had dropped for the rest of the day, only saved from much higher casualties by the fact that they had managed a concerted rush to the canal bank and lay in its shelter with rifle and machine-gun bullets stitching the air just above them. Such was the rate and volume of fire that swept the battlefield from one end to the other that Bloem and those of his contemporaries who survived remained convinced to the end of their days that each British battalion had at least 12 and probably 24 machine-guns apiece.

But there were only 24 machine-guns to a brigade, and only 7,500 men in the BEF altogether – and that number, however well-trained, cannot hold up 200,000 men indefinitely except in circumstances of severe geographic confinement which did not apply at Mons. Inevitably, small groups of Germans reached the bridges over the canal, in one case near Jemappes by driving in front of them a party of little Belgian schoolgirls; it was a ploy which so disconcerted the Northumberland Fusiliers opposite that they lost control of important lock gates and were thus eventually forced out of their position.

German artillery brought up during the late morning blew gaps in the British line, and the Royal Fusiliers and the 4th Middlesex holding the sides of the narrow Mons salient were in an especially dangerous situation once the guns registered on the town. And all the while, more of von Kluck's battalions were flooding down the roads leading to the battle, widening the front until it overlapped the British line and threatened the flanks.

By 16.00, II Corps was being forced back, the rearguards and engineers blowing the bridges as they pulled out (two VCs and a DCM were won in the process) and then later in the evening the true seriousness of the British position was revealed. On their right the French 5th Army had had another disastrous day, Lanrezac had taken fright and ordered a large-scale retirement without, however, informing his allies, despite promises to Sir John French of close liaison.

By 21.00 it was evident that the British had been left on their own, and despite justifiable feelings of confidence throughout all ranks in their ability to beat the enemy, they must now retreat. During that night the tired, frustrated and puzzled men of the BEF began the march back which would end on the Marne.

But they had fought the Battle of Mons, and it would live in history for all time. And they left behind them a confused and depressed enemy. That night Walter Bloem wrote in his diary ' . . . the men all chilled to the bone, almost too exhausted to move and with the depressing consciousness of defeat weighing heavily upon them. A bad defeat, there can be no gainsaying it . . . we had been badly beaten, and by the English – by the English we had so laughed at a few hours before.'

The combination of British infantry training and the SMLE had shot them flat.

Royal Marines in Broderick caps carry No. 1 Mk IIIs during the campaign of open fighting that took place near Ostend in August 1914. They are men of the Royal Marine Light Infantry, who were used to defend the port facilities at Ostend but were later withdrawn from the area.

After Mons the German army pressed on into France, where their great offensive was finally halted on the Marne. German infantry from a Bavarian regiment lie in an extended line that would have been impossible a few months later when the armies had all moved to underground shelter and trenches.

UK
Rifle No. 1 Mks III and III*

During the late 19th century the British army adopted the magazine and bolt system developed by the American engineer James Lee, and through a long process of 'in-house' improvements and trials this led to a series of what were known as Lee-Enfield rifles, the Enfield part of the name coming from the Royal Small Arms Factory at Enfield Lock, Middlesex. This series led in 1907 to a new design known as the **Short Magazine Lee-Enfield (SMLE)**, a rifle with a length between those of a normal rifle and a carbine, for the SMLE was another of the weapons intended for use by all arms from infantry to cavalry. At first SMLE had a rough introduction into service, but improvements and some modifications overcame these and in 1914 the SMLE was taken to France with the BEF; by then it had been re-designated the **Rifle No. 1 Mk III**.

The No. 1 Mk III is another of the candidates for the accolade 'best service rifle of the time'. It was a fully-stocked weapon with a snub-shaped

The onset of winter in 1914 led to the appearance of an astonishing variety of improvised fur coats. In spite of all the vagaries of life in the trenches, some Scottish regiments retained the kilt until the end of the war.

fitting at the muzzle to accommodate a long knife bayonet. The bolt action was of the turn-bolt variety and used rear locking lugs as opposed to the front-locking lugs of the Mauser system. In theory this meant that the Lee system was less safe than that of the Mauser, but in service it caused no problems at all, and the smooth action of the Lee-Enfield mechanism made the British rifle easy and extremely fast. The detachable box magazine in front of the trigger group held 10 rounds, which was twice the capacity of many of its contemporaries. There was also a cut-out device that held all the rounds in the magazine while single rounds were fed into the chamber by hand; this arrangement was supposed to retain the magazine rounds for use only when really needed. The main sights were of the ramp type and calibrated to well over 1,000 yards (914 m), and on the left-hand side of the rifle stock was a peculiar long-range sight that was used to provide really long-range area fire to cover an area; it was used only under careful control when volley fire would be employed.

Above: Two well-laden British soldiers are seen in action holding the south bank of the River Aisne during the battle of May 1918, in the aftermath of the series of German breakthroughs that started during March of that year. The rifle is a No. 1 Mk III*.

The No. 1 Mk III rifle was often known as the SMLE (Short Magazine Lee-Enfield) and was one of the best service rifles of World War I. It could

Australian troops move up into the line near Fricourt in October 1918, carrying the No. 1 Mk IIIs that their descendants were to carry

Below: A cosy scene indicates the Entente Cordiale that was in being in March 1918. The picture was taken well behind the lines, for the No. 1 Mk III* lacks the usual wrappings that would have kept it clean in the dirt and mud of the trenches.

be fired at a rapid rate of over 15 shots a minute as the bolt action was easy to operate, and the magazine could be quickly loaded.

throughout World War II; Australian production of this rifle did not end until 1955 at the Lithgow arsenal. Note the mixture of headgear worn.

While the No. 1 Mk III was an excellent service rifle, it was expensive and time-consuming to make, for virtually everything had to be machined or made by hand. Consequently when trench warfare set in and an ever-increasing number of rifles was needed, some production short cuts were made, including the removal of the magazine cut-out and the long-range sights. The result was the **Rifle No. 1 Mk III***, and this may be regarded as the standard British rifle of World War I. It was produced in tens of thousands, not only in the United Kingdom but also in India and Australia (where it remained in production until 1955). It was a sturdy and sound rifle that was well able to withstand the rigours of trench fighting. All manner of devices were invented to increase its usefulness, these ranging from periscopic sights to grenade-launcher devices. In the hands of a fully-trained soldier it was capable of high rates of fire: a rate of 15 rounds per minute was accepted as the norm and trained soldiers could produce far more. At Mons in 1914 the German forces involved thought they were up against machine-guns at some stages. They were not; it was simply the massed rapid fire produced by the superbly-trained soldiers of the BEF using their No. 1 Mk IIIs to full advantage.

Specification
Rifle No. 1 Mk III*
Calibre: 7.7 mm (0.303 in)
Length: overall 1.133 m (44.6 in); barrel 0.64 m (25.2 in)
Weight: 3.93 kg (8.656 lb)
Muzzle velocity: 634 m (2,080 ft) per second
Magazine: 10-round box

Battle of the Frontiers

Having trusted to defensive tactics in 1870, and lost, the French were determined to attack at all costs in 1914. But the battles on the frontier were to prove that sheer bravery is not enough to defeat modern weapons.

When the French army went to war in 1914 it gloried in its high morale, it considered itself to be superbly equipped, and it was at long last setting out to avenge the defeats and indignities suffered at German hands in the Franco-Prussian War of 1870. Finally it was setting out to regain the lost provinces of Alsace and Lorraine, ceded to the Germans in 1871, and as the marching infantry and the cavalry moved out of their depots they advanced immediately towards these two 'lost' territories with eager anticipation.

They were to be bitterly disappointed, for they were moving into what history was to call the Battle of the Frontiers. In fact there was not one battle but a whole string of them, all ending in French defeats. At the time the French army could do little to analyse why this should have happened, but in time the reasons became clear to all who chose to look for them.

In immediate terms the French were defeated because their military leaders did exactly what the German staff planners wanted them to: they advanced towards Alsace and Lorraine on the eastern sector of the Franco-German border, while the main German moves were being made away to the west in the form of the now-famous Schlieffen Plan. This entailed a massive move by the chief weight of the German army through Belgium, along the Channel Coast and down behind Paris to encounter the French army in the rear to pen it up against the borders. When the French army moved towards the two provinces it was thus doing exactly what the Germans hoped and by so doing considerably assisted the progress of the Schlieffen Plan. The French move was part of the much-vaunted 'Plan 17', but to discover why the French put this plan into effect one has to go back to 1870.

In 1870 the Prussian army defeated the French in such a manner that the French army was all but destroyed. In a series of battles which culminated in the French debacle at Sedan the French military establishment was laid low and the national ego dealt such a blow that it seemed it might never recover. But re-

A French Cuirassier regiment moves through a French town during the very early stages of the war leading up to the Battle of the Frontiers in August 1914. Note the breastplates and the incongruous helmets of an era that was soon to be swept away by the German machine-guns.

cover it did, and in the years after 1871 the French nation and economy entered one of its most prosperous periods, the army being re-established to its former position of national pride and position. Colonial wars enabled it to retrain and to regain confidence, but all the time the shadow of Sedan was still there and it was realized that war with Germany must return sooner or later. But how could this war be fought?

The answer in French eyes was to ignore military realities and assume a philosophy in which the only reaction to any tactical or strategic situation was to advance. The advance became the only manoeuvre that was considered suitable for the French army, and in time this philosophy of the offensive became not just a military reaction to everything but a virtual religion. There appeared writings in which words and phrases like 'morale', 'determination' and 'the will to victory' were liberally spattered, and in time this approach to warfare became the accepted French norm. No form of disagreement or deviation from the advance was allowed in any shape or form, and the French army drilled and equipped itself for the advance. If the army could will itself to win by advancing nothing could stand in its way, or so the philosophy went.

This philosophy went so far that anything that would hold up an advance was simply not acquired. Weapons like heavy artillery were not even considered. Instead the French gunners were provided with the famous '75', a light 75-mm (2.95-in) field gun capable of firing 15 rounds per minute. With this the army could cover any advance by simply blasting away any opposition, or so the philosophy again ran. For the infantry the bayonet was to be the attacking weapon. Rifles were simply things on to which bayonets could be placed. The cavalry would once again regain its place on the battlefield by advancing with the lance and sword. (The lessons of the Boer War in this context were ignored, as too were the even more indicative lessons of the American Civil War and even France's own experiences in 1870.)

As if this was not enough, the French army also did its cause no good by dabbling in politics, a prime example of which was the infamous Dreyfus Case which caused no end of rifts within the army establishment itself. In the short term this led to a rigid adherence to orthodoxy over and above the belief in the advance at all costs. The drill book and the instruction manual became bibles to the extent that on the rifle range it mattered not if the target was missed, for what really mattered was that the exact stance dictated by a chair-borne warrior in an office stated that only so much ammunition was to be carried into action, no deviation was tolerated despite the fact that it was clearly insufficient for more than a single skirmish.

Thus in August 1914 all was not well with the French army, but at the time this unpalatable fact was ignored. At last the French were advancing to Alsace and Lorraine. The bands played as the infantry in their bright uniforms marched east, accompanied by the cavalry some still in shiny breastplates as worn at Waterloo over a century before. The Germans simply waited.

A French patrol at an observation outpost in August 1914, complete with a dog no doubt intended for sniffing out hidden skirmishers. The rifles are Lebel mle 1886/93s, then the standard French service rifle but soon to be supplemented by Berthier rifles, both mle 1907s and mle 1916s.

Above: A section of French infantry guards a canal bank for the camera in September 1914. The rifles are Lebels, and although the Battle of the Frontiers was by then over, the officer still retains his distinctive képi; the soldiers have done their best to tone down the outline of theirs so as not to attract attention.

Below: During the early part of the war tales of German atrocities were rife, to the extent that many hapless prisoners-of-war shared the harsh fate of this unfortunate, who is facing a French firing squad using Lebel rifles. This phase soon passed when trench warfare commenced, and PoWs could then hope for a better fate.

Above: The French began the war in uniforms little changed from those of 1870. Les pantalons rouges, the baggy red trousers worn since the 1830s, were soon exchanged for a less conspicuous kit. The képi *itself was soon replaced by a steel helmet copied from the type issued to the Paris fire brigade.*

The Germans knew all about Plan 17 and had arranged their forces accordingly. They made few advances during the early stages but instead prepared a series of carefully emplaced defences at what they considered to be the right places, and they were not far wrong. The French army advanced on a broad front, and by 20 August the first tentative encounters were under way. The French soldiers usually had to march all the way to the borders, and by the time they got there many were tired. They had to carry much of their personal kit on their backs along with their heavy rifles and at least 100 rounds of ammunition. To this could be added the long and heavy bayonet, at least a part of the day's rations and the long greatcoat, usually worn with the front buttoned open at the bottom. Their enemies were already emplaced and ready, fresh and just as eager as the French to start the forthcoming battles.

The French were arranged in five armies from Lille in the north to Mulhouse in the south. Each army had at least two corps, and such was the confidence of the French that these corps usually advanced to the designated frontier positions side-by-side. They were in for a shock because, once the French scouting parties had discovered the main German positions, the massed French formations simply advanced towards them and there followed what can only be termed a series of massacres rather than battles as the French were cut

down in their tracks.

Much of the damage was done as a result of infantry encounters in which rifles and machine-guns in carefully concealed German positions fired directly into the advancing French ranks. As the French advanced over open fields still covered with the year's harvest, the German machine-gunners could pick them off easily, for the brightly-coloured French uniforms stood out well against the background. The unfortunate French cavalry never got near enough to their destroyers to use their lances and sabres, for a single machine-gun was enough to reduce a battalion to a few uncomprehending men and terrified horses. The French foot soldiers fell in droves, often without

firing a shot, still carrying their bayonet-laden rifles pointing to the east as they fell. The French artillery fared little better. The 75s were supposed to be used well forward with their direct fire supporting the all-important advance. What had not been foreseen was that although the 75s could fire 15 rounds per minute, ammunition had been allocated for a fire rate of only 2.75 rounds per minute. But the 75s did have their successes, for the fighting was not all one-sided. In some places impetuous German officers led their units forward into the fray only to be caught in the open as the French had been, and in some places the piles of German corpses were as high as those of the French.

Battle of the Frontiers

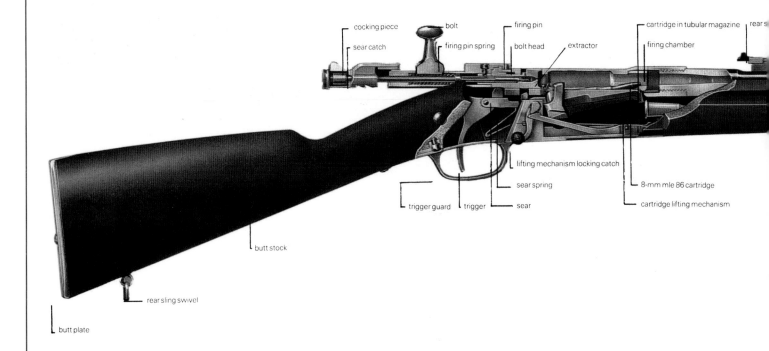

cocking piece · bolt · firing pin · cartridge in tubular magazine · rear s
sear catch · firing pin spring · bolt head · extractor · firing chamber
lifting mechanism locking catch
sear spring · 8-mm mle 86 cartridge
trigger guard · trigger · sear · cartridge lifting mechanism
butt stock
rear sling swivel
butt plate

Where the French were really to suffer was in their overall lack of heavy artillery. In a sharp foretaste of things to come, German artillery spotter aircraft often flew over the advancing French columns to direct the fire of the heavier batteries on to the unsuspecting French, who were killed even before they had joined the battle. It was all too much. The French colonial troops were among the first to break. They were always among the first to move into battle and they accordingly suffered the worst that the Germans could direct against them. The rout of the colonial troops started a general retreat from the frontiers, but at the time this

fact was lost in the mayhem of the advance of the mass of the German army through Belgium and across the northern French plains. The Schlieffen Plan was grinding its way towards Paris and the nation seemed to be in great danger. But the Battle of the Marne lay ahead, and with it the failure of the German plans that led to four years of trench warfare.

The Battle of the Frontiers is now generally seen as a prelude of what was to come after 1914, but at the time it was a disaster for the French. Their long-held theories were seen to be of little worth and they had to revise their strategies and tactics drastically, to suit the

'new' conditions. It also cost them the cream of their armies. The men who fell in the Battle of the Frontiers were the best that the French had. To this day the memorial plaque in the Officer Training College at St Cyr bears the title for the dead of the first year of the war as 'The Class of 1914'. Those officers could never be replaced, and with them perished tens of thousands of the best regular troops that the French army had trained. From then on the war was to be fought with a largely conscript force used en masse in such a way that the casualties of the Battle of the Frontiers were later to be regarded as nothing unusual.

Below: Looking almost like a scene from the Napoleonic Wars, this column of French cavalry moves up to the Battle of the Frontiers in August 1914. These soldiers are among the best-trained of all the French units, but their tactics were of no use against magazine-loading rifles and machine-guns.

Above: The French often used their colonial regiments as shock troops. This squad from the 5ème Tirailleurs Algériens on parade at Aix has Lebel rifles, at a time when many colonial troops were issued with rifles dating back to 1874 to keep modern weapons for the front line.

Right: German troops move up to the newly-established trenches in November 1914 and shoulder the weight of their 4.2-kg (9.26-lb) Gewehr 1898s. Each soldier carried at least 200 7.92-mm (0.312-in) cartridges plus all his personal kit, a greatcoat and at least a day's combat rations.

Lebel mle 1886

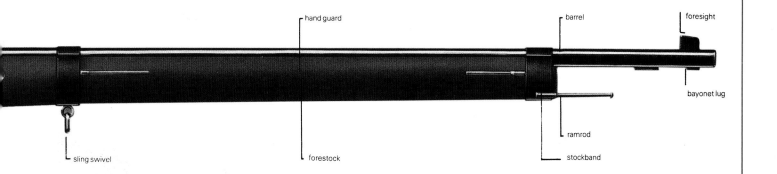

hand guard

barrel

foresight

bayonet lug

ramrod

sling swivel

forestock

stockband

Fusil Lebel mle 1886

By 1886 the French army was in a position to introduce a new 'small' cartridge with a calibre of 8 mm (0.315 in) to fire the new completely smokeless propellant developed by Paul Vielle. With the new cartridge came a new rifle, the **Fusil mle 1886**, usually known as the Lebel after the name of the officer who led the commission that recommended the adoption of the new rifle and round.

The Lebel was for its time only a tentative improvement of the existing Gras mle 1874. The new rifle did indeed have the ability to fire the new 8-mm cartridge, but the bolt action of the Gras design was retained and, in place of the by-then acceptable box magazine, the Lebel used a tubular magazine in which the rounds were loaded nose-to-tail. This magazine was located under the fore-stock and contained eight rounds. It was still possible to load single rounds directly into the chamber and, as loading the tubular magazine was a somewhat slow process, the full loading was usually kept for use only when large amounts of fire were required.

The original mle 1886 underwent a major modification programme in 1893 and the designation was accordingly changed to **mle 1886/93**. Another revi-

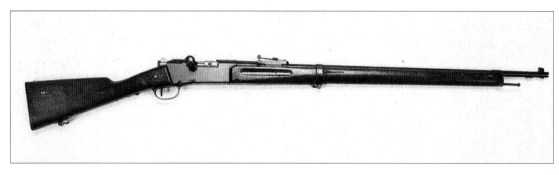

Above: The long mle 1886/93 was basically an 1874 Gras rifle modernized by the use of an eight-round tubular magazine, and was one of the standard French rifles of World War I. It used a straight-action bolt system and fired an 8-mm (0.315-in) cartridge.

Left: Taken on manoeuvres in July 1914, this photograph gives an indication of the French attacking tactics of the Battle of the Frontiers. These massed rushes were supposed to carry all before them, but in the event the soldiers were mown down in heaps.

sion came in 1898 when the ammunition was updated, but the designation remained unaltered.

The original mle 1896 has one major claim to fame, for it was the first service rifle to fire smokeless propellant cartridges. For a short while the French army was thus ahead of all its contemporaries, but this advantage did not last long once the 'secrets' of the propellant became widely known. Within a few years all other major nations had converted to the new propellant and had also adopted the new 'small-calibre' type of cartridge, so the Lebel soon lost its early lead. In fact it assumed something of a back place in rifle development as a result of its anachronistic tubular magazine. One of the major disadvantages of such a

magazine was the relatively long loading time that had already been mentioned; another was the safety aspect, for as the rounds lay nose-to-tail in the magazine there was always the chance that a sudden jolt would cause the nose of one round to hit the primer of the round in front with dire results. Thus there was a gradual move away from the Lebel towards the Berthier rifles, but in 1914 the Lebel remained in service in large numbers, and it was still standard issue to most front-line units. It served throughout World War I and was still in large-scale use in World War II.

The Lebel could mount a long cruciform bayonet, and was by all accounts a pleasant rifle to handle and aim. However, the loading was awkward

and there was always the chance of a magazine explosion when it was least expected. Another drawback was the two-piece bolt which took a degree of maintenance and was prone to clogging with dirt and dust at the earliest opportunity. A special 5.5-mm (0.216-in) training version was produced in small numbers.

Specification
Fusil Lebel mle 1886/93
Calibre: 8 mm (0.315 in)
Length: overall 1.303 m (51.3 in); barrel 0.798 m (31.4 in)
Weight: 4.245 kg (9.35 lb)
Muzzle velocity: 725 m (2,379 ft) per second
Magazine: 8-round tubular

Above: A French Zouave is seen at Vincennes, 1917, standing guard with a mle 1886/93 fitted with the spike-like Epée-bajonette mle 1886. This converted the rifle into a pike for close combat, where it was to prove very effective, but it lacked the general usefulness of the blade-type bayonet.

French troops are shown in action a short distance from the Turkish lines at Gallipoli. The rifle in the foreground can be recognized as a mle 1886/93 by the inline bolt; if it was a Berthier the bolt handle would be turned down. The hardness of the ground has made trench-building impossible; hence the barricades.

French carbines

During World War I the carbine was a widely-used weapon with most armies other than those of the British and the Americans who never favoured the type. As a general rule these carbines were cut-down versions of the standard service rifles of the day and were originally intended for use by cavalry. However, between 1914 and 1918 the carbine was used by many more types of unit, usually in the second line, by signallers, drivers, military police and many others who required some form of weapon but not the long and awkward service rifle.

The carbines used by the French army can be taken as typical of the types in use elsewhere. While the French front-line troops were equipped with the normal service rifle, many other French soldiers carried carbines. At the top of this list inevitably came the cavalry, but after 1914 the French cavalry had little to do and many were used as infantry and were thus given the normal service rifles. Other second-line troops used a variety of weapon types. The oldest of these was the **Mousqueton Gras mle 1874**, like its longer relation a single-shot weapon with no magazine. Surprisingly the mle 1886 Lebel and its derivatives were not produced in carbine form (other than trials models) and most French carbines were based on the Berthier.

The first Berthier carbine was the **Mousqueton Berthier mle 1890** produced for the cavalry. The later **mle 1892** for use by artillery units, and there was also a slightly different version for the Gendarmerie, a branch of the French armed forces. The mle 1892 was probably produced in greater numbers than the mle 1890, and was provided with such accessories such as a bayonet and cleaning rod. From the mle 1892 evolved the mle 1907 rifle. By 1914 the mle 1892 was in service with many arms other than the artillery for which it was originally intended, and the mles 1890 and 1892 met most of the carbine requirements of the French armed forces during World War I. In 1916 they were joined by the **mle 1916** (a carbine version of the Berthier mle 1916 rifle with its five-round box magazine), but relatively few of these were produced.

While carriage of these various carbines was certainly easier than that of the long service rifles, firing them was an unpleasant experience. All the carbine versions of standard rifles had two

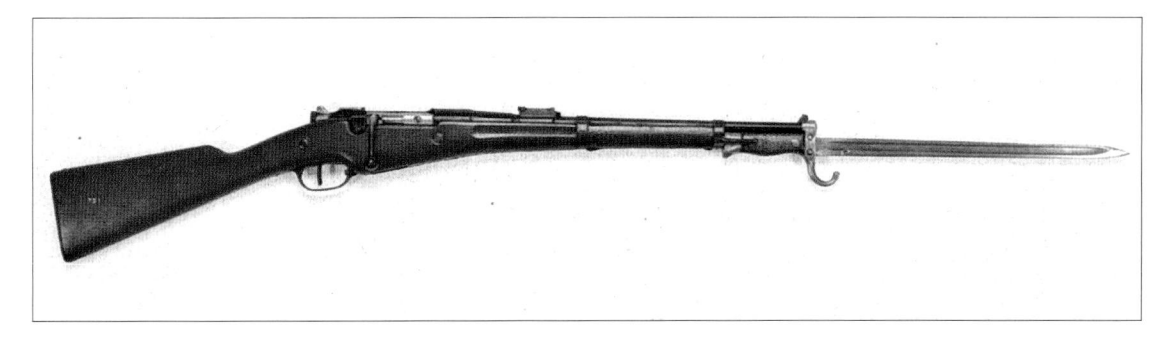

Above: The Mousqueton Berthier 1890 et 1892 was the forerunner of the Berthier rifles, and is seen here with the Sabre-Bajonette mle 92/16 used during World War I. The magazine held only three rounds, but the carbine handled well, retaining, however, the violent recoil 'kick' of all carbines.

nasty drawbacks when fired: excessive flash combined with blast, and heavy recoil giving a pronounced 'kick' as the bullet left the muzzle. Both were produced by the fact that the cartridges were designed for barrels of conventional length. In the carbine some of the firing gases were still unexpended as the bullet left the muzzle, producing the flash and blast that in turn produced the recoil. The carbines were thus not much liked as weapons but were simply carried in lieu of the more awkward rifles. When they were used in action it was very much as a last resort and their performance was at best indifferent when compared with rifles of orthodox size and length.

Specification
Mousqueton Berthier mle 1892
Calibre: 8 mm (0.315 in)
Length: overall 0.945 m (37.2 in); barrel 0.45 m (17.7 in)
Weight: 3.1 kg (6.83 lb)
Muzzle velocity: 634 m (2,080 ft) per second
Magazine: 3-round box

French cavalrymen carrying Berthier carbines pass elements of the 58th (London) Division during April 1918. At that stage of the war the cavalry were still held in reserve in case of the breakthrough that never came, for by then their place had been taken by the tank.

A French soldier in the Dardenelles during 1915 is seen here with a Berthier mle 1892 carbine fitted with a long knife bayonet. The use of such

a carbine would indicate that he is not a foot soldier but possibly some form of specialist such as a signaller.

Fusil Berthier mle 1907

Soon after the Lebel had been adopted for service it was appreciated that the design had several drawbacks, the most important being the use of a tubular magazine. By the time this had been realized the Lebel was in large-scale production so there was little chance of any immediate change-over to a new design. Instead there began a slow and gradual process of introducing a new rifle design known generally as the **Berthier**. This began in 1890 with the introduction of a cavalry carbine and gradually as new requirements arose new Berthier weapons were introduced.

This culminated in 1907 with the adoption of a **Fusil mle 1907** for use in the various French colonies (Indo-

China in particular). The Berthier rifle was typical of the Berthier series for it was a long, slender weapon that used a box magazine and a bolt action based on that already in use on the Lebel. While the change-over to the box magazine was a belated but good move, the Berthier magazine could hold only three rounds, a poor capacity in comparison with those of rifles already in use elsewhere, and therefore something of a disadvantage to the firer.

The mle 1907 was widely used by French troops serving in the colonies, and more were issued to colonial levies. Some were even issued to troops on the mainland of France, but in 1914 the Lebel was still the standard

rifle. The situation was changed by 1915, for by then the French forces were expanding rapidly in numbers and weapons were in short supply. Accordingly the Berthier was rushed into mass production, the mle 1907 being used as the baseline model. Some changes had to be made to the finer design points (especially to the bolt and sights) and the resultant weapon became the **mle 1907/15**. It was soon in service alongside the Lebel, and was used by the French armed forces throughout World War I, and was still in widespread use in 1939.

The mle 1907/15 still retained the three-round box magazine, however, and this was clearly insufficient for the requirements of 1915. Accordingly the

basic design was altered so that a five-round box could be used, and this variant was later placed into production as the **mle 1916**; it could be distinguished by the box magazine protruding from under the fore-stock, whereas on the mle 1907/15 the magazine was flush with the woodwork. The mle 1916 even had the facility to use a charging clip for loading the five rounds, a feature lacking on the mle 1907/15 in which each round had to be loaded individually.

The mle 1907/15 and mle 1916 soon became popular rifles. They certainly had a very attractive appearance for even under wartime production conditions the graceful shape of the long fore-stock was retained. In service the

Berthiers were rather long for the conditions of trench warfare, but they were easy to handle when firing and were usually preferred to the Lebel. The mle 1907/15 was manufactured in large quantities, and at one point was even placed in production by Remington in the United States, but only for French use as the US Army never used the type. The final development of the type occurred in 1934, when mle 1907/15 weapons were modified to fire the 7.5-mm (0.295-in) round developed for light machine-guns. The revised designation was **mle 1907/15 M34**, and the type had a five-round magazine.

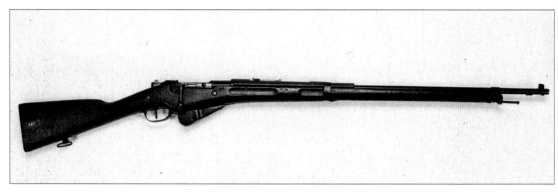

Specification
Fusil Berthier mle 1907/15
Calibre: 8 mm (0.315 in)
Length: overall 1.306 m (51.4 in); barrel 0.797 m (31.4 in)
Weight: 3.8 kg (8.38 lb)
Muzzle velocity: 725 m (2,379 ft) per second
Magazine: 3-round box

Usually known as the Berthier rifle, the mle 1907 was a rifle version of the mle 1890 et 1892 carbine. This example is a mle 1916 modified from the original to take a five-round box magazine. This version was used by many armies after 1918, and was still in widespread use in 1939.

BELGIUM/GERMANY
Fusil FN-Mauser mle 1889

The Belgian **Fusil FN-Mauser mle 1889** is something of an international weapon, for although it was designed in Belgium the action was a direct copy of the Mauser bolt action. It was accepted as the standard Belgian service rifle in 1889 and although some of them came from the Belgian state arsenal, most were produced by an entirely new concern established specifically to manufacture the Model 1889, the Fabrique Nationale, now more commonly known as FN and one of the largest arms manufacturing establishments in the world.

As was then usual the mle 1889 was accompanied by a carbine variant, the **Carabine FN-Mauser mle 1889**, some of which were intended to be used in conjunction with a sword-like bayonet known as a 'Yatagan'; most of these were issued to fortress troops and some Gendarmerie units. In its rifle form the mle 1889 was a very well-made weapon with some unusual features. One was that over its entire length the barrel was encased in a metal tube. This was intended to ensure that the barrel would not come into contact with any of the woodwork, which was prone to warping and could thus impair accuracy. While this feature had some advantages, such as the ability to mount the sights on the tube and not on the barrel, it was rather expensive to manufacture and under some conditions rust could accumulate between the barrel and the tube. But this was a long-term condition and during World War I caused few problems.

When it entered service, the mle 1889 was set for a long life, for it remained in use until 1940, and even after that date the type was taken in German garrison use. Some examples were manufactured for export to Abyssinia and a few nations in South America, but generally speaking the mle 1889 was kept in production for the Belgian army only. When the Germans overran much of Belgium in 1914 the requirements of the remaining Belgian forces

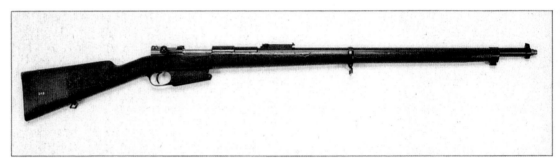

The Belgian mle 1889 was a Mauser design built under licence, and had a distinctive muzzle surround and a pronounced curve to the front of the five-round magazine. It was produced at the FN plant at Herstal and remained the standard Belgian service rifle until World War II.

were met by switching production to Hopkins & Allen in the United States. For much of the war the small Belgian army was stationed on the far left of the Allied trench lines along the River Lys, when conditions were not suitable for large-scale troop movements, and accordingly the Belgian positions remained static for much of World War II.

The mle 1889 may be distinguished from other Mauser weapons by the magazine, which had a distinctive bulge on its forward edge. This bulge accommodated the hinge of the magazine platform that fed the rounds upwards into the bolt mechanism under the control of a leaf spring. The box magazine held five rounds fed into the box from a charger clip, and unlike the practice in later Mauser magazines the rounds were held in a vertical stack. (The later versions used a 'staggered'

arrangement.) Another recognition point is the barrel jacket, which extends to some way behind the muzzle. The usual Mauser cleaning rod was present and a long bayonet could be fitted.

Specification
Fusil FN-Mauser mle 1889
Calibre: 7.65 mm (0.301 in)
Length: overall 1.295 m (51.0 in); barrel 0.78 m (30.6 in)
Weight: 4.01 kg (8.8 lb)
Muzzle velocity: 610 m (2,001 ft) per second
Magazine: 5-round box

Belgian troops armed with mle 1889 Mauser rifles set up a roadblock outside Louvain in a vain attempt to arrest the onrush of the German armies through Belgium during August 1914.

Into the Unknown

Before the war it was assumed that the great increases in firepower produced by the magazine rifle and quick-fire artillery would make battles more bloody but no less decisive. But the new firepower simply drove the armies into the earth, and machine-guns kept them there.

When war broke out in 1914 there were few tacticians on either side who could envisage the manner in which the machine-gun was to dominate infantry tactics in the years to come. That with the better appreciation was the German side, for the Germans alone had taken the care to invest in numbers of these weapons adequate to equip their infantry units, and in 1914 the effect of these weapons was profound. A single machine-gun is sufficient to arrest the movement of an entire infantry or cavalry battalion at times, but in 1914 this simple fact was a novelty and the tacticians of the time could think of nothing other than getting behind some form of protection until a set-piece attack could be mounted. In practice this meant the digging of trenches, but it was to be four years before the infantry could get out of them.

In 1914 armies on all sides were prepared for a war with the usual man-oeuvres and marching warfare that would bring the two sides to battle. Accordingly the infantry trained to march over long distances and when the time came for action the idea was for whole battalions to advance to positions where fire fights would dictate the eventual result. This era did not last long, coming to an abrupt halt with the Battle of the Frontiers for the French, and with Mons and Ypres for the small British Expeditionary Force (BEF). Away in the east the Russian steamroller was annihilated in the vast wheeling battles of Tannenberg and all the others, for on the Eastern Front the static conditions of trench warfare never became fully established and a form of mobile warfare prevailed right until 1917, when the Russians withdrew from the unequal contest.

Once the trench lines were set up on the Western Front, infantry tactics became moribund for some years. And when the 'Old Contemptibles' of the BEF had vanished in the holocaust of Loos in 1915, the greater part of the British army was made up of barely-trained conscripts led by junior officers who were only marginally better trained. The French too had lost their best soldiers in the early stages of the war and were content to base themselves on their trench lines for what were essentially local offensives. For much of the war these operations were confined to local trench raids at night and perhaps the odd company action against limited objectives.

In all these actions apart from the raids the infantry tactics were much the same. A prearranged artillery bombardment was directed against known enemy positions, and at a pre-set time the infantry clambered out of the trenches and walked towards the enemy lines. In the years since 1918 these simple tactics have come in for much criticism, but the fact remains that given the state of manning and training in most armies the protagonists had little alternative. The standard of training and understanding of military basics was such that conscripts had to be used en masse, with little finesse in the way of advancing with mutual fire support between units or the use of flanking support moves. It was quite simply a case of massing enough men, attempting to destroy the enemy's positions and weapons with artillery, and then advancing in a straight line towards the enemy trenches where (if they arrived) the soldiers could engage in hand-to-hand fighting.

The first shot of this ciné film sequence taken during the Battle of the Somme in 1916 shows an officer leading a section of British infantry out of a trench. The officer wears jodphurs and carries a cane, making him an obvious target; later in the war they carried rifles and wore battledress.

Above: The unfortunate man on the right appears to have become one of the many dead, and did not even make it out of the start trench.

Below: His comrades are already on their way through the machine-gun fire, but as so often in 1916 few will actually reach their objective across no-man's land.

The tactics were for many years as crude as that, and as the world now knows in many cases the unfortunate infantry never even made it beyond the middle of the 'no-man's land' that divided the trench lines. Some of the enemy's machine-guns always managed to survive the artillery fire and pop out of the dugouts and bunkers in time to halt the advancing infantry.

However, for much of 1915 the German army was on the defensive while tacticians pondered on how to break the trench-warfare deadlock. In 1916 they came up with the dreadful philosophy of the 'killing ground', which they put into action at Verdun. This philosophy was meant to make the French army defend an area chosen by the Germans in such a manner that the German war machine would simply grind away the strength of its foe. But in order to make the French defend Verdun the Germans had first to attack and this they did in a more sophisticated manner. Instead of the extended lines of walking infantry, the Germans attacked with small sections of infantry supported by light machine-guns, moving forward not in an extended line but in short unco-ordinated rushes that diverted the defenders and dispersed defensive fire. The attack was still preceded by the usual massive artillery action that tore up the ground, but in the main this favoured the attackers. Although the Verdun battles were eventually lost by the Germans, in that their original objectives were not achieved, the novel tactics were noted for future use.

They were certainly not adopted by the British in 1916 when the Somme offensives went ahead in exactly the same manner as those of 1915. Lines of infantry rose out of their trenches at the appointed time and walked forward in extended lines. The only changes from 1915 was that the preliminary artillery barrage was much heavier and that more use was made of chemical warfare. In the latter stages of the offensive the tank appeared on the scene, but only in small numbers that did not make a material contribution.

The tank was nevertheless to have the greatest effect on infantry tactics of the time, but 1918 started with the Germans once more refining their Verdun

This is the type of terrain over which the infantry of both sides had to advance during the many battles of the war. The open, pock-marked landscape was dominated by artillery and the machine-gun, and men could only survive underground or behind protection such as that supplied by tank armour.

If the German machine-guns were not enough of an obstacle in no-man's land, the barbed wire could always be relied on to slow down a rushed attack to a slow walk. The standing infantry made ideal targets for enemy machine-gunners and riflemen, in their relatively safe trenches.

tactics for use during the last major German offensives, arranged to crush the Allies before the Americans could arrive on the scene in vast numbers. In a series of set-piece battles the German infantry were used in small squads that moved forward, taking advantage of cover and ground where possible, to sweep past rather than into the Allied trenches to create mayhem in the rear areas. These new tactics worked wonderfully. Allied formations, conditioned by years of static trench warfare, were suddenly faced with swarms of small infantry squads moving through their lines while gas, artillery and even tanks kept them occupied and seeking what cover there might be to hand. These German tactics created great holes in the Allied lines, and the Germans were halted only when final reserves had been brought up from the rear areas. But it had been a near-run thing, especially for the British forces in front of Amiens.

Eventually the German offensive petered 'out. By the middle of the year the Allies were ready for their final offensive, and this time it was to be different. The years since 1914 had not all been spent in carrying out the same mistakes over and over again, and with the advent of the tank new tactics could be used. The early conscript armies had grown not only in numbers but in skills, and the long series of attacks that finally defeated the Germans on their own terms were made not by the old set-piece attacks but by tactics based on a high degree of inter-arm co-operation. No longer did the artillery simply blast a way through the trench lines: instead it provided a lifting barrage of defensive fire as the infantry and tank advanced in mutual support. Overhead the new Royal Air Force, corrected artillery fire and flew ground-attack sorties. Some units were even supplied at times from the air using parachuted stores and ammunition. No one arm moved forward by itself. It was a balanced and co-operative effort using tactics that were to see their full fruition in World War II. No longer was the foot soldier simply a rifle-carrier. Instead he moved forward with fire support from tanks and artillery to occupy territory and winkle out the enemy from his positions. It was a very long way from the early days of August 1914.

The Second Naval Brigade practise an attack on Imbros, June 1915. The dense rush of men provided an excellent target for those Turks who had survived the British barrage. On the Western Front fluid small-unit tactics were gradually introduced, and contributed greatly to the German breakthrough in March 1918.

Above: After its disastrous performance in the Balkan wars of 1912-3, the Turkish army was once again written off as an effective force. But to the surprise of their enemies, the Turks fought with dogged tenacity when the British and French attacked at Gallipoli. This Turk carries a Mauser rifle and a packed cartridge belt. The cloth hat shaped like a solar topee but without a peak replaced the traditional fez in 1908.

Above: The tactics that were to be used by the German stormtroopers of March 1918 were formulated during 1917 when small squads of infantry attacked using hand grenades as their main weapons. This picture was taken at the German training area at Sedan. Note how rifles were carried slung.

Below: Taken from the German trench lines, this photograph shows troops advancing across open terrain. The troops in the foreground still have their rifles slung, perhaps indicating that they are about to move forward to a support position that cannot be seen from the camera position used.

Mosin-Nagant Model 1891

By the late 1880s the Russian army was in the process of converting its massive forces away from the use of the obsolete Berdan rifles. The army carried out a series of investigations, in the course of which it was attracted by a number of rifles produced by the Belgian Nagant brothers, but it also had on its doorstep a design produced by a tsarist officer known as Sergei Mosin. The planners decided to amalgamate the best features of the two designs and the result was the **Mosin-Nagant** rifle which was introduced into service in 1891; its full Russian title was **Russkaya 3-lineinaye vintovka obrazets 1891g** (Russian 3-line rifle model 1891).

The term '3-line' in the designation denotes that the calibre was gauged in an old Russian linear measurement known as a line, equal to 2.54-mm (0.1 in). This was later changed in 1908 when a new cartridge was introduced and the calibre became 7.62 mm (0.3 in). The original sights were calibrated in the equally old arshins (1 arshin = 0.71 m = 27.95 in), but these too were changed to metres after 1908. Overall the Model 1891 was a sound and rugged rifle design but it did have a few unusual features. One was found in the five-cartridge magazine, for with the system employed the top cartridge was always kept free of magazine spring pressure for the actual bolt-loading process, which had the advantage that feeding jams were less frequent than they might otherwise have been. But this was balanced by the introduction of some complexity in the mechanism. The two-piece bolt was also generally judged to be more complicated than was really necessary, though it gave little enough trouble in use. One other unusual feature was that the rifle was issued with a long bayonet with a screwdriver point that could be used to dismantle parts of the rifle. This bayonet was of the socket type, and during World War 1 it was a virtual fixture on the rifle at all times.

Overall the Model 1891 was a rugged weapon that could take hard knocks and was generally undemanding of care and attention. A **Dragoon Rifle Model 1891** carbine version was produced for use by cavalry and the ubiquitous Russian mounted infantry, but this variant was only slightly shorter than the rifle and much longer than other carbines produced at the time; a genuine **Carbine Model 1910** variant was produced in 1910.

The main problem for the Russians was that they had selected a good service rifle, but there were never enough of them and production facili-

Above: The Russian army went to war in the Slavic uniforms adopted after 1877 and armed with the rugged Mosin-Nagant series of rifles. Lack of competent commanders rather than a shortage of modern equipment was to lead to the heavy defeats of 1914.

ties were overstretched. Those that existed had to make the rifles virtually by hand as the concept of mass production was far from Russian thoughts before 1914. Consequently, when extra Russian army units were formed from the reserves in 1914 there were very often no rifles with which to arm them.

Above: These Russian troops are armed with Mosin-Nagant Model 1891 rifles, all with the long spike bayonets that were such a fixture that the sights were usually adjusted permanently to compensate for their weight. The bayonets used the ancient socket method of fixing.

Part of the Russian contingent is seen at Salonika in July 1916. This was the last year in which the Russian army could adequately sustain combat;

The Model 1891 played its part in the revolutions of 1917 and was again in action during the civil war that followed in 1918. Between the wars the Model 1891 was replaced in production by the shorter **Model 1891/30**, and it was with this that the Red Army was armed in World War II, though some Model 1891s survived after 1941.

the Herculean offensive launched by General Brusilov dealt a savage blow to Austria-Hungary but could not save the tottering Tsarist empire.

Specification
Mosin-Nagant Model 1891
Calibre: 7.62 mm (0.3 in)
Length: overall 1.305 m (51.38 in); barrel 0.802 m (31.6 in)
Weight: 4.37 kg (9.62 lb)
Muzzle velocity: 810 m (2,657 ft) per second
Magazine: 5-round box

Fucile modello 91

The Italian service rifle of World War I was the **Fucile modello 91**, and was of a type known as the **Mannlicher-Carcano**. This was developed at Turin Arsenal between 1890 and 1891 and was an overall amalgamation of a Mauser bolt action taken from the Belgian/German mle 1889, the box magazine arrangement of the Mannlicher system and a new bolt-sleeve safety device produced by one Salvatore Carcano. The Italians thought highly of the resultant weapon and adopted it in 1892; it remained the standard Italian service rifle until World War II.

Unfortunately no else seemed to

share their enthusiasm, for the only sales made outside Italy before World War I were to Japan, and this batch was made to accommodate the Japanese 6.5-mm (0.256-in) round which differed in dimensions from that in Italian use. In service the modello

91s proved sound enough, but the amalgamation of diverse features in the bolt and magazine areas resulted in a design that was rather more complicated than it might have been, and in the field the modello 91 required considerable attention, especially in

This Mannlicher-Carcano carbine is the 6.5-mm (0.256-in) Moschetto modello 91 per cavalleria. As it was meant for use by cavalry troops it has a fixed folding bayonet and the magazine held six rounds, but many were used with other special troops such as gunners and signallers.

the colonial territories in Africa; in particular, the straight-pull bolt action was prone to jamming when dirty.

The modello 91 spawned a whole group of carbine types that were produced in variants for use by cavalry, special troops (including gunners and engineers) and others. While these carbines were handy and easy to carry they suffered from the usual shortcomings inherent on firing short-barrelled weapons, even though the cartridge used was less powerful than many others then in use elsewhere. Some of these carbines were provided with spiked bayonets; the modello 91 rifle used a knife-type bayonet.

As the modello 91 was used only by the Italians during World War I their service use was confined to the border campaigns against Austro-Hungarian troops, coming to a climax with the Battle of Caporetto in 1917. During this action the Italians lost heavily and the resultant withdrawals led to some Brit-

ish divisions being diverted from the Western Front in an attempt to stabilize matters. The outcome of Caporetto was not due entirely to the performance of the modello 91, which was much the same as that of many of its contemporaries, but even at the time it was generally accepted that the Italian 6.5-mm cartridge was rather underpowered and the bullet it fired generally lacked striking power. But these points were marginal, for the modello 91 handled and fired quite well. The small cartridge produced less recoil than was usual among other designs (though the carbine versions kicked as nastily as other types) and the general lack of protrusions and items that could catch on things made the modello 91 a good weapon to use when moving across rough country. But even now the overall impression left by the modello 91 is that it was a rather more complicated weapon than others of the time, and despite the Italians' under-

Troops of the 35th Italian Division march through Salonika during August 1916, carrying their Mannlicher-Carcano modello 91

standable enthusiasm for a national product it was among the 'also rans' in the World War I rifle stakes.

Specification
Fucile modello 91
Calibre: 6.5 mm (0.256 in)

rifles at the trail. Known as the Fucile modello 91, this rifle was still in service in 1940. It differed from the normal Mannlicher rifles only in detail.

Length: overall 1.285 m (50.6 in); barrel 0.78 m (30.7 in)
Weight: 3.8 kg (8.4 lb)
Muzzle veclocity: 630 m (2,067 ft) per second
Magazine: 6-round box

Mannlicher Modell 1895

By the early 1890s the Austro-Hungarian army had in service a number of types of rifle based on the bolt action designed by Ferdinand von Mannlicher. This employed a straight-pull bolt action of two-piece construction, and the first of the type was taken into service as early as 1884. There followed a number of models with various modifications, all of them firing the old black-powder propellant, and it was 1890 before the first 'smokeless' model appeared. It was not until 1895 that the design was finally 'frozen' and it was thus that the **Mannlicher Modell 1895**, also known as the **8-mm Repetier Gewehr Modell 1895** (8-mm repeating rifle model 1895) became the standard rifle of the Austro-Hungarian army.

The Modell 1895 was a sound and straightforward weapon that proved reliable in service. Like so many other rifles of the period the Modell 1895 was rather long but the straight-pull bolt action appears to have produced few problems. It fired the 8-mm (0.315-in) Modell 1890 round-nosed cartridge that was the first Austro-Hungarian round with smokeless propellant, and these were introduced into the five-round integral box magazine by using a cartridge clip and a charger guide on the receiver, in itself something of an innovation for the time.

It was the Modell 1895 that the Austro-Hungarian armies carried when they went to war in 1914. By then the rifles had been joined by a carbine variant known as the **Modell 1895 8-mm Repetier-Stutzen-Gewehr** and issued to troops such as engineers, drivers, signallers and gunners. For once the usual proliferation of carbine types did not occur in the Austro-Hungarian armies and the Stutzen became a familiar sight throughout Central Europe, during World War I and after it, for the Modell 1895 rifle and carbine became virtual fixtures for many armies. One of the first to adopt the Modell 1895 was Bulgaria. After 1918 the type was taken over by Italy in war reparations and the rifle became one of the standard Italian weapons. Others ended up in Greece and Yugoslavia, and of course once the Austro-Hungarian Empire had been split up after 1918 both Austria and Hungary

Above: The Mannlicher Modell 1895 was the standard service rifle of the Austro-Hungarian army and fired a 6.5-mm (0.256-in) cartridge. It was a sound and strong weapon with a five-round box magazine and a straight-pull bolt action. The projection under the muzzle is a cleaning rod.

Below: Austro-Hungarian troops outside Jaroslav carry their Mannlicher Modell 1895s. This rifle used a straight-pull bolt action and was known as the Repetier-Gewehr from its use of a five-round box magazine compared with earlier Mannlicher rifles, such as the Modell 1890.

retained their familiar weapons.

Both the Modell 1895 and the Stutzen are now collector's pieces but for a very long period they were the standard service weapons of much of Central Europe. They were sound if unspectacular weapons that provided good service for over half a century.

Specification
Repetier-Gewehr Modell 1895
Calibre: 8 mm (0.315 in)
Length: overall 1.27 m (50 in); barrel 0.765 m (30.1 in)

Weight: 3.78 kg (8.3 lb)
Muzzle velocity: 619 m (2,031 ft) per second
Magazine: 5-round box

Recruited from a bewildering variety of nationalities, the Austro-Hungarian army proved to be a deceptively fragile instrument. As the war dragged on the Empire was forced to rely on the sort of hapless conscripts epitomized by the Good Soldier Svějk.

Model 1903 Springfield

At the turn of the century the US Army was equipped with a rifle known as the Krag-Jorgensen which had been adopted in 1892. It was not long before the Americans realized that in the rapid developments of the late 1800s the Krag-Jorgensen left a lot to be desired and accordingly decided to adopt a better rifle. They cast around for ideas and were soon impressed sufficiently with the basic Mauser system to negotiate a licence to manufacture Mauser-based rifles in the USA.

The Mauser system was modified to produce a rifle built around a new American cartridge known as the Cartridge, Ball, Caliber .30 in M1903. This had a blunt nose but when the Germans introduced their 'spitzer' sharpnosed bullet with better all-round performance the Americans were quick to follow suit and the rifle was accordingly modified to what was to be its classic form. In fact the rifle was ready in 1903, and was first manufactured at the Springfield Arsenal in Illinois, whence it took its generally-accepted name of the **Springfield** rifle. In appearance it was obviously a Mauser but the length was something new.

The new rifle was officially the **Magazine Rifle, Caliber .30, Model of 1903**, but this was usually abbreviated to **Model 1903** or simply **M1903**. It differed from most of its contemporares by being an interim length between a full-length rifle and a carbine, for it was intended to be the service rifle for all arms from cavalry to infantry. This compromise between lengths resulted in an extremely attractive and well-balanced rifle that was and still is a joy to handle. The bolt action was of the turn-down design with a well-placed bolt handle that was easy to operate rapidly when required; the overall fine standard of finish and detail design made the weapon extremely accurate, and the M1903 and its later versions are still much prized as target rifles. The original Model 1903 was the rifle

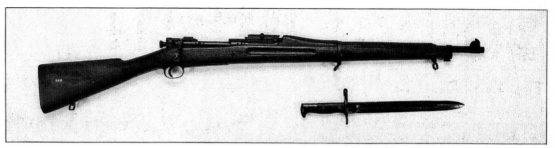

Above: The American M1903 Springfield was a Mauser-based rifle first introduced in 1903 and still in service during the Korean War. It was an excellent weapon and this is the original version, shown with a bayonet from the earlier Krag-Jorgensen Model 1896 service rifle.

the US Army took to France in 1917 but it was soon overtaken on the production lines by later variants including the **M1903 Mk 1**. This was basically a model 1903 adapted to accommodate the ill-fated Pedersen Device, a gadget that was supposed to turn the bolt action rifle into a form of automatic assault rifle by removing the bolt and replacing it with a new receiver firing special 7.62-mm (0.3-in) pistol ammunition fed from an overhead magazine; the rounds were fired using the normal rifle barrel. Although this device was issued, it was produced too late for widespread issue and was held in reserve for the expected offensives of 1919. After the war it was withdrawn from use altogether, the Mk 1 rifles being converted back to normal Model 1903 standards.

After 1918 the Model 1903 was further

The first contingent of American troops that arrived in England in 1917 are seen here with M1903 Springfields piled. They are probably men from the famous

'Rainbow Division' formed from all the states of the Union and the first to be sent to Europe, where their fresh numbers would have ensured an eventual Allied victory.

er modified into various forms, usually with a view to easier production, and it was still in US Army service as a sniper rifle as late as the Korean War. By any standards it is still regarded as one of the best service rifles of its period, and quite apart from its continuing use as a target rifle, the type is now retained as a collector's item.

Specification
M1903
Calibre: 7.62 mm (0.3 in)
Length: overall 1.097 m (43.2 in); barrel 0.61 m (24 in)
Weight: 3.94 kg (8.69 lb)
Muzzle velocity: 853 m (2,800 ft) per second
Magazine: 5-round integral box

Winchester Model 1895

It may seem rather odd to have a rifle more usually regarded as being part of the plains warfare of the American West included in a study of the rifles of World War I, but the fact remains that the **Winchester Model 1895** was for one nation an important part of its World War I inventory. That nation was Russia, which entered the war with a will in 1914 only to suffer a series of catastrophic defeats of which the Battle of Tannenburg was but one. The basic problem for the Russian military planners was that although they had almost bottomless reserves of men they lacked the industrial base to equip them. The Russian economy before 1914 was indeed getting itself on an industrial footing, but it was as yet insufficient to sustain wartime production. Matters got to the point where soldiers were sent into battle without rifles but were expected to obtain them from among the fallen. Things clearly could not continue for long like that.

The easy way out was to purchase weapons from abroad. The Americans duly obliged and in particular the Winchester Repeating Arms Company of New Haven, Connecticut, took the opportunity to use the assembly line

for its well-known range of manually-loaded rifles that used the loading lever beneath the trigger. This was operated by the fingers that gripped the stock; a rapid downwards movement loaded a new round from the tubular magazine under the barrel. By World War I this type of rifle was militarily obsolescent but it suited the Russian requirement and accordingly a 'militarized' version was churned out especially for the Russian army.

This was the Model 1895, which was chambered for the Russians 7.62-mm (0.3-in) cartridge and had sights calibrated in arshins, then the usual method of range measurement used in Russia (1 arshin = 0.71 m = 27.95 in). The resultant rifle could still be recognized as a descendant of the famous Winchester 75 of plains fame, but overall it was longer, heavier and more rugged. It needed to be, for all that

made it to Russia (some were lost as a result of U-boat attacks) were sent straight to the front, and into the hands of rapidly-trained recruits who had little time for maintenance and cleaning. In all 293,816 were actually delivered to Russia and those that survived the rigours of the fighting against German and Austro-Hungarian armies later played their part in the revolutions of 1917 and in the civil war that followed. Moreover, some were captured by the Germans in World War II. It was noticed that some of these 'later' examples had their sights marked in metres, but when this was carried out is uncertain.

By any standard the appearance of the Winchester Model 1895 on the Battlefields of World War I was odd, but it happened nevertheless. Few records actually survive of how the Model 1895 fared in action but no doubt it gave a

good account of itself. It was almost certainly the only lever-action rifle to be used during World War I and on that score alone it is worthy of mention.

Specification
Winchester Model 1895
Calibre: 7.62 mm (0.3 in)
Length: overall 1.175 m (46.25 in); barrel 0.71 m (28 in)
Weight: 4.2 kg (9.26 lb)
Muzzle velocity: not known
Magazine: 5-round tubular

One of the oddest rifles of World War I was the Winchester Model 1895 that still used the Winchester lever action made famous on the American Plains. They were ordered by Russia in 1914 to arm the expanding Tsarist armies. 293,816 were produced and sent to Russia, all in 7.62-mm (0.3-in) calibre.

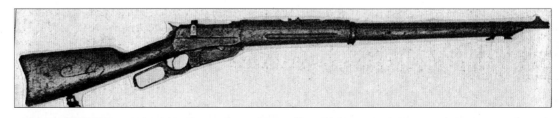

Pistols of the Great War

It was a pistol shot that led to the start of World War I, and once the conflict had engulfed the world, pistol production accelerated. Carried by officers, specialists and airmen, they were used on every front; some weapons stayed in service until after World War II, and a couple are still in production.

An officer of the Worcesters holds a service 0.455 Webley revolver during the battle of the Aisne, May 1918.

World War I was probably the last major conflict in which the pistol was involved as a major weapon of war. Most of the pistol's drawbacks (such as lack of useful range, lack of stopping power at other than close quarters and so forth) were all rendered void by the very nature of the conflict in the trenches. Most soldiers suffered from long-range weapons such as artillery, but often had to fight within the close confines of trenches or in hand-to-hand fighting. Here the pistol retained its combat effectiveness to a greater extent than many other weapons, including the rifle, and it was only when the sub-machine gun came on the scene in 1918 that the days of the combat pistol were numbered.

The number of types of pistol in use during World War I was remarkable. With the introduction of the automatic pistol, small-arms inventors used their considerable ingenuity to produce all manner of automatic self-loading mechanisms. Sometimes the ingenuity was used to get round existing patents while at other times sheer inventiveness won through. The revolver was still around in many forms, some of them getting rather long in the tooth, even by contemporary standards, but such was the state of development of many automatic pistols of the period that revolvers were frequently preferred to the automatic on grounds of reliability.

Some 'classic' pistols will be found in this study, some of them to be just as famous during World War II. The P '08 Luger is included along with the Mauser C/96 and such stalwarts as the Webley revolvers. Oddities such as the Webley Fosbery automatic revolver are also included, along with more orthodox weapons such as the first Beretta automatic pistol.

All these weapons had their part to play in World War I. On the whole they were large and heavy weapons that fired heavy bullets, often with considerable man-stopping power and the ability to produce dreadful wounds. Most of them have now passed from the scene, apart from those in the hands of collectors, but they were formidable weapons during the 'Great War'.

Royal Navy officers use a dangerous combination of weapons: Webley and Scott automatics and Webley revolvers. The mighty 0.456 bullet fired by the automatics was propelled by a fast-burning 7-grain charge, and it fitted the 0.455 revolver. If loaded by mistake it would blow the cylinder out.

Savage Model 1907 and 1915

The **Savage Model 1907** pistol was produced by the Savage Arms Corporation of Chicopee Falls, Massachussets, and other than some commercial sales it was acquired by only one military customer, the Portuguese armed forces. This has led to the Savage pistols being virtually identified with the Portuguese though their origins were definitely American.

The Savage Model 1907 was originally designed to take part in the US Army trials that led to adoption of the Colt M1911 automatic. The Model 1907 showed up well in the trials, and although the decision went elsewhere the Savage Corporation attempted to sell the design abroad. It was not successful until 1914, when the Portuguese found themselves cut off from their usual suppliers in Germany who were selling them versions of the Pistole '08 (the Luger). The Portuguese thus decided to adopt the Savage pistol in its original US Army competition form (as the **M/908**) and in a slightly modified version (as the **M/915**), both rechambered from their original 0.45 in (11.43 mm) to 7.65 mm (0.315 in).

The Model 1907 used a retarded blowback mechanism, an operating system rarely used in pistols. On the Model 1907 this involved the barrel turning through lugs before the slide was allowed to move to the rear after firing, but the system adopted by Savage was only marginally more effective than a simple blowback. It was effective enough with the 7.65-mm cartridge employed but would probably have been less successful with anything heavier over a prolonged period

of firing.

The Portuguese found the Savage pistols effective enough, but the pistol had one unfortunate safety problem. It was possible to rest the striker attached to the cocking spur (the design featured a concealed hammer) in such a way that the striker touched the base of a round in the chamber. Any sudden jar could therefore fire the weapon, often to the user's disadvantage (at best). This led to drills that ensured the pistol was cocked only

when required and if no firing was carried out the pistol had to be unloaded again. This was obviously not a good feature for a combat pistol, so as soon as they could the Portuguese reverted to procuring 9-mm Parabellum pistols of various types; they also used the British 0.455-in Webley revolvers.

Specification
M/908
Calibre: 7.65 mm (0.315 in)
Weight: 0.568 kg (1.252 lb)

This Savage Automatic belongs to the Weapons Museum at the School of Infantry, Warminster. The Savage design originated from the 1904 patent of E.H. Searle and was an entry to the US Army pistol trials of 1907, which were won by Colt.

Lengths: overall 165 mm (6.5 in); barrel 95 mm (3.75 in)
Muzzle velocity: 290 m (950 ft) per second
Magazine capacity: 10 rounds

0.45-in M1917 revolvers

By 1916 the demands for all types of war materials and weapons were outstripping the production capabilities of British and Commonwealth industries, so orders for various items were placed in the USA. Among these items were revolvers, and to save time it was decided to adopt American designs rechambered to accept the British 0.455-in (actually 0.441-in/11.2-mm) pistol cartridge. Many thousands of these pistols were accordingly placed into production by Smith & Wesson and the Colt Firearms Company, and were duly delivered to the British and Commonwealth armed forces.

Then in 1917 the USA entered the war and found itself even shorter of weapons to equip its expeditionary force than the British had ever been. It was time for yet another hasty rearrangement of production priorities and the British 0.455-in revolvers were quickly altered to accommodate the standard American 0.45-in (11.43-mm) pistol cartridge. This caused some problems, not in the pistol designs which remained unchanged (and virtually identical to each other) but in the loading. The British cartridge case had a distinct rim at its base while the American case, intended for use in automatic pistols, did not. Therefore as the cartridges were placed in the cylinder chambers they slipped through. This was avoided by loading the American rounds in 'half-moon' pressed steel clips, each holding three rounds. The clips allowed the rounds to be loaded quickly and held the cases in place for firing and unloading.

Both revolvers were provided with the designation **M1917**, the maker's name being appended to denote the different models. Although the two pistols were virtually identical to the users, there were in fact slight differences. The Colt revolver was based on the 'New Service' model dating from 1897, while the Smith & Wesson pistol was a 'new' design based on the company's existing range of models. Both used swing-out cylinders which, on the M1917 versions, had recesses in their rear face to accommodate the half-moon clips. Both were large and heavy revolvers.

Once in US Army service both pistols proved rugged and reliable. The three-round clip system gave no trouble and proved so successful that it was even adopted for service by other nations such as Brazil, which made large-scale purchases of the Smith & Wesson M1917 in 1938. Both pistols were still in service during World War II, although by then most were used by the British armed forces.

Specification
M1917
Calibre: 11.43 mm (0.45 in)
Weight: (Colt M1917) 1.134 kg (2.5 lb);

The US Army adopted several revolvers in 1917 chambered for 0.45 Auto, like the M1911 Automatic. US enthusiasm for 0.45 calibre stemmed from the failure of 0.38s like this Colt M1892 to stop charging Filipino tribesmen.

(Smith & Wesson M1917) 1.02 kg (2.25 lb)
Lengths: overall 274 mm (10.8 in); barrel 140 mm (5.5 in)
Muzzle velocity: 253 m (830 ft) per second
Cylinder capacity: 6 rounds in two 3-round clips

Pistola Automatica Beretta modello 1915

The **Pistola Automatica Beretta modello 1915** was the first of the Beretta automatic pistols, but it lacked the degree of manufacturing finesse that became the hallmark of later Beretta models. This was mainly because it was produced in a great hurry. When Italy entered World War I in 1914 it did so at a time when the levels of all kinds of weapons were very low, and pistols were no exception to this failing. Italian industry was rushed into production to churn out as many weapons as quickly as possible, and the Beretta modello 1915 was one result of this policy.

For all the rush with which it was placed into production, the modello 1915 showed all the basic features of the Beretta designs. The slide had the cut-away section over the barrel that was to become an instant recognition feature, but the overall appearance lacked the degree of balance and class that were to appear later. Modello 1915s were initially issued in 7.65-mm (0.301-in) calibre, but some were later produced to fire the 9-mm (0.354-in) special Glisenti cartridge; these versions had a more powerful return spring. A relatively small number were also produced to fire the 9-mm Short round, a round much less powerful than the 9-mm Parabellum. The mechanism was simple blowback and the firing mechanism used a concealed hammer. The 7.65-mm version did not use an ejector to force the spent cartridge cases from the weapon after firing: the cases were pushed out by coming into contact with the firing pin that had been forced through the breech block by the hammer at full recoil; the larger 9-mm cartridge versions used a conventional ejector stop.

As was to be expected under wartime conditions, there were several detail variations between models. A large safety catch with differing shapes and locations was one, and there were also changes in butt grip materials and finish. One thing these modello 1915s shared with all users was a general appreciation of the weapon's reliability and good handling. The modello 1915 introduced the basic pattern of what were later to become some of the finest automatic pistols ever produced. Even now the name Beretta stands for sound design and good finish, but examining a modello 1915 today few of these attributes are obvious, due mainly to the rapidity with which they were placed in mass production. But the seeds were there.

Specification
Beretta modello 1915
Calibre: 7.65 mm (0.301 in) or 9 mm (0.354 in) Short
Weight: 0.57 kg (1.25 lb)
Lengths: overall 149 mm (5.87 in); barrel 84 mm (3.31 in)
Muzzle velocity: (9-mm Short) 266 m (873 ft) per second
Magazine capacity: 8 rounds

An Italian 'Deathshead' pioneer, in full trench raiding kit, has a medieval appearance. In the savage close-quarter fighting in the trenches, the entrenching tool and pistol were more sensible weapons than a bulky rifle; the body armour was heavy, but provided good protection. Note the wirecutters carried on the belt.

Pistola Automatica Glisenti modello 1910

The **Pistola Automatica Glisenti modello 1910** was often known just as the **Glisenti**, but an essentially similar pistol was also issued to the Italian army and known as the **Brixia**. The initial pistol, the Glisenti, was designed in Switzerland but initial production was started in Italy in 1905 at the Società Siderurgica Glisenti at Turin. In 1910 the pistol was accepted for Italian army use. Two years later, a **modello 12** produced by the Brixia concern, appeared. This modello 1912 was almost identical to the modello 1910 but lacked the grip safety. For simplicity's sake these two pistols will be treated as one and the same.

The Glisenti modello 1910 used a mechanism that employed a locked-breech system, but for various design reasons this system was not very effective. Therefore it could not use full-power cartridges such as the 9-mm (0.354-in) Parabellum, but instead had to fire its own special cartridge with a less powerful charge. The difficulty with this special cartridge was that it was virtually identical in shape and appearance to the Parabellum round, and that use of the Parabellum round in the Glisenti pistol could, and often did, cause trouble. Some of these troubles could be very hazardous to the firer. Under normal circumstances this potential problem could be avoided but under combat conditions the two types of cartridge could be easily mixed up.

When firing the correct cartridge the modello 10 proved to be reliable enough, but suffered from one basic design weakness. The designers had ensured good maintenance access by allowing almost the entire left-hand side of the pistol frame to be removable. This certainly made for good cleaning and repair, but the removable plate made the entire pistol weak on that side. Under combat conditions the pistol frame could become distorted to an unacceptable degree causing jams and other more potentially severe problems, or the access plate could simply fall off. Thus the modello 1910 was increasingly regarded with suspicion, and whenever possible knowledgeable users plumped for other types of side-arm.

This did not prevent the Glisenti pistols from being carried and used throughout World War I and even during World War II. If looked after and not subjected to too much hard use, the Glisenti/Brixia pistols were sound enough, but under severe combat conditions they often proved to be less than satisfactory.

Specification
Glisenti modello 1910
Calibre: 9 mm (0.354 in)
Weight: 0.8 kg (1.76 lb)

Lengths: overall 211.2 mm (8.315 in); barrel 95 mm (3.74 in)
Muzzle velocity: 258 m (846 ft) per second
Magazine capacity: 7 rounds

The Glisenti was not as popular as the Beretta: the left-hand side of the frame detaches, reducing its strength, and the breech accepted 9-mm Parabellum – far more powerful than the 9-mm Glisenti cartridge, and able to shatter the weapon.

UK

Webley & Scott self-loading pistols

The Webley & Scott self-loading pistols must rank as among the most awkward-looking pistols ever designed, but in use they were reliable. The first of them was accepted for government service in 1912, mainly for police use, and by 1914 the **Webley Self-Loading Pistol Mk I** was in use by Royal Navy and Royal Marine landing or boarding parties. Later more were issued to the newly-formed Royal Flying Corps and to some Royal Horse Artillery battery personnel.

The basic design used a very positive locking system that ran in a series of angled grooves and lugs. This was just as well for the pistol continued to use the 0.455-in (actually 0.441-in/11.2-mm) cartridge but in a much more powerful form, so much so that for many years it remained the world's most powerful pistol cartridge. This cartridge had a charge so heavy that it could cause serious damage to pistol and user if fired from any of the 0.455-in revolvers. Some pistols were produced to fire the 0.38-in (9.65-mm) Super Auto and 9-mm (0.354-in) Browning long cartridges, but few of these appear to have been used by the British military.

The pistol had a a few odd design features all of its own, one being that it was possible to partially withdraw and lock the box magazine to allow single rounds to be fed into the chamber through the ejection slot, leaving the full magazine topped up for emergency use. There was provision on most versions for a flat wooden shoulder stock to be fitted to the butt for more accurate shooting at longer ranges.

These Webley & Scott self-loaders (the term 'automatic' was disliked by the British at the time) were massive pistols that took a lot of careful handling even at short combat ranges. They were well-built with a distinctive 'straight-line' appearance that was not helped by the almost square-set angle of the butt. This butt angle made the pistol rather difficult to fire instinctively, but deliberate shooting by a fully-trained user could be quite accurate. If

all else failed the pistols could be used as clubs as even when unloaded each weighed 1.13 kg (2.5 lb). They were not generally liked. The Royal Horse Artillery got rid of theirs as soon as they could and the Royal Flying Corps were no more enthusiastic. As a result the Webley & Scott self-loaders were never accepted for full military service but the British armed forces continued to use the revolver for many years, officially until well after World War II.

Specification
Webley Self-loading Pistol Mk I
Calibre: 11.2 mm (0.441 in)
Weight: 1.13 kg (2.5 lb)
Lengths: overall(216 mm (8.5 in); barrel 127 mm (5 in)
Muzzle velocity: 236 m (775 ft) per second
Magazine capacity: 7 rounds

Adopted by the Royal Navy in 1914 and later by the artillery and RFC, the ungainly Webley & Scott 0.455 was not wildly popular.

Naval aviation pioneer commander Samson and his Nieuport 10 prepare for another sortie over the Turkish lines at Gallipoli. Pistols were initially carried by airmen for personal defence in case of a forced landing.

Webley 0.455-in revolvers

The 0.455-in cartridge fired by the Webley revolvers had an actual calibre of 0.441 in (11.2 mm), and its design reflected experience gained in colonial warfare. The cartridge was designed to be a certain 'man-stopper' for close-range use against charging native hordes, and the heavy bullet and powerful charge were certainly adequate for the task. The pistol intended for use with this powerful cartridge was produced by Webley & Scott Limited of Birmingham, which produced its first 0.455-in pistol in late 1887.

The **Webley & Scott Mk I** was the forerunner of a host of similar models, many of which are still around. The Mk I had a top-opening frame with an automatic ejecting device that pushed out spent cartridge cases as the frame opened. The butt had a distinctive shape that was termed a 'bird's head', and a lanyard ring was considered essential. A 102-mm (4-in) barrel was used, but later marks also used 152-mm (6-in) barrels.

After the Mk I came a large number of other marks and submarks with detail improvements and/or barrel length changes. The overall mechanism and design did not change much, although by the time the main World War I model appeared in 1915 the butt shape had changed and there had been some alterations to the sights. The Mk VI may be taken as typical of the World War I Webley 0.455-in revolvers, but many of the earlier marks remained in use.

The Mk VI was a very well made and solid revolver. It was also large and something of a handful to tote and fire. The powerful cartridge produced an equally powerful recoil and it was considered to have a useful combat range of only a few metres. For trench warfare this was ideal, and the Webleys were a preferred weapon for trench raids and close-quarter fighting. Under such circumstances the Webleys had one major advantage and that was that they were very forgiving of the dirty and muddy conditions under which they were often used. Even if a Webley jammed or ran out of ammunition it could still be used as an effective club. This attribute was developed by the introduction of the Pritchard-Greener revolver bayonet, a spike-type bayonet/trench knife that fitted over the muzzle with the metal hilt resting against the revolver frame. This fearsome pistol/bayonet combination appears to have been little

Still in service around the world, Webley revolvers are arguably the toughest and most accurate handguns ever made. Their calibre is 0.441 (11.2 mm) but, curiously, they have always been referred to as 0.455 (11.6 mm). Below is the Mk 1, introduced in 1887; above is the Mk 5 of 1913.

used as it was never approved officially. A more useful device was a charger that held six cartridges ready for instant loading into the opened cylinder.

Specification
Webley Mk VI
Calibre: 11.2 mm (0.441 in)
Weight: 1.09 kg (2.4 lb)
Lengths: overall 286 mm (11.25 in); barrel 152 mm (6 in)
Muzzle velocity: 189 m (620 ft) per second
Cylinder capacity: 6 rounds

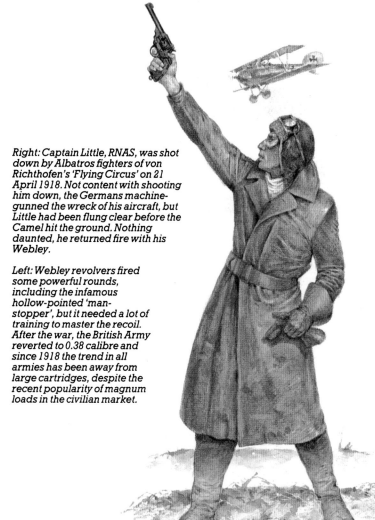

Right: Captain Little, RNAS, was shot down by Albatros fighters of von Richthofen's 'Flying Circus' on 21 April 1918. Not content with shooting him down, the Germans machine-gunned the wreck of his aircraft, but Little had been flung clear before the Camel hit the ground. Nothing daunted, he returned fire with his Webley.

Left: Webley revolvers fired some powerful rounds, including the infamous hollow-pointed 'man-stopper', but it needed a lot of training to master the recoil. After the war, the British Army reverted to 0.38 calibre and since 1918 the trend in all armies has been away from large cartridges, despite the recent popularity of magnum loads in the civilian market.

Webley Fosbery revolver

The **Webley Fosbery** revolver was designed by Colonel G.V. Fosbery VC, and is in a class of its own as it is an automatic revolver. The original patent was taken out in 1896 and production was taken up by Webley & Scott shortly after that, the resultant pistols being chambered for the standard 0.455-in (actually 0.441-in/11.2-mm) cartridge.

The action of the Webley Fosbery was unique. On firing the recoil drove back the barrel, cylinder and top frame along a slide over the butt. This cocked the hammer and a return spring inside the butt then drove the whole assembly back to its initial position. As it did so a stud in the slide ran through an angled groove machined into the cylinder to turn it to the next cartridge position. The system had its attractions to those who thought that they had only to keep pulling the trigger to keep firing rapidly. In practice it was not that simple. One immediate drawback was that the action required a great deal of handling: the entire top frame moving back and forth added to the already considerable movement caused by the heavy recoil, and so made the pistol something of a brute to fire. Another drawback was that the firer had to hold the butt very firmly indeed or the entire system would not function, for the user's grip acted as the anchor for the entire mechanism.

Nevertheless the Webley Fosbery was sold in considerable numbers to British officers who had to supply their own side-arms. Many were sold to Royal Flying Corps personnel who thought that the automatic feature would be of considerable advantage when engaging enemy aircraft from the confines of their cockpits: they soon learned that the considerable

firing movements made in-flight shooting even more difficult than it might otherwise have been.

For all this the Webley Fosbery was never adopted officially, which was just as well for when used in the trenches the type's major drawback became all too obvious. This was that the action relied upon smooth movement through carefully-machined grooves, any clogging of those grooves by dirt or mud resulted in a jam. As most of the grooves involved were fully exposed

they soon became full of all manner of trench debris and it took constant attention to keep them clean. Many officers gave up the task and took up other less troublesome pistols.

Specification
Webley Fosbery
Calibre: 11.2 mm (0.441 in)
Weight: 1.25 kg (2.755 lb)
Lengths: overall 279 mm (11 in); barrel 152 mm (6 in)

The unique Webley Fosbery is an automatic revolver. The barrel and cylinder go back over the frame, cocking the hammer and returning by spring power; the stud on the frame engaged in the prominent grooves in the cylinder rotates it, so completing the action.

Muzzle velocity: 183 m (600 ft) per second
Cylinder capacity: 6 rounds

Browning pistols

The Belgian Fabrique Nationale d'Armes de Guerre (FN) was formed in association with John M. Browning after the latter left Colt, and the association produced many excellent weapon designs. The first pistol produced by the Browning/FN combination was the **Browning Modèle 1900**, a fairly straightforward pistol with few frills and chambered in 7.65 mm (0.301 in). The Modèle 1900 was a pistol that was never officially adopted as a standard service pistol, but it was produced and used in thousands, usually by officers who had to supply their own side-arms. It was also copied in even larger numbers in China and Spain, usually unofficially.

The **Modèle 1903** was the Belgian version of a Browning-designed Colt pistol produced to use an European cartridge known as the 9-mm (0.354-in) Browning Long. The Modèle 1903 employed a straightforward blowback mechanism that could be used because of the relatively low power of the cartridge. The Modèle 1903 was adopted by the Belgian army and was also licence-produced in Sweden. Other user nations were Turkey, Serbia, Denmark and the Netherlands. Some versions could use a shoulder stock that doubled as a holster.

Perhaps the most important of the World War I Browning pistols was the attractive **Modèle 1910**. It was placed on the market in 1912 and was immediately recognized as an ideal

officer's side-arm. It was also accorded the accolade of being copied widely, often without any form of licence agreement. Produced to fire either the 7.65-mm or 9-mm Short (0.354-in, also known as the .380 ACP) cartridge, the Modèle 1910 is still in limited production. The mechanism of the Modèle 1910 is conventional blow-back with the return spring coiled around the barrel. The pistol is still a delight to handle and is easy to aim and fire, having a grip safety. The Modèle 1910 is another pistol that has never been officially adopted as a service weapon, other than by the Belgian army, but it was used in large numbers throughout World War I by many officers who had to purchase their own side-arms. Many Modèle 1910s were still around during World War II. After World War I a slightly enlarged version, the Modèle 1922, was produced but it never replaced the Modèle 1910.

Specification
Modèle 1900
Calibre: 7.65 mm (0.301 in)
Weight: 0.625 kg (1.378 lb)
Lengths: overall 162.5 mm (6.4 in); barrel 102 mm (4.02 in)
Muzzle velocity: 290 m (951 ft) per second
Magazine capacity: 7 rounds

Specification
Modèle 1903
Calibre: 9 mm (0.354 in)

Weight: 0.91 kg (2 lb)
Lengths: overall 203 mm (8 in); barrel 127 mm (5 in)
Muzzle velocity: 320 m (1,050 ft) per second
Magazine capacity: 7 rounds

Specification
Modèle 1910
Calibre: 7.65 or 9 mm (0.301 or 0.354 in)
Weight: 0.57 kg (1.26 lb)

The Modèle 1900 has the distinction of being the first Browning design to be made by FN of Herstal, the beginning of a long and successful association.

Lengths: overall 154 mm (6.06 in); barrel 88.5 mm (3.48 in)
Muzzle velocity: 299 m (981 ft) per second
Magazine capacity: 7 rounds

The shot that shook the world

The assassination of a major political figure often has important repercussions, but the shooting of the heir to the Austro-Hungarian Empire in 1914 led to the Great War. The Austro-Hungarians retaliated by invading Serbia, and the network of alliances dragged the world into conflict. Four empires were to be destroyed, and the world today is still living with the consequences.

Below: The Archduke and his wife walk down to their car, being greeted by assembled Bosnian dignatories. Visiting Bosnia on St Vitus' day enraged Nationalist feeling and has been compared to a member of the British Royal family visiting the most Republican areas of Belfast on St Patrick's Day.

The young conspirators met again shortly after dawn on Sunday, 28 June 1914, the warm sunshine already dispelling the morning mist and promising a radiant summer day. The seven, all young students imbued with that spirit of political idealism which tells them that they must do something, indeed anything, to change society without pausing to consider what to change it into, were members of the 'Young Bosnians' group: Mohamed Mehmedbašić, Vaso Čubrilović, Nedeljko Čabrinović, Cvijetko Popović, Gavrilo Princip, Trifko Grabež were the soldiers of the team, the 'hit men', and Danilo Ilić was the organizer.

They had already been issued with their weapons: pistols and bombs supplied to them by Major Tankosic, one of the leaders of the notorious 'Black Hand' organization under the shadowy command of Colonel Dimitrijevic-Apis, and smuggled across the border from Belgrade; they knew their tasks. Now they took up their stations.

Five of them took position along the bank of the River Miljačka, now in the early summer a mere stream at the bottom of a wide bed. Mehmedbašić, Čabrinović and Čubrilović stood at the junction of the Appel Quay and the Čumuria Bridge, while opposite and facing them was Popović, at first accompanied by Ilić; it was here, they thought, that their tasks would most likely be carried out. Farther along the river bank, at its junction with the Latin Bridge, stood Princip, and farther along the bank towards the Town Hall waited Grabež, the 'last hope' if fortune failed his friends.

They were all in position by 09.00, and had nearly an hour to await their proposed victim's arrival.

The Archduke Franz Ferdinand, heir apparent to the Habsburg empire of Austria-Hungary, had during his life been given so many general warnings of the possibility of assassination that by the age of 51 he listened to even the most specific with an air of tired fatalism.

'I am sure your warning is justified,' he sighed when it was suggested to him that he might meet his end at Sarajevo, 'but I do not let myself be kept under a glass cover. Our life is constantly in danger. One has to rely upon God.' He thus instructed that the programme for his visit to the Bosnian capital should not be curtailed.

As Inspector-General of the Armed Forces of the Empire he was attending the great summer manoeuvres taking place across the provinces of Bosnia and Herzegovina, and his proposed visit to Sarajevo had been announced as early as the previous March. It

Franz Josef, the ageing King and Emperor, takes the salute. Despite his many years he was a powerful political force, and did much to maintain the stablity of his disparate country; Franz Ferdinand was a much more divisive figure, and his accession was awaited with anxiety by many political leaders.

The shot that shook the world

The Royal party at the town hall after the first bomb attack. The Archduke remarked, 'We shall get a few more bullets still' before setting off again. Events were to prove him tragically correct.

would not now be altered because of yet more rumours of yet another attempted assassination, which would yet again doubtless prove to be unfounded. In this opinion it would seem that the Sarajevo police forces were in agreement, as the security measures they were taking were exiguous in the extreme. They seem also totally to have ignored the fact that the visit was taking place on the day of the greatest Serbian festival, St Vitus' Day, a fact which Serbian patriots, ever a fervent body, would almost certainly regard as a gratuitous aggravation of an unnecessary annoyance.

The archducal train arrived at Sarajevo station promptly on time at 10.00, and 10 minutes later the procession of four cars was on its way to the official reception at the town hall. In the leading car were the mayor and the chief of

Then, as now, terrorist bomb outrages attracted ghoulish spectators. The series of guerrilla activities perpetrated by The Black Hand was the first terrorist campaign on modern lines.

police; in the second were the archduke in full uniform with his beloved wife, the Duchess Sophie of Hohenberg, beside him, sitting opposite the governor of Bosnia, General Potiorek, while in the front seat next to the chauffeur was the owner of the car, Count Harrach. In the rear two cars travelled the officers and attendants of the archducal suite.

The cars drove swiftly along the Appel Quay between the houses on their left and low embankment wall on their right, and as they approached the Čumuria Bridge General Potiorek turned and pointed out to his markedly uninterested guests the new barracks they were approaching.

At the same moment, a tall young man in a long black coat and a black hat was asking a nearby policeman in which car the archduke

Death at Sarajevo

Archduke Franz Ferdinand visited the Bosnian town of Sarajevo while attending the summer manoeuvres of the Austro-Hungarian Army. Bosnia and neighbouring Herzegovina had been liberated from Turkish rule in 1878 but never achieved longed-for independence; instead, they were annexed by Austria-Hungary. Nationalist sentiment, stoked by elements within the Serbian government, supported an orchestrated terrorist campaign of the sort we are wearily familiar with today. The Archduke was warned of a possible attempt on his life but refused to have his movements dictated by terrorist threats; he only altered his plans at Sarajevo after a bomb was thrown at his car, bounced off the hood at the back and blew up the following vehicle.

After Čabrinović's failed attack, the Archduke's motorcade was supposed to take a different route from the one planned; the cars would maintain a reasonable speed and hopefully avoid any further attacks. Unfortunately, no-one told the drivers and the Archduke's car went the wrong way, stopped, and reversed past a young student called Gavrilo Princip, who was nervously fingering a Browning pistol in his coat pocket. He shouldered his way past a policeman and shot the Duchess and then Franz Ferdinand before being overpowered. The royal couple were both dead on arrival at hospital, and Europe was plunged into crisis.

The shot that shook the world

was travelling, and upon receiving an answer, he knocked off the cap of a hand-grenade against a lamp post and threw it with admirable accuracy but abysmal luck at his objective, leapt over the embankment wall and fled along the river-bank.

As the bomb flew through the air the archduke's chauffeur saw it and accelerated, so that the bomb landed not in the car but on the folded roof at the back. The archduke also saw it and flung up an arm to protect his wife, and as the car shot forward the bomb dropped on to the road and exploded with sufficent force to wreck the vehicle immediately behind that of the Archduke, and wound some 20 onlookers, some of them seriously, including Colonel Merizzi, Potiorek's aide-de-camp.

Change of plan

With a courage and sympathy which compels admiration, the archduke commanded his car to stop while enquiries were made as to the extent of the damage and casualties, after which the cortege, reduced to three cars, continued to the town hall and the reception. This was somewhat curtailed by the event and the effect they had had on the archduke's composure, increased by the discovery that a piece of the bomb had grazed his wife's neck.

'I came here on a visit and I get bombs thrown at me. It is outrageous!' the archduke said acidly, later commenting to Count Harrach 'Today we shall get a few more bullets still.'

It was in order to avoid this contingency that General Potiorek now suggested that the day's programme be moderated. Instead of visiting the town museum as planned, which would entail returning along the Appel Quay as far as Latin Bridge, then turning right by Schiller's Store and along Franz Josef Street, he suggested that the museum be abandoned and that the party either proceed direct to the governor's residence at Konak, or return instead to Ilidze, both alternatives requiring nothing but a drive at full speed along the Appel Quay. To this the archduke agreed with the proviso that at some point on the journey a small diversion could be arranged to allow him to call at the hospital where Colonel Merizzi was being treated for his wounds, in order for both archduke and duchess to express their sympathy and condolences.

So it was agreed, and it was a great pity that no one thought to inform the chauffeurs of the change in plans.

From his station at the end of the Latin Bridge, Princip had heard Čabrinović's bomb explode, realized soon afterwards that their prime target had escaped unhurt, and seen Čabrinović attempt to escape along the river bed pursued by police who soon caught him. Princip dallied briefly with the idea of pursuing them, shooting Čabrinović in order to ensure his silence and then turning the pistol upon himself. Princip soon abandoned the notion, mixing with the crowd instead and eventually taking post on the opposite side of the Appel Quay, on the corner by Schiller's Store. Here, he and the crowd believed, the cortege would eventually slow in order to turn into Franz Josef Street.

The funeral of Franz Ferdinand took place on 2 July 1914. Austria-Hungary deliberately made demands on Serbia that could not be met in order to go to war. The network of alliances drew the Great Powers into the conflict one by one and across Europe party differences were put aside for the sake of national unity.

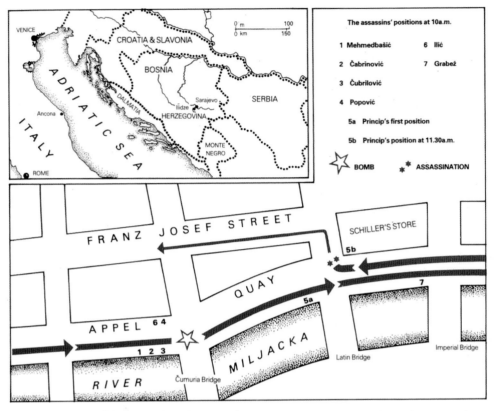

In the event, it did (from Princip's point of view) even better.

The three cars duly approached the crossroads and the chauffeurs, still ignorant of the modifications of programme, swung around the corner. But as the first car turned, Potiorek realized the error and shouted to correct it. The first car sped on but the archduke's slowed in the turn, stopped, and the chauffeur began backing so as to clear again for the passage along Appel Quay. Quite slowly, the car and its occupants reversed past Princip at a distance of some 1.5 m (5 ft).

His arm was grabbed by a policeman who saw the young man produce a pistol but the policeman was then knocked down (probably by another of the conspirators or one of their

At Sarajevo one man with a Browning automatic changed the shape of world history; but if the drivers had been told of the change of route, the Archduke's car would never have slowed down in front of the assassin.

sympathizers) and Princip then fired twice. The first bullet penetrated the side of the car, the duchess's corset and then her right side, while the second went through the archduke's coat collar, severed his jugular vein and lodged in his spine. Both were dead by the time they arrived at the hospital.

It was 11.30 on the morning of 28 June 1914; and the effects of those two shots are still with us.

Austro-Hungarian pistols

The basic pistol of the Austro-Hungarian armies was the **8-mm Rast und Gasser Revolver M.1898**. This was a very robust and well made revolver, and was issued in large numbers to officers and NCOs of the imperial armies. But it was unusual on two counts: one was that it fired its own special 8-mm (0.315-in) cartridge, and the other was the unusual method of stripping. This was carried out by pulling down the trigger guard. In this way the entire interior workings were exposed for cleaning and repair, not that repairs had to be carried out very often for the M.1898 was extraordinarily tough. In fact the standard of production was so high that many were still in use during World War II.

Despite the widespread issue of the M.1898 revolver in 1907, the Austro-Hungarian army decided also to adopt an automatic pistol. This was the **8-mm Repetierpistole M.07** (also known as the **Roth-Steyr**), a pistol that used a unique mechanism that no one has seen fit to copy. The M.07 used a long bolt that initially moved backwards with the barrel on firing and continued to travel to the rear once the barrel was held by stops. A complicated process of ejection and feeding the next round then commenced, ceasing only when the bolt and the barrel were back in their initial position. The process involved a straight travel and at one point rotary movement. Despite all this complexity the M.07 was a sound service pistol but it was never produced for anything other than Austro-Hungarian military service. It too had a cartridge all of its own that was not adopted elsewhere.

The M.07 was difficult to produce and in 1912 the **9-mm Repetierpistole M.12** was introduced. Widely known as the **Steyr-Hahn**, the M.12 used what was probably the strongest pistol action ever made, with a locked-breech mechanism operated by a rotating barrel. The 9-mm (0.354-in) cartridge was again special to the weapon and was used by no other, and another distinction was that the magazine was fixed and had to be reloaded through the top using a charger clip.

The M.12 was officially the standard Austro-Hungarian side-arm of World War I and many were still around during World War II, by then in German

hands. However, the official status did not prevent the earlier M.1898 and M.07 remaining in widespread use.

Specification
M.07
Calibre: 8 mm (0.315 in)
Weight: 1.03 kg (2.27 lb)

The Steyr M1912 was a first-class gun but was adopted only by the Austro-Hungarian army, perhaps because it fired a unique 9-mm cartridge that was more powerful than the increasingly popular 9-mm Parabellum. It was called 'Steyr-Hahn' ('Steyr-Hammer') to distinguish it from the Roth-Steyr.

Superficially similar to the Mauser C/96, the Mannlicher M1903 was a rival weapon produced with the military market in mind, but was rejected as a service pistol as it was not sufficiently reliable.

Lengths: overall 233 mm (9.17 in); barrel 131 mm (5.16 in)
Muzzle velocity: 332 m (1,089 ft) per second
Magazine capacity: 10 rounds

Specification
M.12
Calibre: 9 mm (0.354 in)
Weight: 1.02 kg (2.25 lb)
Lengths: overall 216 mm (8.5 in); barrel 128 mm (5.1 in)
Muzzle velocity: 340 m (1,115 ft) per second
Magazine capacity: 8 rounds

Right: Having begun the Hussar style in the first place, it was only natural that Hungarian hussar uniforms in 1914 retained all the panache of traditional light cavalry, despite the addition of modern weaponry. This officer holds a Steyr-Hahn M12 automatic in classic duelling stance.

Japanese pistols

During World War I the Japanese armed forces used two types of sidearm: the **Pistol revolver Type 26** and the **Pistol Automatic Type 4**.

The 9-mm (0.354-in) Type 26 revolver was adopted in 1893, initially for cavalry use. It was a Japanese design that was typical of its era for it was produced at a time when the Japanese were still studying Western technology to bring their nation forward from the state of generally medieval backwardness. Unfortunately for the small-arms designers they did not know which particular Western designs to follow and so produced an amalgam of several different designs. The overall appearance owed much to the Nagant revolvers, the cylinder swing-out system was borrowed from the Smith & Wessons, the ability to swing open the lock mechanism came from the French Lebel and the action was derived from several European designs. The Japanese decided to add a touch of their own and made the pistol a double-action only weapon. To this they added their own 9-mm ammunition that was not then, or ever since, used by any other weapon. The result was an odd revolver that was at least serviceable and strong enough to last through two world wars.

The Type 4 automatic pistol was de-signed by one Kijiro Nambu and was never officially accepted for Imperial service. However, so many were purchased and used by Japanese officers from the late 1900s onwards that the design was provided with the Type 4 designation. To the West it became known as the **Nambu** and was so widely used that all subsequent Japanese pistols were called Nambus. The Type 4 fired an 8-mm (0.315-in) cartridge, and used an action not un-like that of the Italian Glisenti but mechanically stronger. This action gave the Type 4 a distinctive appearance. There were several variations of the basic Type 4, the most drastic of which was a special 7-mm (0.276-in) 'Baby Nambu' version intended for use by staff officers. Despite its wide-spread use the Type 4 was apparently not a very satisfactory pistol. One constant source of troubles was the striker spring which sometimes became too weak to fire a cartridge. Another was the generally low standard of steel used for some components which often broke under anything other than light use. But the Type 4 remained in service for many years. Many were still in use during World War II despite the provision of a generally-improved design known as the Type 14 (introduced in 1937).

The 8-mm Nambu automatic was purchased by many Japanese officers although it was never adopted as a service pistol. It had a breech-lock similar to that of the Glisenti but suffered from a weak striker spring.

Specification
Type 26
Calibre: 9 mm (0.354 in)
Weight: 0.9 kg (1.98 lb)
Lengths: overall 239 mm (9.4 in); barrel 119 mm (4.7 in)
Muzzle velocity: 277 m (909 ft) per second
Ammunition capacity: 6 rounds

Specification
Type 4
Calibre: 8 mm (0.315 in)
Weight: 0.9 kg (1.98 lb)
Lengths: overall 229 mm (9 in); barrel 120 mm (4.7 in)
Muzzle velocity: 325 m (1,066 ft) per second
Ammunition capacity: 8 rounds

Nagant Model 1895

The **Nagant Model 1895** revolver was originally a Belgian design produced as early as 1878. From then onwards the basic design was procured by Belgium, Argentina, Brazil, Denmark, Norway, Portugal, Rumania, Serbia and Sweden, usually from Belgium and in various calibres (although copies were produced in Spain). However, the number of Nagant revolvers produced in Russia (initially under licence) dwarfed all output carried out elsewhere, to the extent that the Nagant is now regarded as a Russian weapon.

The first Russian production of the Nagant was carried out at the Tula Arsenal in 1895 and continued until 1940. The version involved was the Nagant Model 1895, a model designed to improve the overall efficiency of the basic revolver concept. It was an unusual revolver in many respects, not the least being the unique 7.62-mm (0.30-in) ammunition that used a brass cartridge case with a fully recessed bullet. The idea of this was that as the pistol was fired the cylinder was rammed forward into close contact against the end of the barrel, with the case forming a complete gas seal between the two assemblies. The idea behind this was supposedly to make the cartridge more efficient by minimizing the loss of propellant gases through the small gap between the cylinder and the barrel, but it was a feature of doubtful value that added a degree of complexity to the requirement for a special cartridge, although the Russians thought much of it and retained the feature unchanged until production ceased.

For some reason the Tsarist army decided to perpetuate the differences between the ranks by issuing enlisted men with single-action revolvers while officers received double-action versions. There was also a noticeable dif-

ference between the finish of the two models, the single-action models often being left as bare metal while the officers' versions were plated or blued. Both were extremely sturdy and reliable weapons: they had to be to last under the conditions in which the Russian army usually fought. The frame was solid and the cylinder was fixed, with loading taking place through a gate on the right. A rod was used to eject spent cases.

The Nagant Model 1895 revolvers were produced in hundreds of thousands over the years. The type was used throughout World Wars I and II, and it is possible to encounter some today in odd corners of the world. A few ammunition manufacturers still find it worth their while to produce the special recessed ammunition, although most sales must now be to collectors.

Specification
Nagant Model 1895
Calibre: 7.62 mm (0.3 in)
Weight: 0.795 kg (1.75 lb)

The Nagant was a Belgian design adopted by many different armies but so many were produced under licence in Russia that the revolver is regarded as Russian. It incorporated an unusual gas-seal mechanism which added needless complication for little real benefit.

Lengths: overall 230 mm (9.055 in); barrel 110 mm (4.33 in)
Muzzle velocity: 272 m (892 ft) per second
Cylinder capacity: 6 rounds

9-mm Pistole '08

The 9-mm **Pistole '08** remains one of the 'classic' pistols and it is still almost universally known as the **Luger** after its designer, Georg Luger. The basic design was based on that of a previous pistol, the **Borchardt**, but Luger tidied up that design and developed it into the form manufactured by Deutsche Waffen und Munitionsfabriken (DWM) starting in 1898.

The first Luger pistols were sold to Switzerland in 1900, chambered for the 7.65-mm (0.301-in) cartridge. By 1904 the pistol was being re-chambered for the 9-mm (0.354-in) Parabellum cartridge, and this version was accepted for German navy use. In 1908 a slightly revised model was accepted by the German army and thereafter the P '08 was fabricated in hundreds of thousands. These early models were produced in a variety of barrel lengths, the shortest being 103 mm (4.06 in)

long. Other barrel lengths were 152 mm (6 in), 203 mm (8 in) and even 305 mm (12 in). These long-barrelled versions were usually issued with combined wooden shoulder stock/holster kits and were known as **Artillery Models**. They were frequently used with a 32-round 'snail' magazine.

All the variations of the P '08 used the same mechanisms with its upward-opening toggle lock mechanism. As the pistol was fired all the hinge elements of the toggle were in line to lock the breech. The recoil forces had to overcome the mechanical advantage of the toggle mechanism before it would open, and once open the ejection and reloading processes could be carried out. A return spring in the butt reset everything ready to fire the next round.

The toggle device gave the P '08 a distinctive appearance, and the rake

of the butt made the pistol a good one to aim and fire. The P '08 soon became a prized front-line weapon and war trophy, and throughout World War I there were never enough P '08s being produced to meet the ever-growing demands. It was here that the disadvantages of the P '08 became apparent, for it was a difficult weapon to produce in quantity as virtually all its components had to be hand-made. By 1917 much of the excellent pre-war detail finish had been omitted and the original grip safety was deleted altogether, never to return even after 1918. There was one other drawback to the P '08, and that was the fact that the toggle mechanism was not very tolerant of trench conditions. Mud and dirt could all too easily clog the workings, often at the worst possible times, so the pistols demanded a lot of care.

The soldiers did not seem to mind.

They liked the P '08, and after 1918 the model was kept in service. It was still in production in 1943 and even today many manufacturers find it well worth their while to produce 'look-alike' or direct copies for a seemingly unsatiable market.

Specification
P '08
Calibre: 9 mm (0.354 in)
Weight: 0.876 kg (1.93 lb)
Lengths: overall 222 mm (8.76 in); barrel 103 mm (4.06 in)
Muzzle velocity: 320 m (1,050 ft) per second
Magazine capacity: (box) 8 rounds

A standard Luger P '08 is shown beneath an 'Artillery' Model, thought to have been introduced in 1917. The latter had a 192-mm (7.5-in) barrel and a flat board-like stock.

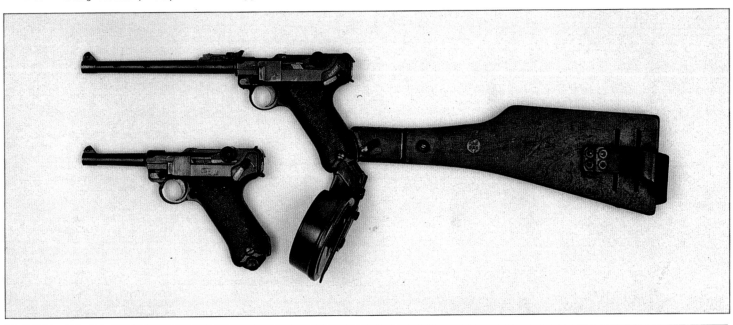

Other German pistols

When trench warfare had set in with a vengeance by the end of 1914, the armies of both sides demanded ever-growing quantities of weapons and war materials. Pistols were no exception to this situation, and as most service pistols then in use had virtually to be hand-made, it was not easy to meet these demands in a hurry. Consequently something else had to be found to equip the soldiers, and many storerooms were examined.

In some of them large numbers of **Reichs-Commissions-Revolver Modell 1879** were found. In fact some of them were still in reserve use by many units, despite their age. They fired an odd and low-powered 10.6-mm (0.417-in) cartridge, but were sturdy weapons as they had solid frames and a gate-load-

One of the first commercial pistols to be produced in 9-mm Parabellum was the RM & M 'Dreyse', which was manufactured only in limited numbers but saw active service nevertheless. The weapon was closely based on this earlier Dreyse Automatic, chambered for the 7.65-mm cartridge.

ing system that required a rod to eject spent cartridge cases. These ancient revolvers were still around in 1918 and for many years after as they did not wear out. There was also a **Modell 1883** with a shorter (126-mm/4.96-in) barrel.

Another typical wartime expedient was the 7.65-mm (0.301-in) **Belholla-Selbsladepistole**. This was really a commercial automatic pistol of undistinguished design, but was available in some numbers and was fairly easy to make. Many were issued to staff officers who had to carry a pistol and for whom the Belholla would be quite sufficient, freeing more useful combat pistols for front-line units. Thousands of Belhollas were made and issued, often under an array of sub-contractor names. The design was so simple that little thought was given to maintenance and the pistol could not be stripped without recourse to a trained armourer with a substantial tool kit.

These two pistols were typical of the mix of commercial and ancient side-arms with which a great deal of the German army (and other services) had to conduct their war. Demand constantly outstripped pistol supply, so a wide range of odd pistols were collected into the German army net. Pistols with such names as the **Dreyse** and the **Langenham** were pressed into service in quantities that ensured that their names would not be entirely forgotten, as they would probably otherwise have been, but few of them were designed for front-line service of the

kind they often had to encounter, so many were less than satisfactory.

Specification
Modell 1879
Calibre: 10.6 mm (0.417 in)

Weight: 1.04 kg (2.29 lb)
Lengths: overall 310 mm (12.2 in); barrel 183 mm (7.2 in)
Muzzle velocity: 205 m (673 ft) per second
Cylinder capacity: 6 rounds

An automatic 7.65-mm pistol designed for the commercial market, the Langenhan was adopted by the German army during the war as demand for weapons exceeded the production capacity of existing guns.

GERMANY
Mauser C/96

The original design of the **Mauser C/96** range of pistols was produced by three brothers named Feederle, who worked on the basic design until 1896 when it was placed in production by Mauser at Oberndorf-Neckar. Thereafter the C/96 and its derivatives were produced in a bewildering array of models to the extent that it is still a veritable minefield for the unwary historian.

The first C/96 pistols were hand guns, but it was not long before later models began to sprout shoulder stocks and other such appendages. Barrels started to increase in length until the weapons became virtual carbines rather than pistols, and some models of the C/96 became very complex pieces of kit together with their shoulder stock/holsters that also carried cleaning tools, spare clips and so on. Only one model needs to be considered at this stage to explain most models.

The **Military Model** was first produced in 1912 and was widely used throughout World War I. It had a 140-mm (5.51-in) barrel and was one of the pistol/carbine versions that used a combination shoulder stock and holster. Originally these pistols were produced to fit a special 7.63-mm (3.01-in) cartridge but during World War I the demand was such that some were issued to fire the 9-mm (0.354-in) Parabellum cartridge: these had a large red number 9 engraved into their butts. Using both these cartridges the

Military Model had a mechanism that can only be described as complicated. Rounds were fed into the magazine situated in front of the trigger using clips fed in from above. At the moment of firing the breech was locked by a locking piece underneath the bolt that moved to and fro in a barrel extension. After firing, a system of tongues and bolt movement delayed the action until the chamber pressure had dropped to a safe level, after which the bolt was allowed to move back to carry out the reloading and recocking operations. The barrel also moved back, but only

to a limited extent. A return spring returned everything for the next round. The mechanism depended on careful machining and exact tolerances, two factors that made the C/96 series difficult to manufacture and which led to its eventual military demise.

The C/96 pistols were certainly formiable military weapons with a certain aura about them that survives to this day, for it seems that every pistol collector wants at least one C/96 in his collection. Such collectors have a wide choice, for the pistols were made in large numbers, not only in Germany

but in Spain and many other nations, including China where the quantities involved were prodigious. Most of this 'overseas' production was entirely unofficial.

Specification
Military Model
Calibre: 7.63 or 9 mm (3.01 or 0.354 in)
Weight: 1.22 kg (2.69 lb)
Lengths: overall 308 mm (12.125 in); barrel 140 mm (5.51 in)
Muzzle velocity: (7.63 mm) 433 m (1,420 ft) per second
Magazine capacity: 10 rounds

The Mauser C/96 has one of the best known profiles of any pistol, and this elegant weapon, already popular at the turn of the century, is today a favourite for collectors.

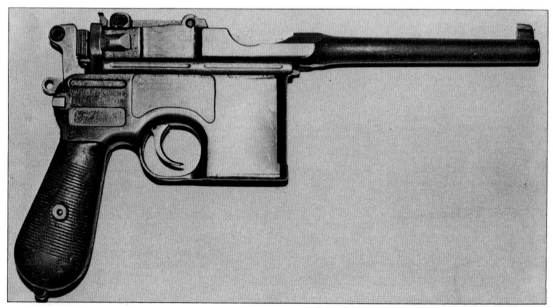

Mauser: the story continues

Designed in 1894 with a hammer intended to be cocked against a horseman's saddle, the Mauser C/96 was carried by Winston Churchill during his army days. Subsequently copied in arsenals around the world, a modified version was marketed by the Chinese as a machine pistol during the 1980s.

The story of the Mauser C/96 'Broomhandle' pistols may have started back in the 1890s, but it is far from over. The C/96 was the world's first truly automatic self-loading pistol, and over the decades has gained a following that has yet to be lost.

The C/96 was first produced in 1896 and immediately became a much desired weapon. The main attraction was its self-loading feature, but many buyers were drawn to the weapon just by its appearance. Simply carrying the weapon seemed to impart some sense of importance to the carrier, but this was offset by the fact that the C/96 was not easy to maintain. It had a complicated mechanism and took some time to understand. The bystander never saw these 'off-stage' requirements, and thus remained impressed.

Anyone on the receiving end was also impressed. The 7.63-mm (0.301-in) cartridge fired by the C/96 was a high-velocity round that could inflict serious damage at quite long ranges compared with other pistols of the era, and Mauser took advantages of this by supplying some models with leaf rearsights calibrated up to as much as 1000 m (1,094 yards), which was rather optimistic. To take advantage of this long-range feature there emerged the use of wooden holsters that could also double as shoulder stocks for more accurate aiming. Originally these accessories were produced for wealthy commercial customers, but it was not long before they attracted the attentions of the military who then decided to take the idea one stage further and add cleaning tools, spare ammunition clips and other items to the holster. In the end the wooden holster was in turn carried in a leather holster with all the extras enclosed.

By the time World War I started the C/96 was in widespread use. Many sales were made to officers of diverse nations, for at that time an officer had to purchase his own side-arm. Many were attracted by the C/96, and many British officers sported them: Winston Churchill carried one during his spell in the World War I trenches. Most of the C/96s used by the German army during the war were a model known as the 'neue Sicherung 1912', this being a simplified variant compared with previous models, and having as standard a barrel 139.7 mm (5.5 in) long. Many were issued with the wooden stock/holsters.

It was with the introduction of this model 1912 that the company made increasingly feasible the use of the C/96 as a specialist assassination weapon by the introduction of a powerful 9-mm (0.354-in) cartridge known as the Mauser Export. This fired a bullet similar to that used in the Parabellum cartridge but at a higher muz-

Right: A German Uhlan sports a Mauser C/96 modified to fire the standard 9-mm Parabellum cartridge instead of the original 7.63-mm round. The weapons were marked on the grip with either a red or (less commonly) a black figure '9'. A few early models made for the army were chambered for the longer-cased 9-mm Mauser Export cartridge.

Below: Most Mauser C/96s were capable of being fitted with the Mauser hollow wooden shoulder stock, which doubled as a holster and carried the cleaning kit. The magazine was an integral part of the pistol and was loaded through the top of the action with the 10 round charger illustrated. Note the figure 9 on the grip of the lower pistol.

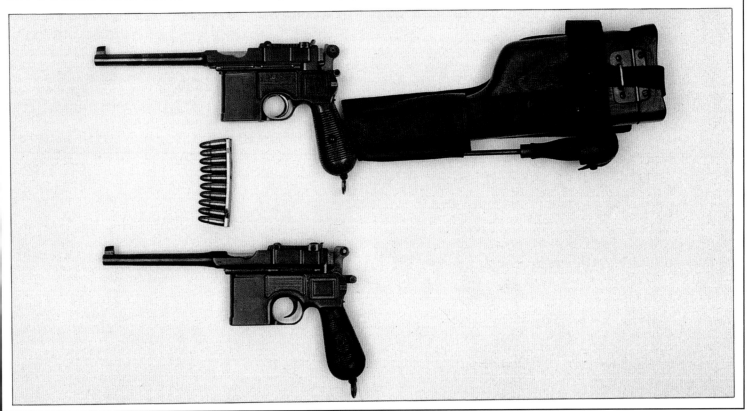

Mauser: the story continues

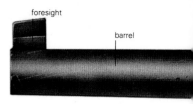

foresight

barrel

Emperor Haile Selassie sits pensively on a log after his epic march back to Ethiopia. His bodyguard carried an extraordinary variety of weapons, including the Mauser C/96 sported by the man on the right.

zle velocity (415 m/1,362 ft per second as opposed to 344 m/1,129 ft per second). This made the pistol/cartridge combination an excellent long-range weapon that could be relatively easily concealed and used at distances well above normal pistol ranges. Thus the Mauser Export pistols were often used for clandestine and assassination missions all around the world, especially in the Balkans where the C/96 was much favoured. The importance of this special cartridge must not be overemphasized, however, for the standard Mauser 7.63-mm cartridge was no mean performer in its own right.

During World War I the C/96 in its various forms did not fare as well as some other pistols when used in the trenches. The complex mechanism did not cope well with mud or dirt getting in its workings, so the C/96s were generally used by second-line units such as the artillery. They were also used with some degree of success by the newly-formed German air arm. It was almost certainly one of the first weapons ever used in air-to-air warfare when German pilots in their otherwise unarmed scout aircraft attempted to shoot at Allied pilots and aircraft flying close by. The C/96 was perhaps better than most pistols in this form of uncertain warfare and promoted Allied pilots to retaliate with pistols or rifles. It was not long before machine-guns were in use and the era of pistols in air-to-air combat passed almost as soon as it had begun.

9-mm Parabellum

In World War I Mauser churned out C/96s (mainly the model 1912) in thousands to meet ever-growing demands. The standard of many of these war-time models suffered, and a change was made in 1916 to enable the pistol to fire 9-mm Parabellum ammunition. These pistols were issued with a large '9' burned into the broomhandle butt and painted red.

After the war Mauser was prevented by the Allies from supplying the German army, and so looked around for new customers. Many commercial sales were made by assembling pistols from spare parts, but the largest post-war customer was the USSR, for which Mauser produced a 7.63-mm model known as the 'Bolo', supposedly after 'Bolshevik'. This version had a barrel 99 mm (3.9 in) long and used a shortened six-round magazine. The overall appearance was cleaned-up and was much smoother than that of earlier models. These Bolos were used extensively by both sides during the Russian Civil War of the early 1920s, and more were purchased in 1926.

Far Eastern version

By the late 1920s Mauser was losing trade to a number of overseas producers of Mauser look-alikes. The attractions of the C/96 were not confined to World War I combatants, and numbers of C/96s were produced before the war for Persia and China, who took to the design with a will. Thus it was not long before nations other than Germany were producing C/96 copies for the market. Spain especially produced direct copies for sales to China and other Far East nations. The Chinese also began to produce Mauser C/96s of all types. Some were direct copies, others were simply look-alikes with differing mechanisms, and still others were produced that were downright dangerous to fire. These Chinese copies were usually liberally sprinkled with Chinese markings to denote their source of origin, and were produced in thousands for local markets.

The Spanish and Chinese also introduced an innovation. By some slight alterations to the trigger mechanism the C/96 could be converted into a form of sub-machine gun, or more correctly a machine pistol, providing fully automatic fire. The value of a weapon the size of the C/96 firing on fully automatic was dubious but its effects could be dramatic, especially at close ranges; the 10-round magazine capacity was soon exhausted and the recoil caused the barrel to climb rapidly away from the target. This did not appear to be any problem to the Chinese, who again took to these new Spanish and locally-produced automatics with a will. The weapons soon became considerable symbols of personal importance, and war lords often equipped their personal bodyguards with the guns in an effort to ensure that the men commanded respect wherever they went. The violent barrel climb was easily overcome by the Chinese: they simply turned the weapons on their side to produce a wide horizontal fan of fire.

New model

Mauser was alarmed by these inroads into its market and soon (1930) produced its own model to meet the situation. The company altered the basic C/96 mechanism slightly to produce the Model 712, almost always known as the 'Schnellfeuer'. This was a more sophisticated firearm than many of the foreign models, with an elongated magazine holding up to 20 rounds and a much superior standard of manufacture; most were produced with fittings for shoulder stocks. This model became just as much a success as many of the earlier models, despite its apparent lack of combat value. It certainly demanded respect for its carrier, and was soon found to be a formidable assassination weapon: King Alexander II of Yugoslavia was killed by one in 1934.

The German military were not so impressed, but nevertheless some were procured for the German armed forces. A few went to the Luftwaffe, more to the Waffen-SS and others to various Hitler Youth units. The German navy also received a number from a batch ordered by the Chinese but not delivered. In German use the Schnellfeuers were not widely used in combat but were generally retained for Waffen-SS activities behind the lines, largely against resistance fighters and partisans.

The C/96 and the Schnellfeur went out of production before the end of World War II. Both were too expensive to produce in large quantities, and other weapons had higher priorities. But the C/96 story did not end there. The Chinese still maintained the production of their various copies and continued to use them all through the campaigns that led to the eventual communist victories of 1948-9. Even then the C/96 was still retained by some, who used it more as a badge of rank rather than a combat weapon.

Mauser C/96 `Broomhandle´

7.63-mm Mauser cartridge

firing pin spring

flip-up rear sight

firing pin

hammer

safety

mainspring plunger

mainspring

10-round magazine

trigger pin

grip screw

magazine floorplate

trigger

grip

Lock mechanism frame

hammer

lanyard ring

sear arm

sear

sear spring and hammer pivot

In the 1980s, the Chinese offered for export the Type 80 machine pistol, which is a version of the C/96 modified for fully automatic fire. It evolved from the Chinese copies of the C/96 produced in the 1920s, when it was a favourite weapon with Chinese warlords.

Lebel revolver

The first French military revolvers were the **Modèle 1873** and **Modèle 1874**. When they were first issued they fired an 11-mm (0.433-in) cartridge that used black powder, although after 1890 a more modern propellant was substituted and some were even converted to fire the new 8-mm (0.315-in) cartridge. The only visual differences between the mles 1873 and 1874 was that the mle 1874 had cylinder flutes while the mle 1873 did not.

These two revolvers with their fixed frames and gate-loaded cylinders were still in use during World War I (indeed, many survived until World War II), but were largely replaced by a more modern design known officially as the **Pistol Revolveur Modele 1892** or the **Modèle d'Ordnance**. To most soldiers it was simply the **Lebel**. The Lebel had evolved via an interim design that fired a new 8-mm cartridge, but this interim model was not considered satisfactory and was redesigned to the mle 1892 standard by the design staff of the Saint Etienne arsenal. The Lebel was the first European revolver to incorporate a swing-out cylinder that considerably assisted rapid reloading: the cylinder swung out to the right and spent cases were ejected using a central hand-operated rod that was normally situated under the barrel.

The Lebel fired a special 8-mm cartridge using a double-action trigger mechanism. The action was very robust and heavy, which was good enough for short-range work but not forgiving enough for target-range accuracy. To clean and repair the action the Lebel had what must be one of the best mechanism access systems of any revolver. A plate at the lower left-hand side of the frame could be hinged open in a forward direction to expose the entire trigger and cylinder operating systems. Changing or cleaning any part was then very simple.

The main drawback to the Lebel when used in close-quarter action was the cartridge. It was seriously underpowered and even at short ranges inflicted wounds that only rarely knocked down an enemy. Unless a bullet found a vital spot an enemy could still continue to function – after a fashion. This drawback did not detract from the in-service popularity of the Lebel during World War I, for many front-line soldiers valued its reliability under adverse conditions more than its hitting power.

Being the first of its kind in Europe the Lebel was copied in both Spain and Belgium.

Specification
Modèle 1892
Calibre: 8 mm (0.315 in)
Weight: 0.792 kg (1.75 lb)
Lengths: overall 235 mm (9.25 in); barrel 118.5 mm (4.665 in)
Muzzle velocity: 225 m (738 ft) per second
Cylinder capacity: 6 rounds

Left: Their catastrophic losses in 1870 notwithstanding, the French cuirassier regiments went to war in 1914 in virtually Napoleonic uniforms, the only difference being that the glittering breastplate and helmet were covered and they carried modern pistols.

Below: The Lebel was the first European revolver to sport a swing-out cylinder for rapid re-loading. Inconveniently, it swung out to the right.

Above: A French officer delivers the coup de grâce to a German prisoner of war, executed by firing squad for fatally knifing one of the guards. This was perhaps the only situation in which the lack of stopping-power of the French 8-mm round was not a problem.

Fighter Aircraft of World War 1

With the outbreak of war in 1914, few could have foreseen that the wire, wood and fabric birdcages with which daring spirits took to the air would evolve within four years into the potent and versatile fighting aeroplane.

No fighter in history was as famous as the Fokker Triplane of Richthofen, the Red Baron. Several replicas have been built of this aircraft.

The whole gamut of air combat came to be realized in the four years of World War I, originally initiated by the need to deprive the enemy of uninterrupted use of the aeroplane as a vehicle of reconnaissance. When it was realized that such aircraft could fly beyond the range of small arms fire on the ground, opposing observers began carrying personal weapons with which to defend themselves in the event that an enemy aircraft appeared in their vicinity. Such was the good use made by the Allies of their early observation aeroplanes that in 1915 the Germans started to introduce purpose-designed aircraft whose pilots were ordered to seek out and destroy the offending intruders; hence the term 'fighting scout' gained universal acceptance to describe the early generation of air combat aeroplane.

Inevitably the next stage was to provide the elderly reconnaissance biplanes (whose lack of power rendered the routine mounting of a defensive gun impractical) with an escort, and in due course (roughly half way through 1915) the first true air combats were being fought in the skies over the Western Front. The first protagonists of the new aerial warfare were the German Fokker monoplanes and the Morane monoplanes, soon to be joined by the British Airco D.H.2, but it was on account of its superior manoeuvrability and front gun that, in the hands of such pilots as Boelcke and Immelmann, the 'Fokker scourge' dominated those skies for nigh on a year.

The second half of the war brought about tremendous advances in technology as well as greatly increased expenditure on the build-up of the aircraft industries of Germany, France and the UK. Perfection of the gun interrupter gear virtually ended the era of the pusher biplane, in which the location of the powerplant behind the pilot removed the chances of the propeller being shot off, and an armament of twin forward-firing, synchronized machine-guns became recognized as standard for almost every fighting scout in service, leaving the aircraft designer free to wring the last ounce of performance from available engines in his search for domination of the dogfight.

Scouts such as the Sopwith Pup, Halberstadt D I and D II, Albatros D I and D II, Fokker D II and D III, and Nieuport XI were but a transient generation, but one in which the elements of air combat were recognized and defined. By mid-1917 all were obsolescent, and during the last year of the war men whose names have passed into the lore of the air were fighting at the controls of such classic aeroplanes as the Sopwith Camel and Triplane, Royal Aircraft Factory S.E.5a, Fokker D VII and Triplane, Pfalz D III, Siemens-Schuckert D III, Nieuport 17 and 28, and SPAD XIII.

Thereafter the term scout was discarded as misrepresenting the purpose for which the aircraft was intended, and the Bristol F.2B Fighter gave its name to the breed whose primary function had already for two years uncompromisingly dominated the skies over France.

Leading American ace of the war, Captain Eddie Rickenbacker, pictured here with his SPAD XIII which he flew with the 94th Aero Squadron in 1918; note the famous 'Hat in the Ring' insignia on the rear fuselage. The mud was a regular feature of a wartime airfield.

Nieuport XVII

Strictly sesquiplanes (that is aircraft with 'one-and-a-half' wings), the Nieuport family of scouts dated back to pre-war months when the naval engineer Gustave Delage began development of a number of observation aircraft which found expression in the Nieuport X, which entered service in 1915, and the **Types XI** and **XII** scouts. All were found to be structurally unsound, but in the **Nieuport XVII** torsional strength in the single spar of the lower, short-chord wing was increased and, with greater power from the 113-hp (84-kW) Le Rhône rotary, the little scout was transformed, the benefits of high lift from the top wing and low drag from the bottom wing being fully exploited.

The Nieuport XVII (Type II) entered service with Escadrille N57 on 2 May 1916, at almost the same time as the D.H.2 with the RFC, spurred by the growing depredations of the 'Fokker scourge', although early versions are said to have served with both French and British units somewhat before this. And it was in the Nieuport XVII that the young Albert Ball rose from obscurity to national fame, flying with No. 11 Squadron and shooting down 44 enemy aircraft between August 1916 and May 1917; there is no doubt that Ball did more than any other single man to restore the flagging British confidence in RFC fortunes in the middle period of the war. At the time of Ball's mysterious death on 7 May 1917 another pilot, Captain William Bishop, was beginning to establish a reputation on Nieuport XVIIs with No. 60 Squadron. In the French air service Guynemer with Escadrille N3 displayed outstanding skill, countering the synchronized gun of the Fokker monoplanes with similar French-developed armament. Among other French scout

pilots who flew Nieuport XVIIs to good effect were Charles Nungesser, Maurice Boyau, Armand Pinsard, René Dorme, Gabriel Guérin, Albert Deullin and Jean Navarre. The great René Fonck transferred direct from Caudron G IVs to SPADs without service in Nieuports.

Nieuports were also widely flown by Belgian *escadrilles*, André de Meulemeester, Edmunds Thieffry, Jan Olieslagers and Francis Jaquet all recording victories while serving with Escadrilles 1 and 5. Macchi-built Nieuport XVIIs were flown by the Italians during 1916-7, when men such as Francesco Baracca, Pier Piccio and Silvio Scaroni all opened their scores on the aircraft. Though largely outclassed late in 1917, Nieuport XVIIs survived to accompany the anti-Bolshevik forces in north Russia in 1918, and also served as trainers with the American Expeditionary Force in France that year.

Flying from Bailleul in 1917, with No. 1 Sqn, RFC, the Nieuport XXVII represented a considerable improvement over the Type XVII.

Albert Ball rose to fame in the Nieuport XVII to become Britain's first well-known ace. This is a Nieuport XVIIbis seen at Yateley in about 1917. They equipped nine squadrons in the RFC and RAF.

Specification
Type: single-seat fighting scout
Powerplant: one 113-hp (84-kW) Le Rhône nine-cylinder air-cooled rotary piston engine
Performance: maximum speed 172 km/h (107 mph) at 2000 m (6,560 ft); climb to 3000 m (9,845 ft) in 9.0 minutes; service ceiling 5300 m (17,390 ft); endurance 2 hours
Weights: empty 375 kg (827 lb); maximum take-off 560 kg (1,235 lb)
Dimensions: span 8.20 m (26 ft 11 in); length 5.75 m (18 ft 10½ in); height 2.33 m (7 ft 7¾ in); wing area 14.77 m² (158.99 sq ft)
Armament: (standard) one fixed 7.7-mm (0.303-in) Vickers machine-gun on nose, synchronized to fire through propeller disc (often replaced by one or two 7.7-mm/0.303-in Lewis machine-guns on Foster mounting on top wing to fire over propeller)

Nieuport XXVIII

The **Nieuport XXVIII** was roughly contemporary with the British Sopwith Camel and, as a direct development of the mid-war scout generation, should have achieved much greater success, continuing as it did the successful Delage sesquiplane formula. Principal design advance in the Type XXVIII lay in the improved fuselage streamlining with additional formers, revision of the vertical tail surfaces to include a fin to which the rudder was hinged in the orthodox manner, and adoption of twin, parallel interplane and centre-section struts in place of the earlier V-type. Power was initially provided by the 160-hp (119-kW) Gnome 9N rotary, though the engine seldom produced this power. However, whereas the Camel lost many of the pleasant handling characteristics of its forebears, those of the Nieuport were somewhat improved, largely as a result of the addition of the fin. Standard armament advanced from single to twin nose guns in the Type XXVIII.

General dissatisfaction with the Gnome engine led to the Le Rhône being adopted as well, and later the Gnome Monosoupape (single-valve) rotary, all engines being equipped with blip-switches which enabled the pilot to cut power momentarily during the glide, although limited throttling was also provided.

The Type XXVIII served with a few

A Nieuport XXVIIIC-1 of the 94th Aero Squadron ('Hat in the Ring'), American Expeditionary Force, in May 1918.

French units towards the end of 1917 but was not generally well received, the aircraft being found to shed fabric from its top wing in any energetic manoeuvre and when flown flat out. It was, however, the only aircraft available in any numbers when the American Expeditionary Force started arriving in France early in 1918 (without any scouts of its own). The first American squadrons to reach the front, the 27th, 94th 95th and 147th Aero Squadrons of the First Pursuit Group, were all equipped with Type XXVIIIs, but because of a low standard of gunnery, success

was slow to be achieved. In due course, victories were chalked up by Lieutenants Alan Winslow, Douglas Campbell, Jimmie Meissner and a few others, but on the other hand two well-known Americans, Quentin Roosevelt and Raoul Lufbery, were shot down and killed while flying the aircraft.

Suspicious that the French had disposed of a 'dud' aircraft on them, the Americans effected a swift changeover to the SPAD XIII in July 1918, but evidence suggests that the Nieuport XXVIII would have been a thoroughly sound combat aeroplane had it not been for the recalcitrant engines, which reflected all the casual attitudes of French manufacturers during the later months of the war.

Specification
Type: single-seat fighting scout
Powerplant: one 160-hp (119-kW) Gnome 9N nine-cylinder air-cooled rotary piston engine
Performance: maximum speed 196 km/h (122 mph) at 2000 m (6,560 ft); climb to 3000 m (9,845 ft) in 11 minutes 30 seconds; service ceiling 5200 m (17,060 ft); endurance 1 hour 30 minutes
Weights: empty 532 kg (1,173 lb); maximum take-off 737 kg (1,625 lb)
Dimensions: span 8.00 m (26 ft 3 in); length 6.20 m (20 ft 4 in); height 2.50 m (8 ft 2½ in); wing area 20.00 m² (215.3 sq ft)
Armament: two fixed 7.7-mm (0.303-in) Vickers machine-guns on nose, synchronized to fire through propeller disc; some American aircraft fitted with Marlin guns or 11-mm (0.43-in) Vickers guns with tracer ammunition for balloon attacks

SPAD VII

Always known by its initials (derived from the name *Société Anonyme Pour l'Aviation et ses Dérivés*) and perpetuating those of the original Deperdussin company, SPAD produced France's finest wartime scouts, most of which owed their success to Marc Birkigt's classic Hispano-Suiza water-cooled engines, of which the broad-V8 version powered both the **SPAD VII** and XIII. First flown in April 1916, the SPAD VII was immediately acknowledged to be greatly superior to the Fokkers and Albatros scouts which still virtually dominated the Western Front. Initial production orders were conservative, but in due course more than 6,000 SPAD VIIs came to be built, about 220 of them subcontracted in the UK. Designed by Louis Béchereau, who had been the designer with the old Deperdussin company, the SPAD VII featured a structure almost entirely of wood with fabric covering, the big engine being entirely enclosed within the contours of the nose cowling which was liberally provided with louvres to allow exit of cooling air from the large frontal radiator.

The SPAD VII owed its reputation to its early service with that most famous of all French scout units, Escadrille SPA 3 *'Les Cicognes'* (The Storks), led in September 1916 (when the first SPAD VIIs arrived) by Alfred Heurteaux, who was himself an ace and who eventually gained 21 victories, of which about 15 were gained in the SPAD VII. Among SPA 3's other famous pilots were René Dorme (23 victories) and Albert Deullin (20 victories) and, most famous of all, Georges Guynemer. When the first SPAD VII arrived in SPA 3, Guynemer had already reached a victory score of nine; by the end of the year this had risen to 30, and by the following July to 50. Emblazoned with the famous stork motif on the rear fuselage, his SPAD was named *Vieux Charles*.

The SPAD VII served with most of the Allied air forces in the last two years of the war, including the RFC. First British squadron to fly the aircraft in France was No. 19 in December 1916, followed by No. 23 in February 1917 and No. 92 in September. No. 17 Squadron flew SPAD VIIs in the Balkans from July to December 1917, while Nos 30, 63 and 72 Squadrons flew the aircraft in Mesopotamia and else-

SPAD VII of Escadrille SPA 81, carrying the squadron's greyhound symbol and the overall grey finish which was favoured by the 'Aviation Militaire' at the time.

For a period in 1917, the SPAD VIIs of the RFC's No. 19 Sqn carried red and white identification bands round the rear fuselage. They flew from La Lovie during July.

where in the Middle East between August 1917 and late 1918. By and large, however, British pilots achieved less success with the SPAD than their contemporaries in the French air services.

Specification
Type: single-seat fighting scout
Powerplant: one 150-hp (112-kW) Hispano-Suiza 8Aa V-8 water-cooled inline piston engine
Performance: maximum speed 192 km/h (119 mph) at 2000 m (6,560 ft); climb to 2000 m (6,560 ft) in 8 minutes 12 seconds; service ceiling 5300 m (17,390 ft); endurance 2 hours 15 minutes
Weights: empty 510 kg (1,124 lb); maximum take-off 740 kg (1,631 lb)
Dimensions: span 7.80 m (25 ft 7¾ in); length 6.15 m (20 ft 2½ in); height 2.12 m (6 ft 11½ in); wing area 17.85 m² (192.14 sq ft)

A SPAD VII of No. 30 Sqn at Baquba, Arabia in mid-1918. These aircraft were used for escorting the RAF

squadron's Martinsydes on bombing duties.

Armament: one fixed 7.7-mm (0.303-in) Vickers machine-gun on nose, synchronized to fire through propeller

disc, and (sometimes) one 7.7-mm (0.303-in) Lewis gun on the top wing

---

FRANCE

SPAD XIII

If the aircraft of World War I are remembered for their brightly-coloured paint schemes, none were so ludicrously daubed as the **SPAD XIII** fighters of the American Expeditionary Force's 94th Aero Squadron (the 'Hat in the Ring' squadron) which achieved a measure of combat maturity with these aircraft in the last four months of the war.

The SPAD XIII, which first flew in August 1917, was principally distinguished from the earlier SPAD VII in having a geared 220-hp (164-kW) Hispano-Suiza 8Ba engine which drove the propeller in the opposite direction to that of the direct-drive Hispano 8Aa. Other differences lay in the inverse tapered-chord ailerons, rounded tailplane tips and larger vertical tail surfaces.

Despite the shattering blow to

French morale with the death of Georges Guynemer, who died in mysterious circumstances while flying one of the first SPAD XIIIs over Poelcapelle in September 1917, the new scout quickly established itself as one of the best Allied aircraft, the great René Fonck reaching his score of 75 victories largely through brilliant marksmanship in the SPAD XIII; one occasion is recorded in which he despatched three enemy aircraft with a total expenditure of just 27 rounds! In the last 14 months of the war the SPAD XIII equipped no fewer than 81 French *escadrilles* as well as numerous units of the Belgian and Italian air service, and Nos 19 and 23 Squadrons of the RFC.

As already mentioned, the Americans decided to adopt the SPAD XIII in July 1918, after experiencing difficulty with the Nieuport 28. The outstanding American pilot was Captain Eddie Rickenbacker of the 94th Aero Squadron. Rickenbacker emerged as top-

The SPAD XIII featured a larger engine than its predecessor and was consequently faster. This example

flew with the American 22nd Aero Squadron in 1918.

scoring ace of the Expeditionary Force, and scored very rapidly in the last few weeks of the war. But no American pilot scored faster than the 'maverick' pilot Frank Luke Jr, whose score of 18 included a number of observation balloons destroyed while

flying the SPAD XIII. These two pilots, both of whom were awarded the Medal of Honor, were the two outstanding American SPAD pilots, yet it must be pointed out that many other highly successful Americans never served with the Expeditionary Force but achieved

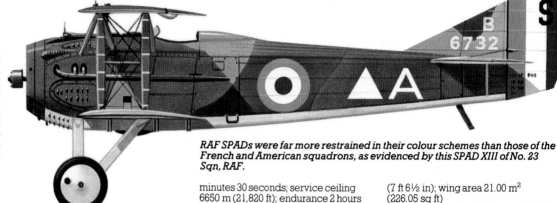

their scores exclusively with the RAF, RFC and French air services. Indeed the veteran Raoul Lufbery, considered by many to be America's finest scout pilot, never flew SPADs and, despite crippling rheumatoid arthritis, remained with the Escadrille Lafayette on Nieuport 28s until his death on 19 May 1918, when he was seen to leap from his blazing scout high over the Western Front; few Allied pilots possessed parachutes.

Specification
Type: single-seat fighting scout
Powerplant: one 220-hp (164-kW) Hispano-Suiza 8Ba V-8 water-cooled inline piston engine
Performance: maximum speed

215 km/h (133.5 mph) at 2000 m (6,560 ft); climb to 2000 m (6,560 ft) in 6

RAF SPADs were far more restrained in their colour schemes than those of the French and American squadrons, as evidenced by this SPAD XIII of No. 23 Sqn, RAF.

minutes 30 seconds; service ceiling 6650 m (21,820 ft); endurance 2 hours
Weights: empty 565 kg (1,245 lb); maximum take-off 820 kg (1,807 lb)
Dimensions: span 8.02 m (26 ft 3¾ in); length 6.20 m (20 ft 4 in); height 2.30 m

(7 ft 6½ in); wing area 21.00 m² (226.05 sq ft)
Armament: two fixed 7.7-mm (0.303-in) Vickers machine-guns on nose, synchronized to fire through propeller disc

 UK

Airco D.H.2

Now generally recognized as the RFC's first true fighter, the **Airco D.H.2** reached France early in 1916. By that time the Fokker monoplane had gained ascendancy over the Western Front on account of its forward-firing machine-gun, to which the RFC had no effective reply as no British interrupter gear had been developed to allow a gun to fire through the propeller disc. Instead the D.H.2, first flown in July 1915, perpetuated the D.H.1's pusher engine layout in which the pilot was seated in the extreme nose. In the new aeroplane he was expected not only to fly the aircraft but also to manhandle his single drum-fed Lewis gun from mounting to mounting, one of which was located on each side of his cockpit. In due course RFC pilots learned to use the Lewis gun as a fixed weapon, aiming the whole aircraft at its target.

Of orthodox fabric-covered wooden construction, the little D.H.2 possessed an all-up weight of no more than 702 kg (1,547 lb) with a Le Rhône engine, the entire tail unit being carried on four struts attached to the wings. Most service aircraft were powered by the 110-hp (82-kW) Gnome rotary driving a two-blade propeller.

First RFC squadron to take its D.H.2s to France was No. 24 Squadron (commanded by Major Lanoe G. Hawker, VC, DSO), which arrived at St Omer with 12 aeroplanes on 7 February 1916. In the next three months Nos 29 and 32 Squadrons followed and these three units participated in the bloody Battle of the Somme, constantly engaging the German Fokker E III monoplanes on fairly equal terms. In due course the type also served with Nos 5, 14, 17, 41, 47 and 111 Squadrons of the RFC, and two aircraft flew with home defence squadrons; one, flown by Captain R.H.M.S. (later Air Marshal Sir Richard, KCB, KBE, MC, DFC, AFC)

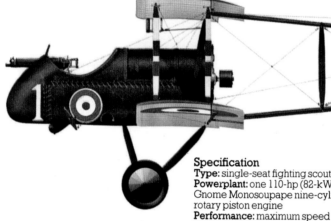

Saundby of the Orfordness Experimental Station, attacked the German airship *L 48* on 17 June 1917. By early 1917 the D.H.2 was outclassed in France, however, and was withdrawn for service with Nos 17 and 111 Squadrons in Palestine, and with No. 47 Squadron in Macedonia.

In the course of 774 combats by D.H.2s in France, No. 24 Squadron pilots destroyed 44 enemy aircraft. In another fight the commander of No. 32 Squadron, Major (later Group Captain) L.W.B. Rees, OBE, MC, AFC, won the Victoria Cross for his single-handed attack on a formation of 10 German aircraft on 1 July 1916. On 28 October that year the great German fighter pilot, Oswald Boelcke, lost his life when his Albatros collided with another German aircraft during combat with D.H.2s of No. 24 Squadron. A few weeks later, in one of the war's longest air combats, the supreme fighter pilot, Manfred Freiherr von Richthofen, fought and eventually killed Major Lanoe Hawker, No. 24 Squadron's gallant commander.

Specification
Type: single-seat fighting scout
Powerplant: one 110-hp (82-kW) Gnome Monosoupape nine-cylinder rotary piston engine
Performance: maximum speed 150 km/h (93 mph) at sea level; climb to 1980 m (6,500 ft) in 12 minutes; service ceiling 4265 m (14,000 ft); endurance 2 hours 45 minutes
Weights: empty 428 kg (943 lb);

An early D.H.2 of Lanoe Hawker's No. 24 Sqn, RFC at the time of the Battle of the Somme. This was the RFC's first true fighter.

maximum take-off 654 kg (1,441 lb)
Dimensions: 8.61 m (28 ft 3 in); length 7.68 m (25 ft 2½ in); height 2.91 m (9 ft 6½ in); wing area 23.13 m² (249.0 sq ft)
Armament: one 7.7-mm (0.303-in) Lewis machine-gun in nose with five 97-round drums of ammunition in cockpit

D.H.2s were flown by RFC squadrons (Nos 14 and 111) in Palestine after they had been withdrawn from operational use on the Western front early in 1917.

 UK

Bristol F.2B Fighter

The origins of the **Bristol F.2B Fighter** may be traced back to the autumn of 1915 when, following the onset of the 'Fokker scourge', the RFC demanded a reconnaissance aircraft 'capable of taking care of itself' in the presence of enemy fighting scouts. The Royal Aircraft Factory produced the thoroughly unsatisfactory R.E.8 (the 'Arry Tate') of which thousands were built, but at the Bristol works Frank Barnwell started

design of his two-seat R.2A 'corps reconnaissance' aircraft. From this stemmed his **F.2A** which, fitted with a synchronized Vickers gun forward and a defensive Lewis gun aft, was regarded more as a fighting machine whose primary task would be armed reconnaissance. And thus was born the reconnaissance fighter. The F.2 was a large aeroplane with a span of over 39 ft (11.9 m) in which the fuselage was

located midway between upper and lower wings; power was to be provided by the Rolls-Royce Falcon engine, but with the eventual build-up of airframe production the supply of engines could not keep pace. Persistent problems arose with the Falcon, moreover, and many of the alternatives suggested (including the Sunbeam Arab) were used.

The first F.2A squadron of the RFC, No. 48, took its aircraft to France in March 1917, but suffered disastrously in 'Bloody April', only two out of six

aircraft returning from the first offensive patrol on 5 April, during the Battle of Arras; the other four had been shot down by Albatros D IIIs of Jasta 11 led by Manfred von Richthofen. Fortunately a revised version, the F.2B, was already in hand with improved lower wing, increased protection for the crew and Scarff ring mounting for the Lewis gun, and with an improved Falcon II engine this new aircraft proved perfectly 'capable of taking care of itself'. In the next few months it re-equipped No. 48 and joined Nos 11, 20 and 22 Squadrons and, being flown as a true dogfighter when attacked by scouts, gave a good account of itself. Top-scoring F.2B crew were the Canadian pilot Lieutenant (later Major) A.E. McKeever and his regular observer Sergeant (later Lieutenant) L.F. Powell of No. 11 Squadron; by the end of 1917, when posted home as an instructor, McKeever had shot down 30 enemy aircraft and Powell's score eventually reached eight. In due course F.2Bs (universally dubbed 'Brisfits') equipped Nos 11, 20, 22, 33, 36, 39, 48, 62, 76, 88 and 141 Squadrons of the RFC/RAF at home and in France, No. 67 Squadron in Palestine, No. 139 Squadron in Italy, and No. 3 Squadron of the Australian Flying Corps in France, as well as being supplied in small numbers to numerous other units. The Bristol fighter survived in RAF front-line service for a dozen years after the war.

Formed only four months before the end of the war, No. 139 Sqn, RAF, at Villaverla in Italy nevertheless destroyed 27 enemy aircraft with its Bristol F.2B Fighters, their aircraft being decorated with strip cartoon characters on the engine cowlings.

Specification
Type: two-seat reconnaissance fighter
Powerplant: one 220-hp (164-kW) Rolls-Royce Falcon II V-12 water-cooled piston engine
Performance: maximum speed 195 km/h (121 mph) at 1525 m (5,000 ft);

climb to 3050 m (10,000 ft) in 13 minutes 15 seconds; service ceiling 6095 m (20,000 ft); endurance 3 hours
Weights: empty 866 kg (1,910 lb); maximum take-off 1297 kg (2,860 lb)
Dimensions: span 11.96 m (39 ft 3 in); length 7.87 m (25 ft 10 in); height 2.97 m (9 ft 9 in); wing area 37.68 m²(405.6 sq ft)

Armament: one fixed 7.7-mm (0.303-in) Vickers machine-gun, synchronized to fire through propeller disc with Constantinesco CC interrupter gear, and one trainable 7.7-mm (0.303-in) Lewis gun on Scarff No. 2 ring on rear cockpit, plus provision for up to 12 9.1-kg (20-lb) Cooper bombs under lower wing

UK
Royal Aircraft Factory S.E.5a

Although conceived at the same time as the **S.E.5**, the improved **Royal Aircraft Factory S.E.5a** followed that aircraft into service some three months later in June 1917 almost simultaneously with the first Sopwith Camels. Designed by H.P. Folland at the Royal Aircraft Factory, Farnborough, in 1916, the aircraft was a beautifully proportioned aeroplane despite its angular lines with semi-rectangular fuselage section and parallel-chord wings and tailplane. Powered by a 200-hp (149-kW) geared water-cooled Hispano-Suiza 8 (which later became the Wolseley Viper), the S.E.5a was dogged in early service by trouble with this engine owing to hastily-manufactured reduction gears, said to have been occasioned by the French Brasier firm's creed that 'engines of incomplete efficiency are better than no engines at all'.

Persistent engine troubles severely delayed production of the S.E.5a and although No. 56 Squadron, RFC, received its first aircraft in June 1917 only five squadrons (Nos 40, 41, 56, 60 and 84), were operating the aircraft by the end of the year, despite the fact that more than 800 S.E.5 and S.E.5a aircraft had by then been completed. The S.E.5a was unusual for its time in being armed with only a single synchronized Vickers gun, to which was added a Lewis gun on a Foster mounting on the top wing, but this slight deficiency in armament (albeit preferred by many pilots) was offset by a high top speed of between 203 and 212 km/h (126 and 132 mph).

Production was widely subcontracted to Austin, Air Navigation Company, Martinsyde, Grahame-White, Vickers, Whitehead and Wolseley, in addition to manufacture at Farnborough. About 5,000 aircraft were prouced, the great majority in 1918, and S.E.5a fighters served on Nos 1, 24, 29, 32, 40, 41, 56, 60, 64, 74, 84, 85, 92 and 94 Squadrons of the RFC and RAF in France, Nos 111 and 145 Squadrons in Palestine, Nos 17, 47 and 150 Squadrons in Macedonia, and No. 72 Squadron in Mesopotamia; they also equipped the 25th and 148th Aero Squadrons of the US Air Service. The most famous of British scout pilots flew the S.E.5 and S.E.5a, of whom the greatest exponent was Major James McCud-

The S.E.5a flown by the highest-scoring British pilot, Captain Edward Mannock VC DSO MC, while serving with No. 74 Sqn.

den, whose total score of 57 air victories included 50 while serving with No. 56 Squadron; Mannock, Bishop, Beauchamp-Proctor and Ball all flew S.E.5 and/or S.E.5a aircraft, although the last-named preferred the Nieuport until eventually becoming reluctantly reconciled to the British aircraft in which he was to lose his life.

Specification
Type: single-seat fighting scout
Powerplant: one 200/240-hp (149/164-kW) Hispano-Suiza 8 water-cooled inline piston engine (of various subvariants)
Performance: maximum speed 212 km/h (132 mph) at 1980 m (6,500 ft); climb to 3050 m (10,000 ft) in 11 minutes 20 seconds; service ceiling 5790 ft (19,000 m); endurance 2 hours 15 minutes
Weights: empty 696 kg (1,535 lb); maximum take-off 930 kg (2,050 lb)

Dimensions: span 8.12 m (26 ft 7½ in); length 6.38 m (20 ft 11 in); height 2.90 m (9 ft 6 in); wing area 22.67 m²(244.0 sq ft)
Armament: one fixed 7.7-mm (0.303-in) Vickers machine-gun, synchronized to fire through propeller disc with Constantinesco CC interrupter gear and 400 rounds, and one trainable 7.7-mm (0.303-in) Lewis gun on Foster mounting on top wing and four 97-round drums

S.E.5as of 'A' Flight, No. 111 Sqn, RAF, serving at Ramleh, Palestine, in 1918; the nearest aircraft is carrying a pair of 20-lb (9-kg) bombs.

Sopwith Pup

UK

Despite all effort by officialdom to the contrary, Herbert Smith's first single-seat scout was known universally as the **Sopwith Pup** for no better reason than that it was so obviously the offspring of the Sopwith 1½-Strutter two-seater. Passed by Sopwith's experimental department in February 1916 on contract to the Admiralty, the prototype Pup, and the next five aircraft (all probably powered by 80-hp/60-kW Clerget rotaries) were delivered for test by the Royal Naval Air Service with whose pilots it was an immediate success. All of them expressed delight with its performance and handling. Production and deliveries were slow to get under way, however, as a result largely of the bickering that broke out between the Admiralty and War Office over priorities, the latter being unable to accept that a commercially conceived design could be superior to one from a government design office, namely the RAF B.E.12 which proved almost useless. At the time of the great Battle of the Somme in mid- to late 1916, RFC squadrons fared badly, and the famous RNAS No. 8 Squadron (or 'Naval Eight') was formed with Pups from units in the Dunkirk area and sent south to assist. So successful was the new squadron that soon both services were crying out for more Pups. By the end of 1916 Nos 54, 46 and 66 Squadrons, RFC, had acquired Pups (now powered by Le Rhône rotaries), and in due course Nos 2, 4, 9, 11 and 12 Squadrons, RNAS, also flew the little scout. As a result of its superb manoeuvrability it avoided the fearsome casualties of other aircraft types during 'Bloody April' 1917 and, despite its relatively modest top speed

and single-gun armament, if handled properly was at least a match for such enemy scouts as the Albatros D III, a view expressed by no less an expert than Lieutenant (later Major) James McCudden, who fitted a Lewis gun in his Pup during early attempts to combat the Gotha bombers whose attacks against south east London started during the summer of 1917. Among the successful Pup pilots at this time was Flight Lieutenant H.S. Kerby of the RNAS who, flying from Walmer, shot down a Gotha on 12 August, and another on 21 August. The Pup was also famous for its early flights from warships, and it was Squadron Commander E.H. Dunning who made the first wartime landing on a ship at sea when he landed a Pup on HMS *Furious* on 2 and 7 August 1917; on his third landing the Pup's engine failed and Dunning was drowned. Thereafter

Pups pioneered the shipboard use of scouts, and eventually served aboard the early aircraft-carriers, as well as several light cruisers and the capital ships HMS *Repulse* and HMS *Tiger*, being launched from platforms over the gun turrets.

Specification
Type: single-seat fighting scout
Powerplant: one 80-hp (60-kW) Le Rhône nine-cylinder air-cooled rotary piston engine
Performance: maximum speed 179 km/h (111.5 mph) at sea level; climb to 1980 m (6,500 ft) in 8.0 minutes; service ceiling 5335 m (17,500 ft); endurance 3 hours
Weights: empty 357 kg (787 lb); maximum take-off 556 kg (1,225 lb)

Sopwith Pup A 635 belonging to No. 46 Sqn, RFC, at Izel-le-Haneau but shot down and captured intact by the Germans.

A few Sopwith Pups were equipped with Le Prieur rockets attached to the interplane struts for anti-Zeppelin combat, but none is thought to have been used operationally.

Dimensions: span 8.08 m (26 ft 6 in); length 5.87 m (19 ft 3¾ in); height 2.87 m (9 ft 5 in); wing area 23.60 m² (254.0 sq ft)
Armament: (normal) one fixed 7.7-mm (0.303-in) Vickers machine-gun on nose, synchronized to fire through propeller disc with Sopwith-Kauper, Scarff-Dibovski or Constantinesco CC interrupter gear; RNAS Pups had one Lewis gun on tripod mounting to fire through top-wing centre-section cutout; RFC Pups had provision for four 11.3-kg (25-lb) bombs

Sopwith Triplane

UK

If Herbert Smith's little Pup was the most appealing combination of aesthetic grace and superb handling chacteristics ever conceived, his **Sopwith Triplane** was an ingenious equation of improved performance and manoeuvrability without significant loss of the splendid design features of the earlier scout. Probably motivated by promise shown by his unattractive three-seat 'Tractor Triplane' (known as the LRTTr), Smith decided to apply the triplane layout to the basic Pup design, employing wings of exactly the same span but of only 99.06-cm (39-in) chord, and single broad I-type interplane and centre-section struts, the latter passing through the roots of the middle wing and fuselage, thereby acting as longeron spacers, bestowing great strength and allowing a minimum of bracing wires. Power was provided by a 130-hp (97-kW) Clerget rotary, and the standard armament was a single synchronized Vickers gun, although some subcontracted Triplanes were armed with a pair of guns. Ailerons were fitted to all wings.

The prototype Triplane passed out of Sopwith's experimental department in May 1916, the test flying being carried out by Harry Hawker at Brooklands. It was then sent to 'A' Squadron, RNAS, in France, for evaluation where it caused a sensation, and was in action within 15 minutes of arrival! Following urgent representations by Sir Douglas Haig, and the appearance of large numbers of Albatros D Is and D IIs, the

Triplane was ordered into production for both the RFC and RNAS, but in the event, to the accompaniment of acrimony between the two services, it served regularly only with RNAS units; by early 1917 it was being delivered to Nos 1, 8, 9, 10, 11 and 12 Squadrons, RNAS, Nos 1, 8 and 10 (Naval) Squadrons being attached to the RFC immediately after 'Bloody April' 1917. At about that time an improvement was being introduced to the Triplane,

namely a shorter-span tailplane which allowed the scout to be dived vertically. Production of the Triplane totalled only about 150 aircraft, as the Camel was already proving its superiority over the Western Front by mid-1917. Nevertheless the Triplane won undying fame in the hands of 'Black Flight' of 'Naval Ten', led by Raymond Collishaw; with such names as *Black Maria, Black Prince, Black Sheep, Black Death* and *Black Roger*, the Triplanes were flown by Collishaw and fellow Canadians, Flight Sub-Lieutenants W.M. Alexander, G.E. Nash, E.V. Reid and J.E. Sharman, and during the summer of 1917 amassed what was probably a victory tally unequalled by any other flight in such a short period. Collishaw himself destroyed 16 enemy aircraft in June.

Specification
Type: single-seat fighting scout
Powerplant: one 130-hp (97-kW)

Clerget 9B nine-cylinder air-cooled rotary piston engine
Performance: maximum speed 188 km/h (117 mph) at 1525 m (5000 ft); climb to 3050 m (10,000 ft) in 11 minutes 50 seconds; service ceiling about 6250 m (20,500 ft); endurance 2 hours 45 minutes
Weights: empty 499 kg (1,101 lb); maximum take-off 699 kg (1,541 lb)
Dimensions: span 8.08 m (26 ft 6 in); length 5.74 m (18 ft 10 in); height 3.20 m (10 ft 6 in); wing area 21.46 m² (231.0 sq ft)
Armament: standard aircraft had one fixed 7.7-mm (0.303-in) Vickers machine-gun on nose, synchronized to fire through propeller disc with Scarff-Dibovski interrupter gear and 500 rounds; some subcontracted examples had two such guns

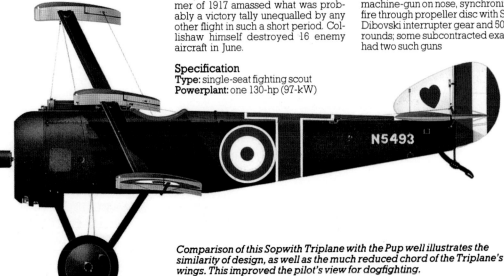

Comparison of this Sopwith Triplane with the Pup well illustrates the similarity of design, as well as the much reduced chord of the Triplane's wings. This improved the pilot's view for dogfighting.

The Evolution of the Dogfight

New skills had to be evolved by pilots to make best use of the greatly increased fighting ability of the aircraft. Failure to master the techniques was almost invariably fatal.

The evolution of aerial dogfighting during World War I was as much the result of increasing flying experience and improved pilot training as of the progressive improvement of aircraft design. Some of the earliest attempts to strike down opponents were dictated by improvization and ingenuity, as witness the resort to a trailing grapnel employed by the Russian pilot Kazakov in attempts to remove his adversary's top wing. Only with the mounting of a machine-gun in the aircraft did the evolution of fighting tactics really begin, a process of jockeying into a position from which the gun could be brought to bear while remaining immune from defensive fire. Thus the first classic manoeuvre was the *stern stalk*, with the attacker approaching unseen beneath the victim's tail; from this position the attacking fighter, whose forward gun could in any case only fire above the propeller, could deliver a lethal burst into the underside of its target with little or no deflection.

Interrupter gear

With the introduction of the gun interrupter gear, which allowed the forward gun(s) to be aimed directly along the attacker's flight path, the whole art of dogfighting advanced, and the Germans (with their Fokker monoplanes) gained a lead in tactics that dominated the air war over the Western Front from mid-1915 until well into 1916. A favourite tactic was the use of a decoy which made feinting attacks just out of range on the beam quarters of the target while, unseen by the defending crew, a scout with synchronized gun would *dive out of the sun* to deliver the coup de grâce.

These tactics gave rise to the first two golden rules of air combat, namely 'Beware of the Hun in the sun', and 'He who has height wins the fight'. Until fairly late in 1916 few fighting scouts possessed sufficient engine power to employ manoeuvres in the vertical plane without fatal loss of speed and control, so that attackers tended to make a single firing pass with front gun before diving away to safety. With the arrival of such aircraft as the Albatros D II and Pup,

power/weight ratios increased so that more and more manoeuvring could be effected by climbing turns, with the result that air combats became protracted affairs, and it was at about this time that *Immelmann* introduced in the Fokker E III the famous climbing turn (in effect a half roll off the top of a loop) that came to bear his name. It was, however, seldom used as a dogfighting manoeuvre but more as a means of escape from an attack from the rear.

Much more practical was the *snap turn* (a manoeuvre which was facilitated either to left or right by the engine's gyroscopic torque) and this formulated the next rule of combat, 'Always turn towards your attacker'. Thus when beset by an attack from, for instance, the rear port quarter the vital action was to turn sharply to port, thereby increasing the attacker's deflection angle and forcing him either into a tighter turn or to break away.

Refinements of basic manoeuvres

As air combat became more and more the functions of flying skill, physical fitness, sharp reactions, keen eyesight and good deflection shooting judgement, so the art of dogfighting came to embrace developments of the basic flying manoeuvres, and the *'split-S'* and *'Lufbery'* came to be employed by the more experienced pilots. Although these never achieved specific definition (owing to individual variations in interpretation) they were essentially variations and extensions of the snap turn in which the target pilot executed several reversing sharp turns so as to force his attacker to overshoot and thus to put him in a firing position on his tail. The Lufbery was a variation of this, but introduced climbing or diving turns, and it was widely averred that the SPAD XIII, as flown by many American pilots in the last year of the war, was the perfect aeroplane to execute this manoeuvre

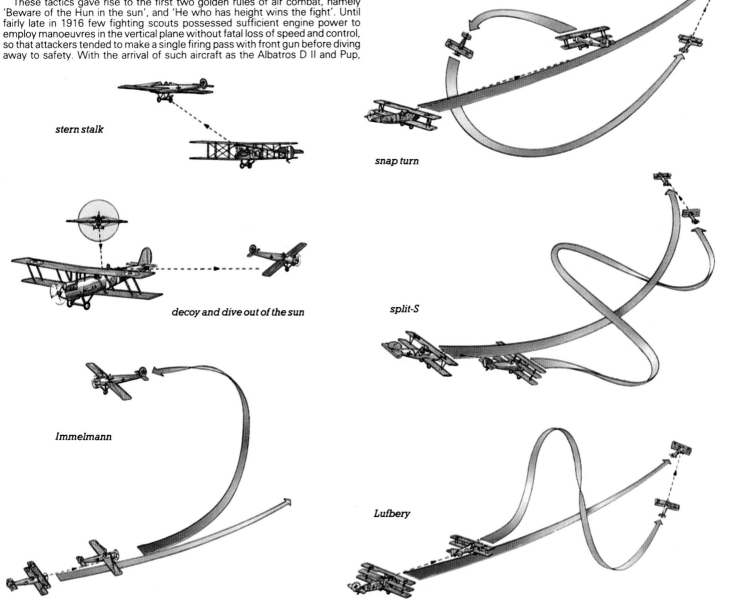

stern stalk

decoy and dive out of the sun

Immelmann

snap turn

split-S

Lufbery

Sopwith 7F.1 Snipe

The ultimate in wartime fighting scouts to reach service status, the **Sopwith 7F.1 Snipe** flew over the Western Front just in time to demonstrate its superiority over all comers, gaining immortality through one epic air battle in the hands of Major W.G. Barker. Intended originally as a relatively simple derivative of the excellent Camel, the prototype Snipe retained the single-bay wings of the earlier aircraft with some modification to the vertical tail in an effort to overcome the Camel's lateral control deficiences. This aircraft was flown well before the end of 1917, but subsequent aircraft employed W. O. Bentley's B.R.2 rotary engine which delivered 230 hp (172 kW) compared with the B.R.1's 150 hp (112 kW), necessitating further increase in fin area. A change was also made to two-bay wings of greater span to enable a greater military load to be carried. As originally tested the Snipe had a Lewis gun in addition to the customary twin Vickers on the nose, but the former was discarded as superfluous. One of the prototypes went to France in February 1918, where it received enthusiastic reports from service pilots. Production orders for 1,700 Snipes were quickly placed, but it was not until September that the first RAF squadrons in France received their initial deliveries, and No. 43 Squadron did good work escorting the Airco D.H.9s of No. 107 Squadron during the last six weeks of the war. Of the three other squadrons to receive Snipes before the Armistice (Nos 78 and 208 of the RAF, and No. 4 of the Australian Flying Corps) only the last was able to prove the Snipe's undisputed superiority, shooting down 36 enemy aircraft in four days (including 13 in a single day). It was Major Barker who, ordered to ferry a new Snipe to France and remain attached to No. 201 (Camel) Squadron for a fortnight, took

A Sopwith 7F.1 Snipe of No. 208 Sqn, RAF, one of only four squadrons to fly the aircraft during the war.

the new scout into the headlines. Unable to find combat during the stipulated fortnight, he was already preparing to return home when, as a last resort, he decided to seek enemy aircraft over the Forêt de Mormal on 27 October. He shot down a two-seater and was then attacked by 15 Fokker D VIIs. Wounded in the thigh, he shot down one of his attackers but fell into a spin; recovering from this he found himself among another group of a dozen D VIIs, one of which he destroyed before being hit in the elbow and again spinning down. He eventually shot his way out of a further group of enemy scouts before crash-landing near a British observation balloon. Barker survived to be awarded the Victoria Cross and his aircraft was recovered and shipped over to his native Canada for permanent preservation and display.

Specification
Type: single-seat fighting scout
Powerplant: one 230-hp (172-kW) Bentley B.R.2 nine-cylinder air-cooled rotary piston engine
Performance: maximum speed 195 km/h (121 mph) at 3050 m (10,000 ft); climb to 3050 m (10,000 ft) in 9 minutes 25 seconds; service ceiling 5945 m (19,500 ft); endurance 3 hours
Weights: empty 595 kg (1,312 lb); maximum take-off 916 kg (2,020 lb)
Dimensions: span 9.14 m (30 ft 0 in); length 6.05 m (19 ft 10 in); height 2.90 m (9 ft 6 in); wing area 25.18 m²

A Boulton & Paul-built Snipe, probably completed only a few days before the war's end. The Snipe was a very capable fighter but was too late to see much action. The aircraft carried on for some years after the war in front-line RAF service.

(271.0 sq ft)
Armament: two 7.7-mm (0.303-in) Vickers machine-guns on nose with Sopwith-Kauper interrupter gear to fire through propeller disc, plus provision for four 11.3-kg (25-lb) bombs

Sopwith F.1 Camel

Following what were universally accepted as 'pilots' aeroplanes', the Pup and Triplane, Herbert Smith's classic **Sopwith Camel** possessed none of the natural grace of the earlier aircraft, yet exuded the power and spite of a fighting machine. In demanding constant watchfulness of its particular traits, it could and did sort the men from the boys. Its capacity to turn with incredible sharpness stemmed largely from the concentration of propeller, engine, pilot, armament and fuel within the front 1.8 m (6 ft) of the aircraft, together with tremendous engine torque and gyroscopic couple. When originally conceived, the **Biplane F.1** was intended to feature equal dihedral on top and bottom wings but, for ease of manufacture, the top wing was made flat and the dihedral of the lower wings arbitrarily doubled, thereby giving to the Camel its distinctive 'tapered gap'. Its name was said to have derived from its characteristic 'hump' over the breeches of the twin Vickers guns, which in turn obviated the need for a windscreen.

Various engines were flown in Camels: 130- and 140-hp (97- and 104-kW) Clergets, the 110-hp (82-kW) Le Rhône, the 150-hp (112-kW) Bentley B.R.1, and the 100- and 150-hp (75- and 112-kW) Gnome Monosoupapes.

The prototype (with 110-hp/82-kW

Clerget 9Z) was completed in December 1916 and was followed by examples for both the RFC and RNAS, the first two squadrons of the former service, Nos 70 and 45, being re-equipped in July 1917. By the end of that year 1,325 F.1 Camels had been completed (of which most were Clerget- and Le Rhône-powered), and early the following year deliveries of the **2F.1 Camel** shipboard variant started. Subcontracting of production was widely undertaken throughout England and before the end of the war Camels served with Nos 3, 28, 43, 45, 46, 54, 65, 70, 71, 73 and 80 Squadrons of the RFC on the Western Front; Nos 28, 45 and 66 Squadrons in Italy; Nos 151 and 152 night-fighting squadrons of the RFC; Nos 1, 3, 4, 6, 8, 9, 10 and 12 Squadrons, RNAS (later with numbers increased by 200 in the RAF); Nos 220, 221, 222, 223, 224, 225, 226 and 227 Squadrons of the RAF's Adriatic and Aegean groups, and many other units; they also flew with the RAF's contingent in Russia at Archangel and with the Slavo-British Aviation Group, as well as the US Air Service's 17th Aero

This photograph serves to emphasize the concentration of weight in the short front fuselage, so characteristic of the Camel. This aircraft has had its guns removed.

Squadron in France. Among the famous fighting exponents of the Camel were Raymond Collishaw (a total of 60 victories), Major D.R. McClaren (54), Major W.G. Barker (53) and Captain H.W. Wollatt (35).

Specification
Type: single-seat fighting scout
Powerplant: one 150-hp (112-kW) Bentley B.R.1 nine-cylinder air-cooled rotary piston engine
Performance: maximum speed 187 km/h (116.5 mph) at 1980 m (6,500 ft); climb to 3050 m (10,000 ft) in 9 minutes 25 seconds; service ceiling 6095 m (20,000 ft); endurance 2 hours 30 minutes
Weights: empty 443 kg (977 lb); maximum take-off 667 kg (1,471 lb)
Dimensions: span 8.53 m (28 ft 0 in); length 5.64 m (18 ft 6 in); height 2.59 m (8 ft 6 in); wing area 21.46 m² (231.0 sq ft)
Armament: two fixed 7.7-mm (0.303-in) Vickers machine-guns on nose with interrupter gear, plus racks for four 20-lb (9.1-kg) Cooper bombs under the fuselage

Sopwith Camel in Action

Nobody could call the Sopwith Camel a graceful aircraft; nor was it easy to fly. Unforgiving in experienced hands, it had one major virtue: it was the most ferocious dogfighter of the war. RFC and RAF Camels alone scored 2880 confirmed victories, far more than any other Allied fighting scout.

Occupying in the affections of World War I scout pilots the same spot as the Supermarine Spitfire in those of a later generation of fighter pilots, the Sopwith Camel was without argument the epitome of classic fighting scouts of the war. Yet, like so many thoroughbreds it could be temperamental and was unforgiving of careless attention in the air, the docile handling of its forebear, the Pup, having been lost in the process of development. Once mastered, however, the Camel was indeed a deadly little fighter; all that was required to change direction quickly in a fight was to pull the nose up, cut the engine and stall turn by use of all controls, and the aeroplane would flick round, especially to the left. Some pilots needing to turn to the right would opt to turn 270° to the left, such was the astonishing speed with which it flicked round! But at the stall, unlike the S.E.5 which was rigged symmetrically and stalled gently without wing drop, the Camel, which had wing incidence washed-out on one side to counteract engine torque, stalled sharply, with a wing dropping into a spin.

Sadly the Camel arrived over the Western Front just too late to avert the catastrophe of 'Bloody April' in 1917, but flew offensive patrols during the 3rd Battle of Ypres which opened on 31 July that year. Indeed, ground-strafing featured prominently in the work performed by Camels over the front, particularly by the aircraft of Nos 3, 28, 46 and 70 Squadrons; casualties were very heavy, losses frequently exceeding 30 per cent, and it was this high rate of attrition that delayed the build-up of Camel strength in France until the end of 1917.

Camel gains respect

It was as a dogfighter that the Camel excelled, however, and long before the end of 1917 the Germans had acquired a healthy respect for the stubby little scout which was easily recognizable from afar by the sharply-tapering wing gap (bestowed by marked dihedral on the lower wing). For example, on 24 March 1918, at the beginning of the big German offensive which was launched in an effort to break the fixed-front deadlock before the Americans could tip the balance, and when the skies over the front filled with swarms of Albatros and Fokker scouts, the pickings were there for those with the stomach for a fight; Captain J.L. Trollope, a Camel pilot of the RFC's No. 43 Squadron, shot down three enemy aircraft in the morning and three more in the afternoon. This record was equalled by another No. 43 Squadron pilot, Captain H.W. Wollatt, who on 12 April also destroyed three German aircraft before lunch and three afterwards. Only nine days later Captain A. Roy Brown, a Canadian Camel pilot on No. 209 Squadron, shot down a red Fokker Dr I near Corbie; when ground parties reached the wreckage they found the body of Manfred Freiherr von Richthofen, Knight of the *Ordre Pour le Mérite*, and victor of 80 air combats. When Brown landed at Bertangles his Camel was found to have 50 bullet holes in it.

Overseas service

Although the Western Front was the Camel's principal killing ground, the little fighter was active in almost every other war theatre. Some, for instance, went to Russia in 1918 to be flown by the Slavo-British Aviation Group against the Bolsheviks, and one was flown with tremendous skill by the veteran Russian ace, Alexander Kazakov who, after his action at Siy Convent in October, was awarded the DSO and promoted major in the British army, Alas, as maintenance of the various foreign aircraft became more difficult owing to a lack of spares, this gallant pilot was killed when his Camel broke up in the air a year later over Bereznik.

Second only to France, the Italian front was the theatre where Camels also saw distinguished service for, following the débâcle at Caporetto on 24 October 1917, the RFC was ordered to deploy three Camel squadrons (Nos 28, 45 and 66) in north Italy. On 30 March 1918 three No. 66 Squadron pilots, Captain P. Carpenter and Lieutenants H. Eycott-Martin and A. Jerrard, were about to attack an Austrian aerodrome when they were set upon by five Albatros scouts, of which Jerrard shot one down. The Camel pilots then got on with their attack on the aerodrome as the Austrians reformed for battle. Eventually 19 enemy aircraft attacked the three Camels, each of whose pilots downed one opponent. Eight aircraft then concentrated on Eycott-Martin and Jerrard went to his aid, shooting down another Austrian and engaging the enemy's attention while his fellow pilots made good their escape. Finally, his own Camel in tatters and with controls all but shot away, Jerrard was obliged to land and surrender. His award of the Victoria Cross (the only one made to a Camel pilot) was announced on 1 May.

William Barker

If only one Victoria Cross was awarded to a pilot for combat in a Camel, another famous RFC pilot, who also received the UK's highest gallantry award, shot down more than 40 enemy aircraft at the controls of a single Camel, surely a record unequalled by any other fighter in history. William Barker, a native of Manitoba in Canada, had already shot down a Roland and held the Military Cross in 1917 when he was appointed a flight commander on No. 28 Squadron in France. In his Camel (B6313) he shot down five more German aircraft before accompanying the squadron to Italy, arriving at Milan on 12 November. By the end of March 1918 he and B6313 had shot down 19 further enemy aircraft, and Barker had been awarded the DSO. In April he took over command of No.

A pair of Beardmore-built 2F.1 Camels based at Turnhouse in 1918 for defence against airship attacks; this naval version had one Vickers and one Lewis gun on the upper wing.

Sopwith Camel

Heavily committed to the air fighting over the big offensives by both sides on the Western Front in 1918, No. 210 Sqn, RAF, flew standard two-Vickers Camels, aircraft passed on from the old RNAS No. 10 (Naval) Sqn. Whereas the Flight had previously been denoted by coloured horizontal bars on the fuselage nose, the RAF Squadron simply retained the Flight letter forward of the fuselage roundel. The CO during this period was Squadron Commander B. C. Bell, RN.

A Sopwith F.1 Camel in post-Armistice colour scheme; with guns removed, it was probably serving as a trainer or hack aircraft.

Painted with 'eagle's plumage' on the wings and given prominent 'eyes' on the engine cowling, this was the 1,000th Camel built by Ruston, Proctor & Co Ltd, Lincoln.

66 Squadron, but retained his favourite Camel, downing 16 Austrian aeroplanes in three months, for which he received another MC and the Italian Silver Medal for Valour. Barker was then given command of a Bristol Fighter squadron, No. 139, but again opted to keep his Camel, in which he went on to destroy six more opponents. In September Barker was posted home to England, and B6313 was deemed to be worn out and had to be scrapped; in it Barker had gained 46 combat victories. (In the last month of the war Barker was ordered to take one of the new Sopwith Snipes, a direct descendant of the Camel, to France. In an epic single-handed combat on 27 October 1918, which earned him the VC, he fought a large number of Fokker D VIIs, estimated at more than 40, over the Forêt de Mormal and, despite numerous severe wounds, shot five down before crashlanding. Barker survived the war with VC, DSO and Bar, MC and two Bars, *Légion d'Honneur, Croix de Guerre*, and two Italian Silver Medals for Valour, a collection of gallantry awards only surpassed by that of 'Mick' Mannnock, and went into business with fellow Canadian ace, Billy Bishop; he was killed in a flying accident on 12 March 1930.

Tricky though the Camel might be to the less initiated, in the hands of an experienced pilot it

Seen at Martlesham Heath in October 1917, this Camel was fitted with a 150-hp (112-kW) Gnome Monosoupape engine. The markings are those of the United States Air Service.

was thus shown to be a deadly weapon. And its special tricks might be thought too difficult to master at night, yet the Camel it was that pioneered the art of night fighting (although earlier aircraft had flown against German Zeppelin airship raiders). Three Camel pilots of No. 44 Squadron, Major G.W. Murlis Green, Captain C.J.Q. Brand and Lieutenant C.C. Banks had, since September 1917, been flying their aircraft at night in the hope of intercepting the German Gotha bombers which were carrying out sporadic raids over south east England. It was Murlis Green who, on the night of 18 December, despite being temporarily blinded by the flashes from his own guns, put one engine of a Gotha out of action, the enemy bomber crashing near Folkestone when its other engine failed. But it was Banks and another No. 44 Squadron pilot, Captain G.H. Hackwill, who on the night of 25 January 1918 were the first to shoot down an enemy aeroplane at night by direct action, bringing down a Gotha in flames at Wickford. Captain Brand gained his first victory while serving with No. 112 Squadron on 19/20 May 1918 when he shot another Gotha down over Faversham. Of these illustrious Camel pilots, Brand (as an Air Vice-Marshal) brilliantly commanded a Fighter Command group in the Battle of Britain 22 years later, at

the same time that Murlis Green was commanding a fighter station.

These were but the first of numerous night victories by Camels, and in August their pilots began flying what in a future war would be termed intruder attacks. On the night of 21/22 August four No. 151 Squadron Camels bombed the enemy aerodromes at Offoy and Moislains, and another pilot of the squadron shot down a

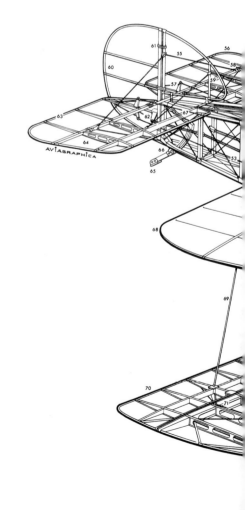

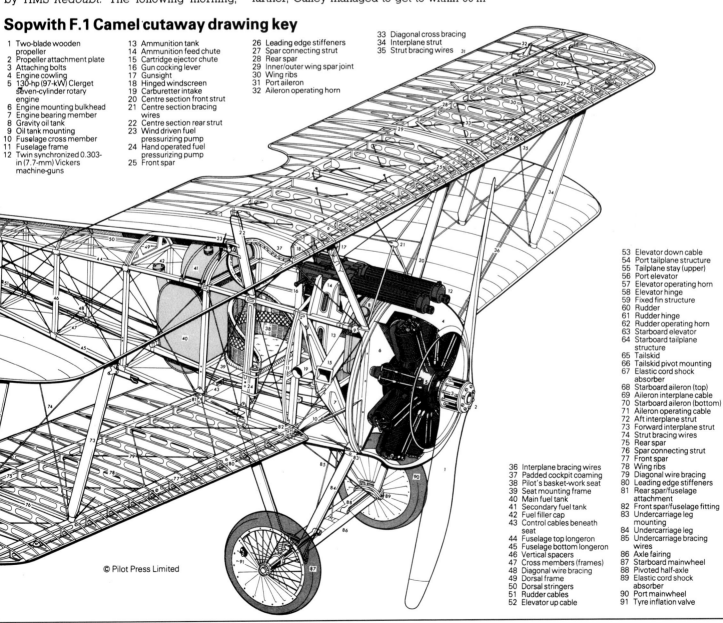

Flown by the Canadian, Captain W. M. Alexander, DSC (17 victories), this Camel of No. 10 (Naval) Sqn displays the horizontal black bars of 'A' Flight when based at Treizennes, shortly before the squadron was renumbered No. 210 when the amalgamation of the RFC and RNAS formed the RAF.

German aircraft which rose to intercept. Three nights later the Camels got amongst German bombers returning to their base and shot two down, and on 17/18 September No. 151 Squadron downed three more.

The last German airship to be brought down during the war was *L53*, shot down by a Camel operated and flown by Lt S.D. Culley RN in a novel manner. For some months trials had been carried out at sea involving a destroyer towing a lighter with a Camel on board. When on 10 August 1918 Admiral Tyrwhitt's Harwich Force set sail for the Heligoland Bight, Culley was in a Camel aboard a lighter being towed by HMS *Redoubt*. The following morning,

when the force was off Terschelling, *L53* (Kapitänleutnant Prölss) appeared on the scene at about 4570 m (15,000 ft). Culley took off from the lighter's deck and half an hour later had reached 5485 m (18,000 ft), by which time the airship had climbed higher. Staggering up further, Culley managed to get to within 90 m

(300 ft) of his victim and opened fire. One of his guns jammed after firing only seven rounds, but the other caused the airship to erupt in a great sheet of flame and to break apart. After Culley had put his aircraft down on the sea and was hoisted aboard his lighter, the Camel was found to have just a pint of fuel left in the tank.

The name Camel, incidentally, was never recognized officially, this being the popular though universally accepted soubriquet for the little scout with its characteristic 'hump' over its two deadly Vickers guns placed less than 0.6 m (2 ft) in front of the pilot's face. To those in Whitehall it was unimaginatively but simply the Sopwith F.1.

Sopwith F.1 Camel cutaway drawing key

1 Two-blade wooden propeller
2 Propeller attachment plate
3 Attaching bolts
4 Engine cowling
5 130-hp (97-kW) Clerget seven-cylinder rotary engine
6 Engine mounting bulkhead
7 Engine bearing member
8 Gravity oil tank
9 Oil tank mounting
10 Fuselage cross member
11 Fuselage frame
12 Twin synchronized 0.303-in (7.7-mm) Vickers machine-guns

13 Ammunition tank
14 Ammunition feed chute
15 Cartridge ejector chute
16 Gun cocking lever
17 Gunsight
18 Hinged windscreen
19 Carburetter intake
20 Centre section front strut
21 Centre section bracing wires
22 Centre section rear strut
23 Wind driven fuel pressurizing pump
24 Hand operated fuel pressurizing pump
25 Front spar

26 Leading edge stiffeners
27 Spar connecting strut
28 Rear spar
29 Inner/outer wing spar joint
30 Wing ribs
31 Port aileron
32 Aileron operating horn

33 Diagonal cross bracing
34 Interplane strut
35 Strut bracing wires

36 Interplane bracing wires
37 Padded cockpit coaming
38 Pilot's basket-work seat
39 Seat mounting frame
40 Main fuel tank
41 Secondary fuel tank
42 Fuel filler cap
43 Control cables beneath seat
44 Fuselage top longeron
45 Fuselage bottom longeron
46 Vertical spacers
47 Cross members (frames)
48 Diagonal wire bracing
49 Dorsal frame
50 Dorsal stringers
51 Rudder cables
52 Elevator up cable

53 Elevator down cable
54 Port tailplane structure
55 Tailplane stay (upper)
56 Port elevator
57 Elevator operating horn
58 Elevator hinge
59 Fixed fin structure
60 Rudder
61 Rudder hinge
62 Rudder operating horn
63 Starboard elevator
64 Starboard tailplane structure
65 Tailskid
66 Tailskid pivot mounting
67 Elastic cord shock absorber
68 Starboard aileron (top)
69 Aileron interplane cable
70 Starboard aileron (bottom)
71 Aileron operating cable
72 Aft interplane strut
73 Forward interplane strut
74 Strut bracing wires
75 Rear spar
76 Spar connecting strut
77 Front spar
78 Wing ribs
79 Diagonal wire bracing
80 Leading edge stiffeners
81 Rear spar/fuselage attachment
82 Front spar/fuselage fitting
83 Undercarriage leg mounting
84 Undercarriage leg
85 Undercarriage bracing wires
86 Axle fairing
87 Starboard mainwheel
88 Pivoted half-axle
89 Elastic cord shock absorber
90 Port mainwheel
91 Tyre inflation valve

© Pilot Press Limited

Albatros D V

Among the most colourful of all World War I fighting scouts were Robert The-lan's sleek **Albatros D V** aircraft, their pilots' bold insignia reflecting their esprit that had been enhanced during 'Bloody April' of 1917, which had witnessed the near total eclipse of the Allied air forces in France.

Unfortunately, although the D V continued in service right up to the end of the war, it never lived up to the expectations of pilots who had ben anticipating an aircraft with a performance much advanced over that of the slightly less streamlined and lower powered **Albatros D III**. From the outset the aircraft gained a bad reputation on account of a suspected wing fault following a number of failures during prolonged dives, a fault later overcome in the strengthened **D Va**.

First flown in the early spring of 1917 in prototype form, the D V was ordered into mass production immediately and deliveries started in May, with *Jasta* strengths building up so quickly that by September the number of D Vs at the front had reached 424. Peak strength of 1,117 D Vs and D Vas was reached in May 1918.

To achieve what was probably one of the most perfectly streamlined fuselage shapes of the war, the semi-monocoque structure comprised lightened plywood formers and eight spruce longerons to which was pinned and screwed a series of carefully shaped plywood panels. The cross-section tapered smoothly from the circular nose section to a knife-edge at the stern post, the rear fuselage being of true elliptic section. The Mercedes engine originally installed was completely enveloped in the nose, but the fairings were later removed so that the top of the engine was exposed.

Introduction of the DV was intended to reverse German fortunes which had suffered following the appearance of the S.E.5 and SPAD in 1917, but this hope was not fulfilled, as a result largely of the fast-improving quality of British and French pilots after 'Bloody April'. Nevertheless it is thought that most of the 80 *Jastas* that were deployed to support the great German offensive of March 1918 flew at least some D Vs and D Vas. Among the famous pilots who flew the aircraft were Manfred von Richthofen, Eduard Ritter von Schleich (*Führer* of Jasta 21), von Der Osten (Jasta 4), Bruno Loerzer (Jasta 26), Karl Thom (Jasta 21), Hermann Goering (then a *Leutnant* with Jasta 27) and Hans Joachim von Hippel,

The striking white and blue diamond pattern adopted by Hauptmann Ritter von Schleich, who served on Jasta 5 at Boistrancourt in 1917 and later commanded Jasta 21.

Albatros D V flown by Oberleutnant Paul Bäumer and Leutnant Wilhelm Lehman, successive commanders of Jasta 5, characterized by an Edelweiss emblem on the rear fuselage.

Albatros D V flown by Leutnant Fritz Rumey of Jasta 5, who went on to gain 45 victories.

whose scarlet dragon-emblazoned D V of Jasta 5 suffered total breakaway of the lower wings in a dive but was nursed down to a crash landing, the pilot surviving to tell the tale.

Specification
Type: single-seat fighting scout
Powerplant: one 180-hp (134-kW) Mercedes D IIIa six-cylinder inline watercooled piston engine
Performance: maximum speed 165 km/h (103 mph) at 1000 m (3,280 ft); climb to 1000 m (3,280 ft) in 4.0 minutes; service ceiling 5700 m (18,700 ft); endurance 2 hours

Weights: empty 687 kg (1,515 lb); maximum take-off 937 kg (2,066 lb)
Dimensions: span 9.05 m (29 ft 8¼ in); length 7.33 m (24 ft 0⅝ in); height 2.70 m (8 ft 10¼ in); wing area 21.20 m² (228.2 sq ft)
Armament: two fixed 7.92-mm (0.31-in) LMG 08/15 machine-guns on the nose, synchronized to fire through propeller disc

An Albatros D Va being inspected by British servicemen after capture. This aircraft was believed to have been later tested by Major James McCudden.

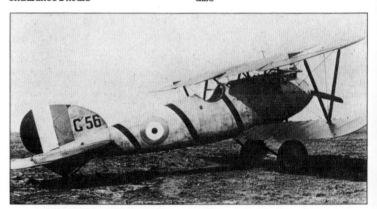

Captured Albatros D V, D 2129/17, previously of Jasta 4, undergoing tests with the British. Aircraft of this type were too late into service to participate in the massacre of Bloody April, 1917.

The Great Fighter Aces of the War

News from the Western Front was of vast casualties and little progress. But now there came a band of heroes, 'knights of the air', whose achievements, though miniscule in the context of the whole war, were applauded around the world.

Pursuing an age-old tradition of fighting prowess, the first great combat aces of the air were necessarily supreme individualists, men who saw themselves as 'knights of the air', whose personal courage transcended wisdom and skill, and whose prowess could be and was spectacularly measured by their tally of enemy aeroplanes struck down in single-handed combat. It was men such as Oswald Boelcke and Lanoe Hawker, however, who quickly recognized that the achievements of individuals would have little bearing on the air war as a whole, and that it would be by personal example and careful coaching that whole squadrons of well-trained pilots would dominate the battle.

Thus it was, after the first generation of pioneering air fighters had fallen in combat, that a new breed of fighter pilots emerged, assisted as they were by more deadly, purpose-designed fighting scouts: men like the greatest pilot of all, Manfred, Freiherr von Richthofen, and Albert Ball, René Fonck, Ernst Udet and many others. Although essentially still individualists (what fighter pilot is not such, even to this day?), these were men who recognized the value of carefully evolved tactics, the use of a formation of aircraft, and of training and experience.

As well as von Richthofen, with his unmatched tally of 80 enemy aircraft destroyed, there was, for example, the superb fighting Frenchman, René Fonck, whose deadly marksmanship frequently enabled him to despatch a foe with no more than half-a-dozen shots placed *comme avec la main* (as if by hand).

These were the men on whom the whole tradition of air combat was founded. Their tactics, evolved in the smoke-filled skies high above the carnage of the Western Front, provided the basis of all air fighting rules for half a century.

THE THREE HIGHEST-SCORING PILOTS OF EACH OF THE WARRING NATIONS

GERMANY
Rittmeister Manfred, Freiherr von Richthofen	80
Oberleutnant Ernst Udet	62
Oberleutnant Erich Loewenhardt	53

FRANCE
Capitaine René Paul Fonck	75
Capitaine Georges Marie Ludovic Jules Guynemer	54
Lieutenant Charles Eugène Jules Marie Nungesser	45

GREAT BRITAIN AND THE BRITISH EMPIRE
Major Edward Mannock, VC, DSO and two Bars, MC and Bar	73
Lieutenant Colonel William Avery Bishop (Canada), VC, CB, DSO and Bar, OBE, DFC, ED	72
Lieutenant Colonel Raymond Collishaw (Canada), CB, DSO and Bar, OBE, DSC, DFC	60

UNITED STATES OF AMERICA
Captain Edward Vernon Rickenbacker, Medal of Honor	26
2/Lieutenant Frank Luke Jr, Medal of Honor	21
Major Gervais Raoul Lufbery	17

ITALY
Maggiore Francesco Baracca	34
Tenente Silvio Scaroni	26
Tenente-Colonello Pier Ruggiero Piccio	24

AUSTRIA-HUNGARY
Hauptmann Godwin Brumowski	c.40
Offizierstellvertreter Julius Arigi	c.32
Oberleutnant Frank Linke-Crawford	c.30

IMPERIAL RUSSIA
Staff Captain Aleksandr Aleksandrovich Kazakov, DSO, MC, DFC	17
Captain P.V. d'Arguev	15
Lieutenant Commander A.P. Seversky	13

BELGIUM
2/Lieutenant Willy Coppens, DSO	37
Adjutant André de Meulemeester	11
2/Lieutenant Edmond Thieffry	10

The Ace System

The 'ace' system, although never officially adopted or recognized by the UK, originated in France where a pilot who was officially credited with the confirmed destruction of five enemy aircraft (including the heavily-defended German observation balloon) was formally named in a specially promulgated communiqué. Such public notification naturally resulted in much national adulation, the men being fêted as heroes, while in Germany, where the term *Oberkanone* (loosely 'top gun') was accorded, there existed a practice of awarding specific decorations on achieving a certain number of air victories; however, no rigid formula existed, and the gratitude of his Fatherland may be seen in the formal style of address bestowed upon Max Immelmann at the time of his death:

The Royal Saxon Reserve-Lieutenant Herr Max Immelmann, Commander of the Order of St Heinrich, Knight of the *Ordre pour le Mérite*, Knight of the Iron Cross, First and Second Class, Knight of the Military Order of St Heinrich, Knight of the Albrecht Order with Swords, Knight of the Höhenzollern House Order with Swords, Knight of the Bavarian Order of Military Merit with Swords, Holder of the Iron Crescent, Holder of the Imbian Medal in Silver, Holder of the Friedrich August Medal in Silver, and Holder of the Hamburg Hanseatic Cross.

On the 'five-victory' criterion to qualify for ace status, British and British Empire air forces produced 532 aces, Germany 364, France 158, the USA (including pilots serving with other air forces) 88, Italy 43, Austria-Hungary about 25 Imperial Russia about 19 and Belgium five.

Fifteen Great Aces

Captain Albert Ball

The first British pilot to be nationally acclaimed on account of his mounting score of air victories, Albert Ball had joined the Sherwood Foresters at the age of 18 in 1914. Transferred to No. 13 Squadron RFC in 1916, Ball flew B.E.2c aircraft on artillery spotting flights before changing to Nieuports with No. 11 Squadron, and by the end of the year had shot down 10 enemy aircraft. He then changed to the S.E.5 (although he always preferred the Nieuport) and before his death on 7 May 1917 had shot down a total of 44 German aircraft. Something of a loner, and an intensely religious young man, he was nevertheless a deadly stalker in the air, pursuing a relentless personal crusade against the enemy. His death in action remains a mystery to this day.

Hauptmann Rudolf Berthold

One of the greatest exponents of the famous Fokker D VII was Rudolf Berthold who, with 44 confirmed victories, was sixth in the roll of German aces. Appointed to command Jagdgeschwader Nr 2 in the last year of the war, Berthold suffered continuous pain from a wound that rendered his right arm useless and prompted him to have his controls altered to allow him to fly at all. At least 16 of his victories were gained during a period when his wound was daily rejecting splinters of suppurating bone. Active in the post-war right-wing *Freikorps*, Berthold was murdered by a band of communist thugs – strangled with the ribbon of his own *Ordre Pour le Mérite*.

Lieutenant-Colonel William Avery Bishop

Originally a subaltern in the Canadian Mounted Rifles, Bishop transferred to the RFC in July 1915, first flying as an observer with No. 21 Squadron. He then trained as a pilot and joined No. 60 Squadron in March 1917, then flying Nieuport 17s. Within two months his score had reached 20 and he already held the DSO and MC. His VC was won for a solo dawn attack on an enemy airfield on 2 June when he destroyed three enemy scouts in the air and shot up others on the ground. He was promoted major, and after a spell off operations took command of No. 85 Squadron in 1918. In one period of 12 days he shot down 25 enemy aircraft, for which he was awarded a second DSO and the DFC. His ultimate score of 72 victories placed him second only to Mannock in the British list of high scoring pilots, and he remained in the Royal Canadian Air Force for many years after the war, eventually dying in Florida in September 1956.

Hauptmann Oswald Boelcke

Universally acknowledged as the first true fighter pilot, Hauptmann Oswald Boelcke is today still commemorated in the honour title of a German air force unit. Born in 1891 he gained his pilot's certificate in August 1914 and served as a reconnaissance pilot (with his brother Wilhelm as observer) during the early months of the war. While serving under Hauptmann Kastner's Feldfliegerabteilung 62 he was fortunate to be selected to fly the new Fokker E I monoplane fighting scout and, after initial instruction by Kastner, set about training promising young pilots in the skills of air combat, invariably by personal trial, error and example, displaying natural gifts of patience and thoroughness. His hand-picked band of pilots, flying the new Albatros D I and D II scouts, became the scourge of the Western Front in 1916-7, and Boelcke himself despatched 40 Allied aircraft. He was killed in combat following collision with a colleague on 28 October 1916 when his aircraft broke up before he could land.

Lieutenant-Colonel Raymond Collishaw

Born in British Columbia in 1893, Collishaw transferred to the Royal Naval Air Service from the merchant service in 1916, first flying Sopwith 1½-Strutters; by the end of that year he had destroyed three enemy aircraft and, after a short spell flying Pups with No. 3 (Naval) Squadron, was appointed 'B' Flight commander on No. 10 (Naval) Squadron, flying Sopwith Triplanes. Under his leadership 'Black Flight' of 'Naval Ten' became one of the most successful of all Allied units in France, all its pilots being Canadians. Although his own score reached 40 by the end of 1917, it was for his brilliant and daring leadership that he was most respected. He subsequently took his victory tally to 60 while commanding Nos 3 and 13 (Naval) Squadrons in 1918. After the war he rose to become an Air Marshal in the RAF and pursued a distinguished career during World War II.

Capitaine René Fonck

René Fonck, whose official victory score was 75 (but whose personal estimate was 127) was unquestionably one of the greatest of all Allied fighter aces of all time. Aged 20 at the outbreak of war, Fonck transferred from the French army to the air service in 1915 and eventually in 1917 joined Escadrille SPA 103, one of the units of the famous Groupe de Combat 12 *'Les Cicognes'*, flying SPADs. His personal score mounted slowly, and he soon acquired a reputation as a thoughtful and analytical fighter, twice destroying six enemy aircraft on single days, and on one occasion three of his victims being found to have crashed within a radius of 400 m (440 yards). He was a master of deflection shooting, his sparing of ammunition bordering on the uncanny. His many decorations included two British Military Crosses and the French *Croix de Guerre* with 28 palms. He died peacefully at his Paris home in June 1953.

Capitaine George Marie Ludovic Jules Guynemer

Born in 1894, Georges Guynemer won an unrivalled place in the hearts of the French public for, as a frail and delicate youth, he had twice been rejected for military service when he enlisted as a pupil-mechanic and was posted to Pau airfield in November 1914. He graduated to flying training, and in June 1915 started flying Morane-Saulnier monoplanes with Escadrille MS 3, scoring his first victory a month later. During the next two years he destroyed a total of 54 German aircraft, the majority while flying Nieuports; it was this prowess, his youth and pale good looks that endeared him to the romantic French people. He was himself shot down seven times, and his health was clearly failing when on 11 September 1917 he failed to return from a flight over Poelcapelle. No claim for his defeat in the air has ever been fully substantiated, nor has any trace of his body or aircraft ever been found.

Reserve-Leutnant Max Immelmann

Widely known as the 'Eagle of Lille', Max Immelmann rose from obscure middle class to lauded officer aristocracy in one short year in step with his advancing fame as a fighter pilot of the revolutionary Fokker E I. He was serving with Feldfliegerabteilung 62 at Douai under Hauptmann Kastner and Oswald Boelcke in 1915 when the first E Is became available. Taught by Boelcke to fly and fight the new aircraft, Immelmann scored a total of 15 victories and was held in awe by friend and foe alike, his nimble fighter permitting the use of a climbing manoeuvre that was for an age to bear his name. With Boelcke and

Captain Albert Ball

Hauptmann Rudolf Berthold

Lieutenant-Colonel William Avery Bishop

Hauptmann Oswald Boelcke

Lieutenant-Colonel Raymond Collishaw

Capitaine René Fonck

Capitaine George Marie Ludovic Jules Guynemer

Reserve-Leutnant Max Immelmann

2/Lieutenant Frank Luke Jr

Major Edward Mannock

Lieutenant Charles Eugène Jules Marie Nungesser

Major James Thomas Byford McCudden

Rittmeister Manfred, Freiherr von Richthofen

Captain Edward Vernon Rickenbacker

Leutnant Werner Voss

other pilots operating in the Lille area, Immelmann did much to create the famous 'Fokker scourge' in 1915-6, but on 18 June 1916 he was shot down and killed by Lieut G.R. McCubbin of No. 25 Squadron, RFC.

2/Lieutenant Frank Luke Jr

Immortal for his exploits as a 'balloon-buster', Frank Luke achieved his score of 21 victories in the six weeks between 16 August and his death on 28 September 1918. A native of Phoenix, Arizona, where he was born in 1897, he arrived in France with a tough self-confidence and an evident contempt for discipline that did not endear him to his fellow pilots on the 27th Aero Squadron. He was, however, a born pilot if something of a loner, and it was this that attracted him to the German observation balloons, particularly hazardous targets on account of their heavy ground defences. On his last mission he destroyed three balloons before being forced to crashland behind the German lines, preferring to resist capture by fighting enemy troops with a pistol, resulting inevitably in his death. Despite his constant flouting of regulations (an order for arrest was awaiting execution at the time of his death), Luke was awarded a posthumous Medal of Honor.

Major Edward Mannock

Son of a soldier, Mannock only transferred to the RFC from the Royal Engineers in August 1916 despite an eyesight deficiency. He joined No. 40 Squadron in April 1917, then flying Nieuports, and was soon shooting down enemy aircraft. Possessed of a ruthless hatred of the Germans, he showed none of the mercy so often ascribed to airmen of World War I, yet made unending efforts to ensure that his own pilots received the best possible combat training, it being said that no patrol by his pilots was ever taken by surprise. From flight commander with No. 74 Squadron he was posted to command No. 85 Squadron, but on 26 July 1918 his aircraft was hit by rifle fire from the ground and he was killed when his score stood at 73, the highest of any British pilot. His grave was never found and, despite the posthumous award of the Victoria Cross, his career attracted no attention until long after his death.

Lieutenant Charles Eugène Jules Marie Nungesser

The fighting career of the Frenchman Charles Nungesser is one of the legendary sagas of air combat as an extraordinary fight to overcome the effects of wounds suffered in battle. Something of a pre-war playboy with a name as a racing driver in South America and a self-taught pilot, he first fought as a hussar in France during 1914 before transferring to the air service. He suffered frequent wounds in combat, necessitating repeated returns to hospital to have fractured bones rebroken and reset yet, flying Nieuports with Escadrille N65 from November 1915 onwards, he amassed a victory total of 45, often being unable to walk and having to be carried to his aircraft. Nungesser survived the war as a darling of Parisian society, only to disappear during an attempt to fly the Atlantic in May 1927. His aircraft insignia in war and peace comprised a black heart charged with a skull and crossbones, two candles and a coffin.

Major James Thomas Byford McCudden

One of the very small number of peacetime rankers who rose to commissioned service and command in the RFC, McCudden transferred to the flying corps in 1913 and served as an NCO until 1916, during which period he made a number of illicit flights as an observer, but winning the Croix de Guerre in the process. He then underwent pilot training, but it was not until August 1916 that he first flew scouts, in the form of D.H.2s with No. 29 Squadron. Receiving his commission on 1 January 1917 he became a flight commander on No. 56 Squadron, flying S.E.5s, and by November his score had reached 20. As a fighter he was instinctively a loner, preferring to stalk his prey so as to attack unseen from close range. He took no leave to return home until April 1918 when, at an investiture, he received his VC, two DSOs and an MC (the highest single collection of awards at a single investiture). He was tragically killed, when his score stood at 57, turning back to his field after an engine failure, an inexplicable error by so brilliant and experienced a pilot.

Rittmeister Manfred, Freiherr von Richthofen

Retaining his cavalry captain's rank during his service with the Luftstreitkräfte, the famous German aristocrat pilot Manfred von Richthofen was 32 when war broke out. He transferred from the cavalry in May 1915 but for some months served without distinction with Feldfliegerabteilung 69. In September the following year he was posted to Jasta 2 and received brief but priceless instruction from the great Oswald Boelcke. Thereafter his score of victories mounted steadily and in January 1917 he earned the coveted Ordre Pour le Mérite. A cold and calculating fighter, von Richthofen nevertheless pursued the instincts of an aristocratic huntsman, maintaining a collection of silver cups each engraved with the name and particulars of a combat victim. As commander of Jasta 11 it was von Richthofen who shot down Major Lanoe Hawker VC, and later personally led the 'Richthofen Flying Circus', an assembly of experienced young pilots that gained a deadly reputation over the Western Front. It was while flying a Fokker Dr I triplane on 21 April 1918 that he met his death, apparently shot down by Captain A. Roy Brown of No. 209 Squadron, RAF, although controversy has raged ever since as to the exact cause of his death. His score of 80 confirmed victories placed von Richthofen ahead of all other fighter pilots of the war.

Captain Edward Vernon Rickenbacker

Born in Columbus, Ohio, in 1890, and a pre-war racing driver, Eddie Rickenbacker was posted to France in 1917 as General Pershing's army chauffeur, but took flying lessons in his spare time. In March 1918 he secured a posting to fly with the 94th Aero Squadron, then commanded by Raoul Lufbery. He had already destroyed several enemy aircraft when given command of the squadron in September. Between then and the Armistice Rickenbacker destroyed 19 further enemy aeroplanes and balloons to take his score to 26 and his name to the top of the American roll of aces. He was awarded the Medal of Honor and continued in aviation as Chairman of the giant Eastern Air Lines.

Leutnant Werner Voss

A born fighter and natural pilot, Werner Voss, whose 48 victories placed him fourth in the German roll of aces, lacked the leadership qualities of Richthofen and Berthold. He flew Albatros D IIIs with Jasta 5 and Jasta 14 early in 1917, one of his aircraft displaying prominent swastikas on the fuselage. It was through friendship with Richthofen that Voss was posted to command Jasta 10 in July 1917, and for a time ranked second only to his friend. He was ultimately killed on 23 September 1917 while flying a Fokker Dr I triplane in a prolonged fight with seven S.E.5a fighters of No. 56 Squadron, RFC, led by Captain J.T.B. McCudden.

Fokker monoplanes

Anthony Fokker's **Eindecker** (literally 'one wing') monoplanes were the manifestation of his design philosophy combining manoeuvrability with a synchronized machine-gun of acceptable reliability. The original **M 5k** prototype was in effect an approximate copy of the pre-war French Morane-Saulnier Type H monoplane and was first flown in 1914, entering production early in 1915 as the **E I**. In this Fokker incorporated the LMG 08/15 7.92-mm (0.31-in) machine-gun with a mechanical interrupter gear designed by the engineers Luebbe, Heber and Leimberger. Fokker himself flew a number of demonstrations with operational units in May 1915, and by mid-July 11 service pilots of Feldfliegerabteilung (FlAbt) 62 at Douai were flying the E I, among them Leutnant Oswald Boelcke. Another pilot soon to be instructed on the E I was Immelmann.

The E I was something of a makeshift aircraft, rushed into production with an 80-hp (60-kW) Oberursel rotary, and was joined in service by the **E II** which had wings of reduced area in an attempt to increase speed, but this resulted in the aircraft being more difficult to fly and so was less popular. The main version was the **E III**, of which the first example reached the Western Front in August with a 100-hp (75-kW) Oberursel U I, and it was at the controls of this version that pilots such as Boelcke, Immelmann, von Althaus, Buddecke, Parschau and Wintgens were to create the legend of the monoplane's invincibility.

Indeed it was only the fast-growing number of victories being gained by the front-line pilots that reversed an order grounding the Fokker following a number of fatal crashes back in Ger-

A standard Fokker E III (factory no. 401) with a single LMG.08 synchronized gun and Oberursel UI engine.

many. One further version, the **E IV**, was produced in small numbers, this being powered by a 160-hp Oberursel two-row rotary, and a special example was prepared for Immelmann equipped with three synchronized guns.

It has been suggested that only when a Fokker E III fell intact into British hands on 8 April 1916 could an antidote be developed to counter the 'Fokker scourge'. This is not correct as the Fokker's decline in fact began as early as January that year with the arrival in service of the excellent little Nieuport XI, and with the arrival in service the following month of the RFC's first D.H.2 unit, No. 24 Squadron, under Lanoe Hawker.

Moreover, contrary to general tradition, the Fokker's gun armament was far from reliable, its ammunition not being wholly suitable for aircraft use, while the gun itself was prone to freezing. Be that as it may, the Eindecker was certainly good enough to hold

sway over France for almost a year.

Specification
Type: single-seat fighting scout
Powerplant: one 100-hp (75-kW) Oberursel U I nine-cylinder rotary piston engine
Performance: maximum speed 140 km/h (87.5 mph) at sea level; climb to 3000 m (9,845 ft) in 30 minutes; service ceiling 3500 m (11,485 ft); endurance 1 hour 30 minutes
Weights: empty 400 kg (882 lb); maximum take-off 610 kg (1,345 lb)

Although impossible to identify with certainty, this is probably a Fokker E II, as the majority of later Eindeckers (E III) had covered wheel centres, but the single machine-gun has interrupter gear fitted.

Dimensions: span 9.52 m (31 ft 2¾ in); length 7.20 m (23 ft 7½ in); height 2.79 m (9 ft 1¾ in); wing area 16.00 m² (172.8 sq ft)
Armament: usually one (sometimes two) forward-firing synchronized LMG 08 7.92-mm (0.31-in) machine-gun

---

Fokker D VII

Unquestionably the best of all German fighting scout aircraft in World War I, the **Fokker D VII** was designed by Reinhold Platz as a natural improvement on the **D VI**, both of which underwent service evaluation at Johannisthal in January 1918. Although service pilots were unanimous in their verdict in favour of the D VII both types entered service. Ironically Albatros Werke, Fokker's arch rival for production contracts and whose scouts were phased out of production after the Johannisthal trials, was ordered to manufacture the D VII in its own factories.

Early production D VIIs were powered by the 160-hp (119-kW) Mercedes D III water-cooled engine with car-type frontal radiator, but later in 1918 the 185-hp (138-kW) BMW was introduced and bestowed a much improved performance. The success enjoyed by the D VII stemmed not only from its straightforward flying characteristics, which were maintained right up to its ceiling and included a docile stall with no sudden wing drop, but also because of simple construction and ease of repair. The wings were of wooden construction covered with fabric, and the fuselage was a braced steel-tube box girder; the nose was metal-clad forward of the lower wing, and plywood-covered aft of this, stretched fabric being applied on top. The lower wing was fabricated as a single unit, the lower fuselage longer-

Displaying the characteristic German lozenge pattern, applied as a pre-painted fabric strip, this Fokker D VII was flown by Josef Raesch, Jastaführer of Jasta 43.

ons being interrupted to allow the wing spars to pass right through the fuselage, an arrangement that gave considerable strength. All interplane and centre-section struts were of streamline-section steel tube.

The first *Geschwader* to receive the D VII was Geschwader Nr 1, deliveries being made to its Jasta 4, 6, 10 and 11 late in April 1918, only days after the death of its illustrious commander, Manfred von Richthofen, in a Dr I triplane. JG 1 was followed by Jastas 12, 13, 15 and 19 of Geschwader Nr 2 and Jasta 2, 26, 27 and 36 of Geschwader Nr 3. In due course a total of 46 *Jastas* were flying D VIIs on the Western and Southern Fronts, roughly 65 per cent of

the German fighting scout strength.

There is no doubt that notwithstanding the excellent quality of Allied scouts which entered service in 1918, such as the S.E.5A and Snipe, the French and British squadrons held a healthy respect for the D VII, with its austere-looking angular wings and

rectangular boxlike fuselage. This respect was evidenced by a clause in the Armistice agreement which speci-

These D VIIs are from Geschwader 3 (individual unit Jasta 2) and are pictured next to an Albatros D Va of Jasta 36.

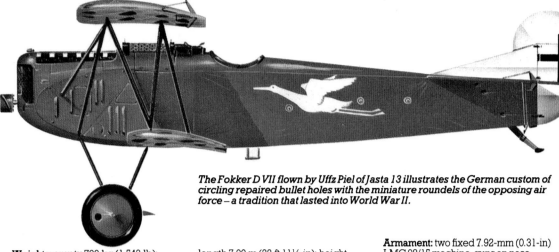

fically required the handing over of all first-line D VIIs to the Allies.

Among the well-known pilots and 'Oberkanonen' whose high scores were achieved in D VII cockpits were men such as Ernst Udet, Rudolf Berthold, von Beaulieu-Marconnay and Georg von Hartelmann, not forgetting Hermann Goering who flew an all-white D VII.

Specification
Type: single-seat fighting scout
Powerplant: one 160-hp (119-kW) Mercedes D III six-cyliojer inline water-cooled piston engine
Performance: maximum speed 187 km/h (116 mph) at 1000 m (3,280 ft); climb to 1000 m (3,280 ft) in 3 minutes 48 seconds; service ceiling 7000 m (22,965 ft); endurance about 1.5 hours

The Fokker D VII flown by Uffz Piel of Jasta 13 illustrates the German custom of circling repaired bullet holes with the miniature roundels of the opposing air force – a tradition that lasted into World War II.

Weights: empty 700 kg (1,543 lb); maximum take-off 850 kg (1,874 lb)
Dimensions: span 8.90 m (29 ft 3½ in);

length 7.00 m (22 ft 11½ in); height 2.75 m (9 ft 2¼ in); wing area 20.50 m² (220.68 sq ft)

Armament: two fixed 7.92-mm (0.31-in) LMG 08/15 machine-guns on nose, synchronized to fire through propeller disc

---

GERMANY
Fokker Dr I

Now long discounted as a 'copy' of the Sopwith Triplane (of which at least one early example fell intact into German hands), Reinhold Platz' **Fokker Dr I** (*Dreidecker*, or three wings) triplane obviously owed its conception to reports of the remarkable manoeuvrability of the British scout. However, when originally produced as the **V 3** prototype, the design featured three cantilever wings without interplane struts, but following severe wing vibration during early trials the **V 4** second prototype was fitted with lightweight hollow steel interplane struts to give added stiffness.

The Dr I was ordered into production during the summer of 1917 and the first two aircraft were delivered to Jagdgeschwader Nr 1 at Courtrai on 21 August where they were immediately taken over as the personal mounts of Manfred von Richthofen and Werner Voss (*Führer* of Jasta 1). The former's aircraft was shot down by Camels of No. 10 Squadron, RNAS, on about 14 September while being flown by Oberleutnant Kurt Wolff of Jasta 11; on the other hand Voss in his Dr I shot down 21 enemy aircraft between 30 August and 23 September, when he was killed in an epic fight with S.E.5s of No. 56 Squadron, RFC.

Disaster struck before the Dr I reached widespread service, a number of fatal accidents following break-up of the top wing. Examination of all Jagdgeschwader Nr 1's aircraft disclosed faulty workmanship, assembly faults and rotting of fabric. This led to the aircraft being grounded and replacement of wings with items of sound construction, a step that seriously delayed general delivery of Dr Is to the front. This said, it is quite incorrect to suggest that the reputation of the aircraft rested solely on the exploits of men like Manfred von Richthofen and Werner Voss. It was an exceptionally nimble fighting scout whose performance exactly suited the style of combat being fought over the Western Front late in 1917, and it was flown by many other rising stars of the German air force, including Lothar von Richthofen, Hermann Goering, Ernst Udet and Adolf Ritter von Tutschek. The delay engendered by the wing replacement played havoc with production plans, however, and although flying restrictions were lifted at the end of November 1917 there were probably only ab-

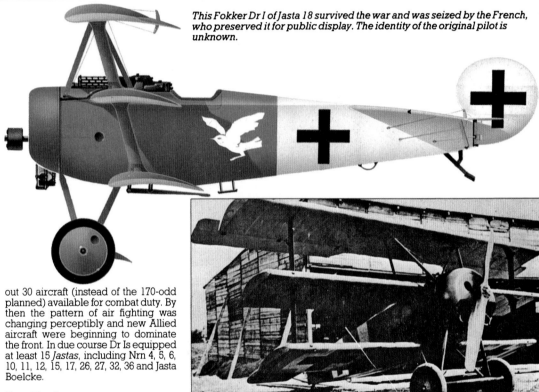

This Fokker Dr I of Jasta 18 survived the war and was seized by the French, who preserved it for public display. The identity of the original pilot is unknown.

out 30 aircraft (instead of the 170-odd planned) available for combat duty. By then the pattern of air fighting was changing perceptibly and new Allied aircraft were beginning to dominate the front. In due course Dr Is equipped at least 15 *Jastas*, including Nrn 4, 5, 6, 10, 11, 12, 15, 17, 26, 27, 32, 36 and Jasta Boelcke.

Specification
Type: single-seat fighting scout
Powerplant: one 145-hp (108-kW) Oberursel UR II nine-cylinder air-cooled rotary piston engine
Performance: maximum speed

185 km/h (115 mph) at 1000 m (3,280 ft); climb to 3000 m (9,845 ft) in 7 minutes 6 seconds; service ceiling 6100 m (20,015 ft); endurance 1 hour 30 minutes
Weights: 430 kg (948 lb); maximum take-off 626 kg (1,380 lb)
Dimensions: span 7.19 m (23 ft 7⅜ in); length 5.77 m (18 ft 11 in); height 2.95 m (9 ft 8¼ in); wing area (including landing gear aerofoil) 18.66 m² (200.86 sq ft)

A standard Fokker Dr I, pictured in 1918; just visible are the ash wing tip skids, omitted from some aircraft, fitted to avoid damage on landing.

Armament: two fixed 7.92-mm (0.31-in) LMG 08/15 machine-guns on nose firing through propeller disc with *Zentralsteuerung* synchronizing gear

All-black Fokker Dr I flown by Leutnant Josef Jacobs of Jasta 7; awarded the Ordre Pour le Mérite, his ultimate score of 41 victories placed him eighth in the list of German aces, equal with Bruno Loerzer.

Pfalz D III

The exceptionally attractive **Pfalz D III** owed much to its manufacturer's experience in the licence production of the LFG Roland D II for the Bavarian *Jastas* early in 1917. When the latter contract ran out the company was able to concentrate on its own design, which emerged in the summer of that year, powered by the popular 160-hp (119-kW) Mercedes D III inline engine. Features of the D II (the parallel-chord wing with sharply raked angular tips and oval-section semi-monocoque fuselage) were perpetuated, and the basic structure, comprising spruce longerons and ply formers spirally wrapped in opposite directions by layers of ply strip, imparted considerable strength. The fin was made integral with the rear fuselage and horn-balanced ailerons provided the little aeroplane with crisp lateral control. The top wing, with twin wire-braced box spars, was built as a single unit without dihedral.

The D III passed its official acceptance test in June 1917, but production was slow to get under way because of the skills required, particularly in building the fuselage. Only three D IIIs had reached the front by the end of August, and thereafter the D IIIa version, with the guns located on top of the nose (instead of being 'buried') to allow simpler access for maintenance, joined the production line. By the end of the year the front-line strength of D IIIs and D IIIas had reached 276 and 114 respectively, but slowly diminished thereafter. Total production has been estimated at around 1,000 aircraft.

As the Pfalz company was financially supported by the Bavarian government it was natural that the first service allocations should be made to the Bavarian Jastas 16, 23, 32, 34 and 35, which were attached to the Bavarian army in the summer of 1917, followed by Jastas 76, 77, 78, 79 and 80. Subsequently the Pfalz served with Jastas 5, 7, 8, 10, 11, 14, 15, 19, 20, 22, 24, 28, 29, 30, 36, 37, 40, 44, 46, 47, 48, 49, 51, 52, 53, 54, 56, 57, 58, 59, 61, 67 and 69, as well as Marine Feld Jastas I, II and III, although few of these units flew the Pfalz exclusively. The redoubtable Werner Voss was posted to command Jasta 10 at the end of July 1917 and while flying the D III scored four victories before moving on to the Fokker Dr I triplane. Hauptmann Paul Bäumer, who was well known for his habit of bouncing his wheels on a hangar to get his wheels spinning before landing and who served with Jasta 2 (Boelcke), notched up a score of 43 victories, most of which were achieved from the cockpit of the Pfalz D IIIa.

Specification

Type: single-seat fighting scout
Powerplant: one 160-hp (119-kW) or 175-hp (130-kW) Mercedes D III or D IIIa six-cylinder water-cooled inline piston engine
Performance: maximum speed 165 km/h (103 mph) at sea level; climb to 1000 m (3,280 ft) in 3 minutes 15 seconds; service ceiling 5450 m (17,880 ft); endurance 2 hours 30 minutes
Weights: empty 725 kg (1,598 lb); maximum take-off 905 kg (1,995 lb)
Dimensions: span 9.40 m (30 ft 10⅛ in); length 6.95 m (22 ft 9¾ in); height 2.67 m (8 ft 9⅛ in); wing area 22.17 m² (238.64 sq ft)
Armament: two fixed 7.92-mm (0.31-in) LMG 08/15 machine-guns on nose, synchronized to fire through propeller disc

The Pfalz D III flown by Vzfw Hecht of Jasta 10 and based near Courtrai; this aircraft was captured intact by the British.

Another Pfalz D III being examined by RFC personnel after capture on the Western Front; the aircraft was later flown in British markings.

Siemens-Schuckert D III

Designed by Dipl.Ing. Harald Wolff, the **Siemens-Schuckert D III** was a good but little-known German fighting scout to reach front-line *Jasta* service before the Armistice, although a handful of the much faster Fokker D VIII monoplanes was flown in combat by some privileged pilots in the last days. Ordered into production after the famous Johannisthal competitive trials of January 1918, the SSW D III was powered by a 160-hp (119-kW) Siemens-Halske Sh III (or IIIa) 11-cylinder geared rotary engine driving a four-blade propeller, giving a top speed of 180 km/h (112 mph).

Despite considerable attention paid to the handling qualities, the SSW D III remained a tricky little aeroplane to fly, there being no pre-stall warning, the stall being accompanied by a sudden wing drop and followed by a vicious spin. However, the counter-rotation by crankshaft and cylinders, though doing nothing to reduce engine torque, did counteract the gyroscopic couple so that, unlike other rotary-powered scouts, the D III did not snap more readily into right or left hand turns. Horn-balanced ailerons on all four wings imparted a brisk rate of roll and, in an effort to counter the considerable tendency to swing on take-off (as a result of engine torque), the fin was of marked asymmetric section.

Arrival at the front was accompanied by a spate of engine failures, piston seizure being attributed to the low-quality castor oil being used in Germany in 1918 (compounded by the high engine speed of the hot-running Sh III), and in May all aircraft were withdrawn for installation of the Sh IIIa with improvements and provision for increased cooling. By the time they were ready for return to the Front a new version, the D IV, was also being delivered; in this the wing chord was markedly reduced, a change that resulted in some improvement in handling and a 10-km/h (6-mph) increase in speed.

Best known of all Siemens-Schuckert D III (and D IV) pilots was Oberleutnant Ernst Udet, who flew the aircraft as *Staffelführer* of Jasta 4 at Metz in the last months of the war. Although few Jastas were equipped exclusively with D IIIs and D IVs, they are known to have flown with Jasta 2, 4, 12, 13, 15, 19, 26, 27 and 36 alongside Fokker D VIIs; the majority was deployed for the defence of the Fatherland with the Kampfeinsitzerstaffeln (Kestas) 2, 4b, 5, 6 and 8 in western Germany, where they are said to have done considerable execution among Allied bombers in the last weeks of the war.

Specification

Type: single-seat fighting scout
Powerplant: one 160-hp (119-kW) Siemens-Halske Sh III (or IIIa) 11-cylinder geared rotary piston engine
Performance: maximum speed 180 km/h (112 mph) at 1000 m (3,280 ft); climb to 3000 m (9,845 ft) in 6.0 minutes; service ceiling 8000 m (26,245 ft); endurance 2 hours
Weights: empty 534 kg (1,177 lb); maximum take-off 725 kg (1,598 lb)
Dimensions: span 8.43 m (27 ft 7¾ in); length 5.70 m (18 ft 8½ in); height 2.80 m (9 ft 2¼ in); wing area 15.12 m² (162.76 sq ft)
Armament: two fixed 7.92-mm (0.31-in) LMG 08/15 machine-guns on nose synchronized to fire through propeller disc

Siemens-Schuckert D III flown by the famous ace, Oberleutnant Ernst Udet, Staffelführer of Jasta 4, Metz, 1918.

Identifiable by its tapered aileron tips, the Siemens-Schuckert D IV was faster than the D III by some 6 mph (10 km/h) but, apart from a top wing of slightly narrower chord, was generally similar.

Bombers of World War 1

Nowhere is the technological impetus provided by war more evident than in aviation. At the start of World War I, aircraft looked as if a boy could tie some string to them and fly them in a breeze, but in four short years the fighting aeroplane was appearing in such diverse forms as the single-seat ground attack fighter and the multi-engined, long-range heavy bomber.

Typical of the first-generation bombers evolved during the early years of war, the Voisin Type VIII and IX two-seat bombers formed the backbone of the French night bombing force. Maximum bombload was 300 kg (660 lb).

The use of the aeroplane to deliver fire and explosive against an enemy on the ground was inevitable from the moment the Wright brothers first achieved controlled flight in 1903. What remained in doubt was the degree and accuracy with which it could be delivered. At the beginning of World War I in the West aerial bombs were confined to nothing bigger than hand grenades as the Russians, who alone possessed large aircraft, started lifting bombs of more than about 68 kg (150 lb) and quickly went on to produce weapons of twice that size, weapons that were obviously able to cause as much damage as a large artillery shell, but capable of delivery over a much greater range.

The regular use of the large high explosive bomb in the West came about through the Germans' employment of airships, whose raids on British and French towns and cities were sanctioned by the Kaiser only in return for assurances by the Imperial Naval Staff that military targets alone would be hit. Inevitably, in the absence of any bomb-aiming equipment, civilian casualties resulted so that any such assurances became purely academic. Within two years bombs of 300 kg (661 lb) were landing among the humble homes of the British and French capitals and elsewhere. Thus arrived total war.

Gradually, however, the value of the airship (progressively shown to be increasingly vulnerable to attack by fighters firing incendiary ammunition) was seen to be of little military significance while at the same time it squandered manufacturing and operating manpower so that, after 1916, it began to take second place to the aeroplane as a

bomber. Apart from the Russians, both the Germans and British (as well as the French and Italians to a lesser extent) pursued the development of large bombers, although only the former, with their huge *Riesen* (giants) managed to get a truly heavy bomber (able to lift a 1000-kg/2,205-lb bomb) into operational service during the war. Yet it was the British who first created a strategic bomber force, the Independent Force under Major General Sir Hugh Trenchard, an element of the RAF that was to dominate British Air Staff philosophies for 50 years.

At the other end of the scale much smaller bomb-carrying aircraft were increasingly used over the front lines in France, Italy, Macedonia and the Middle East against such targets as would otherwise be shelled by artillery. One of the lessons learned was that dropping bombs accurately on anything but sizeable, stationary targets was extremely difficult, especially if the target was shooting back. Towards the end of the war, therefore, as the fighting on the various fronts became more fluid and the soldiers left the sanctuary of their trenches, the machine-gun became the favoured weapon of the ground support aeroplane.

By the end of the war, the Royal Air Force had had more than 400 Handley Page O/400 bombers delivered, with raids of up to 40 aircraft at a time being made on industrial centres in Germany. The O/400 also carried the 750-kg (1,650-lb) bomb, the largest such weapon used by British forces at that time.

ITALY

Caproni Ca.3, 4 & 5

The prototype **Caproni Ca 30** which first flew in October 1914 was a three-engined bomber with a central crew nacelle and twin booms to carry a triple-ruddered tail unit. The powerplant comprised a central engine mounted at the rear of the nacelle (a 100-hp/75-kW Gnome driving a pusher propeller) plus two wing-mounted 80-hp (60-kW) Gnomes each driving a tractor propeller. The definitive model was put into production as the **Ca.3**, and the initial order was for 12 aircraft, although a further 150 were manufactured subsequently.

In 1918 there appeared the **Caproni Ca.4**, a large triplane bomber with the same three-engined nacelle and twin-boom layout of the Ca.3. All but the first three production Ca.4s incorporated a streamlined nacelle, with a gunner's cockpit in the nose, and the early **Ca 41** examples were powered by 300-hp (224-kW) Fiat A.12 or Isotta-Fraschini V.5 engines. Twenty-three aircraft were fitted with 400-hp (298-kW) Liberty engines as the **Ca 42** and six were supplied to the Royal Naval Air Service.

The **Caproni Ca.5** was developed to supersede the Ca.3. The prototype was flown in 1917 and 659 production examples were built between 1917 and 1921, powered by 250-hp (186-kW) Fiat A.12 or Isotta-Fraschini engines, or by the 350-hp (261-kW) Liberty. The type was also selected for manufacture in the United States. However, when the Armistice ended World War I, production plans for 1,500 aircraft were cancelled after just

three had been completed. Nevertheless, the US Army Air Corps' Northern Bombing Group used the Ca.5 over the Western Front, as did the Italians and the French.

Specification
Ca.5 (Ca 44)
Type: heavy bomber
Powerplant: three 250-hp (186-kW) Fiat A.12 piston engines
Performance: maximum speed 150 km/h (93 mph); service ceiling 4600 m (15,090 ft); range 600 km (373 miles)
Weights: empty 3300 kg (7,275 lb); maximum take-off 5300 kg (11,684 lb)
Dimensions: span 23.40 m (76 ft 9.25 in); length 12.60 m (41 ft 4.25 in); height 4.48 m (14 ft 8.33 in); wing area 150.00 m² (1,614.64 sq ft)
Armament: two 7.7-mm (0.303-in) Revelli machine-guns, plus a bombload of 900 kg (1,984 lb)

This Caproni Ca 31 was operated by Escadrille CEP 115, Aéronautique Militaire (French air force) out of Plateau de Malzeville in 1916. More than 700 Ca 31s were built in three main variants.

The Caproni Ca 41 was essentially similar to the Ca 40, but had no nose landing wheels and had a tandem seating arrangement for the two pilots. The unusual bomb arrangement on the sides of the bottom wing nacelle is well displayed, as is the considerable size.

RUSSIA

Sikorsky early aircraft

Following his first unsuccessful experiments with rotary-wing aircraft in 1909-10, the Russian Igor Sikorsky concentrated upon design and development of fixed-wing aircraft. His **Sikorsky S-1** to **S-5** were little more than experimental types, but with the S-2 biplane he achieved a first 12-second hop in 1910. Growing experience and capability gained him an appointment in 1912 as a designer and chief engineer of the Russo-Baltic Wagon Works (RBVZ) and he at once became involved in design and construction of the world's first four-engined aircraft, named officially **Russkii Vitiaz** (Russian knight). This formed a basis for development of the **Ilya Muromets** series of four-engine heavy bombers used by the Imperial Russian army during World War I. The first of between 70 and 80 of these aircraft was flown for the first time in January 1914, and on 12 February 1914 the type established a world height-with-payload record, carrying 16 persons to an altitude of 2000 m (6,562 ft). Few of these production aircraft were identical, improvement and development being continuous, and shortage of engines meant they were flown with a variety of powerplant which, in some cases, involved a mix of engines on one aircraft.

Other designs to enter production

The Sikorsky Ilya Muromets, seen in 1914, was a far cry from the Blériots, Farmans, Taubes and BEs that went to war a year later in the West. The aircraft was without parallel at the time, and the first production model proved capable of flying 16 people.

during the war period included the S-16, a conventional two-seat reconnaissance biplane which, powered by an 80-hp (60-kW) Gnome rotary engine, could be operated on wheel or ski landing gear. The S-20 which entered service in 1917 was a single-seat scout powered by a 110-hp (82-kW) Le Rhône rotary; it was Sikorsky's last design in Russia, for with advent of the revolution in 1917 he emigrated to the USA.

Specification
Sikorky Ilya Muromets B
Type: heavy bomber
Powerplant: four 150-hp (112-kW) Salmson piston engines
Performance: maximum speed 100 km/h (62 mph); service ceiling not known; range 420 km (260 miles)

Weights: empty 3600 kg (7,936 lb); maximum take-off 4850 kg (10,692 lb)
Dimensions: span 34.5 m (113 ft 2.25 in); length 19.0 m (62 ft 4 in); wing area 150.0 m² (1,614.6 sq ft)
Armament: typically 10 16-kg (36-lb) bombs plus a variable defensive armament

Over 80 Ilya Muromets were built, used against German targets on the Eastern Front. They first saw action on the night of 15 February 1915, and were able to operate with relative impunity (although with limited accuracy).

Ground Attack in 1918

The massive strides taken by aviation in the four years of World War I were nowhere more eloquently demonstrated than in the titanic battles of 1918. Tactical air power, at last making a significant contribution to the struggle, had matured into an indispensible tool for the prosecution of modern war.

The AEG DJ 1 was a single-seat armoured ground attack fighter roughly equivalent to the Sopwith Salamander. First flying in September 1918, its fuselage was skinned with aluminium and it had a 195-hp engine; the armistice intervened before it could be developed further.

The use of aircraft to attack targets (troops, transport and artillery batteries) in the front line increased steadily from the occasional opportunist forays of 1915 to the full-scale offensive actions by swarms of aircraft towards the end of the war. Moreover as early as 1916 aircraft, which today would be classified as tactical support aircraft, were being conceived to attack battlefield targets, atlthough by and large these were 'general-purpose' aircraft capable of dropping light bombs on targets of opportunity while they went about other duties, such as gunnery observation and reconnaissance. It was not until 1918 that the 'trench fighter' (a dedicated gun-armed ground-attack fighter) came to be recognized as a weapon in its own right.

Ironically one of the best of Allied aircraft in the tactical support category was brought into service as early as January 1917, was extremely popular with its crews, and continued to give excellent service right up to the Armistice; yet this aeroplane, the Armstrong Whitworth F.K.8 (the 'Big Ack') never attracted the fame of other World War I aircraft. Despite its size the Big Ack was simple to fly, manoeuvrable, strong and capable of withstanding a great deal of damage from ground small arms fire. By early 1918 the manufacturers were producing the type at the rate of four every day.

To illustrate the type of work undertaken by the 'Big Acks' in 1918, as well as the hazards faced, it is worth recording that two of the most outstanding awards of the Victoria Cross were made to pilots of this type. A No. 2 Squadron F.K.8, flown by the 18-year-old Lieutenant Alan McLeod with Lieutenant A.W. Hammond, MC, as his observer, was returning from a bombing attack on enemy forces during the great German offensive of March 1918 when it was attacked by Fokker Dr I triplane. This was shot down by Hammond, but almost immediately seven more Fokkers set on the Big Ack. McLeod shot down one of these with his front gun and Hammond two others, although both British crew members were wounded, the latter six times. The rear cockpit floor fell out and the fuel tank was hit and set on fire. Despite being wounded five more times, McLeod climbed out on to the port wing and with one hand gripping the burning control column managed to crashland the blazing aircraft in no-man's land, Hammond continuing to fire his Lewis gun until the crash knocked him unconscious. German aircraft then started to bomb the wreck, again wounding McLeod, as British troops began dragging the airmen towards their lines. Both

men miraculously survived, Hammond, one of whose legs had to be amputated, receiving a bar to his MC, and McLeod the VC.

The other award of the VC to a Big Ack pilot was made to Captain F.M.F West of No. 8 Squadron who, with Lieutenant J.A.G. Haslam, on 10 August 1918 had just dropped his 51-kg (112-lb) bombs on a German gun position when he was attacked by six enemy scouts while still flying very low over the trenches. Their first burst of fire almost severed West's left leg and wounded him in the right leg yet, faint from loss of blood and half-dead from pain, he managed to hold the F.K.8 level while Haslam drove off their attackers. West succeeded in landing safely in the British lines but refused to be taken to hospital until he had given a detailed report of German gun dispositions to the tank commander with whom No. 8 Squadron was working.

The Junkers CL II was an enlarged version of the J 7 which also formed the basis for the D I monoplane fighter. The Junkers series of dedicated ground-attack aircraft, fitted with armour protection for engines, crew and fuel tanks, could have been the Sturmoviks of the Great War.

Ground Attack in 1918

Above: The Sopwith Salamander was the British answer to the hazards of flying and fighting over the machine-gun laden battlefields of 1918. Heavily armed and armoured, it was the classic British 'Trench Fighter'.

Above: A Liberty-engined D.H.9A is typical of the much-improved aircraft that were to see service against German airfields in the last months of the war. The 'Nine-Ack' also went into US service with the Marine Corps Northern Bombing Group in the weeks before the Armistice.

Below: By 1918, with one of the major tasks assigned to air power being the support of ground forces, many aircraft found themselves trench-bombing and column-strafing. The Sopwith Snipe, an improved version of the Camel, was typical of the scouts co-opted into the task.

Indeed the work being done at this time by No. 8 Squadron foreshadowed the cab-rank tactics by Hawker Typhoons and Supermarine Spitfires during the last two years of World War II. In 1918 the squadron was attached to the Tank Corps, the observers' cockpits often being occupied by tank crew members as the RAF observers travelled in the tanks; early experiments using rudimentary radio telephone for communication soon gave place to wireless telegraphy, but techniques were still being evolved at the time of the Armistice. Another use of F.K.8s, this time of No. 35 Squadron, involved the dropping of 18-kg (40-lb) phosphorus bombs to generate smoke screens. During the attack by the British XIII Corps west of Serain on 8 October 1918 a two-hour screen was maintained by relays of aircraft to conceal the build-up of the attacking forces. F.K.8s were also used to excellent effect in Macedonia, the aircraft (including some D.H.9s) of No. 47 Squadron dropping 2270 kg (5,000 lb) of bombs on the retreating Bulgarian army in the Kosturino Pass on 21 September 1918. On the same day Bristol F.2B Fighters of No. 1 Australian Squadron took very heavy toll of Turkish troops retreating through a valley in Palestine.

Similar German development

German ground-support aircraft followed much the same development pattern as that of British and French aircraft, although their use of bombs tended to give way to guns and grenades. Among the aircraft which commanded the greatest respect among Allied scout pilots were the Halberstadt CL II and CL III, the former being used in close co-ordination with advancing infantry formations during the battles on the Western Front from the late summer of 1917 onwards. So successful were these air support operations during the German counteroffensive of 30 November in the Battle of Cambrai that a subsequent British court of inquiry stated that German aircraft flying below 30 m (100 ft) and firing their machine-guns into the front-line trenches had had a devastating effect on the morale of the defenders, who seemed unable to hit back with the small arms at their disposal. In the German attacks on the Somme bridges of September 1917 the Halberstadts had caused widespread panic on the ground, many of the troops leaping off the bridge parapets to escape the deluge of fire from above.

For such attacks the CL II carried trays of grenades along the outside of the fuselage, the weapons being lobbed overboard at targets of opportunity.

During the last great German 'push' of March 1918 there were no fewer than 38 *Schlachtstaffeln* (battle squadrons), most of which flew Halberstadt CL IIs and CL IVs. These were also employed in an offensive role, flying in groups of about six to strafe enemy trenches and artillery so as to keep opposing troops' heads down at the moment of attack by the German infantry. Until the final months of the war, however, the Germans made much greater use of aircraft machine-guns than the Allies. When warfare became so much more fluid in those final months as the great breakthrough was achieved and the German armies forsook the shelter of their trenches to begin their headlong retreat, British and French scouts (the Sopwith Camels and Snipes, the RAF S.E.5As, the Spads and the Nieuports) dropped down to low level to deliver their own deluge of machine-gun fire on the unprotected columns of troops and horse-drawn transport. Air combats over the routed German armies were commonplace and casualties on both sides were heavy but, as German and Allied pilots were to discover, air combat at low level was exceedingly dangerous and difficult, and it was the Allied superiority of numbers that finally overwhelmed the German air force. Indeed aircraft like the Halberstadts, excellent though they were in support of an infantry attack, were far less effective when forced to defend themselves against the Allied scouts. Nevertheless it was in the offensive tactics formerly flown by those Halberstadts that the seeds of Blitzkrieg were sown: the tight integration of air and ground forces to achieve breakthrough on the battlefield. When, 15 years later a new German air force was born, the Luftwaffe's primary function would be to support the German army on the ground.

By contrast the British, who were hard at work at the end of the war developing the 'trench fighter', such as the Sopwith Salamander (with a battery of forward-firing guns) and Buffalo, dropped the entire concept of high-performance close-support aircraft and reverted to the light bomber. Just 22 years later the wreckage of scores of Fairey Battles in Belgian and French fields lent stark testimony to folly of such a foolish policy.

Breguet 14

The **Breguet 14** two-seat tractor bi-plane began life on the drawing boards at the company's Vélizy-Villa-coublay works in the summer of 1916. It remained in production from March 1917 to 1928, and was not withdrawn from service with France's Aéronautique Militaire until 1932.

Although rather ugly, the Bre.14 was immensely practical and tough. Its angular fabric-covered wings and fuselage were of duralumin, steel and wooden construction, with ailerons on both upper and lower wings. Sturdy cross-axle landing gear was fitted and the Renault engine, which had a rectangular frontal radiator, performed well.

The **Bre.14 A.2** reconnaissance version was equipped with camera, wireless transmitter and racks for four light bombs. It was the first version to make its mark, beginning to replace the obsolescent Sopwith 1½-Strutter during the summer of 1917. The type was issued to a number of well-known reconnaissance *escadrilles*, including the 11e, 35e and 227e, as well as many *escadrilles* attached to heavy artillery regiments of the French army. **Bre.14 B.2** bombers made many impressive formation daylight raids deep behind the German lines. When the November 1918 armistice brought hostilities to an end, Breguet 14 B.2s equipped the 15 *escadrilles* of the 1e brigade de Bombardement, while Bre.14 A.2s were flying with 12 day-reconnaissance *escadrilles* and the 19 *escadrilles* of the Aviation des Corps d'Armées. The five independent army divisions each had a Bre.14 A.2 *escadrille*. A total of 27 Bre.14 A.2 *escadrilles* was attached to heavy artillery regiments. Other wartime verisons of the type included the **Bre.14 B.1** single-seat

bomber, which did not go into large-scale production, and the **Bre.14S** ambulance. A Breguet 14 had been used experimentally for rapid evacuation of casualties from just behind the front line in 1917. In 1918 four Bre.14S ambulances, each carrying two stretcher cases, operated on the Aisne front.

The Breguet 14 served with 14 *escadrilles* in Greece, Serbia and the Middle East at the end of 1918, but it was in the French overseas empire that it was to achieve great distinction over more than a decade in the period between the two world wars. The version utilized in the more far-flung colonies was the **Breguet 14 TOE** (Théâtre des Operations Extérieures).

Specification
Breguet 14 A.2
Type: two-seat reconnaissance aircraft
Powerplant: one 300-hp (224-kW) Renault 12Fe inline piston engine
Performance: maximum speed 184 km/h (114 mph); service ceiling 6000 m (19,690 ft); endurance 3 hours
Weights: empty equipped 1030 kg (2,271 lb); maximum take-off 1565 kg (3,450 lb)
Dimensions: span, upper (original ailerons) 14.36 m (47 ft 1.25 in) or (balanced ailerons) 14.86 m (48 ft 9 in), lower (original ailerons) 12.40 m (40 ft 8 in) or (balanced ailerons) 13.66 m (44 ft 9.75 in); length 8.87 m (29 ft 1¼ in); height 3.30 m (10 ft 10 in); wing area (original ailerons) 47.50 m² (511.30 sq ft) or (balanced ailerons 49.20 m² (529.60 sq ft)
Armament: one fixed 7.7 mm (0.303-in) Vickers machine-gun on port side of fuselage and twin 7.7-mm (0.303-in) Lewis machine-guns on ring mounting in observer's cockpit, plus bombload up to 40 kg (88 lb)

Seen in the colours of the 15e Escadrille, 5e Groupe, 33e Regiment Aérian d'Observation of the French air force in the years after the end of the war, this Bre.14AZ is typical of one of the most famous French aircraft of all time, serving in a multitude of roles until 1932.

Flown in the summer of 1918, the Breguet 17 was an excellent development of the Bre.14 airframe, being more compact and with an uprated engine. The gunner had two conventionally-mounted Lewis guns, and one beneath his cockpit.

Royal Aircraft Factory F.E.2

The **Royal Aircraft Factory F.E.2** represented an initial solution to the problem of providing effective forward-firing capability before the introduction of interrupter gear. It had a two-seat fuselage nacelle in which the powerplant was mounted at the rear to drive a pusher propeller. The pilot had the rear position and the forward cockpit was occupied by the observer/gunner. Initial version was the **F.E.2a**, powered by a 100-hp (75-kW) Green engine, but disappointing performance resulted in the 120-hp (89-kW) Beardmore engine being installed in the **F.E.2b**, which was entering service in small numbers towards the end of 1915. Two **F.E.2c** aircraft were produced by the Factory, these having the pilot seated forward and observer to the rear for a night flying role. The designation **F.E.2d** applied to a version with similar airframe, but a 250-hp (186-kW) Rolls-Royce engine, this provided considerably improved performance.

In operational service the F.E.2b, working in collaboration with the Airco (de Havilland) D.H.2, gradually restricted the menace of the Fokker monoplane, but was in turn to meet its match when confronted by the more advanced Albatros and Halberstadt scouts that became to equip the German air service in late 1916. However, the suitability of the F.E.2b for night flying meant that it was to be deployed for

Above: A Royal Aircraft Factory F.E.2b of No. 22 Sqn, Royal Flying Corps, based in France in 1917. Operating from a number of airfields in the army co-operation role, the squadron took part in the major offensives of the spring of that year before converting to F.2B fighters.

This is thought to be an F.E.2b of No. 25 Sqn preparing for a night raid in 1916, a role which became ever more important to an aircraft vulnerable to each new generation of fighting scouts.

night bombing operations in Europe and for home defence against dirigibles and Gotha bombers, remaining occupied in these roles until the final year of World War I. Production of F.E.2a/F.E.2b aircraft totalled 1,939, and although there is no accurate record of the number of F.E.2d aircraft, it is believed that about 250 were built.

Specification
RAF F.E.2b
Type: two-seat fighter

Powerplant: one 120-hp (89-kW) Beardmore inline piston engine
Performance: maximum speed 129 km/h (80 mph) at sea level; service ceiling 2745 m (9,000 ft); endurance 3 hours
Weights: empty 904 kg (1,993 lb); maximum take-off 1347 kg (2,970 lb)
Dimensions: span 14.55 m (47 ft 9 in); length 9.83 m (32 ft 3 in); height 3.85 m (12 ft 7.5 in); wing area 45.89 m² (494.0 sq ft)
Armament: initially a single 7.7-mm

(0.303-in) Lewis gun, but later a second Lewis gun was added; in a bomber role a maximum of 159 kg (350 lb) of bombs could be carried in various combinations

Introduced in late 1915 to deal with the 'Fokker Scourge', the F.E.2 (in collaboration with the D.H.2) gradually gained an ascendancy, but soon became vulnerable to the Albatros and Halberstadt of 1916. It ended the war as a night bomber.

Handley Page O/100 and O/400
UK

To meet an Admiralty specification of December 1914 for a large twin-engine patrol bomber, Handley Page lost little time in designing an aircraft to meet this requirement and when the **Handley Page O/100** prototype was completed, it was the largest aeroplane that had been built in the UK.

The O/100 was powered by two 266-hp (198-kW) Rolls-Royce Eagle II engines, in armoured nacelles, mounted between the wings just outboard of the fuselage. Accommodation was in a glazed cockpit enclosure, the floor and sides of the cockpit being protected by armour plate. Flown for the first time on 17 December 1915, the O/100 was found to be inadequate in performance, and the second prototype had a revised open cockpit for a crew of two (with provision for a gunner's position forward), the cockpit armour plating and most of that incorporated in the engine nacelles was deleted, and new radiators were introduced for the water-cooled engines.

Formation of the first 'Handley Page Squadron', as it was then known, began in August 1916 and this unit became operational in France in late October or early November; its first recorded bombing attack was made on the night of 16/17 March 1917 against an enemy-held railway junction.

Production deliveries of the O/400 began in early 1918, this being an improved version of the O/100 which differed primarily by having more powerful Rolls-Royce Eagle engines, a revised fuel system and radiators, and the introduction of a compressed-air engine starting system. Although production of O/100s totalled only 46 aircraft, substantial numbers of O/400s became operational before the end of the war and, for example, on the night of 14/15 September 1918 a force of 40 O/400s attacked targets in the Saar. It

O/100 no. 1463 was landed by its RNAS crew on the first good field they saw after breaking cloud on their flight to France on 1 January 1917; it was 13 miles inside enemy territory, near Laon. Among the German evaluation pilots was Manfred von Richthofen.

At the time the RAF was formed, the RFC's standard heavy bomber was the O/400, an aircraft from No. 207 Sqn at Ligescourt, France, in 1918 being shown here. This was the first British squadron used solely for long-range night bombing, and the first to operate Handley Page bombers.

was also at about this same time that these aircraft began to deploy 748-kg (1,650-lb) bombs, the heaviest used by British services during World War I.

More than 400 O/400s were delivered for service with the RAF before the Armistice of November 1918. The type remained in service in reduced numbers until late 1919, when it was replaced by the Vickers Vimy.

Specification
Handley Page O/400
Type: heavy bomber
Powerplant: two 360-hp (268-kW) Rolls-Royce Eagle VIII 12-cylinder Vee piston engines
Performance: maximum speed 156 km/h (97 mph); service ceiling 2590 m (8,500 ft); endurance 8 hours
Weights: empty 3719 kg (8,200 lb);

maximum take-off 6350 kg (14,000 lb)
Dimensions: span 30.48 m (100 ft 0 in); length 19.16 m (62 ft 10.25 in); height 6.71 m (22 ft 0 in); wing area 153.10 m² (1,648.0 sq ft)
Armament: up to five 7.7-mm (0.303-in) Lewis gun on pivoted mounts, plus a maximum bombload of 907 kg (2,000 lb)

The large fuel capacity of the Handley Page O/400 made it a suitable aircraft to blaze the trail for the Empire flying routes to come. This aircraft was used by Borton, Salmond and Smith to survey the airmail route from Egypt to India, and is seen in Delhi on 12 December 1918.

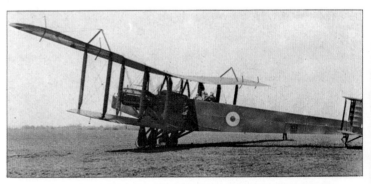

The O/400 replaced the O/100 in production early in 1918, being powered by a pair of 350-hp (261-kW) Rolls-Royce Eagle engines and having improved fuel systems and radiators. Maximum bombload was of the order of 907 kg (2,000 lb), and the heaviest bomb carried was of 750 kg (1,650 lb).

🇬🇧 UK
Handley Page V/1500

Designed and developed to make it possible for the RAF to mount attacks on German targets from bases in the UK, the **Handley Page V/1500** must be regarded as the first practical strategic bomber. Larger in size than the O/100s and O/400s that preceded it, the V/1500 was powered by four Rolls-Royce engines, these mounted in tandem pairs between the wings, outboard of the fuselage, but was in other respects similar in overall configuration to the earlier bombers.

The prototype, assembled by Handley Page from components manufactured by Harland and Wolff, was flown for the first time during May 1918. This differed primarily from production aircraft by having a single large cooling radiator to serve all four engines, the standard installation becoming one hexagonal radiator forward of each pair of engines. This larger aircraft provided accommodation for a crew of five to seven.

When the armistice was signed only three V/1500s were ready for operational use, these standing by with No. 166 Squadron at Bircham Newton, Norfolk, where they had been frustrated by bad weather from attacking targets in Germany. The type saw only limited post-war service with the RAF, gradually being replaced by the Vickers Vimy. One was used to record the first through flight from England to India: taking off on 13 December 1918, the

aircraft flew via Rome, Malta, Cairo, and Baghdad to Karachi, which it reached on 30 December. This aircraft was used in May 1919 to make a bomb attack on Kabul during the problems in Afghanistan. Another V/1500 was shipped to Newfoundland with the object of making a first west-east flight over the North Atlantic, but this project was abandoned when Alcock and Brown achieved the first crossing in a Vickers Vimy. The post-1924 designation was **H.P.15**.

Specification
Handley Page V/1500
Type: long-range heavy bomber
Powerplant: four 375-hp (280-kW) Rolls-Royce Eagle VIII 12-cylinder Vee piston engines
Performance: maximum speed 159 km/h (99 mph) at 1980 m (6,500 ft); service ceiling 3355 m (11,000 ft); range 2092 km (1,300 miles)
Weights: empty 7983 kg (17,600 lb); maximum take-off 13608 kg (30,000 lb)
Dimensions: span 38.40 m (126 ft 0 in); length 19.51 m (64 ft 0 in); height 7.01 m

The Handley Page V/1500 was too late for World War I and too large for the peacetime Royal Air Force, but had the war lasted until 1919 its 2100-km (1,300-mile) range and massive (for the time) bombload would have made a significant contribution.

(23 ft 0 in); wing area 278.70 m² (3,000.0 sq ft)
Armament: single or twin 7.7-mm (0.303-in) Lewis guns in nose, dorsal, ventral and tail positions, plus up to 3402 kg (7,500 lb) of bombs

---

🇬🇧 UK
Vickers F.B.27 Vimy

The **Vickers F.B.27 Vimy** bomber prototype was flown for the first time on 30 November 1917; like the de Havilland D.H.10 Amiens and Handley Page V/1500, it was designed to provide the RAF with a strategic bomber that could attack industrial targets in Germany. Although token numbers of each had arrived in France or were with British squadrons before the Armistice of 11 November 1918, none of them saw operational service in World War I. The **F.B.27A Vimy Mk II** was ordered into large-scale production, but contract cancellations at the war's end limited the total built to about 230. It was not until July 1919 that the Vimy was in full RAF service, equipping first No. 58 Squadron in Egypt, then other squadrons in the Middle East and in the UK. It remained in first-line service until replaced by the Vickers Virginia in 1924-5.

The Vimy is, of course, remembered in aviation history for its pioneering flights, including the first nonstop west-east crossing of the North Atlantic by John Alcock and Arthur Whitten Brown; the first Eng-

land-Australia flight by Ross and Keith Smith and their crew; and the attempted first England-South Africa flight by Pierre van Ryneveld and Christopher Q. Brand, of which the final leg, Bulawayo to Cape Town, was completed in a D.H.9.

Final derivative of the Vimy was the **Vickers Vernon** bomber/transport used by the RAF during its policing of

Seventy-five Vickers F.B.Mk 27A Vimys were ordered from Westland at Yeovil, but only 25 were completed, the second aircraft being depicted here. It was planned to use American Liberty engines, but standard Rolls-Royce Eagle VIIIs were eventually fitted.

Iraq from 1921. Serving with Nos 45 and 70 Squadrons at Hinaidi, they not only carried out their basic tasks, but were used as air ambulances and played a significant role in establishing the Cairo-Baghdad airmail route.

Specification
Vickers Vimy Mk II
Type: heavy bomber

Powerplant: two 360-hp (268-kW) Rolls-Royce Eagle VIII Vee piston engines
Performance: maximum speed 166 km/h (103 mph) at sea level; service ceiling 2135 m (7,000 ft); maximum range 1448 km (900 miles)
Weights: empty 3222 kg (7,104 lb); maximum take-off 4937 kg (10,884 lb)
Dimensions: span 20.75 m (68 ft 1 in); length 13.27 m (43 ft 6.5 in); height 4.76 m (15 ft 7.5 in); wing area 122.44 m² (1,318.0 sq ft)
Armament: one 7.7-mm (0.303-in) Lewis machine-gun on a Scarff ring mounting in both nose and mid positions, plus up to 1123 kg (2,476 lb) of bombs on external racks

The Vickers F.B.27 Vimy was designed to provide a heavy bomber for the RFC, but only a single Vimy Mk IV had reached France by October 1918. It went on to prove a mainstay of the RAF's bombing squadrons, and Alcock and Brown flew one across the Atlantic.

Armstrong Whitworth F.K.8

As a replacement for the B.E.2c, Koolhoven designed the **Armstrong Whitworth F.K.8**, an aircraft of altogether more sturdy appearance, with a considerably larger fuselage to cope with the specialist equipment required for the type's army co-operation role. Produced at the same time as the Royal Aircraft Factory's R.E.8, which was intended for the same task, the F.K.8 was generally considerably superior, but no doubt politics were responsible for the much larger orders for the government-establishment machine.

First flown in May 1916, the F.K.8 was sent to the Central Flying School at Upavon for testing where, although its handling was satisfactory, it fell somewhat short of the specified performance. Nevertheless, substantial orders were placed. Armstrong Whitworth received contracts beginning in August 1916 for more than 700, while another 950 were built by Angus Sanderson in Newcastle. Production at the Armstrong Whitworth factory was be-

tween 80 and 100 F.K.8s per month by the end of 1917, and this continued until July 1918, when the company received contracts for Bristol Fighter production and handed over F.K.8 responsibility to Sanderson.

The F.K.8 served with several squadrons in France, the first to become fully equipped being No. 35, while other squadrons served overseas.

An Armstrong Whitworth F.K.8, one of a run of 200 aircraft ordered from Angus Sanderson & Co, Newcastle upon Tyne, in a contract of 5 July 1918. Sandersons were the largest builder of the type. Two 'Big Ack' (as the type was known) pilots were recipients of the Victoria Cross.

Specification
Armstrong Whitworth F.K.8
Type: two-seat general-purpose aircraft
Powerplant: one 160-hp (119-kW) Beardmore inline piston engine
Performance: maximum speed 153 km/h (95 mph) at sea level; climb to 1980 m (6,500 ft) in 19 minutes; service ceiling 3960 m (13,000 ft); endurance 3 hours

Weights: empty 869 kg (1,916 lb); maximum take-off 1275 kg (2,811 lb)
Dimensions: span 13.26 m (43 ft 6 in); length 9.58 m (31 ft 5 in); height 3.33 m (10 ft 11 in); wing area 50.17 m² (540 sq ft)
Armament: one fixed 7.7-mm (0.303-in) synchronized Vickers machine-gun and one trainable 7.7-mm (0.303-in) Lewis machine-gun in the rear cockpit

Airco D.H.4, 9 and 9A

A major reason for the Allied victory in the air war against Germany was that the Allies managed to develop more and more powerful aero-engines while the German aircraft had to make do with a limited variety of weaker powerplants. It was an engine, the superlative Rolls-Royce Eagle, which endowed an otherwise conventional two-seater called the **Airco D.H.4** with a performance on a par with enemy scouts. The prototype D.H.4 had flown in August 1916 with a different powerplant but delays in placing this unit into production led to early models carrying a 250-hp (186-kW) Rolls-Royce engine; this was later developed into the mighty 375-hp (280-kW) Eagle VII which enabled the D.H.4 to top 225 km/h (140 mph) in level flight and to climb to 1830 m (6,000 ft) in under 5 minutes.

The D.H.4 was first delivered to No. 55 Squadron, RFC, in early 1917 and eventually equipped nine RAF and 13 American squadrons by the Armistice; it also served with the RNAS. Generally armed with a Vickers machine-gun firing forward and one (sometimes two) Lewis guns in the observer's position, the D.H.4 could carry up to 209 kg (460 lb) of bombs on underwing racks. Machines built by Westland for the RNAS carried twin Vickers guns and the observer's Lewis on a pillar mounting. Two D.H.4s were modified as airship interceptors: each sporting a 1½-lb quick-firer mounted to fire nearly vertically upwards, they anticipated some of the night-fighters of World War II but never saw action.

The only flaw in the design of the D.H.4 was the distance separating pilot and observer, which rendered communication almost impossible. Although the layout gave the pilot good downward visibility and the observer a good field of fire, the lack of communication was a serious drawback in air-to-air combat. The D.H.9 rectified this, placing the crew close together in a newly designed fuselage married to the same wings and tail as the D.H.4. Designed as a long-range bomber in mid-1917, the D.H.9 was heralded as an outstanding aircraft but when the machine appeared on the Western

Front in the spring of 1918, its performance fell far short of expectations. Its BHP Puma engine gave endless trouble, and there were not enough Rolls-Royce Eagles to equip the armada of D.H.9s rapidly being assembled. Westland came to the rescue: having manufactured large numbers of D.H.4s and D.H.9s, they redesigned the aircraft to accept the American Liberty engine. The result was the **D.H.9A**, which was a massive improvement and is rightly regarded a one of the best strategic bombers of the 'Great War'. Unlike most of its contemporaries, the D.H.9A continued in production after the war and served with distinction in Iraq and on the troubled North West frontier of India.

Specification
Airco D.H.4
Type: two-seat day bomber
Powerplant: one 375-hp (280-kW) Rolls-Royce Eagle VII inline piston engine
Performance: maximum level speed 230 km/h (143 mph); climb to 1830 m (6,000 ft) in 4 minutes 50 seconds; service ceiling 6705 m (22,000 ft); endurance 3 hours 45 minutes
Weights: empty 1083 kg (2,387 lb); maximum take-off 1575 kg (3,472 lb)
Dimensions: span 12.92 m (42 ft 4.5 in); length 9.35 m (30 ft 8 in); height 3.35 m (11 ft 0 in); wing area 40.32 m² (434.0 sq ft)
Armament: one (RFC) or two (RNAS) fixed forward-firing 7.7-mm (0.303 in) Vickers machine-guns and one or two 7.7-mm (0.303 in) Lewis guns in aft cockpit, plus up to 209 kg (460 lb) of bombs on underfuselage/wing racks; American-built DH-4s had two 7.62-mm (0.3-in) Marlin forward-firing machine-guns, but otherwise were as British production

The D.H.9A served for many years with the RAF, but unlike its predecessor was only used in small numbers by the US Army. It was used in the 37-hour endurance record set on 27/28 August 1923 by the Americans Smith and Richter.

Because of the fuel tank between pilot and observer, the D.H.4 was nicknamed the 'Flaming Coffin' by its crews. Nonetheless, it was built in extremely large numbers, its considerable virtues outweighing that major fault.

Airco D.H.4 and D.H.9 in Action

Geoffrey de Havilland always had a flair for producing aircraft that fitted the bill for a specific requirement. In 1916, with World War I in progress, there was a need for an advanced bombing and reconnaissance aircraft which would give the RFC a 'strategic' bombing capability, being able to hit German targets far beyond the trenches. The aircraft that more than met this need was the D.H.4.

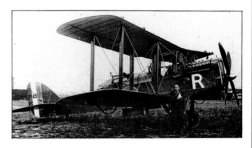

The D.H.4 was a revelation to the pilots of the Royal Flying Corps, giving bomber pilots an advantage in performance over the German scouts that had wrought havoc among the pusher squadrons in 1916.

When Geoffrey de Havilland's D.H.4 first reached Royal Flying Corps squadrons early in 1917 it was greeted with enthusiasm as possessing a performance adequate to outdistance then-current German scouts such as the Albatros and Fokker D III, as well as being able to outmanoeuvre (in experienced hands) all such aircraft. As such it earned lasting fame as the first successful high-performance day bomber.

Early aircraft were powered by 250-hp (186-kW) Rolls-Royce engines and these accompanied No. 55 Squadron to France early in March 1917, followed by No. 57 Squadron in May and by No. 25 Squadron two months later. The first-named unit did not enter combat immediately, being ordered to hold its D.H.4s in reserve so as to achieve the greatest possible surprise in the Battle of Arras which opened on 6 April. On that day and on several subsequent occasions No. 55 Squadron attacked Valenciennes railway station as an important German communications centre. Early in May the targets shifted to the rail junctions at Brebières and Bussigny, where a small number of casualties was suffered from ground fire.

During the Battle of Ypres of May 1917 No. 55 Squadron was joined by the D.H.4s of No. 57, the light bombers being able to operate out of reach of German opposition above 4875 m (16,000 ft). In October that year, by which time No. 18 Squadron had become the RFC's fourth D.H.4 squadron in France, No. 55 was withdrawn from the front to become one of the first three units comprising the RFC's 41st Wing (the others being No. 100 Squadron with RAF F.E.2b pushers and No. 16 (Naval) Squadron with Handley Page O/100s). The 41st Wing, later renamed the VIII Brigade, ultimately became the Independent Force of the RAF on 6

June 1918, and as such the main instrument of strategic bombing by the Allies.

Between October 1917 and the end of the war a year later, No. 55 flew repeated bombing raids over western Germany in daylight, the nature of the raids becoming increasingly of a strategic type. Some 94 such attacks were made against munitions factories and other targets in Cologne, Darmstadt, Düren, Frankfurt, Kaiserslautern, Mannheim, Metz-Sablon and Saarbrücken, some of these objectives involving five and a half hour flights which allowed no margin for air combat. These raids cost No. 55 Squadron a total of 69 D.H.4s.

During the great German offensive of March 1918 the pilots of the 9th Wing (Nos 25 and 27 Squadrons) were ordered to adopt low-flying attacks (despite all risks and bad weather) in harassing enemy troops. Such attacks were accompanied by fairly heavy losses, and at the end of the month the squadrons were allowed to resume operations at higher altitude.

RNAS service

At much the same time as the RFC began flying the D.H.4 over the Western Front in the spring of 1917, the Royal Naval Air Service also started introducing the aircraft for all manner of duties in addition to day bombing over German ports. No. 2 (Naval) Squadron (later to become No. 202 Squadron after amalgamation of the RNAS into the new RAF) was the first to receive the aircraft and was tasked with reconnaissance of the Zeebrugge area in preparation for the famous raid by the Royal Navy on 22/23 April 1918. Captain K.G. Boyd of No. 217 Squadron sank the German submarine *UB-12* with two direct hits with 104-kg (230-lb) bombs.

A handful of D.H.4s was sent to the Middle

East, but rather larger numbers served with RNAS units in the Aegean. Two D.H.4s, which were sent to strengthen 'C' Squadron on Imbros, carried out a number of bombing attacks on the Sofia-Constantinople railway in November 1917. Two months later naval D.H.4 bombers carried out a series of attacks on the German battle-cruiser *Goeben* aground in the Narrows near the Dardanelles until she was withdrawn from danger; thereafter the D.H.4s, specially modified to provide an endurance of seven hours' flying time, were used to keep an eye on the warship as she lay at anchor near Constantinople. At least one of the RNAS aircraft, based at Mudros on the island of Lemnos, was detached to the Greek airfield of Amberkoj to join the Armstrong Whitworth F.K.8s of No. 17 Squadron RAF in bombing attacks on the retreating Bulgars in September 1918. In Italy the D.H.4s of Nos 224, 226 and 227 Squadrons (based at Adrano, Otranto and Taranto) carried out bombing raids on the submarine bases at Cattaro and Durazzo.

The US 11th Aero Squadron (Day Bombardment) pose with their US-built, Liberty-engined D.H.4s at their base at Maulan. By the autumn of 1918 the US Army had significant force in Europe, but the only native-built aircraft used were the British-designed D.H.4.

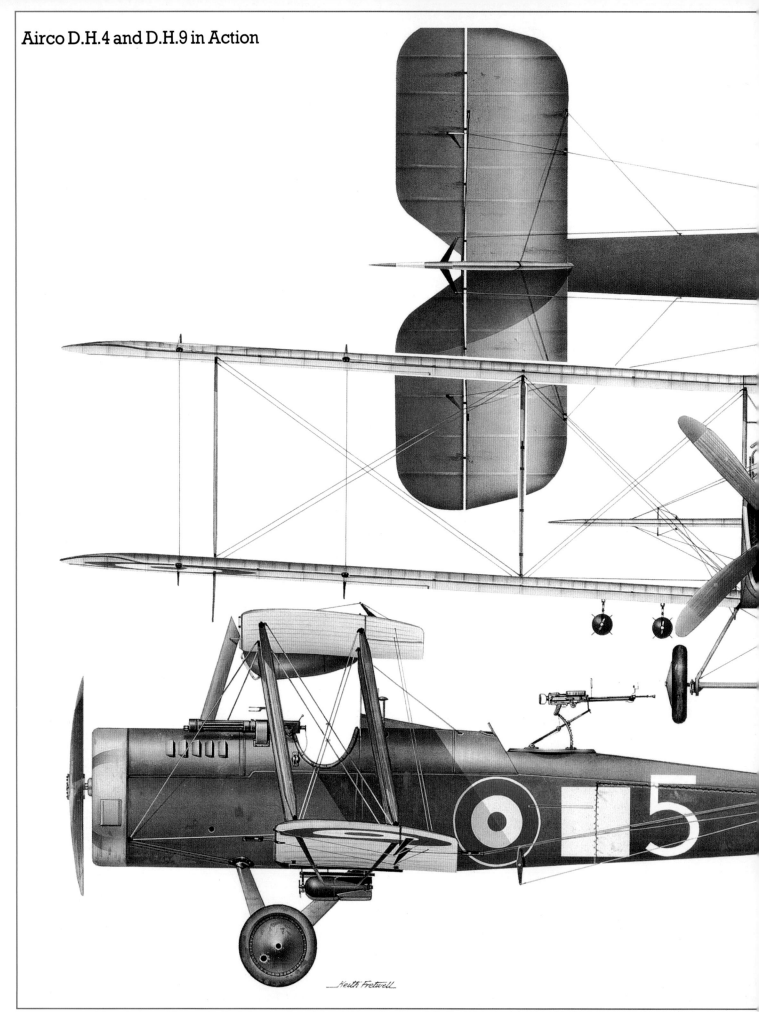

Keith Fretwell

Without doubt the best Airco D.H.4s were those
powered by the 375-hp (280-kW) Eagle VIII, but
this engine was costly and in short supply (and,
because of its bigger propeller, needed longer
landing gears). Many other engines were
therefore fitted, most of the earlier machines
having the RAF.3a, a water-cooled V-12 of only
200 hp (149 kW) produced by the Royal Aircraft
Factory. A7712 was one of the RAF-engined
machines, built by Airco in summer 1917 and
delivered to No. 18 Sqn RFC, which with No. 49 Sqn
used the RAF-engined version exclusively from
June 1917. The frontal radiator tapered slightly
from top to bottom (the reverse of the BHP version)
and had a single exhaust stack. At first the
valuable D.H.4s were kept above 4572 m
(15,000 ft), but during the crucial days of March
1918 No. 18 Sqn was ordered over the front at low
level to harass the advancing enemy troops.

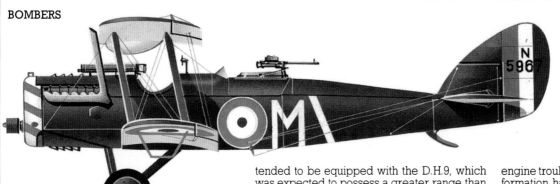

A Westland-built D.H.4, probably serving with No. 5 (Naval) Squadron, Royal Naval Air Service, in the spring of 1918. After the formation of the Royal Air Force on 1 April 1918, this was renumbered No. 205 Squadron, Royal Air Force.

The D.H.4 was the only British aircraft selected for production in the USA to see combat service in France with the American Expeditionary forces; indeed by the end of the war more than twice the number of British-built aircraft had been produced in the USA. Powered mostly by Liberty engines, the American D.H.4s equipped a total of 13 operational squadrons, of which five were bomber units. Among the most famous bombing operations of the last year of the war was the great attack by 200 bombers, commanded by William Mitchell and accompanied by 150 escorting scouts, on the German army as it attempted to concentrate for a counterattack against the Allied offensive in the Argonne-Meuse area. Indeed the effectiveness of this raid was to colour Mitchell's views on the use of bombers and was to have a profound influence on the future policies of the US Army Air Corps.

By the end of the war D.H.4s had equipped 25 squadrons of the RFC, RNAS and RAF; a small number of the aircraft operated with the British forces sent to Archangel in May 1918, while others were sent later to Baku in Azerbaijan to support British naval forces in the Caspian Sea, taking part in bombing attacks on the Bolshevik-held port of Astrakhan at the mouth of the Volga.

The D.H.9 and 'Nine-Ack'

Because the D.H.9A survived in service so much longer than the D.H.4 it gained lasting fame, yet during the war enjoyed a far less distinguished career than the earlier aeroplane, being summed up by the squadrons as a 'D.H.4 which has been officially interfered with to suit it for mass production'. Indeed, except when powered by the 430-hp (321-kW) Lion engine, its performance was markedly inferior.

The raison d'etre of the D.H.9 was to increase the RFC's bombing potential. On 21 June 1917 the War Office decided to increase the number of squadrons from 108 to 200, the majority of the new units being bomber squadrons in-

tended to be equipped with the D.H.9, which was expected to possess a greater range than the D.H.4, thereby extending the area of the RFC's bombing operations. In the final outcome the D.H.9 was no better than the D.H.4 in the matter of range, and could seldom carry as much bombload; only when the improved D.H.9A appeared in service in the last three months of the war was any improvement apparent. The principal weakness of the D.H.9 was its BHP engine, the officially-favoured powerplant which happened not to lend itself to mass production and gave constant trouble in service.

The first aircraft to reach France equipped Nos 98, 206 and 211 Squadrons of the new RAF in April 1918, some of these D.H.9s participating in the Battle of the Lys that month, and dropping more than 600 51-kg (112-lb) bombs in the front-line areas. As with the D.H.4, however, it was with the Independent Force that the D.H.9 saw most service, equipping Nos 99 and 104 Squadrons. Between June and November 1918 these two squadrons flew a total of 83 raids. A measure of the problems being encountered may be judged by the fact that during these attacks no fewer than 123 aircraft had to return early with engine trouble. Moreover, while the D.H.4s were able to hold their own in the face of German scouts, the D.H.9 was exceedingly vulnerable, a fact that was quickly exploited by the defending scouts. On 31 July 12 D.H.9s of No. 99 Squadron set out to bomb Mainz. Three soon returned with engine trouble, another was shot down by scouts over Saarbrücken and three more near Saaralbe; the survivors dropped their bombs on that town and turned for home, but three more were shot down before the leader, Captain A.H. Taylor, and one other survivor landed at their base at Azelot. In an even worse debacle, 29 D.H.9s of Nos. 27 and 98 squadrons took off to bomb the railway junction at Aulnoye on 1 October, but no fewer than 15 turned back with

The D.H.9 (seen here at Eastchurch in 1919) should have been an improvement on the D.H.4, and indeed in terms of design it was. However, powerplant problems gave the new model a performance that was distinctly inferior to that of its predecessor.

engine trouble, with the result that the reduced formation had to abandon its raid.

Frustrated by such raid failures it was not surprising that Trenchard acrimoniously demanded the immediate introduction of the Liberty-powered D.H.9A (the 'Nine-Ack') which had been undergoing leisurely development since late in 1917, although the first American engines did not arrive in the UK until the spring of 1918. No. 110 Squadron with D.H.9As joined the Independent Force at the end of August, but flew only five bombing raids before the end of the war; in the last two months of operations the squadron lost 45 aircraft, and only two of its attacks were deemed successful to any extent. Both the D.H.9 and 9A fared rather better in the eastern Mediterranean and in Palestine, although their operations were generally on a smaller scale than even those of the D.H.4.

The lessons of the bombing operations by relatively small aircraft in daylight, such as the D.H.4 and 9, were there for the learning. The Americans usually employed much larger formations, often with accompanying fighter escort; occasionally losses were suffered, but seldom such as to reduce the effectiveness of the raids by a significant degree. Despite the relatively light bomb loads carried, damage was inflicted out of all proportion when compared with that by the small formations of British aircraft whose squadrons were frequently all but overwhelmed by opposing fighting scouts. Yet it took the RAF 22 more years to learn the folly of committing small formations of unescorted bombers to daylight raids in the likely presence of fighter opposition.

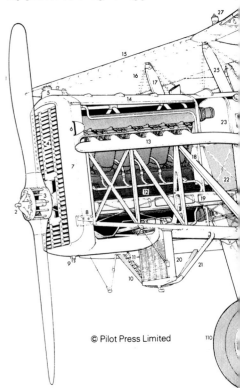

© Pilot Press Limited

110

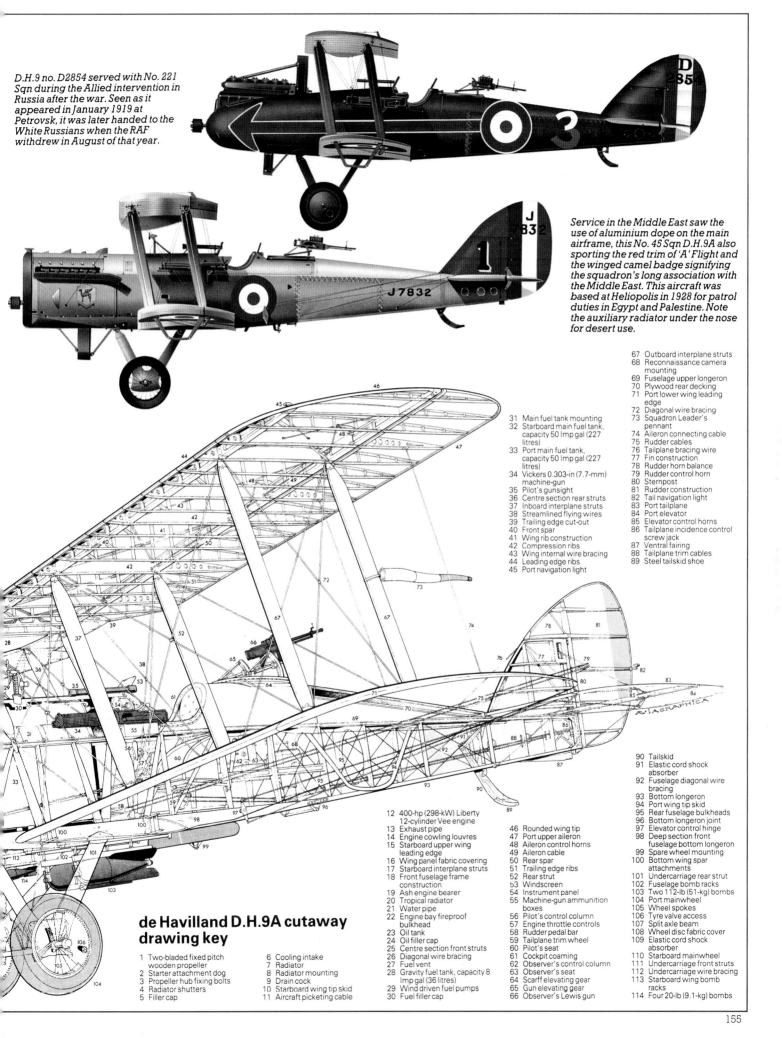

D.H.9 no. D2854 served with No. 221 Sqn during the Allied intervention in Russia after the war. Seen as it appeared in January 1919 at Petrovsk, it was later handed to the White Russians when the RAF withdrew in August of that year.

Service in the Middle East saw the use of aluminium dope on the main airframe, this No. 45 Sqn D.H.9A also sporting the red trim of 'A' Flight and the winged camel badge signifying the squadron's long association with the Middle East. This aircraft was based at Heliopolis in 1928 for patrol duties in Egypt and Palestine. Note the auxiliary radiator under the nose for desert use.

de Havilland D.H.9A cutaway drawing key

1 Two-bladed fixed pitch wooden propeller
2 Starter attachment dog
3 Propeller hub fixing bolts
4 Radiator shutters
5 Filler cap
6 Cooling intake
7 Radiator
8 Radiator mounting
9 Drain cock
10 Starboard wing tip skid
11 Aircraft picketing cable
12 400-hp (298-kW) Liberty 12-cylinder Vee engine
13 Exhaust pipe
14 Engine cowling louvres
15 Starboard upper wing leading edge
16 Wing panel fabric covering
17 Starboard interplane struts
18 Front fuselage frame construction
19 Ash engine bearer
20 Tropical radiator
21 Water pipe
22 Engine bay fireproof bulkhead
23 Oil tank
24 Oil filler cap
25 Centre section front struts
26 Diagonal wire bracing
27 Fuel vent
28 Gravity fuel tank, capacity 8 Imp gal (36 litres)
29 Wind driven fuel pumps
30 Fuel filler cap
31 Main fuel tank mounting
32 Starboard main fuel tank, capacity 50 Imp gal (227 litres)
33 Port main fuel tank, capacity 50 Imp gal (227 litres)
34 Vickers 0.303-in (7.7-mm) machine-gun
35 Pilot's gunsight
36 Centre section rear struts
37 Inboard interplane struts
38 Streamlined flying wires
39 Trailing edge cut-out
40 Front spar
41 Wing rib construction
42 Compression ribs
43 Wing internal wire bracing
44 Leading edge ribs
45 Port navigation light
46 Rounded wing tip
47 Port upper aileron
48 Aileron control horns
49 Aileron cable
50 Rear spar
51 Trailing edge ribs
52 Rear strut
53 Windscreen
54 Instrument panel
55 Machine-gun ammunition boxes
56 Pilot's control column
57 Engine throttle controls
58 Rudder pedal bar
59 Tailplane trim wheel
60 Pilot's seat
61 Cockpit coaming
62 Observer's control column
63 Observer's seat
64 Scarff elevating gear
65 Gun elevating gear
66 Observer's Lewis gun
67 Outboard interplane struts
68 Reconnaissance camera mounting
69 Fuselage upper longeron
70 Plywood rear decking
71 Port lower wing leading edge
72 Diagonal wire bracing
73 Squadron Leader's pennant
74 Aileron connecting cable
75 Rudder cables
76 Tailplane bracing wire
77 Fin construction
78 Rudder horn balance
79 Rudder control horn
80 Sternpost
81 Rudder construction
82 Tail navigation light
83 Port tailplane
84 Port elevator
85 Elevator control horns
86 Tailplane incidence control screw jack
87 Ventral fairing
88 Tailplane trim cables
89 Steel tailskid shoe
90 Tailskid
91 Elastic cord shock absorber
92 Fuselage diagonal wire bracing
93 Bottom longeron
94 Port wing tip skid
95 Rear fuselage bulkheads
96 Bottom longeron joint
97 Elevator control hinge
98 Deep section front fuselage bottom longeron
99 Spare wheel mounting
100 Bottom wing spar attachments
101 Undercarriage rear strut
102 Fuselage bomb racks
103 Two 112-lb (51-kg) bombs
104 Port mainwheel
105 Wheel spokes
106 Tyre valve access
107 Split axle beam
108 Wheel disc fabric cover
109 Elastic cord shock absorber
110 Starboard mainwheel
111 Undercarriage front struts
112 Undercarriage wire bracing
113 Starboard wing bomb racks
114 Four 20-lb (9.1-kg) bombs

AEG C and J series

From 1914, AEG supplied the German air service with a number of unarmed reconnaissance aircraft known as the B series and little real development was necessary for the evolution of the **AEG C I** that was introduced in March 1915. It carried a 150-hp (112-kW) Benz Bz.III inline engine, and a machine-gun for the observer on a flexible mount in the aft cockpit. With the emphasis changing gradually from a stable reconnaissance platform towards a more manoeuvrable aircraft that could evade enemy scouts and fight back, the **C II** of October 1915 was a refined version of the C I.

The most extensively constructed member of the C series was the **C IV**, its development spurred by the German air service's growing appreciation of the importance of aerial reconnaissance. A little larger than the C II, it introduced the more powerful Mercedes D.III engine, a fixed forward-firing machine-gun for the pilot, and a three-position variable-incidence tailplane that was adjustable on the ground. Production figures for the IV are estimated at 400.

In 1916 the German air service introduced *Infanterie-Flieger* units (infantry contact patrol units), which would now be regarded as close support or ground attack squadrons. Proving to be valuable when used on a small

scale during the Battle of Verdun, such units were soon the subject of a high-priority programme of expansion and equipment. AEG's **J I** was developed hurriedly to meet this requirement. The J I was virtually a C IV provided with a 200-hp (149-kW) Benz Bz.IV engine, plus 390 kg (860 lb) of armour plate to protect the crew and powerplant. Two LMG 08/15 machine-guns were mounted in the floor of the aft cockpit, pointing downward and forward at an angle of about 45°, so that they could be used for strafing enemy

trenches or columns of infantry on the march. In addition, the observer had a Parabellum machine-gun on a ring mounting. The **J II** of 1918 was generally similar. More than 600 J I/II aircraft were built.

Specification
AEG C IV
Type: two-seat armed reconnaissance aircraft
Powerplant: one 160-hp (119-kW) Mercedes D.III inline piston engine

The AEG C IV was the most widely produced of the AEG C series of two-seater reconnaissance aircraft, an estimated 400 machines seeing service. Larger than the earlier aircraft, it introduced the Mercedes DIII 119-kW (160-hp) engine and a fixed forward-firing machine-gun for the pilot.

Performance: maximum speed 158 km/h (98 mph); service ceiling 5000 m (16,405 ft); endurance 4 hours
Weights: empty 800 kg (1,746 lb); maximum take-off 1120 kg (2,469 lb)
Dimensions: span 13.45 m (44 ft 1.5 in); length 7.15 m (23 ft 5.5 in); height 3.35 m (10 ft 11.75 in); wing area 39.00 m² (419.81 sq ft)
Armament: one fixed forward-firing 7.92-mm (0.31-in) LMG 08/15 machine-gun, and one 7.92-mm (0.31-in) Parabellum machine-gun for observer on ring mounting

Halberstadt C and CL series

Based on the **Halberstadt B II** two-seater and developed similarly as a reconnaissance aircraft, the **Halberstadt C I** retained the earlier aircraft's slab-sided fuselage, but the crew positions were reversed and the rear (observer's) position was provided with a mounting for a pivoted machine-gun. Towards the end of 1917 the improved **C III** appeared, powered by a 200-hp

(149-kW) Benz Bz.IV engine.

The most prolific of the Halberstadt C series was the **C V** high-altitude reconnaissance aircraft, which appeared in 1918. A camera mounted in the rear cockpit could be directed through a sliding hatch in the floor. Developed to act as escort for the C-type reconnaissance aircraft, the **Halberstadt CL II** appeared in 1917 and soon

entered service with the *Schützstaffeln* (protection flights) of the Imperial German Aviation Service. The single cockpit had tandem accommodation for pilot and observer, the latter being provided with an elevated gun ring which allowed him to fire his Parabellum machine-gun both upward and forward over the upper wing. Trays were fitted on each side of the fuselage

for the carriage of small anti-personnel grenades, or of four or five 10-kg (22-lb) bombs. The CL II soon demonstrated its value to the German high command when, on 6 September 1917, 24 aircraft attacked with great effect British troops crossing the bridges over the Somme at Bray and St Christ. The escort units were then redesignated as *Schlachtstaffeln* (battle flights) for close-support duties and were used extensively during the closing months of 1917, particularly at the Battle of Cambrai on 30 November when the Germans launched a successful counter-offensive.

Specification
Halberstadt CL II
Type: two-seat ground support aircraft and escort fighter
Powerplant: one 160-hp (119-kW) Mercedes D.III 6-cylinder inline piston engine
Performance: maximum speed 165 km/h (103 mph) at 5000 m (16,405 ft); service ceiling 5100 m (16,730 ft); endurance 3 hours
Weights: empty 772 kg (1,701 lb); maximum take-off 1130 kg (2,493 lb)
Dimensions: span 10.77 m (35 ft 4 in); length 7.30 m (23 ft 11.5 in); height 2.75 m (9 ft 0.25 in); wing area 27.50 m² (296.02 sq ft)
Armament: one or two fixed forward-firing 7.92-mm (0.31-in) LMG 08/15 machine-guns and one pivoted 7.92-mm (0.31-in) Parabellum machine-gun, plus four or five 10-kg (22-lb) bombs and grenades

Developed to escort reconnaissance flights, the two-seat Halberstadt CL III proved an effective bomber and, carrying racks of light bombs, played an important part in the German counter-attack at Cambrai in 1917.

Hansa-Brandenburg C I and Phönix C I

One of the earliest designs of Ernst Heinkel for the Hansa und Brandenburgische Flugzeug-Werke GmbH, the **Hansa-Brandenburg C I** was built extensively for its era, being constructed not only by Brandenburg but also under licence by Phönix and Ufag in Austria. A conventional two-bay biplane of wood and fabric construction, it had a slender fuselage with the powerplant mounted in the nose, provided a combined open cockpit for the pilot and observer/gunner, and mounted a braced tail unit at the rear. Landing gear was of tailskid type.

Entering service in 1916, C Is saw wide-scale use by the Austrian forces and some examples continued in service until the end of World War I. In the long period of time over which they were operational, C Is were seen with powerplants ranging from 160 to 230 hp (119 to 172 kW) and with a variety of armaments. Basically this comprised a single machine-gun on a pivoted mount at the rear of the cockpit, but later versions also had a single forward-firing machine-gun mounted in different positions. Some were used for light bombing missions and were equipped to carry up to 100 kg (220 lb) of light fragmentation or incendiary bombs on racks beneath the fuselage or lower wing.

The Austro-Hungarian aircraft manufacturer Phönix Flugzeug-Werke began with licence-manufacture of Albatros and Brandenburg aircraft, turning to aircraft of its own design. The first of these was the **Phönix C I** two-seat armed reconnaissance and general-purpose biplane, which the company developed from the **Hansa-Brandenburg C II**, which it had built under licence. An ugly but practical aircraft, the C I had fixed tailskid landing gear, was powered by a Hiero inline engine, and accommodated pilot

and observer/gunner in tandem open cockpits. Phönix built 110 C Is and these entered service in the spring of 1918, remaining operational until the end of the war.

Specification
Ufag-built C I Srs 169
Type: two-seat armed reconnaissance aircraft
Powerplant: one 220-hp (164-kW) Benz Bz.IVa 6-cylinder inline piston engine
Performance: maximum speed 158 km/h (98 mph); service ceiling 6000 m (19,685 ft)
Weights: empty 820 kg (1,808 lb); maximum take-off 1,320 kg (2,910 lb)
Dimensions: span 12.25 m (40 ft 2.25 in); length 8.45 m (27 ft 8.75 in); height 3.33 m (10 ft 1 in)
Armament: (standard) one Schwarzlöse 8-mm (0.315-in) machine-gun on pivoted mount over rear of combined cockpit

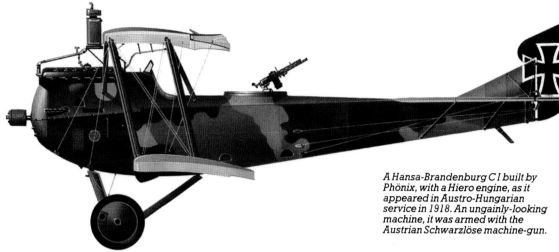

A Hansa-Brandenburg C I built by Phönix, with a Hiero engine, as it appeared in Austro-Hungarian service in 1918. An ungainly-looking machine, it was armed with the Austrian Schwarzlöse machine-gun.

Ernst Heinkel began his career designing biplanes for the Austro-Hungarian Empire, and eventually built jets for Hitler. The Hansa-Brandenburg, one of his early designs, was manufactured under licence by Phönix and Ufag in Austria. It served as a reconnaissance aircraft and light bomber.

Junkers early aircraft

In 1910 the German engineer Dr Hugo Junkers patented a flying-wing aircraft; the thick-section cantilever wing that he designed for it was in the first Junkers aeroplane to fly, the **Junkers J 1**, on 12 December 1915. A mid-wing cantilever monoplane, the J 1 was covered by thin sheet iron, gaining it the nickname 'Tin Donkey'. Six generally similar single-seat **J 2** aircraft were built in 1916, these being armed by a single 7.92-mm (0.31-in) LMG 08/15 machine-gun.

Impressed by Junkers constructional techniques, the German air ministry asked for the development of an armoured biplane. This was the **Junkers J 4**, which entered service as a two-seat close-support aircraft towards the end of 1917 under the military designation **J I**. Powered by a 200-hp (149-kW) Benz Bz.IV engine, the J I was covered by corrugated light alloy skins. Powerplant and crew were enclosed in an armoured capsule, the protection which this provided against

small-arms fire from the ground making the J I popular with its crews. Production totalled 227.

Junkers then turned to a new series of cantilever low-wing monoplanes, the single-seat **J 7** of 1917 serving as prototype for the **J 9** single-seat fighter which, powered by the 185-hp (138-kW) B.M.W. engine and armed with twin forward-firing LMG 08/15 machine-guns, was built in small numbers under the military designation **D I**.

The **Junkers J 10** was a two-seat version of the J 7 powered by a 180-hp (134-kW) Mercedes D.IIIa engine. About 50 examples of this were built before the armistice, entering service as the **Junkers CL I** and carrying the same armament as the D I. Three examples of a floatplane version of this aircraft entered service with the German navy during 1918 under the designation **Junkers CLS I**.

Specification
Junkers J I
Type: two-seat close-support aircraft

Powerplant: one 200-hp (149-kW) Benz Bz.IV 6-cylinder inline piston engine
Performance: maximum speed 155 km/h (97 mph); endurance 2 hours
Weights: empty 1766 kg (3,885 lb); maximum take-off 2176 kg (4,787 lb)
Dimensions: span 16.0 m (52 ft 6 in); length 9.10 m (29 ft 10.5 in); height 3.40 m (11 ft 1.75 in); wing area 49.40 m^2 (533.52 sq ft)
Armament: two fixed forward-firing 7.92-mm (0.31-in) LMG 08/15 machine-guns and one trainable 7.92-mm (0.31-in) Parabellum machine-gun

The innovative Junkers J 1 metal monoplane was followed by six J 2 aircraft in 1916; this is the second of the group. Thin sheet iron covering the machine led to these and later Junkers aircraft being dubbed 'tin donkeys', although dural sheet was soon introduced.

The Birth of Strategic Bombing

From their introduction into military service, aircraft were used to attack enemy ground forces as well as to conduct reconnaissance patrols, but by 1915 designers on both sides were planning large multi-engined machines able to range far beyond the front line; the strategic bomber was born.

No account of the war's strategic bombing efforts by the UK and Germany can begin other than with brief reference to the origins of bombing in the West by lighter-than-air craft, for therein lay the premeditated drift towards total war, if not by deliberate assault on the civilian population then by the knowledge that no means existed to ensure that bombs would only ever fall on military targets.

On the outbreak of war the Kaiser, mindful perhaps of his own family ties with English royalty, had expressed abhorrence at any aerial bombing that might endanger civilians and went so far as to withhold approval for air attacks on targets in England. The Imperial Naval Staff, however, anxious to demonstrate the superiority of its airships in attacks on dockyard and other naval targets in the Thames estuary, managed to persuade the Kaiser to temper his ban on such attacks in return for assurances that such raids would not endanger the civilian population nor indeed the British capital itself. Inevitably, as the navy's (and soon afterwards the army's) airship crews roamed the night skies over England searching for 'military' targets, bombs fell on towns (and London), and civilians were killed. The first such raid occured on the night of 19/20 January 1915 when two Zeppelins dropped bombs on King's Lynn in Norfolk.

Other raids by airships followed, but it was not until the night of 2/3 September 1916 that the first airship was shot down by an aeroplane over the UK when Lieutenant W. Leefe Robinson of No. 39 Squadron RFC brought down a Schütte-Lanz over Hertfordshire (for which he was awarded the VC). Almost three months later two more airships were destroyed in a single night over the East Coast. Later that same day, 28 November 1916, a single German aeroplane flew brazenly over central London and dropped six small bombs in broad daylight and escaped.

Meanwhile Germany, and more particularly the German army, had been at work developing the aeroplane as a bomb-carrier, at first creating several units of Tauben (aircraft with dove-shaped wings) able to reach just beyond the battle front with a few very small bombs.

However, spurred by the achievements of the big Russian Sikorsky bombers which had been active in the East, and frustrated by the inability of the Tauben to reach worthwhile targets in England, the German aircraft industry set to work early in 1915 to evolve much larger bombers, the G-class, *Grosskampfflugzeug* or 'battleplane'. These aircraft, from AEG, Gotha, Friedrichshafen and other makers, started reaching operational units before the end of the year but it was not for another year, after the creation of the Luftstreitkrafte (air force) under an officer of field rank, General Ernst von Hoeppner, that plans were hatched for a sustained air attack by aeroplanes on England. By then improved aircraft, notably the Friedrichshafen G III and Gotha G IV, had flown and the plans included the formation of three *Kampfgeschwader* (bomber wings), of which Kagohl 3 would be committed to raids on England, and the others against targets in France.

Belgian bases

In due course the new bomber wing, comprising six *Staffeln* and commanded by Hauptmann Ernst Brandenberg, occupied its bases in Belgium. On 25 May 1917 23 Gotha G IVs set out to attack London in daylight after losing two aircraft in force landings in Belgium. Crossing the Essex coast near Burnham-on-Crouch, Brandenberg found his path to the capital obscured by cloud so turned south to see if his crews could find worthwhile targets in Kent. Eventually the formation arrived over Folkestone where the Gothas released nearly five tons of bombs, killing 95 and injuring 260. Although the Dover anti-aircraft guns opened fire with a heavy barrage and about 40 British aircraft took off in pursuit, the Gothas escaped,

America's leading bombing exponent was Brigadier-General Mitchell, whose controversial bombing trials during July 1921 involved sinking the German Dreadnought Ostfriesland *by aerial bombing.*

Despite the best endeavours of the RFC and the anti-aircraft guns, landing accidents accounted for the majority of German bomber losses on most raids. This D.H.10 shows that the British encountered similar problems; both sides in fact fitted nose wheels to some aircraft to prevent them nosing in.

only to lose two more of their number in forced landings.

This raid provoked an angry outburst in the British parliament which was still rumbling on when, on 5 June, Brandenberg launched his second raid, this time killing 45 people in the naval dockyard at Sheerness. One week later, on 13 June, 20 Gothas set out for London, their aiming point the railway terminus of Liverpool Street. The formation reached the capital where it dropped more than four tons of bombs; three bombs actually struck the aiming point but another hit an infants' school at Poplar, killing 16 children. In all, this raid killed 162 and injured 432, the highest toll of any single raid on the UK during the war.

The outcry in the British parliament now reached new heights which quickly provoked action to strengthen the defences, and resulted in the formation of a commission headed by the South African, General Jan Smuts, to examine the entire structure of the RFC and RNAS and their ability to provide adequate home defence. The recommendations of this commission were far-reaching and eventually led to the amalgamation of the two 'services' to form the Royal Air Force on 1 April 1918.

In the meantime Kagohl 3 carried out several more attacks on south east England, but on a diminishing scale as a result of losses, mainly from accidents but also to a growing number in combat. This sapping of strength resulted in the decision being taken to switch to night raiding, any pretence at confining attention to military targets having long since dissipated. Ironically, however, the first such raid by only four Gothas on 3/4 September struck the naval barracks at Chatham where a single 51-kg (112-lb) bomb caused the deaths of 131 sleeping ratings and injury to 90 others (the highest toll from any single bomb during the war).

Later the same month the Gothas were joined by a new squadron, Riesenflugzeugabteilung 501 commanded by Hauptmann Richard von Bentivegni, one of two such units now flying the huge R-type 'Giant' bombers. Such was the size of these aircraft (the Zeppelin-Staaken aeroplanes were powered by four, five or even six engines) that each could carry the same bombload as five Gothas. Indeed, when a second raid reached London on 29/30 September with four Gothas and three Giants, the British authorities estimated that 18 Gothas had attacked the capital.

In 1918, however, as the fruits of the RAF reorganization matured, a growing toll was taken of the raiders (though no Giant was ever shot down), and on 19/20 May that year they flew their last attack against England when 28 Gothas and three Giants straggled in over Kent and Essex; no fewer than six Gothas were brought down by night-flying Sopwith Camel and RAF S.E.5A fighters (and one Bristol F.2B) as well as the gun defences. Over the continent sporadic raiding by Kagohl 2, Rfa 500 and Rfa 501 continued until 30 October, when a final attack hit an army supply base at Menin.

The British Independent Force

The German strategic bombing effort reached its climax before the end of 1917 and thereafter declined. By contrast, the British attempts to undertake bombing beyond the immediate area of the Western Front started to gain impetus only at the end of 1917, but increased progressively right up to the end of the war. Another feature of the British bombing

The night of 19/20 May 1918 saw the last of the major night raids on England, when 28 'G' type and three of the giant 'R' type bombers converged on London. Night-flying Sopwith Camels and S.E.5As, together with the ground-based AA artillery, brought down six of the intruders.

The Birth of Strategic Bombing

The Airco D.H.10, like the Vickers Vimy and the Handley-Page V 1500, was designed to conduct a strategic bombing campaign against Germany. Only eight of the 1,295 ordered had been delivered when the war ended. Nevertheless, 220 machines were finally produced for the RAF post-war.

The need to protect bombers from enemy fighter aircraft soon became pressing, and the French developed a long-range fighter, the Caudron R 11, to escort formations of Breguet 14B2s. This is a machine of Escadrille C.46 as it appeared between February and November 1918. It carried five Lewis guns; twin nose and dorsal mounts, and one firing down from the nose.

force was the scale of participation by the Royal Naval Air Service; indeed from the outset the entire heavy bomber force (composed of Handley Page O/100s) was naval-crewed, a predominance that only lost its identity when the RNAS and RFC amalgamated to form the RAF.

The O/100 stemmed from an informal enquiry addressed by Murray Sueter to Frederick Handley Page early in 1915 whether he could produce 'a bloody paralyser', by implication a big aeroplane capable of carrying a large bombload. Already working on such an aircraft that had been loosely defined by the Admiralty, Handley Page modified his design to take more powerful engines, this aircraft, the O/100, being flown in December that year. Entering service with the 5th Naval Wing at Dunkerque the following November, the big bomber could carry up to sixteen 51-kg (112-lb) bombs and started daylight operations with No. 7 (Naval) Squadron in April 1917 along the Belgian coast; soon afterwards the 5th Wing changed its operations to night raiding of targets immediately behind the Western Front; further south the 3rd Wing, also equipping with O/100s, embarked on night raids on German industrial centres up to 95 km (60 miles) behind the front. One aircraft, flown by Flight-Lieutenant John Alcock (who later achieved fame for his transatlantic flight) from Mudros, set out to bomb Constantinople but was forced to ditch in the Sea of Xeros, the crew being taken prisoner.

While 46 O/100s were produced, Handley Page developed an improved version, the O/400; this aircraft achieved considerable production with about 400 completed by Handley Page and a further 107 in the USA before the end of the war. Meanwhile the RFC had begun to assemble a bombing force in France composed of No. 55 Squadron's Airco D.H.4, No. 100 Squadron's F.E.2b and the Naval 'A' Squadron's O/100 aircraft. Commanded by Lieutenant-Colonel Cyril Newall, the 41st Wing was formed on 11 October 1917 to continue the bombing of German industrial targets started by the RNAS' 3rd Wing. Before the month was out the D.H.4s and O/100s had raided the Burbach works near Saarbrücken and the F.E.2b aircraft had bombed railways near Falkenburg. Raiding by these squadrons continued through the winter, and on 1 February 1918 the force was raised to brigade status (becoming

VIII Brigade), and on 6 June it was renamed the Independent Force of the RAF, commanded by Major General Sir Hugh Trenchard. Between then and the end of the war this force increased to 11 squadrons with a total of about 75 D.H.4s, D.H.9s and D.H.9As, some 50 O/400s and a squadron (No. 45) of Camels. Among the targets attacked during the last six months (mostly by night) were Baden, Bonn, Cologne, Koblenz, Darmstadt, Düren, Frankfurt, Heidelberg, Kaiserslautern, Karlsruhe, Ludwigshafen, Mainz, Mannheim, Luxembourg, Offenburg, Saarburg, Saarbrücken, Stuttgart, Wiesbaden and Zweibrücken, as well as numerous airfields and other military targets. The raids involved the dropping of about 550 tons of bombs (compared with less than a tenth of this figure dropped in all the raids on the UK) and a total of 352 aircraft was lost, including 148 D.H.9s and 69 O/400s.

Clearly the achievements of the Independent Force eclipsed those of the relatively small number of German bombers, and from such reports as were produced after the Armistice it is clear that a far higher proportion of bombs fell on strictly military and strategic targets than was the case of the German bomb-

ing; nevertheless, on account of the much greater tonnage of bombs dropped on Germany, civilian casualties were more than double those suffered in the UK.

One other weapon was being prepared for use over Germany when the Armistice brought an end to hostilities. This was the very large Handley Page V/1500, comparable in size to the German Giants but a much more formidable aeroplane. Conceived with the intention of bombing Berlin from bases in the UK, this great aircraft was capable of carrying a 1497-kg (3,300-lb) bomb, and at the moment the Armistice came into effect on 11 November 1918 three V/1500s were standing on Bircham Newton airfield in Norfolk, fully fuelled and bombed-up, awaiting orders to take off for the German capital. As it was, the only such aircraft ever to drop its bombs in anger did so on the city of Kabul during the Afghan War of 1919.

Romanian troops pose beside one of the giant German 'R' class bombers captured in Bessarabia. Romanian troops had been among the first victims of ground attack aircraft, bombarded with water melons by Bulgarian fliers in the Balkan wars. In five years aircraft had become serious fighting machines, and weapons much deadlier.

AEG G series

The introduction of bomber squadrons to the Western Front in World War I was not long delayed, Germany initiating *Kampfstaffel* (battle squadron) units in early 1915. The aircraft that equipped them were used primarily as multi-gun fighters, but the potential of tactical and strategic bombing was soon appreciated. It was in 1915 that the first of AEG's twin-engined bombers appeared. The biplane **AEG G I** powered by two 100-hp (75-kW) Mercedes D.I engines. These powerplants were hardly adequate to confer sparkling performance on what was little more than an enlarged C IV: one that was 75 per cent heavier and yet had only about 24 per cent more power. Perhaps it was not surprising that only a single example was built.

The **G II**, first seen in mid-1915, was slightly larger but had two 150-hp (112-kW) Benz Bz.III engines. Only about 15 of these G IIs were built before the **G III** was introduced, and this also was produced in only limited numbers.

It was not until the end of 1916 that the **G IV** began to enter service. Like its predecessors it had a basic steel-tube structure and fabric covering. All cockpits were interconnected, enabling crew members to change positions in flight if circumstances so dictated. The G IV was hampered by a range that was very limited when the aircraft was carrying a crew of three and a maximum bombload of 400 kg (882 lb).

AEG's G series production totalled almost 550 aircraft, of which about 500 were G IVs, many of them remaining in service until the end of the year. Variants, built in only very small numbers, included the **G IVb** with an increased span three-bay wing; the **G IVK** with a Becker cannon of 20-mm calibre installed in the nose.

Specification
AEG G IV
Type: biplane bomber/reconnaissance aircraft
Powerplant: two 260-hp (194-kW) Mercedes D.IVa inline piston engines
Performance: maximum level speed 165 km/h (103 mph); service ceiling 4500 m (14,765 ft); maximum endurance 5 hours

The AEG G II appeared in July 1915 and paved the way for the G IV. Only about 15 were manufactured, but several did see active service with the Kampfgeschwader over the Western Front. It could carry 200-kg (441-lb) of bombs and mounted two or three machine-guns.

Weights: empty 2400 kg (5,291 lb); maximum take-off 3630 kg (8,003 lb)
Dimensions: span 18.40 m (60 ft 4.5 in); length 9.70 m (31 ft 9.75 in); height 3.90 m (12 ft 9.5 in); wing area 67.00 m² (721.21 sq ft)
Armament: two 7.92-mm (0.31-in) Parabellum machine-guns, one on ring mounting in forward cockpit and one on rail mounting in aft cockpit

Right: At a time when other German twin-engined machines favoured pusher arrangement, AEG installed its engines as tractor units on all its twin-engined aircraft. Five hundred and forty-two G types were produced and were used for short-range missions.

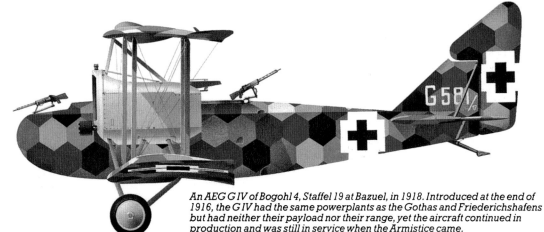

An AEG G IV of Bogohl 4, Staffel 19 at Bazuel, in 1918. Introduced at the end of 1916, the G IV had the same powerplants as the Gothas and Friederichshafens but had neither their payload nor their range, yet the aircraft continued in production and was still in service when the Armistice came.

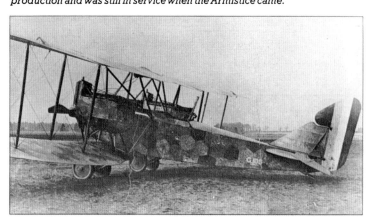

Gotha G II, G III, G IV and G V

During 1917 and 1918 British people generally, and those who lived in London particularly, came to dread air attacks by the 'Gothas', a name which they applied indiscriminately to all German bombers making day or night raids. Development by Gotha of aircraft in this class had started during 1915, and the first of these twin-engine bombers were the **Gotha G II** and **G III** of 1916. Built in only small numbers they were generally similar, differing only in internal detail, but early experience of these aircraft operating in Europe brought development during 1916 of the longer-range **G IV**. Of mixed wood and steel construction,

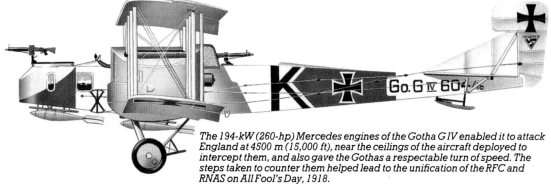

The 194-kW (260-hp) Mercedes engines of the Gotha G IV enabled it to attack England at 4500 m (15,000 ft), near the ceilings of the aircraft deployed to intercept them, and also gave the Gothas a respectable turn of speed. The steps taken to counter them helped lead to the unification of the RFC and RNAS on All Fool's Day, 1918.

The Gotha G VII was developed during 1918 as a long-range photo-reconnaissance aircraft, deleting the nose armament for extra speed. The wings were slightly swept to compensate for the stunted nose.

with plywood and fabric covering, the G IV was of three-bay biplane configuration with a basically square-section fuselage, braced tail unit and tailskid landing gear incorporating twin-wheel main units. The twin-engine powerplant, comprising two Mercedes D.IVa inlines strut-mounted between the wings, directly above the main landing gear, was arranged to drive pusher propellers, a large cut-out being provided in the trailing edge of the upper wing to give the necessary propeller clearance. The G IV was followed by an improved **G V** that was basically the same, but introduced improved equipment and a number of refinements, including cleaner, more streamlined engine nacelles. The **G Vb** was a derivative with a pair of auxiliary wheels mounted forward of each main landing gear unit to reduce

the danger of nosing-over during night operation.

A number of Gotha G series aircraft followed the G V, mostly built in ones or twos.

Specification
Gotha G V
Type: three-seat long-range bomber

Powerplant: two 260-hp (194-kW) Mercedes D IVa 6-cylinder inline piston engines
Performance: maximum speed 140 km/h (87 mph); service ceiling 6500 m (21,325 ft); range 500 km (311 miles)
Weights: empty 2740 kg (6,041 lb); maximum take-off 3975 kg (8,763 lb)

Dimensions: span 23.70 m (77 ft 9in); length 11.86 m (38 ft 11 in); height 4.30 m (14 ft 1.25 in); wing area 89.50 m² (963.40 sq ft)
Armament: two 7.92-mm (0.31-in) Parabellum machine-guns on pivoted mounts in nose and dorsal positions, and a bombload of 300 to 500 kg (661 to 1,102 lb) according to range of mission

---

GERMANY

Zeppelin-Staaken R series

Soon after the beginning of World War I Count von Zeppelin initiated the development of heavy bombers which he could foresee would be of great importance to the nation's war effort. The design of landplane versions began under the leadership of Professor Baumann, the first of them being the **Zeppelin-Staaken V.G.O.I** which established a basic layout and size for the remainder of these giant aircraft. With biplane wings, a slab-sided fuselage and biplane tail unit, the V.G.O.I was supported on the ground by fixed tailskid type landing gear, whose main units had multiple wheels, plus two more wheels beneath the nose. First flown on 11 April 1915, the V.G.O.I was found to be underpowered and was re-engined. The production **R VI**, of which the first was delivered in June 1917, eliminated the powerplant from the fuselage nose. R VI production totalled 18, one being built by the company and the remainder under subcontract by Aviatik (six), Ostdeutsche Albatros Werke (four) and Schütte-Lanz (seven). They were followed into production in 1918 by the similar **R XIV** (three aircraft) and **R XV** (three aircraft), both versions having five Maybach Mb.IV engines. An advanced four-engine version developed by Aviatik, with one 220-hp (164-kW) Bz.IVa and one 530-hp (395-kW) Bz.VI in each nacelle, was allocated the designation **R XVI (AV)**; three were to have been built but only one was completed before the end of the war. Variants included the single **R VII** which differed from the R IV by having two Mercedes D.IIIs in the nose and four Benz Bz.IVs in the nacelles; the **Type L** twin-float seaplane with four

260-hp (194-kW) Mercedes D.IVa engines; and three **Type 8301** twin-float seaplanes which had the same powerplant but introduced an entirely new fuselage.

Specification
Zeppelin-Staaken R VI
Type: seven-crew heavy bomber

The remarkable Zeppelin-Staaken 'R' series was constructed from scratch, there being no experience to draw upon in the design of such gargantuan bombers. By pioneering design work and trial and error, they evolved into seven-man bombers able to carry a substantial payload.

Powerplant: four 245-hp (183-kW) Maybach Mb.IV or 260-hp (194-kW) Mercedes D.IVa inline piston engines
Performance: maximum speed 135 km/h (84 mph); service ceiling 4320 m (14,175 ft); maximum duration 10 hours
Weights: empty 7921 kg (17,463 lb); maximum take-off 11848 kg (26,120 lb)

Dimensions: span 42.20 m (138 ft 5.5 in); length 22.10 m (72 ft 6 in); height 6.30 m (20 ft 8 in); wing area 332.00 m² (3,573.74 sq ft)
Armament: four 7.92-mm (0.31-in) Parabellum machine-guns, plus a maximum short-range bombload of 2000 kg (4,409 lb)

An R IV in flight made an impressive spectacle. Early models suffered terribly from engines blowing up, often during take-off or prolonged climbing, which strained them to the limit. The first R IV to be delivered made a solo attack on London in February 1918, scoring a direct hit on St Pancras railway station.

Airships of World War 1

Airships were the first strategic bombers. Able to carry greater bombloads over far longer distances than early aeroplanes, they were soon employed by the Germans to carry the war to Britain itself. Most belligerent nations used airships, mainly for reconnaissance and observation missions, but today it is the raids of the German Zeppelins that are best remembered.

No. 23 was first of a proposed class of 10 British dirigibles, but arguments about the design took so long to resolve that by the time she was completed she was obsolete. In 1918 No. 23 was experimentally fitted with two Sopwith Camels for defence against hostile aircraft.

In the days immediately preceding World War I, when aeroplane flight had been possible for only 10 years, there existed a large body of opinion that the future of military flying lay as much with lighter-than-air craft as elsewhere. There seemed to be firm foundations for this since the first attempt to construct a guided balloon (a dirigible) had taken place in 1816.

Following this, there had evolved three types of airship: the non-rigid, which depended on inflation for the shape of its envelope; the semi-rigid, which was similar but with a strengthening keel; and the rigid, with a lattice structure of wood or metal surrounding internal gas cells.

In Germany the last proved especially successful, and the first Zeppelin airship was flown in 1900. The years following had seen certain factions concentrating on its military development, so that there had grown up in the public mind the idea of the bombing airship as the ultimate weapon against which there was virtually no defence.

In the UK, France, and later the USA, the tendency to concentrate on the other forms of construction resulted in smaller vessels put to different use. The swift development of a reliable aeroplane broadly altered the whole outlook, although rigid airships of the German pattern continued to attract their supporters even after the Admiralty had abandoned them in 1919. Elsewhere, the US Navy developed the coastal patrol type of smaller airship, even using them in World War II.

L31 flies serenely over the 'Helgoland' class dreadnought SMS Ostfriesland. The German navy made extensive use of Zeppelins for scouting, but communications problems reduced their theoretical effectiveness. L31 and her crew perished over England at the hands of a B.E.2c in 1916.

Parseval PL 18

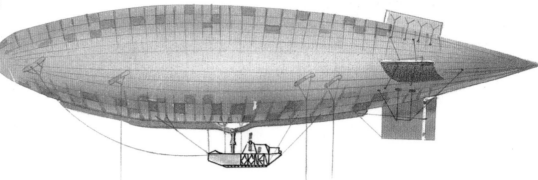

'A new non-rigid airship made its first flight in Germany in May 1906: relatively small with a volume of only 2300 m³ (81,224 cu ft), this airship was of technical interest in that the shape of the envelope was maintained by means of pressurized ballonets fore and aft.

The craft was to the design of former army officer August von Parseval, later a professor at the Berlin Technical Academy, and improved models continued to be produced after their construction was transferred from the Motorluftschiff Studiengesellschaft to the Luftfahrzeug Gesellschaft (LFG) organization in June 1913. In this same year an order was placed by the British government for a single example of the improved type, and **Parseval PL 18** was delivered for use by the Royal Navy where it received the service designation **Naval Airship No. 4 (NA4)**.

On 5 August 1914 this vessel, by a strange stroke of irony, was the first British aircraft to carry out an active war operation when, flying from its base at Kingsnorth, the first RNAS airship station, it was sent to patrol the Thames Estuary. It was used again on 10 August, this time in company with NA3, the only British airship of the period to be armed, another imported design, an Astra-Torres.

The degree to which Parseval designs had advanced in a short time was evident from the fact that the NA4 was a revised type of vessel, which probably promoted the order for a further three before the war, to be built under licence by Vickers at Barrow-in-Furness. These were given the service designations **NA5, NA6** and **NA7** at the beginning of their career, which was entirely confined to use for the instruction of airship crews.

Meanwhile, the NA4 was still employed on sterner duties, and the first months of World War I found it in use as a submarine hunter, although its effect was entirely psychological, providing cover for the convoys ferrying troops of the British Expeditionary Force between Dover and Calais.

An order had been placed with the LFG organization for a further three airships of similar design which would have been the **PL 19, PL 20** and **PL 21**, but the outbreak of war prevented their delivery. They would probably also have been used for training, a role to which the NA4 was finally relegated,

but it is interesting to note that at the time it was in service as a patrol vessel, the German navy had requisitioned the non-rigid PL 6 on 9 August 1914 and also obtained PL 19 on loan on 19 September for sea patrol work over the Baltic from Kiel. This was a duty to which they were well suited, being capable of carrying 590 kg (1,301 lb) of bombs and with a maximum flight time of 11 hours.

Specification
Parseval PL 18
Type: patrol airship
Powerplant: two 134.2-kW (180-hp) Maybach six-cylinder water-cooled piston engines
Performance: maximum speed 72 km/h (45 mph); service ceiling 4000 m (13,123 ft); range 1000 km (621 miles)
Weight: useful lift not known
Dimensions: diameter 15.50 m (50 ft 10.2 in); length 94.00 m (308 ft 4.8 in); volume 10000 m³ (353,147 cu ft)

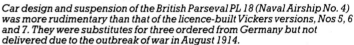

Car design and suspension of the British Parseval PL 18 (Naval Airship No. 4) was more rudimentary than that of the licence-built Vickers versions, Nos 5, 6 and 7. They were substitutes for three ordered from Germany but not delivered due to the outbreak of war in August 1914.

Above: Although enjoying a basic similarity, there were some differences between the Parseval-designed airships. The car of PL 12 is seen here; it was a passenger version, but its lines were to be echoed in those of the three Vickers models built under licence at Barrow-in-Furness.

Left: The first Royal Navy airship station at Kingsnorth was the base of the German-designed Parseval airship, which was ordered in 1912. Seen here on 27 August 1913, it was not to be finally struck off charge until July 1917.

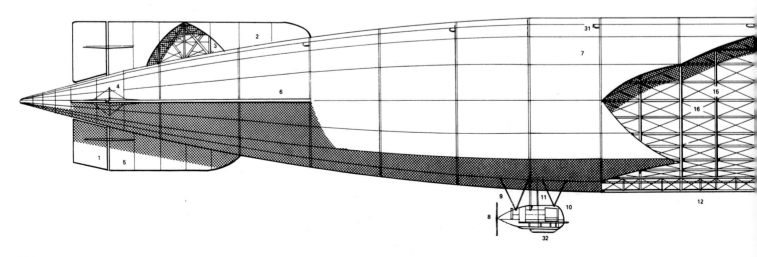

Schütte-Lanz SL11

'A severe shortage of aluminium in Germany had forced her to resort to wood for the construction of her airships.' When **SL11** was brought down by William Leefe Robinson on the night of 3 September 1916 this statement was generally accepted as true, since there was no great metal skeleton to greet the crowds that flocked to Cuffley where the airship fell. In fact wire-braced wooden structures had been used by the Schütte-Lanz company since the design stages of their initial SL1 that had first flown on 17 October 1911.

Conceived from the outset with an alternative construction to rival the metal Zeppelins, the SLs with their rigid ply framework were claimed to be lighter and more flexible than metal-framed airships, and most of those in German military service were operated by the army.

The reason for this is not difficult to discover, because the navy, responsible for most of the raids against the British Isles, rightly claimed that wooden vessels were incapable of lifting a sufficiently large bomb load as their weight would be increased by moisture absorbed while crossing the sea.

SL11 was accepted by the army in June 1916, and after trials was sent to its operational base at Spich in August. At the end of the month its initial operational sortie proved abortive because of the weather, so the attack at the beginning of September was its first and last, such a brief career resulting in the airship having only one commander, Hauptmann Wilhelm Schramm, who had gained experience in charge of three earlier rigids, all of Zeppelin design. On the night of the SL11's destruction, when Schramm died with all his crew, both incendiary and explosive bombs were dropped, but the airship's chief claim to fame now lies in the fact that it was the first enemy aircraft of any kind to be brought down on British soil, in recognition of which Robinson was awarded the Victoria Cross.

Specification
Schütte-Lanz SL11
Type: bombing airship
Powerplant: four 179-kW (240-hp) Maybach HSLu six-cylinder water-cooled piston engines
Performance: maximum speed 95 km/h (59 mph); service ceiling 5400 m (17,717 ft); range 3700 km (2,299 miles)
Weight: useful lift 21500 kg (47,399 lb)
Dimensions: diameter 20.09 m (65 ft 10.9 in); length 173.98 m (570 ft 9.6 in); volume 31900 m^3 (1,126,540 cu ft)
Armament: two 7.92-mm (0.312-in) Parabellum machine-guns on free mountings in single gun position above forward hull, plus bombs

Above: Souvenir pictures of SL11's wreckage and the victor were eagerly sought. That Schütte-Lanz construction used wood instead of the more usual aluminium of the Zeppelins gave rise to the belief in some quarters that there was a shortage of metal in Germany. The structure was wire-braced.

Right: It was reportedly possible to read by the light from the doomed SL11. Here it is seen well alight over north London as it appeared at 2.15 am to a photographer outside the police station at Walthamstow. The wreckage at Cuffley was finally doused by the crew of a horse-drawn fire engine.

German airship SL11 cutaway drawing key

1 Rudder
2 Upper tailfin
3 Fin structure
4 Elevator
5 Lower tailfin
6 Tailplane
7 Outer covering
8 Propeller
9 Engine car supports
10 Engine nacelle
11 Ladder
12 Keel
13 Gangway/catwalk
14 Main ring
15 Intermediate ring
16 Bracing wires
17 Gasbags
18 Ladder
19 Space between bags allowing escaping gas to exit to vents
20 Protective cage to ladder
21 Maybach HSLu engine
22 Control telegraph
23 Radiator
24 Retractable oil radiator
25 Bomb doors
26 Reversing gear
27 Transmission shaft
28 Water ballast tanks
29 Bomb racks
30 Upper observation station
31 Gas venting valve outlets
32 Shock absorber
33 Handrail
34 Control car
35 Wireless aerial
36 Chart table/wireless
37 Nose light
38 Navigator's/bomb aimer's window
39 Helm
40 Elevator wheel
41 Winch cables
42 Telegraphs
43 Switchboard
44 Nose cone

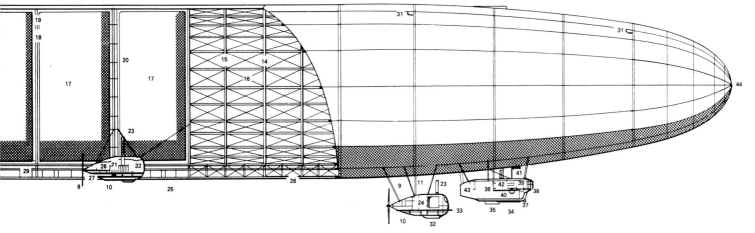

L10 (Zeppelin LZ40)

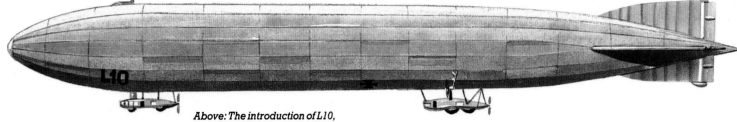

January 1915 was the date set for the introduction of a new type of German bomber airship, the **Zeppelin Typ P.** In point of fact the first of the new vessels was four months late in making its appearance, the lead ship **L10** (builder's designation **LZ40**) being delivered in mid-May. The ship was sent on its attack against targets in England in the following month with a raid on London, it being believed at all levels and on both sides of the North Sea that the selection of individual targets was possible. In point of fact, the weather took a hand, and L10 was able to get only as far as Gravesend, where its bombs chanced to set light to a military hospital with a consequent reaction against such 'frightfulness'.

Another attack was mounted 11 days later when Jarrow and South Shields were the targets, despite heavy fire from the defence batteries on the coast. Three other occasions found the new Zeppelin over the British Isles from a total of 28 military excursions from Nordholz. The German system of organization meant that the flights were usually carried out by the same crews, so that some became more experienced than others, but mindful of the dangers the men tended to live only for the day and to endure bombing trips under thousands of cubic metres of explosive gas and in numbing cold as best they could.

Strangely, it was on what should have been an uneventful flight, a maritime reconnaisance on the afternoon of 3 September 1915, exactly a year before SL11 was destroyed, that the L10's career ended. While the airship was making ready to land back at Nordholz near Cuxhaven, the order to valve off gas was given as a normal preliminary to making landfall. Unfortunately a thunderstorm happened to be raging and the naval airship was struck by lightning. There was a violent explosion before the vessel plunged into the shallow waters below, where it burned for several hours. All aboard perished, Kapitänleutnant Hirsch the commander and his crew of 18. Total production of the Typ P was 10 units, L10 to L19 (builder's designations LZ40, LZ41, LZ43, LZ45, LZ46, LZ48, LZ50, LZ53, LZ52 and LZ54 respectively).

Above: The introduction of L10, together with L11, placed the German navy on an equal footing to that of the army with regard to its ability to mount raids against targets in the British Isles.

Specification
L10 (Zeppelin LZ40)
Type: strategic bomber airship
Powerplant: four 156.6-kW (210-hp) Maybach CX six-cylinder water-cooled piston engines
Performance: maximum speed 95 km/h (59 mph); service ceiling 3900 m (12,795 ft); range 2150 km (1,336 miles)
Weights: empty 21100 kg (46,518 lb); useful lift 26200 kg (57,760 lb)
Dimensions: diameter 18.70 m (61 ft 4.2 in); length 163.50 m (536 ft 5 in); volume 31900 m³ (1,126,540 cu ft)
Armament: two 7.92-mm (0.312-in) Maxim machine-guns on free mountings in single gun position above forward hull, plus bombs

L11 (in the foreground) was one of the Zeppelin fleet participating in the first permitted raid on London that suffered no restrictions on 10 August

1915, and again on 17 August. Behind is L6, once used to take Strasser as an observer, but it was forced back by engine trouble.

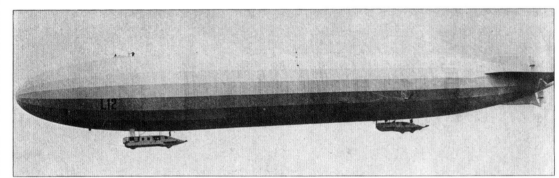

Above: Peterson's L12 passed over Margate, Ramsgate and Deal on 9 August 1915 before bombing Dover in mistake for the naval base of Harwich. All but three of the 92 bombs dropped landed in the sea, and the Zeppelin was damaged by the 76-mm (3-in) naval guns of the defences.

Right: On the night of 9 August 1915 L9, under the command of Odo Loewe, had to take evasive action over Flamborough Head despite a severed rudder cable, before managing to bomb Goole.

L53 (Zeppelin LZ100)

Apart from the historical factors surrounding the last operation carried out by L53, this **Zeppelin Type V** airship was also of some technical prominence. This lay in the fact that her construction embodied an increased spacing of her main frames, which were now 15 m (49 ft 2.5 in) apart compared with the previous norm of 10 m (32 ft 9.7 in). Measures such as these served to lighten the L53, contributing to the fact that her useful lift was some

62.7 per cent of the total, so that on her maiden raid an altitude of 6300 m (20,670 ft) was attained.

Alternatively known by the works designation **LZ100**, this airship made its first flight on 18 August 1917 from Friedrichshafen where she had been built, and became the command of one of Peter Strasser's most senior officers, Kapitänleutnant der Reserve Eduard Proelss. He first brought his new charge over the British Isles on the

night of 24/25 September 1917 when raids were directed against targets in the Midlands and north east, 17 months after his first bombing sortie in L13, his previous command.

However, it would be wrong to give the impression that Zeppelins were entirely directed to bombing missions against land targets. L53 is an illustration of this fact since of the 23 operational sorties made by this vessel between her commissioning date on 21

August 1917 and her fiery end on 11 August of the following year, only four were bombing attacks. The remainder were scouting missions over the North Sea where the endurance of lighter-than-air craft made them superior to any conventional aeroplane of the day. Small wonder therefore that L53 and her nine sister craft (**L55/LZ101, L56/LZ103, L58/LZ105, L60/LZ108, L61/LZ106, L62/LZ107, L63/LZ110, L64/LZ109 and L65/LZ111**) were regarded as a standard scout type. All after L56 were fitted with Maybach motors of the supercharged Mb IVa type.

Specification
L53 (Zeppelin LZ100)
Type: strategic bomber and patrol airship
Powerplant: five 179-kW (240-hp) Maybach HSLu six-cylinder water-cooled piston engines
Performance: maximum speed 106 km/h (66 mph); service ceiling 6400 m (20,997 ft); range 4680 km (2908 miles)
Weights: empty 24500 kg (54,013 lb); useful lift 40460 kg (89,199 lb)
Dimensions: diameter 23.90 m (78 ft 4.9 in); length 196.495 m (644 ft 8 in); volume 55990 m³ (1,977,271 cu ft)
Armament: two 7.92-mm (0.312-in) Maxim machine-guns on free mountings in single position above forward hull, plus bombs

First of the V-type Zeppelins to have new supercharged motors and fourth of the class to be built, L58 was eventually to be destroyed in a mysterious explosion which wrecked four hangars and four other airships at Ahlhorn.

Two victims of sabotage, L42 and L63 lie in their shed at Nordholz after the timber supports and suspension gear had been removed by those

loyal to the old regime on 23 June 1919. L42 had been in use as an advanced training vessel, while L63 had been Gerhold Ratz' command.

GERMANY
L59 (Zeppelin LZ104)

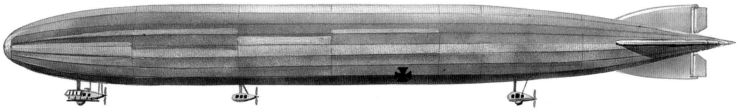

While being built as a Zeppelin Typ V, the L59 (LZ104) was hurriedly lengthened as the second **Zeppelin Typ W**. This was to replace the **L57** which had been chosen for a special mission in November 1917 and, as the **LZ102**, converted from a Typ V to the first Typ W before being damaged in a storm in October. L57 was intended to fly to German East Africa to aid General von Lettow-Vorbeck's forces in the theatre by flying out a sizeable quantity of supplies; the vessel was thereafter to be used as a bomber.

Together with the best men of his crew (the cream of each usually moved with the commander) Kapitän-leutnant Ludwig Bockholt from L57 took charge of L59 without delay, and such was the urgency of the mission that when a member of the crew was discovered to have sold a large part of the rations and made up the cases with the equivalent weight, there was no time to re-provision and the deficit had to be made up with emergency self-heating foods.

Although crews for bombing missions were sometimes reduced to 15 to allow an enlarged offensive load, the full complement of 21 was carried when the vessel set out in November. However, the airship was forced to turn back twice, on the second occasion as a result of damage caused by rifle fire from Turkish railway guards, so that a 32-hour return journey resulted in the next attempt being delayed until suitable weather on 20 November.

In point of fact a large portion of von Lettow-Vorbeck's forces had been forced to surrender on the same day, the commander escaping with a small party to continue the fight after capturing Portuguese supplies, but the recall by radio failed to be picked up in L59. Instead course was set across the Li-

First introduced by the Zeppelin company in August 1917, L59 and its class represented the latest design techniques and established a pattern that was to persist for almost a year, 10 being envisaged by the parent company when the first appeared.

byan desert where the heat made the vessel difficult to control after gas had been lost through the automatic valves; soon after this one engine began to give trouble.

The vessel was beyond the Nile when one of the recall signals was finally heard and the long return trip began. The tropically-kitted crewmen were by now not only exhausted but suffering from the cold at the height where the flight was taking place, but the final leg of the journey was successfully completed and rightly hailed as a triumph by the German Naval Airship Service, which was still regarded as experimental with the officers and men undergoing 'on the job' training.

The problem remained what to do

with the vessel and after a lengthy discussion it was decided to rebuild her for attacks against targets in the Middle East and Italy, and for these she was back at Jamboli (from which the African trips had begun) in February 1918. It was flying from here on 7 April 1918 that L59 mysteriously blew up not far from the heel of Italy.

Specification
L59 (Zeppelin LZ104)
Type: strategic bomber and patrol airship
Powerplant: five 179-kW (240-hp) Maybach HSLu six-cylinder water-cooled piston engines
Performance: maximum speed 108 km/h (67 mph); service ceiling

When L57, a Zeppelin of the W-type, was severely damaged in a storm in October 1917, L59 was placed in the charge of the same commander as a replacement. After being rebuilt following the African flight, she bombed British naval installations on Crete. A month later U-boat U-53 was the sole witness of her end.

8200 m (26,903 ft); range 8000 km (4,971 miles)
Weights: empty 27625 kg (60,903 lb); useful lift 52100 kg (114,861 lb)
Dimensions: diameter 23.95 m (78 ft 6.9 in); length 226.50 m (743 ft 1.3 in); volume 68500 m³ (2,419,059 cu ft)
Armament: provision for up to 10 7.92-mm (0.312-in) Maxim machine-guns above hull, plus bombs

Zeppelins over England: Strasser's Last Mission

The career of Peter Strasser parallels the story of the German airship service. Promoted Leader of Airships in 1913, he led the first strategic bombing campaign in history. The defences eventually mastered the Zeppelin threat, but as Germany's defeat loomed near in August 1918 Strasser personally led another raid. His chosen vessel: L70, the latest and most powerful Zeppelin built.

Peter Strasser, Leader of Airships, poses for a formal portrait wearing the Pour le Mérite *at his throat, an award received from Admiral Scheer at Ahlhorn on 4 September 1917 after commanding airships since 1913. This photograph may have been taken to mark the occasion.*

At the outbreak of World War I it was confidently believed in official circles that the 'terror weapons' of the day, German Zeppelin airships, could not fly during the hours of darkness, and any that crossed the North Sea in daylight would be destroyed with little difficulty by aeroplanes of the Royal Flying Corps.

The fact that airships had been flying sorties after dark for several years made nonsense of the first belief, but there is a ring of truth in the fact that the last Zeppelin to be destroyed by the defences was shot down in daylight at the end of a glorious August afternoon, the finest Bank Holiday in England for seven years it was claimed, the doomed airship taking to his death the revered Fregattenkapitän Peter Strasser, Leader of Airships since 1913.

The formal portraits of this officer, with his heavy moustache and goatee beard of almost theatrical cut above an archaic uniform wing collar, have left to us little impression of what he was really like. But if among a leader's chief qualities is a readiness to share the dangers of his men, then it is easy to see why Strasser quickly gained their respect, and it is certainly true that he was the driving force behind the airship section of the German navy.

Strasser was born on 1 April 1876 at Hanover and at the age of 35, after a career in the Kaiser's navy, he volunteered for aviation duty, a move that in 1913 relieved him from serving as a gunnery specialist in the Naval Airship Division's shipboard ordnance department. Strangely, it was the accident to the naval airship L1 that gave Peter Strasser his first real chance for when this airship, otherwise known by its maker's designation LZ14, crashed into the sea off Heligoland in September 1913, among those who perished was Korvettenkapitän Friedrich Metzing, whose loss left a vacancy filled by Strasser. The leader's role now embraced not only the normal duties of his command, but also participation in design improvements on which first-hand knowledge gained while flying with his men enabled him to comment. There is no doubt that even when the final days of the war cast the shadow of inevitable defeat over Germany, Strasser showed little loss of enthusiasm for the airship in which he still fervently believed. Thus 5 August 1918 found him aboard the very latest type of Zeppelin, prototype of the X-type, heading for the UK.

This vessel was L70 (LZ112) under the command of the inexperienced and impulsive Kapitänleutnant Johann von Lossnitzer, and was then part of the first airship raid to be mounted for four months. It was in company with L53 (LZ100), L56 (LZ102), L63 (LZ110) and L65 (LZ111), flying in a rough 'vic' formation over the North Sea at 5000 m (16,404 ft), at 18.30 only some 100 km (62 miles) from the English coast and thrown into sharp silhouette by the light of the late afternoon.

This is how the crew of the Leman Tail Light-

ship saw them when 48 km (30 miles) from the coast of Norfolk, and is also how one of the Zeppelins appeared to Major Edgar Cadbury, 25-year-old heir to a confectionery empire, as he raced along the sea front at Great Yarmouth.

He had been called from watching his wife who was singing at a charity concert at the Naval Air Station, but his mind was filled now with only two thoughts: surprise at the German appearance in daylight, and how quickly he could reach his car and report to the aerodrome where a two-seat de Havilland D.H.4 stood ready to do duty as an interceptor.

Bringing his Ford to a screaming halt, Cadbury almost fell out of the car, and attempting to put on the helmet and jacket he had seized in his rush he sprinted for the biplane in company with another running figure made awkward by flying kit, namely Captain Robert Leckie, who was to act as gunner in the rear cockpit.

Meanwhile, the German airship formation continued on course, heading for targets specified in their orders as being 'on the south or middle' after a journey that up to then had lasted for about 4½ hours. The commanders were mindful that no bombs were to be dropped on London without orders from Peter Strasser, who was in the leading vessel with its long hull almost entirely covered in an incongruous coat of black, unsuitable for concealment in daylight. Strasser seemingly subscribed to the theory that there was no need to fear being shot down over the sea if one was at an altitude between 4500 and 5500 m (14,765 and 18,045 ft).

The camouflage finish of the airships in fact served some purpose when the interceptors caught up with them, for it was now 22.20 and

the summer light was fading. Even so Cadbury and Leckie had no difficulty in picking out the whole formation, and having done so the pilot flew in the opposite direction to gain extra height, reducing the D.H.4's load by pulling the release to dump into the sea the pair of bombs it was carrying.

Approaching the monster from almost head-on, Leckie, after some ranging shots that went wide since his Lewis gun had no sights, put in a lengthy burst of fire at 550-m (600-yard) range: the burst exhausted a whole drum of Pomeroy explosive ammunition and succeeded in blowing a large hole in the Zeppelin's fabric, starting a fire that swiftly ran the length of the hull. In a moment the airship lifted its nose before turn-

Zeppelins L10 (Wenke); L11 (von Buttlar); L12 (Peterson); and L13 (Mathy) cross the North Sea on 9 August 1915. L10 dropped 12 HE bombs on

Sheppey, but Mathy had to withdraw. L12 was hit by Dover AA fire and force-landed in the Channel; half was later recovered.

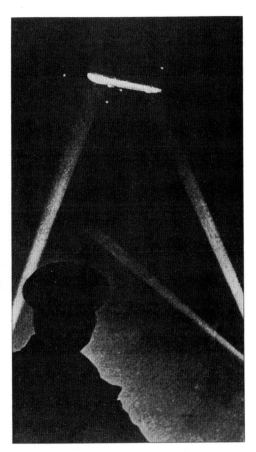

A Zeppelin caught by searchlights. This may be the raider which appeared over the eastern counties on the night of 8 September 1915. If so, it is L13 which penetrated as far as London, dropping 15 high-explosive and 55 incendiary bombs before returning via Norfolk.

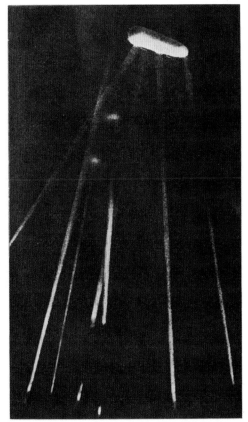

This is the gondola of L54, which was to take part in the famous raid by 13 Zeppelins on 19 October 1917, only to be scattered by high winds. Von

Buttlar's L54 escaped by abandoning the raid, only to be destroyed in its hangar at Tondern after a strike by Sopwith Camels from HMS Furious.

ing over and plunging into the sea as a mass of flame, a smaller fireball being seen to drop away as a fuel tank became detached to make its own meteor-like course into the waves below.

The wreckage did not sink immediately, but lay on the swell, a great burning pyre for the 21 men who had been its crew and for whom there could be no escape. It rested thus for the best part of an hour and if any of the crew members of the airships that accompanied L70 had been ignorant of their leader's immediate fate, none could have failed to see the holocaust now. Their commanders, horrified at what had taken place, abandoned the operation and turned the bows of their Zeppelins towards home, the water ballast of each pouring out as it was dumped to carry out the only manoeuvre that could still give a margin of safety, the rapid gain of height.

That the raiders were within reasonable distance of each other is shown by the fact that Cadbury and Leckie were able to close on a second airship, L64, despite an engine that was giving trouble, and Leckie opened fire: he believed that he scored hits, and even that a fire had been started, but was wrong. However, the weather began to deteriorate and the two returned to base to find not only that they were welcomed as heroes, but also that the bombs, believed to have gone into the sea to lighten the load, were still in place, so that a very different homecoming might have resulted!

It was 7 August when the remains of L70 were found by the trawler *Scomber*. They were promptly buoyed where they lay in only eight fathoms (14.6 m/48 ft) of water, and later

Once caught by searchlights it was difficult for a Zeppelin to conceal its massive bulk from the guns and aircraft seeking to destroy it. Their only real defence was to shed ballast and climb to altitudes out of harm's way.

were salvaged over a period of almost three weeks, the greater part being beached at Immingham. In this mass of twisted metal was discovered the bodies of many of the crew, including that of Peter Strasser from whose clothing some documents, including signal codes, were salvaged and rushed to Naval Intelligence; like the corpse from which they were taken, they were undamaged and not mutilated in any way.

In the days that followed about another half-dozen bodies were washed ashore on the Lincolnshire coast, and these, including the ones recovered from the wreckage and that of Peter Strasser were taken out to sea; there, as befitted naval men, they were committed to the deep, although seemingly with scant ceremony. What remained of L70 was subjected to an examination which revealed such interesting facts as the especially light gauge of some of the metal parts and that silk was substituted for the usual cotton covering; with nothing more to be discovered the wreckage was then dumped into the North Sea.

At home in Germany, the authorities were at first unsure of the fate of Peter Strasser; although realizing the slimness of the chances of escape for the Leader of Airships, several newspapers published tentative obituaries. Few of these failed to mention the respect in which he was held. This was no empty platitude, for Strasser's readiness not only to investigate technical problems, but generally to advance the airship cause, had together with his readiness to share the dangers of operational sorties endeared him to his men, a fact reflected in the manner in which his demise was heard by some. A *Leutnant* entered the room where a group of officers was gathered and stood silent with a look of dumb despair. 'Strasser?' asked one bolder than the others. The *Leutnant* made no reply, merely nodding. Without a word the company removed their caps and stood to silent attention.

Zeppelins over England

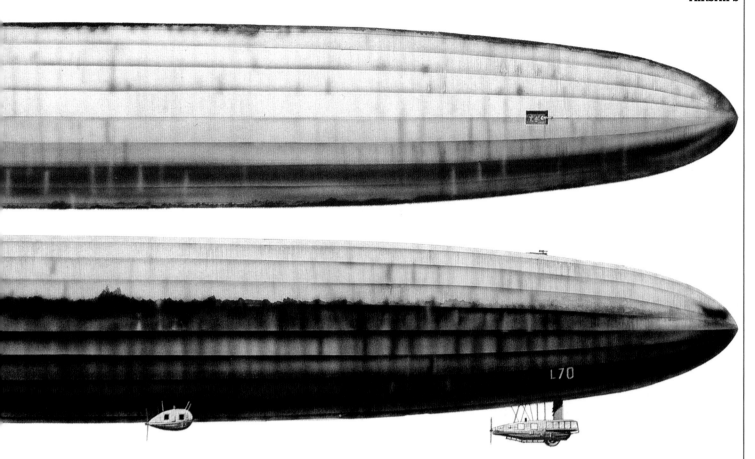

Luftschiffe 70

Above and right: Zeppelin L70, also known by its constructor's designation LZ112, was considered an outstanding vessel and the final version of the 'Super-Zeppelin'. It had been built to a specification which enabled it to climb to an altitude where it might be considered immune from interception. Also, being capable of taking an increased fuel load, it could approach over the coast of Scotland from the circular route across the Atlantic and at the same time provide support for U-boats by remaining in the air for several days.

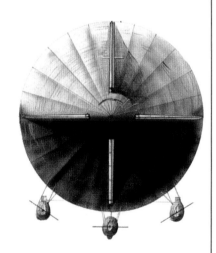

Left: Newly completed, L70 is walked back into Factory Shed II. Less than a month later she was to crash into the sea off the Norfolk coast, a victim of Cadbury and Leckie in their intercepting Airco D.H.4, despite being powered by motors adapted for high-altitude work.

L70 (Zeppelin LZ112)

The **L70** (company designation **LZ112**) represented the final type of military Zeppelin **(Zeppelin Typ X)**, and was conceived around the importance of making an entry to the Atlantic round the north of Scotland and having swift climb characteristics, the emphasis therefore being put on fuel capacity and a lightened structure.

Four airships of this type were planned, of which L70 was the prototype, and the only one to be powered by seven engines, unique among naval lighter-than-air craft. It was work over the Dogger Bank that found L70 on its first operation, a routine patrol during which units of the British fleet were reported. Despite the heavy cloud, course was altered and the targets identified, 10 bombs being dropped on the ships despite concentrated anti-

aircraft fire, an example of the type of action in which lighter-borne interceptors would have been of use.

Zeppelins of this type were not planned for patrol work alone, however, and despite the fact that by 1918 aeroplanes were exhibiting much greater usefulness for attacks on targets in the British Isles, the day of the airship was not completely over. Thus the L70 was committed to a raid on 5 August, an attack that some thought foolhardy since it was planned to take place before it had grown completely dark. This is the action which cost the lives of not only the entire crew, including the commander Kapitänleutnant von Lossnitzer who had been responsible for the attack on the naval vessels, but also Peter Strasser.

Of the planned four units of the Typ

X variants, only two others were built, though only one was commissioned into the Germany navy. This was the **L71 (LZ113)** later handed over to the UK. The **L72 (LZ114)** was completed after the Armistice as the *Dixmude* and was delivered to France as part of war reparations. These vessels differed from the L70 in having six Mb IVa engines and a volume of 68500 m³ (2,419,059 cu ft) in a hull lengthened to 226.5 m (743 ft 1.3 in).

Specification
L70 (Zeppelin LZ112)
Type: strategic bomber and patrol airship
Powerplant: seven 193.9-kW (260-hp) Maybach Mb IVa six-cylinder water-cooled piston engines
Performance: maximum speed

130 km/h (81 mph); service ceiling 7000 m (22,966 ft); range 6000 km (3728 miles)
Weights: empty 28260 kg (62,303 lb); useful lift 43500 kg (95,901 lb)
Dimensions: diameter 23.95 m (78 ft 6.9 in); length 211.50 m (693 ft 10.8 in); volume 62200 m³ (2,196,576 cu ft)
Armament: up to 10 7.92-mm (0.312-in) Maxim machine-guns on free mountings above hull, plus bombs

L70 was the Zeppelin in which Peter Strasser was to die on 5 August 1918. In the interests of weight economy the unshrouded engine exhausts tended to compromise the black dope when they spat flame. She is seen here in July at Friedrichshafen, where she was built.

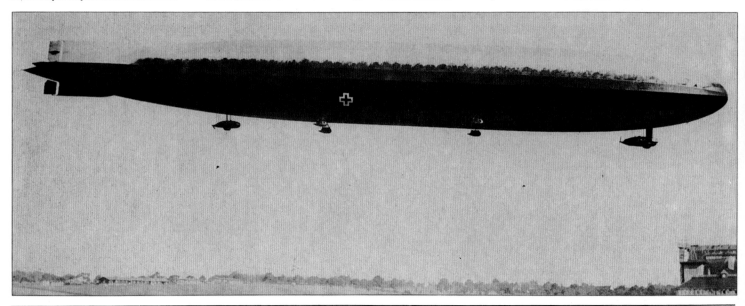

HMA No. 1 (RI) *Mayfly*

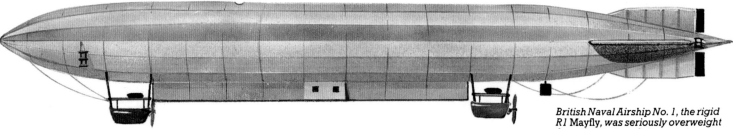

The UK's first rigid airship was proposed in 1908 as a means of evaluating the naval airship as a weapon of war along German lines, and an order was placed with Vickers. The work was to be undertaken by a joint civilian/naval team, few of whose members had much experience in the type of work involved.

Since the vessel was to be flown from water her gondolas were given planing bottoms, although alternative mooring to a mast anticipated German ideas. Construction was to be of the new alloy duralumin as a compromise between those factions who wanted wood or steel.

Engine tests were begun in mid-February 1911, and it was hoped that the maiden flight might coincide with

the Coronation Review of the fleet by King George V. However, the extraction of **HMA No. 1 (RI)** from its floating shed called on the resources of a number of tugs and a hauling party of 300 sailors on the ropes, a difficult task since the airship, now nicknamed *Mayfly*, proved much heavier than expected. This combined with misdirection of the handling party or (according to some reports) a sudden cross-wind, caused the airship to strike one of the uprights of the shed entrance, some damage resulting. This was unfortunate, since an earlier sojourn in the open had seen the airship successfully moored to the short mast provided as the superstructure of a naval vessel (the first use of such equipment in history) and reports speak of the RI thus

riding out a storm with winds rising to as high as 72 km/h (45 mph).

Even so, the damage now sustained had to be repaired, and the airship's return to its shed also provided an opportunity to lighten the structure. It was not until late September that the RI next appeared, fully loaded with hydrogen after a 10-hour inflation of the gas cells and ready for flight. The method of handling was as before, and it was necessary for the airship's nose to be turned. Hardly had the strain been taken on the ropes than a loud crashing was heard from within the centre of the vessel as its back broke. Understandably the crew began to leap overboard as ordered, and with the weight relieved from the rear gondola the stern rose up to complete the

British Naval Airship No. 1, the rigid R1 Mayfly, was seriously overweight from the start, and attempts to lighten the structure only succeeded in weakening it. For security reasons the findings of the investigators were never published.

destruction. The *Mayfly* never flew and was later scrapped.

Specification
HMA No. 1
Type: experimental naval airship
Powerplant: two 119.3-kW (160-hp) Wolseley eight-cylinder water-cooled piston engines
Performance: (estimated) maximum speed 64 km/h (40 mph)
Weight: (estimated) useful lift 20321 kg (44,800 lb)
Dimensions: diameter 14.63 m (48 ft 0 in); length 156.06 m (512 ft 0 in); volume 18774 m³ (663,000 cu ft)

UK 'C' class

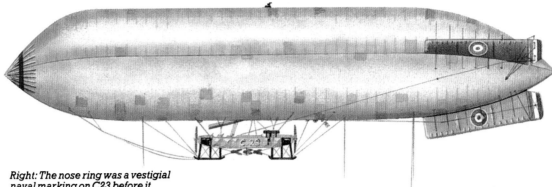

Designated the **'C' class** from its anticipated use as a coastal type (**'Coastal' class** was an alternative name), this non-rigid type was of medium size and constructed with a trefoil envelope section, frequently known as the Astra Torrès type. The first of the pattern was ordered in June 1915 from Kingsnorth, where it was assembled in the following September.

The choice of envelope construction posed problems that were overcome in an interesting manner. Among these was the method of car suspension: the cables for this purpose were attached along the intersection line of the lobes and from here ran through the bottom of the covering to the car. And it is noteworthy that though the gas cells were contained in a non-rigid structure, it was possible to site one of two defensive gun positions on top.

Pembroke was the first naval air station to have the type, and the first flights took place from here in June 1916, other bases being Pulham, Howden, Mullion, East Fortune and Longside. The seas that came under the care of the 'Coastal' class airship patrols were those off the Norfolk coast, Lands End, the mouth of the Humber, the Firth of Forth and Aberdeen.

Although the work of these vessels was largely unspectacular, one was the subject of an interesting set of experiments which were carried out on 6 September 1916. These were made with the first of the type, **C1**, in conjunction with the light cruiser HMS *Canterbury*, and were conducted offshore to look into the question of future developments, whereby an airship might be refuelled from a surface vessel.

A total of only 26 airships of this class was delivered, although these remained in service for lengthy periods. Thus they enjoyed a reputation for longevity as well as for extended flight times, the endurance of the design being as much as 12 hours.

The crew of these airships consisted of five men, four of them in the car which also contained the two engines,

Right: The nose ring was a vestigial naval marking on C23 before it crashed at Folkestone on 21 May 1917, only to be rebuilt and re-enter service as C23A. The type had small variations of airscoop position and car details.

fore and aft, driving tractor and pusher propellers respectively. The men's accommodation was very considerably more comfortable than that of the fifth man, the upper gunner who had a special climbing tube through the envelope to reach his lofty position. 'C' class airships gave good and reliable service once the problems of cooling for the rear engine and blowing in of the nose cone had been solved.

When engines of differing powers were fitted in any one ship, the more powerful was normally that at the rear, while it is interesting to note that the cars were constructed from a pair of Avro 510 fuselages. C1 alone differed from the others in having a 57.9-m (190-ft) envelope with a 3964.4-m³ (140,000-cu ft) capacity.

Specification
'C' class
Type: sea patrol airship
Powerplant: two 111.9-kW (150-hp) Sunbeam six-cylinder water-cooled piston engines, or one 179-kW (240-hp) Fiat and one 82.0-kW (110-hp) Berliet water-cooled piston engines
Performance: maximum speed 80 km/

A 'Coastal' class airship on convoy patrol shows the later location of the ballonet airscoop in the aft position. This differed from that on the

h (50 mph); service ceiling 2134 m (7,000 ft)
Weight: useful lift 1608 kg (3,545 lb)
Dimensions: width 12.04 m (39 ft 6 in);

original model, which was set forward immediately behind the front propeller. Only 27 of this class were delivered before 1918.

length 59.66 m (195 ft 9 in); volume 4813.9 m³ (170,000 cu ft)
Armament: two 7.7-mm (0.303-in) Lewis machine-guns, plus bombs

---

UK 'SS' class

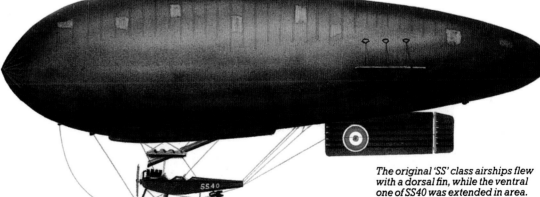

Hurriedly conceived as a composite of the *Willows IV* (HMA No. 4) airship and a car formed from the fuselage of an RAF B.E.2c aircraft, the resultant combination was a simple non-rigid that could be used for submarine hunting and convoy protection. It was first tested in March 1915 and given the designation **'SS' class**, indicating 'Sea Scout' or 'Submarine Scout'.

Alternative cars could be fitted, and although the greater number used the B.E.2c fuselage (these being **SS1** to **SS3**, **SS8** to **SS10A**, **SS12** to **SS20**, and **SS23** to **SS25**), 11 were fitted with Armstrong Whitworth cars and 12 with Maurice Farman cars. Some are on record as going to France and Italy, while they also inspired certain US vessels of similar construction.

The 'SS' class was used for patrols over the Dover Straits and Irish Narrows, the first base to have the type being that established at Capel near Folkestone on 8 May 1915; a second base began operations with the 'SS' on 6 July of the same year, this being at Polegate (Eastbourne) where there were three, compared with five at Capel.

In later models the gas capacity was increased first to 1699 m³ (60,000 cu ft) and later to 1982 m³ (70,000 cu ft) from the original 580.5 m³ (20,500 cu ft). Other more radical variations were introduced to produce the 'SST' class, which had twin engines but of which only six were constructed, and the **'SSP' class** (the last letter indicating pusher propulsion) that was even less

successful, only two being built.

As might be expected these airships, which gave to the English language the word 'Blimp', had the capability to stay aloft for many hours, the normal flight duration being seven hours although records exist claiming up to twice this figure. The type served throughout the war on the same duties and certainly had a deterrent effect on

The original 'SS' class airships flew with a dorsal fin, while the ventral one of SS40 was extended in area. Anticipated work was agent-dropping, but it was actually used for night reconnaissance.

submarine commanders, whose vessels it was possible to see below the surface of the water. Some, with Armstrong Whitworth F.K.3 fuselages doing duty as their cars, were powered with 74.6-kW (100-hp) Green water-cooled motors as an alternative to the standard powerplant, the Hawk engine being particularly associated with the Maurice Farman nacelles. Production was about 150 'SS' class airships.

Specification
'SS' class
Powerplant: one 55.9-kW (75-hp) Renault V-8 or Rolls-Royce Hawk six-cylinder water-cooled piston engine, or one 74.6-kW (100-hp) Green water-cooled piston engine
Performance: maximum speed 48 km/h (30 mph) with Renault or Rolls-Royce engine, or 80 km/h (50 mph) with Green engine

Weight: useful lift 3001 kg (6,615 lb)
Dimensions: diameter 9.75 m (32 ft 0 in); length 43.59 m (143 ft 0 in); volume 1982.2 m³ (70,000 cu ft)
Armament: one 7.7-mm (0.303-in) Lewis machine-gun, plus bombs

An unmarked 'SS' class airship is seen with twin ventral fins and a B.E.2c-type car. A similar envelope was fitted with one of a pair of complete aircraft of this type, in experiments to take an aeroplane aloft to wait for raiding Zeppelins. But these were abandoned when the crew was killed.

UK 'SSZ' class

The final variant of the 'SS' class airship was the **'SSZ' class** (Z indicating the ultimate or zero form), of which no less than 93 were ordered although only 63 of these went to the Royal Navy: **SSZ23** and **SSZ24** were sent to the United States where the latter became A5472, while **SSZ21** and **SSZ22** went to France.

The type was introduced late in 1916 and although the engine was usually the Rolls-Royce Hawk, two were fitted with the Renault V-8 of similar rating, and all were used for similar work to that performed by the earlier 'SS' type. The main visual difference between the two classes was the specially designed car that took the place of the aeroplane fuselages used formerly.

In fact the 'SSZ' was not originally intended for sea patrol, being designed to be towed by surface vessels of the Belgian coast patrol and by monitors, when their role would have been no more than aerial platforms for gunnery spotting after release and under their own power.

The very first airship of this type was in fact built at Capel (Folkestone) and later flown to the Dunkirk area, where it was based at St Pol on 21 September 1916, three months after it had been contructed.

Perhaps the chief claim to history enjoyed by the 'SSZ' is the fact that, despite being of non-rigid construction and therefore capable of being flown only if the weather was suitable, they were responsible for spotting 49 submarines, of which 27 were claimed as sunk. To do this it was necessary for the airships to remain aloft for lengthy

periods and the record for this goes to the crew of **SSZ39**, who remained in the air during the summer of 1918 for a continuous period of 50 hours. This was more than double that of the accepted 'long patrol', which was in the region of 24 hours, although the average was 12.

Specification
'SSZ' class
Type: sea patrol airship
Powerplant: one 55.9-kW (75-hp) Rolls-Royce Hawk six-cylinder or Renault V-8 water-cooled piston engine
Performance: maximum speed 77 km/h (48 mph); service ceiling 2400 m (7,875 ft); normal endurance 12 hours
Weight: useful lift 3300 kg (7,275 lb)
Dimensions: diameter 9.75 m (32 ft 0 in); length 43.59 m (143 ft 0 in); volume 1982.2 m³ (70,000 cu ft)
Armament: one 7.7-mm (0.303-in) Lewis gun for the observer, plus bombs

Particularly on SSZ airships the application of identity markings varied. SSZ65 is seen here as it appeared at Longside in 1918, although some operations were carried out from Auldbar.

Details of the car of SSZ27, which was based at Polegate before moving to Mullion, show the snug crew accommodation and the method of *suspending the bomb load for anti-submarine work. These and other airships were handled behind vast screens to prevent wind damage.*

SSZ37 flies from its station at Pembroke above a minelaying sloop. The cylindrical fuel tanks slung at the sides of the envelope were not *always in evidence. The type was still in production in 1918, when orders for the final 15 were cancelled at the end of the war.*

SSZ3 with its ground party served both at Pulham and East Fortune. Like the 'SS' and 'SSP' vessels, some were fitted with ventral fins of *increased area. SSZ3 here lacks the envelope roundel of many, but has a naval nose ring and flies the White Ensign behind the scoop.*

HMA No. 23
UK

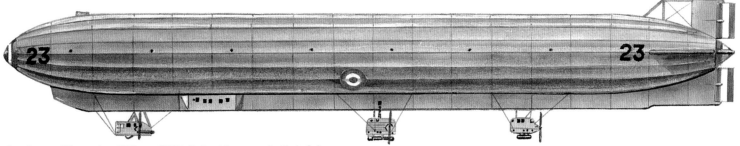

October and November 1918 saw R23 in its best-known role, that of air-launching Sopwith Camels N6622 and N6814. Although used mostly for training, it had carried out North Sea patrols and later participated in the victory celebrations of 1918.

When **His Majesty's Airship No. 9 (HMA No. 9)** was delivered in the closing months of 1916 it was almost obsolete as a result of the lengthy political vicissitudes that had bedevilled its production. It served a useful purpose, however: it had become the basic pattern on which the four rigid airships for the Admiralty were later to be based. The first of these **'23' class** airships, **HMA No. 23**, was subsequently delivered from Vickers Limited, Barrow-in-Furness, to Pulham on 15 September 1917.

Design work had started in June of the previous year, the first flight being planned for that autumn, but considerable redesign had to be carried out when the original specification resulted in a vessel that was something like 3493 kg (7,700 lb) too heavy, the greater part of this excess being attributable to the choice of engines.

The first trial flight of No. 23, four days after delivery, turned out to be something of an anticlimax, for it was clear that she too was at least obsolescent, as might be expected from the original design source, and her modern counterparts had a lifting capacity some nine times greater than that of which she was capable. It is hardly surprising, therefore, that the planned total of 10 airships of this type was finally cut back to six, while No. 23 was relegated to training duties. The other units of the class were **HMA No. 24** (Beardmore), **HMA No. 25** (Armstrong Whitworth), **HMA R26** (Vickers), **HMA**

R27 (Beardmore) and **HMA R29** (Armstrong Whitworth), the last pair being of the improved **'23X' class** without an exterior keel. No. 26 was the first to receive the 'R' prefix for rigid airships.

Mindful that in the mid-months of 1918 there was a possibility of aerial confrontations between airships of the opposing nations, experiments were carried out with Sopwith Camel aircraft suspended beneath the envelope of No. 23; the plan in the event of an attack was for the two fighters to be released to defend the mother vessel. There was no provision at the time for the aircraft to be reclaimed.

In the spring of 1919 No. 23 was strengthened for tests at a mooring mast, but before they could be carried out she was broken up in September.

Specification
HMA No. 23
Type: naval training airship
Powerplant: four 186.4-kW (250-hp) Rolls-Royce Eagle III 12-cylinder water-cooled piston engines
Performance: maximum speed 84 km/h (52 mph); service ceiling 914 m (3,000 ft); range 3219 km (2,000 miles)
Weight: useful lift 6000 kg (13,228 lb) including four 45-kg (100-lb) bombs
Dimensions: diameter 16.15 m (53 ft 0 in); length 163.07 m (535 ft 0 in); volume 26674.4 m³ (942,000 cu ft)
Armament: provision for 7.7-mm (0.303-in) Lewis gun on free mounting above forward portion of hull, plus bombs

Based on the earlier No. 9 of 1916, the No. 23 and its successors were constructed by Vickers at Barrow-in-Furness. The R23 was delivered to the Navy at Pulham on 15 September 1917. It is seen here with a Sopwith 2F.1 Camel underneath and a partially stripped upper fin.

With an observation balloon in the distance, R26 passes over the City of London in 1918. She was the first of five additional vessels of the '23' class ordered for the Royal Naval Air Service in January 1916, to be built by Vickers at Barrow-in-Furness.

In 1918, No. 23 was used for a series of experiments whereby a pair of Sopwith Camel aircraft were air-launched from under the hull, trials that were echoed in the United States and the Soviet Union. The British aircraft involved were drawn from No. 212 Squadron, RAF.

Observation Balloons

As the rival armies faced each other from their trenches, both sides began to employ captive balloons for reconnaissance. Enemy positions could be studied in minute detail, officers could see the terrain over which they were to attack, and artillery fire could be zeroed in. Inevitably, the balloons themselves became targets for attack.

Destroying the heavily-defended balloons called for a high degree of courage, some pilots specializing in the work. One such was Heinrich Gontermann, who accounted for 18 before being killed.

The use of balloons to gather information is old, for such devices were employed during the French Revolution and later by Napoleon on some of his campaigns. Experiments had been conducted in the USA as early as 1784, but it was not until 1840, during the Seminole War, that anything in the nature of an organized balloon corps was planned, and it is interesting to note that in 1863 a youthful Count von Zeppelin made his first flight in the USA.

In the UK, a small balloon factory was established at the Chatham School of Military Engineering as a result of trials that had been begun in 1878 at Woolwich Arsenal, and one year later the British Army had five balloons on charge, complete with winch waggons and horse-drawn gas carts. Small wonder therefore that observation balloons were to be seen above the battlefields of South Africa, Bechuanaland and the Sudan before the end of the century.

At much the same time, experiments in Germany resulted in the Drachenballon combining the principles of both balloon and kite, a design that was used in numbers to observe and direct artillery fire in the opening months of World War I. British reaction was to copy the design or use the unsuitable spherical type; the same type was used by France, which had decided to abandon the use of military balloons in 1912. The final solution was the work of a French officer, Albert Caquot, who designed a new type, albeit based on the German pattern, equipped with three stabilizing fins that enabled it to be used in winds of speeds up to 100 km/h (62 mph).

There were four standard types of Caquot balloon with varying capacities: the smallest was the Type P of 750-m³ (26,486-cu ft), followed by the Type P2 of 820-m³ (28,958-cu ft), the Type M2 of 930-m³ (32,842-cu ft) and the Type R of 1000-m³ (35,314-cu ft). The first three could each carry aloft two men, while the Type R could support three men in its basket. The first two types were used by the French army and also by the French navy from small vessels, while the Type R was capable of being flown from capital ships at altitudes up to 1000 m (3,280 ft), and the smaller M2 to something like half that figure. Five months before the end of World War I the French navy had 200 of all types of balloon on charge, although only 24 vessels were equipped to fly them.

Caquot balloons were soon adopted by France's allies, and over land were capable of being flown to an altitude of 1000 m (3,280 ft) even in a wind of Force 9 (about 100 km/h/62 mph) if the work demanded, both day and night. The observers were very simply equipped, with binoculars and an ordinary field telephone with which to report to the ground what they saw, and since, as might be expected, captive balloons provided a tempting target for enemy aircraft, those aboard also carried parachutes hung over the side of the basket to provide a means of escape. The parachute was opened by a static line as the wearer jumped.

The Germans generally carried out their observation work in the early morning, the British and French in the afternoon. In this way the Germans had the advantage of the morning sun behind them, the afternoon sun fulfilling the same function for the Allies, who as time passed thankfully bade farewell to their Drachens, which more than one observer later recalled as 'damnably unsteady'.

A balloon is used here to train officers in parachute training. Mastery of this was essential if the Caquot could not be winched down sufficiently swiftly in the event of an attack by aeroplanes. Such a victory was considered equal to that over an aircraft.

A row of tethered Caquot balloons clearly show their outlines. These were more elongated fore and aft than those of the World War II barrage balloons used to protect land targets, although these and the present-day parachute training balloons are all related.

That the work made extreme demands on the occupants of the frail suspended baskets is easy to overlook: not only were the duties carried out under extremes of temperature and, if the light was good enough, exposed to the vagaries of the weather, but there was always the danger of attack by opposing fighters. Despite the fact that severe measures were taken to protect the balloons, both sides developed specialists in this type of attack, the Belgian Willy Coppens and the German Heinrich Gontermann being two prime examples. Indeed, the demands of the balloon observers' job had some surprising results, such as the officer who was surprised at the coarseness of his language after a stint aloft, which was accompanied by a stammer and complete deafness that lasted some five minutes after landing. In an attempt to counteract the effects of a swift descent from altitude, some wings developed their own techniques such as that employed by No. 2 Wing, which was to pause at 4270 m (14,000 ft) even if the balloon was being winched down under attack; this was an unnerving practice for passengers unused to balloon work, such as the senior officers taken aloft to become familiar with the terrain over which they were shortly expected to advance!

Observation balloons were flown at first from a variety of motor vehicles, France using either the 32-hp (23.9-kW) or 60-hp (44.7-kW) Delahaye engine driving a Saconney winch, although from 1917 these were replaced by winches of Caquot's own manufacture driven by a 70-hp (52.2-kW) de Dion Bouton that was capable of bringing its charge down at a speed in the region of 6 m (20 ft) per second.

With the Allied observation line running practically the entire length of the Western Front, the demand for crews was of course high, and to meet this the British army set up a series of depots and schools in England at such centres as Larkhill, Lydd and Roehampton, while for a time even the Oval cricket ground was used. At these, and at the artillery schools attended by some observers, special techniques (such as that demanded by the need to keep one's glasses on a target however much the balloon might roll, jerk, leap, soar or sink) were learned. Other techniques (such as that of taking the telephone cable up over the trapeze before running it to the ground, so that it did not foul the parachute of an observer escaping from a balloon set alight by attack on the Caquot) had to be learned at the front as Caquots replaced the Drachens in which the telephone lines were taken direct from the basket to the main cable.

A Caquot captive observation balloon is seen above ruins on the Ypres salient on 27 October 1917. To train personnel, the Royal Flying Corps had opened two training schools in July 1916, plus a balloon depot. There were plans to form two new balloon sections per week.

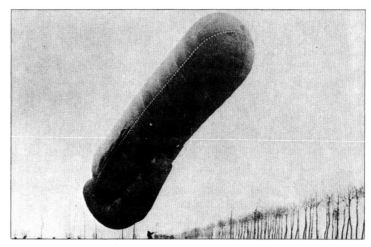

Above: A Belgian Drachen-type kite balloon is seen in Flanders in 1914. The similar Parseval-Sigsfeld pattern had been in use by the German army since 1898 despite its attendant handling problems, in order to direct gunfire and to report its effects.

Right: Willy Coppens, Belgian balloon-attacking specialist, stands in front of his Hanriot HD.1 of 9ème Escadrille. Severe injuries from the dum-dum effect of an incendiary bullet received while attacking a balloon in October 1918 cost him a leg. He had accounted for 26 enemy balloons.

UK 'NS' class

Another trefoil-section vessel, the **'North Sea'** or **'NS'** class was the last non-rigid airship type to be built for the Royal Navy, the first being ordered in January 1916 and delivered to the naval air station at Pulham in February 1917.

The original idea had been for an airship which could carry out convoy duties and also co-operate with naval surface vessels, a concept that was never put into practice, the whole 'NS' fleet being used for patrol duties.

One reason for this decision was the trouble that was experienced with the Rolls-Royce engines first fitted, the problem lying with the over-long shafting, about 3.05 m (10 ft) in length. It was only when this complicated transmission and the engines had been exchanged for direct-drive Fiats, that the type was able to prove its usefulness; previously only 18 were delivered, a mere 12 being with operational units.

Although a variety of car configurations was encountered, all of them were of similar lines, with the powerplant mounted in a separate nacelle joined to the crew quarters by a wooden catwalk. This forward part of the car had been designed with some consideration to the comfort of its occupants. Such additions as a chart table and bunks were now essential, since the 10 men aboard were expected to operate as two watches, five being on duty while the remainder rested.

From July 1917 the small number of North Sea airships then in use were all based on the Firth of Forth at East Fortune, but by the end of the war over 100 had seen service. An early example (**NS14**) had gone to the United States and become A5580, while **NS6** became a familiar sight to Londoners as a result of its frequent appearances over the capital; and in 1919 **NS11** established an endurance record for a non-stop cruise of 6437 km (4,000 miles) in 101 hours.

Although its primary duty was to attack U-boats with its cargo of bombs, an historic use for **NS7** and **NS8** was to

make up the aerial force with the British fleet sent to accept the surrender of the German naval forces on 21 November 1918. All convoy protection and coastal patrol airships carried about 181 kg (400 lb) of bombs with which to attack U-boats, but the useful load varied with the water ballast carried. Earlier models of the 'NS' class were powered by a pair of 186.4-kW (250-hp) Rolls-Royce engines, while latterly **NS12** to **NS18** received 223.7-kW (300-hp) Fiats.

Specification
'NS' class
Type: convoy escort airship
Powerplant: two 186.4-kW (250-hp) Rolls-Royce Eagle III V-12 or 193.9-kW (260-hp) Fiat A.12 six-cylinder water-cooled piston engines
Performance: maximum speed 93 km/h (55 mph); service ceiling about 7010 m (23,000 ft); range 4828 km (3,000 miles)
Weight: useful lift 3810 kg (8,400 lb)
Dimensions: width 17.30 m (56 ft 9 in); length 79.86 m (262 ft 0 in); volume

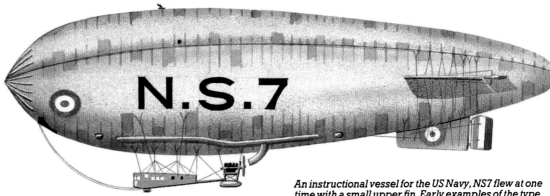

An instructional vessel for the US Navy, NS7 flew at one time with a small upper fin. Early examples of the type carried a row of fuel tanks along the envelope, while NS1 had an enlarged fin and rudder. NS3 retained such a fin but the rudder was discarded.

NS (North Sea) non-rigid No. 4 served at both East Fortune and Longside airship stations. There were detail differences in the car

10194 m³ (360,000 cu ft)
Armament: four or five 7.7-mm (0.303-

design, some having an unfaired connection to the motors. They were larger than the 'Coastal' type but had a trefoil section in common.

in) Lewis machine-guns on free mountings, plus bombs

FRANCE Chalais-Meudon *Fleurus*

When war broke out in 1914, French airship equipment was entirely of the non-rigid pattern, and it was one of these that made history in becoming the first Allied airship to carry out an air raid. This, despite its age, was the *Fleurus*, which had been built (like all French army craft of the lighter-than-air type) in the workshops at Chalais-Meudon two years earlier, being regarded as a smaller sister ship to *L'Adjutant Vincenot* (C.B.IV).

Interestingly, the *Fleurus* (or **C.B.V.** as it was officially known), had for the period a good aerodynamically efficient shape as it had been designed as a result of wind tunnel tests conducted at the Eiffel laboratory. While these results were applied to the contours of the envelope, Clément-Bayard was responsible for the design of the motor and the gondola, hence the initials of the alternative designation.

During the last year of peace, great use was made of the vessel, which participated in the army manoeuvres of that summer. It also left its base at Pau on 23 September at the beginning of a flight to Saint-Cyr, a journey which it completed in 16 hours, averaging a

speed of 54 km/h (33.7 mph), rather less than its maximum, for the distance of 680 km (423 miles) at an altitude never more than 1000 m (3,281 ft).

When making its historic raid from Verdun, the *Fleurus* was officially an army airship, there being no equivalent naval air arm; but with effect from 1 January 1917 this was rectified and the army vessels were handed over to establish the new branch of the navy. Of the six non-rigids involved, four were at once deployed for sea patrol in much the same manner as the British

'North Sea' and similar types, but by now the C.B.V was five years old and obsolescent, so that with another airship it was relegated to training duties. The base for this work was far from the area where the newer airships operated – North Africa's Mediterranean coast – being instead no further afield than Rochefort. It was here the *Fleurus* ended its days when France's most historic non-rigid of World War I was destroyed in a fire as a result of an air raid in June 1918.

National insignia had not been adopted at the time of the first flight to be made by Fleurus, but when it was introduced this vessel was one of the earliest in France to be thus marked.

Specification
Chalais-Meudon *Fleurus*
Type: army bombing airship
Powerplant: two 59.7-kW (80-hp) Clément-Bayard four-cylinder water-cooled piston engines
Performance: maximum speed 58 km/h (36 mph); service ceiling 1000 m (3,281 ft)
Weight: useful lift 5200 kg (11,464 lb)
Dimensions: diameter 12.40 m (40 ft 8.2 in); length 77.00 m (252 ft 7.5 in); volume 6500 m³ (229,546 cu ft)

'M' class

ITALY

The **'M' class** airships of semi-rigid design were extensively used by both the army and navy in Italy, and with them a total of almost 600 wartime sorties of various types were flown. A single example, later designated the **SR.1**, was ordered by the Admiralty for use by the Royal Navy in 1918 and flown from Italy on 28 October of the same year, but it was used only for experimental comparison with various British non-rigid coastal types.

Originally conceived for attacks on targets in Austria-Hungary, the design received special attention with regard to its altitude capability, since the rail junctions and docks which would be attacked were well defended by anti-aircraft guns. Additionally, several innovations were incorporated, such as the manner in which the keel was laid out to support the tailplane and also to meet the bows; wires from the keel connected it to canvas girdles, while bands about the circumference of the envelope in conjunction with parabolic wires took the weight of the car.

As a precaution against excessive leakage the envelope was divided into six sections internally, and the entrance of air to maintain the shape of the covering was through the nose, via a valve containing shutters operating on the principle of a venetian blind. A feature of the motors was the long shafting to the variable-pitch reversible propellers, something of an achievement since the history of motors mounted on outriggers at each side of a gondola (with a consequent demand for complex linkage) had not been happy.

'M' class airships operated by the Italian army were of the standard scouting version, but those with the navy were regarded as special in that they were equipped for bombing; the load of 1000 kg (2,205 lb) was a useful one which might have to be carried on a sortie of six-hour duration, this being the reason why no particular attention was paid to achieving a higher max-

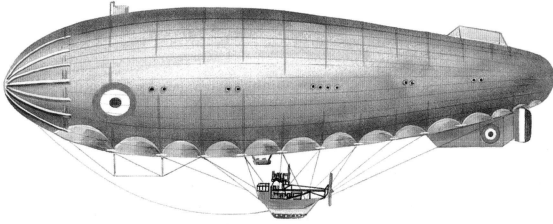

imum speed. Meanwhile, the SR.1 in British service was the target of much criticism, not so much for its capability as for the high costs involved in the trials. The type remained the sole example in the UK, and was not adopted for general use: its designation indicated the type of design, namely semi-rigid, and it was powered by one 149-kW (200-hp) SPA 6A and two 164-kW (220-hp) Italia D.2 engines, all of them water-cooled.

Specification
'M' class
Type: bombing airship
Powerplant: two 186.4-kW (250-hp) or two 208.8-kW (280-hp) Itala-Maybach four-cylinder water-cooled piston engines
Performance: maximum speed 80 km/h (50 mph); service ceiling 2000 m (6,562 ft); range 840 km (522 miles)

Above: Marked by their prominent nose reinforcement, 'M' class airships had biplane horizontal surfaces and elevators supporting outrigged rudders. Photographs show that the navy later marked SR.1 with its number aft of the cockade.

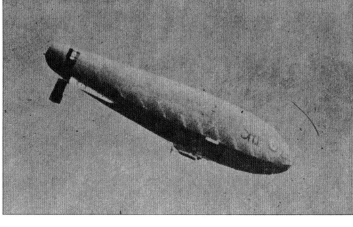

The Royal Navy's semi-rigid No. 1 (SR.1) was similar to those of the same (M) class that were used extensively by the Italian army and

navy during the war years. British experiments with this vessel were designed to compare it with non-rigid 'blimps'.

Weight: useful lift 3800 kg (8,378 lb)
Dimensions: diameter 17.00 m (55 ft 9.3 in); length 83.00 m (272 ft 3.7 in); volume 12500 m³ (441,434 cu ft)

Armament: one 7.7-mm (0.303-in) Lewis gun or equivalent on free mounting above nose of envelope, plus bombs

---

ITALY

'Forlanini' class

Manufactured by the Società Leonardo da Vinci in Milan, the **'Forlanini' class** airships (designed by Enrico Forlanini and the firm's engineer Luigi Crescentini) may be regarded as the most successful of the Italian semi-rigid vessels, winning a number of records during the years immediately preceding World War I.

Early versions had carried their structural girder externally, but this was eventually placed within the hull as a truss from which the central car with its crew compartment, motors and flotation bags protruded, the leading edge being glazed and an unusual triplane set of control surfaces being carried at each side of the **F.3**. To the rear of the car the propellers, arranged as pushers, were carried on outriggers with an extended linkage to the engines, the reversible propellers being capable of variable pitch.

An interesting design feature of the envelope was its double surface with a space between the inner and outer fabric, which served as a ballonet to maintain the shape of the envelope. In addition a climbing well was included together with a ladder by which to gain access to a platform on top of the hull.

There were five initial 'Forlanini' airships with progressively improved performance, the best showing a rate of climb of 1000 m (3,300 ft) per minute. One such airship setting up an endurance record of eight hours, in the

Special constructional features of the Forlanini F.3 were the triplane control surfaces at each side of the car, and five rudders at each side of the stern contained within biplane horizontal surfaces above and below, together with a prominent central fin underneath.

course of which the average altitude maintained was 3960 m (12,992 ft) although at one time 5335 m (17,503 ft) was attained.

Perhaps the most unusual feature of the Forlanini was the construction of

the tail. This did not terminate in the conventional cruciform pattern but had instead a robust ventral fin of thick section. To each side of this and below the centreline a series of high aspect ratio rudders was carried (five to a side) with biplane horizontal surfaces above and below.

A considerably smaller Forlanini airship was the **'P' class** (Piccolo, or small) with a fixed vertical fin and out-rigged rudders at the ends of very wide span elevators. This model was 63.0 m (206 ft 8.3 in) in length, with a diameter of 12.0 m (39 ft 4.4 in).

Specification
Forlanini F.3
Type: sea patrol and bombing airship
Powerplant: two 74.6-kW (100-hp) Fiat A six-cylinder water-cooled piston engines
Performance: maximum speed 80 km/h (50 mph); service ceiling 5480 m (17,979 ft); range 650 km (404 miles)
Weight: useful lift 2720 kg (5,997 lb)
Dimensions: diameter 20.34 m (66 ft 8.8 in); length 90.51 m (296 ft 11.4 in); volume 13800 m³ (487,343 cu ft)

Goodyear/Goodrich 'B' class
USA

It was in 1915 that the US Navy took on charge its first non-rigid coastal patrol airship, a type that was based on the information coming out of Germany and built by the Connecticut Aircraft Company as the DN-1. The **'B' class** which followed the failure of this first design was more closely based on that of British airships used for similar work, the first orders going to Goodyear in March 1917. However in all fairness it should be said that the 'B' class was in no way conceived as a replacement for the earlier type, which had in fact not flown when design work had begun on the Goodyear.

Although the 'B' class shared some of the British features, such as the use of an aeroplane fuselage as its car, there were differences such as the absence of an upper fin, though some 'B' class vessels did have this feature. There were several other differences between individual airships within the same class.

Further variations took place after the first nine examples (**B-1** to **B-9**) had been built by Goodyear, production then being undertaken by the B.F. Goodrich Co. The earlier airships had employed the finger-patch method of fastening the car lines to the envelope, which measured 9.60 m (31 ft 6 in) in diameter, and 48.77 m (160 ft 0 in) in length, but the 'B' class from **B-10** to **B-14** were longer and of greater girth.

It is interesting to note that the later variants (of which two only were built by Connecticut) were the shortest of all but with a greater-diameter envelope, and that the belly-bands which had replaced the finger-patches on the Goodrich were retained.

The B-10, in common with others of its class, proved a sound and reliable vessel; the two-man crew were fairly comfortably accommodated in the individual cockpits of the suspended fuselage, on which the landing gear had been replaced by rigidly-mounted air-filled flotation bags.

The B-10 was among the first batch of Goodyear/Goodrich vessels which were delivered between June 1917 and July of the following year, the former date marking something of a record since the first of the 'B' class made its maiden flight at the end of May, only two weeks after the declaration of war on Germany by the United States. The total number of vessels of this type delivered was only 16, but three were later reconstructed and given new numbers **B-17** to **B-19**. The final **B-20** was sufficiently different, with increased gas capacity and an OXX-3 motor, to be considered a new design.

The Goodyear B-20 had an increased cubic capacity, and the rope lines of earlier models were replaced by cable. Three fins were fitted instead of the five of the early variants, although the car with its typical Avro 504-type lines was unchanged.

Specification
Goodrich B-10
Type: coastal patrol airship
Powerplant: one 74.6-kW (100-hp) Curtiss OXX-2 eight-cylinder water-cooled piston engine
Performance: maximum speed 80 km/h (50 mph); service ceiling 2134 m (7,000 ft); endurance about 16 hours
Weight: useful lift about 2268 kg (5,000 lb)
Dimensions: diameter 10.06 m (33 ft 0 in); length 50.90 m (167 ft 0 in); volume 2265.3 m³ (80,000 cu ft)
Armament: one or two 7.62-mm (0.30-in) Lewis machine-guns

Goodyear 'C' class
USA

The **Goodyear 'C' class** airship was a type which must be counted the most successful design ever produced for the type of work envisaged: the **C-7** became part of technical history and the type as a whole, although of non-rigid pattern, influenced the next generation of rigid vessels.

The first flight of a 'C' class airship took place on 30 September 1918, this and the subsequent five airships being produced by the Goodyear Tire & Rubber Company of Akron, Ohio, where a training establishment and a hydrogen plant had already been set up under contract with the US Navy on 29 May 1917; the 20 trainees in each intake had the advantages of permanent barracks.

The six vessels produced were numbered **C-1** to **C-8**, the omitted designations **C-2** and **C-6** being used for some reason with **C-9** and **C-10** for the quartet of airships of the type ordered from the Goodrich company.

Although the work performed by the 'C' class units proved it an outstanding airship design, the type came into use at a time when World War I was nearing its end, so it is to the design features of the class that one must look for interest. Most obvious of these was the four-crew streamlined car with an engine and pusher propeller mounted at each side. The C-7's claim to history rests on a single incident when, on 1

December 1921, it became the first airship in the world to fly with helium substituted for the normal hydrogen lifting gas. The test was so successful that it was decided that henceforth all US airships would use this inert gas as a fire precaution despite the small loss of lift in comparison with that provided by lighter but inflammable hydrogen.

Other records held by the 'C' class include its use for the first successful release of an aeroplane from a non-rigid airship, and by becoming the first airship to make a coast-to-coast US crossing, this being achieved by one of the pair that were given over to US Army control in 1921. On the other hand the **C-5**, earmarked for a projected transatlantic crossing attempt, was lost in a storm when it was ripped from its moorings.

Specification
Goodyear C-7
Type: coastal patrol and convoy escort airship
Powerplant: two 149.1-kW (200-hp) Hall-Scott L-6 eight-cylinder water-cooled piston engines; reports also mention the 111.9-kW (150 hp) Wright-Hispano as an alternative but supportive evidence is lacking
Performance: maximum speed 97 km/h (60 mph); service ceiling 2438 m (8,000 ft); range about 4828 km (3,000 miles)
Weight: useful lift about 2,404 kg (5,300 lb)
Dimensions: diameter 12.80 m (42 ft 0 in); length 58.52 m (192 ft 0 in); volume 5125.3 m³ (181,000 cu ft)
Armament: one 7.62-mm (0.30-in) Lewis machine-gun

Production of the 'C' class was divided between Goodrich and Goodyear, the type proving highly successful for convoy protection and coastal patrol and exerting a strong influence on future United States design. A boat-like car distinguished all the series.

Battleships of World War 1

Of all the sights to stir the patriotic spirit in the years before World War I, it was the serried steel ranks of Dreadnoughts that most effectively symbolized military potency, and the possession of a strong fleet became a means to glorify the nation.

Looking forward on a 'Kaiser' class battleship in 1917. Though Zeppelins were used extensively by the Germans in co-operation with the High Seas Fleet, they were obviously still rare enough to cause much interest.

If it can be argued that only armies could win World War I, it is beyond doubt that navies could have lost it. To prosecute a war on such a scale meant, for the British in particular, continuous and guaranteed movement of men and materials which, in turn, demanded full control of the sea. Through this it was possible also to effectively deny the sea to the enemy; blockade could cut off the vital raw materials and foodstuffs in which he was not self-sufficient and, by its grinding remorselessness, gradually erode his will to resist.

Close blockade, as practised during the early 19th century, had been rendered impracticable by the submarine, the torpedo and the mine, so this 'front-line' function of the battleship had disappeared. The geographical advantages enjoyed by the UK, however, enabled distant blockade to be rigorously applied by comparatively weak and obsolete ships. These were buttressed by the full might of the Grand Fleet, its main strength lying at Scapa Flow to deter the German High Seas Fleet from either interfering with this slow strangulation or indulging more ambitious deep-sea adventures.

As it happened, however, the Kaiser hedged his cherished fleet with such suffocating operational restrictions that it existed largely as a fleet-in-being, tying down the numerically more powerful Royal Navy and offering battle only on its own terms. Perhaps the greatest disappointment of the battleship fleets was that in this war, during which they could really have justified themselves, they occupied their time largely cancelling out each other's existence. Numbers were important, the need to survive tempering boldness and originality in many commanders. In the end, even as with the French revolutionary navy of over a century before, insufficient real use robbed the High Seas Fleet of its sense of purpose, so that it drifted into deterioration and revolt.

Though, between them, the warring powers could boast many capital ships, few achieved much beyond those involved in the tiny arena of the North Sea. In retrospect it may be said that the Royal Navy, while retaining the Grand Fleet in its main role, could have used its large (and expendable) force of pre-Dreadnoughts far more adventurously in a variety of unorthodox ways.

A late sortie by the High Seas Fleet, probably in 1917 as the 'Bayern' class ship on the right has a mainmast and all have landed their torpedo nets. The Germans successfully preserved the greater part of their battle fleet as a 'fleet-in-being', tying down the superior strength of the British.

'Michigan' class

Had HMS *Dreadnought* not been built precisely when she was, it is conceivable that 'all-big-gun' ships would have been termed 'Michigans', this pair having been approved before the British ship and embodying all the principles of a heavy and homogeneous main battery. The USS *Michigan* and USS *South Carolina* were laid down after the *Dreadnought*, however, and took three years to construct compared with only one. A drawback of the design was that steam turbines were not available for propulsion, but their primary feature was their armament layout. Though the *Dreadnought* carried 10 305-mm (12-in) guns, only eight could be used in broadside as two turrets were sited in the waist. The 'Michigans' had only eight guns but, well before the arrangement became general, mounted them in twinned superfiring turrets at each end.

Sensibly, the Americans also shipped a secondary battery, albeit a lightweight one of 22 76-mm (3-in) guns but, for the greater part, behind protected casemates in the superstructure at a height where they could always be used.

A further innovation was the basket mast. Theoretically combining maximum stiffness with minimum weight it was far from universally loved and was to remain peculiarly American.

Even before the 'Michigans' were in the water, two improved versions (the 'Delaware' class) were laid down. Only one was turbine-driven, but both had

an extra centreline main battery turret and the standard 127-mm (5-in) calibre was readopted for the secondary armament.

Boat booms and awnings rigged, the Michigan and a 'Delaware' class ship lie peacefully at anchor. First with superimposed turrets, she would also have been the first all-big-gun capital ship but for Dreadnought's rushed completion.

Below: Initiated before Dreadnought, but completed well afterwards, the 'Michigans' had all-superfiring main armament. This allowed all guns to fire on both beams, in contrast to the British vessel, which required two extra guns.

Specification
'Michigan' class (as built)
Displacement: 16,000 tons standard and 17,900 tons full load
Dimensions: length 138.07 m (453.0 ft); beam 24.38 m (80.0 ft); draught 7.49 m (24.6 ft)
Propulsion: two quadruple-expansion steam engines delivering 16,500 ihp (12304 kW) to two shafts
Speed: 18.5 kts
Armament: eight 305-mm (12-in) and 22 76-mm (3-in) guns, and two 533-mm (21-in) torpedo tubes
Armour: belt 305 mm (12 in); bulkheads 279 mm (11 in); barbettes 254 mm (10 in); middle deck 19 mm (0.75 in); lower deck 38 mm (1.5 in)
Complement: 870

'Pennsylvania' class

American 'post-Michigan' battleships added firepower in logical steps. The five-turret 'Delawares' and 'Floridas' thus developed into the six-turret 'Wyomings' of 1911. As all of it was sited on the centreline, this armament demanded a long ship with a large area to protect. In 1912, therefore, the trend was halted by a reversion to 10 guns in the 'New Yorks', though these increased the calibre from 305 to 356 mm (12 to 14 in). Again these were grouped in five turrets, but the following pair of 'Nevadas' had much improved protection at little penalty by adopting a four-turret arrangement with twins superfiring triples. It was then but a small step to ship four triples to give a broadside of 356-mm (14-in) guns in the 'Pennsylvania' class. This layout was successful and retained in the following two classes to give a homogeneous seven-ship group, which was not outclassed until the introduction of the 406-mm (16-in) gun with the 'Colorados' of 1921. The 'Penn-

sylvanias' were both completed in 1916 as the USS *Pennsylvania* and USS *Arizona*.

The 'Pennsylvanias' were turbine-driven but, in the 'New Mexico' class that followed them turbo-electric drive was introduced. Inadequacies in American heavy gear production were the overriding reason for this, the turbo-electric machinery requiring neither reduction nor reversing gear. Despite being heavy and expensive, however, the system had advantages in flexibility, with any shaft capable of

being driven from any turbo generator. Further, propulsion motors could be sited well aft, shortening shafts and allowing improved standards of watertight integrity.

Starting their career with characteristic basket masts, small bridge structure and a generally uncluttered appearance, the 'Pennsylvanias' were remodelled between the wars, emerging almost unrecognizable with heavy tophamper, massive tripod masts and the paraphernalia of aircraft operation.

The *Arizona* was shattered by a magazine explosion during the Pearl Harbor attack; with her died nearly 1,200 crewmen. The *Pennsylvania*, further updated, obtained redress in several operations, notably as one of Admiral Oldendorf's gun line at the Surigao Strait; post-war she survived two Bikini nuclear tests and was finally expended as a bombing target.

Specification
'Pennsylvania' class (as built)
Displacement: 31,400 tons standard and 33,000 tons full load
Dimensions: length 185.39 m (608.25 ft); beam 29.62 m (97.17 ft); draught 8.79 m (28.84 ft)
Propulsion: four main and four cruising geared steam turbines delivering 31,500 shp (23490 kW) to four shafts
Speed: 21 kts
Armament: 12 356-mm (14-in) and 22 127-mm (5-in) guns, and two 533-mm (21-in) torpedo tubes
Armour: belt 356 mm (14 in); bulkheads 356 mm (14 in); barbettes 343 mm (13.5 in); upper deck 76 mm (3 in); lower deck 76 mm (3 in)
Complement: 915

The 'Pennsylvanias' were the first US Navy battleships to mount all their main armament in triple turrets, a feature that became a standard American practice.

The Rise of the Dreadnought

The Russo-Japanese war in 1904-5 demonstrated to the world's naval thinkers the need for a radical change of emphasis in warship design. In most of the major maritime nations plans were being advanced, but it was Britain who gave the world the Dreadnought.

On Trafalgar Day, 1904, 63-year-old 'Jacky' Fisher was appointed First Sea Lord, embarking immediately on a series of fundamental changes that would take the Royal Navy from the somnolence of the long, lotus years of the 'Pax Britannica' to the battleworthiness demanded by a war that he saw as inevitable. Within a year the *Dreadnought* had been laid down, her concept the best of a series considered by his 'Committee on Designs'. Fisher claimed to have been refining the idea since 1900 when, as Commander-in-Chief Mediterranean, he had discussed it at length with William Gard, Chief Constructor at Malta.

Fisher was not alone. Professional publications of major naval powers were all familiar with the florid prose of the Italian Vittorio Cuniberti, whose theories cut little ice at home. His dream ship would be fast and carry the greatest number of the largest guns available, choosing her range to 'pour in a terrible converging fire' on any hapless battleship of the time.

Having the world's largest fleet, the UK had no interest in rendering it obsolete by a significant advance, but the impetus came with the improving performance of both torpedoes and guns, forcefully demonstrated by previously unimagined engagement ranges during the Russo-Japanese War of 1904-5. Fisher's sense of urgency may also have been heightened by knowledge that the Americans were about to pre-empt him, the Congress approving plans for Admiral Sim's ideas in the two 'Michigans' early in 1905.

Because of its higher rate of fire and because more barrels could be carried, the 254-mm (10-in) gun was preferred by Fisher to the 305-mm (12-in) weapon but Admiral Bacon, a committee member, convinced him that fewer large guns, married to high speed, would lead to 'scientific and practical shooting'. Once accepted, this argument led directly to the daring adoption of the steam turbine, yet untried in the required power range, together with oil fuelling, that would demand the piercing of bulkheads on a far more modest scale than necessary in coal-fired ships.

In HMS *Dreadnought* the Royal Navy acquired a ship that could steam reliably at high speed and which could fight its armament in all conditions. Firing arcs were good, but the layout reflected Fisher's obsession with chase-fire, tem-

Dreadnought set new standards in capital ships – larger and faster, with 10 large guns of homogeneous calibre. In practice, her lack of secondary armament was a drawback and, despite her turbine propulsion, she proved too slow for the Grand Fleet, from which she was withdrawn in 1916.

pered by the practical considerations of blast effects. A single major gun calibre simplified both magazine arrangements and fire control. The reasoning that resulted in the abandoning of a credible secondary battery was faulty, and rectified in subsequent classes.

The 'Dreadnought Committee' was tasked also with defining a super armoured cruiser, later to be termed the battle-cruiser. As a 30 per cent speed margin was sought over comparable battleships, the result was a large ship, packed with machinery and protected on a scale that was acceptable only when used against conventional armoured cruisers. Carrying the same 305-mm (12-in) main battery calibre as the *Dreadnought* herself, the first of these 'glass-jawed' monsters, HMS *Invincible*, was completed some 15 months later in March 1908.

Right: Though the main battery was better arranged than that of Dreadnought, the 'Michigans' retained reciprocating steam machinery. They were also coal-fired, which meant smoke at higher speeds, as shown by South Carolina making her full 18½ kts.

Below: The four 'Nassaus' were Germany's first Dreadnoughts, yet still contrived to look orthodox. By restricting the main battery calibre to only 280 mm (11 in), six twin turrets could be carried, two of them on either beam. Typical German features are the large gooseneck boat cranes and uncased funnel tops.

'Courbet' class

In spite of the highly individual funnel layout, the French 'Courbets' were not unpleasing in appearance as first built. In the background is an 'Aube' class armoured cruiser completed a decade earlier.

Through a combination of backward naval thought and an inadequate industrial base, France for a while ignored the Dreadnought revolution and built, between 1906 and 1911, the six 18,300-ton 'Dantons' which were obsolete on completion. Only after this, with the four **'Courbet' class** ships, did they acknowlege the inevitable. French designs were hallmarked by their eccentric mast and funnel arrangements, and the 'Courbets' had their three stacks divided between a forward pair and a single much farther aft, a pole mast being planted almost exactly amidships in the resulting gap.

The 'Courbet' class were France's first Dreadnoughts, completed long after the other major maritime nations had entered the battleship-building race.

As the mast carried no control top, there was no valid reason for its siting, particularly as the overall layout was thus incapable of taking a centreline turret. Although superimposed turrets were adopted fore and aft, therefore, two sided turrets had to be incorporated amidships to give the required 10-gun broadside. This in turn meant that the area to be protected was increased and, as the class was already notable for its protected area (the armour being continued unusually low on the hull) the result had to be on the thin side. Torpedo attack had always figured largely in French thought, and the 22 casemated secondary guns were selected for rate of fire rather than weight of metal. Launched in 1911-2, the ships were the **Courbet, France, Jean Bart** and **Paris**.

The *France* was wrecked off Quiberon in 1922, and the remainder were remodelled soon after this. Externally the forward uptakes were paired into a single, larger casing (except in the *Paris*) and a massive tripod foremast with a control top was added over the bridge. This layout, if adopted originally, would have allowed an all-centreline main battery, which was not seen until the following three **'Provence' class** units which, carrying one turret less for the same broadside, could also have the calibre increased to 340 mm (13.4 in).

During the rapid German advance in 1940, both *Courbet* and *Paris* saw brief bombardment action but then shared the fate of many major French units, wasted through the double loyalties of an occupied land.

Specification
'Courbet' class (as built)
Displacement: 23,200 tons standard and 25,850 tons full load
Dimensions: length 168.00 m (551.2 ft); beam 27.00 m (88.58 ft); draught 9.00 m (29.53 ft)
Propulsion: four sets of geared steam turbines delivering 28,000 shp (20880 kW) to four shafts
Speed: 20.5 kts
Armament: 12 305-mm (12-in) and 22 138.6-mm (5.46-in) guns, and four 450-mm (17.7-in) torpedo tubes
Armour: belt 270 mm (10.6 in) barbettes 280 mm (11 in); upper deck 50 mm (1.97 in); lower deck 70 mm (2.76 in)
Complement: 1,110

'Dante Alighieri' class

As Vittorio Cuniberti was one of the earliest protagonists of the 'all-big-gun' capital ship, it is not surprising that Italy's first Dreadnought was a pure embodiment of his ideas. These espoused the greatest possible number of the largest available guns, carried on a fast hull, thus enabling the ship to decide the range at which to pour in an overwhelming fire, the large number of barrels compensating for their slow rate of fire.

Very much a prototype, the *Dante Alighieri* had a layout dictated by the geometry of giving the main battery the best possible firing arcs. Probably because of fears of blast effects or interaction, Cuniberti rejected superimposed turrets, and he wisely avoided sided or echeloned mountings. His all-centreline arrangement could

The Dante Alighieri *bore a resemblance to a battlecruiser in the concentration of the maximum possible firepower on the fastest possible hull. It was one of the first capital ships to employ triple turrets to house the 12 305-mm (12-in) main guns.*

accommodate only four turrets on the length, so he adopted the then advanced concept of the triple turret, copied immediately afterwards by the Austro-Hungarians for their 'Viribus Unitis' class battleships. The forward turret was sited on a raised forecastle, two more were placed amidships and one was located aft, leaving space for only two vestigial superstructure blocks. Kept axially as short as possible, these comprised mainly two severe groups of close-spaced pairs of funnels each separated by a pole mast.

While the resultant firing arcs were exceptionally good, the bridge structure was impractically small and low, and no control top was fitted. The layout also demanded an immense area of protection which thus had to be on the thin side and which would have made the ship vulnerable to attack by a more orthodox Dreadnought.

Modifications during the 1920s increased her bridge size and added a large tripod foremast with top. Even before the *Dante Alighieri* was launched, the three 'Cavours' were laid

down, their design tempering some of Cuniberti's more extreme features. The earlier eccentric paired funnels were, for instance, combined in common casings, and superimposed turrets (twins over triples at each end) allowed an increase of one barrel while reducing the number of amidships turrets to only one.

Specification
'Dante Alighieri' class (as built)
Displacement: 19,500 tons standard and 21,800 tons full load
Dimensions: length 168.10 m (551.5 ft); beam 26.60 m (87.27 ft); draught 9.20 m (30.2 ft)
Propulsion: four sets of geared steam turbines delivering 32,000 shp (23862 kW) to four shafts
Speed: 23 kts
Armament: 12 305-mm (12-in) and 20 120-mm (4.7-in) guns, and three 450-mm (17.7-in) torpedo tubes
Armour: belt 250 mm (9.84 in); barbettes 250 mm (9.84 in); upper deck 30 mm (1.2 in): lower deck 20 mm (0.8 in)
Complement: 970

Development of Fire Control Systems

The advance in fire control systems was made necessary by the rapidly increasing performance of warships and the unprecedented engagement ranges possible with the new, powerful armament then being fitted.

Capital ships toward the end of the 19th century were carrying fewer large guns, so every shot needed to tell. Improved weapons and projectile ballistics also offered consistency and predictability, which enabled forward-thinkers to approach gunnery in a more scientific manner. To hit the enemy before he could hit you demanded centralized gun control from a director, equipped with the means of measuring the range and bearing of the target, together with a prediction of where that target was likely to be after the calculated time of flight of the projectiles.

In 1891 Watkins, using precision optics and telephonic communication, updated the old sailing navy method of measuring range through taking the horizontal angles to the target from the known length of baseline of one's own ship. The system remained vulnerable, however, and accurate only wide on the beam, and was soon superseded by Barr's optical rangefinder which, though of only 1.37-m (4.5-ft) baseline, enabled a single observer to measure range on any bearing.

The target's course and speed could be estimated after a period of observation, and then combined with one's own course and speed to give a firing solution, this having to be modified by other variables such as wind speed and direction. Competitions stimulated the development of instruments to speed the process so, for instance, in 1902 the Dumaresq was introduced, predicting rates of change in target range and bearing. This was followed by the Range Clock, which gave predicted ranges directly and then the complex Dreyer Fire Control Table, which relied on extremely accurately-cut gearing to mix a variety of input variables, the result of which was elevation and training settings that could be transmitted to each gun turret. Once all of these had reported ready, a central firing key was closed to loose a salvo simultaneously.

Practice formed this salvo into a tight group, and fall of shot relative to the target was spotted from the high control top so that corrections could be signalled (up or down, left or right) until subsequent salvoes achieved a 'straddle'.

Gunnery in the Victorian navy envisaged typical engagements at ranges not exceeding 2750 m (3,000 yards). Enthusiasts such as 'Jacky' Fisher and Percy

The Battle of Jutland saw the German and British methods of rangefinding and fire control meet head-on. In rangefinding terms, the German navy was superior; the British were much slower to find the range, but had a more effective fire control system. The main indications of accuracy were the enormous splashes made by the main armament. From the main top, a telescopic view immediately showed whether a salvo was over, under or, as shown here, straddling the range of the target.

Scott changed all this, firing the fleet with a spirit of innovation and competition for challenge trophies. Scott, for instance, daily exercised his gunners with what he termed his 'Dotter', simulating ship movement and firing without the expenditure of ammunition. His commands, HMS *Scylla* and HMS *Terrible*, broke all gunnery records in their time.

Extensive trials on specialized test ranges, followed by regular live battle practices, enabled ships to calibrate their weapons and to prove them in realistic conditions. By 1912, ranges of 13715 m (15,000 yards) were not considered excessive.

American and German practice was generally behind that of the British at this time, but ran roughly parallel. The Germans, however, did have the benefit of superb long-based stereoscopic rangefinders which, in the right hands, could get the range far more rapidly than the well-tried British method of using ranging salvoes. Experience was to show that this difference could be crucial to the outcome of an action.

JAPAN
'Kongo' class

Experience in its recent war with the Russians had shown the Japanese navy the value of superior speed to dictate the course of an action, and the introduction of the battle-cruiser by the British soon after this war caused much interest. Though lacking the necessary expertise, the Japanese required four, ordering the lead ship from Vickers and acquiring the necessary technical support to build three sisters in home yards. Vickers was able to benefit by improving on the design of the 'Lion' class HMS *Princess Royal*, which it was then constructing, so that the **'Kongo' class** for about the same speed carried an eight-gun 356-mm (14-in) main bat-

Completed in 1912, Kongo was a very powerful vessel, with eight 356-mm (14-in) guns and a speed of over 27 kts. Built in England, she was to be drastically rebuilt in the 1930s in order to fill the new role of carrier escort. She was sunk by the US submarine Sealion in November 1944.

tery in place of 10 343-mm (13.5-in) guns, and with better protection. As a result, HMS *Tiger* was built as an anglicized *Kongo*, the latter still looking very British in spite of clipper bow and round-section funnels.

The *Kongo*'s three sisters were built in separate Japanese yards and in very creditable times, the **Hiei** being completed like the *Kongo* in 1912, and the **Haruna** and **Kirishima** in 1913. They

varied only in detail. In the 1920s, with severe treaty limits on new construction, all four were thoroughly rebuilt. Their light horizontal protection was thickened and anti-torpedo bulges added. The latter addition reduced their speed by about 2 kts despite re-boiling.

During the 1930s the Japanese navy was developing its ideas on fast carrier groups and, requiring high speed

heavy escorts, again took the 'Kongos' in hand for remodelling. To improve their lines, their length was increased by about 8 m (26.25 ft) and the original installed power was more than doubled to achieve a 30-kt speed. As a result of advances in machinery technology, this was achieved with a substantial cut in weight.

Extra elevation improved ranges for both primary and secondary armament, aircraft and catapults were added, and the characteristically heavy top hamper was introduced. The job was well done for, although all four were sunk, none was destroyed by the explosion typical of British battle-cruiser design. Notable in this respect was the *Kirishima*, sunk near Savo Island, by the gunfire of two American battleships though, admittedly, at no great range.

Specification
'Kongo' class (as built)
Displacement: 26,320 tons standard

and 27,500 tons full load
Dimensions: length 214.70 m (704.4 ft); beam 28.00 m (91.8 ft) draught 8.40 m (27.6 ft)
Propulsion: four sets of geared steam turbines delivering 64,000 shp (47725 kW) to four shafts
Speed: 27.5 kts
Armament: eight 356-mm (14-in) and 16 152-mm (6-in) guns, and eight 533-mm (21-in) torpedo tubes
Armour: belt 203 mm (8 in); bulkheads 230 mm (9 in); barbettes 254 mm (10 in); deck 51 mm (2 in)
Complement: 1,221

Epitomizing the grace and power of the battlecruiser is the Japanese Kongo soon after completion. She was built in Britain as a model for three home-built copies, but her design was so successful that it formed the basis of the British Tiger.

 JAPAN
'Fuso' class

Launched in 1914-5 the two **'Fuso' class** battleships *Fuso* and *Yamashiro* were contemporaries of the American 'Nevadas' and came between the British 'Iron Dukes' and 'Queen Elizabeths'. The 10-gun broadsides of the two former classes were increased by two further barrels but, lacking experience of constructing triple turrets, the Japanese adopted six centreline twin mountings which, like those in the American 'Wyomings', demanded a long hull. Except for the odd little pairs of 'Satsumas' and 'Kawachis', the Japanese had had no experience of Dreadnought battleship design and construction, and the almost cruiser-like 'Fusos' echoed this with their low, clean lines. Fragility, however, was only apparent as they carried a heavy punch on a well-protected and subdivided hull, turbine-driven for 23 kts. For the first time, most gear was home-built.

As with so many battleships of this era, the 'Fusos' experienced a comparatively uneventful World War I, followed by a period of drastic reconstruction preceding a World War II of hectic activity. Thus in the 1930s they were extensively remodelled, being lengthened by 7.5 m (24.6 ft) to take advantage of a more powerful but lighter set of machinery, with oil firing. Main and secondary armaments had their ranges improved by increased elevation, horizontal protection was thickened against long-range plunging fire, and anti-torpedo bulges were added. Externally the forward funnel,

tripod and bridgework made way for the extraordinary pagoda-like construction that was to become such a Japanese trademark, a structure that grew ever more complex with time.

Despite this thorough remoulding, World War II saw the 'Fusos' (like the *Ise* and *Hyuga*) threatened post-Midway with conversion to hybrid aircraft-carriers. They avoided this further surgery only to be sacrificed together in the dark waters of the Surigao Strait, running the gauntlet to throw themselves at the massed guns of Admiral Oldendorf's battle line in a hopeless attempt to penetrate to Leyte Gulf.

Specification
'Fuso' class (as built)
Displacement: 30,600 tons standard and 31,000 tons full load
Dimensions: length 205.21 m (673.25 ft); beam 28.73 m (94.25 ft); draught 8.69 m (28.5 ft)
Propulsion: four sets of geared steam turbines delivering 40,000 shp (29828 kW) to four shafts
Speed: 23 kts
Armament: 12 356-mm (14-in) and 14

152-mm (6-in) guns, and six 533-mm (21-in) torpedo tubes
Armour: belt 305 mm (12 in); bulkheads 305 mm (12 in); barbettes 203 mm (8 in); upper deck 32 mm (1.25 in); lower deck 51 mm (2 in)
Complement: 1,195

Everybody's idea of the archetypal Japanese battleship, the Fuso is seen here following her 1933 rebuilding. Note how the six centreline turrets break the superstructure into three distinct masses. At this stage, she still carried an aircraft catapult on the roof of 'C' turret, abaft the 'pagoda'.

Fuso as built, displaying her notably slim lines. For the first time, the majority of the equipment fitted to the two 'Fusos' was of Japanese construction. Well protected, both were to be extensively rebuilt during the early 1930s.

 UK
'Canopus' class

Completed at the end of the Victorian era, the six **'Canopus' class** typified contemporary British battleships, with a twin 305-mm (12-in) barbette mounting at either end and a secondary 152-mm (6-in) armament arranged in protected casemates along each side. They had been designed particularly with the China station in mind, and they

needed a restricted draught in order to transit the Suez Canal. Much weight was saved in the design by the incorporation of the new Krupp steel armour which afforded the same protective qualities on only two-thirds the thickness of the Harvey armour in the earlier and similarly sized 'Majestic' class ships. A further weight-saving

measure was the omission of the underwater sheathing and coppering then still customary. Propulsion machinery was the universally-used triple-expansion reciprocating engine, but a 2-knot advantage was gained over the 'Majestics' by the adoption of the water-tube boiler which, size for size, had a far larger

steam-raising surface and could, therefore, develop more energy. The three units completed in 1900 were HMS *Canopus*, HMS *Goliath* and HMS *Ocean* (the latter two being lost in the Dardanelles in 1915), while the three completed in 1901 were HMS *Glory*, HMS *Vengeance* and HMS *Albion*.

Though the Royal Navy in general

greatly underutilized the reserve of strength that it possessed in its older battleships, the 'Canopus' class had its share of action. Comprising the coherent 8th Battle Squadron of the Channel Fleet at the outbreak of war, the ships were rapidly and widely dispersed, *Canopus* going to the South American station. With von Spee's squadron coming eastward across the Pacific, Admiral Cradock took a scratch collection of ships to intercept him. The result was the disaster off Coronel on 1 November 1914. The *Canopus* was not involved in the action, labouring with machinery trouble through heavy seas well to the south.

Specification
'Canopus' class
Displacement: 12,950 tons standard and 14,300 tons full load
Dimensions: length 118.87 m (390.0 ft); beam 22.56 m (74.0 ft); draught 7.87 m (25.85 ft)
Propulsion: two sets of triple-expansion steam engines delivering 13,500 ihp (10067 kW) to two shafts
Speed: 18.5 kts
Armament: four 305-mm (12-in), 12 152-mm (6-in), 10 12-pdr and some smaller

guns, and four 457-mm (18-in) torpedo tubes
Armour: belt 152 mm (6 in) amidships; transverse bulkheads 254-305 mm (10-12 in); barbettes 305 mm (12 in); upper deck 25 mm (1 in); lower deck 51 mm (2 in)
Complement: 680

Right: Though obsolete, the Royal Navy's pre-Dreadnoughts, such as the 'Canopus' class, still played very active roles.

Left: Last British battleships of the Victorian era, the 'Canopus' class had the new Krupp armour and improved water tube boilers. Main armament comprised four 305-mm (12-in) guns.

 UK
'Invincible' class

As the world's first battle-cruisers, the three **'Invincible' class** ships marked a real revolution in warship development. The first of the class, HMS *Inflexible*, was laid down only days before the *Dreadnought* was launched but, where the latter represented logical (if sudden) progression, the newcomers were of an entirely new breed. All major fleets operated armoured cruisers, some of which were comparable with smaller contemporary battleships. Admiral Fisher's brainchildren were to make these their natural prey, being able to sacrifice protection to mount a Dreadnought-scale armament on a Dreadnought-scale hull packed with machinery for unprecedented speed. Used properly, the battle-cruisers would use their speed and range to force or decline action as circumstance demanded. All three units were completed in 1908, the other two being HMS *Indomitable* and HMS *Inflexible*.

The battle-cruisers needed 31 boilers to the *Dreadnought*'s 18, demanding a hull some 12.2 m (40 ft) greater in length, a feature which also permitted extra fineness of line. Three unequally-spaced funnels marked the boiler room layout. Two fewer main battery guns still enabled six to bear

on any target, enough to counter any armoured cruiser, whose scale of protection was also logically adopted.

Admiral Beatty's dramatic intervention at the Heligoland Bight fracas and

Above: This photograph shows the smoke problem that caused Invincible's forefunnel to be lengthened, in 1915.

Below: Designed to combat armoured cruisers, the 'Invincible' class was armoured against fire from such vessels.

Admiral Sturdee's destruction of the two 'Scharnhorsts' (among the finest armoured cruisers afloat) at the Battle of the Falklands confirmed the soundness of Fisher's ideas, which had worked in these instances through correct application. With the offensive doctrine inbred to the Royal Navy, however, it was only a matter of time until these enormous ships had their glass jaws broken by something out of their class. This occurred with horrifying finality at Jutland, when three battle-cruisers, of different classes but including the *Invincible*, were destroyed by magazine explosions caused by hits inflicted at medium range. Further protection was worked in after the battle, but the reputation was shattered and the battle-cruiser's brief day had already reached its evening.

Specification
'Invincible' class
Displacement: 17,400 tons standard and 20,100 tons full load
Dimensions: length 175.56 m (576.0 ft); beam 23.93 m (78.5 ft); draught 7.77 m (25.5 ft)
Propulsion: four sets of geared steam turbines delivering 41,000 shp (30574 kW) to four shafts
Speed: 25 kts
Armament: eight 305-mm (12-in) and 16 102-mm (4-in) guns, and five 457-mm (18-in) torpedo tubes
Armour: belt 152 mm (6 in); transverse bulkhead 178 mm (7 in); barbettes 178 mm (7 in); main deck 25 mm (1 in); lower deck 64 mm (2.5 in)
Complement: 784

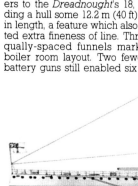

The *Lion* in Action

Embodying all the strengths and weaknesses of Fisher's battlecruiser concept, Lion *was every inch a thoroughbred. Fast and powerful, but vulnerable to fire from heavy vessels, the sight of* Lion *at the head of Beatty's battlecruiser fleet was a stirring sight which disguised the basic frailty of high speed, lightly armoured vessels.*

The magnificent HMS *Lion* was the warhorse of David Beatty, the impetuously courageous genius commanding the Grand Fleet's Battle-Cruiser Squadron. Like all of her kind she carried a punch that could crack a battleship, yet was perilously vulnerable to any plunging return fire. The deficiencies of such battle-cruisers were recognized and accepted as the type could not be used effectively by the cautious, and caution was one word that Beatty never learned.

As a rear admiral, Beatty had been appointed by Churchill in March 1913 and, in the 17 months remaining to the outbreak of war he had infused a real fighting spirit into the squadron with endless gunnery exercises conducted at previously unimagined ranges and speeds. It was as well, for Beatty's battle-cruisers were to be involved in every action of note in the North Sea. In a letter to his wife, Beatty wrote that 'We've lived for 40 years in peace and comfort, and now we are to be put to the test . . . My Captains are splendid and not easily rattled. Whatever comes, the battle-cruisers will give a good account of themselves.' How right he was.

With the war not yet a month old, Commodore Tyrwhitt's Harwich Force was sent deep into the Heligoland Bight to disrupt and destroy any of the enemy light forces that conducted regular patrols. The Harwich Force was itself surprised, several enemy light cruisers arriving unexpectedly and pressing it hard in a very confused action in poor visibility. Thus caught on the Germans' very doorstep, Tyrwhitt called for assistance. He knew that two battle-cruisers

from the Humber were available, but had not been informed of the decision of Admiral Jellicoe, the commander-in-chief, to back these with Beatty's force and Commodore Goodenough's six light cruisers. These were only 65 km (40 miles) from Heligoland and neither commander hesitated. Like the cavalry in a Western drama they surprised Tyrwhitt as much as his tormentors by their entry. Three German light cruisers were sunk, SMS *Ariadne* by the *Lion* herself with three 343-mm (13.5-in) salvoes at barely 4575 m (5,000 yards). Speedily withdrawing before the enemy's heavy forces could cross their tide-bound bars, the British found public acclaim awaiting them but, in truth, it had been a shambles of an encounter, unco-ordinated and poorly planned. Only Beatty's instant acceptance of risk had lifted it from an untidy skirmish to a naval event, doing wonders in the process for the morale of both fleet and nation.

German raid

In December 1914, two of Jellicoe's battle-cruisers were sent south, repeating the exercise on von Spee at the Falklands. The Squadron now had enormous prestige (yet could still attract petty official displeasure at their rate of ammunition expenditure!) but were about to be more severely tested.

Now all too aware of the detachment of the two battle-cruisers, the Germans seized their chance of a bombardment raid on the English east coast, using the battle-cruisers of Beatty's able counterpart, Admiral Hipper. By this provocation, it was hoped to lure Beatty's reduced

force out in pursuit, to be ambushed in turn and destroyed by the main body of the High Seas Fleet which was to render distant support. Decoded radio intercepts had, however, warned the British of the general form of the operation and Beatty sailed to intercept, supported by Vice Admiral Warrender's 2nd Battle Squadron and two cruiser squadrons. In the winter pre-dawn darkness, Warrender's destroyers ran into the German main body which, timidly assuming that it was about to encounter the whole Grand Fleet, turned away. Typically, Beatty gave chase, his four battle-cruisers (led by the *Lion*) actually pursuing a force of 22 battleships, two armoured cruisers, seven light cruisers and 54 destroyers! This farcical situation was ended abruptly by the news that both Scarborough and Hartlepool were being shelled. Hipper had split his battle-cruiser force for the task and was in a disadvantageous position, hard by an enemy coast and able to withdraw safely only eastward through a gap in the defensive minefield. But into this gap were thundering both Beatty and Warrender, their forces separated by the shallow southwest patch of the Dogger Bank. Then the weather, previously fine, turned to rain squalls, with poor visibility. Despite this the inimitable Goodenough latched onto the now-retiring Hipper, only to be disengaged by a totally ambiguous signal originating from the *Lion*. Unbelievably, the Germans slipped through. Beatty was heartbroken ('the blackest week of my life') but, rather unfairly, supported censure of Goodenough rather than his own inadequate signal staff.

Only a month later, in January 1915, both Beatty and the outraged British public had a chance for a measure of revenge. Signal traffic warned of another German operation: Hipper, with a light screen, but backed by the might of the High Seas Fleet, was bound for the Dogger Bank area with a vague brief to deal with any British light forces that may have been out.

Left: Admiral Sir David Beatty is seen aboard Lion *with his Flag Captain, Captain A.E. Chatfield. Beatty served with distinction during the Boxer Rebellion of 1900, when he was promoted to captain at the exceptionally early age of 29. The youngest admiral since Nelson, he led the British battlecruiser squadron, and later the battlecruiser fleet, with all the elan of a light cavalryman. It was on the bridge of* Lion *that Beatty made a classic understatement: having seen the destruction of* Indefatigable *and* Queen Mary, *he turned to Chatfield to say, 'There seems to be something wrong with our bloody ships today'*

Right: 'Lion' class battlecruisers at sea prior to the battle of Jutland. Princess Royal and Lion were both damaged during the battle, but even then escaped the fate of their sister ship. Queen Mary was engaged simultaneously by the German battlecruisers Seydlitz and Derfflinger when hits forward and in Q magazine led to an explosion that took the ship and the lives of 67 officers and 1,209 men, leaving only a handful of survivors. Note the anti-torpedo nets, which were swung out on booms under the threat of torpedo attack.

Above: The Lion's *funnel spacing betrays the manner in which the already generous volume devoted to the 42 boilers and turbine machinery was split by siting the fourth turret amidships. Seen here at Invergordon early in 1915,* Lion *has already landed the boats from the after superstructure. Note the paint scheme.*

Right: Splendid cats – Lion *and* Tiger *exercise with an 'R'-class battleship in the offing. Losses suffered at Jutland, though fully justified when weighed against results, discredited the battlecruiser concept and, lacking any clear cut postwar role, they were among the first to be taken out of service following the Washington Treaty.*

Beatty sailed with five battle-cruisers and Goodenough's 1st Light Cruiser Squadron, rendezvousing with Tyrwhitt's Harwich Force in the grey of dawn south-east of the bank. Virtually at that instant, the latter ran into Hipper's screen and, as day broke, the *Lion* led the British line in a tail chase of the already fleeing enemy, whose force was slowed somewhat by the hybrid cruiser/battle-cruiser SMS *Blücher*. By full daylight, in clear conditions, the *Lion* had closed to within 18300 m (20,000 yards) of the *Blücher* (at the rear of Hipper's line), and opened fire with her forward 343-mm (13.5-in) guns. As the range dropped to 16000 m (17,500 yards), Beatty signalled each ship to engage its opposite number but, as Hipper had only four ships, this was ambiguous and resulted in SMS *Derfflinger*, ahead of the *Blücher*, not being engaged at all. Undisturbed, she made good practice, and undoubtedly contributed to the severe punishment soon sustained by the *Lion*. Her fuel contaminated by holed tanks and power generators failing, the *Lion* slowed, signalling the remainder to close the enemy. This was followed by an order to turn eight points to avoid a totally nonexistent submarine. Beatty, losing touch as the battle moved away, signalled 'Course NE', followed too quickly by 'Engage the enemy's rear'. The two signals were read in conjunction, and taken to mean that the force should engage the hapless *Blücher* which, shattered and ablaze, was falling well behind the remainder. With no power for signal projectors and at a range where flags could no longer be interpreted, Beatty lost control of the battle. In vain did he shift his flag, for Hipper's three survivors were beyond reach and the *Blücher* fought to the very end.

Lion damaged

Though the enemy had lost a useful ship and SMS *Seydlitz* had narrowly missed blowing up, an annihilating victory had been lost through poor gunnery, poor initiative and poor signalling. As a fuming Fisher wrote, 'What excuse

The *Lion* in Action

have we to offer?' The *Lion*, hit by an estimated 16 heavy shells, languished under repair for four months.

On return to service, she was flagship of Beatty's reorganized Battle-Cruiser Fleet of three homogeneous squadrons. A quiet year followed, enlivened only by a couple of seaplane raids on the enemy coast and yet another failure to apprehend a hit-and-run attack, on Lowestoft and Yarmouth in April 1916. Only five weeks later came Jutland.

The battle is covered elsewhere but, during the initial 'run to the south', a shell from SMS *Lützow* removed the better part of the roof of 'Q' turret, the resultant explosion and fire in which would have destroyed the ship except for the courageous action of a mortally-wounded Royal Marine officer who promptly flooded the magazine, earning a Victoria Cross. Within 30 minutes Beatty was to see two more of his ships blow up from the same cause, prompting the famous remark to his flag captain that 'there seems to be something wrong with our bloody ships today'.

The *Lion* and her consorts sighted Admiral Scheer's High Seas Fleet, closed it, reported and then drew it to the north onto Jellicoe's guns, finally forcing round the head of the German line to gain time. After the indecisive battle fleet encounter, in the failing light of late dusk, a frustrated Beatty was still in contact with Hipper, unable to goad Jellicoe into further major contact before darkness.

The anti-climax of the end of Jutland was painful for Beatty after his all-out efforts. The *Lion* had sustained 12 heavy hits, HMS *Tiger* 10 and HMS *Princess Royal* six and, on the passage back to Rosyth, the flagship committed 99 dead to the deep. She reported ready for action within two days and was fully repaired within seven weeks.

Beatty's association with the ship ended early in 1917 on his appointment as Commander-in-Chief of the Grand Fleet. The *Lion* took the

flag of Vice Admiral Pakenham but, although at sea as much as ever, was not again to see action.

A victim of the Washington Treaty conditions, she was scrapped at Jarrow in 1924.

Above: An unusual overhead view of Lion *shows the dominant effect on the layout due to the single turret amidships. Much useful superstructure area is lost due to the need for angling it to give the maximum firing arcs, and little can be mounted on it because of blast damage. Note that her torpedo nets have been landed.*

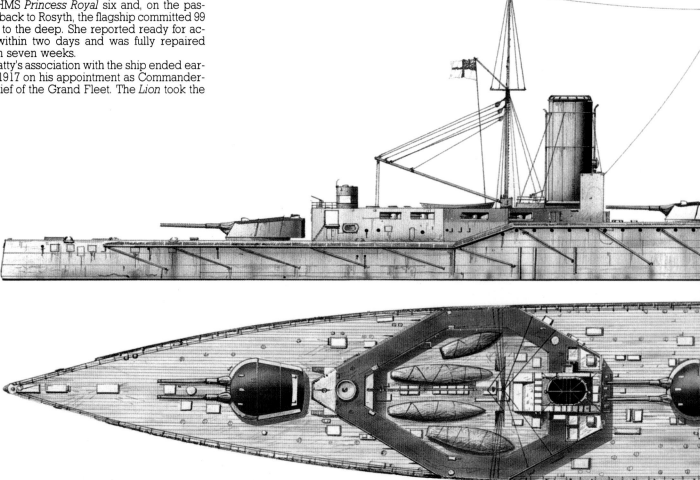

Above: Jutland. Lion is seen steaming at full speed shortly before receiving the near-disastrous hit on 'Q' turret. Bold handling of the battle cruisers by Beatty meant casualties but ensured success in his primary aims of scouting and reporting, containing Hipper and luring the High Seas Fleet onto Jellicoe's massed guns.

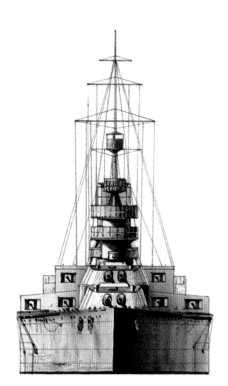

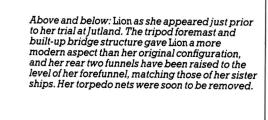

Above and below: Lion as she appeared just prior to her trial at Jutland. The tripod foremast and built-up bridge structure gave Lion a more modern aspect than her original configuration, and her rear two funnels have been raised to the level of her forefunnel, matching those of her sister ships. Her torpedo nets were soon to be removed.

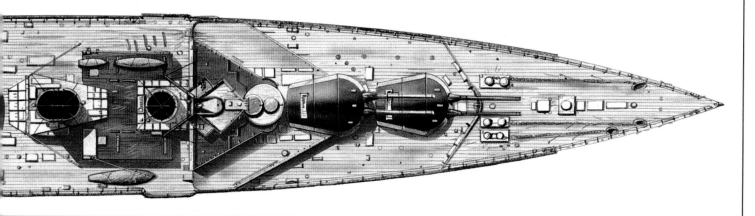

UK
'Renown' class

Orders for the 'Revenge' class battleships were placed in 1914 but then shelved because it was considered that they would not be completed in time for the short war that was anticipated. Following the emphatic success of the battle-cruisers at the Falklands battle of December 1914, however, Admiral Fisher had two units hastily redesigned for delivery in an impossible 15 months as the **'Renown' class**. That they were completed in a little over 18 months as HMS **Renown** and HMS **Repulse** was a credit to the builders, particularly as extra horizontal protection had to be incorporated at a late stage following the awful experiences of Jutland.

The 'Renowns' were the first two-funnelled British battle-cruisers and the first to mount 381-mm (15-in) guns, though only six of these were shipped due to availability over the very short construction period. At a time when the UK was building the fast and well-protected 'Queen Elizabeth' class 'super-Dreadnoughts', the 'Renowns' represented a step backward, though their 32-kt speed placed them in a class of their own.

Their greatest weakness was in vertical protection and, despite subsequent modernizations, this was not easily rectified since the lower edge of the shallow main belt was supported, just below the load waterline, on the upper slope of the large anti-torpedo bulges which, for the first time, had been made an integral part of the hull structure. Another unsatisfactory feature was the reversion to a 102-mm (4-in) secondary armament, most of which was sited in the new triple mounting that was to fall far short of expectations.

Only the *Repulse* saw any real action during World War I, being involved in the messy and indecisive affair in the German Bight in November 1917. Great efforts were made between the wars to rectify the ships' shortcomings, the *Renown* being particularly thoroughly modernized. With improved protection a new secondary armament and a main battery capable of greater elevation, she both took and delivered punishment, being very active as a unit of Force H. The *Repulse* was less fortunate, being sunk with HMS *Prince of Wales* by an overwhelming Japanese air assault that put five torpedoes into her.

Specification
'Renown' class (as built)
Displacement: 27,950 tons standard and 32,725 tons full load
Dimensions: length 242.01 m (794.0 ft); beam 27.43 m (90.0 ft); draught 8.23 m (27.0 ft)
Propulsion: four sets of geared steam turbines delivering 126,000 shp (93958 kW) to four shafts
Speed: 32 kts
Armament: six 381-mm (15-in), 17 102-mm (4-in) and two 76-mm (3-in) AA guns, and two 533-mm (21-in) torpedo tubes
Armour: belt 152 mm (6 in); bulkheads 102 mm (4 in); barbettes 178 mm (7 in); main deck 76 mm (3 in); deck over steering gear 64 mm (2.5 in)
Complement: 970

This late wartime picture shows Renown *(foreground) and* Repulse *in a near-identical phase. Noteworthy is the double row of scuttles along the hull, betraying the absence of any vertical armour belt above the waterline. This was rectified soon after the war.* Renown *particularly was to undergo considerable modification.*

Renown *is seen after the fitting of aircraft flying-off platforms on both 'B' and after turrets, and the searchlights re-arranged on separate towers by the after funnel.*

Even with oil-firing they were still capable of generating vast quantities of smoke, and the forefunnel had to be raised even before completion.

UK
'Bellerophon' class

The three 'Billy Ruffians' would have been four but for a slower-than-expected foreign response to HMS *Dreadnought*. Laid down within months of the latter's completion, they incorporated only minor changes on virtually the same dimensions. Ten 45-calibre 305-mm (12-in) guns were arranged similarly in five turrets; of these the foremost was at forecastle deck level and the remainder one deck lower, two of them sided in the waist and two on the centreline aft. Theoretically, the layout allowed between six and eight guns to bear in any direction. All completed in 1909, the 'Bellerophons' were HMS **Bellerophon**, HMS **Temeraire** and HMS **Superb**.

One great improvement over the *Dreadnought* herself was the substitution of 102-mm (4-in) secondary guns in place of the prototype's near-useless 12-pdr weapons. The 'all-big-gun' doctrine had been taken too literally and the ship was practically helpless against determined torpedo boat attack (a mistake later echoed in the all-missile armaments of the early 1960s). Sixteen larger weapons enabled the 'Bellerophons' to engage such targets at safer ranges, although eight of the guns were sited vulnerably on the turret roofs. That the torpedo was being taken very seriously was evidenced by improved subdivision, notably a 51-mm (2-in) longitudinal bulkhead running the greater length of the ship on each side.

The *Dreadnought*'s masting arrangements had been highly unsatisfactory, a single tripod foremast set abaft the forward funnel and supporting the control top in smoke and heat. The follow-ons had two lofty tripods, each forward of a funnel, with the control tops pre-war providing the base for tall W/T extensions.

The steam turbine machinery was similar to that in the prototype with the boilers accepting coal, oil or patent fuel, all three of which were carried.

Following the Bellerophons were three more virtual repeats, HMS **St Vincent**, HMS **Collingwood** and HMS **Vanguard** of the **'St Vincent'** class, whose major advance was the adop-

Unlike Dreadnought, *the 'Bellerophons' had their foremasts ahead of their forefunnels, which had the great advantage of keeping the control tops out of the smoke. Main and secondary armament was otherwise unchanged from* Dreadnought.

Above: The 'Billy Ruffian' (i.e. Bellerophon) and her two sisters were, essentially, improved Dreadnoughts. They had a similar main battery, similarly disposed.

tion of an improved 50-calibre gun in the main battery. All six ships went through Jutland without a single casualty but the *Vanguard* was destroyed by a magazine explosion in 1917. The remainder fell victim to the terms of the Washington Treaty in the 1920s.

Specification
'Bellerophon' class
Displacement: 18,800 tons standard and 22,100 tons full load
Dimensions: length 160.32 m (526.0 ft); beam 25.15 m (82.5 ft); draught 8.31 m (27.25 ft)

Propulsion: four sets of geared steam turbines delivering 23,000 shp (17151 kW) to four shafts
Speed: 21 kts
Armament: 10 305-mm (12-in), 16 102-mm (4-in) and four 3-pdr guns, and three 457-mm (18-in) torpedo tubes

Armour: belt 254 mm (10 in) amidships; transverse bulkheads 203 mm (8 in); barbettes 228 mm (9 in); upper deck 19 mm (0.75 in); middle deck 76 mm (3 in); lower deck 102 mm (4 in)
Complement: 735

 UK
'Colossus' class

Both 'Colossus' class ships (HMS *Colossus* and HMS *Hercules*, both completed in 1911) were virtual repeats of the single HMS *Neptune*, laid down some six months before, and showed no significant improvements over her. The *Neptune* herself carried the same main battery as the preceding 'St Vincents' but, in answer to foreign practice, this was laid out so that 10-gun broadsides were possible. To achieve this, the two waist turrets were disposed en echelon, enabling them to fire across the deck, albeit on restricted arcs. Considerable extra stiffening and blast-proofing needed to be incorporated as a consequence. The layout also demanded more length, though this was mitigated somewhat by the adoption, for the first time in the Royal Navy, of superimposed turrets aft.

All 16 102-mm (4-in) guns of the secondary armament were sited behind blast screens within the superstructure blocks. The new layout also severely limited the stowage space for the many boats then carried, so distinctive flying decks were introduced for the purpose. As these were deemed likely to be destroyed in action, thus fouling the amidships guns,

Scapa's low hills form the inhospitable backdrop to the Colossus *and the three 'Bellerophons', all of which were serving in the Fourth Battle Squadron.*

one at least was removed in war.

Another effect of the main battery layout was the fragmentation of the ship's internal arrangements. Despite this, the ships were innovatory in being fitted with separate cruising turbines to improve fuel economy at lower speeds.

The superimposition of X-turret decreased the ships' stability range, probably the reason behind the reversion in the two repeat ships to the *Dreadnought*'s layout of a single, lofty tripod. Though often criticized, this arrangement must have proved satisfactory, as it was repeated in further classes. Indeed, the *Neptune*'s after control top was later removed as being almost uninhabitable through smoke and heat. A curious change of thought in the design of the follow-on pair was the abandonment of longitudinal anti-torpedo bulkheads in favour of slightly heavier belt armour. The *Colossus*

herself was the only Grand Fleet battleship of the class to suffer heavy-calibre shell damage, but on an insufficient scale to verify the soundness of this new arrangement.

Specification
'Colossus' class
Displacement: 20,220 tons standard and 23,050 tons full load
Dimensions: length 166.42 m (546.0 ft) beam 25.91 m (85.0 ft); draught 7.70 m (25.25 ft)

Propulsion: four sets of geared steam turbines delivering 25,000 shp (18643 kW) to four shafts
Speed: 21 kts
Armament: 10 305-mm (12-in) and 16 102-mm (4-in) guns, and three 533-mm (21-in) torpedo tubes
Armour: belt 279 mm (11 in); transverse bulkheads 254 mm (10 in); barbettes 279 mm (11 in); main deck 38 mm (1.5 in); middle deck 44.5 mm (1.75 in); lower deck 102 mm (4 in)
Complement: 755

 UK
'Agincourt' class

HMS *Agincourt* was unique. She was ordered from Elswick by Brazil in the course of one of the periodic 'one-upmanship' exercises conducted by the larger South American states to this day. Four impressive designs had been short-listed, that chosen reverting to the 305-mm (12-in) gun (at a time when the British standard was 343-mm/13.5-in) for reasons of commonality with two ships already serving. Even so, no less than 14 barrels were mounted, in seven twin turrets, the most in any battleship. All were sited on the centreline to permit 14-gun broadsides, a spectacle that reportedly was not to be missed. This arrangement demanded a very long hull with, consequently, a reduced standard of protection to cover it. The secondary and tertiary batteries were on an equally lavish scale, with 20 152-mm (6-in) and 10 76-mm (3-in) guns.

Shortly after the ship's launch as the *Rio de Janeiro* in 1913, her owners discovered that their ambitions had outstripped their purse and put her up for sale. She was acquired by Turkey, on

whose account another battleship was being completed in the UK, and renamed *Sultan Osman I*. Both, perhaps unfortunately, were completed in the very month of the outbreak of war and, despite being very much 'odd-balls', were appropriated by the Royal Navy as the *Agincourt* and HMS *Erin*. This windfall was, however, acquired at great cost for the irate Turks were placated by a prompt German offer of immediate replacement, which action greatly influenced Turkey's entering the enemy camp. Despite the undoubted firepower of the ship, it was fortunate that she was never severely tested in action for the hull was weak as well as being underprotected, and three of the seven turrets had res-

Unique in the Grand Fleet, the Agincourt *is seen here at gunnery practice. The immense length of hull*

tricted firing arcs. Offered for sale again to Brazil after the war, she was rejected and prematurely found her way to the breakers in the early 1920s in the company of much other useful tonnage.

to accommodate seven centreline turrets is apparent.

Specification
'Agincourt' class
Displacement: 27,500 tons standard and 30,250 tons full load
Dimensions: length 204.67 m (671.5 ft); beam 27.12 m (89.0 ft); draught 8.23 m (27.0 ft)
Propulsion: four sets of geared steam turbines delivering 34,000 shp (25354 kW) to four shafts
Speed: 22 kts
Armament: 14 305-mm (12-in), 20 152-mm (6-in) and 10 76-mm (3-in) guns, and three 533-mm (21-in) torpedo tubes
Armour: belt 229 mm (9 in); bulkheads 152 mm (6 in); barbettes 229 mm (9 in); main deck 38 mm (1.5 in); middle deck 38 mm (1.5 in); lower deck 25 mm (1 in)
Complement: 1,270

Agincourt is seen in her original form with flying-boat decks. The central turrets had restricted arcs of fire, and the long hull was weak and underprotected.

Jutland

After two years of shadow boxing, the spring of 1916 saw the two greatest fleets in the world at sea and steaming towards each other. If they met, then a battle unlike any previously fought could be expected. The place was Jutland Bank; the date 31 May. Over the following two days some 25 vessels were to be lost, with almost 9,000 sailors dead on both sides.

Indefatigable, with her sister New Zealand, forming the Second Battle Cruiser Squadron at Jutland, is seen at high speed. They could be distinguished from the 'Invincibles' by their equispaced funnels, allowing for improved chances of a full broadside with echeloned amidships turrets. Note the very high boat stowage.

At 14.20 on 31 May 1916, the British light cruiser HMS *Galatea* made an 'enemy in sight' signal and, with her consorts, went on to engage German light units that had stopped a neutral merchantman. The British ships were attached to Admiral Beatty who, with six battle-cruisers and four 'Queen Elizabeth' class battleships, almost immediately came in to assist. But the German ships also possessed heavy backing in the shape of Admiral Hipper's five battle-cruisers: these too bore in, sighting Beatty at 15.20. It was a fine, if hazy, spring afternoon and the position just west of the Jutland Bank. One of the greatest and most contentious of sea battles was about to commence.

Hipper was in fact out to be seen, his task being to lure out a sizable British squadron, preferably Beatty's, and lead it back into the arms of the main body of the High Seas Fleet for destruction. This body, built around 16 Dreadnoughts and six pre-Dreadnoughts under the overall command of Admiral Scheer, was following some 80 km (50 miles) to the south, and if as expected Beatty steered to cut Hipper off from his bases, he would find himself nicely caught between two fires.

Unfortunately for German plans, much of their routine radio traffic was being monitored and decoded by the British who, with adequate warning of an impending operation, had also sailed the full available strength of the Grand Fleet under Admiral Jellicoe, whose 24 Dreadnoughts were about 113 km (70 miles) to the north of Beatty.

For the moment, as they closed each other, neither battle-cruiser admiral was aware of the presence of these enormous concentrations. It was 15.48 before the opposing forces opened fire, the haze not allowing the British to make use of the superior range of their larger guns. Hipper manoeuvred to keep the ranges short, the tracks parallel and the course southward towards Scheer. His shooting was rapid and accurate and, at 16.02, HMS *Indefatigable* at the tail of the British line was smitten by three simultaneous hits, suffered an explosion and began to settle aft. A minute later she took another salvo forward and disintegrated in a massive magazine explosion.

Within minutes, the slower HMS *Queen Elizabeth* had crept within range, and her forward 381-mm (15-in) guns began to punish the tail of the German line. Beatty impetuously strove to close further and paid the price at 16.26, when the enemy gunners found HMS *Queen Mary*: several hits amidships resulted probably in flash penetrating down to 'Q' turret handling room and magazine, the ship breaking in two in a series of colossal explosions. HMS *Lion*, Beatty's flagship, had narrowly missed a similar fate when hit at 16.00.

Throughout the battle the hazy conditions were accentuated by funnel and gun smoke. This was the scene from the light cruiser Birmingham *at about 16.00, just before the* Indefatigable *blew up. Beatty's battle cruisers are to the right and the Fifth Battle Squadron, under fire from Hipper, to the left, with light cruisers beyond.*

Shortly before the end of the *Queen Mary*, both Beatty and Hipper had ordered destroyer torpedo attacks on the other to relieve the pressure. Under this new threat, Hipper broke off the action temporarily at 16.36 by a turn to the eastward. At this juncture, however, the light cruiser HMS *Southampton*, commanded by the admirable Commodore Goodenough, stationed a little ahead of Beatty, sighted the lead ships of Scheer's main body pounding up from the south. Hipper had done his job perfectly and the stage was now Beatty's. Though surprised by the advancing armada, Beatty did not wait to be annihilated, turning on his heel at 16.46 and taking the shortest course to Jellicoe's position, now some 80 km (50 miles) to the north west. Beatty had now become the lure, the means of delivering the unsuspecting Scheer, now in exuberant full cry, into the grateful hands of the Grand Fleet. To do this successfully, he had both to survive and to ensure that Hipper's marauding battle-cruisers did not sight Jellicoe prematurely.

Beatty lures Scheer

Beatty's attached battleships were somewhat tardy in executing their 16-point turn but, falling in astern, covered his rear and, between 16.50 and 17.30, made good practice on the enemy, inflicting 20 hits for only 13 in return. Hipper remained tenaciously in contact with Beatty, the poor visibility which limited their exchanges gradually improving in favour of the latter who, with the lowering sun behind him, succeeded in forcing an enemy disengagement at 17.51. In turning away, however, Hipper faced disaster in running straight into a new opponent in the shape of Rear Admiral Hood's 3rd Battle-cruiser Squadron but succeeded in turning south west and gaining sanctuary at the head of Scheer's force, which was steering about north east. The time was 18.10 and, between them, Beatty and Hood had prevented the sorely-punished Hipper from sighting Jellicoe's van.

Only about 19 km (12 miles) now separated SMS *König* at the head of the German line from HMS *Marlborough*, the closest of Jellicoe's battleships. These were steaming in six parallel columns (each of four ships) and needed to be deployed into line without delay. This manoeuvre would take at least 15 minutes and had to be correct first time. Jellicoe was undecided on account of a dearth of reliable information on the enemy's bearing, speed and disposition. At this juncture (18.14) Beatty, in the rapidly narrowing gap between the two fleets, made contact, the *Marlborough* sighting his gun flashes. Jellicoe acted swiftly, deploying into line on his port column, steering to the east with the port column leader HMS *King George V* at the head and himself, in the flagship HMS *Iron Duke*, lying ninth in line.

With the *Queen Elizabeth* bringing up the rear, the Grand Fleet presented a solid wall of guns some 9.6 km (6 miles) in length, and not a moment too soon. Even as they manoeuvred into position, the 'Queen Elizabeths' of the 5th Battle Squadron sighted the German line at close range. They attracted heavy fire, at which juncture HMS *Warspite*'s helm jammed, causing the ship to describe two complete circles and to sustain 13 large-calibre hits.

At the head of the British line, Beatty and Hood were again jousting with their opposite numbers when HMS *Invincible* was hit, disintegrating even as had the other two battle-cruisers before her. The British line had, by

At 18.30 Hood's flagship Invincible was leading the British line as it forced the head of the High Seas Fleet around to the eastward. At 18.33, under fire from about five enemy ships at short range, she was heavily hit on 'Q' turret amidships. The picture shows the roaring inferno of the magazine fire that preceded the fatal explosion.

As Jellicoe's fleet turned to starboard by divisions at 18.55 following Scheer's 'battle turnaway', the Benbow passed this remarkable sight. Her crew cheered, assuming the wreck was German, but it was that of the Invincible, destroyed 20 minutes earlier. Only three survivors were rescued by the destroyer Badger, also visible.

Hipper's battlecruisers at Jutland, despite suffering more actual hits, showed a remarkable capacity for survival. The Derfflinger (seen at a later date) was instrumental in the destruction of both Invincible and Queen Mary, yet herself survived 21 recorded hits, returning with over 3,000 tons of water in her hull.

now, successfully 'crossed the enemy's T' and was pouring an intolerable fire into the head of Scheer's column, which was in a poor position to reply. At 18.33, therefore, Scheer risked all on a simultaneous 16-point turnaway; peacetime practice paid off as, without collision, the German line just melted from the sight of the British gunlayers. Jellicoe's line swung to the south east by divisions and might have missed the Germans, who were moving westward, but for the tenacity of Goodenough's scouting cruisers.

Jutland

Possibly not appreciating his favourable position, Scheer now surprisingly again turned 16 points, running straight at the British who, with the gloom at their backs, made the most of their chance, inflicting about 35 quick hits virtually without reply. Hipper's *Lützow* had had to retire with severe damage, but Scheer sent the remaining four battle-cruisers, already severely damaged themselves, on a suicidal charge at Beatty, synchronized with a destroyer attack. These diversions worked and, as Jellicoe turned away before the threat of the torpedoes, Scheer was able to make a third about-turn.

Little daylight was left and the British had become disengaged, between 19.35 and 20.00, the Grand Fleet very deliberately coming around onto a westerly course. Sunset was at 20.19 and the enemy was in a ragged line heading southward for the Horns Reef channel and home.

The battle-cruisers were still in contact, and Beatty began to show impatience at Jellicoe's apparent lack of urgency in forcing a decision by cutting off Scheer's line of retreat. Even as Hipper's ships became little but dim silhouettes, Beatty remained, pressing him hard.

Action avoided

Jellicoe did not relish a night action, which would throw away his numerical advantage on a chancy encounter for which the Germans were, in any case, better trained. At 20.45, when a cruiser reported to the British lead ship, *King George V*, that enemy battleships were

only 8 km (5 miles) distant, the contact was not prosecuted on the grounds that they were probably Beatty's ships!

The British admiral made his night dispositions in the belief that Scheer could not slip across his bows and would be prevented from crossing astern through his stationing there of massed destroyer flotillas. Action would be resumed at dawn.

Scheer did not oblige, his line passing in stages through Jellicoe's light forces. These fought bravely and at great sacrifice but in vain;

A 'Nassau' class battleship fires a salvo from her amidships guns. Though six turrets were included in the design, only four could bear on either beam. The four 'Nassaus' formed the Second Battleship Division at Jutland but, being elderly, were positioned well back in the line.

without heavy back-up they could not prevent the enemy bursting through. Quite astoundingly, these furious actions were observed by the end of the British line, the battleships neither intervening nor informing Jellicoe of what was occurring.

The battle reached a decisive point at about 18.30. Scheer's High Seas Fleet, engrossed in chasing Beatty's battle cruisers, was confronted by Jellicoe and the Grand Fleet, some 10 km (6 miles) of heavy guns in a line across his bows. The battleship King George V *headed the British line, followed by* Ajax, Centurion, Erin, Orion, Monarch, Conqueror, Thunderer *and the rest of the fleet led by the flagship,* Iron Duke.

By 01.00 on 1 June Scheer had broken through and, even though still challenged by light forces up to 02.00, no longer had the Grand Fleet athwart his route home. At about 03.00 the *Iron Duke* turned about. Jutland was over.

The British had lost three battle-cruisers, three armoured cruisers and eight destroyers to a battleship, a battle-cruiser, four cruisers and five destroyers. Manpower losses were 6,100 British to 2,550 German dead, but the victory that the latter claimed was hollow for, tactically, no beaten fleet ever chased a victor back into port and, strategically, the situation at sea had not changed.

British gunnery had been the better, many more German ships being heavily damaged, but the latter survived because of their better compartmentation, because a greater proportion of their displacement was devoted to protection and because British shells tended to explode on contact rather than on penetration.

During the night phase, the enemy made good use of his knowledge of British challenges and responses. While the British light forces held fire through lack of positive identification, the Germans would suddenly overwhelm them with searchlights and gunfire. They also bluffed to good effect, saving several damaged ships thereby. Poor British leadership that night was acted upon, and was rectified 25 years later at Matapan.

It has been said that Jellicoe, cautious and heavily aware of his responsibilities, 'fought to make a German victory impossible rather than a British victory certain'. That about sums it up.

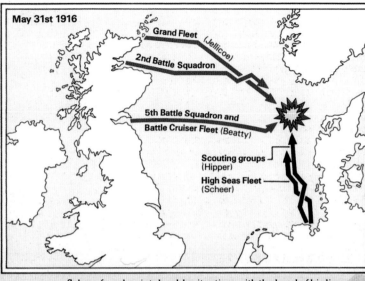

Scheer faced an intolerable situation, with the head of his line receiving severe punishment. Konig, at the head of the line, was losing speed, and was taking water in the bow, and Grosser Kurfurst and Markgraf were also being hit. Scheer's remedy was a manoeuvre practised in peacetime: a simultaneous 16-point (180°) turn, reversing course in as short a time as possible.

UK
'Queen Elizabeth' class

One of the most successful classes of capital ships ever built, the five units of the **'Queen Elizabeth' class** were also the first true fast battleships. This resulted from the decision to mount 381-mm (15-in) guns, the current British 343-mm (13.5-in) weapon being already surpassed by larger foreign calibres. Though there was no question of building ships large enough to take the accepted 10-gun main battery, an eight-gun battery was deemed acceptable as its broadside weight was 6940 kg (15,300 lb) compared with the 6350 kg (14,000 lb) of 10 343-mm (13.5-in) guns. The abandonment of the amidships turret was further advantageous in that the machinery spaces beneath were not fragmented. As a result the 29,000-shp (21625-kW) machinery of the preceding 'Iron Dukes' could be increased to 75,000 shp (55927 kW), giving 24 kts despite a larger hull. With improved speed and gun range, the 'Queen Elizabeths' were judged able to accept protection on a slightly reduced scale and their greatly increased bunker requirements were met by the adoption of all-oil firing. One drawback was that much bunker space lay between the outer skin and the longitudinal 'torpedo bulkheads'. As oil is incompressible this space could no longer satisfactorily absorb an explosion; moreover, if essentially empty it could well be filled with an explosive vapour. The three 1915 units were HMS **Queen Elizabeth**, HMS **Warspite** and HMS **Barham**, while the two 1916 units were HMS **Valiant** and HMS **Malaya**.

The powerful 16 152-mm (6-in) secondary battery was feasible only by siting the majority in casemates, a layout already so completely discredited as to guarantee that only the nameship was thus completed.

Four of the class were present at Jutland as the homogeneous 5th Battle Squadron which, because of its speed, was attached to Beatty's battle-cruiser force rather than to the main body of the Grand Fleet. They thus became heavily engaged at a critical point of the battle. Between them they suffered 27 major calibre hits, the Valiant coming through unscathed but the Warspite taking 13. They were well able to absorb it and all were again fully operational by the following month. All were modified in varying degrees between the wars and all were active in the second, in which only the Barham became a total loss.

Specification
'Queen Elizabeth' class (as built)
Displacement: 29,150 tons standard and 33,000 tons full load
Dimensions: length 196.82 m (645.75 ft); beam 27.58 m (90.5 ft); draught 9.35 m (30.66 ft)
Propulsion: four sets of geared steam turbines delivering 75,000 shp (55927 kW) to four shafts
Speed: 24 kts
Armament: eight 381-mm (15-in), 14 152-mm (6-in) and two 76-mm (3-in) AA guns, and four 533-mm (21-in) torpedo tubes
Armour: belt 330 mm (13 in); bulkheads 152-mm (6-in); barbettes 254 mm (10 in); upper deck 44 mm (1.75 in); main deck 32 mm (1.25 in); middle deck 25 mm (1 in); lower deck 76 mm (3 in)
Complement: 950

The Queen Elizabeth *toward the end of the war, recognizable by her masts of virtually equal height. Soon after this, aircraft flying-off platforms were added to each of the* superimposed turrets. The lighting puts the casemate guns into high relief, only the forward ones being fitted. The spotting balloon lies beyond.

Lying in the stream on a starboard anchor, with the port anchor 'a-cockbill', the Queen Elizabeth *presents a peaceful scene with awnings rigged.*

Possibly the finest class of battleship to see action in World War I, the 'Queen Elizabeths' were fast and well armoured.

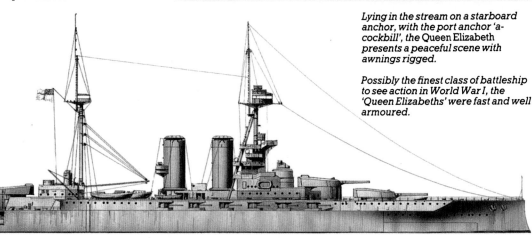

GERMANY
'Deutschland' class

Last of the German pre-Dreadnoughts, the five **'Deutschland' class** ships continued the progression of small battleships dimensioned for the North Sea and Baltic use rather than worldwide deployment. Together with the very similar 'Braunschweigs' that preceded them, they marked a major step forward in the adoption of the 280-mm (11-in) gun in place of earlier classes' 240-mm (9.4-in) weapon. Following contemporary practice, the main battery of four guns was disposed in twin barbette mountings forward and aft. A heavy secondary battery of 14 170-mm (6.7-in) weapons was flawed by being sited in low casemates. Six torpedo tubes were carried (two on each beam, one above the forefoot and one offset beneath the counter). The ships, all completed between 1904 and 1906, were SMS **Deutschland**, SMS **Hannover**, SMS **Pommern**, SMS **Schlesien** and SMS **Schleswig-Holstein**.

Well armoured for their size, the ships had a protective lower deck that ran full length. At main deck level a strip of light horizontal armour ran the length of each side of the central redoubt, protecting the casemates. No torpedo bulkheads were fitted, the inadequacy of the wing coal bunker spaces for protection being demonstrated when the *Pommern* was torpedoed by a British destroyer in the closing stages of Jutland. The resulting magazine explosion destroyed both the ship and her 839 crew.

A funnel originally served each of

Ploughing through a peaceful pre-war sea, the Schleswig-Holstein *was the very last German pre-Dreadnought. Only one 280-mm (11-in) turret is sited at each end, and all seven casemated 170-mm (6.7-in) guns are seen trained on the beam. The 'blisters' of the original bow-chasers have been plated over to give extra accommodation space.*

the three boiler rooms, but in later modernizations of the *Schlesien* and the *Schleswig-Holstein* the two forward stacks were combined in one.

The latter ship had the doubtful distinction of firing the first naval shots of World War II when, on 1 September 1939, she bombarded the Polish positions at Westerplatte, near Danzig (now Gdansk). Both old ships were destroyed in Baltic waters in the final stages of the war.

Specification
'Deutschland' class (as built)
Displacement: 12,980 tons standard and 13,990 tons full load
Dimensions: length 127.60 m

The 'Deutschland' class were made immediately obsolete by HMS Dreadnought. *Two were sunk in the Baltic.*

(418.64 ft); beam 22.20 m (72.83 ft); draught 8.20 m (26.90 ft)
Propulsion: three triple-expansion steam engines delivering 20,000 ihp (14914 kW) to three shafts
Speed: 18 kts
Armament: four 280-mm (11-in), 14 170-mm (6.7-in) and 20 88-mm (3.46-in) guns, and six 450-mm (17.7-in) torpedo tubes
Armour: belt 240 mm (9.45 in); bulkheads 170 mm (6.7 in); barbettes 250 mm (9.84 in); deck 40 mm (1.6 in)
Complement: 743

GERMANY
'Moltke' class

Though Germany's first battle-cruiser SMS *Von der Tann* carried an eight-gun main battery disposed similarly to that in her British contemporaries, the 280-mm (11-in) calibre threw a significantly lower broadside weight than the British 305-mm (12-in) battery. Even before the *Von der Tann*'s launch, therefore, the first of an enlarged pair of follow-ons was laid down. These two examples of the **'Moltke' class** retained the smaller calibre, though in an improved version, but added an extra, superimposed turret aft. The forecastle deck level was continued aft to this point, raising both of the amidships turrets and the casemated secondary armament. SMS *Moltke* was completed in 1911, SMS *Goeben* following in 1912.

Turbine-propelled, their legend speed was inferior to that of their British equivalents though, in practice, they could well hold their own. Better protected than even the later British 'Lion' class, they were shorter but beamier, well subdivided and stable.

The *Moltke* served with Admiral Hipper's battle-cruiser squadron throughout the war, twice surviving torpedoing by British submarines. She was the least damaged of Hipper's ships at Jutland, though receiving four heavy-calibre hits (one 305-mm/12-in piercing her main belt at long range) and taking aboard 1,000 tons of water. She fought at Heligoland Bight and Dogger Bank and achieved notoriety by assisting in the bombardment of British east coast towns, coat-trailing

Ostensibly slower than their British contemporaries, the 'Moltke' class were more effective fighting ships as a result of superior protection. SMS Goeben *entered Turkish waters in 1914, and from then operated under the Turkish flag (although retaining her German crew till 1918).*

exercises designed to entice out elements of the British fleet into prepared ambush.

The *Goeben* became something of a *cause célèbre* when, at the very outset, she evaded the British Mediterranean Fleet to reach Turkey as a replacement for the latter's appropriated battleships (see the *Agincourt* entry). Under Turkish colours, but German-crewed, she spent the war largely 'in-

being', threatening the Black Sea and Levant. In action several times, she survived mining, grounding and bombing. Days before hostilities ended, she was finally handed over, to serve as the Turkish *Yavuz* to as late as 1963.

Specification
'Moltke' class (as built)
Displacement: 22,610 tons standard

Looking distinctly weather-worn, the Moltke *was sister to the* Goeben *and near-sister of* Seydlitz. *Later German battlecruisers had a more compact look, dropping the echeloned amidships turrets in favour of fewer but larger guns, sited in superimposed turrets at either end.*

and 25,000 tons full load
Dimensions: length 186.50 m (611.88 ft); beam 29.50 m (96.78 ft); draught 9.20 m (30.18 ft)
Propulsion: two sets of geared steam turbines delivering 85,500 shp (63757 kW) to four shafts
Speed: 28 kts
Armament: 10 280-mm (11-in) and 12 150-mm (5.9-in) guns, and four 500-mm (19.7-in) torpedo tubes
Armour: belt 270 mm (10.6 in); barbettes 250 mm (9.84 in); deck 50 mm (1.97 in)
Complement: 1,053

'Helgoland' class

Germany's first Dreadnoughts, the four 'Nassaus' of 1907, were remarkable mainly for their conservatism. Limited in length and draught, they were made exceptionally beamy. With the requirement for an eight-gun broadside, yet lacking the length for sufficient centreline turrets, the designers opted for six twin turrets, set in a hexagon. Although the hull was very well compartmented, it was badly broken up by the main battery disposition. The reciprocating engines and 280-mm (11-in) guns of the preceding pre-Dreadnoughts were retained.

The four **'Helgoland' class** units followed in the next year, the ships being essentially 'Nassaus' scaled up to take a 305-mm (12-in) main battery. This was disposed similarly, the ships being almost equally portly. They were also fitted with reciprocating engines, despite the fact that the pioneer battle-cruiser SMS *Von der Tann* had been equipped with steam turbines in the previous year. The machinery had been upgraded, however, from triple to quadruple expansion and, when pushed, the three engines could drive the ships at 21 kts, as fast as their British contemporaries. An odd reversion was to three funnels, particularly surprising as the three boiler rooms were adjacent, whereas in the two-funnelled 'Nassaus' these spaces were divided two-and-one. The first three units were SMS *Thüringen*, SMS *Helgoland* and SMS *Ostfriesland*, all completed in 1911, joined in 1912 by SMS *Oldenburg*.

The topweight of the main battery was probably the reason for the whole 14-gun secondary armament being sited in the casemates too low to be of any practical use.

At Jutland, the *Thüringen* shattered the British armoured cruiser HMS *Black Prince* in a chance night encounter. The *Helgoland* received one heavy hit and the *Ostfriesland* struck a mine during the retirement. All four were disposed of as post-war reparations, the *Ostfriesland* going to the United States and being sunk in celebrated but controversial aerial bombing trials. These would seem to have indicated that topside direct hits could be absorbed but the concussive effect of a near miss could prove fatal.

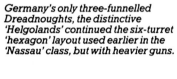

Specification
'Helgoland' class
Displacement: 22,440 tons standard and 24,310 tons full load
Dimensions: length 167.20 m (548.55 ft); beam 28.50 m (93.5 ft); draught 8.90 m (29.2 ft)
Propulsion: three quadruple-expansion steam engines delivering 28,000 ihp (20880 kW) to three shafts
Speed: 20 kts
Armament: 12 305-mm (12-in) and 14 150-mm (5.9-in) guns, and six 500-mm (19.7-in) torpedo tubes
Armour: belt 300 mm (11.8 in); bulkheads 300 mm (11.8 in); barbettes 270 mm (10.6 in); deck 55 mm (2.17 in)
Complement: 1,110

Unlike British Dreadnoughts, the first two classes of all big-gunned ships in the German navy retained the less efficient reciprocating engine. The four vessels in the 'Helgoland' class saw action with Battle Squadron I at Jutland, where Helgoland and Ostfriesland received some damage.

Germany's only three-funnelled Dreadnoughts, the distinctive 'Helgolands' continued the six-turret 'hexagon' layout used earlier in the 'Nassau' class, but with heavier guns.

'Baden' class

Rumours that caused the British to opt for 381-mm (15-in) guns in the 'Revenge' and 'Queen Elizabeth' classes were true, their contemporaries, the **'Baden' class**, receiving the marginally smaller 380-mm weapon. As the Germans had considered their existing 305-mm (12-in) gun to be only slightly inferior to the British 343-mm (13.5-in) gun, they did not develop an equivalent intermediate calibre, so the eventual step was the greater and the results initially disappointing in SMS *Baden* and SMS *Bayern*, each completed in 1916.

The preceding 'Kaiser' and 'König' classes had each shipped a 10-gun main battery, the former with superimposed after turrets and two echeloned mounts amidships, and the latter much improved with superimposition at each end and a single centreline turret in the waist. Like their British counterparts, the designers of the 'Baden' class found that four of the larger twin mountings was the best that could be practically accommodated, the similar arrangement of two superimposed turrets, forward and aft, also requiring a shorter protected citadel. Though very

thoroughly subdivided by virtue of longitudinal bulkheads and coal bunkers stretching continuously from 'A' to 'Y' turrets, the degree of protection in the 'Badens' was afterwards reckoned to be inferior to that of the British 'Revenges'. Coal firing was inferior on several counts (e.g. awkward bunkering and refuelling and large quantities of smoke produced at speed) but necessary because Germany could not guarantee her oil supplies in time of war.

Of the planned class of four, only the *Baden* and *Bayern* were ever completed and neither of these saw much useful action. Both of the others (*Sachsen* and *Württemberg*) could have been finished well before the Armistice, but again like the British, the Germans needed to put their priorities

elsewhere in the prosecution of a 'short' war. In 1919 both ships were scuttled by their crews at Scapa, the *Bayern* successfully and the *Baden* being beached by the Royal Navy. Taken south to Portsmouth, she was thoroughly evaluated before being sunk in the English Channel as a gunnery target.

Specification
'Baden' class
Displacement: 28,060 tons standard and 31,700 tons full load
Dimensions: length 180.00 m (590.55 ft); beam 30.00 m (98.43 ft); draught 9.40 m (30.84 ft)
Propulsion: three sets of geared steam turbines delivering 48,000 shp (35794 kW) to three shafts
Speed: 22 kts
Armament: eight 380-mm (15-in), 16 150-mm (5.9-in) and four 88-mm (3.46-in) guns, and five 600-mm (23.6-in) torpedo tubes
Armour: belt 350 mm (13.8 in); bulkheads 200 mm (7.9 in); barbettes 350 mm (13.8 in); upper deck 120 mm (4.7 in); middle deck 50 mm (1.97 in); lower deck 40 mm (1.6 in)
Complement: 1,170

Developed as a reaction to rumours of the British 'Queen Elizabeth' class, the 'Baden' class was a less successful design. Coal fired, and with a less effective main armament, the two completed saw little in the way of action.

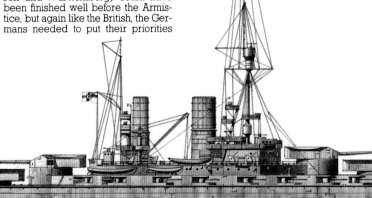

Pre-Dreadnought Battleships

The battleships with which Japan crushed the Russian fleet in 1905 were rendered obsolete just nine months later by the launch of HMS Dreadnought. Capital ship design was revolutionized, and earlier battleships became known as 'pre-Dreadnoughts', but despite their inferiority they saw extensive action during World War I.

To be 'pre-Dreadnought' in August 1914 was to be obsolete, but to be obsolete was not necessarily to be useless. Smaller, slower and far more lightly armed than 'Dreadnoughts', these ships had to be retained in the battle lines until they could be replaced. This, of course, took time; in the Royal Navy for instance, the famous 'Wobbly Eight' were with Jellicoe's main body until the spring of 1915, but the Germans were obliged to keep them in the first team for much longer, a squadron actually serving at Jutland. At the outbreak of World War I, the newest pre-Dreadnoughts were only recently commissioned (e.g. the British 'Lord Nelsons' in 1908, the German 'Deutschlands' 1906-8 and the French 'Dantons' as late as 1911). They were well-built and some of a transitional nature with 'heavy' and 'semi-heavy' batteries rather than the three-tier armament structures of earlier examples. Thus they furnished a valuable and, in some cases, expendable means of establishing and maintaining sea control away from the main area of the North Sea.

About 50 pre-Dreadnoughts were available to the Royal Navy. Not all were in a condition for prolonged active service, and the oldest became guard/training ships, transports or storeships. Those in the active fleet served worldwide, from South America to North Russia, from the Caribbean to Hong Kong, releasing more modern and useful units for the Grand Fleet. No less than 16 were involved with the Dardanelles operation, five being sunk. They were particularly useful here (as off the Belgian coast) in fire support, but were also found leading expeditions

HMS Majestic was the name ship of the largest class of battleships ever built, and set new standards in warship design when she was launched in January 1895. She was the first of what came to be known after 1905 as 'pre-Dreadnoughts' and was torpedoed and sunk by U-21 off Gallipoli in 1915.

against enemy colonies. In at least one case, a conversion was made for minelaying.

Like their German opposite numbers, responsible for securing the Baltic and its approaches, they had little chance for combat against their peers, so the Russo-Japanese and, to a certain extent, the Spanish-American wars remain the best examples of their operational use.

Mikasa was the Japanese flagship at the battle of Tsushima which shattered Russian power in the Pacific and established Japan as a world power. The Japanese navy was trained and heavily influenced by the Royal Navy, and Japanese battleships were built in British yards to British designs. She is preserved today as a museum.

'Charlemagne' class

Contemporary with the later ships of the 'Majestic' class, the three **'Charlemagne' class** units were the first French battleships to adopt the 'two-forward, two-aft' heavy gun layout, favoured for a decade by the British, and a more rational secondary battery down each broadside, the guns separated by splinter-proof screens. Up to and including the *Bouvet* that immediately preceded the 'Charlemagnes', French battleships had a character all of their own, with a single large gun at each end, its muzzles extending to the extremity of the short upper deck to minimize blast effects. From these points both bows and stern extended outward to an exaggerated degree in order to gain sufficient buoyancy and length. Though the 'Charlemagnes' were more moderate in their design they, too, retained a further feature in the pronounced tumblehome that gave the secondary guns a degree of axial fire. Launched in 1895 and 1896, the class comprised the *Charlemagne*, *Gaulois* and *Saint Louis*.

As was usual in French practice, the main belt was very narrow but ran full length. Between its upper edge and the lower edge of the battery armour the swell of the tumblehome was without protection. At this level was set a protective deck and, one level below, a splinter deck, the space between being closely sub-divided ('cellular') to contain flooding following damage. It is doubtful if this cellular layer was of sufficient depth to avoid being submerged by significant water ingress, and thus allowing progressive flooding.

By 1914 the class was of low combat value (like the 'Majestics' the ships just predated the pre-Dreadnoughts) but were nevertheless useful in low-risk areas. On 18 March 1915, the *Charlemagne* and *Gaulois* were operating with the *Bouvet* and *Suffren* as a bombardment group under Admiral Guépratte at the Dardanelles in the battle with the forts. The *Gaulois* had been heavily damaged and was having to withdraw, when the *Bouvet* was mined. Her magazines went and she disappeared in less than three minutes. On this day the British HMS *Irresistible* and *Ocean* were also destroyed, effectively signalling the end of serious attempts to force the strait. The *Gaulois* had to be grounded and, though later refloated and repaired at Toulon, was sunk by submarine torpedo.

Specification
'Charlemagne' class
Displacement: 11,300 tons full load
Dimensions: length 118.0 m (387.1 ft); beam 20.5 m (67.25 ft); draught 8.4 m (27.6 ft)
Propulsion: three sets of triple-expansion steam engines delivering 10810 kW (14,500 ihp) to three shafts
Speed: 18 kts

Armament: two twin 305-mm (12-in), 10 136.8-mm (5.4-in) and eight 100-mm (3.94-in) guns, and two 450-mm (17.7-in) torpedo tubes
Protection: belt 400 mm (15.75 in) tapering to 250 mm (9.84 in); decks 90 and 40 mm (3.54 and 1.57 in); barbettes 400 mm (15.75 in) maximum; casemates 75 mm (2.95 in)
Complement: 725

Pictured here in 1900, Gaulois was obsolete as a battleship by World War I but accompanied Charlemagne to the Dardanelles as part of the Anglo-French fleet which failed to force the straits. Gaulois was badly mauled by Turkish shore batteries on 18 March 1915 and had to withdraw. She was repaired only to be sunk by UB-47 in 1916.

With the 'Charlemagne' class, the French abandoned their quixotic layouts and followed contemporary practice with main armament concentrated in one turret forward and one aft. The main armoured belt was narrow but ran the full length of the hull, which retained the pronounced tumblehome that distinguished French warship design.

'Danton' class

Even in 1907 the possibility of war with Germany occupied the mind of the French services and, though loth to divert money from their army, they proposed a naval building programme that would have resulted in a force of 38 battleships, 20 armoured cruisers, 279 destroyers and torpedo boats, and 131 submarines by 1920. The first class of battleship constructed to implement this grandiose (and never realized) plan were the six **'Danton' class** units of the 1905 programme. The nameship was laid down in 1906, only nine months after the British 'Lord Nelsons'

Seen here at Toulon, Voltaire demonstrated the soundness of the 'Dantons'' extensive subdivision when she took and survived two torpedoes from the German submarine UB-48. Danton herself was not so lucky, succumbing to a single hit from U-64 in 1917.

French naval policy in the 1900s was muddled, wasteful and short-sighted. The 'Danton' class was rendered obsolete by HMS Dreadnought. Whereas the British only built two 'Lord Nelsons', the French obstinately built six 'Dantons'.

and, though they had little in common with the latter, there was a fundamental similarity in that the secondary battery was increased in calibre, rationalized to a single type and fully turreted. Being both beamier and longer, the French ships managed to accommodate three twin secondary turrets per side, but apart from this the

armaments were very similar and, like the British ships, the class represented an intermediate step to the Dreadnought type then just being introduced. Where the 'Lord Nelsons' were wisely terminated at only one pair, however, the French stuck stubbornly to their programme for six hulls, all of which were completed in 1911, when other fleets were building Dreadnoughts. The ships were the **Condorcet, Danton, Diderot, Mirabeau, Verguiaud** and **Voltaire**.

The 'Dantons' were, however, the first French turbine-driven class, with Parsons-built units turning four shafts with a near 30 per cent increase in power compared with the 'Verité' class that preceded them. Their 26

coal-fired boilers exhausted by an impressive five funnels batched, in typically French fashion, in two groups.

While not as extreme in design as earlier French battleships, the 'Dantons' perpetuated the shallow main belt, backed by a large degree of subdivision. This stood the *Danton* herself in good stead when, in 1917, she was heavily damaged by two well-spaced torpedoes from the *U-64*. She eventually succumbed to progressive flooding but gave her crew plenty of time for evacuation. The *Condorcet, Diderot* and *Voltaire* enjoyed long lives, the two latter being scrapped in the late 1930s and the *Condorcet* actually being scuttled in Toulon by the retreating Germans in 1944.

Specification
'Danton' class
Displacement: 18,320 tons standard and 19,760 tons full load
Dimensions: length 146.6 m (481.0 ft); beam 25.8 m (84.6 ft); draught 8.7 m (28.5 ft)
Propulsion: four sets of direct-drive steam turbines delivering 16775 kW (22,500 shp) to four shafts
Speed: 19 kts
Armament: two twin 305-mm (12-in), six twin 240-mm (9.4-in) and 16 75-mm (2.95-in) guns, and two 450-mm (17.7-in) torpedo tubes
Protection: belt 255-200 mm (10-8 in); decks 75 mm (2.95 in); barbettes 280 mm (11 in); secondary turrets 225 mm (8.85 in)
Complement: 920

ITALY
'Vittorio Emanuele III' class

The 'speed is protection' concept has always been a major influence in Italian design, resulting in many highly original warships. In addition the Italians possessed, in Vittorio Cuniberti, the single most influential figure in the movement toward the all-big gun capital ship.

At the turn of the century the Italians' chief designer, Benedetto Brin, produced the two 'Regina Margheritas' which, on a 13,200-ton displacement, shipped a conventional armament mix of four 305-mm (12-in), four 203-mm (8-in) and 12 152-mm (6-in) guns, roughly comparable to the contemporary British 'King Edward VIIs'. What made them different was their high speed, the nameship achieving a trial speed of 20.2 kts. This combination was inevitably reflected in poor protection, the main belt being only a widely-criticized 150 mm (6 in) thick. Interestingly enough, the British 'Triumph' class was similarly afflicted, and for much the same reason.

Cuniberti produced the next class, the four 'Vittorio Emanuele III' class battleships, creating a small transitional masterpiece in the process. On a

marginally smaller displacement than Brin's ships, they were some 3 m (9.8 ft) longer but 1.5 m (4.9 ft) narrower, the resulting fine hull achieving 22 kts on the same power. A two-tier main and secondary battery was favoured, anticipating the British 'Lord Nelsons'. Its great drawback lay in having to accept only two 305-mm (12-in) guns, in single mountings forward and aft; such weak main battery was insufficient for developing a sustained and accurate fire at any range. This penalty was the result of Cuniberti's success in working-in a full-length belt, with 250 mm (9.84 in) of steel over the parts that mattered. Launched beteen 1904 and

1907, the ships were the **Napoli, Regina Elena, Roma** and **Vittorio Emanuele III**.

The Italians, in effect, had built something like a small battle-cruiser ahead of its time. Its immediate influence was with the Japanese, whose recent battle experience had demonstrated the uses of a fast armoured cruiser. As a result they produced the two 'Ibukis' of 1907, slightly longer than the Italian ships and with protection reduced to accommodate a four-gun main battery.

Specification
'Vittorio Emanuele III' class
Displacement: 12,750 tons standard and 14,050 tons full load
Dimensions: length 144.6 m (474.4 ft); beam 22.4 m (73.5 ft); draught 8.3 m (27.2 ft)
Propulsion: two sets of triple-expansion steam engines delivering 14540 kW (19,500 ihp) to two shafts
Speed: 22 kts
Armament: two 305-mm (12-in), six twin 203-mm (8-in) and 12 76-mm (3-in) guns, and two 450-mm (17.7-in) torpedo tubes
Protection: belt 250-100 mm (9.84-3.94 in); transverse bulkheads 200 mm (7.9 in); decks 50-37 mm (1.97-1.46 in); barbettes 250 mm (9.84 in); casemates 80 mm (3.15 in)
Complement: 700

Many Italian warship designs had emphasized speed at the expense of protection, and the Regina Elena and her sisters were no exception. Designed by Vittorio Cuniberti, one of the most important naval architects of the period, they were able to reach 22 kts. During the war with Turkey they bombarded Tripoli and helped capture Rhodes.

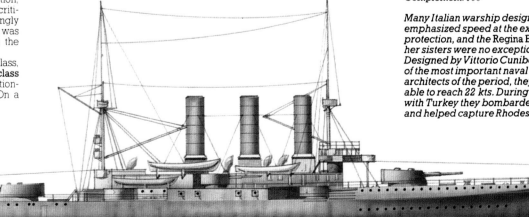

'Royal Sovereign' class

At a time when Royal Dockyards generally took over five years to build a battleship, HMS *Royal Sovereign*, lead ship of the **'Royal Sovereign'** class, was built at Portsmouth in only 32 months. The reason was simply that 'Jackie' Fisher, a newly promoted rear admiral, had been appointed Admiral Superintendent just after her launch in February 1891 and took a personal interest. The other six ships (HMS *Empress of India, Ramillies, Repulse, Resolution, Revenge* and *Royal Oak*) were launched in 1891-2.

In truth, the 'Royal Sovereigns' were a class transitional between the low-freeboard battleship and the true pre-Dreadnought. Since the abandonment of full sailing rig in the Royal Navy, freeboards had been kept low to reduce vulnerability to close-range gunfire and to reduce the necessary area of protection. This lack of freeboard was a great limitation in any sea, and the 'Royal Sovereigns' were built a full deck higher. While this placed the armament of four 343-mm (13.5-in) guns (no satisfactory 305-mm/12-in weapon was available) at a more commanding height, their weight could be accommodated only in open-topped barbettes where the paired guns were mounted on turntables that revolved within a low, armoured redoubt. The two barbettes were separated as widely as possible to allow the installation of a substantial and fully-enclosed secondary armament: these 10 152-mm (6-in) weapons had to be sited on two levels but were of the new quick-firing (QF) type designed to be effective against the growing threat from torpedo craft.

Extra freeboard of course meant extra area needing protection and, while the 'Royal Sovereigns' were not essentially superior to their foreign peers in this respect, they achieved it at reasonable penalty by adopting the new compound steel armour. Seven of the class were built, the eighth (HMS *Hood*) being completed in a modified fashion as the last low-freeboard battleship in order to accommodate the extra weight of turreted main armament.

All had been discarded by 1914 except the *Revenge* which, renamed HMS **Redoubtable** to release the name for a new battleship, was attached to the Dover Command. With her guns relined to reduce the bore to 305 mm (12 in) and her hull heavily bulged both to resist torpedoes and to allow the ship to be heeled by ballasting to increase elevation and range, she was used before the availability of suitable monitors for bombardment of enemy positions in Belgium at up to 14630 m (16,000 yards).

Left: HMS Royal Sovereign *was built a deck higher than contemporary battleships, and the increase in freeboard greatly improved her seakeeping. The last ship of the class, HMS* Hood *was completed in the old style to accommodate a turreted main armament, but was notably inferior.*

Specification
'Royal Sovereign' class
Displacement: 14,150 tons standard and 15,580 tons full load
Dimensions: length 115.8 m (380.0 ft); beam 22.9 m (75.0 ft); draught 8.4 m (27.5 ft)
Propulsion: two sets of triple-expansion steam engines delivering 8200 kW (11,000 ihp) to two shafts
Speed: 16.5 kts

Armament: two twin 343-mm (13.5-in) 10 152-mm (6-in) and 16 6-pdr guns, and seven 457-mm (18-in) torpedo tubes
Protection: belt 457 mm (18 in) tapering to 356 mm (14 in); transverse bulkheads 406 mm (16 in); splinter deck 76 mm (3 in); barbette 432 mm (17 in) maximum; casemates 152 mm (6 in)
Complement: 712

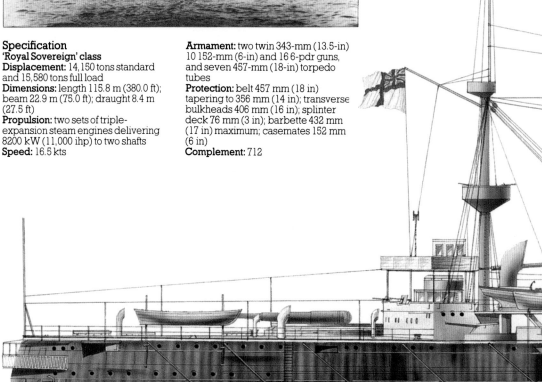

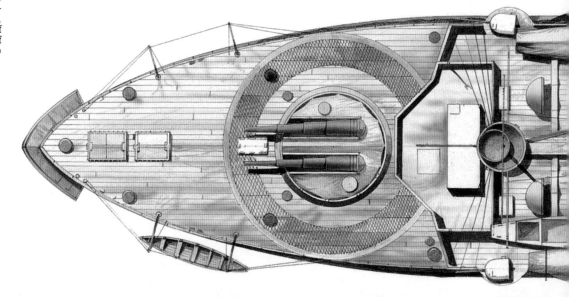

HMS Royal Sovereign *in the magnificent Victorian livery of the 1890s. Thanks to a superlative effort by Portsmouth Dockyard she was completed in just 42 months, a record for the period. HMS* Royal Oak *could be distinguished from her six sisters as her steam pipes were forward of the funnels, but the others were practically identical. By the outbreak of war in 1914 all had been disposed of except HMS* Revenge, *which bombarded German positions on the Belgian coast.*

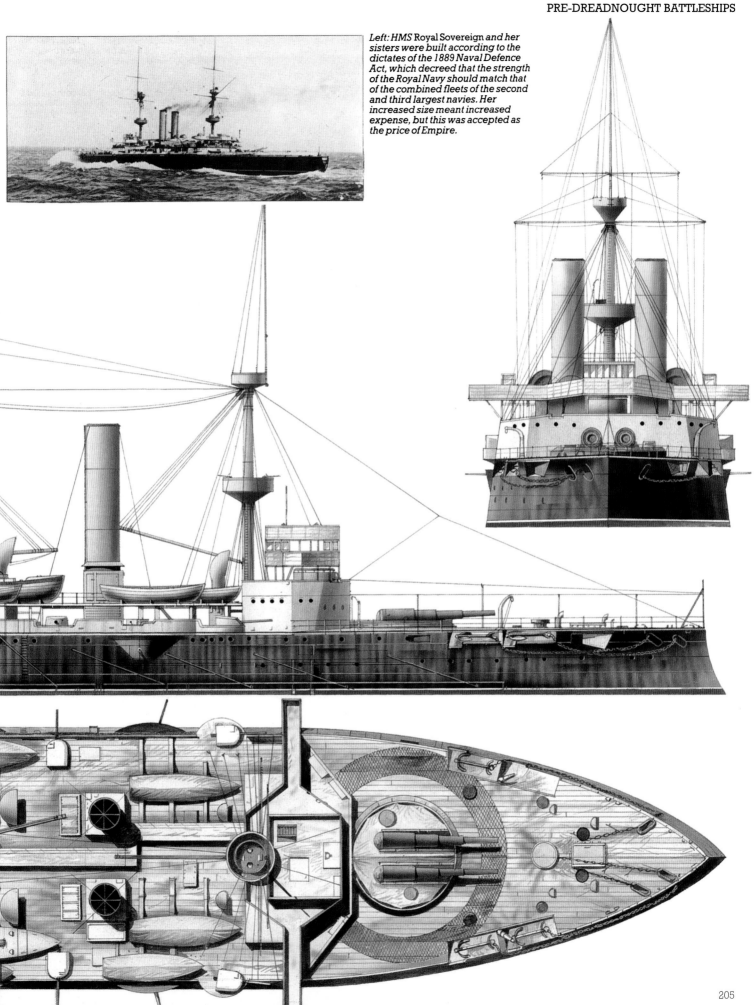

Left: HMS Royal Sovereign *and her sisters were built according to the dictates of the 1889 Naval Defence Act, which decreed that the strength of the Royal Navy should match that of the combined fleets of the second and third largest navies. Her increased size meant increased expense, but this was accepted as the price of Empire.*

'Majestic' class

Where the 'Royal Sovereigns' were offspring of the 1889 Naval Defence Act, the nine **'Majestic' class** ships were begat by the 1893 'Naval Scare' where the combined strength of the French and Russian fleets (in hypothetical alliance) were held to pose a threat which the Royal Navy would find difficult to contain. They were fine ships, seven coming from Royal Dockyards, and combined all the features that set a new standard sufficiently high to give them the palm as the first true pre-Dreadnoughts. Launched in 1895-6, the class comprised HMS *Caesar, Hannibal, Illustrious, Jupiter, Magnificent, Majestic, Mars, Prince George* and *Victorious*.

Superficially they looked rather like enlarged 'Royal Sovereigns', but they benefited greatly from new features. First was the protective deck sloped at the sides to meet the lower edge of the belt. Previously tried in the little HMS *Renown*, this feature was backed by coal bunkers to give improved protection to the machinery spaces as any armour-piercing projectile hitting the belt at an angle that would permit penetration would be deflected by the glacis behind. Secondly, the armour was of 'Harveyized' steel with a face-hardening so effective as to enable the 457-mm (18-in) belts of the 'Royal Quids' to be reduced to a combination of 223-mm (9-in) belt and 102-mm (4-in) deck.

The third important feature also saved weight, this being the adoption of a new-model 305-mm (12-in) gun. This 35-calibre weapon was far lighter than the earlier short 343-mm (13.5-in) gun and the smaller weight of the projectile was offset by 25 per cent greater penetrative power. This was due to the gun being a high-velocity weapon, combining new slow-burning propellants with a long barrel to yield a muzzle velocity of 732 m (2,400 ft) per second compared with the 615 m (2,016 ft) per second quoted for the earlier battleships' 343-mm (13.5-in) guns.

With so much weight saved, the previously open barbettes could be given an armoured hood, bunkers and ammunition capacity could be increased, and the output required of the main machinery could be lowered. The majority of the class were fitted for oil to be sprayed over the coal burning in the furnaces, for a rapid boost of output.

Most of the class saw war duty in home commands and the eastern Mediterranean, where four were involved with the Dardanelles operation. Of these, the *Majestic* was sunk (together with HMS *Triumph*) by Hersing's *U-21* in May 1915. Two torpedoes pierced her protective nets without hindrance and she capsized in seven minutes.

Specification
'Majestic' class
Displacement: 14,900 tons standard and 15,900 tons full load
Dimensions: length 128.3 m (421.0 ft); beam 22.9 m (75.0 ft); draught 8.2 m (27.0 ft)
Propulsion: two sets of triple-expansion steam engines delivering 8945 kW (12,000 ihp) to two shafts
Speed: 17 kts
Armament: two twin 305-mm (12-in), 12 152-mm (6-in) and 16 12-pdr guns, and five 457-mm (18-in) torpedo tubes
Protection: belt 229 mm (9 in); transverse bulkheads 356-305 mm (14-12 in); splinter deck 102-706 mm (4-3 in); barbettes 356 mm (14 in) maximum; casemates 152 mm (6 in)
Complement: 670

HMS Majestic *went into reserve at the Nore in 1906, but was commissioned at Devonport in 1914 and escorted the Canadian troopships. She was Admiral Nicolson's flagship during the Dardanelles operations and took part in the bombardment of 18 March 1915, but was sunk by U-21 the next day.*

The 'Majestic' class was constructed as part of the Admiralty's reaction to the growing naval power of France and Russia. Protected by Harveyized plate, their main armour belt was only half the thickness of that of the 'Royal Sovereigns' but was just as effective. Such weight-saving allowed the main armament to be given an armoured turret.

'King Edward VII' class

The first British battleships to be laid down in the 20th century, the **'King Edward VII' class** ships were also the last of the long line of capital ships (starting with the 'Royal Sovereigns') designed by Sir William White. In truth this basic layout, which had served the Royal Navy well, was now outdated and was really being only refined. The 'King Edward VIIs' were nearly 7 m (23 ft) longer than the preceding 'Duncans', but any seakeeping advantage this might have conferred was offset by reduced freeboard. Particular attention had been paid to manoeuvrability, but the ships proved very quirky on the helm, the rudder pintles wearing rapidly; because of their resulting odd course-keeping while in line, they received the popular name of the 'Wobbly Eight', a title not popular with the

King himself, who had launched the lead ship and who had directed that she should always be a flagship. The final three of the class were built after the plans for the much improved 'Lord Nelsons' had been drafted and were obsolescent on completion. The ships, launched between 1903 and 1905, were HMS *Africa, Britannia, Commonwealth, Dominion, Hibernia, Hindustan, King Edward VII* and *New Zealand*.

Edward VII had decreed that HMS King Edward VII *should always be a flagship and she joined the Grand Fleet in 1914, leading the 3rd Battle Squadron. Here she settles slowly in the water after hitting a mine off Cape Wrath. She capsized after 12 hours.*

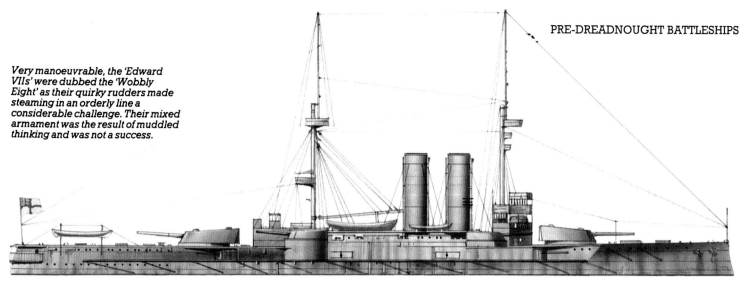

Very manoeuvrable, the 'Edward VIIs' were dubbed the 'Wobbly Eight' as their quirky rudders made steaming in an orderly line a considerable challenge. Their mixed armament was the result of muddled thinking and was not a success.

The innovation of the class was in the mixed secondary armament. At this time the armoured cruiser was reaching the final phase of its design and its 190.5-mm (7.5-in) main battery calibre was giving way to the new 234-mm (9.2-in) type. This latter was an excellent weapon, well capable of piercing the average battleship belt at range then considered normal. Four single weapons were shipped by each of the 'King Edward VIIs' but, in a case of addled thinking, were mixed with the customary 10 152-in (6-in) guns.

Thus not enough of the heavier guns were carried to make their inclusion worthwhile and the smaller-calibre weapons were squeezed into a box battery, behind the side armour but separated from each other by only a thin splinter screen. Their protection, redistributed because of the revised secondary and tertiary battery arrangements, was also downgraded almost immediately by the introduction of the APC projectile, an armour-piercing shell with a soft cap that prevented it shattering on hitting the hard

surface of cemented armour. The *New Zealand* was later renamed *Zealandia* to free the original name for a battle-cruiser, and the *Britannia* and *King Edward VII* were lost in World War I.

Specification
'King Edward VII' class
Displacement: 16,350 tons standard and 17,100 tons full load
Dimensions: length 138.3 m (453.75 ft); beam 23.8 m (78.0 ft); draught 7.8 m (25.5 ft)

Propulsion: two sets of triple-expansions steam engines delivering 13420-kW (18,000 ihp) to two shafts
Speed: 18.5 kts
Armament: two twin 305-mm (12-in), four 234-mm (9.2-in), 10 152-mm (6-in) and 14 12-pdr guns, and four 457-mm (18-in) torpedo tubes
Protection: belt 229-192 mm (9-4 in); transverse bulkheads 305-203 mm (12-8 in); decks 51, 51 and 64 mm (2, 2 and 2.5 in); barbettes 305 mm (12 in) maximum; battery 178 mm (7 in)
Complement: 780

 UK
'Lord Nelson' class

Together with her sister HMS *Agamemnon*, HMS *Lord Nelson* was the last of the British pre-Dreadnoughts. Having been preceded by the frigate *Nelson* of 1876 and followed by the battleship *Nelson* of 1925, it is not clear why the 'Lord' was added. The **'Lord Nelson' class** was the logical extension of the 'King Edward VIIs', but the ships' construction was commenced only just before that of HMS *Dreadnought*, their guns were purloined for the latter's swift completion and, finally, the two were not completed until nearly two years after, already obsolete.

An interesting point is that these, the last of the old school, cost little more than contemporary armoured cruisers at about £1.54 million each, while the revolutionary newcomer seemed comparatively inexpensive at £1.78 million.

The main lessons of the Russo-Japanese engagements, still in progress in 1905, was that the big-calibre gun looked set to dominate and dictate the course of an action before secondary armaments were even in range. The decision to uprate the whole secondary battery to 234-mm (9.2-in) calibre was, therefore, vindicated, though an apparent suggestion to re-cast the ships to an all 305-mm (12-in) layout fell on deaf ears. Ten 234-mm (9.2-in) guns were carried, an unusual number due to the centre turrets hav-

ing to be singles. This was in order to restrict the beam, comparatively arbitrarily, to fit certain drydocks. One strength of German equivalents was, of course, their excellently subdivided hulls and large beams, so that this restriction was certainly inhibiting. As it was, the two 'Lord Nelsons' were shorter than their predecessors and, being designed to the maximum beam, proved remarkably handy.

By tight design, they achieved improved protection at almost no weight penalty, the area of armour being kept to an absolute minimum. One-third of their bunker capacity was for oil but they were the last British battleships equipped with steam reciprocating engines. Externally, they could immediately be recognized by their high superstructure topped-off by short funnels of unequal section. The mainmast also reintroduced the tripod bracing that was to remain a feature in British

warships for many years to come. Both ships performed valuable service in the eastern Mediterranean, particularly the Dardanelles, but were always overshadowed by their successors.

Specification
'Lord Nelson' class
Displacement: 16,500 tons standard and 17,750 tons full load
Dimensions: length 135.2 ft (443.5 ft); beam 24.2 m (79.5 ft); draught 7.9 m (26.0 ft)
Propulsion: two sets of triple-

expansion steam engines delivering 12490 kW (16,750 ihp) to two shafts
Speed: 18 kts
Armament: two twin 305-mm (12-in), four twin and two single 234-mm (9.2-in), and 24 12-pdr guns, and five 457-mm (18-in) torpedo tubes
Protection: belt 305-102 mm (12-4 in); transverse bulkheads 203 mm (8 in); decks 38, 102 and 76 mm (1.5, 4 and 3 in); barbettes 305 mm (12 in) maximum; secondary turrets 178 mm (7 in)
Complement: 810

Agamemnon adopted this unusual colour scheme while in the East Mediterranean in 1915. Uprating the secondary battery to 9.2-in calibre was a logical step in view of the lessons of the Russo-Japanese war, but arguably the vessels were over-armed for their displacement. The real answer was the all-big gun ship.

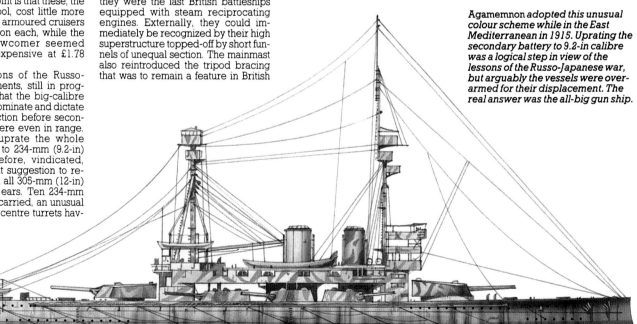

UK
'Swiftsure' class

From time to time in emergency the British Admiralty appropriated warships building to foreign account, but the compulsory purchase of two Chilean battleships in 1903 could only have been because of a suspicion that the customer might default and offer the ships to a rival fleet (that of Russia). Certainly they were of little use to the Royal Navy as they were underarmed and too lightly built to take their place in the main line. They had been ordered as a counter to the Chilean's usual rivals, the neighbouring Argentines, which were building the final pair of a group of fast ships carrying both 254- and 203-mm (10- and 8-in) guns. As these were rated armoured cruisers, the Chileans opted for a pair of battleships, whose scantlings and armament would be scaled for local, rather than European, disputes.

The Royal Navy already had three small 254-mm (10-in) gunned battleships, but these were sized especially for foreign flag duties, particularly in China. In the case of the **'Swiftsure' class**, the hulls were about 30.5 m (100 ft) longer but of the same beam to achieve the required 20 kts. Interestingly, the small battleships in the Far East had seen both Jellicoe and Beatty make their mark in more junior ranks,

while Fisher preferred HMS *Renown* in the Mediterranean. Indeed, with the high speed of the 'Swiftsures' (the first in the Royal Navy to exceed 20 kts) and their mixture of 254- and 190.5-mm (10- and 7.5-in) guns, they very much followed the Fisher ideal of the 'smallest effective big gun and the largest possible secondary gun'. On such narrow-gutted ships, the large casemates demanded by the 190.5-mm (7.5-in) guns dominated the amidships layout. Corners were cut in overall protection which, while permissible with Argentine 254-mm (10-in) shells in mind, would have proved vulnerable to an unlucky hit by a 305-mm (12-in) round. This was particularly true of those parts of the barbette structure behind the main armoured bulkheads. The ships' two tall, symmetrical funnels and gooseneck boatcranes gave them a very distinctive silhouette.

Both ships were active in the Dardanelles campaign, HMS *Swiftsure* having already seen service in the Suez area and the Red Sea and HMS *Triumph* commissioning from reserve in Hong Kong. The latter was torpedoed and sunk while assisting with fire support. Her loss, together with that of HMS *Majestic*, signalled the end of the Royal Navy's traditional close invest-

ment policy.

Specification
'Swiftsure' class
Displacement: 11,800 tons standard and 13,850 tons full load
Dimensions: length 146.2 m (479.75 ft); beam 21.6 m (71.0 ft); draught 7.7 m (25.33 ft)
Propulsion: two sets of triple-expansion steam engines delivering 9230 kW (12,500 ihp) to two shafts
Speed: 19 kts
Armament: two twin 254-mm (10-in), 14 190.5-mm (7.5-in), 14 14-pdr and two 12-pdr guns, and two 457-mm (18-in)

torpedo tubes
Protection: belt 178-76 mm (7-3 in); transverse bulkheads 152 mm (6 in); decks 76-25 mm (3-1 in); barbettes 254-mm (10 in) maximum; casemates 178 mm (7 in)
Complement: 800

Easily distinguished from other British battleships by her gooseneck cranes, HMS Triumph and her sister were being built for Chile by Armstrong, but the Admiralty issued a compulsory purchase order after it seemed they were to be sold to Russia by Chile.

GERMANY
'Kaiser' class

The immediate result of the accession of the naval-minded Kaiser Wilhelm II in 1888 was the laying down of the first group of four seagoing battleships, the **'Brandenburg' class**. Though these were exactly contemporary with the British 'Royal Sovereigns', they were remarkably different in layout. Of the same length, they were of less beam and, though of less power, were reasonably fast. Their major feature was a six-gun main battery of 280-mm (11-in) guns in a twin mounting at each end and a third in a gap in the superstructure, the last with barrels of reduced length. Despite this, the ships had a unique six-gun broadside at a time when four was the norm, an example of advanced thinking but at the cost of inadequate protection.

To a certain extent, therefore, the following five-ship **'Kaiser' class** launched between 1896 and 1900 was something of a disappointment as, in endeavouring to rectify the earlier ships' deficiencies, their designers produced something little different from contemporaries abroad. The interesting decision was not to increase the calibre of guns to match the 305-mm (12-in) usual in foreign battleships, but to reduce it to 240-mm (9.4-in) and to cut the number to four, set in the usual manner, with a twin mounting both forward and aft. The penetrative power of these guns was the equal of most vertical belts only at close ranges, and the anticipated compensation of a high rate of fire evidently did not materialize. Again, protection was below par, with a very shallow belt that extended over only the forward 80 per cent of the length, and

linked across top and bottom by protective and splinter decks. The reason for this economy was the shipping of a heavy secondary armament of 16 150-mm (5.9-in) guns. Only four of these were mounted in casemates, the remainder being grouped at main deck level in a superstructure protected only at each end but so shaped as to permit a maximum of axial fire. Reconstructed in 1906, the ships lost their four casemated weapons, which were of little use in a seaway but, in doing so, increased freeboard to the extent that the belt was virtually clear of the surface. Of low fighting value by 1914, SMS *Kaiser Barbarossa, Kaiser Friedrich III, Kaiser Karl der Grosse, Kaiser Wilhelm II* and *Kaiser Wilhelm der Grosse* were used for training and accommodation during World War I.

Specification
'Kaiser' class
Displacement: 10,970 tons standard
Dimensions: length 125.0 m (410.1 ft); beam 20.2 m (66.3 ft); draught 7.8 m (25.6 ft)
Propulsion: three sets of triple-expansion steam engines delivering 9880 kW (13,250 ihp) to three shafts
Speed: 18 kts
Armament: two twin 240-mm (9.4-in), 19 150-mm (5.9-in) and 12 88-mm (3.46-in) guns, and six 457-mm (18-in) torpedo tubes
Protection: belt 300 m (11.8 in); transverse bulkheads 200 mm (7.9 in); decks 75 and 60 mm (2.95 and 2.36 in); barbettes 250 mm (9.8 in) maximum; casemates and secondary turrets 150 mm (5.9 in)
Complement: 670

Seen here in 1902, SMS Kaiser Friedrich III represented a step backwards for German naval architecture after the bold and innovative 'Brandenburg' class. The heavy secondary armament of 16 150-mm (5.9-in) guns could not compensate for the weak choice of four 240-mm (9.4-in) weapons as the main armament.

When commissioned, the 'Kaiser' class formed the 1st Squadron of the Heimatflotte (Home Fleet), as the German navy was then called. By 1914 they had been placed in reserve, but were mobilized on the outbreak of war to form the 5th Squadron of the High Seas Fleet. They were withdrawn from the active list for the second and final time in 1915.

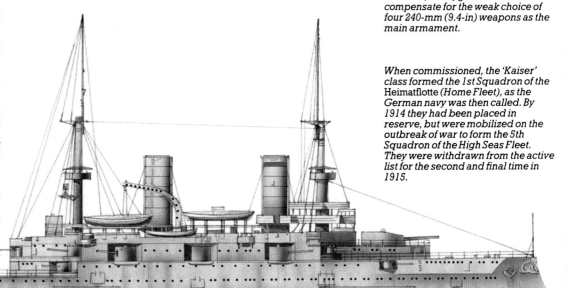

'Wittelsbach' class

Like the preceding 'Kaisers', there were five 'Wittelsbach' class battleships which, though of the same armament, had a very different layout. Launched in 1900-1, the ships were SMS *Mecklenburg, Schwaben, Wettin, Wittelsbach* and *Zahringen*. They retained the small 240-mm (9.4-in) main battery gun, paired fore and aft, but differed in having a flush main deck which effectively raised the after turret by one level. The forward turret remained elevated a further level on a high barbette. The hull was some 5 m (16.4 ft) longer and commensurately beamier but, in adopting the more effective Krupp cemented armour in place of the earlier ships' Harvey nickel steel, a greater area of thinner plate was incorporated for the same degree of protection. Where the earlier ships had a narrow belt over about 80 per cent of the length with only armoured trunks to the turrets above, the 'Wittelsbachs' could accommodate full-length protection and, surprisingly, resurrect the old central battery concept. Its weight precluded extending this battery to any height, so that the eight 150-mm (5.9-in) guns that it contained were carried at a low level. Two further weapons were sited in protected casemates at the same level farther aft, the height of the forward 240-mm (9.4-in) guns, which must have been greatly affected by blast. Thus, to obtain the exceptionally heavy chase fire of two main and eight secondary barrels, the layout left much to be desired in a seaway and blast interference.

'Wittelsbach' class battleships in line ahead, seen from the Zeppelin L.54. They were mobilized in 1914 to form the 4th Battle Squadron but soon left the fleet as they were too vulnerable to stand in the line of battle. After the war, all were scraped save Zahringen, which survived until 1944.

German battleships of this period were still aimed primarily at North Sea and Baltic operations, their dimensions and draught being limited to suit tidal restrictions and sizes of locks to basins and the Kiel Canal. The class was too old to play any significant role in World War I and all survived it. For a period between the wars the *Zahringen* operated as a radio-controlled target ship.

Specification
'Wittelsbach' class
Displacement: 11,775 tons standard and 12,790 tons full load
Dimensions: length 126.8 m (416.0 ft); beam 22.8 m (74.8 ft); draught 8.0 m (26.2 ft)
Propulsion: three sets of triple-expansion steam engines delivering 11185 kW (15,000 ihp) to three shafts
Speed: 18 kts
Armament: two twin 240-mm (9.4-in), 18 150-mm (5.9-in) and 12 88-mm (3.46-in) guns, and four 450-mm (17.7-in) torpedo tubes
Protection: belt 225-100 m (8.86-3.94-in); protective deck 75 mm (2.95 in); barbettes 250 mm (9.84 in); secondary guns 150 mm (5.9 in)
Complement: 688

The Imperial German Navy's third class of battleships, the 'Wittelsbachs' were armed like the 'Kaisers' but adopted a very different layout, featuring a flush main deck and larger hull. Krupp-cemented (KC) armour was used in place of the Harvey nickel steel, allowing full-length protection.

'Braunschweig' class

Tirpitz's First Navy Bill of 1898 had provided for the basis of a German fleet headed by 19 battleships by 1904. The UK, though not directly threatened, took notice. It was the Second Navy Bill, of 1900, that started the naval race, calling as it did for 38 capital ships with an extension eventually to 48. Germany intended now to be a colonial power and would need to challenge the British to do it; her ships, therefore, began to change in character.

The five 'Wittelsbachs' had been essentially 'home waters' ships, accepting a small-calibre main battery as a necessary consequence of an acceptable rate of fire. At the battle ranges then considered normal, the 240-mm (9.4-in) guns could, in any case, penetrate the belts of any likely opponent. British ideas were already, however, moving toward increasing ranges, which would have rendered the German guns ineffective. The latter, therefore, urgently improved the rate of fire of the 280-mm (11-in) gun and increased the size of the second class, the five 'Braunschweig' class battleships, to accommodate such guns. The dimensions and displacement were to the maxima compatible with the Wilhelmshaven locks and the

Preussen, seen here in 1910, was the fourth of the 'Braunschweig' class, which began construction after Tirpitz's Second Navy Bill (1900) and the beginning of the Anglo-German naval race which was to do so much to bring about World War I.

Kiel (Nordsee-Ostsee) Canal. The ships, launched between 1902 and 1904, were SMS *Braunschweig, Elsass, Hessen, Lothringen* and *Preussen*.

Secondary armament was also upgraded, from the preferred 150-mm (5.9-in) gun to an unusual 170-mm (6.7-in) type, with a loss of four barrels. As the hull was able to accept a greater area of armour, the secondary weapons were better grouped amidships, though the majority were in a main deck battery that was still too low to be fought properly in a seaway. The primary reason for this upgrading was the growing need to stop torpedo craft at ranges that were rapidly increasing with the improved technology of the torpedo. To achieve the same 18-kt speed as the earlier class, installed power had to be increased by about 15 per cent, though the endurance of about 6300 km (3,915 miles) at 16 kts

was only a marginal improvement. Boilers were divided between six cylindrical and eight Thornycroft-Schulz water tube types, a combination that required three funnels. Up to 1,600 tons of coal and 200 tons of oil fuel could be carried.

Specification
'Braunschweig' class
Displacement: 12,990 tons standard
Dimensions: length 127.6 m (486 ft); beam 22.5 m (73.8 ft); draught 7.45 m (24.4 ft)
Propulsion: three sets of triple-expansion steam engines delivering 1252 kW (16,800 ihp) to three shafts
Speed: 18.5 kts
Armament: two twin 280-mm (11-in), 14 170-mm (6.7-in) and 12 88-mm (3.46-in) guns, and six 450-mm (17.7-in) torpedo tubes
Protection: belt 225-100 mm (8.86-3.94-in); transverse bulkheads 150 mm (5.9 in); protective deck 75 mm (2.95 in); barbettes 250 mm (9.84 in); casemates 150 mm (5.9 in)
Complement: 660

Guns and Armour

From the launch of the first ironclad to the eclipse of the battleship as the final arbiter of war at sea, warship design was dominated by the struggle between guns and armour. Guns steadily grew in range and power, but engineers continued to devise new types of armour plate to defeat them.

As a term, 'pre-Dreadnought' dates of course from the completion of HMS *Dreadnought* herself and thus invariably bears overtones of obsolescence. In their day, however, such vessels were the best capital ships afloat, but what is often uncertain is the precise definition of that day.

From the transitional types of capital ship in the 1860s, where steam-driven hulls still retained a broadside armament and full rig, development took off in a variety of directions, with a literal trial of strength emerging between the gun and armour plate. As massive protection kept out heavy projectiles, larger guns had to be carried but there had to be fewer of them. Properly arranged, these occupied less space and, therefore, demanded a smaller area of protection which, in turn, could be thicker. Such arrangements rapidly took the gun from its traditional carriage to pivot mountings, which could be trained through one of several embrasures, and then to the powered barbette, where the weapons were sited on a revolving turntable, firing over and protected by, a fixed and heavy circular redoubt. While the latter allowed guns to be trained rapidly through wide arcs, they were of little use if obstructed by a full set of rigging. So until machinery was reliable enought to make the 'mastless' warship accept-able, central battery ships were popular, built around armoured boxes extending often through two decks and projecting beyond the sides to maximize axial fire. This latter feature was important as powered opponents could either flee or possibly work themselves into a decisive raking position.

Adequate protection was so heavy that when the 'mastless' turret ship became a reality, its freeboard was exceedingly low. While this kept the belt area to a minimum, it gave a poor stability range and seakeeping was rapidly degraded by a deteriorating sea state. Attempts to increase freeboard resulted immediately in greater areas of thinner armour and the heavy guns sited so high that they had to be mounted in barbettes rather than turrets. Thus mounted, both guns and crews were vulnerable to fragments, though heavy projectiles were still fired at such close ranges that their trajectories were flat, armour being concentrated into heavy vertical belts to defeat them.

Early armour was of wrought iron, usually sandwiched with teak and proprie-

HMS Conqueror, *launched in 1881, was a product of a misinterpretation of the battle of Lissa in 1866 which seemed to demonstrate that the ram was an effective means of sinking ironclad battleships. Conqueror's armament was concentrated forward to support the ramming attack.*

tory compounds to improve resilience and to resist fragmentation. This phase lasted approximately from 1860 to 1880, by which time it was possible to find two 305-mm (12-in) layers of wrought iron, secured back-to-back. With new guns soon able to pierce even this, however, the next move was to steel armour which, while showing greater resistance to penetration, was liable to shatter under the smashing effect of large shot.

From 1880 to 1890, therefore, compound armour evolved. This was iron, faced with harder steel, which was either poured molten or hot-rolled to produce a composite slab which, itself, could be rolled further. While this combined the projectile-shattering quality of steel with the toughness of iron, the hard face did

A close-up of the open barbette mounting of the 13.5-in guns of HMS Royal Sovereign. Able to fire one round every 2½ minutes, which could penetrate nine inches of KC plate at 5,000 yards, they were the most effective guns of their day. Later British battleships reverted to higher-velocity 12-in guns.

tend to peel from its substrate when impacted, while improved types of chilled and capped armour-piercing shot again soon proved compound armour's equal.

The decade from 1890 to 1900 was that of the metallurgist. First, Harvey 'carbonised' the face of nickel steel plate, quenching it and annealing it to produce a very hard surface. While a great step forward, such armour had the tendency to spall on the inside when struck, a deficiency rectified by Krupp who reinstated toughness by the addition of chrome. The resultant 'Krupp Cement', or KC, plate became the new standard. Compared with wrought iron KC could offer the same level of protection at only 40 per cent of the weight, so freeboards could be significantly increased with small effect on vulnerability.

The big gun, meanwhile, kept pace. Up to the 1880s, large calibres were shipped for their 'smashing' capabilities rather than superior range. Belts and supporting structures were to be shattered at close quarters, with medium calibre guns simultaneously riving the softer superstructure, starting fires and maintaining a rapid rate of fire to demoralize the other ship's crew.

To engineers, however, it was readily apparent that, while the energy of a projectile is directly proportional to its mass, it is also proportional to its velocity squared. In short, increases in muzzle velocity were of far greater import than increases in calibre, which had the attendant penalties of greater weight and slower rates of fire.

Several factors combined to capitalize on this relationship. In about 1890 cordite replaced black powder as a propellant. In place of a near explosive detonation on firing, which was inefficient and put enormous stresses into the gun chamber, the slower-burning cordite released rapidly-expanding gases that smoothly accelerated a projectile along the barrel. Far higher muzzle velocities were possible, but only with longer barrels which did not 'droop'. Cast weapons thus gave way to a construction with concentrically shrunk tubes, and this in turn to the greatly superior wire-wound variety. The length of the latter could be accepted only because a reliable breech mechanism was produced finally to displace muzzle-loading. Hydraulic power was applied to handling, loading and training to increase firing rates.

Thus, in the early 1890s, the standard 305-mm (12-in) British naval gun was increased from 35 to 40 calibres in length, muzzle velocity rising from 640 m (2,100 ft) to 792 m (2,600 ft) per second. Better penetrating power and longer range were coupled with more consistent ballistics and a much-reduced smoke nuisance. Rather than smash an opponent in a risky close-range brawl, it was now possible to destroy him scientifically from beyond the range of his secondary battery. This possibility resulted immediately in the beginning of fire control, the provision of heavier horizontal and oblique armour to defeat the plunging shell, and an increase in secondary armament calibres.

Fuji was the first battleship ordered from Britain by the young Japanese navy. An improved 'Royal Sovereign' design, she shipped 12-in 40-calibre guns which, because of their higher muzzle velocity, were more effective weapons than the 13.5-in guns of the British vessels.

A sequence of fundamental improvements thus came together in the early 1890s to produce a new strain of capital ship, seakindly yet capable of both inflicting and receiving punishment. In a period of British naval pre-eminence, the Royal Navy led the way with HMS *Majestic* of 1895 and, by the time that the next fleet, that of the Russians, completed its first in 1902, had commissioned a further 17 and built four more for the client, Japan.

The 'pre-Dreadnought' as a type was supreme for just a decade. By the time that the Americans (1902), the Germans (1904), the Italians (1904) and the French (1906) followed suit, they were barely in time to be eclipsed by the next and greater revolution, the introduction of the Dreadnought battleship itself.

The forecastle of HMS Majestic *at the turn of the century, a period when paintwork and polish seemed more important to some Royal Navy officers than gunnery and manoeuvre. Her 12-in guns fired 850-lb shells which could penetrate 11½ in of KC armour at 5,000 yards.*

'Kearsage' class

Early American battleships were aimed primarily only at coastal defence, but the 1898 US war against Spain was rapidly successful because of naval power. By virtue of the war and following annexations, the USA acquired the Philippine Islands, Hawaii, Wake Island, Puerto Rico and part of Samoa. Anti-imperialist consciences proved elastic enough to accept these new responsibilities and to expand the fleet to a level that would not only safeguard the new territories but would, eventually, be second only to that of the UK.

Limited size and draught, coupled with a heavy armament of 330- and

USS Kearsage *was a step toward the all-big gun ship as she, like the 'King Edwards' in Britain, carried an intermediate battery. Fourteen 5-in guns were also shipped in long broadside batteries, separated by splinter screens, the calibre being chosen because it was the largest available in fixed ammunition.*

203-mm (13- and 8-in) primary and secondary batteries respectively, put the three 'Indiana' class ships (BB-1 to BB-3) of 1893 ahead of European contemporaries on paper but, practically, resulted in great limitations as a result of low freeboard and blast effects. The USS *Iowa* (BB-4) of 1896 aimed to rectify this with a higher freeboard for better seakeeping, saving weight on the more elevated turrets by accepting a cut in calibre to 305 mm (12 in), the European norm. This back-tracking was not at all in favour with the new navy, which limited the class to one ship and opted for the innovative but extraordinary pair of 'Kearsage' class ships (BB-5 and BB-6) as follow-ons.

Launched in 1898, these were the USS *Kearsage and Kentucky*.

Although the *Iowa* had suffered a reduction in main battery calibre, she had retained a heavy secondary armament of eight 203-mm (8-in) guns set sensibly but weightily in twin turrets. The 'Kearsages' reverted to the 330-mm (13-in) gun at the cost of four of the 203-mm (8-in) weapons but, to save weight further in the quest for freeboard, the remaining four 203-mm (8-in) weapons were paired on the top of the main turrets in houses rigidly fixed to the lower element. Thus the two batteries had to be trained together on a common roller path. Fourteen 127-mm (5-in) guns (the

largest calibre that could use 'fixed' QF ammunition) were shipped in two long broadside batteries, the guns separated by splinter screens. Speed was sacrificed for wide beam (for steadiness) and heavy protection, the cofferdams backing the belt (419 mm/16.5 in thick amidships) being filled with 'compressed American corn pith cellulose' to limit flooding following damage.

Specification
'Kearsage' class
Displacement: 11,540 tons standard
Dimensions: length 114.4 m (375.25 ft); beam 22.0 m (72.25 ft); draught 7.2 m (23.5 ft)
Propulsion: two sets of triple-expansion steam engines delivering 8950 kW (12,000 ihp) to two shafts
Speed: 16.5 kts
Armament: two twin 330-mm (13-in), two twin 203-mm (8-in) and 14 127-mm (5-in) guns, and four 457-mm (18-in) torpedo tubes
Protection: belt 419-241 mm (16.5-9.5 in); protective decks 127-70 mm (5-2.75 in); barbettes 432 mm (17 in) maximum; secondary guns 229 mm (9 in)
Complement: 554

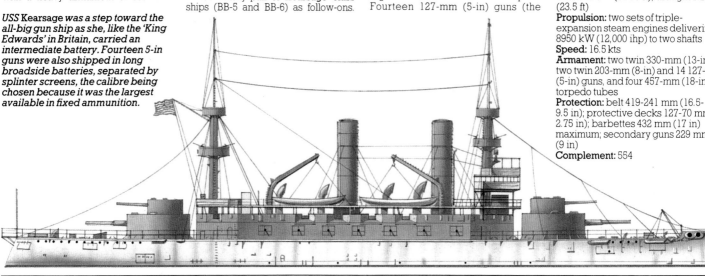

'Mississippi' class

The US Navy has always firmly believed in the virtues of acquiring the largest affordable ships; the current (1986) arguments regarding future aircraft-carriers and attack submarines demonstrate a continuing conviction. The argument is a powerful one as the designer has freedom to make his ship more battleworthy in terms of armament, speed and protection, while the larger ship can better keep the seas.

As the US Navy moved toward the inception of the Dreadnought era it had a very heavy building programme. Six 15,000-ton 'Virginias' and the first two of the enlarged but very similar 'Connecticuts' were launched in 1904 alone. Of these, the former again tried a two-storey turret arrangement, with both 305-mm (12-in) twin turrets crowned by a paired 203-mm (8-in) gunhouse. The layout was again unsatisfactory but left the conviction that superimposed guns mounted on the centreline were the obvious way ahead. With this in mind, the plans for the two all-big-gun 'South Carolinas' went ahead. At this point, however, Congress put on the financial brakes, allowing the UK to steal the race and complete HMS *Dreadnought* first.

Another unsatisfactory result of

these economies was the pair of 'Mississipi' class diminutives built in the middle of the 'Connecticut' series, which ran from the USS *Connecticut* (BB-18) herself to the USS *New Hampshire* (BB-25), the standard 139.1-m (456.3-ft) hull permitting a powerful three-tier armament of four 305-mm (12-in) guns, eight 203-mm (8-in) guns in paired turrets and 12 178-mm (7-in) guns in casemates. In 1905, however, Cramp of Philadelphia launched the USS *Mississippi* (BB-23) and USS *Idaho* (BB-24) 'economy versions' cut down to 116.4 m (382 ft). By actually increasing the beam very slightly, however, they managed still to economize in armament to the extent of only four casemated 178-mm (7-in) guns.

The major loss was in power, 12300 kW (16,500 ihp) for 18 kts being reduced to only 7455 kW (10,000 ihp) for 17 kts. Thus the final evocation of the American pre-Dreadnought was deemed unsatisfactory, the pair serv-

ing only six years before being sold to the Greeks. Renamed *Lemnos* and *Kilkis*, they must have strained the facilities of the Greek navy to the utmost, but *Kilkis* lasted to be sunk in 1941 in a different war.

Specification
'Mississippi' class
Displacement: 13,000 tons standard
Dimensions: length 116.4 m (382.0 ft); beam 23.5 m (77.0 ft); draught 7.6 m (25.0 ft)
Propulsion: two sets of triple-

expansion steam engines delivering 7455 kW (10,000 ihp) to two shafts
Speed: 17 kts
Armament: two twin 305-mm (12-in), four twin 203-mm (8-in) and eight 178-mm (7-in) and 12 76-mm (3-in) guns, and two 533-mm (21-in) torpedo tubes
Protection: belt 229-102 mm (9-4 in); transverse bulkheads 178 mm (7 in); splinter deck with 64-mm (2.5-in) slopes; barbettes 305 mm (12 in); casemates 152 mm (6 in)
Complement: 800

USS Mississippi *and her sister* Idaho *were cut-down versions of the 'Vermont' class, and merely proved that a smaller hull contains less space than a larger one. They were sold to Greece as soon as decently possible, and the money was used to buy another 'New Mexico' class Dreadnought instead.*

Armoured Cruisers of World War 1

Six years before the outbreak of World War I the battle-cruiser was introduced. Too slow to intercept their lighter brethren but too weak to stand in the line of battle, armoured cruisers nevertheless fought throughout the war.

HMS Hampshire was one of the six-strong 'Devonshire' class of armoured cruisers built between 1902 and 1905.

As a type, the armoured cruiser was reckoned obsolete by 1914, its development having been halted abruptly by the introduction of the battle-cruiser in 1908. In fact, the latter was initially referred to as an 'armoured cruiser' but this was a ploy to disguise its true nature. It outclassed the older type so conclusively that its qualities put it in another bracket entirely and it could be argued that, if used with common sense, the more traditional armoured cruiser could still have had a role complementary to that of the battle-cruiser. Had this been the case, evolution would probably have taken the better qualities of each and fused them into a third, and probably more healthy, type. War, however, has a habit of interrupting normal evolutionary processes.

The origins of the armoured cruiser go back to HMS *Shannon* of 1877 and, therefore, almost to the introduction of the ironclad itself. Clearcut categories such as 'battleship' and 'cruiser' did not exist in modern terms and, for long, an armoured cruiser was reckoned on a par with a third- (or even second-) class battleship, with protection and armament reduced in scale for the benefit of speed. The indifferent quality of contemporary armour plate still, however, meant enough weight to offset any effective gain in speed. To the Royal Navy they were a failure, banished

as flagships to distant imperial stations and the type was discontinued. Only with improvements in armour could the class be resurrected with a view to discharging its designed functions of reconnaissance in force, support for smaller friendly cruisers, frustrating the aims of the enemy's cruisers and finishing damaged ships of superior size.

Upon the advent of the battle-cruiser these aims should have been modified as, in a fleet context, they tended to throw the armoured cruiser at the very ships that were designed to destroy it. That this was not recognized led directly to the disaster suffered by Arbuthnot at Jutland. Coupled with Coronel and the Falklands battles and a very high loss rate from a variety of other causes, this led to the armoured cruiser once again being banished to trade protection. The UK had disposed of its remaining 19 hulls by 1922, but the type lingered in the fleets of France, Italy and the USA.

A classic armoured cruiser, the Russian Rurik was built by Vickers; her design incorporated the lessons of the Russo-Japanese war. She carried a heavy armament of four 254-mm (10-in) and eight 203.2-mm (8-in) guns and her defensive protection included a 152-mm (6-in) belt, armoured magazines and torpedo defence.

USA
'Brooklyn' class

Brooklyn was a 'one-off' vessel, essentially an improved version of Saratoga. Her uniform armament of eight 203.2-mm (8-in) guns foreshadowed later heavy cruiser armament.

Though a 'one-off', the single **'Brooklyn' class** ship USS **Brooklyn** launched in 1895 had a profile so distinctive that she is probably the best-remembered American armoured cruiser. She was an improved version of the USS **New York** (later **Saratoga**) of four years earlier though, in truth, neither was more than a protected cruiser with a very shallow belt running only the length of the machinery spaces. This lack of depth was possible largely because of the low vertical height of the small reciprocating engines that were installed. The two shafts each had two prime movers, directly-coupled and arranged in tandem. Most cruising could be achieved on one engine to each shaft, making for economy and endurance, and foreshadowing the COGAG and CODAG arrangements in current practice.

Also prophetic was the armament mix, the eight 203.2-mm (8-in) and 12 127-mm (5-in) guns being typical of a ship four decades later. The earlier *New York* had had only six 203.2-mm weapons, twin turrets forward and aft, together with a single in a shield-protected barbette on each side amidships. With an increase in length of 6.1 m (20 ft) but none in the beam, the *Brooklyn*'s designers substituted a twin turret for each barbette mounting and added a forecastle deck. With her extremely high freeboard, exaggeratedly curved ends, pronounced tumblehome and tubular masts of varying section, the ship clearly owed much to French influences, though the three spindly funnels of unusual height were the designer's own.

Both the *Brooklyn* and *New York*

participated in the Battle of Santiago de Cuba in 1898, the former as Schley's flagship. In the course of the Spanish-American War an inferior Spanish squadron, blockaded in the port, was forced out to avoid capture by land operations. Ineptly handled, they were destroyed by superior gunfire as they emerged, all ending as grounded, gutted wrecks.

Specification
'Brooklyn' class
Displacement: 9,215 tons standard and 10,100 tons full load
Dimensions: length 122.68 m (402.5 ft); beam 19.71 m (64.67 ft); draught 8.00 m (26.25 ft)
Propulsion: four sets of triple-expansion steam engines delivering 13795 kW (18,500 ihp) to two shafts
Speed: 22 kts
Armament: eight 203.2-mm (8-in), 12 127-mm (5-in) and 12 6-pdr guns, and five 457.2-mm (18-in) torpedo tubes
Armour: belt 203.2 mm (8 in) tapering to 76.2 mm (3 in); protective deck 152.4 (6 in) tapering to 76.2 mm (3 in); barbettes 203.2 mm (8 in); casemates 101.6 mm (4 in)
Complement: 718

Above: Brooklyn was so lightly armoured as to almost warrant classification as a protected cruiser, having only a 76.2-mm (3-in) armour *belt with no bulkheads at the ends. The low height of her reciprocating engines allowed the belt to be equally shallow.*

Brooklyn as she appeared before her 1909 reconstruction, the high freeboard and pronounced tumblehome imparting a distinctly French look. However, the incongruous ochre and white colour scheme was wholly American.

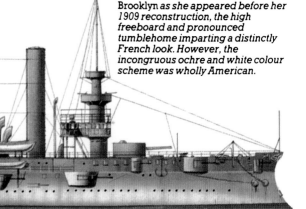

USA
'Pennsylvania' class

Six **'Pennsylvania' class** armoured cruisers (USS **Pennsylvania**, USS **West Virginia**, **California**, **Colorado**, **Maryland** and **South Dakota**, later renamed **Pittsburgh**, **Huntingdon**, **San Diego**, **Pueblo**, **Frederick** and **Huron**) were launched in 1903-4 and represented not only a great leap in sheer size but also a transition to European style of armament balance. They also typified the American love for completely symmetrical armament layout, a trait that continued right through to the various standard designs of World War II. For

their size, their armament was on the light side in a vain attempt to reduce weight and improve speed to the European norm of 23 kts. This was because they (together with the follow-on 'Tennessee' class ships) were meant, like their British contemporaries, to be used as a fast wing of the main battle-fleet. Though they were longer than

Displacing over 15,000 tons, the 'California' class were the first US armoured cruisers built on a European scale.

contemporary battleships, they had a common problem of inadequate speed margin.

In terms of protection, the amidships armour, 127 mm (5 in) thick, rose sufficiently high to protect the 152.4-mm (6-in) casemates but was long enough only to cover the boiler and machinery spaces. Though 88.9-mm (3.5-in) belts extended both to bow and stern, these were very shallow and typically of the type that reinforced the British ideas that, unless it could effectively keep out 152.4-mm shell fire, its weight was better incorporated in the protective deck behind it.

War experience resulted in their armaments being considerably modified, 14-pdr AA guns being added and, in at least one case, an aircraft catapult being temporarily added. Most had their pole foremasts replaced by the 'basketwork' cage masts, which enabled their spotting tops to be considerably elevated without incurring a vibration penalty to upset the instruments, while also improving the visibility by being clear of the ship's smoke.

The *Pittsburgh* emerged from her mid-life refit with only three funnels, giving her the looks of a 'Connecticut' class battleship. Only one, the *San Diego*, was lost, running on a mine in home waters. The port machinery spaces flooded and, though steam was available, there was reluctance to counterflood the starboard spaces and the ship capsized.

Specification
'Pennsylvania' class
Displacement: 13,700 tons standard
Dimensions: length 153.62 m (504.0 ft); beam 21.18 m (69.5 ft); draught 7.39 m (24.26 ft)
Propulsion: two sets of triple-expansion steam engines delivering 17151 kW (23,000 ihp) to two shafts
Speed: 22 kts
Armament: four 203.2-mm (8-in), 14 152.4-mm (6-in) and 18 76.2-mm (3-in) guns, and two 457.2-mm (18-in) torpedo tubes
Armour: belts 152.4 mm (6 in) tapering to 88.9 mm (3.5 in); transverse bulkhead 101.6 mm (4 in); protective deck 38.1 mm (1.5 in) with 101.6-mm (4-in) slopes; barbettes 152.4 mm (6 in); casemates 127 mm (5 in)
Complement: 829

Above: For their size, the 'Pennsylvannia' class were lightly armed, partly in an attempt to give them a good margin of speed over contemporary battleships.

Below: During the war Pittsburgh *acquired a basketwork cage foremast allowing spotting tops to be higher but without incurring a weight penalty.*

'Tennessee' class

Four **'Tennessee' class** armoured cruisers (USS *Tennessee*, USS *Washington*, USS *North Carolina* and USS *Montana*, later renamed *Memphis*, *Seattle*, *Charlotte* and *Missoula*) were built, the last completed in 1908. Except for the underarmed Charlestons of 1904-5, no more of the type were built as a result of the introduction of the battle-cruiser. Like earlier armoured cruisers, they eventually yielded the 'state' names in favour of battleships.

In size and in armament the 'Tennessees' equated fairly to the contemporary British 'Warriors' though they carried also 22 14-pdr 76.2-mm (3-in) guns for use in repelling torpedo craft. A major difference as compared with the British ships was their bulk: like the French, the Americans believed in plenty of freeboard and, though six of each ship's 152.4-mm (6-in) guns were casemated on each side, they were sufficiently high to be fought satisfactorily. Above them, at upper deck level, four more 152.4-mm guns were set in casemates, one at each corner of the superstructure.

A feature of the Tennessees was their large expanse of armour plating.

The main belt, 127 mm (5 in) thick, extended from before the forward turret to abaft the after turret, being continued in a shallower 76.2-mm (3-in) belt to the extremities, this being backed by a 0.91-m (3-ft) cofferdam filled with a 'water-excluding material'. The 127-mm (5-in) side armour was taken high enough to enclose all of the secondary guns, which were able, via re-entrant ports, to be stowed within its protection. The protective deck had 101.6-mm (4-in) slopes.

The main battery consisted of a twin 254-mm (10-in) turret at each end, the largest calibre carried by any armoured cruiser of this generation.

Unlike the triple-screwed French and Germans, the Americans followed the British twin-screw layout, with their engines in separate compartments and their 16 boilers in no less than eight separate compartments.

Wartime alterations saw the replacement of the foremast pole by the cage-type structure then common in American battleships, the landing of much of the secondary armament and the acquisition of aircraft catapults by two ships. The *Memphis* was the sole war loss of the class.

Specification
'Tennessee' class
Displacement: 14,500 tons standard
Dimensions: length 153.62 m (504.0 ft); beam 22.25 m (73.0 ft); draught 7.92 m (26.0 ft)
Propulsion: two sets of triple-expansion steam engines delivering 17897 kW (24,000 ihp) to two shafts
Speed: 22 kts
Armament: four 254-mm (10-in), 16 152.4 mm (6-in) and 22 76.2-mm (3-in) guns, and four 533.4-mm (21-in) torpedo tubes
Armour: belt 127 mm (5 in) tapering to 76.2 mm (3 in); transverse bulkhead 152.4 mm (6 in); protective deck 25.4 mm (1 in) with 88.9-mm (3.5-in) slopes; barbettes 228.6 mm (9 in); casemates 127 mm (5 in)
Complement: 857

The wartime camouflage of Tennessee *makes a dramatic change from the pre-war panoply of* Brooklyn. *The 'Tennessees' were the last armoured cruisers to be built by the USA.*

Jutland-Twilight of the Armoured Cruiser

The battle of the Falklands demonstrated that even the best armoured cruisers were no match for battle-cruisers, yet May 1916 found two cruiser squadrons scouting for the Grand Fleet. Under the impetuous Rear-Admiral Arbuthnot four vessels, Defence, Warrior, Duke of Edinburgh and Black Prince, steamed ahead to engage the German 2nd Scouting Group, but they were steering straight for the German line.

At 18.00 on 31 May 1916 the Battle of Jutland was at a critical juncture. The long line of the German High Seas Fleet had been lured northward by Admiral Sir David Beatty's battle-cruisers and its head was only 21 km (13 miles) from Admiral Sir John Jellicoe's nearest battleship, within gunshot but hidden in the haze. But Britain's Grand Fleet was still steaming south east in cruising formation, six parallel columns of four ships, its commander-in-chief yet unable to deploy into battle line for want of firm information. His immediate 'eyes' were the 1st and 2nd Cruiser Squadrons, each consisting of four armoured cruisers, deployed on each forward wing of the fleet. Their task was to support the fleet and its light cruisers, to reconnoitre in force and to deal with enemy cruisers.

Aware of the need to prevent premature contact of the two fleets, Beatty at some cost barged across the head of the German line, forcing it from its near northerly course to about east. By this time the die was cast and the Grand Fleet was deploying correctly onto a battle line roughly paralleling that of the enemy. Between the two fleets the calm sea had been cut up by the manoeuvrings of both battle-cruiser forces and their attendant scouting groups of light cruisers. The already fickle visibility had deteriorated with the smoke from a hundred funnels.

On the nearer side to the enemy was the 1st Cruiser Squadron, under the spirited command of Rear-Admiral Sir Robert Arbuthnot. His flag was in HMS *Defence*, supported directly by HMS *Warrior*. Farther out was HMS *Duke of Edinburgh* with HMS *Black Prince* on the wing. Immediately before the Grand Fleet's deployment began, Arbuthnot signalled to the *Warrior* (timed 17.53) 'Open fire and engage enemy.' It is not known which of the enemy he had sighted; probably it was light cruisers of the German's 2nd Scouting Group at a point just before they were savaged by the guns of Rear-Admiral Sir Horace Hood's battle-cruisers.

Even as Jellicoe deployed, the German line remained invisible to him, with Beatty's battle-cruisers storming across his view. For his part, Beatty was aware of two British armoured cruisers (they were the *Defence* and *Warrior*) closing on his port bow and firing at an unknown target. He was more than surprised when the two held their course, passing close under his bows, forcing him to alter course and lose sight of the enemy line.

Arbuthnot was, at this stage, after SMS *Wiesbaden*, an enemy light cruiser that had been disabled just before by Hood's gunfire but still afloat and in a good position to launch torpedoes at Jellicoe's line.

Had Arbuthnot been able to finish her off, together with the rest of her group and gather up-to-date information on the main German line, it would have been in accordance with battle instructions. The precipitate manner in which he went about it was true to his character.

At this time, Beatty was exchanging fire with the enemy main body, but when Arbuthnot turned his head and went away at a closer range and on a reciprocal course, the German gunlayers were presented with a far more attractive target. From the bigger British ships, Arbuthnot's ships were virtually hidden by the walls of water thrown up by salvoes from at least four enemy capital ships.

Visibility was such that even from the *Warrior*, 400 m (440 yards) astern of the *Defence*, the source of the fire could not be made out but, at 18.19, as he was forced to alter slightly away under the sheer weight of fire, Arbuthnot was struck by two heavy salvoes in succession. The *Defence* staggered but was still proceeding at high speed when she suddenly erupted in a cataclysmic explosion. The *Warrior*, herself under heavy fire, was so close astern that she steamed straight through the smoke and falling debris. Burning at each end, hydraulic power lost and guns in local control, she finally took a smashing blow in the port machinery space. Both spaces were filled with live steam and evacuated by those still able to, but with steam still feeding to the engines she kept her way and crept toward the protection of the 5th Battle Squadron. Already hit by an estimated 15 major- and six lesser-calibre projectiles, she would probably have shared the fate of the *Defence* but for the jamming of HMS *Warspite*'s helm. Describing two complete circles out of control, the battleship drew the fire of the enemy gunners.

The Grand Fleet assembled at Scapa. The armoured cruisers were now ships without a role: their reconnaissance task usurped by lighter vessels and battlecruisers, they were relegated to low-risk operations after Jutland.

The battle moved away and the *Warrior*, with 68 dead, concentrated on survival. At 18.40 the seaplane carrier HMS *Engadine* hove in sight and stood by. An hour later the cruiser signalled that she was still trying to turn off steam but, at 19.45, ordered 'Stand by to tow me.' the *Engadine*, a lightly-built converted cross-Channel packet, passed a light line by skiff and then winched over a heavy towline. In deteriorating weather conditions, the tow slowly got under way and, once the *Warrior*'s hard-over rudder had been centred, built up to an estimated 7 kts (with the *Engadine* doing revolutions for 19 kts). Despite all efforts at damage control, the *Warrior* slowly settled by the stern and, although 160 km (100 miles) had been made good towards the Scottish coast, daybreak found the cruiser in a parlous state. In a rising sea the bulkheads were yielding under the strain and, at 07.15, the *Warrior* hoisted flag 'K', the pre-arranged signal for immediate evacuation. It was followed by her last signal, by semaphore: 'Slip wire – Never mind buoying it.' The *Engadine* ranged alongside and conducted an orderly transfer; with no way of sinking the cruiser she left her, quarter deck already awash, to founder. She had been about 320 km (200 miles) from the safety of Cromarty.

At the point in the battle where Arbuthnot had started his impetuous dash, the neighbouring *Duke of Edinburgh*, having received his signal, made to conform. Fortunately, the risky dash under Beatty's bows could not be undertaken and the cruiser lost touch with her leader. At 19.17 she joined up with the 2nd Cruiser Squadron and survived intact.

As wing ship of the 1st Cruiser Squadron, the *Black Prince* was some 21 km (13 miles) distant from Jellicoe and out of sight. At 17.33 she was sighted by the light cruiser HMS *Falmouth*: as the latter was attached to Beatty's force, this was the first link between the two groups. Nine

Crippled in the evening action, the unfortunate Black Prince *blundered into the dreadnought SMS* Thuringen *during the night. The battleship put 15 305-mm (12-in) shells into her before the blazing hulk drifted into the night.*

A cruiser is seen under large-calibre shell fire at Jutland. A murky day, visibility was further reduced by the vast volumes of smoke produced by coal-fired ships.

minutes later the *Black Prince*, as requested, relayed to Jellicoe a situation report from the *Falmouth* but, almost immediately, was observed to make a major change of course. It was known that she was suffering from an earlier electrical breakdown but now, strangely, she 'disappeared'; she was not seen again until after midnight. At this time the German main body was breaking through the light forces massed at the tail of Jellicoe's column. The unfortunate cruiser, in what must have been a semi-crippled condition, blundered into a very alert enemy rearguard. At a range of only 1000 m (1,100 yards) she was suddenly illuminated by the searchlights of the old battleship SMS *Thüringen* which, subsequently, claimed to have put 15 305-mm (12-in) shells into her without reply. Blazing fiercely, she passed from sight.

Also engaged in the desperate encounters of that night was the destroyer HMS *Spitfire*, which had carried the fight so well to the enemy that she had been in violent collision with the German battleship SMS *Nassau*. While engaged in patching up her considerable damage, the *Spitfire* was nearly run down by a large ship on fire 'from foremast to mainmast, on deck and between decks . . .' so close was she that the *Spitfire*'s crew could both hear and feel the fire. The wreck had two, widely-spaced funnels and was taken to be a battle-cruiser, but was almost certainly the *Black Prince* with her two centre stacks shot away. A massive explosion was observed soon afterwards but neither trace nor survivor was ever found.

The disaster to Arbuthnot's squadron accelerated the final decline of the armoured cruiser. Coronel and the Falklands had underlined the obvious, that older ships were no match for newer ones and that the newer ones themselves were easy prey for the battle-cruiser.

Jutland had shown in turn that armoured cruisers no longer had a role as the reconnaissance wing of the fleet: too slow, they could now become victims of battleships as well. For the remainder of the war they were used in low-risk operations and areas, and for the most part, survived the peace only by months.

'Rurik' class

The *Rurik* that served during World War I should not be confused with the ship of the same name completed in 1896. This latter vessel, a 10,950-tonner built like her near-sister *Rossia* in St Petersburg, so outclassed contemporary British protected cruisers that the two 'Powerfuls' were hurriedly constructed as a counter. Though potentially a challenge she was lost, like so much of the Russian fleet, in the war with Japan, being sunk in August 1904 in the battle of the Korea Strait.

Obviously the Russians thought the name to be worth continuing, for another armoured cruiser (more correctly rendered *Riurik*, after the founder of a long dynasty of early tsars) was ordered soon afterwards from Vickers at Barrow, the first of two projected. Completed in 1907, she was of unique appearance with three funnels of equal height and a single, crossed mast which was stepped abaft them. Of a size with the contemporary British 'Minotaurs', she was slower but more heavily armed, capable of putting four 254-mm (10-in) and four 203-mm (8-in) guns on each broadside, compared with four 233.7-mm (9.2-in) and five 190.5-mm (7.5-in) guns, or about 20 per cent by weight. As the two major-calibre batteries were all housed in twin mountings, there was space also for 20 120-mm (4.7-in) QFs mounted singly in protective casemates, for the most part at upper-deck level. The *Rurik*'s protection was impressive in the large area covered, the only 'soft' zones being the extreme counter and

Her three stubby funnels gave Rurik a unique silhouette. All her major batteries were housed in twin mountings which allowed space for 20 119.3-mm (4.7-in) quick-fire guns to be fitted in single casemates along the level of the upper deck.

the accommodation spaces on the two upper decks right forward.

The Russian fleet of 1914-8 was little better used than its predecessor of a decade before. The *Rurik* belonged to the Baltic Fleet, numerically superior to the Germans that opposed it. Both sides were actively engaged in mine-laying, in the course of which the *Rurik* twice badly grounded. In July 1915 the Russians encountered an inferior German force east of Gotland and the *Rurik* claimed to have hit the *Roon* several times in an indecisive action. The *Rurik* was broken up in a general 'thinning' of the fleet in the later 1920s, after the Revolution.

Specification
'Rurik' class
Displacement: 15,200 tons standard
Dimensions: length 149.35 m (490 ft 0 in); beam 22.86 m (75 ft 0 in); draught 7.92 m (26 ft 0 in)
Propulsion: two sets of triple-expansion steam engines delivering 14690 kW (19,700 ihp) to two shafts
Speed: 21 kts
Armament: four 254-mm (10-in), eight 203-mm (8-in) and 20 120-mm (4.7-in) guns, and two 457-mm (18-in) torpedo tubes
Protection: vertical belt 152 mm (6 in) tapering to 76.2 mm (3 in); topsides 76.2 mm (3 in); transverse bulkheads 76.2 mm (3 in); protective deck 38.1 mm (1.5 in); barbettes 203 mm (8 in); casemates 177.8 mm (7 in)
Complement: 800

The Russian fleet was handled with much the same ineptitude and lethargy in World War I as it had been in 1905. Rurik spent the war in the Baltic largely inactive, a sad waste of her potential.

'Blücher' class

SMS *Blücher* (only unit of the **'Blücher' class**) affords a prime example of a misfit warship produced rapidly to meet a mistakenly-perceived threat from a rival power. The British built their first battle-cruisers in great secrecy, referring to them (deliberately misleadingly) as 'armoured cruisers'. Of the latter, true current examples were displacing upwards of 13,500 tons, with a mix of 233.7- and 190.5-mm (9.2- and 7.5-in) guns, and it was easy to make the Germans accept the idea of a 16,000-tonner with eight 233.7-mm guns when, in fact, the 'Invincibles' were to be 17,230-tonners with eight 304.8-mm (12-in) guns.

Committed to 'reply', the uncertain Germans prudently laid down a 'one-off', the *Blücher*. By adopting a 12-gun main battery, set in a six-turret hexagonal layout similar to that of the contemporary 'Nassau' class battleships, her designers expected a broadside advantage: not only did their 210-mm

The design of the Blücher stemmed from a clever deception by the British, who gave out that the new 'Invincibles' were to be conventional cruisers mounting 233.7-mm (9.2-in) guns. The Germans built Blücher with a much superior armament.

(8.27-in) gun outrange the British 233.7-mm guns, but the available eight-gun broadside weighed nearly 1134 kg (2,500 lb) against the 862 kg (1,900 lb) of the five 233.7-mm guns expected to bear in a single-gun layout.

On their part the British, stimulated by their own deviousness, credited the *Blücher* with more than she had. As late as 1908 the authoritative *Brassey's Naval Annual*, though properly reporting six turrets, listed them as being four twin and two single 280-mm (11.02-in) mountings, tempering this with the observation that eight guns of this size 'at most' should be expected on the displacement.

Even when the true nature of the 'Invincibles' was known, the Germans had little choice but to complete the ship, a super armoured cruiser with full length belt, two protective decks and a speed of 26 kts. Unfortunately, the *Blücher*'s size found her tied to Hipper's battle-cruiser force despite the fact that her speed and armament were inferior to those of her companies. At the Dogger Bank in 1915 she was placed at the tail of the fleeing German line, slowing it down. As Beatty's ships came into range their 304.8-mm shells, impacting at steep angles, drilled through both protective decks to guarantee her destruction.

Blücher's 210-mm (8.2-in) guns not only outranged the standard British cruiser armament, but her eight-gun broadside threw a far heavier weight of shell than the five-gun broadside of typical British designs.

Above: Blücher was undoubtedly the finest armoured cruiser ever built, but she had no place among battle-cruisers. Attached to Hipper's squadron at Dogger Bank, she was shot to pieces by Beatty's squadron. With flag still flying she capsizes, crewmen scrambling for safety.

Specification
'Blücher' class
Displacement: 15,500 tons standard
Dimensions: length 161.61 m (530.22 ft); beam 24.52 m (80.45 ft); draught 8.07 m (26.48 ft)
Propulsion: three sets of triple-expansion steam engines delivering 32 811 kW (44,000 ihp) to three shafts
Speed: 26 kts
Armament: 12 210-mm (8.27-in), eight 150-mm (5.91-in) and 16 88-mm (3.46-in) guns, and three 450-mm (17.72-in) torpedo tubes
Armour: belt 185 mm (7.28 in) tapering to 90 mm (3.54 in); upper protective deck 35 mm (1.38 in); lower protective deck 50 mm (1.97 in); barbettes 150 mm (5.91 in)
Complement: 850

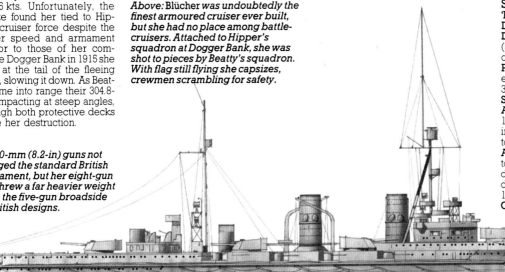

 GERMANY
'Scharnhorst' class

Under the Naval Act of 1900, with later additions, the German navy was set at 38 battleships, 20 armoured cruisers, 38 small cruisers and 144 torpedo boats; but the programme was rather spoiled by the advent of the Dreadnought. It was perceived that there was a need for 'at least one squadron of efficient armoured cruisers' for use outside home waters.

As in light cruisers so in larger cruisers, the Germans evolved continuously, producing mainly 'one-offs' and pairs of ships. Thus, in 1900, they launched their first pair, SMS *Fürst Bismarck* and SMS *Prinz Heinrich* of the 'Bismarck' class which, though of similar dimensions, varied in displacement because of two separate standards of protection. Each incorporated two of the older battleships' guns of 240-mm (9.45-in) calibre. These were followed closely by the two 'Prinz Adalbert' class units SMS *Prinz Adalbert* and SMS *Friedrich Karl* which, again of similar size, adopted the lighter scheme of protection, greater installed horsepower and doubled the number of main battery guns by changing to the excellent 210-mm (8.27-in) gun. Despite this, their speed was barely 20 kts.

The two 'Roon' class units SMS *Roon* and SMS *Yorck*, launched in 1903-4,

stretched the design minimally to improve the power by about 8 per cent. This, predictably, increased their speed by less than a knot. An improved layout of the secondary 150-mm (5.91-in) guns (five to a side, set on two levels) enabled the protection to be better distributed. The result of more boilers was an increase in funnels from three to four.

Although their armament was excellent, the 'Roons' were inferior in speed and protection (marginally) compared with their Royal Navy yardsticks. This was rectified in the two 'Scharnhorst' class units SMS *Scharnhorst* and SMS *Gneisenau* of 1906, which achieved 22.5 kts with 30 per cent more power. The Germans resisted the temptation to increase the scale of armament (except to substitute four 210-mm guns for casemated 150-mm guns) and improved the protection, the belt armour being thickened slightly at the expense of the protective deck. Their application was sound, for the ships both absorbed tremendous punishment before being sunk, as related elsewhere, at the Falklands.

SMS Gneisenau, together with her sister Scharnhorst, formed the principle striking power of von Spee's East Asiatic squadron. The two cruisers represented a considerable improvement over the earlier 'Roons' and gave Germany the victory in the first major naval battle of the war.

Dimensions: length 144.55 m (474.25 ft); beam 21.63 m (70.96 ft); draught 7.46 m (24.48 ft)
Propulsion: three sets of triple-expansion steam engines delivering 19 388 kW (26,100 ihp) to three shafts
Speed: 22.5 kts
Armament: eight 210-mm (8.27-in), six 150-mm (5.91-in) and 20 88-mm (3.46-in) guns, and four 450-mm (17.72-in) torpedo tubes
Armour: belt 150 mm (5.91 in) tapering to 80 mm (3.15 in); protective deck 50 mm (1.97 in); barbettes 170 mm (6.69 in)
Complement: 770

Specification
'Scharnhorst' class
Displacement: 11,500 tons standard

The *Scharnhorst* in Action

Scharnhorst was the flagship of Graf von Spee's East Asiatic squadron based at Tsingtao in China. Given the British dominance, the meteoric career of von Spee and his vessels could only end one way, but before he was cornered he administered the Royal Navy's first major defeat for two and a half centuries.

In the early years of the 20th century, Germany's imperial trading interests in China were administered from an enclave at Tsingtao, which acted also as a base for river gunboats and the powerful East Asiatic Squadron. Commanded by Vizeadmiral Graf von Spee, the latter was a highly efficient force consisting of the 11,400-ton armoured cruisers SMS *Scharnhorst* and *Gneisenau*, and the light cruisers SMS *Emden*, *Leipzig* and *Nürnberg*, averaging about 3,500 tons apiece. All had been completed between 1906 and 1909.

Germany recognized the fact that, in the case of general war with the colonial powers and (probably) Japan, Tsingtao would be indefensible and it was not surprising, therefore, that von Spee's ships were widely dispersed at the outbreak of war in August 1914. His two major ships, unknown to the Allies, were at Ponape in the Carolines, where they were rapidly joined by the *Nürnberg* from the US west coast. Good-class mercantile ships were requisitioned and armed, and added as auxiliaries. Last out of Tsingtao was the *Emden*, which left on 3 August 1914 with four colliers. The *Leipzig* was recalled from the Mexican coast.

Though there was great Allied concern about his presence, threatening as it did a large number of trooping convoys, their activity kept von Spee lying low. He proceeded to Pagan Island, where he was joined by the *Emden*. Deciding that offensive activity in the Pacific would certainly result in the disablement and destruction of his squadron, which lacked any base, von Spee detached the *Emden* for her raid into the Bay of Bengal and embarked on a leisurely and rambling trek eastwards across the Pacific. With little hostile presence in the theatre, his progress was not opposed and he aimed to work down the Chilean coast, disrupting trade and breaking for home by way of the Horn. He was off the South American coast by

On 1 November 1914 off the coast of Chile, von Spee was intercepted by Rear-Admiral Cradock's scratch force led by HMS Good Hope.

27 October, his cruiser strength supplemented by the arrival of SMS *Dresden*, which had been hustled out of the South Atlantic by an ominous increase in British naval presence.

On 31 October von Spee had the *Leipzig* detached in the neighbourhood of the small port of Coronel, where she detected the presence of the British cruiser HMS *Glasgow*. As there seemed a good chance of destroying the latter the German admiral came south, and the afternoon of the following day found him 80 km (50 miles) north west of the port. His two armoured cruisers were in line ahead, closely followed by the *Leipzig*. Some distance astern was the *Dresden*, with the *Nürnberg* out of sight to the north. The ragged line was pounding at 14 kts into a lumpy sea caused by the

residue of a southerly gale when, at about 16.30, the smoke of two warships was sighted to the south west.

The approaching ships were identified as British and, not knowing their intentions, von Spee steered inshore to cut them off from any sanctuary in neutral waters. Some degree of concentration was desirable and neither side pushed for an immediate conclusion, von Spee particularly not knowing the British strength backing the *Glasgow*.

By 18.00 the Germans were running roughly parallel with a four-funnelled 'Drake' class armoured cruiser and a three-funnelled 'County'. These were HMS *Good Hope* and *Monmouth*, the former wearing the flag of Rear-Admiral Sir Christopher Cradock, who had come round from the Atlantic with a scratch-crewed squadron with the ambitious intention of finding and stopping von Spee. The German gunlayers were looking westward at targets indistinct against the dazzle of a lowering sun, which broke through occasional wrack. Themselves well illuminated, the Germans manoeuvred at this stage to keep well out of range, and the British seemed unwilling to seize their temporary advantage.

Sunset was about 19.00 and, anticipating the reversal of conditions, von Spee had closed to about 11000 m (12,030 yards). Once the sun had dipped, the British were sharply silhouetted against the afterglow while his own force rapidly merged with the increasing gloom in the east. The *Scharnhorst*'s opening three-gun salvo put a neat group into the sea 500 m (550 yards) short of the *Good Hope*. Her third salvo put out of action, the *Good Hope*'s forward 233.7-mm (9.2-in) guns, and 12 210-mm (8.27-in) guns were now bearing against a solitary 233.7-mm and a variety of 152-mm (6-in) guns, many of which were in wave-immersed casemates.

From the outset, the unpractised British gunnery was wretched and, with the advantage of light, von Spee closed in. By 19.30 the range was down to 'sixty hectometres' (about 6,500 yards) and the rapid German fire was smothering the opposition. At the cost of four hits, the *Gneisenau* forced the *Monmouth* out of line, badly on fire, with her burning interior visible in places through rents in her glowing plates. The *Gneisenau* then shifted to the difficult and fleeting target of the *Glasgow*, and the *Nürnberg* was detailed to find and sink the stricken *Monmouth*.

Good Hope destroyed

The *Scharnhorst*, meanwhile, had sustained only two hits in inflicting an estimated 37 on the *Good Hope*. The latter, badly on fire forward, was still gamely replying when she was suddenly shattered by a magazine explosion, disintegrating in what von Spee described as a 'splendid firework display'. The *Glasgow* disengaged to the west and the completeness of victory became apparent later when the *Nürnberg* reported having despatched the *Monmouth* which, by the time she was found in fleeting moonlight at 21.00, was listing too far to work the majority of her remaining guns.

Scharnhorst *sustained only two hits in reply from* Good Hope *but achieved nearly 40 hits, setting the British cruiser on fire and disabling most of her guns.*

Panzer-Kreuzer SMS *Scharnhorst*

Armed with eight 210-mm (8.27-in) 40-calibre and six 152-mm (6-in) 40-calibre guns, Scharnhorst was more than a match for her opponent at Coronel. Powered by three sets of vertical triple-inverted expansion steam engines, her designed 19388 kW (26,000 hp) gave her a maximum speed of 22.5 kts, although she was never able to steam as well as her sistership after badly grounding in 1909. Meeting a vastly superior opponent at the Falklands, Scharnhorst fought to the last and went down with all hands.

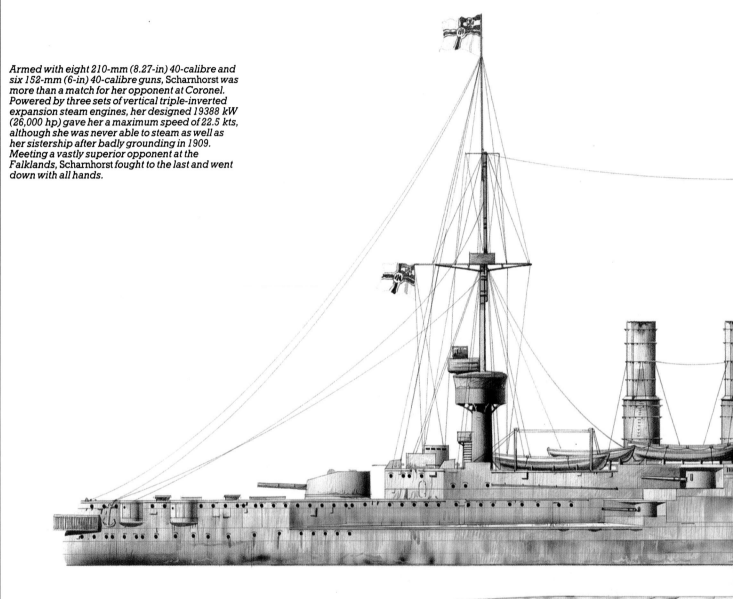

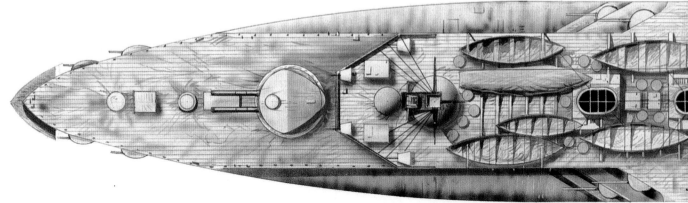

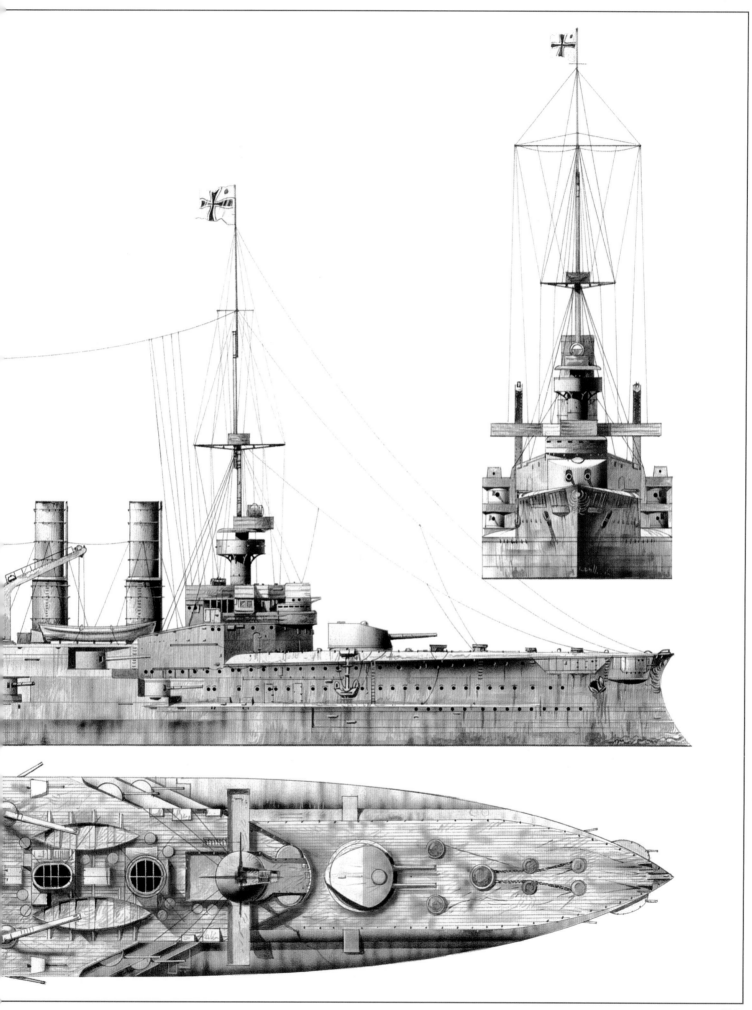

The *Scharnhorst* in Action

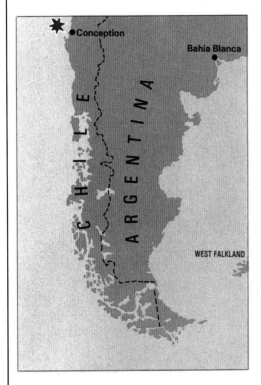

Map labels: Conception, Bahia Blanca, CHILE, ARGENTINA, WEST FALKLAND

Map labels (right): Good Hope, Glasgow, Monmouth, Otranto, 19.00 hours, Nürenburg, Scharnhorst, Gneisenau, Leipzig, Dresden, Glasgow escaping, 19.00 hours, 21.18 hours Monmouth sank, 20.00 hours, Otranto escaping, 19.57 hours Good Hope lost, 20.00 hours, 21.25 hours, Miles 0 10 15 20

Leipzig located HMS Glasgow *alone at Coronel and von Spee brought his squadron south to attack her.*

Running into the whole British squadron, von Spee closed in at dusk; the British were silhouetted

against the setting sun, the Germans hidden in the murk by the Chilean coast.

Like the *Good Hope* the *Monmouth* left no survivors, the seas being, in any case, too fierce to permit the lowering of boats.

Von Spee seemed far from elated by his success. Though he had suffered no significant damage, he had expended almost half of his major-calibre ammunition. There was little prospect of obtaining more, he was 16000 km (10,000 miles) from home and he was all too aware that the world's greatest seapower, stung by its reverse, would be seeking him out to redress the score. The day after the action he entered Valparaiso for coal but refused to attend the general celebrations.

Falklands encounter

Possibly a quick break round the Horn and into the vastness of the South Atlantic would have spelled success at this point, but again von Spee seemed to be afflicted by indecision, hanging around at the isolated island of Mas-a-Fuera and then an anchorage on the desolate Chilean coast, north of the Magellan Strait. Only on 26 November, 25 days after the action off Coronel, did he sail at full strength for the Falklands. There he expected to destroy its important radio station, the survivors of Cradock's squadron and any stocks that were superfluous to his own needs.

Though summer in these latitudes, the weather was atrocious and the squadron did not round the Horn until the night of 1/2 December. Early on the morning of 2 December a British sailing vessel, laden with coal, was sighted. Ever mindful of his long run home, von Spee took her into sheltered waters and spent three days transferring her cargo.

8 December dawned bright and clear. It found the *Gneisenau*, supported by the *Nürnberg*, following the coast of East Falkland toward Stanley; von Spee was hull-down to the south. Main batteries were being trained on the radio station when suddenly the great splashes of a two-gun, major-calibre salvo

erupted in the morning sun. It was followed by a second, close enough to put fragments onto the *Gneisenau*'s upper deck. Standing farther out, the two German ships eventually rounded the bluff that screened the harbour. At 09.40 could be seen a great smoke cloud and tall, tripod masts. These could mean only British capital ships. Von Spee had wasted too much time.

After the disaster at Coronel the British Admiralty had moved rapidly, despatching three battle-cruisers from the Grand Fleet strength. Two of them, HMS *Invincible* and *Inflexible*, had just arrived with four cruisers and were still coaling. Fortunately for Vice-Admiral

Sturdee, in command, the old battleship HMS *Canopus* had been beached as a static harbour defence and had bought time for the disadvantaged force by firing indirectly on the *Gneisenau*.

The *Gneisenau* and *Nürnberg* closed on von Spee and the whole squadron made all haste away to the south-east in loose formation. None could make designed speed through foul hulls and machinery problems. Even before they

Scharnhorst enters Valparaiso the day after the battle. Although elated by his victory, von Spee knew he was nearly 16000 km (10,000 miles) from home and the Royal Navy would be seeking revenge.

were over the horizon the Germans could see the first British ships leaving Stanley. Visibility was perfect, the day was young and Nemesis was but a matter of time.

The *Leipzig* began to lag, but urgency was maintained by the constant sight of the pursuers who, in no hurry, overhauled them inexorably under a dense cloud of funnel smoke. At 12.47 came the ranging 304.8-mm (12-in) salvo from the leading battle-cruiser, the *Invincible*. By 13.00 the Germans were surrounded by splashes yet still unable to reply. At 13.20, still without significant damage, von Spee detached his light cruisers to shift for themselves but could see their British counterparts peel off in pursuit while his own ships were still suffering at the hands of the two battle-cruisers. He needed to close the range so turned abruptly and, at 13.30, got to within his 12000-m (13,125-yard) maximum. Opening fire, the *Scharnhorst* rapidly hit the *Invincible*, but the British reply was merely to sheer further off and continue the bombardment. The British were obviously content to stay at long range and expend as much ammunition as it took, even though the *Gneisenau* was having a light time with her big adversary, the *Inflexible*, blinded by her leader's smoke.

The kill

Long periods elapsed with no firing on either side, as each manoeuvred for advantage. By 15.00 the weather was deteriorating and the British obviously went for a decision. The range fell to 10975 m (12,000 yards) which, while allowing von Spee's ships to use their secondary 150-mm (5.9-in) guns, began to prove decisive. The *Scharnhorst* was burning heavily forward and had lost her third funnel. As her shooting began to fall off the *Gneisenau* also started to list. Ignoring a call to surrender, von Spee's ship suddenly ceased fire 'like a light blown out' and foundered at 16.17. There were no survivors.

The *Gneisenau* fought on though, through the mist of drizzling rain now falling, she could see her two opponents had been joined by a four-funnelled armoured cruiser, HMS *Carnarvon*. The murk offered no sanctuary from punishment. Reportedly hit by over 50 large-calibre rounds, the cruiser had her foremost funnel leaning drunkenly against the second, her foremast was missing and she was faltering to a stop in a cloud of her own smoke. Ammunition had run out and a British battle-cruiser closed the range and put 15 deliberate rounds into the wreck. The survivors formed up on deck, gave three cheers for the Kaiser and abandoned; only 200 were saved from the freezing water.

Of the light cruisers, only the *Dresden* was to escape for a further brief existence. Coronel

Above: Von Spee's squadron as seen from the Falklands, 8 December 1914. After a lucky shot from HMS Canopus, *Spee made off at speed, but before he was over the horizon the battlecruisers were leaving Port Stanley in pursuit.*

Below: Her turbines giving her a 5-kt advantage over the German cruisers, Invincible *opened fire with her forward 304.8-mm (12-in) guns shortly before 13.00 hours.* Scharnhorst *and* Gneisenau *swung towards their mighty enemy to give their consorts a chance to escape.*

Scharnhorst went down at 16.17 with all 770 of her crew and the gallant von Spee. Gneisenau *did not survive her sister for long; flags still flying and out of ammunition, she was battered into submission by 18.00. The battle-cruisers stopped, and saved 200 men from the freezing water.*

had been terribly avenged but, besides proving the obvious supremacy of the battle-cruiser over the armoured cruiser, the Falklands battle demonstrated also the toughness of German ships, the surprising range of their armament and the fighting spirit of their crews.

'Blake' class

Closely related to the 'Edgar' and 'Crescent' classes, the **'Blake' class** together with the 'Powerful' class ships were protected cruisers but are included to show the stem from which grew the later armoured cruiser. 'First-generation' armoured cruisers had ceased in the UK with the 'Orlando' class of 1886-7 which, on a limited displacement, had been unhandy to the point where the ships were of nearly similar performance to the battleships for which they were supposed to be scouting. Weight-saving by the suppression of vertical belts led to a dozen years of ascendancy for the protected cruiser.

The Royal Navy's cruiser force was expanded rapidly through the Naval Defence Act of 1889. Of first-class cruisers, designed to act as flagships and to hold their own in the interests of trade protection on distant stations, the two 'Blakes' of 1889-90, HMS *Blake* and *Blenheim* were a sound design. Protection of the ship proper was vested in the arched armoured deck, with vertical armouring introduced only around vitals such as the conning tower, casemates and ammunition hoists. What was to become a standard armament layout of heavy chase guns for and aft, backed by a casemated secondary battery, was also incorporated. It was, in fact, in the 'Blakes' that the maindeck casemate was introduced. With their two lofty funnels and original rig they looked particularly imposing in Victorian livery.

Between 1890 and 1892 was built a first derivative in the form of the seven slightly shorter **'Edgar' class** first-class cruisers with an armament similar to that of the 'Blakes'. The 'Edgars' were HMS *Edgar*, *Endymion*, *Gibraltar*, *Grafton*, *Hawke*, *St George* and *Theseus*. The two **'Crescent' class** units HMS *Crescent* and *Royal Arthur* were built in the same period, much

the same but, curiously, with the forward 233.7-mm (9.2-in) gun replaced by an extra pair of 152.4-mm (6-in) guns. All were reliable ships, with proven machinery and excellent for colonial service.

By the outbreak of war all were considered old and outdated, and the two original pairs, together with two 'Edgars', had been demoted to use as various types of depot ship. The *Hawke* was sunk by submarine in 1914 (the same *U-9* that sank three 'Cressys'). The remaining four rendered sterling service in the blockading 10th Cruiser Squadron and, after being bulged in 1914-5, at the Dardanelles.

Specification
'Blake' class
Displacement: 9,150 tons standard
Dimensions: length 114.30 m (375.0 ft); beam 19.81 m (65.0 ft); draught 7.85 m (25.75 ft)
Propulsion: two sets of triple-expansion steam engines delivering 9694 kW (13,100 ihp) to two shafts
Speed: 21.5 kts
Armament: two 233.7-mm (9.2-in), 10 152.4-mm (6-in) and 16 3-pdr guns, and four 355.6-mm (14-in) torpedo tubes
Armour: protective deck 152.4 mm (6 in) tapering to 76.2 mm (3 in); casemates 152.4 mm (6 in); barbettes 177.8 mm (7 in)
Complement: 570

The Naval Defence Act of 1889 led to a considerable expansion of the Royal Navy's cruiser force. HMS Blake was the precursor of the armoured cruiser designs of the turn of the century, introducing maindeck casemates and what was to be standard British armament.

Designed primarily as flagships for squadrons on distant stations and trade protection, the 'Blakes' were armed with 233.7-mm (9.2-in) chasers fore and aft and a main battery of 10 152.4-mm (6-in) guns. Obsolete by 1914, they were destined never to see action.

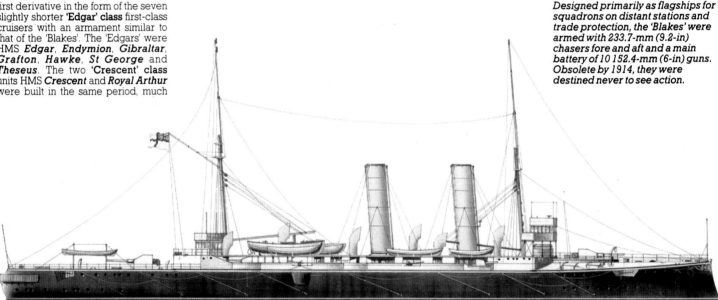

'Cressy' class

With the six **'Cressy' class** ships (HMS *Aboukir*, *Bacchante*, *Cressy*, *Euryalus*, *Hogue* and *Sutlej*), the armoured cruiser proper re-entered the Royal Navy list, though the type had continued to be built abroad during the 13-year British hiatus. These were belted and improved 'Diadems', their longer hulls allowing more efficient driving. They also continued the fashion of the 'Powerfuls', with a major-calibre chase gun forward and aft, and an entirely casemated secondary battery which, while protected, had its

lower casemates so low as to be unusable in any sea. This basic design fault was common through many classes.

Extra armour amounted to about 1,200 tons, absorbed mostly by a 152.4-mm (6-in) belt, stretching from a point 36.6 m (120 ft) from the bows to another some 27.4 m (90 ft) from the stern, tied athwartships by 127-mm (5-in) bulkheads. The 'soft' ends, of no more than 50.8-mm (2-in) plate, were widely criticized. The main protective deck was lighter than in the 'Diadems' as it was no longer considered the primary

shield. Armour was made by the Krupp cemented process and, strength-for-strength, was lighter than earlier plate, the ships were launched between 1899 and 1901.

On some of the class, windscoops replaced the ranks of familiar cowl ventilators; the idea was to reduce the profile offered to high-explosive shells. Another innovaton was the use of fire-proofed wood which, reportedly, was unpopular on the grounds that, if uniforms were stored in furniture made of it, their gold braid deterio-

rated!

It is the tragic record of this class that it is remembered most often for having lost three of its number within 90 minutes. Five of them were attached to the 7th Cruiser Squadron at the Nore, with the primary duties of supporting the Harwich Force and covering the northern approaches to the English Channel. On 22 September 1914, with a disdainful disregard of the already well-appreciated threat from submarine attack, the *Aboukir*, *Cressy* and *Hogue* were patrolling a narrow corri-

Origins of the Armoured Cruiser

Cruisers were not only the 'eyes of the fleet' but were designed to exercise, or indeed challenge, control of the ocean trade routes. Their design was a delicate balance between speed, protection and armament, with varying emphasis leading to a bewildering variety of cruiser categories.

As battlefleets of the 19th century were built to decide both wars at sea and the destiny of the states whose flags they wore, it was here that the money was spent and here that the great revolutions in warship development had most effect.

Less glamorous were the considerable fleets of cruising ships maintained by imperial powers to police their overseas possessions and guarantee free navigation on their vital trade routes. For these 'cruisers' the principal assets were self-sufficiency, flexibility and endurance. Heavy armament was not deemed necessary as their main defence lay in their flag and the power it represented. With machinery still inefficient and coal stocks uncertain, sail was still retained for both utility and smartness. Wooden hulls were undeniably more comfortable than iron under the hot sun of the tropics. Thus had developed a heterogeneous collection of powered and unpowered frigates, corvettes and sloops.

Mainstream evolution, meanwhile, had produced the steam-powered singledecker of metal construction which, though technically a frigate, completely outclassed any line-of-battle ship of the traditional navy. The cost and effort involved in the rapid increase in the numbers of these was another reason for the Royal Navy's cruising fleet to remain little changed.

The American Civil War saw effective use of the large cruiser that could be used not only against commerce but also to hunt down other cruisers. Always keen on the ideas of war against seaborne trade, the French also built the type, though it took the powerful Russian 'General Admiral' design of 1870 to prompt a British reply. This was HMS *Shannon* of 1877 which, in contrast with earlier steam frigates, was heavily protected, having not only a substantial vertical belt but also a protective deck. She began the vogue for ships as large as second-class battleships and capable of dispute with one. On paper their ultimate defence lay in their speed but, practically, the margin was negligible, the scale of armour and armament making them extremely sluggish. This lack of performance precluded their practical use with the main battlefleet and guaranteed their employment as flagships on distant stations.

Speed could be bought only at the expense of protection and, for a period, the

HMS Powerful *was built in response to a perceived Russian cruiser threat. Fast and long-ranged, she was under-armed, and the imbalance of her design led to the 'Diadem' class and thence to a generation of armoured cruisers proper.*

protected cruiser held sway. Typical of these were the two 'Blenheims' of 1889-90, comparable in length with a 'Royal Sovereign' class battleship but lacking her heavy main battery, the hull being slimmer and packing in a 50 per cent increase in power.

No longer able to engage a modern battleship, the large cruiser was beginning to bear the same relationship to it as had a sailing frigate to a ship of the line.

With the introduction of improved armour at the turn of the century, it was again possible to think in terms of adding a vertical belt in addition to protective decks. Thus the 'Cressy' class adopted the basic 'Diadem' design of protected cruiser of 1896-8 but with redistributed armour which added considerably to the displacement. Further weight was added in shipping centreline guns of a calibre larger than those mounted in casemates. This fashion for two major calibres was justified on the grounds that the ships would need to work with the battlefleet, and the fashion persisted until the armoured cruiser was superseded in 1908 by the battle-cruiser.

With the Cressy *and her five sisters, the armoured cruiser reappeared in the Royal Navy. The armament of the 'Powerfuls' was retained – two large chase guns and a casemated secondary battery – but the lower casemates were so low as to be unusable in any sea.*

dor between minefields and the Dutch coast, unescorted, at low speed and without zigzagging. At 06.30 the *Aboukir* was torpedoed. Assuming that she had been mined the others stopped to render assistance. All were torpedoed, all were sunk, and nearly 1,500 men died. Weddigen's old submarine *U-9* had done for them all, greatly influencing both British and German ideas on the possibilities of submarine warfare.

The fate of Cressy *was a terrible portent for the future. Steaming slowly in a straight line off the Dutch coast with two of her sisters,* Hogue *and* Aboukir, *she was attacked by the German submarine U-9. All three cruisers were sunk, one after the other, with the loss of 1,500 men.*

Specification
'Cressy' class
Displacement: 11,700 tons standard
Dimensions: length 143.87 m (472.0 ft); beam 21.18 m (69.5 ft)
Propulsion: two sets of triple-expansion steam engines delivering 15660 kW (21,000 ihp) to two shafts
Speed: 21 kts
Armament: two 233.7-mm (9.2-in), 12 152.4-mm (6-in) and 13 12-pdr guns, and two 457.2-mm (18-in) torpedo tubes

Armour: belt 152.4 (6 in) tapering to 50.8 mm (2 in); transverse bulkheads 127 mm (5 in); protective deck 76.2 mm (3 in) tapering to 38.1 mm (1.5 in); barbettes 152.4 m (6 in); casemates 127 mm (5 in)
Complement: 755

'Drake' class

Where the 'Cressys' had managed to stow the armament of the 'Powerfuls' on a considerably shorter and cheaper hull, they were too short to be capable of more than 21 kts. Battleships were getting faster, so armoured cruisers were still experiencing a speed problem and, to accommodate power for the desired 23 kts (HMS *King Alfred* averaged 24.8 kts for eight hours in 1907) the four **'Drake' class** that followed were again of a size with the 'Powerfuls'. Together with the *King Alfred* these were HMS **Drake**, **Good Hope** and **Leviathan**. They lacked the great freeboard and general bulky appearance of the 'Powerfuls', helped by being cut-down by one deck aft and adopting the new all-grey paint scheme. The four tall funnels were well-proportioned and uninterrupted by ventilator cowls, giving the profile a feeling of grace and power, yet emphasizing the almost complete lack of superstructure. As with all of their type, when completed in 1902-3 the masts were of enormous height and of three sections to give elevation to radio aerials, semaphore and gaffs and yards for flag signals. Though double-decked casemated armament was, from exercises, already well understood to be of little use, they were still included to house the 16 152.4-mm (6-in) guns deemed necessary. Another carry-over from mistaken thinking of the past was the ram bow; its existence

Despite the poor showing of her sister Good Hope *at Coronel,* Drake *was a worthy successor to the 'Cressys'. But her design was still bedevilled by outdated ideas; the ram served no serious purpose, and the ineffective lower casemates were retained regardless of their proven failure.*

had never and was never to be justified, and its only real use was to increase the waterline length of the ship.

The poor showing of the *Good Hope* at Coronel has been described elsewhere. Outclassed as she was, she could have done better with a fully worked-up regular crew and a better tactical sense on the part of Craddock. The only other loss in the class was the *Drake* herself. With the greater majority of the now-obsolete armoured cruisers, she was involved in the Atlantic convoy business. On 2 October 1917, having just dispersed an inward convoy, she was torpedoed by a submarine near Rathlin Island. A substantial escort materialized for her and she actually reached a secure anchorage, only to capsize and become a total loss.

Specification
'Drake' class
Displacement: 14,100 tons standard
Dimensions: length 161.39 m (529.5 ft); beam 21.64 m (71.0 m); draught 8.23 m (27.0 ft)

Propulsion: two sets of triple-expansion steam engines delivering 23117 kW (31,000 ihp) to two shafts
Speed: 23 kts
Armament: two 233.7-mm (9.2-in), 16 152.4 (6-in) and 14 12-pdr guns, and

two 457.2-mm (18-in) torpedo tubes
Armour: belt 152.4 mm (6 in) tapering to 76.2 mm (3 in); transverse bulkhead 127 mm (5 in); protective deck 76.2-50.8 mm (3-2 in)
Complement: 900

'Black Prince', 'Warrior' and 'Minotaur' classes

Between 1906 and 1908 (when its first battle-cruiser was commissioned), the Royal Navy received its last nine armoured cruisers. These were of three closely-related groups: two **'Black Prince' class** units (HMS *Black Prince* and *Edinburgh*), four **'Warrior' class** units (HMS *Achilles*, *Cochrane*, *Natal* and *Warrior*) and three **'Minotaur' class** units (HMS *Defence*, *Minotaur* and *Shannon*). Though the design was based on that of the 'Drakes', the hulls were beamier yet appreciably

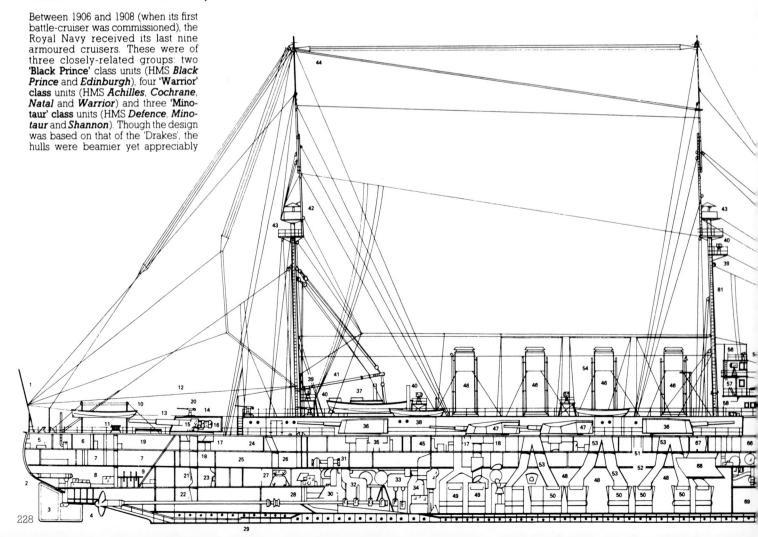

UK 'County' class

The only three-funnelled armoured cruisers in the Royal Navy, the high sided 'County' class were second-class ships aimed primarily at commerce protection. As such they had 152.4-mm (6-in) armament, a total of 14 guns being carried. Of these, however, four were in two experimental and trouble-prone twin turrets and six were in uselessly low casemates, factors which contributed to the poor showing of the Monmouth at Coronel. During the war, several had their lower casemated guns resited on the upper deck.

As trade-protection cruisers, the armour of the 'Counties' was also on a light scale. The belt was a maximum 101.6 mm (4 in) in thickness, tapering to half that forward and terminating beyond the after casemates. Speed was a major consideration, and most could manage 24 kts when pressed. As their length was limited, the production of lines capable of being driven at this speed did credit to the still-developing science of ship hull design. The class comprised HMS *Bedford*, *Berwick*, *Cornwall*, *Cumberland*, *Donegal*, *Essex*, *Kent*, *Lancaster*, *Monmouth* and *Suffolk*. Of the 10 built one, the *Bedford*, was wrecked in 1910; the *Monmouth*, disabled by SMS *Gneisenau* at Coronel, was finished off by the light cruiser SMS *Nürnberg*. It fell to her sister, the *Kent*, to avenge her at the Falklands in December

Lying peacefully in Vladivostok, HMS Suffolk (left) is seen here with USS Brooklyn. The 'County' class had a chequered history: Monmouth was lost at Coronel, but Kent took part in the battle of the Falklands, where by exceeding her designed speed she caught and sank the Nürnberg.

1914. With Sturdee's battle-cruisers devoted to the pursuit and destruction of von Spee's two armoured cruisers, the smaller British units were sent on a general chase after the enemy light cruisers, detached to shift for themselves. The *Kent*, a poor steamer, found herself chasing the *Nürnberg*, nominally faster but long out of dock. The *Kent* forced her fires with wood, reputedly the wardroom furniture, and managed a previously unheard-of 25 kts, slowly overhauling her quarry. For a while there was discomfiture when it was found that the forward 152.4-mm guns, superior in both calibre and elevation, were being outranged by the *Nürnberg*'s after 105-mm (4.1-in) armament. For some time the *Kent* was unable to reply to increasingly accurate fire but the German's ailing machinery finally failed under the strain and she was overwhelmed and sunk. The *Cornwall*, meanwhile, had assisted the *Glasgow* in despatching SMS *Leipzig*.

Specification
'County' class
Displacement: 9,800 tons standard
Dimensions: length 141.27 m (463.5 ft); beam 20.12 m (66.0 ft); draught 7.47 m (24.5 ft)
Propulsion: two sets of triple-expansion steam engines delivering 16405 kW (22,100 ihp) to two shafts
Speed: 23 kts

Armament: 14 152.4-mm (6in) and 10 12-pdr guns, and two 457.2-mm (18-in) torpedo tubes
Armour: belt 101.6 mm (4 in) tapering to 50.8 mm (2 in); transverse bulkheads 127 mm (5 in); protective deck 50.8 mm (2 in); barbettes 127 mm (5 in); casemates 101.6 mm (4 in)
Complement: 687

---

shorter, with the belt continued on a lighter scale right to the stern.

Like the 'Drakes', the 'Black Princes' completed in 1906 had a mixed 233.7-mm and 152.4-mm (9.2-in and 6-in) armament, but took six of the former arranged in single turrets in a hexagon layout. Ten 152.4-mm guns were set impossibly low in single casemates at maindeck level but, as long as this number of single mountings was required, there was little alternative to this defective layout. Later in the war, the casemate were plated-in and some of their weapons resited on the upper deck.

In the 'Warriors' that followed a year later, the hulls were similar but with

slightly improved horizontal protection. The great difference was in the reduction of the number of guns. Six 233.7-mm guns were carried in a similar arrangement to that of the previous class, but with two 190.5-mm (7.5-in) guns on each beam in single turrets. These could be sited at upper deck level, worked in any weather and still throw 80 per cent of the broadside weight of the earlier five 152.4-mm weapons. If, however, it is accepted

Black Prince and her sister were the last British armoured cruisers to carry a secondary battery of 152.4-mm (6-in) guns that could not be worked in any seaway; neither were very good sea boats. With the 'Warrior' and 'Minotaur' classes that followed, a sensible gun layout was adopted at last.

HMS *Achilles* cutaway drawing key
(vessel shown as completed, with short funnels and original tall masts)

1 Ensign mast
2 Stern torpedo tube (1904 model)
3 Balanced rudder
4 Twin screws
5 Captain's cabin
6 Captain's pantry
7 Stores etc
8 Steering engine
9 Winch engine
10 Gig
11 Capstan
12 Middle awning ridge
13 234-mm (9.2-in) Mk XI 50-calibre gun barrel
14 Turret
15 Saddle
16 Breech
17 Turntable
18 Turret machinery
19 Wardroom
20 3-pdr semi-automatic gun
21 Ammunition hoist
22 Magazine
23 Hoist machinery
24 Officers' quarters
25 Engineers' quarters
26 Armoured access tube
27 Auxiliary engine
28 Inspection pit
29 Double bottom
30 Turbine reduction gear
31 Dynamo
32 Starboard engine room
33 Four-cylinder triple expansion engine
34 Feed water tank
35 Barbette
36 Twin 234-mm (9.2-in) gun turret
37 Steam launch
38 Lifeboat
39 Searchlight platform
40 Searchlight
41 Boat handling derrick
42 Mainmast
43 Spotting top
44 Wireless aerials
45 Machine shop
46 Funnel
47 Twin 190-mm (7.5-in) Mk II 50-calibre guns
48 Boiler room
49 Cylindrical boilers
50 Yarrow large tube boilers
51 Upper armoured deck
52 Lower armoured deck
53 Funnel uptakes
54 Steam pipes
55 Upper bridge
56 Compass platform
57 Navigation room
58 Wireless room
59 Chart room
60 Armoured conning tower
61 Access to conning tower
62 Lower armoured command centre
63 Auxiliary machine shop
64 Dynamo
65 Fuel pump
66 Sailors' mess
67 Upper armour belt
68 Lower armour belt
69 Coal bunkers
70 Ammunition hoist machinery
71 Sailors' quarters
72 Canteen
73 Main deck
74 Cable store
75 Anchor wells
76 Anchors
77 Paint store
78 Waterline
79 Sloping armoured deck
80 Ram bow
81 Foremast

that the main function of the secondary battery was to fight off torpedo attacks then five well-sited 152.4-mm QF had to be superior to two 190.5-mm guns.

The final refinement came with the 'Minotaurs', which carried four 233.7-mm guns in two twinned centreline turrets, allowing four guns in broadside fire, the same as that possible for six singles. This arrangement left the waist along each side free for the mounting of five single 190.5-mm guns. Somewhat longer and beamier than their predecessors, the 'Minotaurs' had a 13 per cent increase in power for the same speed.

Though all rendered good wartime service, their record is forever overshadowed by the disaster of Arbuthnot's impetuosity at Jutland, where the *Black Prince*, *Warrior* and *Defence* were sunk, and the loss of the *Natal* to a magazine explosion in 1915. The *Cochrane* was wrecked in 1918.

Specification
'Minotaur' class
Displacement: 14,600 tons standard
Dimensions: length 158.19 m (519.0 ft); beam 22.71 m (74.5 ft); draught 8.23 m (27.0 ft)
Propulsion: two sets of triple-expansion steam engines delivering 20134 kW (27,000 ihp) to two shafts
Speed: 23 kts

Armament: four 233.7-mm (9.2-in), 10 190.5-mm (7.5-in) and 14 12-pdr guns, and five 457.2-mm (18-in) torpedo tubes
Armour: belt 152.4 mm (6 in) tapering to 76.2 mm (3 in); protective deck 38.1-19.1 mm (1.5-0.75 in); barbettes 203.2 mm (8 in)
Complement: 755

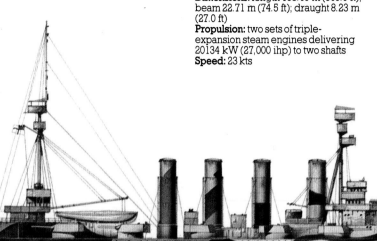

The 'Minotaurs' were the last class of British armoured cruisers, but were not as successful as the 'Warriors'. This is Shannon in her late war colour scheme. As designed, the class had short funnels but the uptakes were heightened by 4.5 m (15 ft) in 1909.

FRANCE
'Amiral Charner' class

Most elderly of the armoured cruisers to wear the French tricolore flag in World War I were the three 'Amiral Charner' class ships *Amiral Charner*, *Bruix* and *Latouche-Tréville*, completed in 1895-6. A fourth, *Chanzy*, had been lost in 1907. Their design was derived directly from that of the pioneering *Dupuy de Lôme* of 1893. The UK was having a 'holiday' from armoured cruiser construction at this time and, despite the fact that these ships were openly constructed with *guerres de course* (commerce-raiding campaigns) in mind, it was considered that the British protected cruisers of the day could match them. This was hardly true for though their contemporaries, the 'Hermiones', had a knot or so speed advantage they also had far lighter armament and, to tackle a Frenchman, would have needed to approach close enough to rue the lack of a vertical belt.

French ideas included a vertical belt over the complete length, employing exaggerated 'tumblehome' to give guns the maximum fields of fire, and protruding bows and sterns of hysterical aspect to increase the waterline length.

Where the *Dupuy de Lôme* had considerable armoured freeboard and was powered for a useful 20 kts, the 'Charners' were more modest and used a low-freeboard protected hull with wide side decks flanking a full-length unarmoured deckhouse. Along the length of the side decks were deep armoured casemates for guns of some 138-mm (5.43-in) calibre. In the accepted style, two large guns (194-mm/7.64-in calibre) were sited one forward and one aft; so short was the forecastle that the muzzle of the gun protruded almost to the stemhead. A similar armament layout was adopted later by the British, though the 'Charners' did not follow the example of the *Dupuy de Lôme* which had its two large guns sited amidships and the six smaller weapons in groups of three on both foredeck and quarterdeck.

The design was taken one stage further in the one-off *Pothuau*, which

was higher-powered and slightly larger, and equipped with a further pair of secondary-calibre guns on each side. Four were casemated and two were set in shields on pronounced sponsons.

Specification
'Amiral Charner' class
Displacement: 4,700 tons standard
Dimensions: length 110.0 m (360.89 ft); beam 14.0 m (45.93 ft); draught 6.0 m (19.69 ft)
Propulsion: two sets of triple-expansion steam engines delivering 6189 kW (8,300 ihp) to two shafts
Speed: 18.5 kts
Armament: two 194-mm (7.64-in) and six 138-mm (5.43-in) guns, and four 450-mm (17.72-in) torpedo tubes
Armour: belts 90 mm (3.54 in) tapering to 70 mm (2.76 in); protective deck

65 mm (2.56 in) with 55-mm (2.17-in) ends; barbette and casemates 90 mm (3.54 in)
Complement: 380

Above: Latouche-Treville *was one of three commerce-raiding cruisers built in the 1890s which were still in service during World War I.*

Seen here off Salonika in December 1915, Bruix displays the exaggerated tumblehome that was the hallmark of French warship design. When completed, Bruix was more than a match for contemporary British cruisers like the Hermiones.

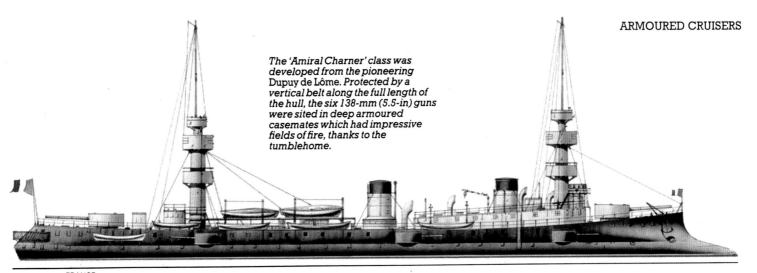

The 'Amiral Charner' class was developed from the pioneering Dupuy de Lôme. Protected by a vertical belt along the full length of the hull, the six 138-mm (5.5-in) guns were sited in deep armoured casemates which had impressive fields of fire, thanks to the tumblehome.

 FRANCE

'Kléber', 'Gueydon' and 'Aube' classes

In 1899 the French launched the *Jeanne d'Arc*, an equivalent to the British 'Powerfuls'. Though smaller she was, like the latter, a prodigious eater of coal, and she exerted a strong influence on later ships.

Launched in 1900-2, the three '**Kléber' class** armoured cruisers (*Dupleix*, *Desaix* and *Kléber*) were intermediate between this monster and the *Pothuau* and, by the standards of the day, were quite lightly armed, their eight main-battery guns being disposed in four twin turrets, one forward, one aft and one on each beam. This adoption of the twin mounting was exactly contemporary with that in the Royal Navy's 'Counties'. By Gallic standards quite pleasing in appearance, the 'Klébers' had four funnels in two widely-spaced pairs, each pair exhausting a space containing 10 boilers. The *Kléber* was a war loss.

Contemporary with the 'Klébers' were the three larger '**Gueydon' class** cruisers. With a length of 138 m (452.76 ft), these 9,500-ton ships had a thick belt of greater depth than that of the 'Klébers' and running nearly the length of the ship. Indeed, the 'Klébers' ran contrary to normal French practice with their meagre area of belt. The 'Gueydons', too, had eight 164.4-mm (6.47-in) guns, but all were casemated effectively at upper deck level on a

high-freeboard hull. In addition they had a single centreline 194-mm (7.64-in) piece at each end. Though the *Dupetit-Thouars* was torpedoed and sunk in 1918 her two sisters, surprisingly, survived in auxiliary capacities until World War II.

The five '**Aube' class** ships of 1900-2 were derivatives of the 'Gueydons'. The *Marseillaise, Gloire, Sully, Condé* and *Amiral Aube* were slightly longer, beamier and better protected. These carried four of their secondary guns at a level one deck higher. Like their predecessors they were triple-screwed, an arrangement that made them handle unpredicatably at low speeds. The *Sully* was wrecked in 1905, and the others were deleted in the 1920s.

Specification
'Kléber' class
Displacement: 7,650 tons standard
Dimensions: length 130.0 m (426.51 ft); beam 17.75 m (58.23 ft); draught 7.40 m (24.28 ft)
Propulsion: three set of triple-expansion steam engines delivering 13050 kW (17,500 ihp) to three shafts
Speed: 21 kts
Armament: eight 164.4-mm (6.47-in), four 100-mm (3.94-in) and 10 47-mm (1.85-in) guns, and two 450-mm (17.72-

in) torpedo tubes
Armour: belt 100 mm (3.94 in) tapering to 75 mm (2.95 in); protective deck

Gloire was one of the 'Aube' class, good steamers that were derived from the 'Gueydons'. A fifth member

of the class, Sully, was wrecked in February 1905 but the other four served throughout the war.

65 mm (2.56 in); barbettes 90 mm (3.54 in)
Complement: 570

 FRANCE

'Léon Gambetta' class

With the 164.4-mm (6.47-in) gun paired successfully into twin turrets in the 'Kléber' class, the French were encouraged to go on to produce the twin 194-mm (7.64-in) mounting, thus doubling firepower with minimum penalty on displacement and dimensions. The result was successful, and was to be the primary armament of French armoured cruisers until the end of their development.

With the 'Gambetta' class the French mounted 194-mm (7.6-in) guns in twin turrets, an eminently sensible development.

First recipients of the new mounting were the four 'Léon Gambetta' class cruisers *Jules Ferry, Léon Gambetta, Victor Hugo* and *Jules Michelet*, launched in 1902-5. With a twin 194-mm mounting at each end, three twin 164.4-mm mountings along each side at the same upper-deck level, and four more singles in casemates set at each corner, the armament of the first three ships was considerable; it was, indeed, superior to that of the contem-

porary British 'Devonshires', with the further advantage of being set much higher. Speed, however, was one parameter against which the French set much store and, in this, they were deficient compared with the smaller Royal Navy ships. Supposedly, therefore, to improve speed, the fourth and last unit, the *Jules Michelet*, sacrificed four secondary barrels but, as this was done by substituting eight single turrets for six twins, there was a net increase of displacement. One can only conclude, therefore, that the measure was aimed primarily at dispensing with the twin turret, an opinion reinforced by the delay in the completion of the *Jules Michelet* until 1908, the same year as the one-off follow-on **Ernest Renan**, which carried a precisely similar armament. As a measure to increase the speed of the latter, however, she had about 28 per cent greater installed power, requiring a 9-m (29.5-ft) increase in length and two groups of three funnels. A feature of all

the French armoured cruisers was their large bunker capacity for colonial service. Above the long armour belt the sides were pierced with numerous large, rectangular scuttles to improve habitability. Their war service was active but none was ever given the chance to prove its merits in a gunnery duel with an equivalent surface target. The sole loss was the class nameship, *Léon Gambetta*.

Specification
'Léon Gambetta' class
Displacement: 12,350 tons standard
Dimensions: length 148.0 m (485.56 ft); beam 21.40 m (70.21 ft); draught 8.20 m (26.9 ft)
Propulsion: three sets of triple-expansion steam engines delivering 20505 kW (27,500 ihp) to three shafts
Speed: 22 kts
Armament: four 194-mm (7.64-in), 16 164.4-mm (6.47-in), two 65-mm (2.56-in) and 22 47-mm (1.85-in) guns, and four 450-mm (17.72-in) torpedo tubes

Armour: belt 170 mm (6.69 in) tapering to 90 mm (3.54 in); upper protective deck 35 mm (1.38 in); lower protective deck 65 mm (2.56 in); main barbettes 200 mm (7.87 in); secondary barbettes 140 mm (5.51 in)
Complement: 730

The 'Gambetta' class were excellent steamers, able to make over 17 kts on half boilers and to maintain 18 kts for 72 hours continuously. Noted for their very clear gun decks, the 'Gambettas' were better armed than their British contemporaries.

 FRANCE
'Waldeck Rousseau' class

As a result of the introduction by the British of the dreadnought in 1906, followed by the battle-cruiser in 1907, the established armoured cruiser with its dual-calibre armament and comparatively low speed found itself a dated concept. The French had been very keen on the type and had developed it in a sound manner. The *Ernest Renan* was to have been the first of a trio of improved 'Gambettas', but events in the UK ensured that only the one ship was completed as planned, the other two being delayed pending developments. In the event there was little that the designers could do to revamp the hulls except install a single-calibre main battery. This they did by retaining the twin 194-mm (7.64-in) turrets at each end, by siting three single 194-mm turrets along each side, and by adding single casemated 194-mm guns at each corner. The resultant 14 barrels of this **'Waldeck Rousseau' class** (*Edgar Quinet* and *Waldeck Rousseau*, launched in 1907-8) were not insignificant, with nine bearing on each broadside, but its weight of 777 kg (1,713 lb) was inferior to that of the contemporary 'Minotaurs' (1143 kg/2,520 lb) or even 'Warriors' (871 kg/1,920 lb). The British ships were also credited with a similar speed on considerably less power.
Externally, the 'Waldeck Rousseaus' were immediately distinguishable from the *Renan* and *Jeanne d'Arc* by the fully-cased funnels of equal height and unequal section. Again six were set in two groups of three, exhausting 40 Niclausse large-tube boilers which had been reintroduced following

many problems with the small-bore du Temple Guyots, of which only half the number needed to be carried.
The wide separation of the boiler spaces was due to the engine room being set between them. Above this, all French armoured cruisers had a prominent rectangular 'pillbox' for the forced ventilating system, an alternative to the many cowls or windscoops on British ships.
Obsolete or not, the ships were still far from old at the Armistice and were kept on until the 1930s, the *Edgar Quinet* being wrecked off Algeria in 1930 while serving as a training ship.

Specification
'Waldeck Rousseau' class
Displacement: 13,750 tons standard
Dimensions: length 159.0 m (521.65 ft); beam 21.40 m (70.21 ft); draught 8.40 m (27.56 ft)
Propulsion: three sets of triple-expansion steam engines delivering 27218 kW (36,500 ihp) to three shafts
Speed: 23 kts
Armament: 14 194-mm (7.64-in) and 14 65-mm (2.56-in) guns, and two 450-mm (17.72-in) torpedo tubes
Armour: belt 170 mm (6.69 in) tapering to 90 mm (3.54 in); upper protective deck 35 mm (1.38 in); lower protective deck 130 mm (5.12 in); transverse bulkhead 130 mm (5.12 in); barbettes 150 mm (5.91 in); casemates 120 mm (4.72 in)
Complement: 840

Above: Waldeck Rousseau *lies peacefully at anchor off Algiers. Although fine cruisers, the class was rendered obsolete by the new battle-cruisers.*

Below: Waldeck Rousseau *broke with French tradition by adopting a uniform armament of 14 194-mm (7.6-in) guns instead of the usual combination.*

Although the 'Waldeck Rousseaus' could bring nine guns to bear on either beam, their broadside was inferior to that of the British 'Minotaurs'.

Light Cruisers of World War 1

The principle task of light cruisers during World War I was to scout ahead of the main battlefleet. But, in the weather conditions of the North Sea, this often meant that these weakly-protected vessels had to venture within range of the enemy battleships' main armament.

HMS Southampton *sank the German cruiser* Frauenlob *and the torpedo boat S 35 at Jutland but suffered severe damage during the night action.*

'We crouched behind the tenth of an inch plating and ate bully beef, but it didn't seem to go down very easily. It seemed rather a waste of time to eat beef, for surely in the next ten minutes one of those 11-inch shells would get us, they couldn't go on falling just short and just over indefinitely and, well, if one did hit us – light cruisers were not designed to digest 11-inch high explosives. . .' This laconic eyewitness account was by an officer aboard HMS *Southampton* at Jutland, but could equally well have come from a thousand others on either side.

The older fleet concept of pushing forward armoured cruisers to gain intelligence of the enemy had been bankrupted by the arrival of the battle-cruiser and the fast battleship, the job passing to the new generation of light cruisers. To do their job required getting to within clear visual range and this, in typical visibilities, meant well within heavy gun range of the enemy line. It took dedication and nerve to press such a reconnaissance well home with half the bridge observing the enemy line and the other half watching the navigator who manoeuvred the ship rapidly away from where he judged the next salvo would land. He usually got it right.

Virtually unprotected cruisers, relying on their agility to keep out of trouble, were initially difficult for the British Admiralty to accept although, historically, they were close in concept to Nelson's frigates. Once in service, however, both British and Germans found them indispensible. They were deeply involved in every major action and in all the humdrum, unseen and uncomfortable drudgery that lies behind the simple expression 'sea control'. Many were lost but all were valiantly served. Despite their apparent fragility they proved remarkably resistant to gunfire and the endless 'dripping' of their crews concealed a deep-felt love for their ships, few envying those with 'cushier' billets on the big ships.

Nelson said he would die with the words 'want of frigates' engraved on his heart; the Royal Navy's problem before 1914 was a shortage of cruisers fast enough to work ahead of the new generation of fast battleships.

'Friant' class

Intended primarily for colonial duties, the three **'Friant' class** cruisers dated from that splendidly silly period when French ships were unique in the world. Despite their modest size they were built on the same 'fierce face' principles that also governed the armoured cruisers and battleships. Each featured the exaggerated ram bow and bulbous stern that gave extra buoyancy at either end and extra length to improve the lines. Their high freeboard hulls were two levels deep over their entire length and pierced liberally with rectangular ports rather than the usual scuttles, to improve living conditions in the tropics. The sides were given a pronounced tumble-home.

For their size and date, they were respectably armed with a main battery of six 164-mm (6.4-in) guns. Though these were only 30-calibre weapons, the muzzles of the two sited at each end were virtually in line with the deck limits. The remaining four guns were sited on sponsons 'growing' from the steeply-sloping sides, thus gaining a measure of axial chase-fire. The narrow upper deck was sponsoned further to accommodate a 100-mm (3.9-in) gun at each 'corner' and 10 47-mm quickfirers were also supposed to be fitted. At least one unit, the nameship, originally had some of these weapons sited on 'military masts', both guns and masts having to be removed as a result of stability problems.

They were protected cruisers with a full-length 30-mm (1.18-in) armoured deck, arched over the machinery and thickened on the flanking slopes to 80 mm (3.15 in). No less than 20 boilers were divided between three spaces.

The original class consisted of the magnificently-named *Chasseloup-Laubat, Bugeaud* and *Friant*, followed by the slightly modified *du Chayla, Cassard* and *d'Assas*. A good idea of the breadth of scope open to the older ships in 1914-8 is given by their service in the Caribbean, the Red Sea, the Levant coast and the Dardanelles, the Indian Ocean and the Black Sea.

Specification
'Friant' class
Displacement: 3,880 tons standard
Dimensions: length 95.0 m (311.7 ft); beam 13.0 m (42.7 ft); draught 6.4 m (21.0 ft)
Propulsion: two sets of triple-expansion steam engines delivering 9,500 ihp (7085 kW) to two shafts
Speed: 18.5 kts
Endurance: 11125 km (6,915 miles) at 10 kts
Armament: six single 164-mm (6.4-in), four single 100-mm (3.94-in) and 10 single 47-mm guns, and two 450-mm (17.7-in) torpedo tubes
Armour: 80-mm (3.15-in) belt
Complement: 375

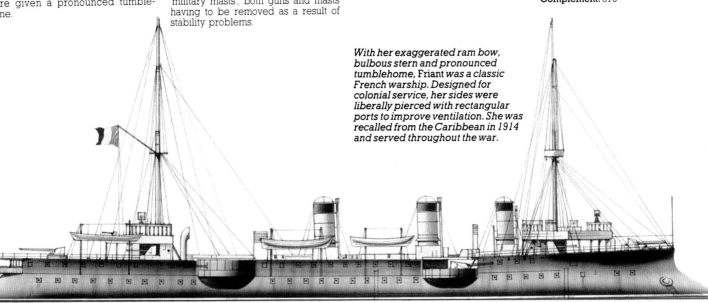

With her exaggerated ram bow, bulbous stern and pronounced tumblehome, Friant was a classic French warship. Designed for colonial service, her sides were liberally pierced with rectangular ports to improve ventilation. She was recalled from the Caribbean in 1914 and served throughout the war.

'Jurien de la Gravière' class

As the American USS *St Louis* was to be a diminutive of the 'California' design, so was the *Jurien de la Gravière* scaled down from the 'Gueydon' class armoured cruiser, but at an early date. That she was one-off is interesting itself, representing probably the last gasp of the so-called Jeune Ecole movement. This stemmed largely from the beliefs of Admiral Aube during the 1880s that, as the UK was the most likely enemy of France, the latter's fleet should be recast with this in mind. It would be easier, he argued, to adopt a

guerre de course, defeating the UK economically through the destruction of her mercantile marine rather than her battlefleet. What, therefore, was required were coast defence ships and a large number of corsairs (privateering had been declared internationally illegal by the Congress of Paris in 1856 but, run by the government, it was presumably respectable), the money for them being made available by the scrapping of the redundant battle fleet and its expensive infrastructure. A number of commerce-raiding

cruisers were constructed but, by the end of the century, it was obvious that war was now far more likely with the Triple Alliance than with the UK and Aube's influence waned. It was at this point that the *Jurien* was built.

Of virtually the same length as the 'Gueydons', whe was nearly 5 m (16.4 ft) smaller in the beam, a considerable amount that called for a lighter and lower superstructure in compensation, with poles in place of military masts. Further topside weight was saved by lighter calibre guns and use

of casemates rather than sided turrets. There was no belt, the volume beneath the waterline being covered by a 65-mm (2.56-in) protective deck and flanked by cellular sub-division. Though having less installed power than the larger ships, her finer lines and lighter displacement were supposed to realize 23 kts. This speed was never achieved. As with most French cruisers in the war, her potential was under-utilized, the *Jurien* being employed primarily in containing a largely quiescent Austrian fleet in the Adria-

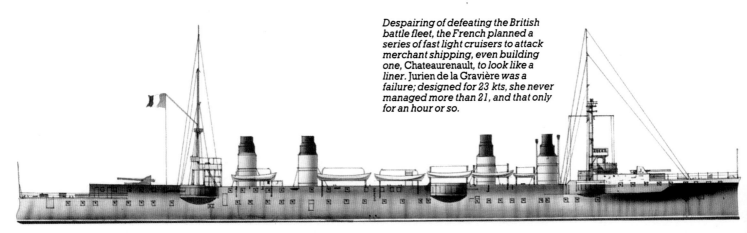

Despairing of defeating the British battle fleet, the French planned a series of fast light cruisers to attack merchant shipping, even building one, Chateaurenault, to look like a liner. Jurien de la Gravière was a failure; designed for 23 kts, she never managed more than 21, and that only for an hour or so.

tic and in minor operations with the British in Greek and Turkish waters.

Specification
Jurien de la Gravière
Displacement: 5,650 tons standard
Dimensions: length 137.0 m (449.5 ft); beam 15.0 m (49.2 ft); draught 6.4 m (21.0 ft)
Propulsion: three sets of triple-expansion steam engines delivering 17,000 ihp (12675 kW) to three shafts
Speed: 22 kts
Endurance: 1150 km (7,145 miles) at 10 kts
Armament: two twin and four single 164-mm (6.4-in) and 10 single 47-mm guns, and two 450-mm (17.7-in) torpedo tubes
Armour: 65-mm (2.56-in) deck and 50-mm (1.98-in) gunhouses and casemates
Complement: 511

Jurien de la Gravière was designed as a commerce raider, her intended victims British merchantmen, but détente between Great Britain and France left her without a role. She is seen here entering Toulon for a refit in September 1916.

ITALY

'Quarto' class

Italian fleet operations have always been limited largely by the confines of the Mediterranean; this has combined with close rivalry with the neighbouring French to exert great influence on their warship design over the years. Typically, endurance and protection have been subordinated to speed and armament. Like other fleets before 1914, the Italians flirted with the idea of the scout cruiser once the steam turbine and oil-firing were available to produce sufficient power in a small hull. Unusually, where this beginning might well have been expected to result in a series of ever larger classes, the Italians initially progressed downward to the large destroyer and, though the difference was fine, this was recognized in the categorization of *esploratori* rather than *incrocitori leggeri*.

Typical of ships built in the age of the reciprocating engine were the two 1,300-ton 'Agordats' which, as scouts, were poorly served by their 22 kts and, when the **Quarto** was completed in 1913, she marked something of a revolution. Of about the same size as the earlier British scouts, her later machinery permitted a maximum of over 29,000 shp (21620 kW) on four shafts, resulting in a trial speed of nearly 29 kts. Her turbines were of Parsons manufacture and were reliable throughout her comparatively long career (she was not finally stricken until 1939). Long and low with a raised forecastle, she was a classic scout, her

three low but evenly sized and spaced funnels imparting a somewhat Japanese appearance.

Before *Quarto* was even launched, however, and obviously not appreciating her excellent design, the Italians laid down two 'improved' and enlarged versions, the **Marsala** and **Nino Bixio**. These had lower installed power and were triple-screwed, yet still contrived four funnels which were oddly spaced and, together with the masts, given a pronounced rake. Their more Italianate appearance was not matched by performance, however, their Curtiss machinery typically producing power for about 3 kts less than the *Quarto*, and they were discarded in the late 1920s. The sheer cost of speed is well illustrated by the quoted endurance figures of *Quarto*: at 15 kts she could cover some 4265 km (2,645 miles) but at 28 kts less than 1110 km (690 miles).

Specification
'Quarto' class
Displacement: 3,275 tons standard and 3,450 tons full load
Dimensions: length 131.6 m (431.8 ft); beam 12.9 m (42.3 ft); draught 4.1 m (13.4 ft)
Propulsion: four sets of steam turbines delivering 25,000 shp (18640 kW) to four shafts
Speed: 28.5 kts
Armament: six single 120-mm (4.7-in) and six single 76-mm (3-in) guns, two 450-mm (17.7-in) torpedo tubes, and up to 200 mines
Armour: 40-mm (1.57-in) and 20-mm (0.79-in) decks
Complement: 247

Long, low, and fast, Quarto had the characteristic speed and grace of an Italian warship, although her three small funnels made her look a little like the Japanese destroyers operating in the Mediterranean during World War I.

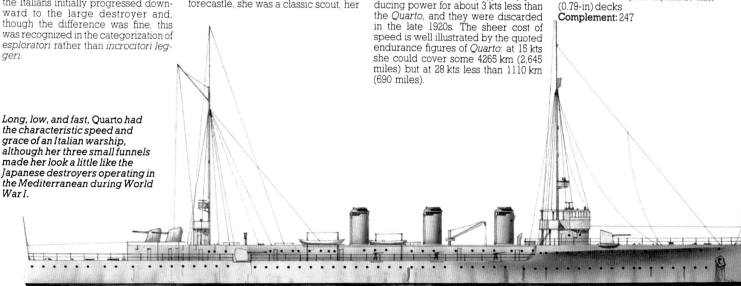

'Gem' class

Though strictly protected cruisers, the **'Gem' class** ships (HMS *Amethyst, Diamond, Sapphire* and *Topaze*) mark the point of departure for the light cruiser in the Royal Navy. Protected cruisers relied primarily on an arched armoured deck, running the full length of the ship, below the waterline at each end but higher amidships to clear the top of the high reciprocating engines and boilers. Such ships came in a variety of sizes but, like the armoured cruisers, possessed too little (if any) speed margin over the fleet's main body with which to act as scouts. The four 'Gems', launched in 1903-4, were built in parallel with the two 'Challengers' but, where the latter displaced

5,900 tons on a 145 by 17.1 m (376 by 56 ft) hull, the 'Gems' on virtually the same length displaced only 3,000 tons by virtue of a slender 12.2-m (40-ft) beam. The 'Challengers' had a slightly heavier deck but needed 12,500 ihp (9320 kW) to make 21 kts while the 'Gems' could manage 22 kts on only 9,800 ihp (7310 kW). More significantly, one of their number, *Amethyst*, was the first smaller ship to be fitted with steam turbines. By fitting her with cruising, in addition to main, turbines, Parsons nearly overcame the machinery's greatest weakness, an economy inferior to that of reciprocating engines at lower speed. Even so, comparative trials against the similar-hulled *Topaze* saw the turbine ship consuming 1315 kg (2,900 lb) of coal per hour at 10 kts against the *Topaze's* 1043 kg (2,300 lb). At 14 kts consumption was about equal while, at the upper end, the more compact turbines developed 12,000 hp (8945 kW) compared with 9,800 hp (7305 kW) for only 11068 kg (24,400 lb) per hour against 11839 kg

(26,100 lb). Thus the lighter machinery for a three per cent greater economy produced power for an extra 1.5 kts.

These slender little ships were also armed only with 102-mm (4-in) guns (possibly influenced by German cruisers with the superior 105-mm (4.13-in) gun, a much-criticized move. Though not officially described as 'scouts', the 'Gems' closely paralleled the first scout-type cruisers then also being built, which sacrificed armament and some protection to accommodate machinery for 25 kts. *Sapphire* was very active in the Dardanelles campaign and to *Topaze* and *Diamond*, as 'attached cruisers', fell the melancholy task of rescuing the few survivors of the battleship HMS *Formidable* off Portland at the turn of the year in 1914. No 'Gems' were lost.

Specification
'Gem' class
Displacement: 3,000 tons standard
Dimensions: length 114.0 m (374.0 ft); beam 12.2 m (40.0 ft); draught 4.4 m (14.5 ft)
Propulsion: two sets of triple-expansion steam engines delivering 10,000 ihp (7455 kW) to two shafts, or (*Amethyst*) two sets of geared steam turbines delivering 12,000 shp (8945 kW) to two shafts
Speed: 22 kts or (*Amethyst*) 23.5 kts
Armament: 12 single 102-mm (4-in) and eight single 3-pdr guns (later altered to two single 152-mm/6-in and eight 102-mm guns), and two 457-mm (18-in) torpedo tubes
Armour: 51-mm (2-in) deck
Complement: 296

The 'Gems', Topaze, Amethyst, Diamond and Sapphire, were the predecessors of the Scouts, carrying only 4-in guns and light protection to gain speed. HMS Amethyst had turbines which gave her a 1⅓-kt advantage over her sisters and lower coal consumption at high speed. She was leader of the Harwich Force and Destroyer Command in 1914, but left for the Grand Fleet in August.

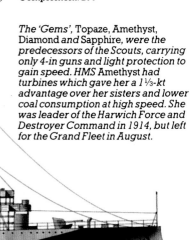

Scout types

Like the 'largest gun' on the 'highest speed', the idea of the 'fast scout' was firmly entrenched and, though of questionable worth, was resurrected by naval staffs from time to time to plague the naval architect. British involvement probably stemmed from the classic urge to 'reply' to any foreign lead. In this case it was the *Novik*, a 3,000-tonner built in Germany to Russian account, which inspired Elswick to offer a similar but enlarged design to the Admiralty. Impressed by the 26-kt Russian, this authority put out a general specification for a small, fast cruiser that could serve for the safe observation of an enemy port as the 'eyes' of a blockading squadron. The requirement was to maintain 25 kts for eight hours, and a 5560-km (3,450-mile) endurance at 10 kts. Armament was to include two torpedo tubes but only 12-pdr (76-mm/3-in) guns. The light scale of protection was to be a protective deck 'at least 1½ inches in thickness' or its equivalent in a vertical belt, an interesting lack of commitment in context with designed function. Four proposals were accepted, a pair of ships being built by each of Armstrong (Elswick), Fairfield, Laird and Vickers, all of them being completed in 1905.

On a light displacement limit, all looked low and lean, with single, sided torpedo tubes three-quarters aft, four 12-pdr guns along each side and one more forward and aft. These were later up-rated to nine 102-mm (4-in) weapons. All had raised forecastles

and the two **'F' class** ships from Fairfield had a poop in addition. Only the two **'A' class** ships from Armstrong had four funnels, the remainder three. Both the Fairfield ships and the two **'P' class** ships from Laird worked in a 51-mm (2-in) vertical patch in addition to a light protective deck. The last pair comprised the two **'S' class** ships from Vickers. An unusual feature at the time was a single, tall mast. All averaged over 25 kts on an eight-hour full-power trial, HMS *Attentive* maintaining 26.25 kts for an hour, well up to destroyer speeds of the time and a record for a ship of her size. Their cost of around £275,000 apiece attracted criticism, particularly as their function was seen to be capable of being equally well performed by destroyers in the narrow seas and by merchant cruisers in the open oceans. In the event, they performed admirably attached to line squadrons or as flotilla leaders to destroyers. Only HMS *Pathfinder* was lost.

Specification
'A' class
Displacement: 2,670 tons standard and 2,940 tons full load
Dimensions: length 114.0 m (374.0 ft); beam 11.7 m (38.25 ft); draught 4.1 m (13.5 ft)
Propulsion: two sets of triple-expansion steam engines delivering 16,000 ihp (11930 kW) to two shafts
Speed: 25.5 kts
Armament: 10 single 12-pdr and eight single 3-pdr guns (later altered to nine

single 102-mm/4-in and one 76-mm/3-in guns), and two 457-mm (18-in) torpedo tubes
Armour: 51-mm (2-in) deck
Complement: 270

HMS *Foresight* cutaway drawing key

1 Captain's quarters
2 Quarterdeck
3 Skylight
4 Wardroom
5 12-pdr (28-cwt) quick-firing gun
6 Engineers' quarters
7 Steering compartment
8 Steering engine
9 Balanced rudder
10 Twin screws
11 12-pdr shell room
12 Searchlight platform
13 Searchlight
14 Stove
15 Flag locker
16 Officers' quarters
17 Pantry
18 Gig
19 Cutter
20 Magazine
21 Dynamo room
22 Dynamo room
23 Double bottom
24 Auxiliary engine room
25 Twin 14-in Mk XI torpedo tubes
26 Main feedwater tank
27 Engine room
28 15,800 hp twin six-cylinder engines
29 Store
30 3-pdr quick-firing guns
31 Funnel
32 Steam pipe
33 Funnel casing
34 Super heaters
35 Funnel uptake
36 No. 1 boiler room
37 No. 2 boiler room
38 No. 3 boiler room

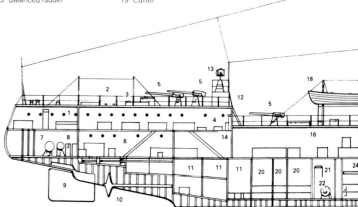

Following the completion of the first eight scouts, there was a period of appraisal. This was a time of rapid German building and they had just completed SMS *Bremen*, the first of a new 'light cruiser' type derived, like the British ships, from the small protected cruiser. Similar in length but beamier, the German ships had the advantage of continuous high freeboard and their influence resulted eventually in the British 'Towns'. The Admiralty decided to develop the smaller cruiser further in parallel, however: not only could such ships maintain their speed longer than a destroyer in deteriorating weather, but they had the firepower to dispose of it. Further, the large destroyer flotillas of the time needed a leader with accommodation for Captain (D) and his staff. These, then, rather than scouting, became their roles.

The ships of the second, extended series of small cruisers were thus not termed 'scouts' and were constructed, not by private yards, but by Pembroke Dockyard. This single small yard did well to complete the four 'Boadiceas' in 1909-11 and the three follow-on 'Active' class ships (HMS *Active, Amphion* and *Fearless*) in 1912-3. The first pair, though given 102-mm (4-in) guns, received only six of them. Only three could fire on the broadside, which was inadequate to sink a small target from a lively platform, so later ships were given 10 guns, of which six could fire on the broadside. The first two units had a light protective deck but the remainder had what was de-scribed as a 'double skin' amidships: vertical, spaced plating to defeat sensitively-fused projectiles. All were turbine-driven and carried dual coal/oil fuel: the oil was sprayed onto the already burning coal in the furnace and, at the cost of rather too much smoke, gave a rapid boost in heat energy to the boiler.

While *Amphion* was mined and lost only two days after the outbreak of war, the reminder survived despite being very actively involved. The four 'Boadiceas' served as 'attached cruisers' to each of the four Grand Fleet battle squadrons and the three 'Actives' as leaders to three of the four Grand Fleet destroyer flotillas, an arduous duty from which they were relieved by the larger 'Arethusas' as they became available. Of these flotillas, the 1st with 20 destroyers and the 3rd with 15 were part of Tyrwhitt's Harwich Force.

Specification
'Active' class
Displacement: 3,440 tons standard
Dimensions: length 123.4 m (405.0 ft); beam 12.6 m (41.5 ft); draught 4.0 m (13.0 ft)
Propulsion: two sets of steam turbines

HMS Active *cruises off Queenstown in 1917 before her deployment to the Mediterranean. The 'Active' class was the third group of Scouts, distinguishable from its predecessors by the plough bows.*

delivering 18,000 shp (13420 kW) to two shafts
Speed: 26 kts
Armament: 10 single 102-mm (4-in) and four single 3-pdr guns, and two 533-mm (21-in) torpedo tubes
Armour: none
Complement: 320

39 Three-quarter White-Forster cylindrical boiler
40 Bulkhead
41 Inlet valve
42 Circulation pump
43 Coal bunker
44 3-pdr ready store
45 Wireless office
46 Wireless aerial
47 Ventilators
48 Foremast
49 Lookout station
50 Compass platform
51 Compass
52 Bridge
53 Chart room
54 Crew quarters
55 Steam pipe for heating living spaces
56 Stokers' quarters
57 Dynamo room/machine shop
58 Lobby
59 Paint store
60 Capstan
61 Ram
62 Torpedo store
63 3-pdr shell room
64 Foredeck
65 Feed water tanks
66 2-in armour belt
67 ⅝-in armoured deck (ends)
68 1½-in armoured deck (amidships)
69 Waterline
70 Ventilator to crew's quarters

Below: When she was completed in early 1905, HMS Foresight *carried 10×12-pdr guns and a pair of 14-in torpedo tubes. Her gun armament was later changed to 10×4-in weapons. Of the 'scout' types, only* Foreward *and* Foresight *had poops and could further be distinguished from the 'A', 'P' and 'S' classes by having high funnels and no cowls. On trials,* Foresight's *engines developed 15,800 ihp, making 25.28 kts.*

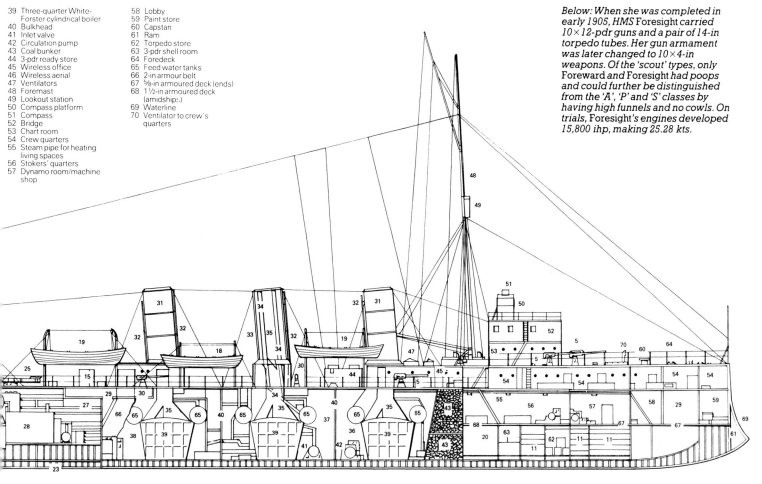

UK 'Chatham' class

Contemporary with the 'Active' class, the British built a quintet of larger ships, the 'Bristols', which looked like a cross between the smaller ships and the big armoured cruisers whose construction had ceased about four years before. It had been the supersession of such ships by battle-cruisers that produced the requirements for the 'Towns', big enough to cruise with the fleet and fast enough to work ahead of it. But while armed sufficient to look after themselves, they were unable to undertake the heavier duties of the armoured cruiser.

The 4,800-ton 'Bristols' suffered again from a mixed armament, a meagre pair of 152-mm (6-in) guns being supplemented by 10 102-mm (4-in) guns. A 76-mm (3-in) protective deck was fitted. For their duties, they were criticized as being greatly underarmed, and the four 'Weymouths' that followed had an all-152-mm main battery. Their size was little increased, however, so their protection suffered, a significant loss in view of the fact that their speed had not been improved and that they could be run down by a battle-cruiser.

The six 'Chatham' class ships (HMS *Chatham, Dublin, Southampton, Brisbane, Melbourne* and *Sydney*) of 1911-12 were improved Weymouths, their eight single 152-mm mountings still not superimposed but mainly sided, so that a broadside was of only five guns. They did have a partial 76-mm belt worked in, but again enjoyed no increase in speed, the main reason for which being that they were the last of the coal-fired ships, for which the only way to produce more energy was to increase the size of the ship and install more boilers.

It is interesting to note that German light cruiser construction had followed an almost exactly parallel path, also adopting a belt at this time. In general they were slenderer, of higher power and usefully faster. Their power was absorbed by triple propellers and reflected the difficulties that the British were having in that one ship of each class was twin-screwed with the remainder quadruple. Three ships of the class served in the British Royal Navy, three in the Australian. Of the former

the *Southampton* earned fame wearing Goodenough's broad pennant in a faultless performance at Jutland while, of the latter, the *Sydney* will be remembered for disposing of the raider SMS *Emden*.

Specification
'Chatham' class
Displacement: 5,400 tons standard
Dimensions: length 139.6 m (458.0 ft); beam 14.9 m (48.75 ft); draught 4.6 m (15.0 ft)
Propulsion: four sets of geared turbines delivering 25,000 shp (18640 kW) to four (*Southampton* two) shafts
Speed: 25.5 kts
Armour: eight single 152-mm (6-in), one 76-mm AA and four single 3-pdr guns, and two 533-mm (21-in) torpedo tubes
Armour: 76-mm (1-in) belt
Complement: 490

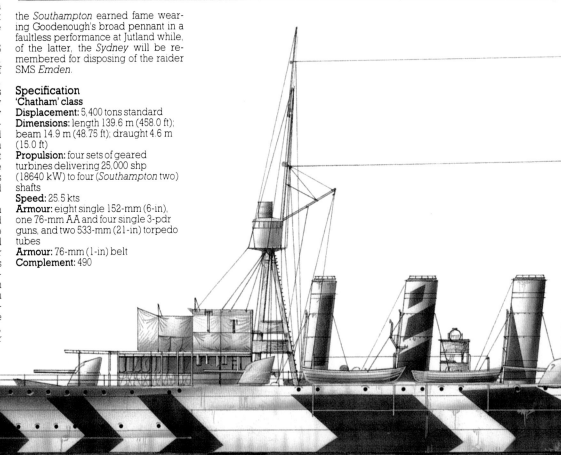

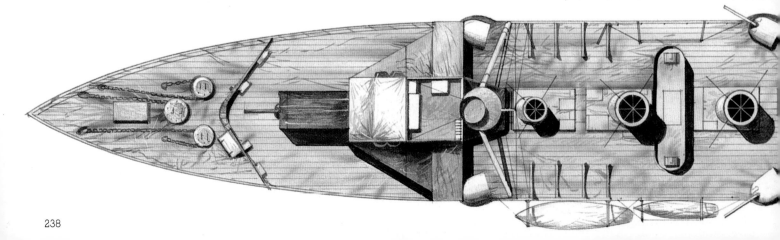

Left: The mixed armament of the 'Bristol' class did not prove a success, and the 'Chathams' were armed with eight 6-in guns which gave Sydney *overwhelmingly superior broadsides in her fight with the* Emden. *Three of the class served with the Royal Navy and three with the Australian Navy.*

HMS Southampton *as she appeared in July 1919 when operating off Murmansk during the Allied intervention in Russia. The 'Chatham' class were superior sea-boats to the preceding British cruiser classes, as the forecastle was extended down more than half the length, and lower metacentric height reduced rolling. Horizontal armour was supplemented by a thin armour belt. The high velocity guns of the 'Weymouth' class had proved unsatisfactory, and the 'Chathams' mounted a new, lower-velocity 6-in gun which was considerably lighter yet could still score hits at up to 14,000 yards. After an active wartime career which included action at Heligoland, Dogger Bank and Jutland, she left Russian waters in 1919 to lead the 7th Light Cruiser Squadron in South America. After service there and at the Cape she spent 1921-4 in the East Indies before going into reserve at the Nore.*

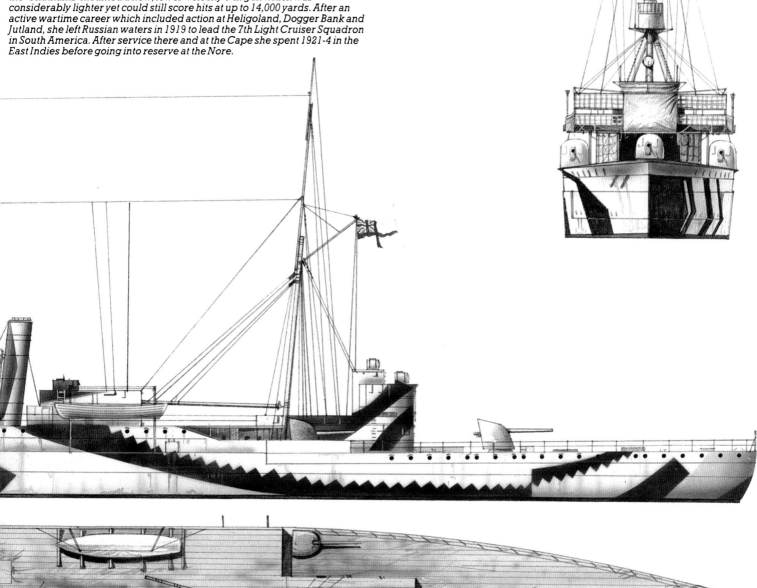

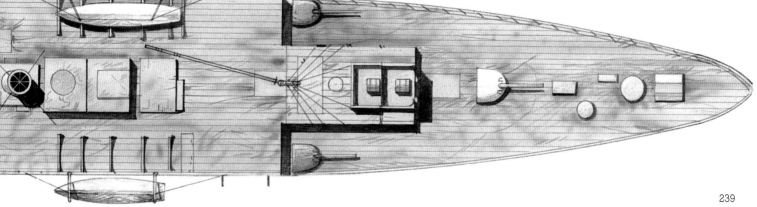

'Caroline' class

The success of the 'Actives' pointed up the advantages of a larger and higher-powered class that could better operate with the fleet main force, the 'Boadiceas', for instance, suffering badly by having to keep station on the battle squadrons in heavy weather. Higher power was now a real possibility with the rapid advances in steam turbine engineering and the eight 'Arethusas' followed in rapid succession. They were powered for 30 kts (a 120 per cent increase in shaft horse-power over the 'Actives') though their actual speeds were up to 1.5 kts slower. A major function being still seen as countering the ever-larger destroyer, they were given an oddly-mixed armament of two centreline 152-mm (6-in) guns, with eight 102-mm (4-in) weapons in single, sided mountings. They also carried a quadruple 533-mm (21-in) torpedo tube bank on either side. The extra machinery demanded a much larger hull but this was further improved by adding a 76-mm (3-in) vertical belt to the 25-mm (1-in) protective deck.

Six 'Caroline' class cruisers (HMS Caroline, Carysfort, Cleopatra, Comus, Conquest and Cordelia) then followed in quick succession, five of them from royal dockyards. A 3-m (10-ft) increase in length was of less consequence than 0.5 m (1.6 ft) extra on the beam, improving stiffness. As with the 'Arethusas', the mixed armament proved decidedly unpopular and most were re-armed with a varying number of 152-mm (6-in) guns as refits permitted. A 'first' for both classes was the inclusion of a high-angle 76- or 102-mm (3- or 4-in) gun for use against aircraft.

Some earlier units were later fitted with a runway over the forecastle gun to fly off a fighter for use against the enemy's spotting Zeppelins.

Ultimately 28 'C' class cruisers were built but, with the last completing after the war, they varied quite widely in design. All following the initial 'Carolines' had only two funnels and main armaments were rationalized to five 152-mm (6-in) centreline mountings. Later ships had guns superimposed both forward and aft, a few taking an aircraft hangar beneath the bridge. To counteract the wetness of hard driving, they were also fitted with a so-called 'trawler bow' having a knuckle and marked sheet. Thirteen went on to see service in World War II, in which six were lost. Some were used early-on in the new Northern Patrol but had to be replaced for the same reasons as the 'Talbots' in World War I.

Specification
'Caroline' class
Displacement: 3,750 tons standard
Dimensions: length 135.9 m (446.0 ft); beam 12.6 m (41.5 ft); draught 4.2 m (14.0 ft)
Propulsion: four sets of geared turbines delivering 40,000 shp (29825 kW) to four shafts
Speed: 29 kts
Armament: two single 152-mm (6-in), eight single 102-mm (4-in) and one or two single 76-mm (3-in) AA guns, and two twin or quadruple 533-mm (21-in) torpedo tube mountings
Armour: 25-mm (1-in) deck and 76-mm (3-in) belt
Complement: 325

HMS Caradoc engages Bolshevik forces in Kaffa Bay during the British intervention in Russia. On 26 December 1918, together with her sister Calypso and three destroyers, she captured two Bolshevik destroyers. Caradoc survived to serve again in World War II and was finally sold in 1946.

Above: The Royal Navy's apparently insatiable demand for light cruisers (there were over 40 in service or nearing completion by 1915) led to six 'improved Centaurs' being ordered in 1915. Twenty-eight 'C' type cruisers were eventually built, all with similar armament. HMS Cassandra, seen here, was mined in the Gulf of Finland in 1918.

As completed, HMS Caroline mounted two more 4-in guns than the preceding 'Arethusas', but the superiority of 6-in weapons had already been established. Some of the 4-in guns were removed in 1916 and all had gone by the next year, replaced by a uniform armament of four 6-in guns.

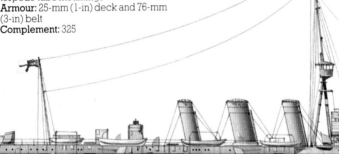

'D' class

Where the 'C'-type cruisers passed through several stages to reach the ultimate 'Carlisle' type, the **'D' class** ships were really the next logical step. Destroyers by the latter part of the war had advanced to the stage where they were big enough to outdistance a cruiser in all but the worst sea states

Below: Rumours that the Germans were building new and more powerful light cruisers led to the 'Danae' class mounting a sixth centreline 6-in gun and, taking advantage of the increased beam, they also mounted a heavy torpedo armament of 12 × 21-in weapons in four triple mountings.

and the 'Ds' did not therefore suffer a significant increase in size to accommodate up-rated machinery. They were, however, about 6 m (20 ft) longer to take a sixth, centreline 152-mm (6-in) mounting, squeezed between the forefunnel and the bridge. As such they were the last class to take the all-single mount main battery that was extremely demanding of axial length. Advantage was also taken to double the torpedo armament to four triple mountings. Only the three 'Danae' class units HMS *Danae*, *Dauntless* and *Dragon* of the first group were completed in time to see active service, joining a selection of 'C' class cruisers in the Harwich Force.

Five more were completed postwar (HMS *Delhi*, *Despatch*, *Diomede*, *Dunedin* and *Durban*) and a further four were cancelled. With light cruiser building resumed only in the 1930s, the 'Cs' and 'Ds' were an important compo-

nent of the fleet between the wars. Most of the 'Cs' that saw service in World War II had been usefully converted to AA cruisers, with the new twin HA 102-mm (4-in) mountings and the requisite fire control (though it was generally agreed that they could fire ammunition far more efficiently than they could stow it). The 'D' class ships, on the other hand, were never so converted and, being decidedly old-fashioned by 1939, were used in low-hazard duties such as patrolling the more distant trade routes or hunting raiders' supply ships. One, the *Dunedin*, was sunk in the South Atlantic by *U-124* (with one of the longest recorded torpedo runs) in November 1941, the Royal Navy's blackest month.

A high-speed stretched version of

the 'Ds' was started during World War I as the planned trio of 'E' class cruisers (only two were completed), doubling the machinery to achieve an astonishing 33 kts. They were completed in 1919-20. One, HMS *Enterprise*, carried a prototype twin 152-mm mounting. Both she and HMS *Emerald* had also an aircraft and catapult, and a record 16 torpedo tubes. They had the thick-and-thin funnels of the 'C' and 'D' classes, but were distinctive by having also a third funnel set well aft.

Specification
'Danae' subclass
Displacement: 4,650 tons standard
Dimensions: length 143.6 m (471.0 ft); beam 14.0 m (46.0 ft); draught 4.6 m (15.0 ft)
Propulsion: two sets of geared steam turbines delivering 40,000 shp (29825 kW) to two shafts
Speed: 28.5 kts
Armament: six single 152-mm (6-in) and two single 102-mm (4-in) AA guns, and four triple 533-mm (21-in) torpedo tube mountings
Armour: 25-mm (1-in) deck and 76-mm (3-in) belt
Complement: 375

The 'D' class survived the war and, in the case of Despatch, *a scheme to convert her into a royal yacht, and found themselves in action once again in 1939. They were generally used to patrol the most distant waters, although HMS* Dunedin *was torpedoed and sunk by U-124 off Brazil in 1941.*

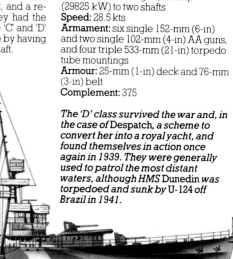

 GERMANY
'Gazelle' class

The 10 **'Gazelle' class** cruisers (SMS *Amazone*, *Ariadne*, *Arkona*, *Frauenlob*, *Gazelle*, *Medusa*, *Niobe*, *Nymphe*, *Thetis* and *Undine*) bore roughly the same relationship to German light cruiser development as the 'Gem' class did to the British. They were evolved from the single SMS *Hela*, completed in 1896 (sunk by Max Horton's *E 9* a month after the outbreak of war). This ship, which was later reconstructed, was a useful prototype, limited in speed by the low rating of her cylindrical boilers, but demonstrating that a heavier armament could be shipped and that the protective deck could be uprated.

On the same length, therefore, the 'Gazelles' had another 1 m (3.3 ft) of

beam and their horizontal protection doubled in thickness to 50 mm (1.98 in). Water-tube boilers produced a 40 per cent increase in power at no penalty while the main battery was improved to 10 105-mm (4.13-in) guns. These weapons probably influenced the British in their choice of 102-mm (4-in) weapons for their equivalent ships, though the German gun was more powerful, with a muzzle velocity that enabled it to outrange even the older 152-mm (6-in) gun of the Royal Navy.

The class was produced by the Germans as a fusion between earlier concepts of 'fleet' and 'overseas' cruisers, and were sized accordingly. Their initial duties were to screen the fleet

against the attentions of torpedo craft, but as they were rapidly superseded by improved classes, they soon found themselves serving worldwide in Germany's burgeoning imperial interests. They were smart little ships, weatherly and with good freeboard, featuring an exaggerated ram bow which, like the French, gave extra buoyancy forward and improved lines on a limited length.

Despite their age they were well used during the war and suffered accordingly. *Ariadne* was shattered by close-range salvoes from Beatty's flagship HMS *Lion* at the Heligoland Bight action. *Frauenlob* was also there but was eventually sunk by a torpedo from HMS *Southampton* during the confused night action after Jutland. *Un-*

dine was sunk in the Baltic in 1915 by the British submarine *E 19*.

Specification
'Gazelle' class
Displacement: 2,605 tons standard
Dimensions: length 105.0 m (344.5 ft); beam 12.1 m (39.7 ft); draught 5.35 m (17.6 ft)
Propulsion: two sets of triple-expansion steam engines delivering 8,500 ihp (6,340 kW) to two shafts
Speed: 21 kts
Armament: 10 single 105-mm (4.13-in) guns and three 450-mm (17.7-in) torpedo tubes
Armour: 50-mm (1.98-in) deck
Complement: 260

The 10 'Gazelle' class cruisers built between 1897 and 1903 established the basic pattern for German cruisers. Handsome vessels, with a good freeboard, their exaggerated ram bow endowed them with extra buoyancy forward. This is Frauenlob, *which was torpedoed and sunk by HMS* Southampton *at Jutland.*

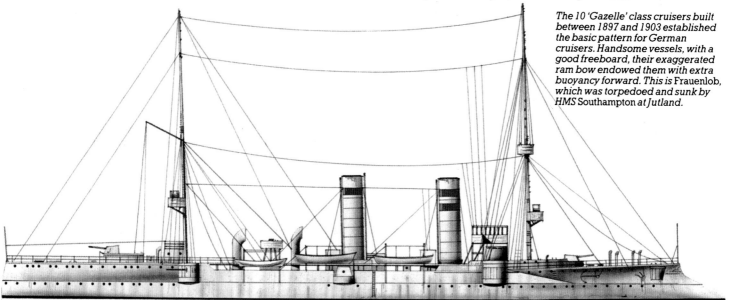

'Berlin' class

Besides the British, the German was the only fleet to build light cruisers in any numbers in time to make a significant contribution to the war. The 10 'Gazelles' had proved to be excellent prototypes and follow-on ships were heavily based on them, thence developing very logically from class to class. By the Kaiser's instruction the earlier mixed bag of names had to give way to uniformity, all new light cruisers being named after cities. Thus the five **'Berlin' class** cruisers, completed in 1904-5, were named after the capital (SMS *Berlin*) the three Hanseatic city-states and München (Munich). They were essentially 'Gazelles' stretched by 6 m (20 ft) to accommodate 40 per cent more power, which necessitated a third funnel. They retained the same armament and scale of protection, also the characteristic positioning of the foremast forward of the bridge structure and the extreme 'ram bow'. Of this group SMS *Lübeck* became the first German cruiser to be propelled by steam turbines, her 14,000-shp (10440-kW) outfit being of Parsons' design; they were not geared at this time and, to absorb the power at high revolutions, an original multi-propeller arangement was tried on two shafts. The system was not particularly successful with the screw technology of the time and, pending evaluation, the three follow-ons in 1906-7 reverted to the well-tried triple expansion engine. Of these, SMS *Danzig* and *Leipzig* were virtual repeats but the one-off but similar SMS *Königsberg* was again

lengthened, by 4 m (13.1 ft), to increase power to over 13,000 shp (9695 kW). It is of note that this extra size was not used to load the ship with any more armament and the 105-mm (4.13-in) gun was retained for its high rate of fire: up to 20 rounds per minute with a well-drilled crew. Compared with British ships of similar length, the Germans were a full 2 m (6.6 ft) wider in the beam, improving stability and also bunker capacity. Both the latter and the conservatively-rated machinery contributed to the ships' designed alternative role as commerce raiders. The *Königsberg* herself escaped from

Dar-es-Salaam to operate in the Indian Ocean simultaneously with SMS *Emden*, but her major success was in surprising and overwhelming the little crusier HMS *Pegasus* off Zanzibar before tamely allowing herself to be blockaded and, eventually destroyed in the Rufiji delta.

Specification
SMS *Königsberg*
Displacement: 3,350 tons standard and 3,950 tons full load
Dimensions: length 115.25 m (378.1 ft); beam 13.33 m (43.7 ft); draught 5.1 m (16.7 ft)

Königsberg, seen here in pre-war panoply, was at Dar-es-Salaam in 1914 and caught HMS Pegasus with her fires drawn off Zanzibar, sinking her in just 15 minutes.

Propulsion: two sets of triple-expansion steam engines delivering 13,200 ihp (9840 kW) to two shafts
Speed: 23.5 kts
Armament: 10 single 105-mm (4.13-in) guns and two 450-mm (17.7-in) torpedo tubes
Armour: 50-mm (1.98-in) deck
Complement: 320

'Dresden' class

To follow the lone SMS *Königsberg*, the German navy built the three **'Stettin' class** and two **'Dresden' class** cruisers, which though officially of two classes were very similar. SMS *Nürnberg*, *Stettin* and *Stuttgart* were all completed in 1908, with SMS *Dresden* and *Emden* following in 1908-9. On the same beam as the earlier *Königsberg*, they were longer by about 3 m (10 ft), allowing a better machinery arrangement and slightly improved lines. The 'Stettins' were unique in the fleet in having a unequal spacing to their three funnels, while the nameship essayed a further experiment in steam turbines, the compact nature of which enabled the development of over 50 per cent more power for an extra 2 kts. In

general, the machinery of German cruisers appears to have been conservatively rated as they were often capable of exceeding their legend speeds.

The two 'Dresdens' offered a better appearance with three equi-spaced funnels and a cleaner hull, from which the earlier sponsons (*Schwalbennster* or swallows' nests) had disappeared. The *Emden* was the last triple-expan-

Right: Dresden *lies at Mas a Fuera. Cornered by HMS* Kent, *HMS* Glasgow *and the AMC* Orama, *she hoisted a white flag after the British opened fire and while the future Admiral Canaris, then a lieutenant, negotiated with the Royal Navy, her captain blew up her forward magazine.*

SMS Emden *as she appeared in the Pacific, 1909-1914. On the outbreak of war she slipped out of Tsingtao and steamed for the Indian Ocean to prey on British merchant ships in classic corsair tradition.* Emden *was the last cruiser built by Germany with reciprocating engines, perhaps because they were easier to maintain on so distant a station.*

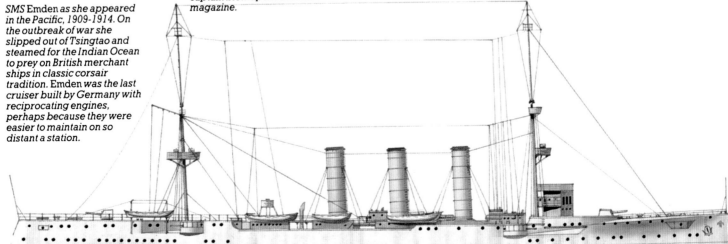

sion engined cruiser built by the Germans, the simple reliability of the machinery being a positive asset for the necessary self maintenance undertaken during her raiding cruise. Her turbine-driven sister *Dresden*, however, was the only one of von Spee's ships to be so fitted and was able to develop the extra speed necessary to out-distance Sturdee's cruisers at the Falklands and survive, while the very similar but reciprocating-engined *Nürn-*

berg was run down and destroyed by HMS *Kent*, whose stokers had worked miracles. It was very obvious that the almost universally 105-mm (4.13-in) gunned Germans were always at a disadvantage when unable to escape the British with their 152-mm (6-in) weapons. The *Dresden's* existence was a lonely one. This was no area for raiding and she went into hiding in the desolate inlets of Tierra del Fuego for two months until, with her boiler in

poor condition, she broke out to Juan Fernandez where, on 14 March 1915 she was cornered and sunk by HMS *Glasgow* and *Kent*.

Specification
'Dresden' class
Displacement: 3,590 tons standard and 4,270 tons full load
Dimensions: length 118.25 m (388.0 ft); beam 13.33 m (43.7 ft); draught 4.8 m (15.75 ft)

Propulsion: (*Dresden*) four sets of steam turbines delivering 10,800 shp (8,050 kW) to two shafts, or (*Emden*) two sets of triple-expansion steam engines delivering 14,500 ihp (10810 kW) to two shafts
Speed: 26 kts
Armament: 10 single 105-mm (4.13-in) guns and two 450-mm (17.7-in) torpedo tubes
Armour: 50-mm (1.98-in) deck
Complement: 360

 GERMANY
'Breslau' class

The four 'Kolbergs', completed in 1909-10, were a full 12 m (39.4 ft) longer than the 'Dresdens' despite being the first all-turbine class. They doubled the installed power of the earlier ships, increased bunker space and took another two 105-mm (4.13-in) guns. This was contemporary with the British 'Boadicea' class, smaller ships with only six to 10 102-mm (4-in) weapons. When, the following year, the Royal Navy replied with the first 'Town' group (the 'Bristol' class) they built them slightly larger than the 'Kolbergs', though similar in power and scale of protection. Significantly, however, they also put aboard a pair of 152-mm (6-in) guns.

The deliberately-developing German series continued almost without a break with the four **'Breslau' class** cruisers (SMS *Breslau, Magdeburg, Stralsund* and *Strassburg*). These were comparable in size to the Bristols and, interestingly, the quartet included double-, triple- and quadruple-shaft propulsion, for evaluation purposes. Both power and speed differed considerably, the ships (like the British units) adopting a four-funnel layout. The stacks were typically German, being cased for only half their height. Boiler efficiency was improved somewhat by adopting oil burners to supplement the coal in the furnace. While retaining the gun armament of the 'Kolbergs', they increased the torpedo armament from two 450-mm (17.7-in) to four 500-mm (19.7-in) tubes. Another innovation was to reduce the protective deck from the previously universal 50 mm (1.98 in) to only 15 mm (0.6 in) while introducing a new feature in a 70-mm (2.76-in) belt. This was a fundamental change of heart, not born of battle experience. War, however, was to show that the fast rate of fire of the 105-mm guns was still no match for the fewer and slower British 152-mm guns and several groups of German cruisers

were regunned with 150-mm (5.9-in) weapons.

Magdeburg was lost as early as 26 August 1914, being destroyed by the Russians after grounding in the Gulf of Finland. The recovery of her codebooks proved priceless to the Allies. Her sister *Breslau* was something of a *cause célèbre* when, with the battle-cruiser SMS *Goeben*, she reached Turkey at the outbreak of war. As the *Yavuz Sultan Selim* and **Midilli** they were an endless threat to both the Russians in the Black Sea and the Anglo-French forces outside the Strait. *Midilli* was sunk by running into a British minefield in January 1918.

Specification
'Breslau' class
Displacement: 4,550 tons standard and 5,590 tons full load
Dimensions: length 138.5 m (454.4 ft); beam 13.5 m (44.3 ft); draught 5.1 m (16.7 ft)
Propulsion: two (*Strassburg*), three (*Magdeburg* and *Stralsund*) or four (*Breslau*) sets of steam turbines delivering between 22,300 and 33,500 shp (16625 and 24980 kW) to two, three or four shafts
Speed: 28 to 30 kts
Armament: 12 single 105-mm (4.13-in) guns (later altered to seven single 150-mm/5.9-in guns) and four 500-mm (19.7-in) torpedo tubes
Armour: 15-mm (0.6-in) deck and 70-mm (2.76-in) belt
Complement: 365

Right: Breslau *at Constantinople with* Goeben. *Their passage across the Mediterranean represented a humiliating defeat for the Allied navies and was a stunning strategic victory for Germany, since the imposing presence of the squadron enabled pro-German elements in Turkey to pitch the Ottoman Empire into the war against the Allies.*

Like Goeben, Breslau *'joined' the Turkish navy; styling herself* 'Midilli', *she and the battle-cruiser threatened Russian forces in the Black Sea and Allied units in the Aegean. She perished when a sortie in January 1918 went disastrously wrong;* Breslau *struck five British mines and sank, while* Goeben *was mined too, stranded, and had to be towed to safety.*

Breslau *introduced several innovations: the new bow improved seakeeping, she had a cleaner hull and, unusually, an armoured belt. The cut-down quarterdeck provided a platform for mines, and each vessel of the class had a different set of turbines.* Magdeburg *was the most crucial German loss of the war: grounded in the Baltic, the Russians captured her code book.*

GERMANY
'Frankfurt' class

The four 'Breslaus' were followed in 1913 by the pair of twin-screwed 'Karlsruhes', nearly identical except for the almost-obligatory slight increase in length and beam. Improved boiler and layout enabled the next pair (SMS *Graudenz* and *Regensburg*) of 1914 to revert to three funnels, being otherwise similar. Both of these pairs were later rearmed with 150-mm (5.9-in) guns, but the first to take them from the outset were also the first to be completed during the war and after the early lesson of the Heligoland Bight action, SMS *Frankfurt* and *Wiesbaden* of the 'Frankfurt' class. War experience not only decided their main battery of eight larger guns, but added a pair of HA 88-mm (3.46-in) weapons for use against aircraft. The new belt and splinter deck protection was also confirmed as correct and repeated subsequently in all other war-built light cruisers. A small increase in beam enabled them to ship 120 mines on deck, another improvement to be repeated in later ships. An innovation in machinery led to the 'Frankfurts' being fitted with reduction gears for their steam turbines (contemporary with the same addition in the British 'Cs').

With shared priorities, the early severe losses in light cruisers sustained by the German fleet were hardly recovered during the war, only six more actually being completed (and repeating names of lost ships), together with a pair of 'windfalls' building to Russian account, and a further pair of specialist cruiser-minelayers. Eight more, launched or building at the Armistice, were never completed.

Frankfurt and *Wiesbaden* participated at Jutland as part of the 2nd Scouting Group. Both, with SMS *Pillau*, were badly treated when they ran into Hood's battle-cruisers, the *Wiesbden* becoming a total wreck in being an immobilized 'Aunt Sally' between both fleets though remaining afloat for nearly 12 hours after having sustained a fearful battering. *Frankfurt* survived the war to be surrendered with the High Seas Fleet. She was not sunk in the general scuttling of 21 June 1919 at Scapa Flow, being one of the ships beached in time by the Royal Navy. She was eventually transferred to the Americans and expended in 'Billy' Mitchell's controversial aerial bombing trials.

Specification
'Frankfurt' class
Displacement: 5,150 tons standard and 6,600 tons full load
Dimensions: length 145.3 m (476.7 ft); beam 13.9 m (45.6 ft); draught 6.1 m (20.0 ft)
Propulsion: two sets of geared steam turbines delivering 37,500 shp (27960 kW) to two shafts
Speed: 28 kts
Endurance: 8900 km (5,530 miles) at

12 kts
Armament: eight single 150-mm (5.9-in) and two 88-mm (3.46-in) guns, four 500-mm (19.7-in) torpedo tube and 120 mines
Armour: 20-mm (0.79-in) deck and 70-mm (2.76-in) belt
Complement: 500

Frankfurt and Wiesbaden were the first German light cruisers to receive 150-mm (5.9-in) guns for their main armament. They also mounted a pair of 88-mm (3.4-in) anti-aircraft guns. A modest increase in beam allowed them to carry 120 mines on deck.

 RUSSIA
'Askold' class

To the Russians Askold was an early Varangian chieftain, but to the Royal Navy that knew her well, the ship *Askold* was simply the 'Packet of Woodbines', one of the few ships outside the French navy boasting more than four funnels. The ship was launched in 1899 by the Krupp-Germania Werft at Kiel and, though contemporary with the German 'Gazelle' class was closer in concept to the earlier 'Freyas'. In common with others of the date, she was truly a protected cruiser in the sense that her armour was horizontal, in the form of a full-length protective deck and an armoured glacis over the high cylinder tops of the reciprocating engines. Her major function differed from her German contemporaries in that she, like her compatriots *Bogatyr* and *Variag*, was designed for commerce raiding. The 23-kt contract speed was high for its time and demanded a long, fine hull and nine double-ended watertube boilers, whose compartmentation resulted in the five funnels. Three engines were required and over two-thirds of the hull was devoted to machinery.

All main battery guns were mounted singly, eight with light shields and on the open deck and four casemated. The forecastle was very short and the concentration of weight forward gave her a reputation for wetness and, in order to meet the demands of the specification, her builders (not familiar with this class of ship) underestimated for scantlings in some areas of the hull. Nevertheless, she had a successful and useful career.

As part of the Port Arthur squadron during the Russo-Japanese war, *Askold* broke out of the beleaguered base in August 1904 by imperial decree and was one of the few to escape, arriving at Shanghai considerably damaged. She was here interned, thus escaping the debacle of Tsushima. In

the Far East at the outbreak of World War I, she came under British operational control, taking part in the search for von Spee, escorting convoys in the Indian Ocean and then serving in the Mediterranean, on the Levant coast and at the Dardanelles. Following the 1917 revolution and with the UK siding against the Bolsheviks, she was taken over by the British and lay rusting until returned and scrapped in 1922.

Specification
Askold
Displacement: 5,910 tons standard
Dimensions: length 132.1 m (433.4 ft); beam 15.0 m (49.2 ft); draught 6.2 m (20.3 ft)
Propulsion: three sets of triple-

expansion steam engines delivering 19,650 ihp (14650 kW) to three shafts
Speed: 23.5 kts
Armament: 12 single 152-mm (6-in) and 12 single 76-mm (3-in) guns, and six 380-mm (15-in) torpedo tubes
Armour: 50-mm (1.98-in) deck, and patches of 100-mm (3.94-in) and 38-mm (1.5-in) armour over the machinery spaces
Complement: 500

Askold, seen as completed in 1901, had a very active career; her beautiful colour scheme replaced by a coat of grey, she fought the Japanese off Port Arthur in 1904 and broke out to Shanghai and internment. In 1914 she joined the hunt for von Spee's squadron.

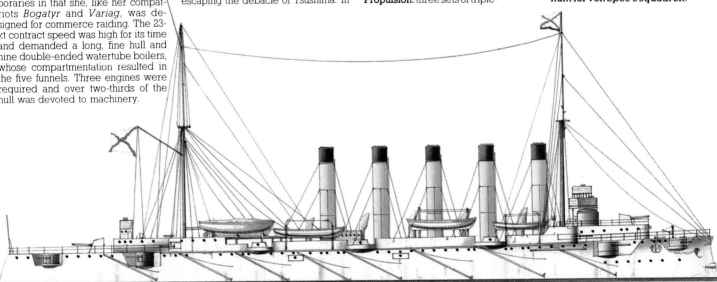

Emden's Epic Raid

In August 1914 Germany's Pacific squadron gathered in the Marianas, and at the suggestion of her captain the cruiser Emden *was detached to raid British commerce in the Indian Ocean. Conducted in the classic corsair tradition, her cruise attracted worldwide attention, and the chivalry and daring of her captain won praise even from his enemies.*

Safeguarding Germany's interests in the Far East was Vice-Admiral Graf von Spee's East Asiatic Squadron, based on the limited facilities of Tsingtau in northern China. Its major units comprised the armoured cruisers SMS *Scharnhorst* and *Gneisenau*, and the light cruisers SMS *Emden, Nürnberg* and *Leipzig*.

His area of responsibility being vast, von Spee spent considerable time at sea. Following the Sarajevo affair in June 1914, war looked inevitable and, taking the practical view that Tsingtau would be indefensible against Allied naval power, he decided to get 'lost' in the Pacific, thus avoiding the fate of the Russian Port Arthur squadron a decade before.

Only the *Emden* remained and, on the receipt of the warning telegram on 30 July her captain, von Müller, put to sea to await events. Hostilities against Russia commenced on 3 August and the *Emden* captured the new auxiliary *Rjasan*, which she took back to Tsingtau for rapid conversion to a raider (*Kormoran*). By now the UK and France were also hostile, and Japan was also expected to declare, so von Müller wasted no time, topped up and sailed on 6 August with two auxiliaries to rendezvous with von Spee in the Marianas. A conference there on 12 August decided that the squadron should make for Germany via the Pacific and the Horn but von Müller, having convinced his senior of the great prospects open to a cruiser in the Indian Ocean, was allowed his own way.

'My dutiful thanks for the confidence placed in me. Success to the Squadron and Bon Voyage': with this valedictory signal *Emden* left von Spee to his separate fate of Coronel and the Falklands. Von Müller moved at a leisurely pace through the myriad islands of Indonesia, honing both ship and crew to peak efficiency. As they passed Celebes on 23 August they heard of war with Japan and the pursuing of old scores in her investment of Tsingtau. *Emden* was now without friends or facilities.

A first problem was the failure of a collier to make a pre-arranged rendezvous off Timor and bunkers were taken from an auxiliary. On 27 August the little cruiser came through the Lombok Strait and entered the Indian Ocean. British radio discipline was slack, von Müller rapidly becoming aware of major activity in the area. During the week spent running the length of Java and Sumatra, a dummy fourth funnel was contrived to give the appearance of a British 'Town'. A second coaling stop at the northern end of Sumatra also failed and had to be resolved as before, the ships almost running foul of the British cruiser HMS *Hampshire*, one of a force seeking another German, SMS *Königsberg*.

From here, von Müller struck out across the Indian Ocean but, despite crossing major trade routes, arrived north east of Ceylon on 10 September having taken only a Greek ship, loaded with contraband (and invaluable) British coal. *Emden* then followed the Colombo-Calcutta route northward and was immediately rewarded. Her first prize was the British ship *Indus*, which was stripped of useful items (particularly soap that was in very short supply) before being sunk. Four other ships were taken in rapid succession but their crews were becoming an embarrassment in numbers. A passing neutral Italian was stopped and requested to take them to land but refused, afterwards warning the British *City of Rangoon* of the *Emden*'s presence. This ship broadcast a general raider warning, the first confirmation of von Müller's whereabouts. While the latter realized that to dally would be disastrous, he took the British *Kabinga*, sparing her to transport his 250-odd captives and, incidentally, beginning his great reputation for fairness and humanity.

Dangerously close to the Sandheads he captured the empty collier *Trabbock*. To sink her without delay he used his guns rather than charges but, in the depth of night, the dust-

Captain Karl Friederich Max von Müller became the most famous German sea captain, his name a byword for chivalry and enterprise. He joined Emden *in the Far East in 1913 and soon made a name for himself dealing with brigands on the Yangtse. It was he who suggested a campaign in the Indian Ocean, and he executed it with rigorous professionalism.*

Emden's *graceful profile soon began to haunt the minds of ship owners in the Indian Ocean; her raid on Madras sent shock waves across India, and* 'Emden' *came to be used in the local Tamil dialect to mean 'an ingenious person'.*

Emden's Epic Raid

laden atmosphere inside the ship's holds was inadvertently detonated in a shattering explosion. This brought the *Clan Matheson* to the scene to offer assistance, this ship and her valuable piece-goods cargo also being lost as a consequence. With ample radio evidence of British, French and Japanese cruisers on her trail, *Emden* was now obliged to vacate the lucrative Calcutta approaches, heading south eastward toward Rangoon. The movement had been anticipated and the raider found the area clear of shipping, though the radio traffic was ever more threatening. Von Müller therefore turned to the west, again narrowly missing the *Hampshire* as he set out across the Bay of Bengal.

Oil tank attack

At about 22.00 on 22 September *Emden* boldly appeared off Madras, approaching to within 3000 m (3,300 yards) to bombard and destroy the extensive tank storage facilities of the Burmah Oil Compnay. Dazzling the port battery with his searchlights, von Müller got off 125 rounds in short order and was away. The material gain was small compared with the effect on British morale.

Heading southward, the *Emden* cheekily looked in to the French ports of Pondicheri and Cuddalore, rounded Ceylon and arrived at the traffic focal point south of Cap Conmorin just ahead of the chase. Half a dozen prizes were taken, one (the British *Buresk*) being taken along for her cargo of first-quality steaming coal.

Expecting von Müller to double back to the Indies the Allies sent cruisers to the area but were frustrated as the German moved south to Diego Garcia for a period of self maintenance. Following this, the *Emden* returned to claim another seven victims before finally heading

Having spread fear and confusion along the Indian coast, Emden raided Penang at dawn on 28 October 1914. Sporting a fake fourth funnel to make her resemble HMS Yarmouth, she entered harbour flying the British flag. When she reached Zhemchung, down went the false colours, up went the German ensign and Emden opened fire. In just 15 minutes the Russian cruiser exploded and sank.

westward for a coaling rendezvous in the Nicobars.

A raider bereft of facilities needs to avoid damage at all costs, and von Müller's next step seems almost foolhardy. Intelligence indicated an old French cruiser at Penang, and resolving to attack her *Emden*, with her fourth 'funnel' rigged, entered through the outer anchorge at first light on 28 October. What she found was the little Russian cruiser *Zhemchug* which, totally surprised, was overwhelmed at close range by a hail of gunfire and torpedoes. Understandably, von Müller pulled out rapidly but, two hours out, stopped an inward-bound British Glen liner. His action was interrupted by a small French destroyer, the 300-ton *Mousquet* which, with more courage than tactical sense, bore straight in. Her two torpedoes were coolly avoided by the German, which shattered her with 12 close-range salvoes. Even here, however, von Müller stopped to rescue her survivors, many of whom were severely injured.

09.30 hrs, 10 November 1914: Emden's losing battle with the Sydney could be watched from the roof of the wireless station on the island and von Mücke decided to seize the schooner anchored offshore and escape with the landing party.

The *Emden* rounded the northern tip of Sumatra and ran southward along the island's coast. Allied efforts to catch her were diluted by necessary operations against the *Königsberg*, off the African coast, and the need to cover vast movement of troops by sea. Having peeped briefly and unrewardingly into the Sunda Strait, von Müller resolved to complete-

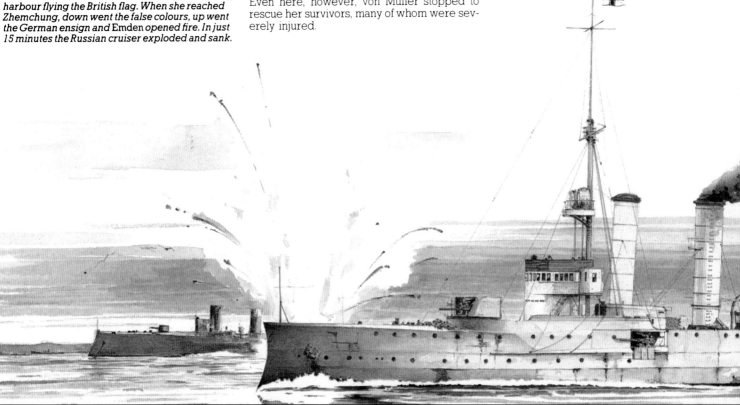

ly change his area to the Red Sea approaches. On his way he made a fateful decision to detour and destroy the important British Cable and Wireless station in the Cocos-Keelings.

Warning broadcast

This move had long been anticipated and an alert staff rapidly saw through the German's four-funnel disguise when she approached early on 9 November and broadcast a powerful warning en clair. To avoid possible bloodshed through shelling, von Müller put a 50-strong landing party ashore but these were almost immediately marooned when the *Emden* suddenly got under way. A British cruiser had been sighted. She was, in fact, the Australian 152-mm (6-in) ship HMAS *Sydney* which, observing radio silence, had been just below the horizon, covering a convoy. Besides her heavier main battery, the newcomer was clean and had at least a 4-kt speed advantage which her captain, Glossop, used to full advantage to dictate the range and the course of the action.

The German policy of lighter-calibre but faster-firing gun sometimes, as here, worked to their disadvantage. Despite accurate return fire, the heavier vessel's salvoes soon began to tell. The *Emden*'s rangefinder was destroyed and her steering gear damaged, the latter problem being compounded by loss of speed following the toppling of two funnels. The foremast went by the board and the ship began to flood from damage sustained below the protective deck. In the lightly-protected gun positions, the carnage caused by fragments and blast was appalling and, after 100 minutes of hopeless action, von Müller ran his wrecked command onto the reef of North Keeling. Nearly half his crew was dead and most of the remainder wounded, while the Australian had suffered only slight damage and four fatal casualties in disposing of this most successful of the German raiders. She had caused the British great material damage, but this was of little consequence compared with the associated disruption to movements and tying down of much Allied naval strength in her apprehension.

Kapitänleutnant Hellmuth von Mücke, Müller's 'Number One', was a resourceful extrovert whose epic journey back to Germany made a dramatic postscript to the sinking of the Emden. *It was his idea to rig a fourth funnel on the ship to give her a silhouette resembling that of HMS* Yarmouth.

Von Mücke brought the landing party to Constantinople where they were received by Admiral Wilhelm Souchon. They had sailed across the Indian Ocean, evading the Royal Navy, survived Turkish double-dealing and fought off Arab brigands in a battle in the desert.

This is the end: shot to pieces by Sydney's *heavier broadsides,* Emden *was run ashore on North Keeling Island; over 60 per cent of her crew became casualties. In her raiding career she had covered 30,000 miles, sunk 16 British ships and inflicted damage to the tune of about £5,000,000 – some 15 times the cost of building* Emden.

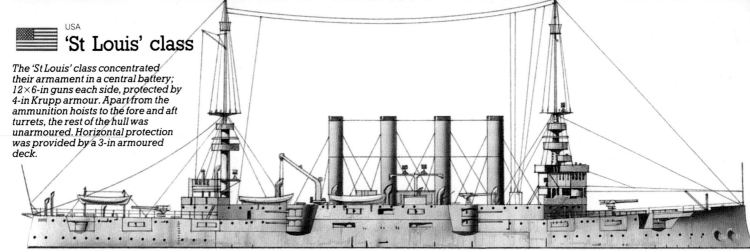

'St Louis' class

USA

The 'St Louis' class concentrated their armament in a central battery; 12×6-in guns each side, protected by 4-in Krupp armour. Apart from the ammunition hoists to the fore and aft turrets, the rest of the hull was unarmoured. Horizontal protection was provided by a 3-in armoured deck.

Until rendered obsolete by the introduction of the battle-cruiser, the armoured cruiser looked set to be an important feature of the US fleet, initially indeed taking the state names reserved at that time for capital ships. Since 1892 the fleet had, by policy, built almost entirely 'first-class battleships and first-class cruisers', so second- and third-class cruisers were produced in only small numbers in the 1890s for coastal defence and to maintain a presence at the few American colonial possessions. Following the war of 1898 with Spain and the acquisition of more foreign territory, two Elswick cruisers were taken over from Brazilian account, but the workmanlike design of these little ships had no influ-

ence whatsoever on the six 'Denver' class colonial cruisers (Nos 14-19) that followed in 1901-3. It was, therefore, a considerable change of policy that suddenly produced the three **'St Louis' class** ships (USS **Charleston, Milwaukee** and **St Louis**) which though they took the next pendants (20-22) had nothing else in common.

In 1899 the British had effectively introduced the armoured cruiser by adding a belt to the design of the 'Diadem' class protected cruisers then just completed. In a neat reversal of this move the Americans created a diminutive of the 'California' (later 'San Diego') class armoured cruisers and of a size with the contemporary British 'Monmouths' with whom they shared a

common main battery of 14 152-mm (6-in) guns. Where the British policy was to work in a shallow 102-mm (4-in) belt over the greatest possible length and protect otherwise only the two level casemates the Americans carried on the central battery idea from the 'Californias', encasing it in 102-mm steel with a short extension both forward and aft to cover the machinery spaces. Predictably, the navy considered them underarmed but, though they also carried light horizontal protection, their primary drawback was in their being no faster than armoured cruisers. As their economy was not seen as a virtue they were to languish along with them. The *Milwaukee* was a war loss.

Specification
'St Louis' class
Displacement: 9,700 tons standard
Dimensions: length 123.0 m (426.5 ft); beam 20.1 m (66.0 ft); draught 6.9 m (22.5 ft)
Propulsion: two sets of triple-expansion steam engines delivering 24,000 ihp (17895 kW) to two shafts
Speed: 22 kts
Armament: 14 single 152-mm (6-in) and 18 single 76-mm (3-in) guns
Armour: 76-mm (3-in) deck and 102-mm (4-in) belt
Complement: 668

'Omaha' class

USA

Perhaps surprisingly, the US Navy launched no cruisers between 1907 and 1920. By the time that isolationism had turned to active involvement in the war in 1917, the maritime threat from Germany was primarily through her submarines rather than her battlefleet, and it was on building destroyers that USA concentrated. Even so, the gap in cruiser construction is difficult to justify.

A long series of armoured cruisers, powerful enough to rank as third-class battleships, had been rendered rudely obsolescent in 1906 by the introduction of the battle-cruiser. Further, while the Civil War had demonstrated the value of both the blockade-runner and commerce raider, the fast cruiser descendent of the latter had no place

in the war likely to be fought by 20th-century USA.

Thus, the only likely role for the cruiser to a nation lacking a real empire was that of scouting for the main body of the fleet. The UK had introduced the steam turbine-driven light cruiser with HMS *Amethyst*, completed in 1904, and the possibilities posed by this new form of compact but powerful machinery led the US Navy to build the three 3,750-ton 'Chesters' (CL 1-3), all launched in 1907, to evaluate reciprocating machinery against direct-drive and geared turbines. The US Navy, however, did not (and indeed does not) like small ships and the American cruiser thus languished for lack of a raison d'être.

Probably more because both the UK

and Germany made good use of light cruisers rather than through a perceived need, a new class of 10 cruisers had been authorized in 1916, classified as 'scouts' despite being half as large again as any light cruiser in Europe. The **'Omaha' class** ships (CL 4-13) were not, however, to be completed until after the war. They were interesting vessels with the large number of boilers for their 34 kts in two groups, resulting in two distinctive pairs of funnels, giving them the appearance of overgrown flushdecked destroyers. Their original eight 152-mm (6-in) guns (including some in the last casemates recorded) were augmented by two twin turrets at a late stage. All went through World War II, emerging with varying degrees of modification, to be

scrapped with the 1940s. The ships were the USS *Cincinnati, Concord, Detroit, Marblehead, Memphis, Milwaukee, Omaha, Raleigh, Richmond* and *Trenton*.

Specification
'Omaha' class
Displacement: 7,050 tons standard
Dimensions: length 169.3 (555.5 ft); beam 16.8 m (55.25 ft); draught 4.5 m (14.75 ft)
Propulsion: four sets of geared turbines delivering 90,000 shp (67105 kW) to four shafts
Speed: 33.5 kts
Armament: two twin and eight single 152-mm (6-in) and four single 76-mm (3-in) guns, and 10 533-mm (21-in) torpedo tubes
Armour: none
Complement: 360

The 'Omaha' class cruisers were built to complement the proposed 35-kt battle-cruisers of the 1916 programme. The design was modified after the US Navy worked with the Royal Navy in 1917-8; extra guns and torpedoes were added, which meant more crew and a rather crowded vessel.

Submarines of World War 1

From 1914 to 1918 submarines progressed from being short-range coastal craft to large ocean-going vessels capable of extended cruises. Germany soon realized their value and launched a submarine campaign against Great Britain which came close to winning the war.

The major navies consistently attempted to design submarines with long range and high surface speed to operate in close support of the battlefleet, but experience proved this to be unworkable. J7, seen right, was built for the Royal Australian Navy in 1917.

In the course of a British naval exercise in the early years of the 20th century, a submarine informed the opposing admiral that he had just been 'sunk'. The latter replied to the effect that he 'would be damned if he was', and carried on. Such entrenched attitudes were typical, despite the fact that similar evolutions had consistently demonstrated the submarine's potential: the truth was unpalatable and was therefore best ignored. (A current parallel exists in the average warship's totally inadequate defences against a wide variety of aerial threats.)

It is fair to say that by August 1914 submariners understood their craft's potential but had failed to convince those who mattered in the conduct of the surface war. This was the more strange in the UK, where the redoubtable 'Jacky' Fisher remained in close touch with submarine development: indeed, they were contemptuously dismissed as 'Fisher's toys' by Admiral Lord Beresford, who really should have known better.

Within weeks of the outbreak of war, the British *E9* under Horton had sunk the cruiser *Hela* near Heligoland, and Weddigen's *U-9* had disposed of three 'Cressy' class cruisers before breakfast, followed shortly by HMS *Hawke*. The British *B11* penetrated the Dardanelles defences to knock out the *Messoudieh*, offset by the loss to submarine attack of the first battleship, HMS *Formidable*, off Portland. In the Adriatic, Austrian boats dealt as harshly with the French and Italians, and the long British tradition of close blockade came to a bloody finale when Hersing's *U-21* sank two more battleships off Gallipoli, having made the long passage from Germany for the occasion. In a bare nine months, the submarine had firmly stated that war at sea would never again be the same. Under the German flag it went on to the controversial war against merchant shipping. In sinking nearly eight million gross registered tons of British shipping it nearly won the war but, in the process, so outraged the neutral Americans that they finally declared for the Allied cause. Germany's war-winning weapon ultimately worked against her own interests and brought about her downfall.

Detail of one of the Royal Navy 'E' class boats off the Dardanelles with a French submarine in the background. It fell to E2 to make the last patrol there in January 1916 as the Allied evacuation was completed. The land campaign may have been a disastrous failure, but the submarine operations were a credit to the Royal Navy.

GERMANY
'UB' classes

The *UB classes* were coastal submarines which stemmed initially from a requirement for a boat of limited performance that could be transported by rail to its area of operations. Though the hull would need to be divided into three main sections to achieve this, the major restriction was on diameter. For this reason, the initial 17 boats completed in 1915 (and later designated the '**UB I' class**) were single-hulled, with diving, trimming and fuel tanks inboard. They were also single-screwed and, with the diesel in the unreliable early days of its development, this proved a mechanical drawback. Sections were round, flattening forward to an ellipse to allow two 450-mm (17.7-in) tubes to be carried side by side. As there was space for only two spare torpedoes, the lack of a proper deck gun was a real limitation, but those operating from Bruges (following assembly at Antwerp) were a nuisance off the British east coast, particularly to the fishing fleet, at that time composed mainly of sailing craft. Several operated from Pola on the

Adriatic, and one of these, von Heimburg's *UB-14*, sank the troop transport *Royal Edward* near Kos in August 1915 with the loss of almost 1,000 lives. In the November he sank also the British submarine *E20*, which was keeping a compromised rendezvous.

Though the 'UB Is' met their designed aims, they inevitably proved inadequate with the war stalemated on land and, therefore, becoming of greater importance at sea. Their 1915-6 follow-ons, the '**UB II' class** boats, were therefore considerably enlarged to allow for twin-screw propulsion, together with greater power and range. As there was no longer any prospect of rail transportation, they could be given saddle-tanks, the double-hulled construction allowing some

tanks to be carried outboard, thus increasing space within. This in turn permitted two 500-mm (19.7-in) tubes to be carried forward, vertically disposed, together with four reloads. A 50-mm (1.97-in) deck gun and a radio installation were also fitted in the class, which ran to 30 boats (*UB-18* to *UB-47*). Beginning in 1917, the first of 85 '**UB III' class** boats (*UB-48* to *UB-132*) came into service. Compared with the 263/292 tons of the 'UB IIs', these were of 516/651 tons and large enough for unrestricted operations around the whole of the UK. With five tubes and an 88-mm (3.46-in) gun, they were comparable in size to earlier sea-going U-boats. Eight 'UB Is' became war losses, as did 21 'UB IIs' and 40 'UB IIIs'.

Specification
'UB I' class
Displacement: 127 tons surfaced and 142 tons dived
Dimensions: length 28.10 m (92 ft 2.5 in); beam 2.97 m (9 ft 9 in); draught 2.90 m (9 ft 6 in)
Propulsion: one diesel delivering 44.7 kW (60 bhp) and one electric motor delivering 89.5 kW (120 hp) to one shaft
Speed: 6.5 kts surfaced and 5.5 kts dived
Range: 3000 km (1,864 miles) at 5 kts surfaced, and 85 km (53 miles) at 4 kts dived
Armament: one machine-gun, and two 450-mm (17.7-in) torpedo tubes (bow) with four torpedoes
Complement: 14

Short-range coastal submarines originally intended to be transported by rail to their area of operations, the little 'UB I' class boats had only two torpedo tubes and four torpedoes. This is UB-4, which operated in the Channel before meeting its end at the hands of the Q-ship Inverlyon.

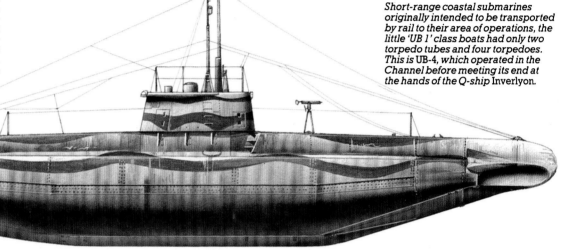

GERMANY
'UC' classes

The **UC** (later '**UC I') class** was built in parallel with the 'UB I', taking its hull as a basis but stretching it for duty as a pure minelayer, no torpedo tubes being fitted. Mining the teeming coastal traffic lanes of the UK was a particularly cost-effective form of warfare but fraught with problems in the narrow and constricted channels, and a small boat was essential. Something under 6 m (19.7 ft) longer than the 'UB I', the minelayer employed a new principle in having six centreline minetubes passing right through the hull forward of the fin. From the bottom these tubes sloped aft at about 30° and were free-flooding. Each could accommodate two mines which, being negatively buoyant when attached to their sinkers, could be dropped out of the bottom of the tubes with the boat moving slowly ahead. Fifteen of the class (*UC-1* to *UC-15*) were built for assembly elsewhere during 1915, and the hazards of their trade were such that only one survived to the end of the war. Not the least problem was a boat's liability to strike her own mines, two (and possibly as many as five) of the class being so lost. A further drawback was that the depth-setting for the mines could not be altered once at sea.

UC-5 was stranded and captured by the Royal Navy; she is seen here on display at Temple Bar pier in 1916. She carried no torpedoes, just 12 mines launched via six vertical tubes which passed right through the hull.

During 1915 foreign public opinion obliged the Germans to restrict their U-boat operations, and minelaying took on a greater significance. Further specialized boats were required and, as in the 'UBs', the size was increased. The resulting 'UC II' class was of 49.4 m (162.1 ft) overall length, had twin screws and was of 417/493 tons displacement. Each of the six tubes could take an extra mine by virtue of a deep casing forward and a wide and substantial keel. A further improvement was to include also three 500-mm (19.7-in) torpedo tubes and an 88-mm (3.46-in) gun to permit offensive operations on the completion of the lay. Two of the tubes were external to the pressure hull, flanking the tops of the mine chutes in the forward casing; the third was inboard and right aft, cramping the rudder and hydroplane gear. Sixty-four 'UC IIs' were built (UC-16 to UC-79), 43 becoming war losses, and these were followed by 25 'UC III' class boats (UC-90 to UC-114) which improved upon the poor surface seakeeping qualities of the 'UC II' and had a 105-mm (4.13-in) gun.

Two types of ocean minelayer, the 10 boats of the 655/830-ton 'UE I' class and the 10 boats of the 1,165/1,512-ton

Above: UC-74 was one of the longest-ranged vessels of the 'UC-II' class minelayers. Bigger boats than their predecessors, the class carried six 100-cm (39.4-in) mine tubes with 18 UC200-type mines. Her sister UC-65 sank HMS Ariadne off Beachy Head in 1917, but was herself sunk by the British C-15 later in the year.

'UE II' class, were also available with capacities of 32 and 48 mines respectively, laid from a dry-storage chamber through two tubes aft.

Specification
'UC I' class
Displacement: 168 tons surfaced and 183 tons dived
Dimensions: length 34.00 m (111 ft 6.5 in); beam 3.20 m (10 ft 6 in); draught 3.00 m (9 ft 10 in)
Propulsion: one diesel delivering 67 kw (90 bhp) and one electric motor delivering 130.5 kW (175 hp) to one shaft
Speed: 6 kts surfaced and 5 kts dived
Range: 1400 km (870 miles) at 5 kts surfaced, and 95 km (59 miles) at 4 kts dived
Armament: 12 mines
Complement: 16

Submarine-launched mines accounted for many Allied warships, including HMS Hampshire, mined by U-75 (Lord Kitchener was among the dead); the Italian battleship Regina Margherita (mined by the Austro-Hungarian UC-14); and the French cruiser Kléber (mined at the entrance to Brest by UC-61).

 GERMANY
'U-19' class

The U-19 was not a great technical advance over the 14 U-boats that preceded her, all of which were to play a war role; what she did introduce when completed in 1913 was the diesel engine. Earlier boats had been propelled on the surface usually by Köting engines which burned paraffin or heavy oil, deemed safer than the petrol engine used in earlier British boats though, interestingly, the latter had started to use diesels in the 'D' class boats some three years earlier. Though the Germans had the diesel, they were still proving its long-term reliability. Diesels, besides being safer, were far more economic, an important factor with respect to operational radius. One diesel per shaft could also develop more power than the two Körting engines previously used in tandem, saving greatly on overall length.

The design continued the tried four-tube layout, with two forward and two in the cramped after sections, but increased the calibre from 450 to 500 mm (17.7 to 19.7 in). This arrangement was to be favoured for the majority of the following war-built classes. An important innovation was the adoption of a deck gun, an 88-mm (3.46-in) weapon. The circular-section pressure hull was flanked by substantial saddle tanks with flattened top surfaces, usually awash, and the narrow centreline casing had a sheer forward to assist in better surface seakeeping. Light, folding masts were carried to spread the wireless aerials.

Only four 'U-19' class boats were built (U-19 to U-22), the design then being stretched by 0.5 m (1.64 ft) to up-rate the diesels by a cylinder apiece. With only minor variations, U-23 to U-41 followed this arrangement, accounting for sea-going U-boat deliveries until early 1915. Of the original group, U-21 became known under her commander, Hersing, who inflicted the first loss on the Royal Navy by submarine attack when, on 5 September 1914 he sank the scout cruiser HMS Pathfinder in the North Sea. On 29 January 1915 he cheekily surfaced off Walney Island to bombard the Barrow works of Vickers, only to be chased off by a shore battery. Surviving the war, U-21 'foundered' en route to surrender.

Specification
'U-19' class
Displacement: 650 tons surfaced and 837 tons dived
Dimensions: length 64.20 m (210 ft 7.5 in); beam 6.10 m (20 ft 0 in); draught 3.60 m (11 ft 10 in)
Propulsion: two diesels delivering 1268 kW (1,700 bhp) and two electric motors delivering 895 kW (1,200 hp) to two shafts
Speed: 15.5 kts surfaced and 9.5 kts dived
Range: 13900 km (8,637 miles) at 8 kts surfaced, and 150 km (93 miles) at 5 kts dived
Armament: one 88-mm (3.46-in) gun, and four 500-mm (19.7-in) torpedo tubes (two bow and two stern) with six torpedoes
Complement: 37

U-23 to U-41 were stretched versions of the 'U-19' class submarines. Of the four built in the class, U-21 had an exceptional record, sinking HMS Pathfinder in 1914 – the first Royal Navy loss to submarine attack. She went on to sink the French cruiser Amiral Charner and later, off the Dardanelles, the British battleships Goliath and Triumph, both on the same day.

The Great War beneath the waves

In 1914 the submarine was regarded by many naval officers as a short-range defensive weapon manned by grubby engineer types, and not even the Germans appreciated its potential as a war-winner. In fact the development of underwater weapons revolutionized naval warfare; battleships remained the final arbiters of war at sea, but the submarine was evolving rapidly.

It was fortunate for the UK that pre-war German exercises had failed to highlight the great potential of the U-boat. The UK herself had already committed considerable resources to submarines, so that their possibilities were more widely appreciated. But the manner of their wartime use and an accurate definition of the threat that they posed to individual warships, to the battlefleet and, equally importantly, to merchant shipping, was far from formulated. Peacetime exercises tended to be set-piece affairs, modifying established doctrine rather than evolving new concepts, particularly any as revolutionary as using submarines in an aggressively offensive role.

Probably the submarine's greatest drawback was in its being viewed as a piece of machinery rather than a ship, a device for engineers rather than seamen at a time when 'oily rags' were viewed as an inferior race. Submariners were of a closed order (known defensively in the Royal Navy as 'The Trade') and their craft were looked upon as near-seas defensive weapons with little relevance to fleet matters. Just as the Germans had failed to foresee their submarine arm's offensive qualities, so had the British failed to develop suitable effective means for their detection and destruction.

Even by 1914 the submarine itself had progressed from the single-hulled, 'spindle' type to larger saddle-tanked or double-hulled varieties that possessed far greater usable internal volume and vastly improved seakeeping. The latter point was of great importance for submarines (or 'submersibles'), with their poor submerged performance, diving for evasion or attack. Little thought had been devoted to the problems posed by extended patrols or to equipping them for use against their most likely targets. Thus, for instance, when the Germans discovered (to their own surprise as much as anybody's) that the U-boat's range and endurance was considerably greater than anticipated, an immediate limitation was imposed by the few torpedoes carried. This, with existing boats, would result in fruitful patrols being curtailed and inordinate time spent in transit if a way could not be found to resupply on station or develop other modes of attack. In practice, torpedoes were reserved for high-value or difficult targets while merchantmen, the protection of which Germany rapidly discovered to be the UK's weak point, could be sunk by gun or demolition charge. In turn, however, this robbed the U-boat of its greatest advantage, stealth, and resulted in countermeasures such as 'Q' ships. Slow submergence had been seen in peacetime as of little consequence, but proved gravely disadvantageous when the tables were suddenly turned. Improvements could often be made simply by cutting extra limber holes in the casing structure.

Torpedoes in general worked well for their time, but the lack of range and killing power of the British 457-mm (18-in) and the German 450-mm (17.7-in)

U-8 was the first U-boat lost, being sunk by HMS Maori and HMS Gurkha on 4 March 1915. The ram was a favourite method of submarine destruction: U-29 was the unluckiest in this respect, being rammed by the 18,000-ton bulk of HMS Dreadnought two weeks later.

weapons led to the introduction of 533-mm (21-in) and 500-mm (19.7-in) calibres. These, inevitably, demanded larger boats but could strike from a safer range. The extra size brought about the abandoning of athwartships tubes by the British and less stress on manoeuvrability for rapid disengagement.

As British boats would likely be operating against warships, guns were little in evidence at the outset. Inadequate 6-pdr guns were superseded by 12-pdr weapons and later boats carried one or two 102-mm (4-in) guns as the best means of countering surfaced U-boats. As an alternative to the torpedoing of merchantmen, the Germans found the gun indispensible, its calibre jumping from 50 mm (1.97 in) progressively to 88 mm (3.46 in), 105 mm (4.13 in) and eventually 150 mm (5.9 in), with sometimes two guns fitted. Though aircraft attacks were mounted on submarines, the latter's light automatic weapons

Armed with a single torpedo tube and crewed by eight men, the 113-ton HM Submarine No. 2 was the first submarine to enter service with the Royal Navy. No. 1 foundered while on tow in 1913, only to be found again in 1981; she is being restored at the submarine museum at Gosport.

One of the victims: submarine attack accounted for the loss of 11 heavy cruisers during World War I. The 14,000-ton cruiser HMS Drake was torpedoed and sunk by U-79 off Rathlin Island, Northern Ireland. U-79 was primarily a minelayer but had two external torpedo tubes.

A U-boat in an interesting camouflage scheme surrenders in 1918. While most of the High Seas Fleet mutinied, one U-boat crewed by volunteer officers attempted to enter the Royal Navy anchorage at Scapa Flow on a last do-or-die mission, and became the only submarine to be destroyed by a shore station.

were not viewed specifically in an AA context. Large-calibre weapons, as fitted in 'monitor' submarines, were an aberration and contributed nothing to mainstream submarine development.

Minelaying was taken seriously by the Germans, who appreciated its cost-effectiveness far more than did the British. Where the latter converted a few standard boats, the former built many coastal and ocean boats configured for the task. Both sides used roughly the same system, with mines laid from free-flooding stowage chutes; it was hazardous and slow, however, and the British changed to mine stowage in the length of the casing and laid over the stern.

Wireless communication was, for the most part, of unpredictable range and quality, so that the sort of centralized command exercised over the U-boats of World War II was not possible in World War I. Aerials demanded that submarines were encumbered with two tall telescopic or folding masts.

Communications between a submerged boat and a surface ship were in the experimental stage in 1914 and merged with research already being conducted into the detection of submarines by passive acoustic means. Directional hyro-

planes were widely deployed, particularly by the British, both from shore station and surface ship, but contributed little of note. Perhaps surprisingly, in these days of 'towed arrays', hydrophones were being towed astern of ships in 'fish' and multi-unit arrays as early as 1917, but the big breakthrough, active detection by Asdic (later Sonar), achieved operational status just too late to be of use. At this time, nearly all submarines were very cluttered externally, had inefficient propellers and were extremely noisy, but detection still tended to occur only after they had broken cover to attack, leaving them firmly with the initiative.

Ramming and gunfire were both used against surfaced submarines but, as these could usually submerge quickly enough to avoid damage, the depth charge rapidly came into its own. Initially, British production was slow, with an average of only 200 being expended each month in 1917, but by the war's end

A U-boat makes a dramatic addition to a Sussex beach in 1919. After their victory the Allies divided the surviving German fleet amongst themselves, but many U-boats 'accidentally' foundered when German sailors were supposed to be delivering them to their new owners.

The Great War beneath the waves

Periscope depth aboard a Royal Navy submarine. Once at sea, World War I submarine commanders were very much left to their own devices, since the radio technology which allowed the Germans to control their U-boats from ashore during World War II was only in its infancy.

Seamen rest in the cramped interior of a British submarine. As the boats became larger so did their crews, and space was always at a premium. It became noticed that submarines invariably smelt of stale cabbage, which has remained a disagreeable feature of submariners' lives ever since.

Seen here at Scapa Flow among the pride of the Grand Fleet, G14 was one of a 14-strong class of submarines ordered before the war in response to exaggerated rumours of the performance of German submarines. Royal Navy submariners acquitted themselves very well in World War I.

this number had increased tenfold. In the end the U-boat was not so much defeated by hardware as frustrated by tactics, for the tardy introduction of convoy reduced the horrifying 5.75 million gross registered ton mercantile loss of 1917 to a manageable 2.65 million for the first 10 months of 1918.

Early German research to produce a reliable diesel engine benefitted their boats with excellent machinery, only a few of the very earliest having the smoky Körting engine that burned high flashpoint fuel. Only with the 'D' class had the British switched from the more hazardous petrol engine though, in its defence, it could be pointed out that it was more compact and had a significantly better power-to-weight ratio. Diesels were started, and often reversed, by using the main propulsion motors. Storage battery technology of the time permitted submerged ranges typically less than 185 km (100 miles).

All types of submarine grew considerably in size during the war. They were less agile as a result and easier to detect, but both endurance and habitability were greatly improved so that patrols of six and seven weeks were possible.

Left: The 'K' class was designed as fleet submarines capable of 24 kts surfaced. No contemporary diesels were equal to the task so steam turbines were fitted together with a diesel to drive the generator. Over a third of the hull was devoted to machinery.

Above: The short-range coastal C-class boats were the first class to be built in large numbers for the Royal Navy. Despite their short range and petrol engines, they saw extensive war service.

'U-139' class (Type UA or U-Kreuzer)

Resumption of unrestricted submarine warfare by the Germans in February 1917 went far toward obliging the USA to declare war in April 1917. Failing to anticipate this result, the Germans were caught short of boats suitable to carry the mercantile war to the American eastern seaboard, and the rearming of the slow and vulnerable *Handels U-Boote* emphasized this predicament. The construction of these large boats had, however, yielded useful experience and enabled a programme of large cruising submarines to be undertaken with confidence. Already being built at the US declaration were the big ocean minelayers and a pair of cruiser classes, the larger by far of which were the **'U-139' class** boats. Despite their size, these cruiser submarines could still carry only 13 spare torpedoes, so much debate was given to surface armament for the purpose of despatching 'soft' targets. Eventually they were given two 150-mm (5.9-in) guns and were fitted for, but not necessarily with, a further 88-mm (3.46-in) piece abaft the fin. A low bulwark around the amidships section was designed to keep down the amount of free water that would otherwise have swilled about to hamper gunlaying, and a retractable 4-m (13.1-ft) rangefinder was housed in the after end of the superstructure. A respectable surface speed was as important as long endurance, but diesels of high enough power were only in the development stage. Steam propulsion was considered but wisely rejected, and a speed of 16 kts had to be accepted, though even this was not achieved in

practice.

It was then too late to build such submarines in any numbers, because of shortages of skilled labour and materials, and of conflicts of priorities, and the three boats were not commissioned until 1918. A planned follow-on 'U-142' class was even larger at 2,160/2,785 tons (dwarfing anything used in World War II), adding a second 88-mm gun, 18 reload torpedoes and a 40750-km (25,320-mile) cruising range. Only the lead ship of a planned nine was ever completed. Also planned, but never built, was an even larger 110-m (360.9-ft) boat with an armament of four 150-mm and two 88-mm guns, with topsides armoured for surface combat.

Only a handful of corsairs ever

reached the Western Atlantic operationally. Their success was limited but their nuisance value was considerable, particularly in obliging the Americans to adopt a convoy system, with its attendant delays.

Specification
'U-139' class
Displacement: 1,930 tons surfaced and 2,483 tons dived
Dimensions: length 92.00 m (301 ft 10 in); beam 9.10 m (29 ft 10.25 in); draught 5.30 m (17 ft 5 in)
Propulsion: two diesel-electric drives delivering 2946 kW (3,950 bhp) and two electric motors delivering 1268 kW (1,700 hp) to two shafts

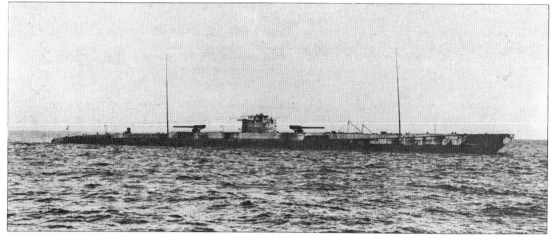

The shape of things to come: a 'U-139' type long-range cruiser submarine, which displaced over 2,000 tons. The powerful gun armament of two 150-mm (5.9-in) weapons was important, as despite their size they could only accommodate 19 torpedoes.

Speed: 15.5 kts surfaced and 7.5 kts dived
Range: 23150 km (14,385 miles) at 8 kts surfaced, and 92.5 km (57.5 miles) at 5 kts dived
Armament: two single 150-mm (5.9-in) guns, and six 500-mm (19.7-in) torpedo tubes (four bow and two stern) with 19 torpedoes
Complement: 70

'U-151' class (Handels U-Boote)

Germany, blockading the UK with her U-boats was, in turn, blockaded by the Royal Navy. Only a short war had been planned by the Germans so, even by 1915, shortages were appearing in vital commodities, notably nickel and rubber, both of which were freely available in the still-neutral USA. Official plans to bring across small quantities in existing submarines were replaced by a commercial proposal to build specialized, unarmed, cargo-carrying U-boats (**Handels U-Boote**). Investment was underwritten by the state and an operating company, the Deutsche-Ozean Red. GmbH was established. A degree of urgency attended the construction of the first two boats, the largest yet ordered: hulls were built in one yard and fitted out in another; machinery was made available from official sources in the form of auxiliary machinery from capital ships then under construction; and completion took only 6½ months. Two internal cargo spaces were provided, and the free-flooding volume between the pressure hull and the outer casing was utilized for further stowage for such as raw rubber while providing scope for further deep-framing of the

large-diameter hull. About 350 tonnes could be carried in total. Access to the inner cargo spaces was understandably poor but, for such a venture, timely arrival took precendence over speed of handling. Surfaced, the hull had a high freeboard, double-ended appearance, the stern particularly having a quite mercantile form with a deep skeg supporting a simplex-type rudder separating the twin screws, which were fully bossed. The first boat, *Deutschland*, made two successful trips to the USA with great attendant propaganda value but the second, *Bremen*, disappeared on her maiden voyage. Nevertheless, six more boats were ordered. By then (1916-7) they had to share priorities with other pro-

jects and were delivered late. This, together with the USA's entry into the war and possibly with doubts regarding the structural strength following the loss of the *Bremen*, resulted in a change of role. The **'U-151' class** boats were armed with two 150-mm (5.9-in) guns and two torpedo tubes and used as long-range cruisers. *Deutschland* became the *U-155* and alone took six tubes. These big boats had a two-month endurance and operated largely in the central Atlantic where, though their tally was small, they caused the British much anxiety because of the difficulty in providing countermeasures in so remote a region.

Specification
'U-151' class
Displacement: 1,512 tons surfaced and 1,875 tons dived
Dimensions: length 65.00 m (213 ft 3 in); beam 8.90 m (29 ft 2.5 in); draught 5.30 m (17 ft 5 in)
Propulsion: two diesels delivering 597 kW (800 bhp) and two electric motors delivering 597 kW (800 hp) to two shafts
Speed: 12.5 kts surface and 5 kt dived
Range: 38900 km (24,171 miles) at 6 kts surfaced, and 120 km (75 miles) at 3 kts dived
Armament: two single 150-mm (5.9-in) guns, two single 88-mm (3.46-in) guns, and two 500-mm (19.7-in) torpedo tubes (bow) with 18 torpedoes
Complement: 56

The 'U-151' class began life as submarine freighters (with names) built to carry vital cargo from the neutral USA to Germany, avoiding the Royal Navy blockade which was slowly strangling the German economy. After their fellow submarines had brought America into the war, the 'U-151's were used as long-range submarine cruisers.

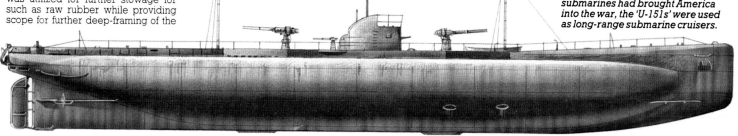

First of the Aces

U-35 remains to this day the most successful submarine of all time. She sank 224 ships, totalling 535,900 tons, most of them while under the command of Lothar von Arnauld de la Perière; by comparison, the most successful submarine of World War II (the German U-48) sank 52 ships totalling 310,000 tons. After two years in the Mediterranean her commander returned to Germany and took over one of the latest U-boats, but the war ended before he could substantially improve his score.

On 12 November 1915, the German submarine *U-35* returned to its forward base in the then Austro-Hungarian port of Cattaro. Her commander, Kophamel, in a month ranging the eastern Mediterranean, had sunk about 49,000 gross tons of shipping. He was now appointed to command the new refitting base at Pola, being relieved by an unknown with an unlikely background.

Lothar Eugen George von Arnauld de la Perière, not yet quite 30 years of age, had French aristocratic antecedents traceable to the early 15th century. His father was a State Auditor in Potsdam but a great grandfather had earned a Pour le Mérite with Oakleaves while serving as a *Generalleutnant* under Frederick the Great in 1757.

The 10-year-old Lothar was placed as a naval cadet at Wahlstatt, joining the Kaiserliche Marine seven years later. Specializing in torpedoes, he served in the cruiser *Emden* in the Far East in 1911-3 before being drafted to the staff of Admiral von Pohl, soon to be C-in-C of the High Seas Fleet. His next move was to the *U-35*.

Ominously, Kophamel had reported the Mediterranean eastern basin to be a good hunting ground, with 'few patrols' and 'shipping (following) prescribed courses'. After a short refit, U-35 sailed on 20 February 1916 to operate between Malta and Crete. His first kill, on 26 February, was the French auxiliary *Provence II*, over half the 1,800 troops aboard

perishing. Her status allowed a submerged attack with no warning but, in order to conserve torpedoes, von Arnauld had wisely conscripted a good gunner from the fleet. While, in the next two days, two ships were sunk by gunfire, a third escaped because the boat's movement made shooting difficult. On 29 February four torpedoes were expended in sinking the British sloop HMS *Primula*. The first took her bows off, but the little ship went full astern, not only evading two further shots but also attempting to ram the submarine. Respecting her two 102-mm (4-in) guns, the German drew off and sank her with his last torpedo, which obliged him to return to Cattaro after a patrol of only one week.

Returning immediately, von Arnauld found the area almost devoid of shipping, a month's patrol yielding only one respectable prize, the 13,540-ton British transport *Minneapolis*, which took two days to founder.

Following rectification of machinery defects, *U-35* appeared in the western Mediterranean in June 1916. Between 10 and 24 June he sank 40 ships, mostly small French and Italian traders, but aggregating 57,000 grt. With so many targets available, it was noteworthy that when the British ship *Clodmoor* made a spirited defence, she survived. On 21 June von Arnauld entered Cartagena to deliver a letter from the Kaiser to King Alfonso of Spain and finally returned only when 520 rounds of ammunition had been expended.

U-35 *receives dispatches from a Friederikshafen seaplane in the Mediterranean. The Kaiser once used* U-35 *to deliver a personal message to the King of Spain. On his way to and from Cartegena, Von Arnauld expended over 500 rounds of ammunition against Allied merchantmen.*

On 26 July he sailed again for the same area on what was to be the war's most productive U-boat patrol. In 25 days he destroyed 54 ships totalling about 90,000 grt, all of which were attacked with the *U-35* surfaced. Von Arnauld took considerable risks to abide by the rules. On 14 August, for instance, in sinking no less than 11 small Italian traders rounding northern Corsica, he was jumped by the same number of French anti-submarine ships. Next day, having stopped a small vessel, he was approached by another, large and unmarked, which suddenly opened a heavy fire at '60 hectametres' (about

U-35 *lies on the surface observing four warships steaming over the horizon in April 1917; von Arnauld had the mortifying experience of missing the large French cruiser* Waldeck Rousseau *the previous year. Most of U-35's kills were achieved by surface action, which was not forgotten by the veterans joining the inter-war Kriegsmarine.*

U-35 makes a rendezvous with a later-model U-boat. Lack of radio equipment meant that 'Wolfpack tactics' were not yet possible, but on the other hand surface vessels had few weapons or sensors and the Allied navies took a long time to mount a serious ASW effort.

6,500 yards). Von Arnauld submerged rapidly but the ship, the Italian decoy *Città di Sassari*, pulled away. On his return he had expended over 900 rounds of 105-mm (4.13-in) ammunition but only four torpedoes, one of which had missed the French armoured cruiser *Waldeck-Rousseau*.

His next patrol netted 22 ships of over 70,000 grt. Typical of the larger victims was the 3,840-ton *Benpark*, on passage from North America to Genoa, with a manifest including 5,000 tons of piece goods, manufactured steel, machine tools, 900 bars of copper and 1,000 tons of coke. During this operation he again called at Cartagena to pick up a party of German officers engaged on an undisclosed mission; among them, interestingly, was a 'Lt Cdr Canaris', later head of German military intelligence. Von Arnauld was awarded the Pour le Mérite and, patrol by patrol, steadily added to

his total. With the convoy system becoming organized, however, lack of targets gradually forced him to operate outside Gibraltar.

Early in 1918, with 195 ships totalling over 500,000 grt to his credit, von Arnauld returned to Germany to take command of the big U-Kreuzer *U-139* to spearhead the assault on American waters. Though others, including Kophmel's *U-140*, arrived in the summer, von Arnauld was recalled and, operating subsequently west of Spain, had little luck against well escorted convoys, and the new experience of being heavily depth-charged. Though he had received the honour of being personally received by the Kaiser, he returned to Kiel on 14 October 1918 to find the fleet in a state of revolt, and shared in its joint shame.

With no submarines in the postwar fleet, von Arnauld found himself until 1925 commanding the equivalent of naval brigades in Stralsund

Von Arnauld de la Perière ended the war in command of U-139, one of the large ocean-going cruiser submarines which could range right across the Atlantic. Here his former command U-35 lies amongst other surrendered boats at Harwich in 1918.

and Stettin. There followed a year as navigating officer in the old battleship *Elsass* before being appointed to the Naval Staff in Wilhelmshaven. In 1931, as a *Korvettenkapitän*, he joined the new submarine command; still only 45 years of age, his experience was grafted onto the rootstock of a new generation of submarine heroes.

U-35 receives visitors in the shape of the crew of a small 'UB' class submarine during a cruise in the Mediterranean. The small size of the UB boat is obvious. The figure in British uniform on U-35 forward of the 88-mm gun is Captain Wilson, King's Messenger, taken prisoner by von Arnauld earlier in the patrol.

U-boats increased in size and armament throughout the war. Early boats carried so few torpedoes that their offensive capacity was severely limited, whereas the later units of the 'U-93' class could carry up to 16 torpedoes and mounted a heavy gun armament.

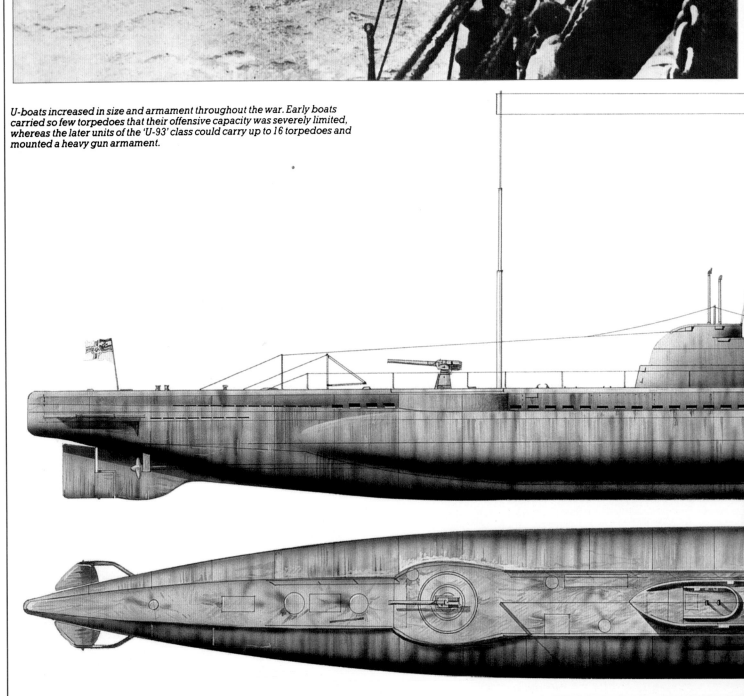

Unterseeboot U-160

By 1918 U-boats had evolved to a size and shape foreshadowing that of the boats that fought the second battle of the Atlantic during World War II. Displacing 820 tons surfaced and 1,000 tons submerged, the 'U-160' group was a logical development of the earlier U-boats. Like the 'U-87' class they were fitted with a heavy bow armament of six 500-mm (19.7-in) torpedo tubes, and ended the war mounting 105-mm (4.1-in) and 88-mm (3.46-in) dual-purpose guns. Commerce raiding was hedged with a series of restrictions imposed by the Hague Convention to which both Great Britain and Germany were signatories; for submarines, these conditions posed very serious problems because of their vulnerability when surfaced. The convention was violated early in the war by the Royal Navy as well as by the Germans. Neutral opinion was upset by the actions of both sides, the Germans achieving greatest opprobrium only as their sink-on-sight policy gathered pace. The U-boats soon inflicted terrible damage on the Allied merchant marine; it is often forgotten that fatal damage was already being done before the Germans embarked on unrestricted submarine warfare. U-160 was not launched until February 1918 when the U-boats had been all but defeated, and unrest in the German fleet would soon lead to mutiny.

American submarines

Pre-war emphasis in US submarine design had been based largely on the needs of coastal defence, with submerged handiness and rapid diving important considerations. This rather insular approach was rudely shaken from 1914 when German U-boats demonstrated their capabilities in ocean warfare. Until 1913, almost all boats had been of Holland design, excepting only the three 'G' class boats of 1911-3 (built to the design of Simon Lake but held by the navy to be too complex) and a single Laurenti type, the G-4 of 1912 (found to be unstable in practice, a problem discovered also by the British in their boats built to Laurenti design). The navy had little confidence in submarines in general but, being obviously so far behind European practice, characteristically began to build, though increasing the size of successive classes with great caution.

All American submarines after 1910 had diesels for surface propulsion; those built pre-war were typically of 300 tons or less but the excellent 'H' class of about 360 tons was available in 1913, the British Admiralty having many more built than the American's nine. Eleven 'L' class boats between 1915 and 1917 raised the surface tonnage to beyond 450 and, for the first time, the boats mounted a 76-mm (3-in) deck gun; when not in use this retracted, barrel vertical, into a space-

The US Navy developed its submarine arm at a leisurely pace, and at the end of the war was surprised at the superiority of the U-boats it inspected; close examination of U-111 revealed a dry bridge and a sound propulsion system. Many US vessels, like the 'K' class, suffered from unreliable diesels.

consuming stowage in the pressure hull. The 'L' class boats were followed by an assortment of largely similar 'N', 'O' and 'R' class boats, all of the same armament and constructed by the Electric Boat Company. They were rated for operations down to 61-m (200-ft) submergence.

At the USA's entry into the war her navy had a respectable 50 boats in service, but many of these were obsolete and little was to be achieved by them. In October 1917 a flotilla of 'L' class boats was sent to the Azores and a further flotilla (labelled 'ALs' to void confusion with the British 'L' class) operated in western Irish waters against U-boats, for German surface targets were by this time virtually nonexistent. They had no direct success, although the German UB-65 possibly torpedoed herself and was lost while trying to sink the AL-2.

Specification
'L' class
Displacement: 456 tons surfaced and 524 tons dived
Dimensions: length 50.29 m (165 ft 0 in); beam 4.50 m (14 ft 9 in); draught 4.04 m (13 ft 3 in)
Propulsion: two diesels delivering 895 kW (1,200 bhp) and two electric motors delivering 597 kW (800 hp) to two shafts
Speed: 14 kts surfaced and 10 kts dived
Range: not known
Armament: one 76-mm (3-in) gun, and four 457-mm (18-in) torpedo tubes (bow) with eight torpedoes
Complement: 28

The 'O' class were typical of the submarines constructed in America before the USA entered the war. Displacing just over 500 tons, they carried a crew of 28 and were fitted with four 457-mm (18-in) torpedo tubes.

'Dupuy de Lôme' class

At the outbreak of war in 1914 France had over 120 submarines in service. Many were obsolete, however, and more modern examples were so plagued by mechanical trouble as to spend long periods under repair. One cause was an insatiable urge to experiment in design without consolidating on proven technology. Steam propulsion was popular from an early date and remained so for surface navigation, largely because of the unreliability of French-designed diesels of that date. 'Overseas'-type boats were more numerous than in the Royal Navy, their size being sympathetic with Laubeuf double-hulled construction, with the outer hull used for running on the surface. Diving took typically five minutes but this was not thought to be detrimental and an acceptable

tradeoff for seaworthiness. Steam propulsion in itself was a handicap in diving, with the boilers having to be shut down, funnels secured and blanked-off, and electric propulsion run up.

The early 'Pluviôse' type sea-going boats of 1907-10 had two sets of triple-expansion steam engines, and all their torpedoes were carried in the unsatisfactory external drop-collars rather than tubes. They were followed by one-off larger steam-propelled boats, the generally similar Archimède of 1909 and the improved Gustave Zédé of 1913. The latter had two tubes for torpedoes but retained dropping gear, as did the ultimate pair, the 'Dupuy de Lôme' class boats, Dupuy de Lôme and Sané of 1915-6. Like all French submarines, they were constructed in state dockyards, in this case at Toulon.

Their size enabled them to maintain 17 kts on the surface but it must be doubtful if they ever reached their claimed 11 kts submerged. After the war they were re-engined with 895-kW (1,200-bhp) diesels removed from ceded German boats. This gave them a greatly increased radius and more internal space as a result of the compactness of the machinery. They also received eight torpedo tubes and served through until 1935.

Specification
'Dupuy de Lôme' class (as built)
Displacement: 833 tons surfaced and 1,287 tons dived
Dimensions: length 75.00 m (246 ft 1 in); beam 6.40 m (21 ft 0 in); draught 4.60 m (15 ft 1 in)
Propulsion: two sets of triple-expansion steam engines delivering 1305 kW (1,750 ihp) and two electric motors delivering 611 kW (820 hp) to two shafts
Speed: 17 kts surfaced and 8 kts dived
Range: 4250 km (2,640 miles) at 10 kts surfaced (after re-engineering), and 200 km (124 miles) at 5 kts dived
Armament: one 75-mm (2.95-in) gun, one 47-mm (1.85-in) gun, and 10 450-mm (17.7-in) torpedoes
Complement: 43

Serving with the Morocco flotilla of the French navy in 1917-18, based at Gibraltar, Dupuy de Lôme was an enlarged version of the successful 'Archimède' design. She reached 19 kts on her reciprocating engines on trials. These engines were replaced after the war by a 1200-bhp Krupp diesel taken from an ex-German submarine.

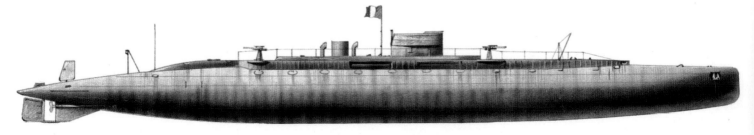

UK

'C' class

SUBMARINES

As a lengthened and improved 'B' class, the 'C' class submarines ran to the considerable number of 38 boats though, in the four years of their construction programme, various improvements were incorporated. In practice there were two main groups, *C1* to *C18* (completed 1906-8) and *C19* to *C38* (completed 1909-10). Costing something like £47,000 to £50,000 each, all except six were built by Vickers, which firm had the monopoly of constructing, in concert with the Royal Dockyards, any submarine for which the company had provided the major design input. The hull design was of spindle form with poor characteristics on the surface (where the boats of the day spent the greater part of their time). It is interesting that the concept of these early forms, which were aimed at the best submerged performance, was gradually abandoned over the years, to be readopted and refined only in the high-speed submarine developments post-1950. Improvements to both casing and tower resulted not only in better seakindliness but also in increasing periscope length from 3.76 m (12 ft 4 in) to 6.40 m (21 ft 0 in), an important consideration with respect to depth-keeping in a sea. In the earlier boats, two periscopes were fitted for the first time.

Reserve of buoyancy was greater than in earlier boats but was still limited, decreasing further over the years to the extent that, eventually, the choice often had to be made between spare torpedoes or fuel capacity. Compared with that of the 'B' class boats, battery power was increased by 50 per cent, but the submerged endurance of 93 km (58 miles) at 4.5 kts still needs to be compared with 37 km (23 miles) at 5 kts for the earliest 'A' boats.

A drawback to all these early classes was their total lack of main internal watertight bulkheads; to reduce the danger of rapid flooding, a collision bulkhead was later fitted to some. Habitability was of a very low standard and the adherence to the petrol engine perpetuated the explosion risk from vapour.

Despite their obvious limitations, the 'C' boats were active in the war. Because of their small size four were shipped to North Russia, broken into sections, transported overland and reassembled for use in the Gulf of Finland. At a time when smaller U-boats were pestering the British North Sea fishing fleet, 'C' boats were occasionally towed submerged by decoy trawlers, a ruse that resulted in the destruction of two of the enemy before detection caused its abandonment. War losses totalled four, and the four boats in the Gulf of Finland were all eventually blown up.

A remarkable series of photos taken from one of Oberleutnant Friederich Christiansen's Hansa-Brandenburg W.29 floatplanes, which attacked C-25 off Harwich on 6 July 1918. The pressure hull was pierced and the CO, Lieutenant Bell, was killed along with five of his crew.

Specification
'C' class (second series)
Displacement: 290 tons surfaced and 320 tons dived
Dimensions: length 43.36 m (142 ft 3 in); beam 4.14 m (13 ft 7 in); draught 3.51 m (11 ft 6 in)
Propulsion: one petrol engine delivering 447 kW (600 bhp) and one electric motor delivering 224 kW (300 hp) to one shaft
Speed: 13.5 kts surfaced and 8 kts dived
Range: 2414 km (1,500 miles) at 8 kts surfaced, and 101 km (63 miles) at 5 kts dived
Armament: two 457-mm (18-in) torpedo tubes (both bow) with two or four torpedoes
Complement: 16

Right: The figure by the periscope is believed to be Leading Seaman Barge, who was mortally wounded while firing a Lewis gun back at the aircraft. He shouted for the submarine to dive, unaware that she had already sustained prohibitive hull damage.

The 'C' class of submarine was the first type to be produced in substantial numbers for the Royal Navy, 38 examples being built. Small coastal craft with limited endurance and with petrol engines, they were perhaps intended for ill-defined harbour defence tasks but saw widespread action, four serving in the Baltic.

Above: Bullets impact into the water as C25 vainly tries to manoeuvre. She was rescued by the appearance of the minelaying submarine E51, which towed her back to Harwich despite the continued attentions of Christiansen's aircraft. Christiansen added C25 to his kill total nevertheless.

261

'E' class

UK

The eight-boat **'D' class**, completed in 1909-12, rectified many of the shortcomings of the 'C' class. Though 5.79 m (19 ft) longer, they were better seaboats and they were also equipped with saddle tanks, which accommodated most ballast capacity outside the pressure hull and increased the reserve of buoyancy. They also had diesel propulsion on twin shafts (so improving manoeuvrability), could carry a 12-pdr gun and shipped a third torpedo tube aft. It was felt that while the design was successful, the 'D' class boats would experience difficulty in getting clear following an end-on torpedo attack at close range, even though fitted with an upper, separate rudder. Two transverse tubes were, therefore, added to a new design to permit beam attacks, and it was the length of these tubes, located amidships, that decided the main dimensions of what was to become the **'E' class**.

Completed from 1913 through to 1916, the 'E' class ran to 55 hulls whose construction, once war was declared, was shared between 13 private yards. They fell into five major groups, differences being primarily in torpedo layout and the adaption of six boats to carry 20 mines in place of their amidships tubes. The stowage of the mines in external vertical chutes anticipated later French practice. Two, sometimes three, internal bulkheads were added, increasing the safety margin but giving problems in reloading the forward tubes.

The diesels fitted were of Vickers' own design, usually built under licence. They were single-acting, four-stroke units with blast injection, started by either compressed air or electric motor. In the 'D' class the engines had six cylinders and in the 'E' class eight.

With their heavy operational involvements, the 'E' class boats had an important yet extraordinarily varied surface armament. Early boats had nothing or one 2-pdr, while later examples had both a 12- and 2-pdr. One, *E20*, was fitted with a 152-mm (6-in) howitzer. Improvements necessary for longer-range radio communication required some 'E' class boats to surrender an amidships tube to make room for a wireless telegraphy cabinet.

The class was active in the North Sea, Baltic and eastern Mediterranean. Just before Jutland, *E22* became one of the earliest submarines to carry aircraft, in the course of experimenting with Sopwith seaplanes for operations against Zeppelins. Some 22 of the boats were lost in World War I.

Specification
'E' class ('E21' type)
Displacement: 667 tons surfaced and 807 tons dived
Dimensions: length 55.17 m (181 ft 0 in); beam 6.91 m (22 ft 8 in); draught 3.81 m (12 ft 6 in)
Propulsion: two diesels delivering

1193 kW (1,600 bhp) and two electric motors delivering 626 kW (840 hp) to two shafts
Speed: 14 kts surfaced and 9 kts dived
Range: 6035 km (3,750 miles) at 10 kts surfaced, and 121 km (75 miles) at 5 kts dived
Armament: one 12-pdr gun, and five 457-mm (18-in) torpedo tubes (two bow, two amidships and one stern) with 10 torpedoes
Complement: 30

In 1911 the Admiralty ordered six enlarged 'D' class submarines. This modified design became known as the R-1 group; eight were built for the Navy and two for Australia. E1, seen here, was shipped to Murmansk and taken overland to operate in the Gulf of Bothnia and the Baltic. She was eventually scuttled at Helsingfors in April 1918 to avoid capture by the advancing Germans.

E11 as she appeared during her operations in the Dardanelles; like the British boats in the Mediterranean in World War II she adopted a blue camouflage to conceal herself in the shallow, clear waters. The lack of a deck gun on the 'E' class was keenly felt and a variety of improvised gun fits were tried.

'K' class

UK

With HMS *Swordfish* building but anticipated to reach nothing like her designed surface speed, there came a requirement direct from the Grand Fleet for a class of 24-kt submarines to work tactically with surface forces. Such a speed was quickly demonstrated to need 7457 kW (10,000 shp) on a surface displacement of 1,700 tons. No contemporary diesels could deliver such power from anything less than eight units, and there was thus no alternative to steam. With two boilers and a turbine room the hull of the **'K' class** needed to be of a good size but, with the poor economy of steam plant and the need to provide power when steam was shut down, a 597-kW (800-bhp) diesel was also installed to drive a generator. This could either charge the batteries or power the main drive motors for a surface speed of about 9.5 knots. Over one-third of the hull was thus devoted to machinery. The two funnels exhausting the boilers hinged downward into the casing before a dive was commenced, their orifices being simultaneously shut off by sealing plates. Diving took up to five minutes.

While 533-mm (21-in) torpedo tubes were specified for the class, they could not be made available in time and 457-

mm (18-in) tubes were fitted except in the single improved boat, K26, completed in 1923. Four fixed athwartships tubes were sited in a torpedo room immediately forward of the boiler space and two further, trainable tubes (later removed) were set behind screens in the large superstructure, for use in surface action. Two 102-mm (4-in) guns were mounted at (usually) lower casing level, with a 76-mm (3-in) high-angle gun sited on the superstructure, but individual armament fits varied. Some 17 boats were completed in 1917 and 1918.

The 'K' class boats met the fleet requirements for surface speed but needed the addition of a flared and bulbous bow casing (known euphemistically as a 'swan bow') to maintain speed in any sea. Such hard driving damaged the addition of bow shutters and, more critically, funnel mechanisms. The boats' complexity made them extremely troublesome, and they acquired an evil name, not fully justified. In particular, the so-called Battle of May Island in January 1918, when two were lost in collisions, demonstrated the underlying fallacy of operating large submarines on the surface in high-speed fleet manoeuvres at night, not shortcomings in the boats themselves.

Above: K6 is seen before the addition of the ungainly bow casing, politely termed the 'swan bow'. Sealing the boat before diving proved difficult, as ventilators could be jammed open by only a small obstruction. The planned 21-in torpedoes were abandoned in favour of 18-in ones.

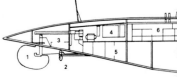

UK 'J' class

In 1912 requirements were framed for likely future types of submarine, and these included an 'overseas' craft, of an appropriate size and habitability for extended operations. It was hoped to achieve a speed of 21 kts on the surface which, in conjunction with a double-hulled design (the outer of which could be given a suitable configuration unrestricted by the pressure-tight requirements of the inner hull) would enable it to operate with the main body of the fleet. A prototype, HMS *Nautilus*, was built by Vickers and completed in 1917 in slow time. The company produced two new 1380-kW (1,850-bhp) diesels for the purpose, but it was apparent from model testing that the boat would never be able to exceed 17 kts. For this reason, Scotts were given the task of building a steam-propelled alternative in HMS *Swordfish*. Both were very large boats compared with the 'E' type but experience with them was still lacking and, as longer-range submarines were needed, it was decided to follow German practice and build a smaller double-hulled design without the requirement for a high surface speed. This was the 14-strong 'G' class.

The two, experimental boats were still incomplete when it became known (incorrectly) that the Germans were building a 22-kt class, and there was suddenly a pressing need to match them. Existing machinery had to be used and, with the largest available diesel being the 12-cylinder 895-kW (1,200-bhp) Vickers unit, three of these were incorporated in what became the 'J' class. These were the longest boats yet and could manage over 19 kts on the surface. To attain the necessary fineness of line the seven boats (six completed in 1916 and one in 1917) were double-hulled over only some 56 per cent of their length. This length was determined largely by the demands of the machinery, though only the wing shafts were driven when submerged. Their beam needed to accommodate the two transverse amidships tubes and the pressure hull itself needed to be locally bulged to suit. They were the first British submarines with four tubes forward and a unique arrangement aft allowed the *J1* (only) to release depth charges. Only one was lost and that by accident to the 'Q' ship HMS *Cymric* just before the Armistice. The remainder were transferred to the Royal Australian Navy.

Specification
'J' class
Displacement: 1,204 tons surfaced and 1,820 tons dived
Dimensions: length 83.97 m (275 ft 6 in); beam 7.01 m (23 ft 0 in); draught 4.27 m (14 ft 0 in)
Propulsion: three diesels delivering 2685 kW (3,600 bhp) and two electric motors delivering 1007 kW (1,350 hp) to three shafts
Speed: 19.5 kts surfaced and 9.5 kts dived
Range: 9254 km (5,750 miles) at 10 (?) kts surfaced, and 101 km (63

The handful of 'J' class boats was one of several attempts to produce a 'fleet submarine': that is, a submarine capable of over 20 kts able to operate in conjunction with the battlefleet. J1 was later fitted to drop depth charges from her after casing.

miles) at 5 kts dived
Armament: one 76- or 102-mm (3- or 4-in) gun, and six 457-mm (21-in) torpedo tubes (four bow and tow amidships) with 12 torpedoes
Complement: 44

The steam turbine-powered 'K' class gained a reputation for bad luck and bad design culminating in the so-called 'battle of May Island' when K4 and K17 both sank in collisions while on manoeuvres. In fact they were tremendous technical achievements, the problems stemming from the concept of a fleet submarine, not the actual design.

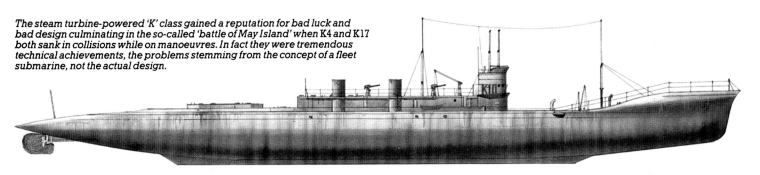

Specification
'K' class
Displacement: 1,980 tons surfaced and 2,566 tons dived
Dimentions: length 103.32 m (339 ft 0 in); beam 8.10 m (26 ft 7 in); draught 5.18 m (17 ft 0 in)
Propulsion: two sets of geared steam turbines delivering 7830 kW (10,500 shp) or one diesel delivering 597 kW (800 bhp) via a generator, and two electric motors delivering 1074 kW (1,440 bhp) to two shafts
Speed: 24 or 9.5 kts surfaced (steam or diesel) and 8.5 kts dived
Range: 23175 km (14,400 miles) at 9.5 kts surfaced, and 56 km (35 miles) at 4 kts dived
Armament: two single 102-mm (4-in) guns, one 76-mm (3-in) gun, and 10 later eight (four bow, four amidships and two superstructure) 457-mm (18-in) torpedo tubes with 16 torpedoes
Complement: 59

Modified 'K' class submarine cutaway drawing key

1. Rudder
2. Twin screws
3. Hydroplanes
4. Steerage compartment
5. Trim tanks
6. Crew compartment
7. Engine room
8. Eight-cylinder diesel engines
9. Main motor
10. Motor control room
11. 10-ton aft keel weight (to be dropped in emergency)
12. Gearbox
13. Escape hatch
14. Superstructure
15. High-pressure/low-pressure steam turbine
16. Hinged funnel
17. Oil-fired boiler
18. Hatches (closed when submerged)
19. Three-inch AA gun
20. Four-inch gun
21. Hinged air intakes
22. Dinghy
23. Derrick for boat handling or stowing torpedoes
24. Battery compartment
25. Control room
26. Conning tower
27. Forced draft fan
28. Search periscope
29. Attack periscope
30. Bridge with streamlined screen
31. Wheelhouse
32. Dome
33. Hatch
34. Compass tube
35. Wireless aerial
36. Retractable wireless mast
37. Periscope wells
38. Batteries
39. Inner pressure hull
40. Double hull
41. Crew mess area/quarters
42. Derrick
43. Ballast tanks
44. 10-ton forward keel weight
45. Auxiliary ballast tanks
46. Air bottles
47. Raised swan bow
48. Buoyancy chamber
49. Torpedo room
50. 18-inch torpedoes
51. Torpedo tubes

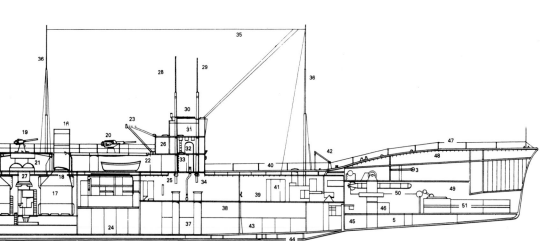

Holbrook's B11 opened the Dardanelles campaign in tremendous style, making the first deep-water penetration of the strait on 13 December 1914 and diving beneath the Turkish mines. Finding the Turkish battleship Messoudieh lying at anchor, he hit her with a single torpedo at 800 m; she went down quite rapidly but opened a heavy fire on B11, which had trouble submerging in the very shallow water. B11 escaped down the straits in an epic nine-hour submerged journey. When she finally surfaced in the open sea the air aboard was so foul that the petrol engine refused to run. Holbrook received a well-earned VC.

Victory in the Straits

The Turkish fleet had good reason to feel safe in 1914; although it was committed to war with the world's most powerful navy, its vessels sheltered at the end of the Sea of Marmora, a hundred miles of shallow waters with treacherous currents, sown with mines and protected by forts. Yet Allied submariners took up the challenge and sailed their frail craft into the straits, one British boat entering Constantinople itself.

When on 30 October 1914 Turkey declared for the Central Powers, business began in earnest for a small Anglo-French submarine force based on the Greek island of Tenedos. Handily-placed close to the entrance to the Dardanelles, the boats had been familiarizing themselves with the approaches ever since the German battle-cruiser *Goeben* and light cruiser *Breslau* had disappeared up the strait in the previous August. Together with the makeshift depot ship *Hindu Kush* were, initially, three French boats and the British *B9, B10* and *B11*.

The Dardanelles is a narrow strait about 58 km (36 miles) in length and leads to the land-girt Sea of Marmora, about 160 km (100 miles) from end to end. At the far end of this water was the magnet of the Turkish capital, Constantinople, but to reach it a submarine had to negotiate the strait, which was heavily defended by forts, batteries and searchlights, its waters possessing unpredictable currents of up to 5 kts at the Narrows and also strewn with nets and mine barriers.

Of the Allied submarines, Holbrook's *B11* had been recently equipped with new batteries and was elected to make the first deep penetration of the strait. Thus on 13 December 1914, equipped with improvised mine guards,

the little boat dived inside Cape Helles just before daylight. Holbrook kept to the European side to cheat the tide and (except when taking frequent periscope checks) ran as far as possible at 18 to 24 m (60 to 80 ft) to keep below the mines. Four hours after going down and after various alarms and excursions, *B11* had negotiated the first mine barriers off Kephez and was approaching the second, below the Chanak narrows. To his delight, her commander sighted the aged armoured cruiser *Messoudieh* lying unconcernedly at anchor. Considering the date and conditions, his hitting her with a single torpedo at the range of 800 m (880 yards) was a fine feat. She settled rapidly but opened a brisk fire on the submarine, which was experiencing difficulty in remaining hidden in very shallow water. With no compass, Holbrook bumped and bored his way back down the iron gullet of the strait. Successful, he surfaced in the open sea after nine hours submerged, the air in the boat so foul that his petrol engine refused to run. The obsolete little boat had opened unlimited prospects, and her commander received a well-merited Victoria Cross.

With the opening of the main Dardanelles campaign early in 1915, there was a rapid

build-up in the joint fleets, the British submarine force being boosted by the arrival of modern 'E' class boats. As the Turkish land communication system was virtually nonexistent, supply and reinforcement of their front would depend greatly on sea transport down the Sea of Marmora and it was vital to disrupt the route. The first attempt to force the strait, by *E15*, was disastrous: the submarine stranded near Kephez and was finally destroyed only after a heroic foray by boats from the battleships HMS *Majestic* and *Triumph*.

It fell to the Australian boat *AE2* to be the first through the strait, on 25 April 1915, followed the very next day by *E14* which bored through mainly on the surface, taking advantage of darkness. Strong nerves were required as the boat was held by the cold fingers of the searchlights and subjected to a continuous bombardment. Boyle, the commander, submerged when things became too hot but, finding the scraping of mine cables along the hull even more unpleasant, kept popping up. Like the Australian, Stoker before him, Boyle found a gunboat to torpedo but, in the process, had a periscope shot through and the other grasped rudely by a Turk in an open boat!

Australian vessel sunk

Activity was intense, it being the third day before Boyle could fully charge his batteries. He was rewarded by being able to force aground one of two transports under destroyer escort. The same evening he met up with *AE2*, which was down to one torpedo, having had the cruel experience of firing six duds. On the very next day the Australian was caught on the surface by a Turkish destroyer and sunk.

The British boat had a lean time, for the Turks cut their sailings to a minimum and put refugees on those that did move so that they could not be sunk. Then, the first legitimate target was hit by a torpedo that failed to explode. At last on 10 May Boyle sank a laden troopship hard by Constantinople and, reduced to one faulty torpedo (he had no deck gun), he then harassed local shipping for a week with threats and rifle fire until recalled on 17 May. Hunted persistently whilst coming down the strait with the stream, he avoided much trouble by passing the various barriers close astern of an enemy patrol. He returned after a 22-day absence with much intelligence regarding the defences and anti-submarine measures, to be awarded the second Victoria Cross gained by the force. During his time away, two French submarines had attempted the passage; of these the *Bernouilli* was unable to stem the current and was forced to return while the *Joule* was sunk in a minefield. Two more French boats, the *Saphir* and *Mariotte*, were also to be lost, similarly or following technical troubles.

Boyle was immediately relieved by Nasmith in the *E11*, the latter already a veteran of North Sea operations. Profiting by the *E14*'s experiences, Nasmith negotiated the Dardanelles successfully and made for the eastern end of the Sea of Marmora. He, too, began by sinking

a Turkish patrol craft which also succeeded in putting a 6-pdr shot through his periscope. This was followed by a couple of transports, the loss of which caused traffic to cease. Nothing daunted, Nasmith took the *E11* right into the Golden Horn, the harbour of Constantinople, and torpedoed a freighter alongside the arsenal.

The lack of a deck gun was keenly felt and transports were sunk by demolition charge whenever possible. Nasmith developed the technique of setting his torpedoes to float at the end of their run, so that 'misses' could be later recovered, disarmed and manoeuvred carefully back into the bow tubes with the boat suitably trimmed, a precarious business that left them very vulnerable for a time. Even when torpedoed, however, a large well-found ship could survive the explosion of a 457-mm (18-in)

warhead, and several were thus beached. Sailing craft were burned in numbers. Not until 7 June did the condition of the *E11*'s machinery oblige withdrawal, the passage down the strait seeing another ship torpedoed and a mine towed for some distance, its cable caught in a hydroplane. Nasmith's extended cruise had bagged seven large ships and earned a further Victoria Cross.

British sub penetration

Despite the fact that the Turks and Germans continuously improved the Dardanelles defences, the Sea of Marmora was inhabited by at least one British submarine throughout 1915. Maritime traffic, though hard hit and often stopped had, of necessity, always to resume because of the endless needs of the front and the dreadful land communications. German engineers laboured on a new rail line but this took time. Knowing the British boats' small torpedo reserve it is surprising that the enemy never capitalized more on their requirement to surface to attack commerce by other means. By this time the Q-ship stratagem was well publicized, and German 'UBs' were being assembled at Pola.

The experiences of Bruce's *E12* were typical. In passing up the strait in June 1915 the boat was enmeshed in a newly-added net and survived only by flooding everything and crashing her motors alternately into ahead and reverse thrust. All but burned out, they thereafter gave endless trouble, obliging Bruce to operate largely on the surface. In one encounter he tackled two merchantmen towing five sailing

Nasmith took his submarine E11 right into the Golden Horn, the harbour of Constantinople, and torpedoed a freighter. During this patrol he set his torpedoes to float at the end of their run so that if he missed, he could surface and recover the torpedo for re-use. After sinking seven large enemy vessels he took E11 back through the straits but snagged a mine on the way, towing it for some distance. After some hairy moments it floated free and E11 escaped.

Victory in the Straits

Above: The waterfront in Constantinople is seen after the British submarine E11, commanded by Nasmith, entered the harbour and unleashed a salvo of torpedoes, sinking a large merchantman and shattering this section of dock. Nasmith even took time to take a photograph through his periscope to record his visit for posterity.

Right: The straits had dangerous currents and were heavily mined by the Turks; passing through on the surface meant braving the powerful forts. Here the triumphant crew celebrate their return. Note the damage to the periscope.

Above: E11 returns from her most successful patrol, having sunk the Turkish battleship Heireddin Barbarossa on 8 August 1915. The battleship (ex-German 'Brandenburg' class, Kurfürst Friedrich Wilhelm) had had an active career in Ottoman service, fighting the Greek fleet in 1912-3, when she was the Turkish flagship.

Left: The commander of E2 poses by his gun after returning from a successful patrol in the Sea of Marmora. E2 began life with a 12-pdr weapon but received a 4-in gun at Malta.

craft. Spurning the aid of his toy 6-pdr he ran alongside one ship, only to have somebody above heave a bomb at him (it bounced off the foredeck without exploding) and direct a sustained fusillade of rifle fire. In a very exposed situation, Bruce had his gun crew put shots along the length of the ship's hull at a range where half-bricks would have been more appropriate. Simultaneously, others of his crew used rifles to fight off two of the tows, which were endeavouring to snare his propellers with a cable. After a Henty-type scrap the submarine disposed of its tormentors and pursued the second ship until it ran under the protection of a shore battery.

As the 'E' boats gained 12-pdr guns they developed also a taste for annoying targets ashore, duelling with artillery and shelling such railways as existed. During the August, Nasmith and Boyle, in *E11* and *E14*, shared a parti-

cularly fruitful patrol. Off Gallipoli town the *E11* sank the Turkish battleship *Heireddin Barbarossa*, following which her first lieutenant, d'Oyly Hughes, swam ashore one night and blew up a railway line. Hotly pursued by the vengeful enemy, he was fortunate to survive the escapade.

The Sea of Marmora remained no sinecure. In the September *E7* had to be scuttled after having become hopelessly fouled by nets off Nagara. Of the French submarines, only the *Turquoise* ever succeeded in negotiating the strait, operating in the Sea of Marmora for a short period in October 1915. Returning, however, she stranded and was captured intact. Not only did the Turks recommission her (as the *Mustadieh Ombashi*) but her papers compromised a planned rendezvous with the British *E20*, which was thus simply ambushed by the German *UB-14*, torpedoed and sunk

with all but nine of her crew.

Only Nasmith in the E11 was then left in the Sea of Marmora but, in a cruise of 47 days, he created such mayhem that he was rewarded by promotion to captain's rank after only one year as a commander. In mid-December he was joined by Stock's *E2*, which was the final boat in the area as the decision to abandon the whole Dardanelles campaign had been taken. When this boat returned down the strait on 2 January 1916 some obstructions had already been removed and the Allied evacuation was almost complete.

For the loss of four British and four French boats, the force had proved that submarines could sustain an effective campaign in disputed waters. In addition to disruption ashore, they had sunk two armoured ships, six flotilla ships, 37 merchantmen and nearly 200 assorted sailing craft.

🇬🇧 UK 'R' class

Had they not arrived so late in the war, the 10 **'R' class** boats may well have advanced the overall concept and use of submarines considerably. They were designed from the outset as hunters of U-boats which, in these early days of electronics, needed to be attacked on the surface. It was, of course, difficult to approach surfaced U-boats unseen and, once these had observed an enemy and had submerged, it was virtually impossible to detect them again. The 'L' class boats, then (1918) entering service, carried a 10-mm (4-in) gun in the tower for the purpose, but what was needed was to have the speed to approach U-boats submerged, and it was with this in mind that the 'R' class was designed.

Not large boats, they carried a reasonable but not excessive battery capacity. This was allied to a very clean hull which, itself, was largely responsible for their then-phenomenal underwater speed of 15 kts. The design was single-hulled with casing only at the bows and as a fairing to the small tower. They were the first single-shaft boats since the 'C' class, the propeller being driven by either a single diesel or two electric motors in tandem. The torque from the propeller was such as to require horizontal stabilizers aft, these serving also to support the outboard ends of the hydroplanes. An interesting feature was the provision of a

Far ahead of their time, the 'R' class comprised specialist hunter-killer submarines intended to overtake and torpedo enemy submarines. Their streamlined hull and large rudder gave them good underwater performance and the bow compartment contained five hydrophones.

further 18.6-kW (25-hp) electric motor right aft for 'creeping' at low speed, repeated in the 'L' class boats.

In some, the amidships superstructure was extended forward for the purposes of mounting a 102-mm gun, but as this weapon would have done nothing for the streamlining, it is doubtful if it was ever fitted. The boats relied on their powerful forward battery of six 457-mm (18-in) tubes, the first in the Royal Navy. An advanced feature was an array of five externally-mounted hydrophones for obtaining the position of a submerged enemy. It was the tragedy of the 'R' class boats that they began to commission only weeks before the Armistice, so that their adv-

anced features were never fully appreciated and post-war construction reverted to the cluttered exterior that characterized the 'O' class.

Specification
'R' class
Displacement: 410 tons surfaced and 503 tons dived
Dimensions: length 49.91 m (163 ft 9 in); beam 4.80 m (15 ft 9 in); draught

The uncluttered appearance of R7 is in sharp contrast to that of her contemporaries and gave her an outstanding submerged speed. Sadly, the 'R' class was only completed at the end of the war and their revolutionary design passed unnoticed.

3.50 m (11 ft 6 in)
Propulsion: one diesel delivering 179 kW (240 bhp) and two electric motors delivering 895 kW (1,200 hp) to one shaft
Speed: 9.5 kts surfaced and 15 kts dived
Range: 3701 km (2,300 miles) at 9 kts surfaced, and 27.75 km (17.25 miles) at 15 kts dived
Armament: six 457-mm (18-in) torpedo tubes (all bow) with 12 torpedoes
Complement: 12

🇮🇹 ITALY 'S' class

In its 'D' and 'E' classes, completed from 1910, the British Admiralty changed from the earlier spindle form to the saddle-tanked submarine. Foreign yards had, in the meantime, begun to produce another type with a double hull, i.e. with the pressure hull entirely surrounded by external tank spaces. As this outer hull could be given a shape sympathetic with surface seakeeping, the type was known at this time as a 'submersible', to differentiate it from the earlier 'submarine' in which the outer form was more in harmony with submerged operation. There was much to be said for the idea: ballast tanks and frame could be sited external to the pressure hull, increasing useful space within; with deeper framing, strength was increased; and the flat top of the casing allowed the crew to exercise away from the fetid conditions within the hull. The inherently greater buoyancy reserve of the type was desirable from the safety aspect but had the drawback of sluggish diving.

Laubeuf in France and Laurenti in Italy were foremost in this type of craft and, following a visit in 1911 to Fiat-San Giorgio, the British ordered a single

Laurenti from Scotts, followed by a further two in 1913. They were known as the **'S' class** boats *S1* to *S3*, the letter indicating the builder and with the added implication of their being viewed as prototypes. They were only marginally larger than the earlier British 'C' class and were classed as coastal submarines.

Both tubes were sited forward and, to preserve the upper lines of the hull, they were set very low, almost at keel level, the pressure hull adopting an odd cross-section to suit. Indeed, one great failing of the design was the number of discontinuities (and, therefore, weaknesses) in the pressure hull. There were no less than 10 internal watertight bulkheads and the reserve of buoyancy, at 47 per cent, was effectively double that of any previous British boat. The machinery was of Fiat design and, being two-stroke, the engines were capable of direct reversal. An interesting feature was that both forward and after planes could be housed. The boats proved unpopular and unsuitable for the Royal Navy, and were transferred to Italy on the latter's entry into the war in 1915. They were discarded in 1919.

Specification
'S' class
Displacement: 265 tons surfaced and 324 tons dived
Dimensions: length 45.16 m (148 ft 2 in); beam 4.39 m (14 ft 5 in); draught 3.17 m (10 ft 5 in)
Propulsion: two diesels delivering 485 kW (650 bhp) and two electric motors delivering 298 kW (400 hp) to two shafts
Speed: 13 kts surfaced and 8.5 kts dived
Range: 2960 km (1,839 miles) at 8.5 kts

S1 enters Brindisi in 1916. Built in England to an Italian design, she had served for a year with the Royal Navy before being transferred. Similar in size to the British 'C' class, the 'S' boats were slightly slower but had a high reserve of buoyancy.

surfaced, and 16 km (10 miles) at 8.5 kts dived
Armament: two 457-mm (18-in) torpedo tubes (bow) with four torpedoes
Complement: 18

INDEX

Numbers in *italics* refer to photographs.